CHILTON BOOK COMPANY

REPAIR MANUAL

BUICK CENTURY/ REGAL 1975-87

All U.S. and Canadian models of rear wheel drive BUICK Century and BUICK Regal

President GARY R. INGERSOLL
Senior Vice President, Book Publishing and Research RONALD A. HOXTER
Publisher KERRY A. FREEMAN, S.A.E.
Editor-In-Chief DEAN F. MORGANTINI, S.A.E.
Senior Editor RICHARD J. RIVELE, S.A.E.
Editor JOHN M. BAXTER, S.A.E.
Editor ANTHONY C. TORTORICI

CHILTON BOOK COMPANY
Radnor, Pennsylvania
19089

CONTENTS

DRIVE TRAIN

SUSPENSION and STEERING

BRAKES

BODY

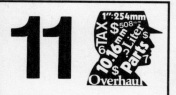

MECHANIC'S DATA

SAFETY NOTICE

Proper service and repair procedures are vital to the safe, reliable operation of all motor vehicles, as well as the personal safety of those performing repairs. This book outlines procedures for servicing and repairing vehicles using safe, effective methods. The procedures contain many NOTES, CAUTIONS and WARNINGS which should be followed along with standard safety procedures to eliminate the possibility of personal injury or improper service which could damage the vehicle or compromise its safety.

It is important to note that repair procedures and techniques, tools and parts for servicing motor vehicles, as well as the skill and experience of the individual performing the work vary widely. It is not possible to anticipate all of the conceivable ways or conditions under which vehicles may be serviced, or to provide cautions as to all of the possible hazards that may result. Standard and accepted safety precautions and equipment should be used when handling toxic or flammable fluids, and safety goggles or other protection should be used duirng cutting, grinding, chiseling, prying, or any other process that can cause material removal or projectiles.

Some procedures require the use of tools specially designed for a specific purpose. Before substituting another tool or procedure, you must be completely satisfied that neither your personal safety, nor the performance of the vehicle will be endangered.

Although information in this guide is based on industry sources and is as complete as possible at the time of publication, the possibility exists that the manufacturer made later changes which could not be included here. While striving for total accuracy, Chilton Book Company cannot assume responsibility for any errors, changes, or omissions that may occur in the compilation of this data.

PART NUMBERS

Part numbers listed in this reference are not recommendations by Chilton for any product by brand name. They are references that can be used with interchange manuals and aftermarket supplier catalogs to locate each brand supplier's discrete part number.

SPECIAL TOOLS

Special tools are recommended by the vehicle manufacturer to perform their specific job. Use has been kept to a minimum, but where absolutely necessary, they are referred to in the text by the part number of the tool manufacturer. These tools can be purchased, under the appropriate part number, from the Service Tool Division, Kent-Moore Corporation, 29784 Little Mack, Roseville, MI 48066-2298,or an equivalent tool can be purchased locally from a tool supplier or parts outlet. Before substituting any tool for the one recommended, read the SAFETY NOTICE at the top of this page.

ACKNOWLEDGMENTS

The Chilton Book Company expresses its appreciation to the General Motors Corporation, Detroit, Michigan, for their generous assistance.

Information has been selected from shop manuals, owners manuals, service bulletins and technical training manuals.

Chilton's Repair Manual: Buick Century/Regal 1975–87
ISBN 0-8019-7823-8 pbk.
Library of Congress Catalog Card No. 87-47943

General Information and Maintenance

HOW TO USE THIS BOOK

This book covers all Buick Century and Regal rear wheel drive models from 1975 through 1987.

The first two chapters will be the most used, since they contain maintenance and tune-up information and procedures. Studies have shown that a properly tuned and maintained car can get at least 10% better gas mileage (which translates into lower operating costs). Furthermore, periodic maintenance will catch minor problems before they turn into major repair bills. The other chapters deal with the more complex systems of your car. Operating systems from engine through brakes are covered to the extent that the average do-it-yourselfer becomes mechanically involved. This book will not explain such things as rebuilding the differential for the simple reason that the expertise required and the investment in special tools make this task uneconomical. It will give you the detailed instructions to help you change your own brake pads and shoes, tune-up the engine, replace spark plugs and filters, and do many more jobs that will save you money, give you personal satisfaction and help you avoid expensive problems.

A secondary purpose of this book is as a reference guide for owners who want to better understand their car and/or what their mechanic has to say. In this case, no tools at all are required. Knowing just what a particular repair job requires in parts and labor time will allow you to evaluate whether or not you're getting a fair price quote and help decipher itemized bills from a repair shop.

Before attempting any repairs or service on your car, read through the entire procedure outlined in the appropriate chapter. This will give you the overall view of what tools and supplies will be required. There is nothing more frustrating than having to walk to the bus stop on Monday morning because you were short one gasket on Sunday afternoon. So read ahead and plan ahead. Each operation should be approached logically and all procedures thoroughly understood before attempting any work. Some special tools that may be required can often be rented from local automotive jobbers or places specializing in renting tools and equipment. Check the yellow pages of your phone book.

All chapters contain adjustments, maintenance, removal and installation procedures, and overhaul procedures. When overhaul is not considered practical, we tell you how to remove the failed part and then how to install the new or rebuilt replacement. In this way, you at least save the labor costs. Backyard overhaul of some components (such as the alternator or water pump) is just not practical, but the removal and installation procedure is often simple and well within the capabilities of the average car owner.

Two basic mechanic's rules should be mentioned here. One, whenever the left side of the car or engine is referred to, it is meant to specify the driver's side of the car. Conversely, the right side of the car means the passenger's side. Secondly, most screws and bolt are removed by turning counterclockwise, and tightened by turning clockwise.

Safety is always the most important rule. Constantly be aware of the dangers involved in working on or around an automobile and take proper precautions to avoid the risk of personal injury or damage to the vehicle. This means that you must always work slowly and visualize what is going to happen, rather than rushing into a job. See the section in this chapter, "Servicing Your Vehicle Safely", and the SAFETY NOTICE on the acknowledgment page before attempting any service procedures and pay attention to the instructions provided. There are 3 common mistakes in mechanical work:

1. Incorrect order of assembly, disassembly or adjustment. When taking something apart or putting it together, doing things in the wrong order usually just costs you extra time; however it CAN break something. Read the entire procedure before beginning disassembly. Do everything in the order in which the instructions say you should do it, even if you can't immediately see a reason for it. When you're taking apart something that is very intricate (for example a carburetor), you might want to draw a picture of how it looks when assembled at one point in order to make sure you get everything back in its proper position. We will supply exploded views whenever possible, but sometimes the job requires more attention to detail than an illustration provides. When making adjustments (especially tune-up adjustments), do them in order. One adjustment often affects another and you cannot expect satisfactory results unless each adjustment is made only when it cannot be changed by any other.

2. Overtorquing (or undertorquing) nuts and bolts. While it is more common for overtorquing to cause damage, undertorquing can cause a fastener to vibrate loose and cause serious damage, especially when dealing with aluminum parts. Pay attention to torque specifications and utilize a torque wrench in assembly. If a torque figure is not available remember that, if you are using the right tool to do the job, you will probably not have to strain yourself to get a fastener tight enough. The pitch of most threads is so slight that the tension you put on the wrench will be multiplied many times in actual force on what you are tightening. A good example of how critical torque is can be seen in the case of spark plug installation, especially where you are putting the plug into an aluminum cylinder head. Too little torque can fail to crush the gasket, causing leakage of combustion gases and consequent overheating of the plug and engine parts. Too much torque can damage the threads or distort the plug, which changes the spark gap at the electrode. Since more and more manufacturers are using aluminum in their engine and chassis parts to save weight, a torque wrench should be in any serious do-it-yourselfer's tool box. There are many commercial chemical products available for ensuring that fasteners won't come loose, even if they are not torqued just right (a very common brand is Loctite®). If you're worried about getting something together tight enough to hold, but loose enough to avoid mechanical damage during assembly, one of these products might offer substantial insurance. Read the label on the package and make sure the product is compatible with the materials, fluids, etc. involved before choosing one.

3. Crossthreading. This occurs when a part such as a bolt is screwed into a nut or casting at the wrong angle and forced, causing the threads to become damaged. Crossthreading is more likely to occur if access is difficult. It helps to clean and lubricate fasteners, and to start threading with the part to be installed going straight in, using your fingers. If you encounter resistance, unscrew the part and start over again at a different angle until it can be inserted and turned several times without much effort. Keep in mind that many parts, especially spark plugs, use tapered threads so that gentle turning will automatically bring the part you're threading to the proper angle if you don't force it or resist a change in angle. Don't put a wrench on the part until it's been turned in a couple of times by hand. If you suddenly encounter resistance and the part has not seated fully, don't force it. Pull it back out and make sure it's clean and threading properly.

Always take your time and be patient; once you have some experience, working on your car will become an enjoyable hobby.

TOOLS AND EQUIPMENT

NOTE: *Special tools are occasionally necessary to perform a specific job or are recommended to make a job easier. Their use has been kept to a minimum. When use of a special tool is indicated, it will be referred to by the manufacturer's part number and, where possible, an illustration of the tool will be provided so that an equivalent tool may be used.*
GM special tools are available from:
Service Tool Division
Kent-Moore
29784 Little Mack
Roseville, MI 48066-2298
This is the source GM uses to supply its dealers. You will find other sources from which they are available by cross-referencing the GM part number.

Naturally, without the proper tools and equipment, it is impossible to properly service your vehicle. It would be impossible to catalog each tool that you would need to perform each or every operation in this book. It would also be unwise for the amateur to rush out and buy an expensive set of tools on the theory that he may need one or more of them at some time.

The best approach is to proceed slowly, gathering together a good quality set of those tools that are used most frequently. Don't be misled by the low cost of bargain tools. It is far better to spend a little more for better quality. Forged wrenches, 10 or 12 point sockets and fine tooth ratchets are by far preferable to their less ex-

This basic collection of hand tools will handle most service needs

pensive counterparts. As any good mechanic can tell you, there are few worse experiences than trying to work on a car with bad tools. Your monetary savings will be far outweighed by frustration and mangled knuckles.

Certain tools, plus a basic ability to handle tools, are required to get started. A basic mechanic's tool set, a torque wrench, and, for 1976 and later models, a Torx® bits set. Torx® bits are hexlobular drivers which fit both inside and outside on special Torx® head fasteners used in various places on GM and other vehicles.

Begin accumulating those tools that are used most frequently; those associated with routine maintenance and tune-up.

In addition to the normal assortment of screwdrivers and pliers you should have the following tools for routine maintenance jobs (your car, depending on the model year, uses both SAE and metric fasteners):

1. SAE/Metric wrenches, sockets and combination open end/box end wrenches in sizes from ⅛" (3mm) to ¾" (19mm); and a spark plug socket (¹³⁄₁₆")

If possible, buy various length socket drive extensions. One break in this department is that the metric sockets available in the U.S. will all fit the ratchet handles and extensions you may already have (¼", ⅜", and ½" drive).

2. Jackstands for support
3. Oil filter wrench
4. Oil filter spout for pouring oil
5. Grease gun for chassis lubrication
6. Hydrometer for checking the battery
7. A container for draining oil
8. Many rags for wiping up the inevitable mess.

In addition to the above items there are several others that are not absolutely necessary, but handy to have around. These include an absorbent powder to soak up spilled oil, a transmission funnel and the usual supply of lubricants, antifreeze and fluids, although these can be purchased as needed. This is a basic list for routine maintenance, but only your personal needs and desires can accurately determine your list of necessary tools.

The second list of tools is for tune-ups. While the tools involved here are slightly more sophisticated, they need not be outrageously expensive. There are several inexpensive tach/dwell meters on the market that are every bit as good for the average mechanic as a $100.00 professional model. Just be sure that it goes to at least 1,200-1,500 rpm on the tach scale and that it works on 4, 6 and 8 cylinder engines. A basic list of tune-up equipment could include:

1. Tach/dwell meter
2. Spark plug wrench
3. Timing light (a DC light that works from

the car's battery is best, although an AC light that plugs into 110V house current will suffice at some sacrifice in brightness)

4. Wire spark plug gauge/adjusting tools
5. Set of feeler blades.

Here again, be guided by your own needs. A feeler blade will set the point gap as easily as dwell meter will read dwell, but slightly less accurately. And since you will need a tachometer anyway ... well, make your own decision.

In addition to these basic tools, there are several other tools and gauges you may find useful. These include:

1. A compression gauge. The screw-in type takes more time to use, but reduces the possibility of a faulty reading due to escaping pressure
2. A manifold vacuum gauge
3. A test light
4. An induction meter. This is used for determining whether or not there is current in a wire. These are handy for use in checking if a wire is broken somewhere in a wiring harness.

As a final note, you will probably find a torque wrench necessary for all but the most basic work. The beam type models are perfectly adequate, although the newer click (breakaway) type are more precise, and you don't have to crane your neck to see a torque reading in awkward situations. The breakaway torque wrenches are more expensive and should be recalibrated periodically.

Torque specification for each fastener will be given in the procedure in any case that a specific torque value is required. If no torque specifications are given, use the following values as a guide, based upon fastener size:

Bolts marked 6T
6mm bolt/nut – 5-7 ft.lb.
8mm bolt/nut – 12-17 ft.lb.
10mm bolt/nut – 23-34 ft.lb.
12mm bolt/nut – 41-59 ft.lb.
14mm bolt/nut – 56-76 ft.lb.
Bolts marked 8T
6mm bolt/nut – 6-9 ft.lb.
8mm bolt/nut – 13-20 ft.lb.
10mm bolt/nut – 27-40 ft.lb.
12mm bolt/nut – 46-69 ft.lb.
14mm bolt/nut – 75-101 ft.lb.

Special Tools

Normally, the use of special factory tools is avoided for repair procedures, since these are not readily available for the do-it-yourself mechanic. When it is possible to perform the job with more commonly available tools, this fact will be pointed out, but, occasionally, a special tool was designed to perform a specific function and should be used. Before substituting another tool, you should be convinced that neither your safety nor the safe operation or performance of the vehicle will be compromised.

Some special tools are available commercially from major tool manufacturers. Others can be purchased through your car dealer.

SERVICING YOUR VEHICLE SAFELY

It is virtually impossible to anticipate all of the hazards involved with automotive maintenance and service, but care and common sense will prevent most accidents.

The rules of safety for mechanics range from "don't smoke around gasoline," to "use the proper tool for the job." The trick to avoiding injuries is to develop safe work habits and take every possible precaution. It is also vitally important to work at a sensible pace and to think ahead so that you can anticipate what is going to happen.

Dos

• Do keep a fire extinguisher and first aid kit within easy reach.

• Do wear safety glasses or goggles when cutting, drilling or prying, even if you have 20-20 vision. If you wear glasses for the sake of vision, they should be made of hardened glass that can also serve as safety glasses, or wear safety goggles over your regular glasses.

• Do shield your eyes whenever you work around the battery. Batteries contain sulphuric acid; in case of contact with the eyes or skin, flush the area with water or a mixture of water and baking soda and get medical attention immediately.

• Do use safety stands for any undercar service. Jacks are for raising vehicles; safety stands are for making sure the vehicle stays raised until you want it to come down. Whenever the vehicle is raised, block the wheels remaining on the ground and set the parking brake.

• Do use adequate ventilation when working with any chemicals. Like carbon monoxide, the asbestos dust resulting from brake lining wear can be poisonous in sufficient quantities.

• Do disconnect the negative battery cable when working on the electrical system. The primary ignition system can contain up to 40,000 volts.

• Do follow manufacturer's directions whenever working with potentially hazardous materials. Both brake fluid and antifreeze are poisonous if taken internally.

• Do properly maintain your tools. Loose hammerheads, mushroomed punches and chisels, frayed or poorly grounded electrical cords, excessively worn screwdrivers, spread wrenches (open end), cracked sockets, slipping ratchets, or faulty droplight sockets can cause accidents.

• Do use the proper size and type of tool for the job being done.

• Do when possible, pull on a wrench handle rather than push on it, and adjust your stance to prevent a fall.

• Do be sure that adjustable wrenches are tightly adjusted on the nut or bolt and pulled so that the face is on the side of the fixed jaw.

• Do select a wrench or socket that fits the nut or bolt. The wrench or socket should sit straight, not cocked.

• Do strike squarely with a hammer—avoid glancing blows.

• Do set the parking brake and block the drive wheels if the work requires that the engine be running.

Don'ts

• Don't run an engine in a garage or anywhere else without proper ventilation—EVER! Carbon monoxide is poisonous; it takes a long time to leave the human body and you can build up a deadly supply of it in your system by simply breathing in a little every day. You may not realize you are slowly poisoning yourself. Always use power vents, windows, fans or open the garage doors.

• Don't work around moving parts while wearing a necktie or other loose clothing. Short sleeves are much safer than long, loose sleeves and hard-toed shoes with neoprene soles protect your toes and give a better grip on slippery surfaces. Jewelry such as watches, fancy belt buckles, beads or body adornment of any kind is not safe working around a car. Long hair should be hidden under a hat or cap.

• Don't use pockets for toolboxes. A fall or bump can drive a screwdriver deep into you body. Even a wiping cloth hanging from the back pocket can wrap around a spinning shaft or fan.

• Don't smoke when working around gasoline, cleaning solvent or other flammable material.

• Don't smoke when working around the battery. When the battery is being charged, it gives off explosive hydrogen gas.

• Don't use gasoline to wash your hands; there are excellent soaps available. Gasoline may contain lead, and lead can enter the body through a cut, accumulating in the body until you are very ill. Gasoline also removes all the natural oils from the skin so that bone-dry hands will suck up oil and grease.

• Don't service the air conditioning system unless you are equipped with the necessary tools and training. The refrigerant, R-12, is ex-

Always use support stands when working under your car

tremely cold and when exposed to the air, will instantly freeze any surface it comes in contact with, including your eyes. Although the refrigerant is normally non-toxic, R-12 becomes a deadly poisonous gas in the presence of an open flame. One good whiff of the vapors from burning refrigerant can be fatal.

• Don't use screwdrivers for anything other than driving screws! A screwdriver used as a prying tool can snap when you least expect it, causing injuries. At the very least, you'll ruin a good screwdriver.

• Don't use a bumper jack (that little ratchet, scissors, or pantograph jack supplied with the car) for anything other than changing a flat! These jacks are only intended for emergency use out on the road; they are NOT designed as a maintenance tool. If you are serious about maintaining your car yourself, invest in a hydraulic floor jack of at least 1½ ton capacity, and at least two sturdy jackstands.

SERIAL NUMBER IDENTIFICATION

Vehicle Identification Number (VIN)

It is important for servicing and ordering parts to be certain of the vehicle and engine

Thirteen Digit Vehicle Identification Number (VIN)

Model Year Code		Engine Code					
Code	Year	Code	Displacement Cu. in.	Liters	Cyl.	Fuel Delivery ③	Eng. Mfg.
5	1975	C	231	3.8	6	2	Buick
		H	350	5.7	8	2	Buick
		J	350	5.7	8	4	Buick
6	1976	C	231	3.8	6	2	Buick
		H	350	5.7	8	2	Buick
		J	350	5.7	8	4	Buick
7	1977	C	231	3.8	6	2	Buick
		H	350	5.7	8	2	Buick
		J	350	5.7	8	4	Buick
		L	350	5.7	8	4	Chev.
		R	350	5.7	8	4	Olds.
		K	403	6.6	8	4	Olds.
8	1978	C	196	3.2	6	2	Buick
		A	231	3.8	6	2	Buick
		G	231 ①	3.8	6	2	Buick
		3	231 ①	3.8	6	4	Buick
		H	305	5.0	8	2	Chev.
		U	305	5.0	8	4	Chev.
		L	350	5.7	8	4	Chev.
9	1979	C	196	3.2	6	2	Buick
		A	231	3.8	6	2	Buick
		2	231	3.8	6	2	Buick
		3	231 ①	3.8	6	4	Buick
		Y	301	4.9	8	2	Pontiac
		W	301	4.9	8	4	Pontiac
		H	305	5.0	8	4	Chev.
		L	350	5.7	8	4	Chev.
A	1980	A	231	3.8	6	2	Buick
		3	231 ①	3.8	6	4	Buick
		S	265	4.3	8	2	Pontiac
		W	301	4.9	8	4	Pontiac
		H	305	5.0	8	4	Chev.

The thirteen digit Vehicle Identification Number can be used to determine engine application and model year. The 6th digit indicates the model year, and the 5th digit identifies the factory-installed engine.

① Turbocharged engine ② Diesel engine—fuel-injected ③ 2—2 barrel carburetor; 4—4 barrel carburetor

identification. The VIN (vehicle identification number) is a 13 digit number (1987-80) or 17 digit number (1981 and later) visible through the windshield on the driver's side of the dash and contains the vehicle and engine identification codes.

Thirteen digit Vehicle Identification Number (VIN)

Vehicle identification number (VIN) located on the driver's side of the dash

Seventeen digit Vehicle Identification Number (VIN)

Seventeen Digit Vehicle Identification Number (VIN)

Model Year Code		Engine Code					
Code	Year	Code	Displacement Cu. In.	Liters	Cyl.	Fuel Delivery ③	Eng. Mfg.
B	1981	A	231	3.8	6	2	Buick
		3	231 ①	3.8	6	4	Buick
		S	265	4.3	8	2	Pontiac
		J	267	4.4	8	2	Chev.
		W	301	4.9	8	4	Pontiac
		H	305	5.0	8	4	Chev.
		X	350	5.7	8	4	Buick
C	1982	A	231	3.8	6	2	Buick
		3	231 ①	3.8	6	4	Buick
		4	252	4.1	6	4	Buick
		V	263	4.3	6	②	Olds.
		N	350	5.7	8	②	Olds.
D	1983	A	231	3.8	6	2	Buick
		3	231 ①	3.8	6	4	Buick
		4	252	4.1	6	4	Buick
		V	263	4.3	6	②	Olds.
		N	350	5.7	8	②	Olds.
E	1984	A	231	3.8	6	2	Buick
		9	231 ①	3.8	6	SFI	Buick
		4	252	4.1	6	4	Buick
		V	263	4.3	6	②	Olds.
F	1985	A	231	3.8	6	2	Buick
		9	231 ①	3.8	6	SFI	Buick
		V	263	4.3	6	②	Olds.
G	1986	A	231	3.8	6	2	Buick
		7	231	3.8	6	SFI	Buick
		Y	307	5.0	8	4	Olds.
H	1987	A	231	3.8	6	2	Buick
		7	231	3.8	6	SFI	Buick
		Y	307	5.0	8	4	Olds.

The seventeen digit Vehicle Identification Number can be used to determine engine application and model year. The 10th digit indicates the model year, and the 8th digit identifies the factory-installed engine.
① Turbocharged engine ② Diesel engine—fuel-injected ③ 2—2 bbl. carburetor; 4—4 bbl. carburetor.
SFI—Sequential port fuel injected

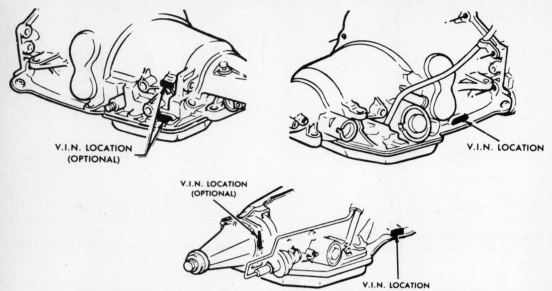

Various optional serial number locations on the Turbo Hydra-Matic transmissions

Engine Serial Number Location

On all V8 engines and the V6 231 engine through 1979, the serial number is found on a pad at the front/right or left hand side of the cylinder block, just below the cylinder head. On the 1980 and later V6 231 and 252 engines, and the 1984 and later V6 260 diesel engine, the serial number is found on the left/ rear of the block.

Transmission Serial Number Location

A transmission serial number is stamped on a plate which is attached to either the right or left side of the transmission case on all automatic transmissions. On manual transmissions, the serial number is stamped on a pad on the top/ right side of the case.

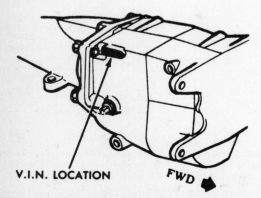

V.I.N. LOCATION **FWD** ➤

Manual transmission serial number location

Rear Axle

The code for the rear axle is stamped on the right side of the axle housing tube.

ROUTINE MAINTENANCE

Air Cleaner

The air cleaner has a dual purpose. It not only filters the air going to the carburetor, but it also acts as a flame arrester if the engine should backfire through the carburetor. If an engine maintenance procedure requires the temporary removal of the air cleaner, remove it; otherwise, never run the engine without it. Operating a car without its air cleaner results in some throaty sounds from the carburetor giving the impression of increased power but will only cause trouble. Unfiltered air to the carburetor will eventually result in a dirty, inefficient carburetor and engine. A dirty carburetor increases the chances of carburetor backfire and, without the protection of an air cleaner, fire becomes a probable danger.

The air cleaner assembly consists of the air cleaner itself, which is the large metal container that fits over the carburetor, the element contained within, and the flame arrester located in the base of the air cleaner. The air filter should be inspected at its first 12,000 miles, rechecked every 6,000 miles thereafter, and replaced at 30,000 mile intervals. Inspections and replacements should be more frequent if the car is operated in a dirty, dusty environment. When inspecting the element, look for dust leaks, holes

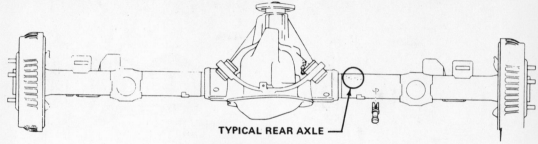

TYPICAL REAR AXLE

Rear axle code location

or overly dirty appearance. If the element is excessively dirty, it may cause a reduction in clean air intake. If air has trouble getting through a dirty element, the carburetor fuel mixture will become richer (more gas, less air), the idle will be rougher, and the exhaust smoke will be noticeably black. The catalytic converter may also overheat, if the degree of clogging exceeds the ability of the oxygen sensor and electronic fuel control systems to compensate.

To check the effectiveness of your paper element, remove the air cleaner assembly and, if the idle speed increases, then the element is re-

stricting airflow and should be replaced. The flame arrester, located at the base of the air cleaner, should be cleaned in solvent (kerosene) once every 12,000 miles.

Fuel Filter

REMOVAL AND INSTALLATION

Carbureted Gasoline Engines

The fuel filter is located behind the fuel inlet connection on the carburetor. 1976 and later fuel filters incorporate a check valve and are not interchangeable with earlier years. Replace

Unscrew the wing nut and remove the cover

Check the small crankcase breather

Remove and discard the old filter

Using a clean rag or paper towel, wipe out the inside of the air cleaner

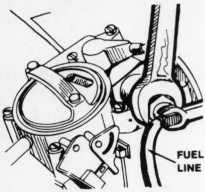

FUEL LINE

The fuel filter is located behind the large fuel line inlet nut on the carburetor

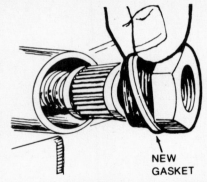

NEW GASKET

Install the new filter and spring. Certain early models use a bronze filter element, but most are made of paper

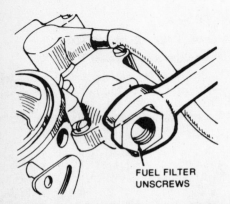

FUEL FILTER UNSCREWS

Remove the retaining nut and the filter will pop out under spring pressure

the fuel filter every 15,000 miles, or sooner if engine flooding is a problem.

1. Using an open-end wrench (preferably a line or flare nut wrench), disconnect the fuel line connection from the larger fuel filter nut. You will have to hold the other nut with a wrench to keep it from turning. Most of the time these units are quite difficult to break loose. It is a good idea to first apply a lot of penetrating oil to the threads and then tap the nut very, very lightly with a hammer.

2. Once you have the fuel line disconnected from the carburetor, remove the larger nut from the carburetor with a box-end wrench or socket.

3. Remove the filter element and spring from the carburetor.

4. Check the element for dirt blockage by blowing through the fuel inlet end. If the element is good, air should pass through easily.

5. Once you have checked and/or replaced the filter, reinstall the carburetor nut and the fuel line. Be careful not to strip the threads on the fuel line nut.

Fuel Injected Gasoline Engines

WARNING: *Do not disconnect the fuel lines at the fuel filter until the system has been depressurized. Failure to heed this warning could produce a dangerous, high pressure spray of fuel that is highly combustible. Keep all sources of ignition, including smoking, away from the area, as fuel can drain from open lines or the filter even after the system is depressurized.*

The fuel system retains full operating pressure after the engine is shut off due to the action of check valves. Fuel must be cleared from the system to avoid a high pressure spray. First, disconnect the power supply to the fuel pump as follows:

• Throttle Body Injection Units--Remove the fuse labeled "Fuel Pump" from the fuse block in the passenger compartment.

• Multiport Fuel Injection Units--Disconnect the fuel tank electrical harness connector.

Now, start the engine and allow it to run until it stalls. Then, engage the starter again for at least three seconds to make sure all fuel has been removed from the system. It must be possible to crank the engine for three seconds without it firing.

These systems use inline filters located on one of the frame rails or on the rear crossmember. Using a backup wrench, loosen the filter attaching nut at either end. Once the lines are disconnected, pull the filter out of the bracket. Be careful to collect fuel that may drain from the filter or lines in a metal container. Supply new O-rings with the new filter. Reconnect the lines and tighten the connections with a backup wrench, torquing the fittings to 22 ft.lb.

Diesel Engines

On diesel engines the fuel filter is located at the back of the engine above the intake manifold between the mechanical fuel pump and the

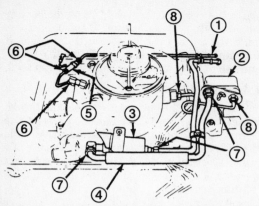

Replacing the diesel fuel filter (1984 350 diesels)

injection pump. The filter should be replaced at least every 30,000 miles. You'll need crow'sfoot wrenches to loosen the connections. Disconnect the fuel lines from the filter, replace with a new filter and reconnect the fuel lines. Torque the inlet connection to 19 ft.lb. and the outlet connection to 11 ft.lb.

Because of air that got into the system while you were changing the filter, the engine will take much longer to start than it does normally. If the engine is warm (above about 105°F. on '85 models and 125°F. on the others), you should use a jumper wire to bypass the Housing Pressure Cold Advance to reduce the length of time the starting process will take.

To bypass the HPCA, first locate the two-lead connector at the engine temperature switch. Follow the wiring from the injection pump to the Thermal Vacuum Switch on the manifold or near a cylinder head bolt. Disconnect the two-prong connector at the temperature switch and then jumper the connector with a jumper wire.

Crank the engine pausing for 30 seconds after each cranking period of 20 seconds. When the engine starts, disconnect the jumper and reconnect the electrical connector to the TVS.

Positive Crankcase Ventilation (PCV) Valve

LOCATION

V6 Engines

The PCV valve is located in the right hand valve cover on V6 engines through 1980. On 1981 and later engines, it is located in the rear of the intake manifold.

V8 Engines

The PCV valve is located in one of the valve covers depending on the engine. Replace the PCV valve every 30,000 miles. The PCV filter,

located in the air cleaner, is replaced when the air cleaner element is replaced.

REMOVAL AND INSTALLATION

Pull the PCV and hose straight out of the valve cover or manifold. Use a pair of pliers to slide the hose clamp back down the hose and off the valve connector. Then, twist the valve gently to break it loose from the hose and pull it out. Inspect the hose and valve cover grommet and replace them if they are hard and brittle or cracked. Clean the hose with solvent if it is clogged. When installing the new valve, make sure it seats fully in the hose, that the clamp is situated on the narrow portion of the hose connector, and that the valve seats fully in the valve cover grommet.

For further details on PCV valve operation see Chapter 4.

Evaporative Canister

The evaporative canister is part of a system, standard since 1970, which prevents the release of unburned fuel vapors into the atmosphere.

SERVICING

Check the connecting lines of the system for kinks or other damage and deterioration periodically. Lines should only be replaced with quality fuel line or special hose marked **evap**. On models up to 1985, every 24 months/30,000 miles the filter in the bottom of the carbon canister, which is located in the engine compartment, should be removed and replaced. On '86-'87 models, replacement is not necessary unless the filter becomes visibly clogged. Inspect and replace it, on these models, if the system appears to be malfunctioning, for example by leaking gasoline from the bottom of the canister.

Battery

Loose, dirty, or corroded battery terminals are a major cause of "no-start." Every 3 months or so, remove the battery terminals and clean them, giving them a light coating of petroleum jelly when you are finished. This will help to retard corrosion.

Check the battery cables for signs of wear or chafing and replace any cable or terminal that looks marginal. Battery terminals can be easily cleaned and inexpensive terminal cleaning tools are an excellent investment that will pay for themselves many times over. They can usually be purchased from any well-equipped auto store or parts department. Side terminal batteries require a different tool to clean the threads in the battery case. The accumulated white powder and corrosion can be cleaned from the top of the battery with an old toothbrush and a solution of baking soda and water.

Unless you have a maintenance-free battery, check the electrolyte level (see Battery under Fluid Level Checks in this chapter) and check the specific gravity of each cell. Be sure that the vent holes in each cell cap are not blocked by grease or dirt. The vent holes allow hydrogen gas, formed by the chemical reaction in the battery, to escape safely.

REPLACEMENT BATTERIES

The cold power rating of a battery measures battery starting performance and provides an approximate relationship between battery size and engine size. The cold power rating of a replacement battery should match or exceed your engine size in cubic inches.

FLUID LEVEL (EXCEPT MAINTENANCE FREE BATTERIES)

Check the battery electrolyte level at least once a month, or more often in hot weather or during periods of extended truck operation. The level can be checked through the case on translucent polypropylene batteries; the cell caps must be removed on other models. The electrolyte level in each cell should be kept filled to the split ring inside, or the line marked on the outside of the case.

If the level is low, add only distilled water, or colorless, odorless drinking water, through the opening until the level is correct. Each cell is completely separate from the others, so each must be checked and filled individually.

If water is added in freezing weather, the truck should be driven several miles to allow the water to mix with the electrolyte. Otherwise, the battery could freeze.

SPECIFIC GRAVITY (EXCEPT MAINTENANCE FREE BATTERIES)

At least once a year, check the specific gravity of the battery. It should be between 1.20 in.Hg and 1.26 in.Hg at room temperature.

The specific gravity can be check with the use of an hydrometer, an inexpensive instrument available from many sources, including auto parts stores. The hydrometer has a squeeze bulb at one end and a nozzle at the other. Battery electrolyte is sucked into the hydrometer until the float is lifted from its seat. The specific gravity is then read by noting the position of the float. Generally, if after charging, the specific gravity between any two cells varies more than 50 points (0.50), the battery is bad and should be replaced.

It is not possible to check the specific gravity in this manner on sealed (maintenance free) batteries. Instead, the indicator built into the top of the case must be relied on to display any signs of battery deterioration. If the indicator is dark, the battery can be assumed to be OK. If the indicator is light, the specific gravity is low, and the battery should be charged or replaced.

CABLES AND CLAMPS

Once a year, the battery terminals and the cable clamps should be cleaned. Loosen the clamps and remove the cables, negative cable first. On batteries with posts on top, the use of a puller specially made for the purpose is recommended. These are inexpensive, and available in auto parts stores. Side terminal battery cables are secured with a bolt.

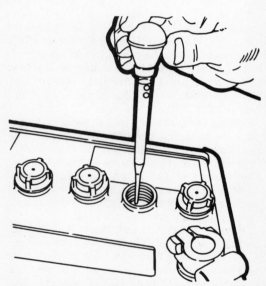

Specific gravity can be checked with an hydrometer

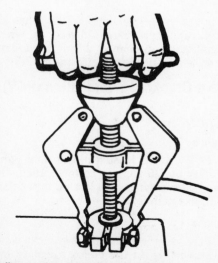

Pullers make clamp removal easier

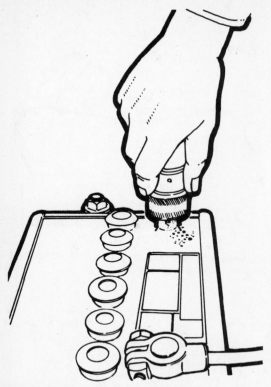

Clean the post with a wire brush, or a terminal cleaner made for the purpose (shown)

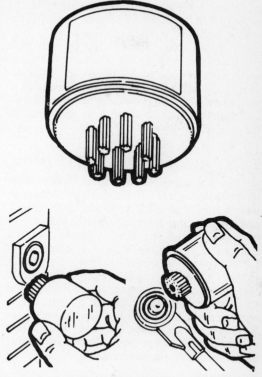

Special tools are also available for cleaning the posts and clamps on side terminal batteries

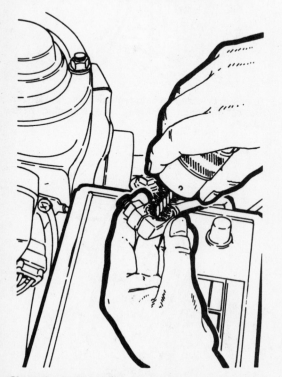

Clean the inside of the clamps with a wire brush or the special tool shown

Clean the cable clamps and the battery terminal with a wire brush, until all corrosion, grease, etc., is removed and the metal is shiny. It is especially important to clean the inside of the clamp thoroughly, since a small deposit of foreign material or oxidation there will prevent a sound electrical connection and inhibit either starting or charging. Special tools are available for cleaning these parts, one type for conventional batteries and another type for side terminal batteries.

Before installing the cables, loosen the battery holddown clamp or strap, remove the battery and check the battery tray. Clear it of any debris, and check it for soundness. Rust should be wire brushed away, and the metal given a coat of anti-rust paint. Replace the battery and tighten the holddown clamp or strap securely, but be careful not to overtighten, which will crack the battery case.

After the clamps and terminals are clean, re-install the cables, negative cable last; do not hammer on the clamps to install. Tighten the clamps securely, but do not distort them. Give the clamps and terminals a thin external coat of grease after installation, to retard corrosion.

Check the cables at the same time that the terminals are cleaned. If the cable insulation is cracked or broken, or if the ends are frayed, the cable should be replaced with a new cable of the same length and gauge.

CAUTION: *Keep flame or sparks away from the battery; it gives off explosive hydrogen gas. Battery electrolyte contains sulphuric acid. If you should splash any on your skin or in your eyes, flush the affected area with plenty of clear water. If it lands in your eyes, get medical help immediately.*

Early Fuel Evaporation (EFE) System

This is a more effective form of heat riser which is vacuum actuated. It is used on all carbureted models built in 1975 and later years. It heats incoming mixture during the engine warm-up process, utilizing a ribbed heat exchanger of thin metal that is located on the floor of the intake manifold. This preheating of mixture allows the choke to open more rapidly, and thus helps reduce emissions. Problems in this system might be indicated by poor engine operation during warm-up. Operation of the EFE system should be checked initially at 6 months/7500 miles and, thereafter, at 18 month/22,500 mile intervals.

SERVICING

To check, move the valve through its full stroke by hand, making sure that the linkage does not bind and is properly connected. If the valve sticks, free it with a solvent. Also check that all vacuum hoses are properly connected and free of cracks or breaks. Replace hoses or broken or bent linkage parts as necessary.

Belts

INSPECTION

Check the drive belts every 7,500 miles or six months for evidence of wear such as cracking, fraying, and incorrect tension. Determine tension as described below.

ADJUSTING

Standard Belts

Determine belt tension at a point halfway between the pulleys by pressing on the belt with moderate thumb pressure. If the distance between the pulleys (measured from the center of each pulley) is 13-16", the belt should deflect ½" at the halfway point or ¼" if the distance is 7-10". If the deflection is found to be too much or too little, loosen the mounting bolts and make the adjustments. Before you attempt to adjust any of your engine's belts, you should take an old rag soaked in solvent and clean the mounting bolts of any road grime which has accumulated there. On some of the harder-to-reach

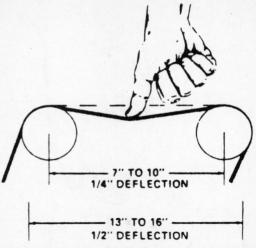

7" TO 10"
1/4" DEFLECTION

13" TO 16"
1/2" DEFLECTION

A gauge is recommended, but you can check belt tension with thumb pressure

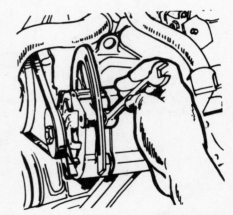

To adjust belt tension or to replace belts, first loosen the component's mounting and adjusting bolts slightly

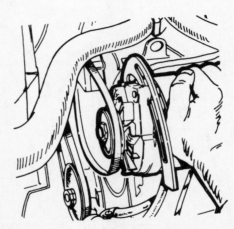

Push the component toward the engine and slip off the belt

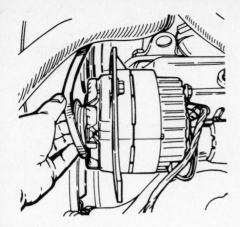

Slip the new belt over the pulley

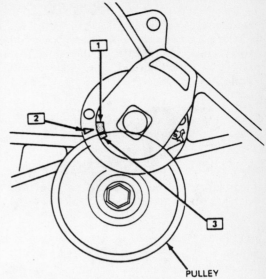

PULLEY

1. Minimum tension range
2. Pointer
3. Maximum tension range

Automatic belt tensioner used with serpentine belts

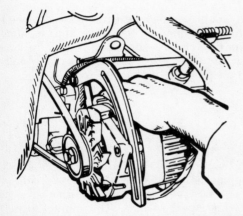

Pull outward on the component and tighten the mounting bolts

bolts, an application of penetrating oil will make them easier to loosen. When you're adjusting belts, especially on late model V8's with air conditioning and power steering, this is especially helpful in getting to those hard-to-reach bolts.

NOTE: *When adjusting the air pump belt, if you are using a pry bar, make sure that you press against the cast iron end cover and not against the aluminum housing. Excessive force on the housing will damage it.*

Serpentine Belt (3.8 L V6)

A single, serpentine belt is used to drive all the engine accessories. The accessories are bolted to the engine without the usual slotted adjusting brackets. A spring loaded tensioner keeps belt tension constant. It is normal for the belt to squeak slightly for an instant when stopping or starting the engine. However, if the belt is slipping on a regular basis, you should check to see if excessive belt wear or a lack of spring force in the tensioner is causing the problem.

A special tool, Belt Tensioner BT-7825 or J-23600B is used to check belt tension. Even if you do not decide to buy this special tool, you can check to see if the belt is slipping because it is excessively worn (a worn and therefore stretched belt runs at reduced tension with this type tensioner).

To determine whether or not the belt is excessively stretched look at the alignment of the pointer in relation to the range mark on the front of the tensioner. The mark should point at an area of the tensioner well within the range mark. If it aligns with the area of the tensioner above the mark, the belt should be replaced.

To check the tension of the belt (tensioner performance) with the special tool, proceed as follows:

1. Turn all the accessories off and then start the engine and idle it until it is warmed up. Then, shut it off and read the belt tension with the special tool. Position the tool half way between the generator and A/C compressor on air conditioned cars and halfway between the power steering pump and the crankshaft pulley on non-air conditioned cars. The tension should be 67 lbs.

2. Now, start the engine (with the accessories still off) and run it for 15 seconds to stabilize all the systems. Turn the engine off. Then, with an 18mm box wrench, exert force so as to attempt to turn the tensioner pulley bolt clockwise. Release the force and then immediately

HOW TO SPOT WORN V-BELTS

V-Belts are vital to efficient engine operation—they drive the fan, water pump and other accessories. They require little maintenance (occasional tightening) but they will not last forever. Slipping or failure of the V-belt will lead to overheating. If your V-belt looks like any of these, it should be replaced.

This belt has deep cracks, which cause it to flex. Too much flexing leads to heat build-up and premature failure. These cracks can be caused by using the belt on a pulley that is too small. Notched belts are available for small diameter pulleys.

Cracking or weathering

Oil and grease on a belt can cause the belt's rubber compounds to soften and separate from the reinforcing cords that hold the belt together. The belt will first slip, then finally fail altogether.

Softening (grease and oil)

Glazing is caused by a belt that is slipping. A slipping belt can cause a run-down battery, erratic power steering, overheating or poor accessory performance. The more the belt slips, the more glazing will be built up on the surface of the belt. The more the belt is glazed, the more it will slip. If the glazing is light, tighten the belt.

Glazing

The cover of this belt is worn off and is peeling away. The reinforcing cords will begin to wear and the belt will shortly break. When the belt cover wears in spots or has a rough jagged appearance, check the pulley grooves for roughness.

Worn cover

This belt is on the verge of breaking and leaving you stranded. The layers of the belt are separating and the reinforcing cords are exposed. It's just a matter of time before it breaks completely.

Separation

read the tension and remember or record it (make sure you don't disturb the tensioner's position).

3. Now, apply a counterclockwise force to the tensioner pulley bolt so as to raise the pulley to the "install" position. Lower the pulley in a gradual, controlled manner to its natural position. Remove the wrench. Now, read the tension again and remember or record it.

4. Average the three readings (add them together and divide by 3). Then, note the position of the pointer in relation to the range mark on the front of the tensioner. If the mark is in the proper area of the tensioner, the belt is okay; if not, replace the belt. Compare the reading of the belt tension to the specification of 67 lbs. If the belt is within specified length limits and the tension reading is below the specification, replace the tensioner.

REMOVAL AND INSTALLATION

To remove a drive belt, simply loosen the accessory being driven and move it on its pivot point to free the belt. Then, remove the belt. If an idler pulley is used, it is often necessary, only, to loosen the idler pulley to provide enough slack the remove the belt.

It is important to note, however, that on engines with many driven accessories, several or all of the belts may have to be removed to get at the one to be replaced.

Hoses

REMOVAL AND INSTALLATION

1. Remove the radiator cap.
2. Drain the coolant from the radiator by opening the radiator petcock, if so equipped, or by disconnecting the lower radiator hose. If your car is equipped with a petcock it might be a good idea to squirt a little penetrating oil on it first.
CAUTION: *When draining the coolant, keep in mind that cats and dogs are attracted by the ethylene glycol antifreeze, and are quite likely to drink any that is left in an uncovered container or in puddles on the ground. This will prove fatal in sufficient quantity. Always drain the coolant into a sealable container. Coolant should be reused unless it is contaminated or several years old.*
3. To replace the bottom hose drain all the coolant from the radiator but if only the top hose is to be replaced drain just enough fluid to bring the level of the top hose. If the fluid is over a year old discard it.
4. Most hoses are attached with a screw type hose clamps. If the old clamps are badly rusted or damaged in any way it is always best to replace with new ones.

5. When installing the new hose slide the clamps over each end of the hose then slide the hose over the hose connections. Position each clamp about ¼" from the end of the hose and tighten.
CAUTION: *Do not over tighten at the radiator connections as it is very easy to crush the metal.*
6. Close the petcock and refill with the old coolant if it is less than a year old or with a new mixture of 50/50, coolant/water.
7. Start the engine and idle it for 15 minutes with the radiator cap off and check for leaks. Add coolant if necessary and install the radiator cap.

Cooling System

CAUTION: *Never remove the radiator cap under any conditions while the engine is running! Failure to follow these instructions could result in damage to the cooling system or engine and/or personal injury. To avoid having scalding hot coolant or steam blow out of the radiator, use extreme care when removing the radiator cap from a hot radiator. Wait until the engine has cooled, then wrap a thick cloth around the radiator cap and turn it slowly to the first stop. Step back while the pressure is released from the cooling system. When you are sure the pressure has been released, press down on the radiator cap (still have the cloth in position) turn and remove the radiator cap.*

At least once every 2 years, the engine cooling system should be inspected, flushed, and refilled with fresh coolant. If the coolant is left in the system too long, it loses its ability to prevent rust and corrosion. If the coolant has too much water, it won't protect against freezing.

The pressure cap should be looked at for signs of age or deterioration. Fan belt and other drive belts should be inspected and adjusted to the proper tension. (See checking belt tension).

Hose clamps should be tightened, and soft or cracked hoses replaced. Damp spots, or accumulations of rust or dye near hoses, water pump or other areas, indicate possible leakage, which must be corrected before filling the system with fresh coolant.

CHECK THE RADIATOR CAP

While you are checking the coolant level, check the radiator cap for a worn or cracked gasket. It the cap doesn't seal properly, fluid will be lost and the engine will overheat.

Worn caps should be replaced with a new one.

CLEAN RADIATOR OF DEBRIS

Periodically clean any debris — leaves, paper, insects, etc. — from the radiator fins. Pick the

HOW TO SPOT BAD HOSES

Both the upper and lower radiator hoses are called upon to perform difficult jobs in an inhospitable environment. They are subject to nearly 18 psi at under hood temperatures often over 280°F., and must circulate nearly 7500 gallons of coolant an hour—3 good reasons to have good hoses.

A good test for any hose is to feel it for soft or spongy spots. Frequently these will appear as swollen areas of the hose. The most likely cause is oil soaking. This hose could burst at any time, when hot or under pressure.

Swollen hose

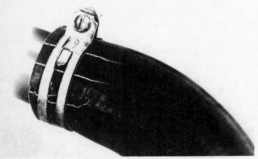

Cracked hoses can usually be seen but feel the hoses to be sure they have not hardened; a prime cause of cracking. This hose has cracked down to the reinforcing cords and could split at any of the cracks.

Cracked hose

Weakened clamps frequently are the cause of hose and cooling system failure. The connection between the pipe and hose has deteriorated enough to allow coolant to escape when the engine is hot.

Frayed hose end (due to weak clamp)

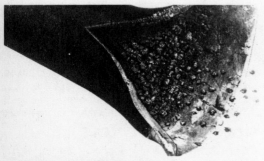

Debris, rust and scale in the cooling system can cause the inside of a hose to weaken. This can usually be felt on the outside of the hose as soft or thinner areas.

Debris in cooling system

large pieces off by hand. The smaller pieces can be washed away with water pressure from a hose.

Carefully straighten any bent radiator fins with a pair of needle nose pliers. Be careful — the fins are very soft. Don't wiggle the fins back and forth too much. Straighten them once and try not to move them again.

DRAIN AND REFILL THE COOLING SYSTEM

Completely draining and refilling the cooling system every two years at least will remove accumulated rust, scale and other deposits. Coolant in late model trucks is a 50/50 mixture of ethylene glycol and water for year round use. Use a good quality antifreeze with water pump lubricants, rust inhibitors and other corrosion inhibitors along with acid neutralizers.

1. Drain the existing antifreeze and coolant. Open the radiator and engine drain petcocks, or disconnect the bottom radiator hose, at the radiator outlet.

NOTE: *Before opening the radiator petcock, spray it with some penetrating lubricant.*

2. Close the petcock or reconnect the lower hose and fill the system with water.

3. Add a can of quality radiator flush.

4. Idle the engine until the upper radiator hose gets hot.

5. Drain the system again.

6. Repeat this process until the drained water is clear and free of scale.

7. Close all petcocks and connect all the hoses.

8. If equipped with a coolant recovery system, flush the reservoir with water and leave empty.

9. Determine the capacity of your coolant system (see capacities specifications). Add a 50/50 mix of quality antifreeze (ethylene glycol) and water to provide the desired protection.

10. Run the engine to operating temperature.

11. Stop the engine and check the coolant level.

12. Check the level of protection with an antifreeze tester, replace the cap and check for leaks.

Air Conditioning System
SAFETY WARNINGS

There are two particular hazards associated with air conditioning systems and they both relate to the refrigerant gas. First, the refrigerant is in liquid form in every area of the system. When exposed to air, it will instantly boil, freezing any surface it comes in contact with, including your eyes. The other hazard relates to fire. Although normally non-toxic, refrigerant gas becomes highly poisonous in the presence of an open flame. One good whiff of the vapor formed by burning refrigerant can be fatal. Keep all forms of fire (including cigarettes) well clear of the air conditioning system.

Any repair work to an air conditioning system is best left to a professional. Do not, under any circumstances, attempt to loosen or tighten any fittings or perform any work other than that outlined here.

SYSTEM INSPECTION
Checking for Oil Leaks

Refrigerant leaks show up as oily areas on the various components because the compresser oil is transported around the entire system along with the refrigerant. Look for oil spots on all the hoses and lines, and especially on the hose and tubing connections. If there are oily deposits, the system may have a leak, and you should have it checked by a qualified repairman.

NOTE: *A small area of oil on the front of the compressor is normal and no cause for alarm.*

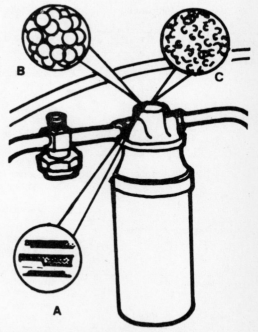

Oil streaks (A), constant bubbles (B) or faom (C) indicate there is not enough refrigerant in the system. Occasional bubbles during initial operation is normal. A clear sight glass indicates a proper charge of refrigerant or no refrigerant at all, which can be determined by the presence of cold air at the outlets in the car. If the glass is clouded with a milky white substance, have the receiver/drier checked professionally

Troubleshooting Basic Air Conditioning Problems

Problem	Cause	Solution
There's little or no air coming from the vents (and you're sure it's on)	• The A/C fuse is blown • Broken or loose wires or connections • The on/off switch is defective	• Check and/or replace fuse • Check and/or repair connections • Replace switch
The air coming from the vents is not cool enough	• Windows and air vent wings open • The compressor belt is slipping • Heater is on • Condenser is clogged with debris • Refrigerant has escaped through a leak in the system • Receiver/drier is plugged	• Close windows and vent wings • Tighten or replace compressor belt • Shut heater off • Clean the condenser • Check system • Service system
The air has an odor	• Vacuum system is disrupted • Odor producing substances on the evaporator case • Condensation has collected in the bottom of the evaporator housing	• Have the system checked/repaired • Clean the evaporator case • Clean the evaporator housing drains
System is noisy or vibrating	• Compressor belt or mountings loose • Air in the system	• Tighten or replace belt; tighten mounting bolts • Have the system serviced
Sight glass condition Constant bubbles, foam or oil streaks Clear sight glass, but no cold air Clear sight glass, but air is cold Clouded with milky fluid	 • Undercharged system • No refrigerant at all • System is OK • Receiver drier is leaking dessicant	 • Charge the system • Check and charge the system • Have system checked
Large difference in temperature of lines	• System undercharged	• Charge and leak test the system
Compressor noise	• Broken valves • Overcharged • Incorrect oil level • Piston slap • Broken rings • Drive belt pulley bolts are loose	• Replace the valve plate • Discharge, evacuate and install the correct charge • Isolate the compressor and check the oil level. Correct as necessary. • Replace the compressor • Replace the compressor • Tighten with the correct torque specification
Excessive vibration	• Incorrect belt tension • Clutch loose • Overcharged • Pulley is misaligned	• Adjust the belt tension • Tighten the clutch • Discharge, evacuate and install the correct charge • Align the pulley
Condensation dripping in the passenger compartment	• Drain hose plugged or improperly positioned • Insulation removed or improperly installed	• Clean the drain hose and check for proper installation • Replace the insulation on the expansion valve and hoses
Frozen evaporator coil	• Faulty thermostat • Thermostat capillary tube improperly installed • Thermostat not adjusted properly	• Replace the thermostat • Install the capillary tube correctly • Adjust the thermostat
Low side low—high side low	• System refrigerant is low • Expansion valve is restricted	• Evacuate, leak test and charge the system • Replace the expansion valve
Low side high—high side low	• Internal leak in the compressor—worn	• Remove the compressor cylinder head and inspect the compressor. Replace the valve plate assembly if necessary. If the compressor pistons, rings or

Troubleshooting Basic Air Conditioning Problems (cont.)

Problem	Cause	Solution
Low side high—high side low (cont.)		cylinders are excessively worn or scored replace the compressor
	• Cylinder head gasket is leaking	• Install a replacement cylinder head gasket
	• Expansion valve is defective	• Replace the expansion valve
	• Drive belt slipping	• Adjust the belt tension
Low side high—high side high	• Condenser fins obstructed	• Clean the condenser fins
	• Air in the system	• Evacuate, leak test and charge the system
	• Expansion valve is defective	• Replace the expansion valve
	• Loose or worn fan belts	• Adjust or replace the belts as necessary
Low side low—high side high	• Expansion valve is defective	• Replace the expansion valve
	• Restriction in the refrigerant hose	• Check the hose for kinks—replace if necessary
	• Restriction in the receiver/drier	• Replace the receiver/drier
	• Restriction in the condenser	• Replace the condenser
Low side and high side normal (inadequate cooling)	• Air in the system	• Evacuate, leak test and charge the system
	• Moisture in the system	• Evacuate, leak test and charge the system

Checking the Compressor Belt

Refer to the section in this chapter on Drive Belts.

Checking Refrigerant Level

There are two ways to check the refrigerant level, depending on how your model is equipped.

WITH SIGHT GLASS

The first order of business when checking the sight glass is to find it. It will either be in the head of the receiver/drier, or in one of the metal lines leading from the top of the receiver/drier. In some cases, it may be covered by a small rubber plug designed to keep it clean. Once you've found it, remove the cover, if necessary, wipe it clean and proceed as follows:

1. With the engine and the air conditioning system running, look for the flow of refrigerant through the sight glass. If the air conditioner is working properly, you'll be able to see a continuous flow of clear refrigerant through the sight glass, with perhaps an occasional bubble at very high temperatures.

2. Cycle the air conditioner on and off to make sure what you are seeing is a pure stream of liquid refrigerant. Since the refrigerant is clear, it is possible to mistake a completely discharged system for one that is fully charged. Turn the system off and watch the sight glass. If there is refrigerant in the system, you'll see bubbles during the off cycle. Also, the lines going into and out of the compressor will be at radically different temperatures (be careful about touching the line going forward to the condenser in front of the radiator, as it will be very hot). If the bubbles disappear just after you start the compressor, there are no bubbles when the system is running, and the air flow from the unit in the car is delivering cold air, everything is OK.

3. If you observe bubbles in the sight glass while the system is operating, the system is low on refrigerant. Have it checked by a professional.

4. Oil streaks in the sight glass are an indication of trouble because there is no liquid refrigerant in the system (otherwise, the oil would mix with the refrigerant and would be invisible). Most of the time, if you see oil in the sight glass, it will appear as a series of streaks, although occasionally it may be a solid stream of oil. In either case, it means that part of the charge has been lost.

WITHOUT SIGHT GLASS

On vehicles that are not equipped with sight glasses, it is necessary to feel the temperature difference in the inlet and outlet lines at the receiver/drier/accumulator to gauge the refrigerant level. Use the following procedure:

1. Locate the accumulator. It will generally be near the evaporator. It is shaped like a small fire extinguisher and will always have two lines connected to it. One line comes from the evaporator and the other goes to the suction side of the compressor.

2. With the engine and the air conditioner

running, hold a line in each hand and gauge their relative temperatures. Hold the line going into the compressor as far as possible from the accumulator and as close as possible to the compressor. If they are both cold and at the same approximate temperature, the system is probably overcharged. It should be noted that overcharge is an extremely rare condition.

3. If the line from the evaporator to the accumulator is a somewhat colder than the line from the accumulator to the compressor, and the compressor clutch cycles in a consistent way and at a reasonable frequency, then the system is properly charged.

4. If both lines are fairly warm and the compressor cycles very frequently, the system is undercharged. If the system is undercharged or overcharged, have it checked by a professional air conditioning mechanic.

KEEP THE CONDENSER CLEAR

Periodically inspect the front of the condenser for bent fins or foreign material (dirt, bugs, leaves, etc.) If any cooling fins are bent, straighten them carefully with needlenosed pliers. You can remove any debris with a stiff bristle brush or hose.

OPERATE THE A/C SYSTEM PERIODICALLY

A lot of A/C problems can be avoided by simply running the air conditioner at least once a week, regardless of the season. Simply let the system run for at least 5 minutes a week (even in the winter), and you'll keep the internal parts lubricated as well as preventing the hoses from hardening. This is especially important because lubricating the compressor seal by running the compressor helps keep the refrigerant from leaking out of the system.

USING THE BAR GAUGE MANIFOLD

WARNING: *Refrigerant work is usually performed by highly trained technicians. Improper use of the gauges can result in a leakage of refrigerant liquid, damage to the compressor, or even explosion of a system part. The do-it-yourselfer must be very careful to insure that he proceeds with extreme care and understands what he is doing before proceeding. The best insurance for safety is a complete understanding of the system and proper techniques for servicing it. A careful study of a complete text such as CHILTON'S GUIDE TO AIR CONDITIONING SERVICE AND REPAIR, book part No. 7580, is the best insurance against either dangerous or system damaging problems. It is also recommended that you wear goggles during all refrigerant system work as, when it comes to refrigerant,*

the eyes are the most easily damaged part of the human body.

To use the bar gauge manifold, follow the procedures outlined below.

1. It is first necessary to clear the manifold itself of air and moisture, especially if the fittings have been left open. You should follow this procedure, unless you know that the hoses and gauge manifold have recently been bled with refrigerant and capped off tightly. Otherwise, you may actually force air and moisture into the system when you are testing or charging it.

a. First, tap a can of refrigerant. Unscrew the tap's cutting tool all the way. Turn the rotatable locking lever so it leaves one side of the collar assembly open. Then, slide the tap onto the top of the can so the collar tabs fit over the rim that runs around the top of the can. Turn the locking lever so that it secures the collar. Then, turn the cutting tool all the way down to tap the can.

b. Remove any plugs that may be present and then screw the *center* hose to the screw fitting on top of the tap. Now, slightly loosen the plugs in the ends of the other two lines.

c. Sit the can of refrigerant down right side up on a flat surface. *Make sure the can does not get pulled up off the surface as you work, or you could be splattered by liquid refrigerant.* Then, open the tap by unscrewing the tapping tool handle all the way. Crack both of the bar gauge manifold valves just a little-- just until you hear a slight hiss at the plug at the end of the hose on either side. Allow the refrigerant to enter the system until you are sure it has reached the ends of the hoses (30 seconds). Tighten the plugs at the bottom of the hoses and then *immediately* turn off both manifold valves.

2. Using a wrench if the cap has flats, uncap the low and high pressure, Schrader valve type fittings for the system. The low pressure fitting is usually on the (large) POA valve or accumulator tank (located on the large line coming out of the evaporator); the high pressure fitting is located on the smaller line coming from the receiver/drier or condenser and connecting to the line leading into the (small) expansion valve or a coiled up tube which is mounted on the front of the evaporator. There is a low pressure gauge on the left side of the manifold, which shows pressures up to about 100 psi *and* vacuum. Connect the line on this side to the low pressure side of the system. The gauge on the right or high pressure side of the manifold reads only pressure and, typically, the scale goes up to 500 psi. or higher. On many newer systems, the threads on high and low pressure Schrader

valves are of different sizes to prevent improper hookup.

If you have an older set of gauges, you can get an adapter or a different hose that will convert your gauges to the new thread sizes. Consult a heating, air conditioning and refrigeration supply source.

WARNING: *When making connections, start the threads carefully and, once you are sure they are not crossthreaded, turn the fitting as fast as you can in order to avoid getting sprayed by refrigerant. Sometimes the Schrader valve will open early--before the fitting is tight, and this will cause a little refrigerant to be sprayed out.*

3. Use of the gauges once they are bled and installed typically includes reading high and low side pressures with both valves closed, charging the system with the low side valve cracked partly open, and discharging it with both valves partly open. Refer to the section just below on "Charging the System" for specifics.

4. To disconnect the gauges, turn the fittings as quickly as possible so as to close the Schrader valves as quickly as possible. Note that liquid refrigerant and oil may be sprayed out for a short time as this is done, especially on the low pressure side. Turn the fittings by reaching down from above, as liquid will be sprayed out underneath the gauge connection. Less refrigerant will be sprayed out on the high side if the connection is broken a few minutes after the system is turned off. Cap the open ends of the gauges immediately. If, for any reason, the ends are left open for a minute or two, repeat the bleeding procedure above. Tightly cap the system openings right away.

DISCHARGING THE SYSTEM

NOTE: *To perform this procedure, you'll need a glass bottle.*

1. Connect the gauges to the high and low sides of the system, as described above. Do not connect a refrigerant can to the center hose.

2. Insert the center hose into a glass bottle with an opening that is slightly larger in diameter than the hose. *Do not attempt to cap or seal the opening in the top of the bottle in any way.* This bottle will collect oil discharged from the system so that it can be measured and replaced when the system is recharged. Make sure you keep the bottle upright to avoid spilling this oil out.

3. Make sure the compressor is turned off and remains off throughout the procedure. Crack the low side manifold valve until refrigerant gas is expelled at a steady, moderate rate. Don't open the valve all the way, or too much

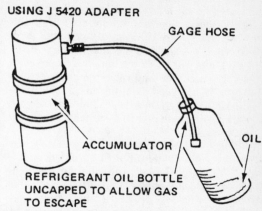

USING J 5420 ADAPTER

GAGE HOSE

ACCUMULATOR

OIL

REFRIGERANT OIL BOTTLE UNCAPPED TO ALLOW GAS TO ESCAPE

Discharge the A/C system into a bottle to collect system oil for later measurement

refrigerant oil will be expelled from the system.

4. As refrigerant pressure drops and the gas begins to be expelled only very slowly, open the low side manifold valve more and more to compensate and keep the refrigerant moving out of the system.

5. Once *all* the pressure is discharged, open the high side service valve to make sure the system is clear. Close it after any pressure has escaped. Note that if there is a significant flow of refrigerant out of the high side at this point and the system uses an orifice tube rather than an expansion valve, the orifice tube may be clogged. This problem must be corrected by replacing the tube or cleaning the system.

6. Disconnect the gauges and recap the openings. Retain the bottle of oil. If you have the system evacuated and recharged by a professional, give him the bottle of oil. He will measure the amount it contains and replace it with a like amount.

CHARGING THE SYSTEM

WARNING: *Charging the system can prove to be very dangerous. You must satisfy yourself that you are fully aware of all risks before starting. Although most systems use a high pressure cutoff switch for the compressor, overcharging the system, attempting to charge it when it contains air, or charging it when there is inadequate cooling of the condenser could cause dangerous pressures to develop if this switch should fail. Overcharging could also damage the compressor.*

The safest way to charge the system is with a set of gauges installed and reading both low and high side pressures so that you can monitor pressures throughout the procedure. It is best to refer to a text on refrigeration and air conditioning first, so that you understand what will happen. Using the simple hose sold for do-it-yourself charging of the system can be safe, provided three precautions are taken:

a. Make sure the system has been completely evacuated and recharged by a professional with a good vacuum pump. Eliminating air in the system is a vital step toward maintaining safe pressures during the charging process.

b. Charge the system with precisely the amount of refrigerant it is specified to use *and no more*. Consult the label on the compressor. Purchase the right number of cans. You can precisely estimate what percentage of a can has been charged into the system by noting the frost line on the can.

c. Run the engine at a moderate speed during charging (not too fast), valve the refrigerant into the system at a controlled rate, and keep a fan blowing across the condenser at all times.

Charge the system by following these steps:

1. Make sure the system has been completely evacuated with a good vacuum pump. This should be done with gauges connected and the pump must be able to create a vacuum of 28-29 in.Hg near sea level. Lower this specification 1 in.Hg for each 1,000 feet above sea level at your location.

2. Connect the gauges as described above, including tapping in a new can of refrigerant. If you are using a gaugeless hose that is part of a charging kit, follow the directions on the package; in any case, make sure to hook up the hose to the low pressure side of the system--to the accumulator or POA valve.

3. Situate a fan in front of the condenser and use it to blow air through the condenser and radiator throughout the charging process.

4. Unless the system has a sight glass, get the exact refrigerant capacity off the compressor label. Make sure you have the proper number of cans available to help avoid unnecessary overcharge.

5. It will speed the process to place the cans, top up, in warm water. Use a thermometer and make sure the water is *not over 120°F*. You will need to warm the water as the process goes on. Monitor the temperature to make sure it does not go too high, as warm water will almost immediately create excessive pressure inside the can. Make sure the cans *always* stay top up. This requires a lot of attention because as the cans run low on refrigerant, they being to float and may turn upside down. Charging the system with the can upside down may cause liquid refrigerant to enter the system, damaging the compressor. If the bar gauge manifold or charg-

ing line suddenly frosts up, check the position of the can!

6. Start the process with the engine off. Open the charging valve (if you are using a kit) or the low side bar gauge manifold valve slightly until the pressures equalize. Then, start the engine and run it at idle speed or just very slightly above. If you have a bar gauge manifold, turn the low side valve off. Turn the air conditioner on in the normal operating mode. If the system uses an expansion valve (it has a sight glass), turn the blower to the lowest speed. If it has no sight glass, set the fan on the highest speed.

7. If you're working with a bar gauge manifold, note the operating pressure (the average if the compressor is cycling). Then, open the manifold valve until system low side pressure rises 10 psi. Throughout the charging procedure, maintain this pressure by opening or closing the valve to compensate for changes in the temperature of the refrigerant can. Also, keep your eye on the high side pressure and make sure it remains at a moderate level (usually less than 200 psi.)

8. When the first can runs out of refrigerant, close off the manifold valve or charging line valve. Tap in a new can, immerse it in liquid, keeping it right side up, and then open the charging line valve if you're working without gauges. If you are working with gauges, open the valve on the tap and then open the low side manifold valve to maintain the same pressure as before.

9. Continue with the process until the last can is hooked up. Measure in a fraction of a can, if necessary, by watching the frost line on the can and stopping appropriately. Also, watch for signs of overcharge at the accumulator as described above and stop if liquid refrigerant is traveling back to the compressor (the suction line to the compressor frosts up). On systems with a sight glass, watch continuously for the time when bubbles just disappear from the glass and stop charging just after this occurs. On these systems, turn off the charging valve or low side manifold valve and then run the system with the fan on high and the engine accelerated to about 1,500 rpm to check the charge. If bubbles appear, charge the system slightly more until just after all the bubbles disappear.

10. When charging is complete, turn off the manifold or charging line valves and any valve on the can. Disconnect the low side line *at the accumulator or suction line and not at the gauges*, grabbing the connection from above, watching for liquid refrigerant to spray out, and unscrewing the connection as fast as you can. Turn off the engine and allow the pressure on the high side to drop until it stabilizes. Then,

disconnect the high side gauge connection (if necessary) as quickly as possible. Cap both system openings and all gauge openings as soon as possible.

Windshield Wipers

Intense heat from the sun, snow and ice, road oils and the chemicals used in windshield washer solvents combine to deteriorate the rubber wiper refills. The refills should be replaced about twice a year or whenever the blades begin to streak or chatter.

WIPER REFILL REPLACEMENT

Normally, if the wipers are not cleaning the windshield properly, only the refill has to be replaced. The blade and the arm usually require replacement only in the event of damage. It is not necessary (except on new Tridon® refills) to remove the arm or the blade to replace the refill (rubber part), though you may have to position the arm higher on the glass. You can do this by turning the ignition switch on and operating the wipers. When they are positioned where they are accessible, turn the ignition switch off.

There are several types of refills and your vehicle could have any kind, since aftermarket blades and arms may not use exactly the same type refill as the original equipment.

Most Anco® styles use a release button that is pushed down to allow the refill to slide out of the yoke jaws. The new refill slides in and locks in place. Some Trico® refills are removed by locating where the metal backing strip or the re-

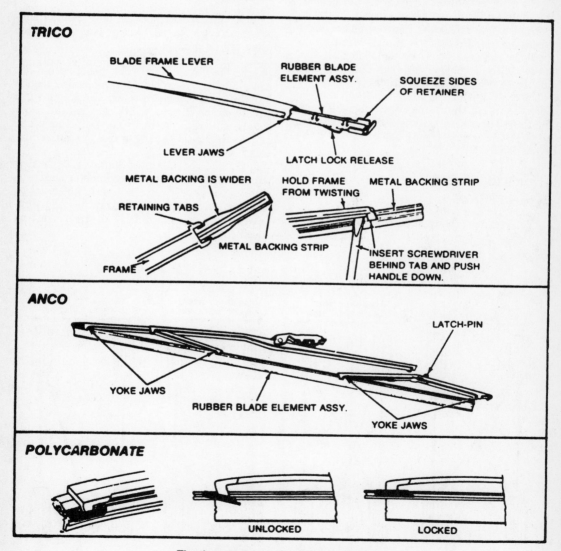

The three types of wiper blade retention

fill is wider. Insert a small screwdriver blade between the frame and metal backing strip. Press down to release the refill from the retaining tab.

The Trico® style is unlocked at one end by squeezing 2 metal tabs, and the refill is slid out of the frame jaws. When the new refill is installed, the tabs will click into place, locking the refill.

The polycarbonate type is held in place by a locking lever that is pushed downward out of the groove in the arm to free the refill. When the new refill is installed, it will lock in place automatically.

The Tridon® refill has a plastic backing strip with a notch about an inch from the end. Hold the blade (frame) on a hard surface so that the frame is tightly bowed. Grip the tip of the backing strip and pull up while twisting counterclockwise. The backing strip will snap out of the retaining tab. Do this for the remaining tabs until the refill is free of the arm. The length of these refills is molded into the end and they should be replaced with identical types.

No matter which type of refill you use, be sure that all of the frame claws engage the refill. Before operating the wipers, be sure that no part of the metal frame is contacting the windshield.

Tires and Wheels

TIRE ROTATION

Tire wear can be equalized by switching the position of the tires about every 6,000 miles. In-cluding a conventional spare in the rotation pattern can give up to 20% more tire life.

CAUTION: *Do not include the new Space-Saver or temporary spare tires in the rotation pattern.*

There are certain exceptions to the standard rules of tire rotation, however. Studded snow tires should not be rotated, and radials should be kept on the same side of the car (Maintain the same direction of rotation). The belts on radial tires get set in a pattern. If the direction of rotation is reversed, it can cause rough ride and vibration.

NOTE: *When radials or studded snows are taken off the car, mark them, so you can maintain the same direction of rotation.*

TIRE DESIGN

1. All four tires must be of the same construction type. Radial, bias, or bias-belted tires must not be mixed.

2. The wheels must be the correct width for the tire. Tire dealers have charts of tire and rim compatibility. A mismatch can cause sloppy handling and rapid tire wear. The tread width should match the rim width (inside bead to inside bead) within an inch. For radial tires, the rim width should be 80% or less of the tire (not tread) width.

3. The height (mounted diameter) of the new tires can greatly change speedometer accuracy, engine speed at a given road speed, fuel mileage, acceleration, and ground clearance. Tire manufacturers furnish full measurement specifications.

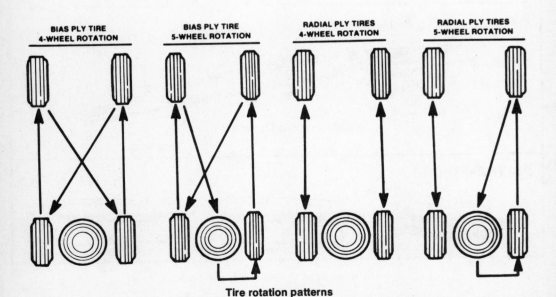

Tire rotation patterns

NOTE: *Dimensions of tires marked the same size may vary significantly, even among tires from the same manufacturer.*

4. The spare tire should be usable, at least for low speed operation, with the new tires.

5. There shouldn't be any body interference when loaded, on bumps, or in turning.

TIRE INFLATION

Tire inflation is the most ignored item of auto maintenance. Gasoline mileage can drop as much as 0.8% for every one 1 pound per square inch (psi) of underinflation.

Two items should be permanent fixtures in every glove compartment; a tire pressure gauge and a tread depth gauge. Check the tire air pressure (including the spare) regularly with a pocket type gauge. Kicking the tires won't tell you a thing, and the gauge on the service station air hose is notoriously inaccurate.

The tire pressures recommended for your car are usually found on a Tire Placard, located on

Troubleshooting Basic Wheel Problems

Problem	Cause	Solution
The car's front end vibrates at high speed	• The wheels are out of balance • Wheels are out of alignment	• Have wheels balanced • Have wheel alignment checked/ adjusted
Car pulls to either side	• Wheels are out of alignment • Unequal tire pressure • Different size tires or wheels	• Have wheel alignment checked/ adjusted • Check/adjust tire pressure • Change tires or wheels to same size
The car's wheel(s) wobbles	• Loose wheel lug nuts • Wheels out of balance • Damaged wheel • Wheels are out of alignment • Worn or damaged ball joint • Excessive play in the steering linkage (usually due to worn parts) • Defective shock absorber	• Tighten wheel lug nuts • Have tires balanced • Raise car and spin the wheel. If the wheel is bent, it should be replaced • Have wheel alignment checked/ adjusted • Check ball joints • Check steering linkage • Check shock absorbers
Tires wear unevenly or prematurely	• Incorrect wheel size • Wheels are out of balance • Wheels are out of alignment	• Check if wheel and tire size are compatible • Have wheels balanced • Have wheel alignment checked/ adjusted

Troubleshooting Basic Tire Problems

Problem	Cause	Solution
The car's front end vibrates at high speeds and the steering wheel shakes	• Wheels out of balance • Front end needs aligning	• Have wheels balanced • Have front end alignment checked
The car pulls to one side while cruising	• Unequal tire pressure (car will usually pull to the low side) • Mismatched tires • Front end needs aligning	• Check/adjust tire pressure • Be sure tires are of the same type and size • Have front end alignment checked
Abnormal, excessive or uneven tire wear See "How to Read Tire Wear"	• Infrequent tire rotation • Improper tire pressure • Sudden stops/starts or high speed on curves	• Rotate tires more frequently to equalize wear • Check/adjust pressure • Correct driving habits
Tire squeals	• Improper tire pressure • Front end needs aligning	• Check/adjust tire pressure • Have front end alignment checked

the driver's door or on the glove compartment door. Ideally, inflation pressure should be checked when the tires are cool. When the air becomes heated it expands and pressure increases. Every 10 degree rise (or drop) in temperature means a difference of 1 psi, which also explains why the tire appears to lose air on a very cold night. When it is impossible to check the tires cold, allow for pressure build-up due to heat. If the hot pressure exceeds the cold pressure by more than 15 psi, reduce your speed, load or both. Otherwise, internal heat is created in the tire. When the heat approaches the temperature at which the tire was cured, during manufacture, the tread can separate from the body.

CAUTION: *Never counteract excessive pressure build-up by bleeding off air pressure (letting some air out). This will only further raise the tire operating temperature.*

Before starting a long trip with lots of luggage, you can add about 2-4 psi to the tires to make them run cooler, but never exceed the maximum inflation pressure on the side of the tire.

CHECKING TREAD DEPTH

All tires made since 1968 have built-in tread wear indicator bars that show up as ½" wide smooth bands across the tire when $\frac{1}{16}$" of tread remains. The appearance of tread wear indicators means that the tires should be replaced. In fact, many states have laws prohibiting the use of tires with less than $\frac{1}{16}$" tread.

You can check your own tread depth with an

Tire Size Comparison Chart

"Letter" sizes			Inch Sizes	Metric-inch Sizes		
"60 Series"	"70 Series"	"78 Series"	1965–77	"60 Series"	"70 Series"	"80 Series"
			5.50-12, 5.60-12	165/60-12	165/70-12	155-12
		Y78-12	6.00-12			
		W78-13	5.20-13	165/60-13	145/70-13	135-13
		Y78-13	5.60-13	175/60-13	155/70-13	145-13
			6.15-13	185/60-13	165/70-13	155-13, P155/80-13
A60-13	A70-13	A78-13	6.40-13	195/60-13	175/70-13	165-13
B60-13	B70-13	B78-13	6.70-13	205/60-13	185/70-13	175-13
			6.90-13			
C60-13	C70-13	C78-13	7.00-13	215/60-13	195/70-13	185-13
D60-13	D70-13	D78-13	7.25-13			
E60-13	E70-13	E78-13	7.75-13			195-13
			5.20-14	165/60-14	145/70-14	135-14
			5.60-14	175/60-14	155/70-14	145-14
			5.90-14			
A60-14	A70-14	A78-14	6.15-14	185/60-14	165/70-14	155-14
	B70-14	B78-14	6.45-14	195/60-14	175/70-14	165-14
	C70-14	C78-14	6.95-14	205/60-14	185/70-14	175-14
D60-14	D70-14	D78-14				
E60-14	E70-14	E78-14	7.35-14	215/60-14	195/70-14	185-14
F60-14	F70-14	F78-14, F83-14	7.75-14	225/60-14	200/70-14	195-14
G60-14	G70-14	G77-14, G78-14	8.25-14	235/60-14	205/70-14	205-14
H60-14	H70-14	H78-14	8.55-14	245/60-14	215/70-14	215-14
J60-14	J70-14	J78-14	8.85-14	255/60-14	225/70-14	225-14
L60-14	L70-14		9.15-14	265/60-14	235/70-14	
	A70-15	A78-15	5.60-15	185/60-15	165/70-15	155-15
B60-15	B70-15	B78-15	6.35-15	195/60-15	175/70-15	165-15
C60-15	C70-15	C78-15	6.85-15	205/60-15	185/70-15	175-15
	D70-15	D78-15				
E60-15	E70-15	E78-15	7.35-15	215/60-15	195/70-15	185-15
F60-15	F70-15	F78-15	7.75-15	225/60-15	205/70-15	195-15
G60-15	G70-15	G78-15	8.15-15/8.25-15	235/60-15	215/70-15	205-15
H60-15	H70-15	H78-15	8.45-15/8.55-15	245/60-15	225/70-15	215-15
J60-15	J70-15	J78-15	8.85-15/8.90-15	255/60-15	235/70-15	225-15
	K70-15		9.00-15	265/60-15	245/70-15	230-15
L60-15	L70-15	L78-15, L84-15	9.15-15			235-15
	M70-15	M78-15				255-15
		N78-15				

Note: Every size tire is not listed and many size comparisons are approximate, based on load ratings. Wider tires than those supplied new with the vehicle, should always be checked for clearance.

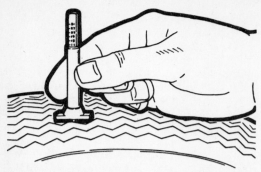

Check the tread depth with an inexpensive depth gauge

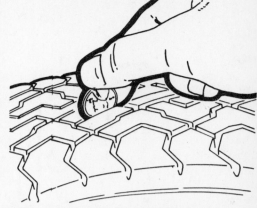

A Lincoln penny can be used to approximate tread depth. If the top of Lincoln's head is visible in two adjacent grooves, replace the tire

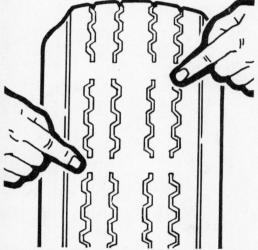

Since 1968, tread wear indicators have been built into the tire tread and appear as ½ inch wide bands when ¹⁄₁₆ inch of tread remains

The special coating may be abraded by repeated washing of the car in an automatic car wash using certain types of brushes. Once the finish abrades, it will provide less protection and normal exposure to either caustic cleaners or road salt will cause the process to continue. If the wheel reaches the point where it requires refinishing, it must be specially prepared and then coated with R-M® 893 2K Enamel Clearcoat and 894 Catalyst Hardener or equivalent products from other sources. This is an extremely lengthy process and every step must be performed in precisely the right way. Special protective gear must be worn to protect the person performing the refinishing operation from the solvents in the cleaners and coatings. We therefore suggest that you have a professional paint shop perform the work for best and safest results.

inexpensive gauge or by using a Lincoln head penny. Slip the Lincoln head penny into several tread grooves. If you can see the top of Lincoln's head in 2 adjacent grooves, the tires have less than ¹⁄₁₆" tread left and should be replaced. You can measure snow tires in the same manner by using the tails side of the Lincoln penny. If you can see the top of the Lincoln memorial, it's time to replace the snow tires.

CARE OF ALUMINUM WHEELS

Normal appearance maintenance of GM aluminum wheels includes frequent washing and waxing. However, you *must be careful to avoid the use of abrasive cleaners*. Failure to heed this warning will cause the protective coating to be damaged.

FLUIDS AND LUBRICANTS

Fuel Recommendations

All the gasoline engines covered in this guide are designed to use only unleaded gasoline. Unleaded gasoline must be used for proper emission control system operation. Its use will also minimize spark plug fouling and extend engine oil life. Using leaded gasoline can damage the emission control system and could result in loss of emission warranty coverage.

The use of a fuel too low in octane (a measurement of anti-knock quality) will result in spark knock. Since many factors such as altitude, terrain, air temperature and humidity af-

Maintenance Intervals in Thousands of Miles*

Item	'75	'76	'77	'78	'79–'80	'81	'82–'83	'84–'85	'86–'87
Clean air cleaner element or oil bath	15	—	—	—	—	—	—	—	—
Replace air cleaner paper element	15 six/ 30 V8	30	30	30	30	30	30	30	30
Replace or clean air cleaner PCV element or flame arrestor	30	30	30	30	30	30	30	30	30
Replace PCV valve	30/24 mo	30/24 mo	30	30	30	30	30	30	30
Replace evaporative canister filter	30/24 mo	30/24 mo	30	30/24 mo	30/24 mo	30/24 mo	30/24 mo	30/24 mo	⑥
Check EFE Valve	8/6 mo	8/6 mo	12	12	12	12	12	12	—
Rotate tires	8/15 radial	as needed	8①	6②	6②	6②	15	15	7.5
Replace spark plugs	22.5	22.5	22.5	22.5	⑤	⑤	30	30	30
Replace fuel filter	15/12 mo	15/12 mo	15	15/12 mo	15/12 mo	15	30	30	30
Change engine oil and filter	7/6 mo	7/6 mo	7/12 mo	7/12 mo④	7/12 mo③,④	7/12 mo③	7.5/12 mo③	7.5/12 mo③	7.5/12 mo⑧

Change automatic transmission fluid and filter	30	60	60	60	100	100	100	100	100	100
Check manual transmission, and axle fluid levels	8/6 mo	8/6 mo	7	7	7	7	7/12 mo	7/12 mo	7/12 mo	7/12 mo
Grease chassis	8/6 mo	8/6 mo	8/12 mo	7/12 mo	7/12 mo	7/12 mo	7.5/12 mo	7.5/12 mo	7.5/12 mo	15/24 mo
Grease front wheel bearings	30	30 2WD/12 4WD	30	30	30	30	30	30	30	30
Change engine coolant	30/24 mo	30/24 mo	30/24 mo	30/24 mo	30	30	30	30	30	30

*Minimum intervals for a truck driven the average 12,000 miles per year under ideal conditions. Intervals given only in thousands of miles can be roughly converted to months: 12,000 mi =12 mo. Halve service intervals for severe use such as trailer towing or off-road driving. If both miles and months are given, use whichever interval elapses first.

① 15,000 miles for radial tires
② 12,000 miles for radial tires
③ 5,000 miles for diesel engines
④ 3,000 miles for turbocharged engines
⑤ 1979—All except turbocharged engines—22,500 miles, Turbocharged engines—15,000 miles
1980–81—All except turbocharged engines—30,000 miles, Turbocharged engines—22,500 miles
⑥ No periodic replacement is required. Inspect the canister if there is fuel leakage or there are operating problems; replace the filter if it is obviously dirty.
⑦ Rotate tires initially at 7,500 miles.
⑧ Change engine oil at 3,000 miles/3 mos. when driving short trips, trips of moderate length (10 miles) in below-freezing temperatures, or when towing a trailer.

fect operating efficiency, knocking may result even though the recommended fuel is being used. If persistent knocking occurs, it may be necessary to switch to a higher grade of fuel. Continuous or heavy knocking will almost always result in engine damage.

NOTE: *Your engine's fuel requirement can change with time, mainly due to carbon buildup, which will increase the compression ratio slightly and raise the temperature of the mixture during compression. If your engine pings, knocks, or runs on, switch to a higher grade of fuel. Sometimes just changing brands will cure the problem. If it becomes necessary to retard the timing from the specifications, don't change it more than about two degrees. Retard timing will reduce power output and fuel mileage, in addition to increasing the engine temperature.*

All diesel engines in temperatures above 20°F (–7°C), are to use Number 2 diesel fuel. In temperatures below 20°F (–7°C), Number 1 diesel fuel is recommended. In some areas of the country, a combination of Number 1 and Number 2 diesel fuel (known as "blended fuel") is available and is recommended for winter use.

The reason that Number 2 diesel fuel is not recommended for cold weather operation is that, at temperatures below 5°F (–13°C), paraffin wax flakes form that thicken the fuel and block the fuel filter.

OPERATION IN FOREIGN COUNTRIES

If you plan to drive your car outside the United States or Canada, there is a possibility that fuels will be too low in anti-knock quality and could produce engine damage. Send to Buick Owner Relations Department the Vehicle Identification Number, compression ratio of your engine and the countries in which you plan to operate and they will send you details of adjustments or modifications that can be made to your engine. It is also wise to consult with local authorities upon arrival in a foreign country to determine the best fuels available.

Engine Oil Recommendations

The SAE (Society of Automotive Engineers) grade number indicates the viscosity of the engine oil and thus its ability to lubricate at a given temperature. The lower the SAE grade number, the lighter the oil; the lower the viscosity, the easier it is to crank the engine in cold weather.

Oil viscosities should be chosen from those oils recommended for the lowest anticipated temperatures during the oil change interval.

Multi-viscosity oils (10W-30, 20W-50 etc.) offer the most important advantage of being adaptable to temperature extremes. They allow

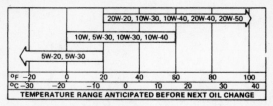

Recommended oil viscosities for gas engines used in cars built in 1975–83

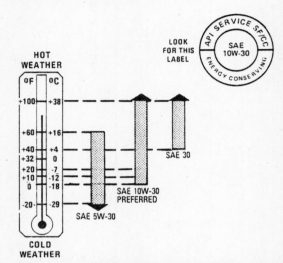

Revised oil viscosity chart for 1984 and later vehicles, showing GM's revised findings and preference for 10W–30 oils

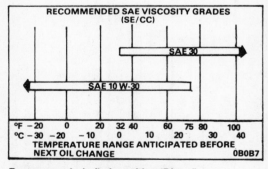

Recommended oil viscosities (Diesel)

easy starting at low temperatures, yet they give good protection at high speeds and engine temperatures. This is a decided advantage in changeable climates or in long distance touring.

The API (American Petroleum Institute) designation indicates the classification of engine oil used under certain given operating conditions. Use only oils with API service designation SF, SF/CC or SF/CD for gasoline engines and for diesel use only SF/CC and SF/CD. Oils of this type perform a variety of functions inside the engine in addition to their basic function as a lubricant. Through a balanced system of metallic detergents and polymeric dispersants, the oil prevents the formation of high and low temperatures deposits and also keeps sludge and particles of dirt in suspension. Acids, particularly sulfuric acid, as well as other byproducts of combustion, are neutralized. Both the SAE grade number and the API designation can be found on top of the oil can.

For recommended oil viscosities, refer to the charts.

After extensive testing of 10W-40 oils, General Motors recently concluded that they should be replaced by oils that offer a narrower viscosity range. Note that 10W-30 or 15W-40 oils are preferred for use by GM on 1984 and later models, as shown in the appropriate chart. While this is not a standard that has been adopted widely in the petroleum and auto industries, GM found that these oils maintain rated viscosities especially well in long oil change intervals.

OIL LEVEL CHECK

Every time you stop for fuel, check the engine oil as follows:

1. Make sure the car is parked on level ground.

2. When checking the oil level, it is best for the engine to be at normal operating temperature, although checking the oil immediately after stopping will lead to a false reading. Wait a few minutes after turning off the engine to allow the oil to drain back into the crankcase.

3. Open the hood and locate the dipstick, which will be on either the right or left side depending upon your particular engine. Pull the dipstick from its tube, wipe it clean and then reinsert it all the way (make sure it bottoms out).

4. Pull the dipstick out again and, holding it horizontally, read the oil level. The oil should be between the **FULL** and **ADD** marks on the dipstick. If the oil is below the **ADD** mark, add oil of the proper viscosity through the capped opening in the top of the cylinder head cover. See the Oil and Fuel Recommendations chart in this chapter for the proper viscosity and rating of oil to use.

5. Replace the dipstick and check the oil level again after adding the oil. Be careful not to overfill the crankcase. Approximately one quart of oil will raise the level from the **ADD** mark to the **FULL** mark. Excess oil will generally be consumed at an accelerated rate.

OIL AND FILTER CHANGE

Change your oil according to the Maintenance Interval Chart shown in this chapter. The mileage figures given are the Buick recommended intervals assuming normal driving and conditions. If your car is used under dusty, polluted or off-road conditions, change the oil and

filter more often than specified. The same goes for cars driven in stop-and-go traffic or only for short distances at a time. Always drain the engine oil after the engine has been running long enough to bring it up to normal temperature. Hot oil will flow easier and more contaminants will be removed along with the oil than if it were drained cold.

Note that GM factory maintenance intervals specify changing the filter at every second oil change after the initial service. This is a standard widely accepted in the industry and has been proven adequate by repeated testing. However, common operating patterns for many cars make changing the filter every second oil change somewhat risky in our opinion. Short trips, especially in combination with cold weather tremendously increase the amount of foreign material the filter must trap. Further, when you leave the filter in place, a quart or more of dirty oil, which may be partially broken down by heat, and which may contain depleted additives, stays in the filter and the engine oil galleries. We therefore recommend replacing the filter with every oil change simply because of the extra insurance this affords. You can buy a great many filters and quarts of oil for the price of one mechanical repair that may result from neglect!

To change the oil and filter:

1. Run the engine until it reaches normal operating temperature.

2. Jack up the front of the car and support it on safety stands, if necessary, for clearance.

3. Slide a drain pan of at least 6 quarts capacity under the oil pan.

4. Loosen the drain plug. Turn the plug out by hand. By keeping an inward pressure on the plug as you unscrew it, oil won't escape past the threads and you can remove it without being burned by hot oil. Place the drain plug in a clean, safe place and then allow the oil to drain while you perform the next several steps, which involve replacing the filter.

5. Using a strap wrench, remove the oil filter. Keep in mind that it's holding about one quart of dirty, hot oil.

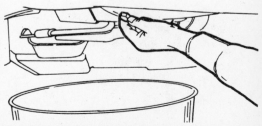

By keeping inward pressure on the plug as you unscrew it, oil won't escape past the threads

Remove the oil filter with a strap wrench

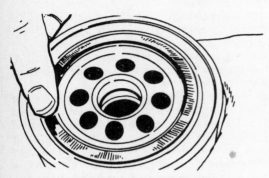

Coat the new oil filter gasket with clean oil

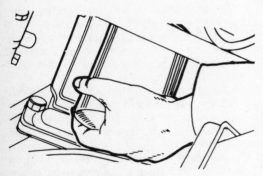

Install the new oil filter by hand

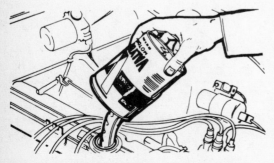

Add oil through the capped opening in the cylinder head cover

6. Empty the old filter into the drain pan and dispose of the filter.

7. Using a clean rag, wipe off the filter adapter on the engine block. Be sure that the rag doesn't leave any lint which could clog an oil passage. Also, be sure the old gasket has come off with the old filter.

8. Coat the rubber gasket on the new filter with fresh oil. Spin it onto the engine by hand; when the filter touches the adapter surface, give it another ½-¾ turn (the instructions on the filter box or body will tell you just how tight to turn the filter). Don't turn in farther than specified, or you'll squash the gasket and it will leak.

9. If there is still a steady drip of oil from the pan, allow the oil to drain completely and then install the drain plug. Don't overtighten the plug, or you'll be replacing the oil pan or buying a trick replacement plug for stripped threads.

10. Refill the engine with the correct amount of fresh oil. See the Capacities chart.

11. Check the oil level on the dipstick. It is normal for the level to be a bit above the full mark. Start the engine and allow it to idle for a few minutes.

CAUTION: *Do not run the engine above idle speed until it has built up oil pressure, indicated when the oil light goes out.*

12. Shut off the engine, allow the oil to drain for a minute, and then check the oil level. Check around the filter and drain plug for any leaks, and correct as necessary.

Manual Transmission
FLUID RECOMMENDATIONS

In all manual transmissions, use only standard GL-5 hypoid gear oil of SAE 80W or SAE 80W/90 viscosity.

LEVEL CHECK

1. With the car parked on a level surface, remove the filler plug from the side of the transmission housing.

2. If the lubricant begins to trickle out of the hole, there is enough and you need not go any further. Otherwise, carefully insert your finger (watch out for sharp threads) and check to see if the oil is up to the edge of the hole.

3. If not, add oil through the hole until the level is at the edge of the hole. Most gear lubricants come in a plastic squeeze bottle with a nozzle; making additions simple. You can also use a common kitchen baster. Use only standard GL-5 hypoid-type gear oil-SAE 80W or SAE 80W/90.

4. Replace the filler plug, run the engine and check for leaks.

WESTERN AUTO STORE 02
4566 W TUSCARAWAS
CANTON, OHIO 44708

MSS VER 5.03A

EXCHANGE 13   40 52613 27976
               0004 07/24/92 10:14 AM

SALESPERSON NO.
          99
ITEMS SOLD
    7440449   10.95
    7307 BUICK 1975-87   10.95
         SUB-TOTAL   0.66

    513 6%   TAX
                           0.00
RETURN OR TRADE-IN
         SUB-TOTAL   0.00
    513 6%   TAX $11.61
         TOTAL   12.00-
         CASH
         DUE CUSTOMER
         CHANGE   0.39

Receipt required to return merchandise

Thank you - WESTERN AUTO

DRAIN AND REFILL

NOTE: *To perform this procedure, you'll need a turkey baster in order to put transmission fluid into the case through the filler plug. You may also purchase the fluid in a plastic squeeze bottle with a nozzle top, which is specially designed for adding fluid to gearboxes and differentials.*

1. The gearbox will drain faster if it is warm. So, especially in cold weather, you may want to drive the car five miles or so to warm up the fluid. The unit uses a filler plug on its side and a drain plug located at the low point on the case. If you need clearance to get underneath the transmission, raise one end of the vehicle and support it securely on axle stands. If the drain plug is located more toward the rear of the transmission, support the front of the car and vice-versa.

2. Place a drain pan of capacity larger than the figure shown in the Capacities Chart for the transmission fluid capacity underneath the transmission case. Place the pan so that is is under both the drain plug and the filler plug.

3. The filler plug typically has a square indentation into which a socket wrench extension will fit. Wipe the area around both of the plugs and the top of the plugs themselves to remove dirt. Remove the filler plug to vent the transmission. Then, remove the drain plug. Allow the fluid to drain until the dripping stops.

4. Wipe the threads of the drain plug clean and reinstall it, tightening it until it is just snug.

5. Using a syringe, refill the case with the specified fluid until it runs out the filler hole. Wipe the threads of the filler plug and install it, tightening just until snug. Inspect the area around the drain plug to make sure it does not leak.

Automatic Transmission

FLUID RECOMMENDATIONS

All automatic transmissions use only Dexron®II automatic transmission fluid.

LEVEL CHECK

The fluid level should be checked only when the transmission is hot (normal operating temperature). The transmission is considered hot after about 20 miles of highway driving.

1. Park the car on a level surface with the engine idling. Shift the transmission into Neutral and set the parking brake.

2. Remove the dipstick, wipe it clean and then reinsert it firmly. Be sure that it has been pushed all the way in. Remove the dipstick and check the fluid level while holding it horizontally. With the engine running, the fluid level

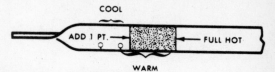

Automatic transmission dipstick marks; the proper level is within the shaded area

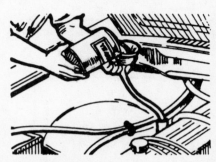

Add automatic transmission fluid through the dipstick tube

should be between the second notch and the **FULL HOT** line. If the fluid must be checked when it is cool, the level should be between the first and second notches.

3. If the fluid level is below the second notch (engine hot) or the first notch (engine cold), add Dexron®II automatic transmission fluid through the dipstick tube. This is easily done with the aid of a funnel. Check the level often as you are filling the transmission. Be extremely careful not to overfill it. Overfilling will cause slippage, seal damage and overheating as the working parts will churn the fluid and make it foam. Approximately one pint of ATF will raise the fluid level from one notch/line to the other.

NOTE: *Always use Dexron®II ATF. The use of AFT type F or any other fluid will cause severe* damage to the transmission.

The fluid on the dipstick should always be a bright red color. If it is discolored (brown or black), or smells burnt, serious transmission troubles, probably due to overheating, should be suspected. The transmission should be inspected by a qualified technician to locate the cause of the burnt fluid.

DRAIN, REFILL, AND FILTER SERVICE

1. The fluid should be changed with the engine warm. Raise the car in the air and support it with jackstands.

2. Place a large pan under the transmission. Remove all the front and side bolts. Loosen the rear bolts about four turns. Pry or tap the pan loose and let it drain.

3. Remove the pan and gasket. Clean the pan thoroughly with solvent and air dry it. Be very careful not to get any lint from rags in the pan.

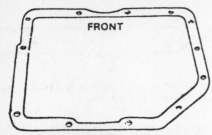

Turbo-Hydramatic® 250, 350, 375B pan shape

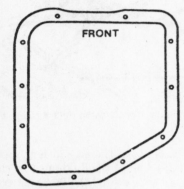

Turbo-Hydramatic 200 pan shape

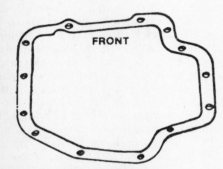

Turbo Hydra-matic 400 pan shape

4. The transmission will be equipped either with a replaceable filter or a strainer which must be cleaned. Turbo 400 transmissions will have a filter. All others may have either a filter or a strainer.

5. Remove the strainer-to-valve body screws, the strainer and the gasket. On the 400 transmission, remove the filter retaining bolt, filter, and intake pipe O-ring. If there is strainer, clean it in solvent and air-dry it.

6. Install the new filter or cleaned strainer with a new gasket. On the Turbo 400, install a new intake pipe O-ring along with the new filter.

7 Install the pan with a new gasket. Tighten the bolts evenly to 10-13 ft.lb.

8. Lower the car and add five pints of DEXRON®II automatic transmission fluid through the dipstick tube.

9. Start the engine and let it idle in Park. Do not race the engine. Shift through each of the gears, then shift back to Park. Check the fluid level on the dipstick. The fluid level will probably be one pint low. Add fluid as necessary. Do not ovefill the transmission.

10. Drive the car long enough to thoroughly warm up the transmission. Recheck the fluid level and add fluid as necessary.

Drive Axle
FLUID RECOMMENDATIONS

For standard differentials, use only standard GL-5 hypoid-type gear oil--SAE 80W or SAE 80W/90. For positraction/limited slip differentials, GM recommends only a special GM lubricant designed for this type of unit that is available only at your Buick parts department. Limited slip differentials have clutch packs that have special lubrication requirements. Of course, you may find alternative sources for such a lubricant. You should satisfy yourself that the lubricant is specifically applicable and thoroughly tested for use in GM limited slip differentials.

LEVEL CHECK

Most gear oils come in a plastic squeeze bottle with a nozzle end, which makes adding lubricant a simple job. You can also use a common turkey baster to draw the fluid out of a standard container and pump it into the side of the differential.

The oil in the differential should be checked routinely at each engine oil change (7,500 miles); check the level immediately if you notice any leakage.

Park the car on a level surface and place a drain pan under the filler plug, located on the front of the differential carrier. Clean the outer surface of the plug and the area around it with a rag. Remove the filler plug. If the lube begins to trickle out the hole when the plug is removed, the differential is full and you can simply replace the plug, tightening it just until it is snug.

If no oil trickles out, carefully insert your finger, *being careful not to cut yourself on the threads, which may be sharp.* Check that the oil is up to the level of the filler hole. If it is not, add oil until the lube just begins to run out. Replace the plug, tightening it just until it is snug.

DRAIN AND REFILL

NOTE: *Before performing this procedure, get a gasket designed to seal the axle housing cover.*

There is no recommended change interval for

the rear axle lubricant, but it is always a good idea to change the lube if you have purchased the car used or if it has been driven in water high enough to reach the axle. To change the fluid:

1. Park the car on a level surface and set the parking brake.

2. Place a large drain pan underneath the rear axle.

3. Remove the rear axle filler plug on the front side of the differential housing.

4. Unscrew the retaining bolts and remove the rear axle cover. The lube will now drain out of the case through the opening.

5. Coat both sides of the new gasket with sealant, and install the cover over the gasket with all the boltholes lined up.

6. Install the cover retaining bolts and tighten them in several stages and in a criss-cross pattern.

7. Refill the axle with the proper quantity of the fluid recommended above (see the Capacities Chart for the fluid quantity).

8. Replace the filler plug and tighten it until it is just snug. Take the car for a short ride and then make sure there are no leaks around the plug or rear cover.

Master Cylinder

FLUID RECOMMENDATIONS

When making additions of brake fluid, use only fresh, uncontaminated brake fluid which meets or exceeds DOT 3 standards.

LEVEL CHECK

The brake master cylinder is located under the hood, in the left rear section of the engine compartment. It is divided into two sections (reservoirs) and the fluid must be kept within

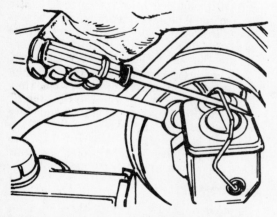

Pry the retaining bail from the master cylinder reservoir cap to check the fluid level

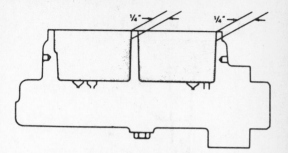

The fluid level in the master cylinder reservoir should be within ¼ in. of the top edge

¼″ of the top edge of both reservoirs. The level should be checked at least every 7,500 miles.

WARNING: *Any sudden decrease in the level of fluid indicates a possible leak in the system and should be checked out immediately.*

To check the fluid level, simply pry off the retaining bail and then lift off the top cover of the master cylinder. Be careful not to spill any brake fluid on painted surfaces, as it eats paint. Do not allow the brake fluid container or the master cylinder reservoir to remain open any longer than necessary; brake fluid absorbs moisture from the air, reducing its effectiveness and causing corrosion in the lines.

NOTE: *The reservoir cover on some later models (1978 and later) may be without a retaining bail. If so, simply pry the cover with your fingers.*

Power Steering Pump

FLUID RECOMMENDATIONS

Use DEXRON® Automatic Transmission Fluid on 1976 cars. 1977 and later cars require GM power steering fluid or an equivalent specifically tested and approved for operation in GM power steering systems.

LEVEL CHECK

Power steering fluid level should be checked at least once every 7,500 miles. To prevent possible overflowing, check the fluid level only when the fluid has warmed to operating temperature and the wheels are turned straight ahead. If the level is low, fill the pump reservoir until the fluid level measures full on the reservoir dipstick. Low fluid level usually produces a moaning sound as the wheels are turned (especially when standing still or parking) and increases steering wheel effort.

Chassis Greasing

There are only two areas which require chassis greasing; the front suspension components and the steering linkage. These

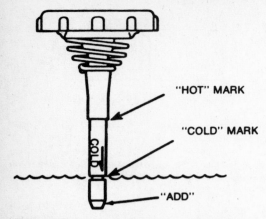

"HOT" MARK

"COLD" MARK

"ADD"

Use the dipstick to check the power steering fluid

parts should be greased every 12 months or 7,500 miles (12,000 Km.) with an EP grease meeting G.M. specification 6031 M.

If you choose to do this job yourself, you will need to purchase a hand operated grease gun, if you do not own one already, and a long flexible extension hose to reach the various grease fittings. You will also need a cartridge of the appropriate grease.

Wipe the grease nipple clean of all road dirt with a clean rag. Press the fitting on the grease gun hose onto the grease fitting on the suspension or steering linkage component. Pump a few shots of grease into the fitting, until the rubber boot on the joint begins to expand, indicating that the joint is full.

When greasing idler arms, it may be difficult to get grease into the bearing area. If this condition, called "grease lock" occurs, push the unit upward and pull it downward hard to break the lock.

Remove the gun from the fitting. Be careful not to overfill the joints, which will rupture the rubber boots, allowing the entry of dirt.

Chassis and Body Lubrication

Every 12 months or 7,500 miles (12,000 km.), the various linkages and hinges on the chassis and body should be lubricated, as follows:

TRANSMISSION SHIFT LINKAGE

Lubricate the manual transaxle shift linkage contact points with the EP grease used for chassis greasing, which should meet G.M. specification 6031M. The automatic transaxle linkage should be lubricated with clean engine oil.

HOOD LATCH AND HINGES

Clean the latch surfaces and apply clean engine oil to the latch pivot bolts and the spring anchor. Use the engine oil to lubricate the hood hinges as well. Use the same grease used for the chassis to lubricate all the pivot points on the latch release mechanism.

DOOR HINGES

The gas tank filler door, car door, and trunk lid hinges should be wiped clean and lubricated with clean engine oil. Silicone spray also works well on these parts, but must be applied more often. Use engine oil to lubricate the trunk or hatch lock mechanism and the lock bolt and striker. The door lock cylinders can be lubricated easily with a shot of silicone spray or one of the many dry penetrating lubricants commercially available.

PARKING BRAKE LINKAGE

Use chassis grease on the parking brake cable where it contacts the guides, links, levers, and pulleys. The grease should be a water resistant one for durability under the car.

ACCELERATOR LINKAGE

Lubricate the carburetor stud, carburetor lever, and the accelerator pedal lever at the support inside the car with clean engine oil.

Front Wheel Bearings

The bearings should be repacked every 30,000 miles. After repacking, the bearings must be adjusted properly. See Chapter 8 for procedures. While it is advisable (even essential) to ensure that the front wheel bearings are repacked at stated intervals, the most efficient way to handle their maintenance is to repack them in conjunction with normal brake repair work. Repack the bearings whenever removing the rotors to machine them. Then, keep careful records to ensure that the bearings are repacked when required.

Properly adjusted bearings have a slightly loose feeling. Wheel bearings must *never* be preloaded! Preloading will damage the bearings and eventually the spindles. If the bearings are too loose, they should be cleaned and inspected. If their condition is satisfactory, they can then be repacked and adjusted; otherwise, they should be repaired as described in Chapter 7.

Hold the tire at the top and bottom and move the wheel in and out on the spindle. If the movement is greater than 0.005″ or 0.127mm (more than just barely perceptible), the bearings are too loose.

ADJUSTMENT

Before handling the bearings, there are a few things that you should remember to do and not to do.

Remember to DO the following:
- Remove all outside dirt from the housing before exposing the bearing.
- Treat a used bearing as gently as you would a new one.
- Work with clean tools in clean surroundings.
- Use clean, dry canvas gloves, or at least clean, dry hands.
- Clean solvents and flushing fluids are a must.
- Use clean paper when laying out the bearings to dry.
- Protect disassembled bearings from rust and dirt. Cover them up.
- Use clean rags to wipe bearings.
- Keep the bearings in oil-proof paper when they are to be stored or are not in use.
- Clean the inside of the housing before replacing the bearing.

Do NOT do the following:
- Don't work in dirty surroundings.
- Don't use dirty, chipped or damaged tools.
- Try not to work on wooden work benches or use wooden mallets.
- Don't handle bearings with dirty or moist hands.
- Do not use gasoline for cleaning; use a safe solvent.
- Do not spin-dry bearings with compressed air. They will be damaged.
- Do not spin dirty bearings.
- Avoid using cotton waste or dirty cloths to wipe bearings.
- Try not to scratch or nick bearing surfaces.
- Do not allow the bearing to come in contact with dirt or rust at any time.

1. Raise the car and support it securely by the lower control arm.
2. Remove the wheel cover. Remove the dust cap from the hub. You can pry it outward using a small, conventional screwdriver against the ridge on the cap.
3. Remove the cotter pin and then turn the spindle nut off.
4. Spin the wheel forward by hand and make sure it keeps spinning. Then, use a wrench to tighten the nut as the wheel spins until it is snug to fully seat the bearings. It's best to use a torque wrench and torque the nut to 12 ft.lb.
5. Back the nut off ¼-½ turn so that it will be loose (no bearing preload). Then, tighten it just finger tight.
6. Loosen the nut until either hole in the spindle lines up with a slot in the nut and then insert the cotter pin. This may appear to be too loose, but is the correct adjustment. The nut must not be even finger tight. This adjustment will create 0.001-0.005" end play.

REMOVAL AND INSTALLATION

1. Remove the hub/disc assembly (refer to Chapter 9).
2. Remove the outer roller bearing assembly from the hub.
3. Pry out the inner seal and discard it. Remove the inner bearing assembly.
4. Wash all parts in a safe solvent and air dry. Check for visible damage (brinneling or roughness on a race or roller surface). Replace parts as necessary. Knock bad races out with a hammer and brass drift, using the groove in the hub.
5. Install a new race by tapping the race with a soft steel drift, working slowly and going all around the race so it stays square. Make sure the race bottoms on the locating lip of the hub recess all around.
6. Pack the bearing full of grease as described below under "Repacking".
7. Place the inner bearing cone and roller into the hub. Place grease on your finger and then place an additional quantity of wheel bearing grease in the grooved area outboard of the bearing. Make sure this groove is filled.
8. Use a flat plate to install a new grease seal so the seal is flush with the outer surface of the hub. Lubricate the lip of the seal with a thin layer of wheel bearing grease.
9. Install the hub or the hub/rotor assembly, being careful not to disturb the grease you have worked into the various recesses in the assembly. Position the outer bearing assembly into the outer bearing cup. Install the washer and nut, tightening the nut finger tight. Now, run another ring of grease around the outside diameter of the washer out to the outer edge of the rotor.
10. Install the rotor (if it is separate from the hub). Install the caliper, as described in Chapter 9.
11. Install the wheel and adjust the wheel bearing as described above and then securely replace the grease cap. Install the wheel cover.

REPACKING

Bearings must be cleaned in solvent and inspected before repacking. They may be dried with compressed air, but *you must not* spin the bearings when doing this, as this will damage them, due to their unlubricated condition. Inspect as specified in Step 2 of the procedure above. Replace parts as necessary. If the races need replacing, replace them as described above.

Use a high quality, wheel bearing grease designed for use in high temperatures (i.e. with disc brakes). The grease must meet the specification of GM part No. 1051344, although dif-

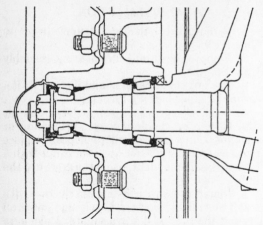

Apply grease to the darkened areas shown when repacking front wheel bearings

ferent brands are available for this purpose. Note that there are critical differences between ordinary chassis grease and wheel bearing grease.

Apply a small quantity of grease in a ring, inboard of each bearing cup in the hub, using your finger. This will help to keep grease in the bearing and also provide an additional supply.

Now, you must work very hard to fill the bearing cone and roller assemblies absolutely 100% with grease. There is a special device called a "cone greaser" which can force the grease in mechanically by trapping it around the bearing. This is the best means of ensuring efficient bearing packing, so you might want to invest in this device. If you pack the bearing by hand, work the grease very thoroughly into the areas of the bearings between the rollers, the cone, and the cage. Force the grease through repeatedly until you are sure all air has been eliminated.

When the bearings have been thoroughly packed with grease, reassemble them and adjust the wheel bearing play as described above under "Removal and Installation".

TRAILER TOWING

Trailer towing puts a great deal of extra load and stress on your car. If you're planning on towing frequently, especially if your trailer is heavy (more than 1,000 lbs.), you should explore the possibility of having a transmission oil cooler and heavy duty cooling system installed.

Trailer Weight

Maximum trailer weight, even if your car has various towing options, is 3,000 lbs. GM recommends that you *do not* tow anything if your car

has a turbocharged engine. This is because turbo engines work harder and are much more easily overloaded.

Tire Inflation And Total Weight of The Car

Make sure your tires are inflated to the pressure specified on the driver's door before towing a trailer. Check the maximum weight figure shown there. Reduce the weight of passengers and luggage carried in the car by the amount of weight that is on the trailer tongue, if you are approaching the maximum load for the car.

Maintenance

More frequent maintenance is required when you tow a trailer for many reasons, especially the tendency for engine oil, transmission fluid, and rear axle lube to run hotter and therefore break down chemically. See the Maintenance Intervals Chart in this chapter. You should also be extra careful about checking the belts, cooling system, and brakes.

It is also *vitally important* that you check frequently that all trailer hitch bolts and nuts are tight.

We also recommend you check your owner's manual for specific directions on factory standards relating to: brake system capacity and performance; connecting trailer brakes to the car's brake system; engine break-in when you plan to tow a trailer; and special driving and parking techniques appropriate when you are towing a trailer.

PUSHING

This is the least recommended method of starting a car and should be used only in an extreme case. Chances of body damage are high, so be sure that the pushcar's bumper does not override your bumper. If your Buick has an automatic transmission, it cannot be push started. In an emergency, you can start a manual transmission car by pushing. Make sure the bumpers are evenly matched. Get in your car, switch on the ignition, and place the gearshift in Second or Third gear. Do not engage the clutch, but depress the pedal all the way, instead. Start off slowly. When the speed of the car reaches about 15-20 mph, release the clutch gradually.

TOWING

A car with an automatic transmission may be towed (in Neutral, of course) for up to 15 miles at speeds up to 35 mph. If these conditions will not provide necessary distance or speed, disconnect the driveshaft or tow with the rear wheels off the ground (many tow trucks have a special dolly for this purpose). Note that the steering wheels must be locked in the straight ahead position if the car is to be towed by the rear. This must be done with a special device and not the car's integral steering wheel lock. Otherwise, safety cannot be guaranteed and it may not be possible to get the wheels set to the straight-ahead position.

JUMP STARTING

Jump Starting a Dual Battery Diesel

All GM diesels are equipped with two 12 volt batteries. The batteries are connected in a parallel circuit (positive terminal to positive terminal, negative terminal to negative terminal). Hooking the batteries up in parallel increases the total battery power *without* increasing the voltage.

WARNING: *It must be understood that hooking up the batteries in series (with the positive terminal of one connected to the negative of another) would double the voltage to 24 volts. Trying to run any portion of the car's electrical system at 24 volts would cause immediate, severe damage. It could even start a FIRE!*

In the event a dual battery diesel must be jump started, use the following procedure:

1. Open the hood and locate the batteries. You can use either one, so choose the one which is more accessible to the donor car. Park the cars so they do not touch. Of course, the donor car must have a 12 volt, negative ground system.

2. Shut off all electrical equipment on both cars to conserve power. Turn the engine of the donor car *off*.

3. Set the parking brakes on both cars and put manual transmissions in neutral, automatic transmissions in Park. Block the wheels.

4. Using the red jumper cable, (if they are color coded), connect the cable between the positive (+) terminal of the battery in the donor car to the positive (+) terminal of the battery in the car being jump started.

5. Then, connect the negative (black) cable between the negative (grounded or – terminal) of the donor car's battery and a solid, stationary, and unpainted metallic ground area of the car being jumped. Good examples are alternator or power steering brackets. If you can only find painted areas, you can often get good contact by clamping the jaws of the cable on the part and rotating them back and forth to scratch through the paint. Just make sure the connection is not too close to the battery.

6. Check to make sure that the cables are clear of all parts, especially the fans of both cars.

7. Start the engine of the donor car and run it at slightly above idle speed.

8. Turn the ignition switch of the diesel on and allow it to preheat the glow plugs. Then, when the amber light goes off, crank the diesel. If the engine will not crank, you might want to turn off the ignition switch of the car being jumped and continue running the donor car for a few minutes to put a slight charge into the batteries of the other car. Then try again to start the stalled car.

9. When the operation is completed, disconnect the cables in *exact reverse* order. This means that you must disconnect the ground cable at the jumped car first, then at the donor car; then, disconnect the cable from the positive terminal of the battery of the car that was jumped, and finally, disconnect the other end of this cable at the positive terminal of the battery of the donor car.

JACKING

There are certain precautions which should be observed when jacking the vehicle. They are as follows:

1. Always jack the car on a level surface.

2. Set the parking brake if the front wheels are to be raised. This will keep the car from rolling backward off the jack.

3. If the rear wheels are to be raised, block the front wheels to keep the car from rolling forward.

4. Block the wheel diagonally opposite the one which is being raised.

5. If the vehicle is being raised in order to work underneath it, support it with jackstands. Do not place the jackstands against the sheet metal panels beneath the car or they will become distorted.

The service operations in this book often require that one end or the other, or both, of the car be raised and safely supported. The ideal method, of course, would be a hydraulic hoist. Since this is beyond both the resources and the requirements of the do-it-yourselfer, a small hydraulic, screw or scissors jack will suffice for the procedures in this guide. Two sturdy jackstands should be acquired if you intend to work under the car at any time. An alternate method of raising the car would be drive-on ramps. These are available commercially or can

JUMP STARTING A DEAD BATTERY

The chemical reaction in a battery produces explosive hydrogen gas. This is the safe way to jump start a dead battery, reducing the chances of an accidental spark that could cause an explosion.

Jump Starting Precautions

1. Be sure both batteries are of the same voltage.
2. Be sure both batteries are of the same polarity (have the same grounded terminal).
3. Be sure the vehicles are not touching.
4. Be sure the vent cap holes are not obstructed.
5. Do not smoke or allow sparks around the battery.
6. In cold weather, check for frozen electrolyte in the battery. Do not jump start a frozen battery.
7. Do not allow electrolyte on your skin or clothing.
8. Be sure the electrolyte is not frozen.

CAUTION: *Make certain that the ignition key, in the vehicle with the dead battery, is in the OFF position. Connecting cables to vehicles with on-board computers will result in computer destruction if the key is not in the OFF position.*

Jump Starting Procedure

1. Determine voltages of the two batteries; they must be the same.
2. Bring the starting vehicle close (they must not touch) so that the batteries can be reached easily.
3. Turn off all accessories and both engines. Put both cars in Neutral or Park and set the handbrake.
4. Cover the cell caps with a rag—do not cover terminals.
5. If the terminals on the run-down battery are heavily corroded, clean them.
6. Identify the positive and negative posts on both batteries and connect the cables in the order shown.
7. Start the engine of the starting vehicle and run it at fast idle. Try to start the car with the dead battery. Crank it for no more than 10 seconds at a time and let it cool off for 20 seconds in between tries.
8. If it doesn't start in 3 tries, there is something else wrong.
9. Disconnect the cables in the reverse order.
10. Replace the cell covers and dispose of the rags.

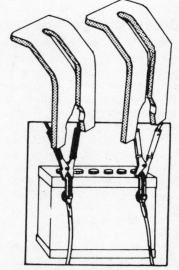

Side terminal batteries occasionally pose a problem when connecting jumper cables. There frequently isn't enough room to clamp the cables without touching sheet metal. Side terminal adaptors are available to alleviate this problem and should be removed after use.

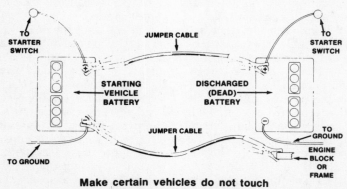

TO STARTER SWITCH

JUMPER CABLE

TO STARTER SWITCH

STARTING VEHICLE BATTERY

DISCHARGED (DEAD) BATTERY

TO GROUND

JUMPER CABLE

TO GROUND

ENGINE BLOCK OR FRAME

Make certain vehicles do not touch

This hook-up for negative ground cars only

WAGONS

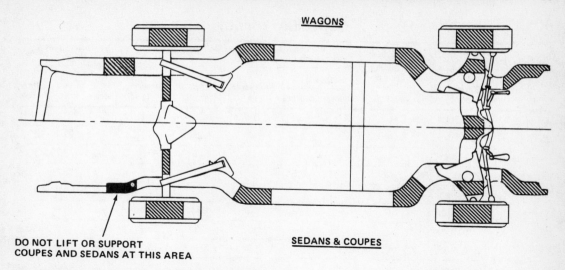

DO NOT LIFT OR SUPPORT
COUPES AND SEDANS AT THIS AREA

SEDANS & COUPES

Vehicle lifting points. Note that on 1986 and later models, the vehicle may be lifted by the wheels, axle, A-arms, or center frame, but *not* by those portions of the frame in front of or behind the wheels.

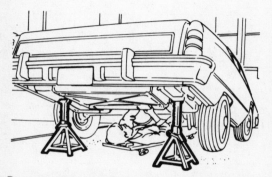

Do not work beneath a vehicle supported only by a tire changing jack. Always use jack stands which are properly positioned under the car

be fabricated from heavy boards or steel. Be sure to block the wheels when using ramps. Never use concrete blocks to support the car. They may break if the load is not evenly distributed.

Regardless of the method of jacking or hoisting the car, there are only certain areas of the undercarriage and suspension you can safely use to support it. See the illustration below, and make sure that only the shaded areas are used. In addition, be especially careful that you do not damage the catalytic converter. Remember that various cross braces and supports on a lift can sometimes contact low hanging parts of the car.

Capacities

Year	Engine No. Cyl. Displacement (cu. in.)	Engine Crankcase Add 1 Qt For New Filter	Transmission Pts to Refill After Draining — Manual 3-Speed	4-Speed	Automatic ●	Drive Axle (pts)	Gasoline Tank (gals)	Cooling System (qts) With Heater	With A/C	Heavy Duty
'75–'76	6-231 Buick	4	3.5	—	6	4.25	22	15.5	15.4	—
	8-350 Buick	4	—	—	6	4.25	22	17.9	18.5	—
'77	6-231 Buick	4	3.1	—	6	4.25	22	12.9	12.7	—
	8-350 Buick	4	—	—	6	4.25	22	14.9	16.4	—
	8-350 Olds.	4	—	—	6	4.25	22	15.0	15.6	—
	8-350 Chev.	4	—	—	6	4.25	22	14.8	16.9	—
	8-403 Olds.	4	—	—	6	4.25	22	16.4	18.5	—

Capacities (cont.)

Year	No. Cyl. Displacement (cu. in.)	Engine Crankcase Add 1 Qt For New Filter	3-Speed	4-Speed	Automatic ●	Drive Axle (pts)	Gasoline Tank (gals)	With Heater	With A/C	Heavy Duty
'78	6-196 Buick	4	3.5	—	3.0	4.25	18.1	13.1	13.2	13.1
	6-231 Buick	4	3.5	3.5	⑤	4.25	18.1	13.1	13.2	13.1
	6-231 Buick	4	3.5	—	3.0	4.25	20.8	13.6	13.7	13.5
	6-231 Buick	4	—	3.5	3.0	3.75	18.5	11.7	12.1	12.6
	8-305 Chev.	4	—	—	⑤	4.25	18.1	19.2	18.9	19.6
	8-350 Chev. ②	4	—	—	3.0	4.25	18.1	19.2	18.9	19.6
'79	6-196 Buick	4	3.12	—	②	3.5	18.1	13.5	13.5	13.4
	6-231 Buick	4	—	3.5	②	—	18.1	13.4	13.4	—
	8-301 Pont.	4	—	—	②	③	18.1	17.6	17.9	17.9
	8-305 Chev. ④	4	—	—	②	③	18.1	15.7	15.6	16.4
	8-350 Chev. ④	4	—	—	②	③	18.1	15.7	16.4	17.9
'80	6-231 Buick	4	3.5	—	②	③	18.1	13.4	13.4	—
	8-265 Pont.	4 ①	—	—	②	③	18.0	N.A.	N.A.	—
	8-301 Pont.	4 ①	—	—	②	③	18.0	20.3	21.0	20.8
	8-305 Chev.	4	—	—	②	③	18.0	17.6	—	18.1
'81	6-231 Buick	4	3.5	—	②	③	18.1	13.4	13.4	—
	8-265 Pont.	—	—	—	②	③	18.1 ④	20.2	20.2	—
	8-267 Chev.	—	—	—	②	③	18.1	20.6	20.6	—
	8-301 Pont.	—	—	—	②	③	18.1	N.A.	N.A.	—
	8-305 Chev.	—	—	—	②	③	18.1	16.5	16.5	—
	8-350 Buick	—	—	—	②	③	18.1	N.A.	N.A.	—
'82	6-231 Buick	4	—	—	⑥	③	18.1	13	13.1	—
	6-252 Buick	4	—	—	⑥	③	18.1	13	13.1	—
	6-263 Olds. (Diesel)	6	—	—	⑥	③	18.1 ⑤	—	14.8	—
	8-350 Olds. (Diesel)	6	—	—	⑥	③	18.1 ⑤	—	17.3	—
'83	6-231 Buick	4	—	—	⑥	③	19	13	13.1	—
	6-252 Buick	4	—	—	⑥	③	19	13	13.1	—
	6-262 Olds. (Diesel)	6	—	—	⑥	③	19	—	14.8	—
	8-350 Olds. (Diesel)	6	—	—	⑥	③	19	—	17.3	—
'84	6-231 Buick	4 ⑦	—	—	⑥	③	19 ⑤	12.9	13	13
	6-252 Buick	4	—	—	⑥	③	19 ⑤	13	13	13
	6-263 Olds. (Diesel)	6	—	—	⑥	③	19 ⑤	13.6	14.4	14.4
'85	6-231 Buick	4 ⑦	—	—	⑥	③	19 ⑤	12.9	13	13
	6-263 Olds. (Diesel)	6	—	—	⑥	③	19 ⑤	13.6	14.4	14.4

Capacities (cont.)

Year	Engine No. Cyl. Displacement (cu. in.)	Engine Crankcase Add 1 Qt For New Filter	Transmission Pts to Refill After Draining Manual 3-Speed	4-Speed	Automatic ●	Drive Axle (pts)	Gasoline Tank (gals)	Cooling System (qts) With Heater	With A/C	Heavy Duty
'86	6-231 Buick	4	—	—	7	③	18.1	12.9	13	13.5
	6-231 Buick	5	—	—	7	③	18.1	13	13	13.5
	8-307 Olds.	4	—	—	7	③	18.1	14.9	15.6	15.5
'87	6-231 Buick	4	—	—	7	③	18.1	12.9	13	13.5
	6-231 Buick	5	—	—	7	③	18.1	13	13	13.5
	8-307 Olds.	4	—	—	7	③	18.1	14.9	15.6	15.5

* Specifications do not include torque converter
① 4 quarts total
② THM 200—6; THM 350—3
③ 7.5 in. ring gear—3.5; 8.5 in. ring gear—4.25; 8.75 in. ring gear—5.4
④ Station wagon—22 gal.
⑤ Station wagon—18.2 gal.
⑥ THM 200 & 200R-4—7 pts.; THM 250C—8 pts.; THM 350C—6.3 pts.
⑦ Turbocharged engine—5 qts.
N.A.—Not Available
—: Not applicable

Engine Performance and Tune-Up 2

TUNE-UP PROCEDURES

In order to extract the full measure of performance and economy from your car's engine it is essential that it be properly tuned at regular intervals. Although the tune-up intervals for the newer models have been stretched to limits which would have been thought impossible a few years ago, periodic maintenance is still required. A regularly scheduled tune-up will keep your car's engine running smoothly and will prevent the annoying minor breakdowns and poor performance associated with an a tuned engine.

A complete tune-up should be performed at the interval specified in the Maintenance Intervals chart in Chapter 1. This interval should be halved if the car is operated under severe conditions, such as trailer towing, prolonged idling, continual stop-and-start driving, or if starting and running problems are noticed. It is assumed that the routine maintenance described in the first chapter has been kept up, as this will have a decided effect on the results of a tune-up. All of the applicable steps should be followed in order, as the result is a cumulative one.

If the specifications on the tune-up label in the engine compartment of your Buick disagree with the Tune-Up Specifications chart in this chapter, the figures on the sticker must be used. The label often reflects changes made during the production run.

Spark Plugs

Spark plugs ignite the air and fuel mixture in the cylinder as the piston reaches the top of the compression stroke. The controlled explosion that results forces the piston down, turning the crankshaft and the rest of the drive train.

The average life of a spark plug in your Buick is 22,000-30,000 miles. Part of the reason for this extraordinarily long life is the exclusive use of unleaded fuel, which reduces the amount of deposits within the combustion chamber and on the spark plug electrodes themselves, compared with the deposits left by the leaded gasoline in the past. An additional contribution to long life is made by the HEI (High Energy Ignition) System, which fires the spark plugs with over 35,000 volts of electricity. The high voltage serves to keep the electrodes clear, and because it is a cleaner blast of electricity than that produced by conventional breaker-points ignitions, the electrodes suffer less pitting and wear.

Nevertheless, the life of a spark plug is dependent on a number of factors, including the mechanical condition of the engine, driving conditions, and the driver's habits.

When you remove the plugs, check the condition of the electrodes; they are a good indicator of the internal state of the engine. Since the spark plug wires must be checked every 15,000 miles, the spark plugs can be removed and examined at the same time. This will allow you to keep an eye on the mechanical status of the engine.

A small deposit of light tan or rust-red material on a spark plug that has been used for any period of time is to be considered normal. Any other color, or abnormal amounts of wear or deposits, indicates that there is something amiss in the engine.

The gap between the center electrode and the side or ground electrode can be expected to increase not more than 0.001" every 1,000 miles under normal conditions.

When a spark plug is functioning normally or, more accurately, when the plug is installed in an engine that is functioning properly, the plugs can be taken out, cleaned, regapped, and reinstalled in the engine without doing the engine any harm.

When, and if, a plug fouls and begins to misfire, you will have to investigate, correct the cause of the fouling, and either clean or replace the plug. There are several reasons why a spark

Tune-Up Specifications

(When analyzing compression test results, look for uniformity among cylinders rather than specific pressures)

Year	Engine V.I.N. Code	Engine Type (No. of cyl- C.I.D.)	Engine Manufacturer	Spark Plugs Type (A.C.) [1]	Gap (in.)	Ignition Timing (deg. B.T.D.C.) [2] Manual Transmission [3]	Automatic Transmission [3]	Intake Valve Opens (°B.T.D.C.)	Fuel Pump Pressure (psi)	Idle Speed (rpm) [4] Manual Transmission [3]	Automatic Transmission [3]
'75	C	6-231	Buick	R44SX	.060	12B	12B	17	3-4½ [13]	800/600	700
	H,J	8-350	Buick	R45TSX	.060	12B	12B	19	4¼-5¾	—	600
'76	C	6-231	Buick	R44SX	.060	12	12	17	4¼-5¾	800/600	600
	H,J	8-350	Buick	R45TSX	.060	—	12	13½	5-6½	—	600
'77	C	6-231	Buick	R46TS or R46TSX	.040 .060	—	12	17	4¼-5¾	—	600
	H,J	8-350	Buick	R46TS or R46TSX	.040 .060	12	12	13½	7½-9	600	600
	L	8-350	Chev.	R45TS	.045	8	8(6)[6]	28	7½-9	700	650/500
	R	8-350	Olds.	R46SZ	.060	—	200 @ 1100 [6]	16	5½-6½	—	650/550 [650/600]
	K	8-403	Olds.	R46SZ	.060	—	24(20)[20] @ 1100	16	6-7½	—	650/550 [650/600]
'78	C	6-196	Buick	R46TSX	.060	15 @ 800	15	18	4½-5½	800/600	600
	A	6-231	Buick	R46TSX	.060	15 @ 800	15	17	4½-5½	800/600	670/600
	G	6-231	Buick	R44TSX	.060	—	15 @ 600	17	4½-5½	—	650
	3	6-231	Buick	R44TSX	.060	—	15 @ 600	17	4½-5½	—	650
	H,U	8-305	Chev.	R45TS	.045	—	4 @ 500 (6 @ 500) [8 @ 600]	28	7½-9	—	600/500 (650/500) [700/600]
	L	8-350	Chev.	R45TS	.045	—	8 @ 500 [8 @ 600]	28	7½-9	—	600/500 [650/600]
'79	C	6-196	Buick	R45TSX or R46TSX	.060 .060	15 @ 800	15 @ 600	16	4½-5¾	800/600	670/550
	A	6-231	Buick	R45TSX or R46TSX	.060 .060	15 @ 800	15 @ 600	16	4¼-5¾	800/600	670/550 (600) [600]

Tune-Up Specifications (cont.)

(When analyzing compression test results, look for uniformity among cylinders rather than specific pressures)

Year	Engine V.I.N. Code	Engine Type (No. of cyl-C.I.D.)	Engine Manufacturer	Spark Plugs Type (A.C.) [1]	Gap (in.)	Ignition Timing (deg. B.T.D.C.) [2] Manual Transmission [3]	Automatic Transmission [3]	Intake Valve Opens (°B.T.D.C.)	Fuel Pump Pressure (psi)	Idle Speed (rpm) [4] Manual Transmission [3]	Automatic Transmission [3]
	2	6-231	Buick	H45TSX or R46TSX	.060 / .060	—	15 @ 580	16	4¼–5¾	—	670/580
	3	6-231	Buick	R44TSX	.060	—	15	16	4¼–5¾	—	650
	Y	8-301	Pont.	R46TSX	.060	—	12 @ 650	27	7–8½	—	650/500
	W	8-301	Pont.	R45TSX	.060	—	12 @ 650	27	7–8½	—	650/500
	H	8-305	Chev.	R45TS	.045	—	4 @ 500 [8 @ 600]	28	7½–9	—	600/500 [650/600]
	L	8-350	Chev.	R45TS	.045	—	8 @ 600 [8 @ 500]	28	7½–9	—	600/500 [650/600]
'80	A	6-231	Buick	R45TSX	.060	15 @ 550	15 @ 550	16	3 min.	800/600	670/550 [8] (620/550) [9] 550 [10]
	3	6-231	Buick	R45TS	.040	—	15 @ 650	16	5 min.	—	650
	W	8-301	Pont.	R45TSX	.060	—	12 @ 500	27	7–8½	—	650/500 [11] 550 [10]
	H	8-305	Chev.	R45TS	.035	—	4 @ 550	28	7½–9	—	650/550 [11] 550 [10]
'81	A	6-231	Buick	R45TS8	.080		—[12]	16	5½–6½		450/900 [12]
	3	6-231	Buick	R45TS	.040		—[12]	16	5½–6½		450/900 [12]
	S	8-265	Pont.	R45TSX	.060		—[12]	27	5½–6½		400/1200 [12]
	W	8-301	Pont.	R45TSX	.060		—[12]	27	5½–6½		
'82	A	6-231	Buick	R45TS8	.080		—[12]	16	5½–6½		See Sticker
	3	6-231	Buick	R45TSX	.060		—[12]	16	5½–6½		See Sticker
	4	6-252	Buick	R45TS8	.080		—[12]	16	5½–6½		See Sticker
'83	A	6-231	Buick	R45TS8	.080		—[12]	16	5½–6½		450/900 [12]
	3	6-231	Buick	R45TSX	.060		—[12]	16	5½–6½		450/900 [12]

Year	No.	Engine C.I.D.	Brand	Spark Plug Type	Gap (in.)	Ignition Timing (Man.)	Ignition Timing (Auto.)	Fuel Pump	Pressure	Idle Speed
'84	4	6-252	Buick	R45TS8	.080		—⑫	16	5½-6½	470/900 ⑫
	A	6-231	Buick	R45TS8	.080		—⑫	16	5½-6½	450/1000 ⑫⑬
	9	6-231	Buick	R45TSX	.060		—⑫	16	26-51	—
'85	4	6-252	Buick	R45TS8	.080		—⑫	16	5½-6½	470/900 ⑫⑬
	A	6-231	Buick	R45TS8	.080		—⑫	16	5½-6½	450/1000 ⑫⑬
	9	6-231	Buick	R45TSX	.060		—⑫	16	26-51	—
'86	A	6-231	Buick	R45TSX	.060	15B⑭	—⑫	N.A.	4.3-5.8	450/900 ⑫⑬
	7	6-231	Buick	R44TS	.035	—	—⑫	N.A.	37-43	⑫
	Y	8-307	Olds.	FR3LS6	.060	20B⑮	—	N.A.	6.0-7.5	450/725 ⑫⑬
'87	A	6-231	Buick	R45TSX	.060	15B⑭	—⑫	N.A.	4.3-5.8	450/1000
	7	6-231	Buick	R44TS	.035	—	—⑫	N.A.	25-35	⑫
	Y	8-307	Olds.	FR3LS6	.060	20B⑮	—	N.A.	6.0-7.5	450/700 ⑫⑬

NOTE: The underhood specifications sticker often reflects tune-up specification changes made on production. Sticker figures must be used if they disagree with those on this chart.

All models use electronic ignition systems.
B.T.D.C.—Before top dead center (No. 1 cylinder)
C.I.D.—Cubic inch displacement
N.A. Not Available
Min.—Minimum

① Part numbers in this chart are not recommendations by Chilton for any product by brand name.
② On some models, the engine must be held at a specific rpm to accurately check and adjust the ignition timing. See the text for specific procedures.
③ Figure in parenthesis ( ) indicates a special figure for California models; figure in brackets [] indicates a special figure for high-altitude models.
④ Most 1979 and later carburetors have idle mixture screws concealed with hardened steel plugs. Normal idle mixture adjustments are not required on these carburetors. Plug removal should be performed only by professional technicians.
⑤ Must be checked at 1100 rpm. Note that engines having codes QA and QD should be set at 16°B.T.D.C. @ 1100 rpm.
⑥ Except California LeSabre and Skylark coupes and sedans, which should be set at 18°B.T.D.C. @ 1100 rpm.
⑦ With the solenoid energized, set the solenoid screw to 600 rpm; with the solenoid de-energized, set the carburetor screw to 550 rpm for models with air conditioning, 500 for models without air conditioning.
⑧ With air conditioning, 49 states models only
⑨ With air conditioning, California models only
⑩ All models with air conditioning
⑪ All models with air conditioning
⑫ On vehicles equipped with computerized emissions systems (which have no distributor vacuum advance unit), the idle speed and ignition timing are controlled by the emissions computer. The computer actuates the Idle Speed Control or Idle Load Compensator on carbureted engines only. See text for adjustment procedures for these devices. There are no idle speed adjustments on fuel injected engines.
⑬ In Drive
⑭ At idle speed in Drive
⑮ 1100 rpm in Park

Diesel Tune-Up Specifications

Year	Engine No. of cyl.- Displacement- Manufacture	Fuel Pump Pressure (psi)	Compression Pressure (psi) ②	Intake Valve Opens (°B.T.D.C.)	Idle Speed (rpm)
'81–'83	8-350 Olds	5.5–6.5	275 minimum	16	①
'82–'85	6-263 Olds	5.8–8.7	275 minimum	16	①

NOTE: The underhood specifications sticker often reflects tune-up specification changes made in production. Sticker figures must be used if they disagree with those in this chart.

B.T.D.C.—Before top dead center (No. 1 cylinder)
① See the underhood specifications sticker
② The lowest cylinder reading must not be less than 70% of the highest cylinder reading.

plug will foul and you can learn which is at fault by just looking at the plug.

A few of the most common reasons for plug fouling, and a description of the fouled plug's appearance, are listed in the Color Insert Section, which also offers solutions to the problems.

Spark plugs suitable for use in your car's engine are offered in a number of different heat ranges. The amount of heat which the plug absorbs is determined by the length of the lower insulator. The longer the insulator, the hotter the plug will operate; the shorter the insulator, the cooler it will operate. A spark plug that absorbs (or retains) little heat and remains too cool will accumulate deposits of oil and carbon, because it is not hot enough to burn them off. This leads to fouling and consequent misfiring. A spark plug that absorbs too much heat will have no deposits, but the electrodes will burn away quickly and, in some cases, pre-ignition may result. Pre-ignition occurs when the spark plug tips get so hot that they incompletely ignite the fuel/mixture before the actual firing of the plug. This premature/partial ignition will usually cause a pinging sound under conditions of low speed and heavy load. In severe cases, the heat may become high enough to start the fuel/air mixture burning throughout the combustion chamber rather than just near the plug. In this case, the resultant explosion (detonation) will be strong enough to damage pistons, rings, and valves.

In most cases the factory recommended heat range is correct; it is chosen to perform well under a wide range of operating conditions. However, if most of your driving is long distance, high speed travel, you may want to install a spark plug one step colder than standard. If most of your driving is of the short trip variety, when the engine may not always reach operating temperature, a hotter plug may help burn off the deposits normally accumulated under those conditions.

```
      1  2  3   4   5
      ‾  ‾  ‾   ‾   ‾
      R  4  5   T   S   X

1 — R--INDICATES RESISTOR-TYPE PLUG.
2 — "4" INDICATES 14 mm THREADS.
3 —    HEAT RANGE
4 — TS--TAPERED SEAT.
       S--EXTENDED TIP
5 — SPECIAL GAP
```

Spark plug coding using a AC-R45TSX as an example

REMOVAL

1. Remove the wires one at a time and number them so you won't cross them when you replace them.
2. Remove the wire from the end of the spark plug by grasping the wire by the rubber boot. If the boot sticks to the plug, remove it by twisting and pulling at the same time. Do not pull the wire itself or you will most certainly damage the core, or tear the connector.
3. Use a $^{13}/_{16}$" or ⅝" spark plug socket (this is a very long, deep well socket) to loosen all of the plugs about two turns.
4. If compressed air is available, blow off the area around the spark plug holes. Otherwise, use a rag or a brush to clean the area. Be careful not to allow any foreign material to drop into the spark plug holes.
5. Remove the plugs by unscrewing them the rest of the way from the engine.

INSPECTION

Check the plugs for deposits and wear. If they are not going to be replaced, clean the plugs thoroughly. Remember that any kind of deposit will decrease the efficiency of the plug. Plugs can be cleaned on a spark plug cleaning machine, which can sometimes be found in service stations, or you can do an acceptable job of cleaning with a stiff brush.

Check spark plug gap before installation. The ground electrode must be aligned with the cen-

Troubleshooting Engine Performance

Problem	Cause	Solution
Hard starting (engine cranks normally)	• Binding linkage, choke valve or choke piston	• Repair as necessary
	• Restricted choke vacuum diaphragm	• Clean passages
	• Improper fuel level	• Adjust float level
	• Dirty, worn or faulty needle valve and seat	• Repair as necessary
	• Float sticking	• Repair as necessary
	• Faulty fuel pump	• Replace fuel pump
	• Incorrect choke cover adjustment	• Adjust choke cover
	• Inadequate choke unloader adjustment	• Adjust choke unloader
	• Faulty ignition coil	• Test and replace as necessary
	• Improper spark plug gap	• Adjust gap
	• Incorrect ignition timing	• Adjust timing
	• Incorrect valve timing	• Check valve timing; repair as necessary
Rough idle or stalling	• Incorrect curb or fast idle speed	• Adjust curb or fast idle speed
	• Incorrect ignition timing	• Adjust timing to specification
	• Improper feedback system operation	• Refer to Chapter 4
	• Improper fast idle cam adjustment	• Adjust fast idle cam
	• Faulty EGR valve operation	• Test EGR system and replace as necessary
	• Faulty PCV valve air flow	• Test PCV valve and replace as necessary
	• Choke binding	• Locate and eliminate binding condition
	• Faulty TAC vacuum motor or valve	• Repair as necessary
	• Air leak into manifold vacuum	• Inspect manifold vacuum connections and repair as necessary
	• Improper fuel level	• Adjust fuel level
	• Faulty distributor rotor or cap	• Replace rotor or cap
	• Improperly seated valves	• Test cylinder compression, repair as necessary
	• Incorrect ignition wiring	• Inspect wiring and correct as necessary
	• Faulty ignition coil	• Test coil and replace as necessary
	• Restricted air vent or idle passages	• Clean passages
	• Restricted air cleaner	• Clean or replace air cleaner filler element
	• Faulty choke vacuum diaphragm	• Repair as necessary
Faulty low-speed operation	• Restricted idle transfer slots	• Clean transfer slots
	• Restricted idle air vents and passages	• Clean air vents and passages
	• Restricted air cleaner	• Clean or replace air cleaner filter element
	• Improper fuel level	• Adjust fuel level
	• Faulty spark plugs	• Clean or replace spark plugs
	• Dirty, corroded, or loose ignition secondary circuit wire connections	• Clean or tighten secondary circuit wire connections
	• Improper feedback system operation	• Refer to Chapter 4
	• Faulty ignition coil high voltage wire	• Replace ignition coil high voltage wire
	• Faulty distributor cap	• Replace cap
Faulty acceleration	• Improper accelerator pump stroke	• Adjust accelerator pump stroke
	• Incorrect ignition timing	• Adjust timing
	• Inoperative pump discharge check ball or needle	• Clean or replace as necessary
	• Worn or damaged pump diaphragm or piston	• Replace diaphragm or piston

Troubleshooting Engine Performance (cont.)

Problem	Cause	Solution
Faulty acceleration (cont.)	• Leaking carburetor main body cover gasket	• Replace gasket
	• Engine cold and choke set too lean	• Adjust choke cover
	• Improper metering rod adjustment (BBD Model carburetor)	• Adjust metering rod
	• Faulty spark plug(s)	• Clean or replace spark plug(s)
	• Improperly seated valves	• Test cylinder compression, repair as necessary
	• Faulty ignition coil	• Test coil and replace as necessary
	• Improper feedback system operation	• Refer to Chapter 4
Faulty high speed operation	• Incorrect ignition timing	• Adjust timing
	• Faulty distributor centrifugal advance mechanism	• Check centrifugal advance mechanism and repair as necessary
	• Faulty distributor vacuum advance mechanism	• Check vacuum advance mechanism and repair as necessary
	• Low fuel pump volume	• Replace fuel pump
	• Wrong spark plug air gap or wrong plug	• Adjust air gap or install correct plug
	• Faulty choke operation	• Adjust choke cover
	• Partially restricted exhaust manifold, exhaust pipe, catalytic converter, muffler, or tailpipe	• Eliminate restriction
	• Restricted vacuum passages	• Clean passages
	• Improper size or restricted main jet	• Clean or replace as necessary
	• Restricted air cleaner	• Clean or replace filter element as necessary
	• Faulty distributor rotor or cap	• Replace rotor or cap
	• Faulty ignition coil	• Test coil and replace as necessary
	• Improperly seated valve(s)	• Test cylinder compression, repair as necessary
	• Faulty valve spring(s)	• Inspect and test valve spring tension, replace as necessary
	• Incorrect valve timing	• Check valve timing and repair as necessary
	• Intake manifold restricted	• Remove restriction or replace manifold
	• Worn distributor shaft	• Replace shaft
	• Improper feedback system operation	• Refer to Chapter 4
Misfire at all speeds	• Faulty spark plug(s)	• Clean or replace spark plug(s)
	• Faulty spark plug wire(s)	• Replace as necessary
	• Faulty distributor cap or rotor	• Replace cap or rotor
	• Faulty ignition coil	• Test coil and replace as necessary
	• Primary ignition circuit shorted or open intermittently	• Troubleshoot primary circuit and repair as necessary
	• Improperly seated valve(s)	• Test cylinder compression, repair as necessary
	• Faulty hydraulic tappet(s)	• Clean or replace tappet(s)
	• Improper feedback system operation	• Refer to Chapter 4
	• Faulty valve spring(s)	• Inspect and test valve spring tension, repair as necessary
	• Worn camshaft lobes	• Replace camshaft
	• Air leak into manifold	• Check manifold vacuum and repair as necessary
	• Improper carburetor adjustment	• Adjust carburetor
	• Fuel pump volume or pressure low	• Replace fuel pump
	• Blown cylinder head gasket	• Replace gasket
	• Intake or exhaust manifold passage(s) restricted	• Pass chain through passage(s) and repair as necessary
	• Incorrect trigger wheel installed in distributor	• Install correct trigger wheel

Troubleshooting Engine Performance (cont.)

Problem	Cause	Solution
Power not up to normal	• Incorrect ignition timing • Faulty distributor rotor • Trigger wheel loose on shaft • Incorrect spark plug gap • Faulty fuel pump • Incorrect valve timing • Faulty ignition coil • Faulty ignition wires • Improperly seated valves • Blown cylinder head gasket • Leaking piston rings • Worn distributor shaft • Improper feedback system operation	• Adjust timing • Replace rotor • Reposition or replace trigger wheel • Adjust gap • Replace fuel pump • Check valve timing and repair as necessary • Test coil and replace as necessary • Test wires and replace as necessary • Test cylinder compression and repair as necessary • Replace gasket • Test compression and repair as necessary • Replace shaft • Refer to Chapter 4
Intake backfire	• Improper ignition timing • Faulty accelerator pump discharge • Defective EGR CTO valve • Defective TAC vacuum motor or valve • Lean air/fuel mixture	• Adjust timing • Repair as necessary • Replace EGR CTO valve • Repair as necessary • Check float level or manifold vacuum for air leak. Remove sediment from bowl
Exhaust backfire	• Air leak into manifold vacuum • Faulty air injection diverter valve • Exhaust leak	• Check manifold vacuum and repair as necessary • Test diverter valve and replace as necessary • Locate and eliminate leak
Ping or spark knock	• Incorrect ignition timing • Distributor centrifugal or vacuum advance malfunction • Excessive combustion chamber deposits • Air leak into manifold vacuum • Excessively high compression • Fuel octane rating excessively low • Sharp edges in combustion chamber • EGR valve not functioning properly	• Adjust timing • Inspect advance mechanism and repair as necessary • Remove with combustion chamber cleaner • Check manifold vacuum and repair as necessary • Test compression and repair as necessary • Try alternate fuel source • Grind smooth • Test EGR system and replace as necessary
Surging (at cruising to top speeds)	• Low carburetor fuel level • Low fuel pump pressure or volume • Metering rod(s) not adjusted properly (BBD Model Carburetor) • Improper PCV valve air flow • Air leak into manifold vacuum • Incorrect spark advance • Restricted main jet(s) • Undersize main jet(s) • Restricted air vents • Restricted fuel filter • Restricted air cleaner • EGR valve not functioning properly • Improper feedback system operation	• Adjust fuel level • Replace fuel pump • Adjust metering rod • Test PCV valve and replace as necessary • Check manifold vacuum and repair as necessary • Test and replace as necessary • Clean main jet(s) • Replace main jet(s) • Clean air vents • Replace fuel filter • Clean or replace air cleaner filter element • Test EGR system and replace as necessary • Refer to Chapter 4

Check the spark plug gap with a wire feeler gauge

ter electrode and the specified size wire gauge should pass through the gap with a slight drag. If the electrodes are worn, it is possible to file them level.

INSTALLATION

1. Lubricate the threads of the spark plugs with a drop of oil or a shot of silicone spray. Insert the plugs in the spark plug hole and tighten them hand tight. Take care not to crossthread them. This means that you should make sure they are straight going in to the spark plug hole and then start them very gently with your fingers. If you don't force them, and you allow each plug to find the threads in the head, you won't damage them. Just make sure they turn freely by hand before applying a wrench to them.

2. Tighten the plugs to the torque figure specified in the Tune-Up section at the end of this chapter.

NOTE: *While over-tightening the spark plug is to be avoided, under-tightening is just as bad. If combustion gases leak past the threads, the spark plug will overheat and rapid electrode wear will result. So, it really pays to use a torque wrench. If you don't have one, turn the socket handle with a comfortable amount of torque--don't strain yourself, but make sure you can feel some tension.*

3. Install the spark plug wires on their plugs. Make sure that each wire is firmly connected to each plug. You will be able to feel them click into place. Spark plug wiring is shown in the firing order diagrams if you get into trouble.

Adjust the electrode gap by bending the side electrode

Spark Plug Wires
CHECKING AND REPLACING

Every 15,000 miles, inspect the spark plug wires for burns, cuts, or breaks in the insulation. Check the boots and the nipples on the distributor cap. Replace any damaged wiring.

Every 45,000 miles or so, the resistance of the wires should be checked with an ohmmeter. Wires with excessive resistance will cause misfiring, and may make the engine difficult to start in damp weather. Generally, the useful life of the cables is 45,000-60,000 miles.

To check resistance, remove the distributor cap, leaving the wires in place. Connect one lead of an ohmmeter to an electrode within the cap; connect the other lead to the corresponding spark plug terminal (remove it from the spark plug for this test). Replace any wire which shows a resistance over 30,000 ohms. The following chart gives resistance values as a function of length. Generally speaking, however, the resistance figure shown is considered to be the outer limit of acceptability; so, if the wire approaches the maximum, you should replace it to prevent trouble in the future.

- Up to 15": 3,000-10,000
- 15-25": 4,000-15,000
- 25-35": 6,000-20,000
- Over 35": 25,000

It should be remembered that resistance is also a function of length; the longer the wire, the greater the resistance. Thus, if the wires on your car are longer than the factory originals, resistance will be higher, quite possibly outside these limits.

When installing new wires, replace them one at a time to avoid mixups. Start by replacing the longest one first. Install the boot firmly over the spark plug. Route the wire over the same path as the original. Insert the nipple firmly onto the tower on the distributor cap, then install the cap cover and latches to secure the wires.

Firing Orders

To avoid confusion, replace spark plug wires one at a time.

High Energy Ignition (HEI) System

The General Motors HEI system is a pulse-triggered, transistor-controlled, inductive discharge ignition system. The engine HEI system is contained within the distributor cap.

The distributor, in addition to housing the mechanical and vacuum advance mechanisms, contains the ignition coil (except on some inline six cylinder engines), the electronic control module, and the magnetic triggering device.

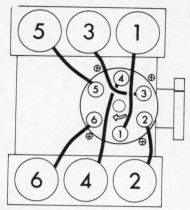

GM (Buick) 231, 252 V6
Engine firing order: 1-6-5-4-3-2
Distributor rotation: clockwise
V6 harmonic balancers have two timing marks: one is ⅛ in. wide, and one is ¹/₁₆ in. wide. Use the ¹/₁₆ in. mark for timing with a hand held light. The ⅛ in. mark is used only with a magnetic timing pick-up probe

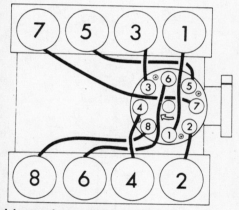

Buick-manufactured V8 engines
Engine firing order: 1-8-4-3-6-5-7-2
Distributor rotation: clockwise

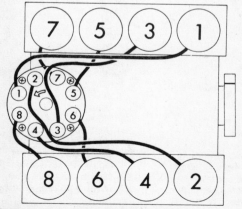

Oldsmobile-manufactured V8 engines
Engine firing order: 1-8-4-3-6-5-7-2
Distributor rotation: counterclockwise

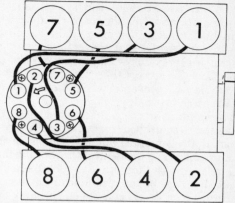

Pontiac-manufactured V8 engines
Engine firing order: 1-8-4-3-6-5-7-2
Distributor rotation: counterclockwise

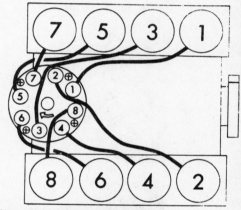

Chevrolet-manufactured V8 engines
Engine firing order: 1-8-4-3-6-5-7-2
Distributor rotation: clockwise

The magnetic pick-up assembly contains a permanent magnet, a pole piece with internal teeth, and a pick-up coil (not to be confused with the ignition coil, but, in fact, a part that helps replace the ignition points).

On cars built from 1981-87, an HEI distributor with Electronic Spark Timing is used (for more information on EST, refer to Chapter 4). This system uses a one piece distributor with the ignition coil mounted in the distributor cap, similar to 1980.

All spark timing changes in the 1981-87 distributors are controlled electronically by the Electronic Control Module (ECM), which monitors information from various engine sensors, computes the desired spark plug timing and then signals the distributor to change the timing accordingly. No vacuum or mechanical advance systems are used whatsoever.

In the HEI system, as in other electronic ignition systems, the breaker points have been replaced with an electronic switch - a transistor - which is located within the control module. The switching transistor performs the same function the points did in a conventional ignition system; it simply turns coil primary current on and off at the correct time. Essentially, then, electronic and conventional ignitions operate on the same principle.

The module which houses the switching transistor is controlled (turned on and off) by a magnetically generated impulse induced in the pick-up coil. When the teeth of the rotating timer core align with the teeth of the pole piece, the induced voltage of the pick-up coil signals the electronic module to open the coil primary circuit. The primary current then decreases, and a high voltage is induced in the ignition coil secondary windings which is then directed through the rotor and high voltage leads (spark plug wires) to fire the spark plugs.

In essence then, the pick-up coil module system simply replaces the conventional breaker points and condenser. The condenser found within the distributor is for radio suppression purposes only and has nothing to do with the ignition process. The module automatically controls the dwell period, increasing it with increasing engine speed. Since dwell is automatically controlled, it cannot be adjusted. The module itself is non-adjustable and non-repairable and must be replaced if found defective.

HEI SYSTEM PRECAUTIONS

Before going on to troubleshooting, it is a good idea to take note of the following precautions:

Timing Light Use

Inductive pick-up timing lights are the best kind to use with HEI. Timing lights which con-

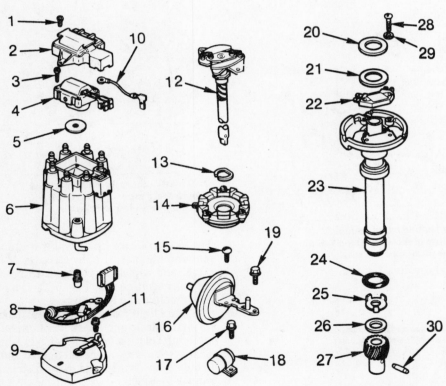

1. Cap cover attaching screw
2. Distributor cap cover
3. Coil attaching screw
4. Distributor coil
5. Coil to distributor cap seal
6. Distributor cap
7. Resistor brush
8. Module coil harness
9. Distributor rotor
10. Distributor ground lead
11. Rotor screw
12. Distributor mainshaft
13. Pole piece and plate retainer
14. Distributor pole piece and plate
15. Vacuum control attaching screw
16. Distributor vacuum control
17, 18. Capacitor and attaching screw
19. Vacuum control attaching screw
20. Felt washer
21. Distributor housing seal
22. Module
23. Distributor housing
24. Housing stem washer
25. Shaft spacer washer
26. Shaft thrust washer
27. Distributor drive gear
28. Module attaching screw
29. Washer
30. Gear attaching pin

HEI integral coil electronic ignition distributor—1975–80

nect between the spark plug and the spark plug wire occasionally (not always) give false readings.

Spark Plug Wires

The plug wires used with HEI systems are of a different construction from conventional wires. When replacing them, make sure you get the correct wires, since conventional wires won't carry the voltage. Also, handle them carefully to avoid cracking or splitting them and never pierce them.

TACHOMETER USE

Not all tachometers will operate or indicate correctly when used on a HEI system. While some tachometers will give a reading, this does not necessarily mean the reading is correct. In addition, some tachometers hook up differently from others. If you can't figure out whether or not your tachometer will work on your car, check with the tachometer manufacturer. Dwell readings, of course, have no significance at all.

HEI SYSTEM TESTERS

Instruments designed specifically for testing HEI systems are available from several tool manufacturers. Some of these will even test the module itself. However, the tests given in the following section will require only an ohmmeter and a voltmeter.

ADJUSTMENTS

While no adjustment of the distributor primary components is required as a matter of routine maintenance, there is one check to be made if the Pickup Coil or Hall Effect switch has been replaced; you might want to check this adjustment if the mounting screws on either of these components have loosened up.

Remove the distributor as described in Chapter 3, being careful to position the engine and mark the rotor, distributor, and block to ensure easiest reassembly. Rotate the distributor shaft and make sure the pickup coil and Hall Effect switch teeth do not touch the signal generator located on the distributor shaft. If there is any touching, loosen the attaching screws for the component whose teeth touch, reposition it to ensure adequate clearance, and then retighten the mounting screws. Rotate the rotor to check that the teeth clear one another.

TROUBLESHOOTING THE HEI SYSTEM

NOTE: *This book contains simple testing procedures for your car's electronic ignition system. Such systems are extremely complex. An exhaustive testing procedure would be too difficult for the typical backyard mechanic to* *follow. It would also occupy a great deal of space that would be better used for more easily understood types of repairs and checks. If you're interested in learning more about electronic ignition, you might want to consider purchasing CHILTON'S GUIDE TO ELECTRONIC ENGINE CONTROLS, book part number 7535 which is available in many bookstores and at auto parts retailers.*

The symptoms of a defective component within the HEI system are exactly the same as those you would encounter in a conventional system. Some of the symptoms are:

- Hard or No Starting
- Rough Idle
- Poor Fuel Economy
- Engine misses under load or while accelerating

If you suspect a problem in your ignition system, there are certain preliminary checks which you should carry out before you begin to check the electronic portions of the system. First, it is extremely important to make sure the vehicle battery is in a good state of charge. A defective or poorly charged battery will cause the various components of the ignition system to read incorrectly when they are being tested. Second, make sure all wiring connections are clean and tight, not only at the battery, but also at the distributor cap, ignition coil, and at the electronic control module.

Since the only differences between electronic and conventional ignition systems are in the distributor component area, it is imperative to check the secondary ignition circuit first. If the secondary circuit checks out properly, then the engine condition is more than likely not the fault of the ignition system. To check the secondary ignition system, perform a simple spark test. Remove one of the plug wires and insert some sort of extension in the plug socket. An old spark plug with the ground electrode removed makes a good extension. Hold the wire and extension about ¼" away from the block and crank the engine. If a normal spark occurs, then the problem is most likely not in the ignition system. Check for fuel system problems, or fouled spark plugs.

If, however, there is no spark or a weak spark, then further ignition system testing will have to be done. Troubleshooting techniques fall into two categories, depending on the nature of the problem. The categories are (1) Engine cranks, but won't start or (2) Engine runs, but runs rough or cuts out. To begin with, let's consider the first case.

Engine Fails to Start

NOTE: *You'll need either a voltmeter or a test light for this test.*

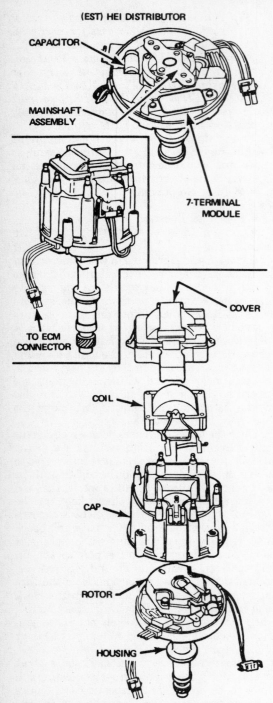

(EST) HEI DISTRIBUTOR

CAPACITOR

MAINSHAFT ASSEMBLY

7-TERMINAL MODULE

TO ECM CONNECTOR

COVER

COIL

CAP

ROTOR

HOUSING

HEI EST distributor components—1981 and later (note absence of vacuum advance unit)

If the engine won't start, perform a spark test as described earlier. This will narrow the problem area down considerably. If no spark occurs, check for the presence of normal battery voltage at the battery (BAT) terminal in the dis-

tributor cap. The ignition switch must be in the ON position for this test. Connect the test light wire to ground and the probe end to the BAT terminal at the distributor. If you're using a voltmeter, connect its positive (red) probe to the BAT terminal of the distributor and the black lead to a good ground. If the light comes on (or there is a reading near 12 volts), you have voltage to the distributor. If the light fails to come on or there is almost not voltage indication, this indicates an open circuit in the ignition primary wiring leading to the distributor. In this case, you will have to check wiring continuity back to the ignition switch using the test light or voltmeter. If there is battery voltage at the BAT terminal, but no spark at the plugs, then the problem lies within the distributor assembly. Go on to the distributor components test section.

Engine Runs, But Runs Roughly or Cuts Out

1. Make sure the plug wires are in good shape first. There should be no obvious cracks or breaks. You can check the plug wires with an ohmmeter, but do not pierce the wires with a probe. Check the chart for the correct plug wire resistance.

2. If the plug wires are OK, remove the cap assembly and check for moisture, cracks, chips, or carbon tracks, or any other high voltage leaks or failures. Replace the cap if any defects are found. Make sure the timer wheel rotates when the engine is cranked. If everything is all right so far, go on to the distributor components test section following.

DISTRIBUTOR COMPONENTS TESTING

If the trouble has been narrowed down to the units within the distributor, the following tests can help pinpoint the defective component. An ohmmeter with both high and low ranges should be used. These tests are made with the cap assembly removed and the battery wire disconnected. If a tachometer is connected to the TACH terminal, disconnect it before making these tests.

1. Connect an ohmmeter between the TACH and BAT terminals in the distributor cap. The primary coil resistance should be less than one ohm.

HEI Plug Wire Resistance Chart

Wire Length	Minimum	Maximum
0–15 inches	3000 ohms	10,000 ohms
15–25 inches	4000 ohms	15,000 ohms
25–35 inches	6000 ohms	20,000 ohms
Over 35 inches		25,000 ohms

2. To check the coil secondary resistance, connect an ohmmeter between the rotor button and the BAT terminal. Note the reading. Connect the ohmmeter between the rotor button and the TACH terminal. Note the reading. The resistance in both cases should be between 6,000 and 30,000 ohms. Be sure to test between the rotor button and both the BAT and TACH terminals.

3. Replace the coil only if the readings in Step 1 and Step 2 are infinite.

NOTE: *These resistance tests will not disclose shorted coil windings. This condition can only be detected with scope analysis or a suitably designed coil tester. If these instruments are unavailable, replace the coil with a known good coil as a final coil test.*

4. To test the pick-up coil, first disconnect the white and green module leads. Set the ohmmeter on the high scale and connect it between a ground and either a white or green lead. Any resistance measurement less than infinity requires replacement of the pick-up coil.

5. Pick-up coil continuity is tested by connecting the ohmmeter (on low range) between the white and green leads. Normal resistance is between 650 and 850 ohms, or 500 and 1500 ohms on 1977 and later models. Move the vacuum advance arm while performing this test. This will detect any break in coil continuity.

Ohmmeter 1 shows the primary coil resistance connection. Ohmmeter 2 shows the secondary resistance connection (1980 shown, most models similar)

Such a condition can cause intermittent misfiring. Replace the pick-up coil if the reading is outside the specified limits.

6. If no defects have been found at this time, and you still have a problem, then the module will have to be checked. If you do not access to a module tester, then the only possible alternative is a substitution test. If the module fails the substitution test, replace it.

HEI SYSTEM MAINTENANCE

Except for periodic checks of the spark plug wires, and an occasional check of the distributor cap for cracks (see Steps 1 and 2 under Engine Runs, But Runs Rough or Cuts Out for details), no maintenance is required on the HEI system. No periodic lubrication is necessary; engine oil lubricates the lower bushing, and an oil filled reservoir lubricates the upper bushing.

COMPONENT REPLACEMENT

Integral Ignition Coil

1. Disconnect the feed and module wire terminal connectors from the distributor cap.
2. Remove the ignition set retainer.
3. Remove the 4 coil cover-to-distributor cap screws and the coil cover.
4. Remove the coil-to-distributor cap screws.
5. Using a blunt drift, press the coil wire spade terminals up out of distributor cap.
6. Lift the coil up out of the distributor cap.
7. Remove and clean the coil spring, rubber seal washer and coil cavity of the distributor cap.
8. Coat the rubber seal with a dielectric lubricant furnished in the replacement ignition coil package.
9. Reverse the above procedures to install.

Distributor Cap

1. Remove the feed and module wire terminal connectors from the distributor cap.
2. Remove the retainer and spark plug wires from the cap.
3. Depress and release the 4 distributor cap-to-housing retainers and lift off the cap assembly.
4. Remove the 4 coil cover screws and cover.
5. Using a finger or a blunt drift, push the spade terminals up out of the distributor cap.
6. Remove all 4 coil screws and lift the coil, coil spring and rubber seal washer out of the cap coil cavity.
7. Using a new distributor cap, reverse the above procedures to assemble being sure to clean and lubricate the rubber seal washer with dielectric lubricant.

Rotor

1. Disconnect the feed and wire module wire connectors from the distributor.
2. Depress and release the 4-distributor cap-to-housing retainers and lift off the cap assembly.
3. Remove the two rotor attaching screws and rotor.
4. Reverse the above procedures to install.

Vacuum Advance (1975-80)

1. Remove the distributor cap and rotor as previously described.
2. Disconnect the vacuum hose from the vacuum advance unit.
3. Remove the two vacuum advance retaining screws, pull the advance unit outward, rotate and disengage the operating rod from its tang.
4. Reverse the above procedure to install.

Module

1. Remove the distributor cap and rotor as previously described.
2. Disconnect the harness connector and pick-up coil spade connectors from the module. Be careful not to damage the wires when removing the connector.
3. Remove the two screws and module from the distributor housing.
4. Coat the bottom of the new module with dielectric lubricant supplied the new module. Reverse the above procedure to install.

HEI SYSTEM TACHOMETER HOOKUP

There is a terminal marked TACH on the distributor cap. Connect one tachometer lead to this terminal and the other lead to a ground. On some tachometers, the leads must be connected to the TACH terminal and to the battery negative terminal. Always consult the instructions that came with the instrument, as tachs differ as to the correct hookup and the tach or ignition system can be damaged if you do it wrong! CAUTION: *Never ground the TACH terminal; serious module and ignition coil damage will result. If there is any doubt as to the correct tachometer hookup, check with the tachometer manufacturer.*

Tachometer Hook-up - Diesel Engines

A magnetic pickup tachometer is necessary because of the lack of an ignition system. The tachometer probe is inserted into the hole in the timing indicator.

Ignition Timing

Ignition timing is the measurement, in degrees of crankshaft rotation, of the point at which the spark plugs fire in each of the cylin-

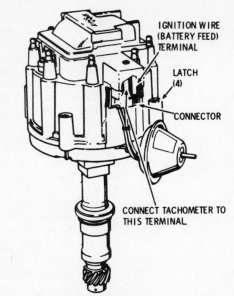

Tachometer connection for the HEI system

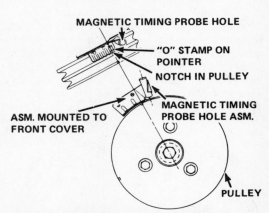

Magnetic timing probe hole (diesel engines)

ders. It is measured in degrees before or after Top Dead Center (TDC) of the compression stroke.

Because it takes a fraction of a second for the spark plug to ignite the mixture in the cylinder, and to create the maximum pressure on the downstroke, the spark plug must fire a little before the piston reaches TDC. Otherwise, the full power of the explosion will not be used by the engine.

The timing measurement is given in degrees of crankshaft rotation before the piston reaches TDC (BTDC). If the setting for the ignition timing is 5 degrees BTDC, the spark plug must fire 5 degrees before each piston reaches TDC. This only holds true, however, when the engine is at idle speed.

As the engine speed increases, the pistons go faster. The spark plugs have to ignite the fuel even sooner if it is to burn at the optimum time and complete the combustion cycle early enough. To do this, the distributor has two means to advance the timing of the spark as the engine speed increases. This is accomplished by centrifugal weights within the distributor, and a vacuum diaphragm mounted on the side of the distributor.

If the ignition is set too far advanced (BTDC), the ignition and expansion of the fuel in the cylinder will occur too soon and tend to try to force the piston down while it is still traveling up, while also creating excessive temperatures. This causes engine ping. If the ignition spark is set too far retarded, after TDC (ATDC), the piston will have already passed TDC and started on its way down when the fuel is ignited. This will cause the combustion to occur too late, which prevents the creation of maximum pressures and the most effective use of the engine's compression ratio. The fuel burns so late that excess heat is left in the exhaust. This will result in poor engine performance, poor fuel economy, and overheating, especially of the exhaust valves.

Timing marks consist of a notch on the rim of the crankshaft pulley and a scale of degrees attached to the front of the engine. The notch corresponds to the position in the number 1 cylinder. A stroboscopic (dynamic) timing light is used, which is hooked into the circuit of the No. 1 cylinder spark plug. Every time the spark plug fires, the timing light flashes. By aiming the timing light at the timing marks, the exact position of the piston within the cylinder can be read, since the stroboscopic flash makes the mark on the pulley appear to be standing still. Proper timing is indicated when the notch is aligned with the correct number on the scale.

There are three basic timing lights available. The first is a simple neon bulb with two wire connections (one for the spark plug and one for the plug wire, connecting the light in series). This type of light is quite dim, and must be held closely to the marks to be seen, but it is quite inexpensive. The second type of light operates from the car's battery. Two alligator clips connect to the battery terminals, while a third wire connects to the spark plug with an adapter. This type of light is more expensive, but the xenon bulb provides a nice bright flash which can even be seen in sunlight. The third type replaces the battery source with 110 volt house current. Some timing lights have other functions built into them, such as dwell meters, tachometers, or remote starting switches. These are convenient, in that they reduce the tangle of wires under the hood, but may duplicate the function of tools you already have.

If your car has electronic ignition, you should use a timing light with an inductive pickup. This pickup simply clamps onto the No. 1 spark plug wire, eliminating the adapter. It is susceptible to crossfiring or false triggering, which may occur with a conventional light, due to the greater voltages produced by electronic ignition.

CHECKING AND ADJUSTING

1. Warm the engine to normal operating temperature. Shut off the engine and connect the timing light to the No.1 spark plug (left front). Do not, under any circumstances, pierce a wire to hook up a light.

2. Clean off the timing marks and mark the pulley or damper notch and the timing scale with white chalk or paint. The timing notch on the damper or pulley can be elusive. Bump the engine around with the starter or turn the crankshaft with a wrench on the front pulley bolt to get it to an accessible position.

3. Disconnect and plug the vacuum hose at the distributor to prevent any distributor advance. The vacuum line is the rubber hose connected to the metal cone shaped canister on the side of the distributor. A short screw, pencil, or golf tee can be used to plug the hose.

NOTE: *1981 and later models with Electronic Spark Timing have no vacuum advance, therefore you may skip the previous step, but you must disconnect the four terminal EST connector before going on.*

4. Start the engine and adjust the idle speed to that specified in the Tune-Up Specifications chart. Some cars require that the timing be set with the transmission in Neutral. You can disconnect the solenoid, if any, to get the speed down. Otherwise, adjust the idle speed screw. This is to prevent any centrifugal advance of timing in the distributor. Make sure that major accessories such as air conditioning are off and that the engine is at operating temperature, with the choke fully open on carbureted models.

On HEI systems, the tachometer connects to the TACH terminal on the distributor. Some tachometers must connect onto the TACH terminal and to the positive battery terminal. Some tachometers won't work at all with HEI. Consult the tachometer manufacturer if the instructions supplied with the unit do not give the proper connection.

WARNING: *Never ground the HEI TACH terminal; serious system damage will result including module burnout.*

5. On 1986-87 3.8L carbureted engines, verify that the "CHECK ENGINE" light is not on after connecting the timing light. Then, disconnect the distributor four-wire electrical connector. The "CHECK ENGINE" light will now

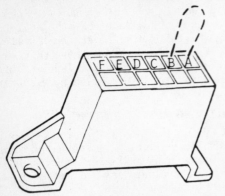

On 1986 and later 5.0 L V8, ground the diagnostic terminal of the ALCL plug as shown.

come on. On 1986-87 5.0L carbureted V8 engines, disconnect and then ground the diagnostic terminal of the 12-terminal ALCL connector, as shown.

6. Aim the timing light at the timing marks. Be careful not to touch the fan, which may appear to be standing still. Keep your clothes and hair, and the light's wires clear of the fan, belts, and pulleys. If the pulley or damper notch isn't aligned with the proper timing mark (see the Tune-Up Specifications chart), the timing will have to be adjusted.

NOTE: *TDC or Top Dead Center corresponds to 0 degrees; B, or BTDC, or Before Top Dead Center, may be shown as BEFORE; A, or ATDC, or After Top Dead Center, may be shown as AFTER.*

7. Loosen the distributor base clamp locknut. You can buy special wrenches which make this task a lot easier on V8s. Turn the distributor slowly to adjust the timing, holding it by the body and not the cap. Turn the distributor in the direction of rotor rotation (found in the Firing Order illustration in this chapter) to retard, and against the direction of rotation to advance.

NOTE: *The 3.8L V6 engine has two timing marks on the crankshaft pulley. One timing mark is 1/8" wide and the other, four inches away, is 1/16" wide. The smaller mark is used for setting the timing with a hand-held timing light. The larger mark is used with the magnetic probe and is only of use to a dealer or a garage. Make sure you set the timing using the smaller mark.*

8. Tighten the locknut. Check the timing, in case the distributor moved as you tightened it.

9. Replace the distributor vacuum hose, if removed. Correct the idle speed.

10. On the 3.8L V6, where the four wire electrical connector was disconnected, reconnect it. Turn the engine off and then momentarily disconnect the battery to cancel stored trouble codes. On the 1987-87 5.0L V8, remove the ground wire and reconnect the ALCL plug before shutting down the engine. On all models except the late model 3.8L V6, turn off the engine and disconnect the light.

Valve Lash

Hydraulic valve lifters rarely require adjustment, and are not adjusted as part of normal tune-up. The valves on Buick engines cannot be adjusted. If there is excessive clearance in the valve train, look for worn push rods, rocker arms, valve springs or collapsed or stuck lifters. Chevrolet engines require initial lash adjustment whenever rocker arms are removed or major repairs are made. In case of excessive wear due to inadequate engine maintenance, adjusting the valves on a Chevrolet engine may correct excessive lifter lash. (See Chapter 3)

Idle Speed and Mixture Adjustment

NOTE: *For idle speed adjustments on the diesel engines refer to the Diesel Engine Fuel System in Chapter 5.*

1975-76 V6 and V8

NOTE: *Idle speed and mixture must be set with the engine at normal operating temperature, the air conditioner OFF, the air cleaner on, and the transmission in Drive.*

1. Set the parking brake and block the wheels.

2. Disconnect the evaporative hose at the air cleaner. Disconnect and plug the distributor vacuum line at the distributor. Disconnect and plug the EGR vacuum line at the EGR valve on all 1976 V6s.

3. Adjust the idle speed to that specification in the Tune Up Specifications chart. First adjust the idle speed screw with the solenoid disconnected to get the lower speed, then adjust the solenoid screw with the solenoid connected to get the higher speed on models so equipped. If there is no solenoid, adjust the idle speed with the idle speed screw.

4. Cut the tabs off the mixture screw caps then turn them out to obtain the maximum idle speed.

5. Using the solenoid screw (if equipped), or the idle speed screw, adjust the idle speed to the higher speed specified on the underhood sticker, which is usually 60-100 rpm above the normal idle speed.

6. Turn in the mixture screws equally until the engine returns to the normal idle speed. On the V6, reset the idle speed with the solenoid de-energized, if necessary.

7. Reconnect all the hoses removed in Step 2.

1977

NOTE: *Engines produced by several GM divisions are used in Buicks. The vehicle emission control information sticker in the engine compartment should be checked for the individual engine specifications.*

1. With the engine at normal operating temperature, set the parking brake and block the wheels.

2. Remove the air cleaner to gain access to the idle air screws, but leave the vacuum lines connected.

3. Disconnect and plug the vacuum lines as indicated by the emission control sticker.

4. Connect a tachometer and a timing light to the engine, and if necessary, adjust the ignition timing to specifications. Disconnect the vacuum advance line, if directed by the instructions on the emission control sticker.

5. Carefully remove the idle mixture screw limiter caps. Lightly seat the screws by turning them into the carburetor base, and then back the screws out equally until the engine will run without stalling.

6. If the car has an automatic transmission, place the selector lever in Drive.

7. Back out the idle mixture screws, ⅛ of a turn at a time, until the maximum idle speed is obtained.

8. Adjust the engine idle speed to 25-50 rpm over the specified low rpm setting. Repeat Step 7, if necessary.

NOTE: *Two idle speed adjustments are normally required. One is the normal rpm setting, controlled by the adjustment of the electric solenoid screw, and the second adjustment, or low setting, is controlled by a screw on the carburetor throttle shaft lever. If the car has air conditioning, the solenoid may be used as an idle speed up control. To determine the type used, turn the air conditioning on; if the engine idle speed increases, the solenoid is used as a speedup device. The idle speed is then adjusted by the screw on the throttle shaft lever.*

9. Turn each screw in, ⅛ of turn at a time, until the idle speed reaches the specified idle rpm.

10. Reset the idle speed.

11. Connect all the vacuum lines and install the air cleaner. Recheck the idle speed and correct as necessary.

Idle Speed Adjustment

1978 2GC, 2GE Carburetor

1. Run the engine to normal operating temperature. Make sure that the choke is fully opened, set the parking brake, block the drive wheels, turn the air conditioning Off and connect a tachometer to the engine according to the manufacture's instructions.

2. Disconnect and plug the vacuum hoses at the vapor canister and EGR valve.

3. Place the transmission in Park (AT) or Neutral (MT).

4. Disconnect and plug the vacuum advance hose at the distributor. Set the ignition timing.

5. Reconnect the vacuum advance hose and turn the idle speed screw to obtain the specified rpm.

6. Connect all hoses and remove the tachometer.

1978-80 M2ME/M2MC/E2ME-210 Carburetor

1. Run the engine to normal operating temperature.

2. Make sure that the choke is fully opened, set the parking brake, block the wheels, connect a tachometer to the engine according to the manufacturer's instructions, disconnect the compressor clutch wire, turn the A/C Off, place the transmission in Drive, and disconnect and plug the vacuum advance hose at the distributor.

NOTE: *If instructions on car's underhood sticker differ from these, follow underhood sticker.*

3. Set the ignition timing, if necessary.

4. Reconnect the vacuum advance hose.

5. Disconnect the purge hose at the vapor canister.

6. On cars without A/C: set the idle speed screw to the specified rpm. Turn the A/C on. Open the throttle momentarily to extend the solenoid plunger, then adjust the solenoid screw to obtain the solenoid speed shown on the underhood sticker. Turn the A/C off.

7. Connect all hoses, and remove the tachometer.

1978-80 M4MC-M4ME Carburetor

1. Run the engine to normal operating temperature.

2. Make sure that the choke is fully opened, turn the A/C Off, set the parking brake and block the wheels.

3. Connect a tachometer to the engine according to the manufacturer's instructions.

4. Disconnect the purge hose from the vapor canister. On the 350, plug the purge hose.

5. Disconnect and plug the EGR vacuum hose at the valve. Disconnect and plug the vacuum advance hose.

6. Place the transmission in Park.

7. Check and adjust the timing.

8. Reconnect the vacuum advance hose.

9. Place the transmission in Drive.

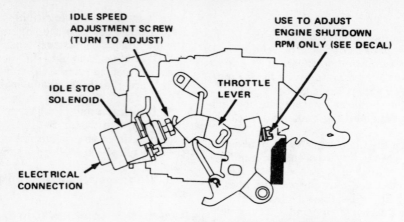

(MODELS NOT EQUIPPED WITH A/C)

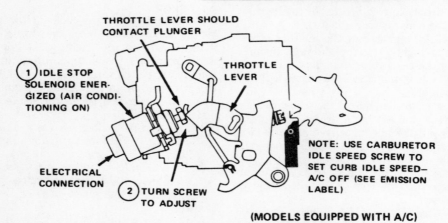

(MODELS EQUIPPED WITH A/C)

Typical 2 bbl idle speed adjustment locations

NOTE: *If the instructions on the underhood sticker differ from these, follow the underhood sticker.*

10. On cars without A/C: Turn the idle speed screw to obtain the specified rpm. On cars with A/C: Turn the idle speed screw to set the specified curb idle speed. Turn the A/C ON and disconnect the compressor clutch wire. Open the throttle momentarily to extend the solenoid plunger. Adjust the solenoid screw to obtain the solenoid idle speed shown on the underhood sticker. Reconnect the compressor clutch and turn the A/C Off.

11. Reconnect all hoses and remove the tachometer.

1981 and Later

Most 1981 and later models are equipped with an Idle Speed Control (ISC) mounted on the float bowl. Idle speeds are computer controlled by the ECM.

On some V8 models an Idle Load Compensator (ILC) is mounted on the float bowl to control the curb idle speed. The ILC is adjusted at the factory and capped.

If an idle problem is suspected on either of the above systems it is recommended that it be first verified that the idle speed is incorrect. You should verify that all basic engine systems are operational, that other tune-up adjustments and parts replacements have been performed within a reasonable length of time, and that there are no vacuum leaks or operating problems such as a clogged fuel filter or defective thermostat. You may want to refer adjustment to a qualified technician because a special tool is required to adjust the unit.

On cars that do not include either an ISC or ILC, but are equipped with air conditioning, an idle speed solenoid is used to maintain idle speed. For adjustment of these models refer to the 1978-80 adjustment procedures.

NOTE: *The underhood sticker specifies which idle system your car is equipped with.*

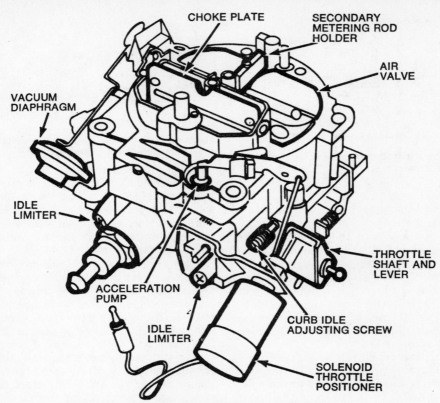

CHOKE PLATE

SECONDARY
METERING ROD
HOLDER

AIR
VALVE

VACUUM
DIAPHRAGM

IDLE
LIMITER

THROTTLE
SHAFT AND
LEVER

ACCELERATION
PUMP

IDLE
LIMITER

CURB IDLE
ADJUSTING SCREW

SOLENOID
THROTTLE
POSITIONER

Typical 4 bbl idle speed adjustment locations

Idle Load Compensator Adjustment

NOTE *:To accomplish this adjustment, you'll need a tachometer, a special adjusting tool J-29607, BT-8022 or the equivalent, a hex ³⁄₃₂" hex key, and a spare rubber cap, drilled so you can adjust the control with the cap in place.*

1. Prepare the car for adjustment by following all the instructions on the engine compartment sticker.

2. Connect a tachometer to the distributor TACH connector. Remove the air cleaner. Disconnect and plug the vacuum hoses going to the: Thermal Vacuum Valve, EGR valve, the canister purge port, and the Idle Load Compensator (ILC).

3. Back out the idle stop screw on the carburetor three turns. Make *sure* the A/C is off. Set the parking brake, put the transmission in PARK, and block the drive wheels.

4. Start the engine. If necessary, idle it until it is hot (warm water flows through the radiator). Hold the jam nut with a wrench while you turn the plunger as necessary to obtain 725 rpm ± 50 rpm on 1985 and 1986 models, and 700 ± on '87 models. Make sure to hold the nut

securely because, if it turns, this could damage the guide tabs.

5. Measure the distance from the jam nut to the tip of the plunger (Dimension A). It must be 1" or less. If the distance is too great, there is a problem in the engine electronics that is trying to drive the ILC to a low idle position. This must be corrected by someone familiar with diagnosing and repairing these systems before the ILC can be adjusted. Otherwise, proceed with the rest of the procedure.

6. Now, remove the plug and reconnect the ILC vacuum hose to the ILC port. Have a helper apply and hold the brake pedal and put the car in Drive. Read the idle speed on the tach. It should be 450 ± 25 rpm. If the reading meets specification, proceed to Step 12. Otherwise, proceed with the steps below.

7. Stop the engine. You must use a ³⁄₃₂" hex key wrench to adjust the ILC. Modify the wrench by cutting portions of it off, as necessary, so that you can adjust the valve on the car.

8. Remove the rubber cap from the center outlet tube of the ILC. Install the rubber cap through which you have drilled a hole. Install the hex wrench, passing through the hole in the

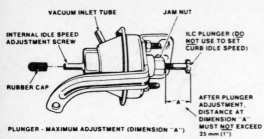

Adjusting the idle load compensator used on 1983 and later V8 engines

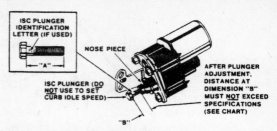

Measuring ISC plunger length ("Dimension A") and maximum adjustment ("Dimension B")

cap, engaging the wrench with the adjusting screw inside the ILC.

9. Have a helper start the engine with the brake applied and put the transmission in Drive. Then, turn the adjusting screw with the wrench until the rpm is 450. Turn the screw counterclockwise to increase speed and clockwise to decrease it. One turn equals about 75-100 rpm. When 450 rpm is attained, remove the wrench and the drilled cap. Install the undrilled rubber cap onto the fitting.

10. If the rpm is not correct, you'll have to repeat the adjustment, allowing for the amount and direction of the discrepancy. For example, if the rpm is 400, turn the screw one half turn counterclockwise. The adjustment is not correct until the engine runs at 450 rpm with the complete rubber cap installed.

11. Turn off the ignition switch. Then, disconnect the power feed to the ECM for at least 10 seconds. This is necessary for the ECM to reset the TPS value. The ECM is a large, flat black box located in front of the right side door. There are two multi-prong plugs located above the unit itself. Pull out the locking tabs and disconnect the plugs by pulling them upward and off.

12. Disconnect and plug the vacuum hose again. Apply a vacuum source such as a vacuum pump or a direct line to full intake manifold vacuum to the port to fully retract the plunger. Now, adjust the idle stop screw on the carburetor float bowl to give 450 rpm in Drive. Then, put the transmission in Park and turn the engine off.

13. Remove the plugs and reconnect all vacuum hoses. Install the air cleaner.

Idle Speed Control Adjustment

This device controls idle speed electronically via the Electronic Control Module. It is factory adjusted and does not require adjustment as a matter of routine maintenance. If diagnostic work indicates that idle speed is not to specification, and all the basic engine adjustments are correct, it may be adjusted. A special tool J-

29607, BT-8022 or equivalent is required to make the adjustment. The reason for this is that the plunger has an unusual head to discourage tampering. You will also need a tach and separate dwell meter and two jumper wires.

CAUTION: *Put the transmission in Park, apply the parking brake securely, and block the wheels before starting the engine.*

1. Look at the unthreaded portion of the adjustable plunger, just below the head, for a letter code. If there is a letter, note what it is for later use, and then go on to the next step. Except on the 3.8L V6 in 1986-87, if there is a letter, use the special wrench to remove the plunger by unscrewing it. Then, measure the length (Dimension A) from the threaded end to the inner surface of the head. Note and record this dimension for later use. On the 3.8L V6 in 1986-87, use the second line of the Idle Speed Control Adjustment chart, showing dimensions of $\frac{41}{64}"$ and $\frac{5}{16}"$.

2. Prepare the engine for adjustments as detailed on the engine compartment sticker. Connect a tachometer, using the distributor side of the TACH filter, if one is used.

3. Connect a dwell meter to the mixture control solenoid (M/C) dwell lead. Set the meter on the six cylinder scale, regardless of the type of engine.

4. Turn the A/C off.

5. Start the engine and run it until the ECM system enters closed loop operation. At this point, the dwell meter reading will begin to vary, indicating that the oxygen sensor is regulating fuel flow through a solenoid in the carburetor.

6. Now, turn the ignition switch off and unplug the connector going to the ISC motor.

7. Ground the **D** terminal of the motor connection (see illustration) with a jumper wire. Then, connect another jumper wire from the battery positive terminal to the **C** connection while simultaneously applying pressure with your finger to the plunger to help it retract.

WARNING: *If the plunger is not assisted in this way, the internals of the ISC may be damaged. As soon as the plunger has retracted, remove the 12 volt jumper to prevent dam-*

Idle Speed Control Adjustment Chart

Identification Letter	Plunger Length (in.)	Dimension "B" (in.)
NONE	$9/16$	$7/32$
NONE	$41/64$	$5/16$
X	$47/64$	$5/16$
A	$49/64$	$27/64$
Y	$51/64$	$15/32$
S	$27/32$	$1/2$
Z	$7/8$	$35/63$
G	$29/32$	$37/64$
E	1	$43/64$
L	$13/32$	$3/4$
J	$13/16$	$27/32$
N	$1\,17/64$	$59/64$
T	$1\,11/32$	1

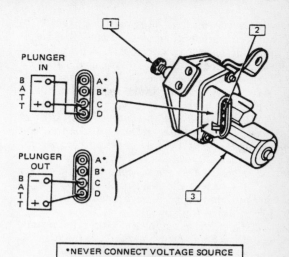

PLUNGER IN

PLUNGER OUT

*NEVER CONNECT VOLTAGE SOURCE ACROSS TERMINALS "A" AND "B"

1. ISC plunger (do not use to set curb idle speed)
2. Electrical connector
3. Motor

Making connections to retract and extend the plunger on the Idle Speed Control

age to the ISC. Make sure you make the right connections. If you were to connect across terminals **A** *and* **B**, *this, also, would cause ISC damage.*

8. Block the drive wheels and apply the parking brake. Start the engine and run it until the dwell meter reading varies. Then, put the transmission (if it's automatic) in Drive. Make sure the carburetor is off the fast idle cam.

9. Now, note the rpm on the tach and adjust the carburetor slow idle stop screw (minimum authority) to the lower figure shown in the tune-up chart. Then, if the car has an automatic transmission, put it back in Park.

10. Now, ground terminal **C** again, and jumper the 12 volt source to terminal **D** to fully extend the plunger. Leave the power connected **only long enough** to extend the plunger, or the ISC may be damaged. Again, doublecheck to make sure you are making the right connections.

11. On cars with manual transmissions:

Use the special tool to turn the plunger until the engine runs at the higher rpm (Maximum Authority) shown on the Engine Tune-Up chart.

On cars with automatic transmissions: with the transmission in Park, use the special tool to preset the plunger for 1,500 rpm. Then, set the parking brake and block the drive wheels and put the transmission in Drive. Now, use the special tool to turn the plunger to get the higher figure (Maximum Authority) shown in the Engine Tune-Up chart.

For both types of transmissions, re-apply power now as described in Step 10 to make sure the plunger is fully extended. Recheck the Maximum Authority rpm to make sure it is still correct. Readjust if necessary.

12. Now measure dimension **B**, as shown in the illustration. This is the distance from the back side of the plunger head to the front surface of the nose piece--the portion of the assembly the plunger fits into. This is the dimension you determined in Step 1. If the dimension is too great, adjust the plunger with the special tool until it is within the specified limit.

13. Fully retract the plunger by jumping the connections described in Step 7. Put the transmission in Park if it's an automatic. Turn the ignition switch off. Remove all instruments and jumper wires and reconnect the ISC motor connector. On engines using the E2ME 2-bbl carburetor, an INTERMITTENT trouble code will be sent. To clear this, you must remove battery voltage from the ECM (Electronic Control Module), a metal box located under the dash in the passenger compartment. With the ignition off, unplug the connector from this box or pull the fuse from the fuse box which is labeled ECM. The power must be interrupted for 10 seconds and **must be interrupted only with the ignition switch off**.

Idle Mixture Adjustment
1978-80

Changes in the carburetor for 1978-80 cars have made the adjustment of idle mixture impossible without the use of a propane enrichment system not available to the general public. Most 1979 and later carburetors have mixture screws concealed by staked-in plugs in order to discourage tampering. Backing out the mixture screw, of itself, will have very little effect on the mixture anyway. It is impossible to determine whether or not the adjustment is correct without a propane enrichment system. However, if you purchase a special tool, GM propane enrichment tool J–26911 or equivalent, you *can* perform this procedure. Follow these steps:

1. Set the parking brake securely and block the drive wheels.

WARNING: *On cars equipped with a vacuum parking brake release, disconnect and plug the actuation hose at the brake to prevent accidental release.*

2. Consult the engine compartment sticker and disconnect those hoses it says should be disconnected to perform propane enrichment idle mixture adjustment.

3. Operate the engine until it reaches normal operating temperature so that the choke is wide open, and at normal idle speed. Turn off the air conditioner, if the car has one.

4. Connect an accurate tachometer according to manufacturer's instructions.

5. Disconnect and plug the hose to the vacuum advance unit. Set the ignition timing according to the sticker specifications. If the car has electronic timing, merely check that the system is working as the sticker specifies. Then, unplug and reconnect the advance hose.

6. Disconnect the PCV tube at the air cleaner. Insert the hose with the rubber stopper coming from the propane valve into the crankcase ventilation opening in the air cleaner. Make sure the propane cartridge is in a vertical position.

7. Make sure the engine is idling and that, if the car has an automatic transmission, it is in Drive; if it has a manual transmission, make sure it is in Neutral. While holding the button on the propane control valve down, slowly open the valve as you watch the tach until maximum rpm is reached. Occasionally check the propane flow meter to make sure the cartridge is full, giving a good flow.

NOTE: *Make sure you open the valve very, very gradually. If you turn it out too fast and the mixture goes too rich, you will reach a point where increasing the valve opening will slow the rpm instead of speeding it up. If this should happen, close the valve, allow the engine to clear out the propane gas, and then start over with the gradual opening of the valve.*

8. Adjust the idle speed screw to give the enriched rpm setting shown on the engine compartment sticker. After changing the setting, readjust the propane valve very gradually either opening or closing it to get maximum rpm.

Then, reset the speed, if necessary. Repeat these procedures until you get the enrichment rpm setting with the optimum amount of propane.

9. Turn off the propane. Put the transmission in Neutral and then run the engine at 2,000 rpm for 30 seconds to clear it out. Return the engine to idle speed and put it back in gear (if equipped with an automatic).

10. Check the idle speed with the tach and observe whether or not the engine is idling smoothly. If the speed is correct, go to the last step. If the speed is correct but there is still rough idle, check for any vacuum leaks and repair them as necessary; then proceed to Step 13. If the idle is smooth but speed is either low or high, proceed with Step 11.

11. If idle speed is too low, back both idle screws out equally ⅛ turn at a time until the speed on the emission control label is reached. If the speed is too high, turn the screws in equally ⅛ turn at a time until until the correct idle speed is obtained. If either of these adjustments has been performed, now repeat the propane enrichment test to verify that the correct enriched idle speed specification is obtained when propane enrichment maximizes rpm (Step 8). If the specification is not reached, then readjust the idle speed screw as specified in Step 8.

12. Turn off the propane valve. Put the car in Neutral and clear out the engine by running it at 2,000 rpm for 30 seconds. Release the throttle and recheck idle speed (with the car in Drive if it has an automatic). If idle speed is incorrect, repeat the adjustment of the mixture as described in Step 11.

13. If the idle is still rough, turn the mixture screws in *very slowly and cautiously* until they seat *very lightly, counting the turns as you go*. Add the two figures for numbers of turns and then divide by two to get the average, i.e. 3 turns + 2 turns = 5 turns divided by two = 2½ turns. Turn each screw back out the average number of turns so that they are both backed out the same distance. Then, repeat the adjustment procedure, starting with Step 7.

14. Turn the engine off. Remove the propane enrichment testing equipment and reconnect the PCV system and other hoses.

1981 AND LATER

On these models the air/fuel mixture is controlled by the electronic control module of the computer command control system. No adjustment should be attempted.

ENGINE ELECTRICAL

Understanding the Engine Electrical System

The engine electrical system can be broken down into three separate and distinct systems: (1) the starting system; (2) the charging system; and (3) the ignition system.

BATTERY AND STARTING SYSTEM

The battery is the first link in the chain of mechanisms which work together to provide cranking of the automobile engine. In most modern cars, the battery is a lead-acid electro-chemical device consisting of two six-volt (2 V) subsections connected in series so the unit is capable of producing approximately 12 V of electrical pressure. Each subsection, or cell, consists of a series of positive and negative plates held a short distance apart in a solution of sulfuric acid and water. The two types of plates are made of dissimilar metals. This causes a chemical reaction to be set up, and it is this reaction which produces current flow from the battery when its positive and negative terminals are connected to an electrical appliance such as a lamp or motor. The continued transfer of electrons would eventually convert the sulfuric acid in the electrolyte to water, and make the two plates identical in chemical composition.

As electrical energy is removed from the battery, its voltage output tends to drop. Thus, measuring battery voltage and battery electrolyte composition are two ways of checking the ability of the unit to supply power. During the starting of the engine, electrical energy is removed from the battery. However, if the charging circuit is in good condition and the operating conditions are normal, the power removed from the battery will be replaced by the generator (or alternator) which will force electrons back through the battery, reversing the normal flow, and restoring the battery to its original chemical state.

The battery and starting motor are linked by very heavy electrical cables designed to minimize resistance to the flow of current. Generally, the major power supply cable that leaves the battery goes directly to the starter, while other electrical system needs are supplied by a smaller cable. During the starter operation, power flows from the battery to the starter and is grounded through the car's frame and the battery's negative ground strap.

The starting motor is a specially designed, direct current electric motor capable of producing a very great amount of power for its size. One thing that allows the the motor to produce a great deal of power is its tremendous rotating speed. It drives the engine through a tiny pinion gear (attached to the starter's armature), which drives the very large flywheel ring gear at a greatly reduced speed. Another factor allowing it to produce so much power is that only intermittent operation is required for it. Thus, little allowance for air circulation is required, and the windings can be built into a very small space.

The starter solenoid is a magnetic device which employs the small current supplied by the starting switch circuit of the ignition switch. This magnetic section moves a plunger which mechanically engages the starter and electrically closes the heavy switch which connects it to the battery. The starting switch circuit consists of the starting switch contained within the ignition switch, a transmission neutral safety switch or clutch pedal switch, and the wiring necessary to connect these with the starter solenoid or relay.

A pinion, which is a small gear, is mounted to a one-way drive clutch. This clutch is splined to the starter armature shaft. When the ignition switch is moved the start position, the solenoid plunger slides the pinion toward the flywheel ring gear via a collar and spring. If the teeth on the pinion and flywheel match properly, the pinion will engage the flywheel immediately. If the gear teeth butt one another, the spring will be compressed and will force the gears to mesh as soon as the starter turns far enough to allow them to do so. As the solenoid plunger reaches the end of its travel, it closes the contacts that connect the battery and starter and then the engine is cranked.

As soon as the engine starts, the flywheel ring gear begins turning fast enough to drive the pinion at an extremely high rate of speed. At this point, the one-way clutch begins allowing the pinion to spin faster than the starter shaft so that the starter will not operate at excessive speed. When the ignition switch is released from the "Start" position, the solenoid is de-energized, and a spring contained within the solenoid assembly pulls the gear out of mesh and interrupts the current flow to the starter.

Some starters employ a separate relay, mounted away from the starter, to switch the motor and solenoid current on and off. The relay thus replaces the solenoid electrical switch, but does not eliminate the need for a solenoid mounted on the starter used to mechanically engage the starter drive gears. The relay is used to reduce the amount of current the starting switch must carry.

THE CHARGING SYSTEM

The automobile charging system provides electrical power for operation of the vehicle's ignition and starting systems and all the electrical accessories. The battery serves an electrical surge or storage tank, storing (in chemical form) the energy originally produced by the engine-driven generator. The system also provides a means of regulating generator output to protect the battery from being overcharged and to avoid excessive voltage to the accessories.

The storage battery is a chemical device incorporating parallel lead plates in a tank containing sulfuric acid-water solution. Adjacent plates are slightly dissimilar, and the chemical reaction of the two dissimilar plates produces electrical energy when the battery is to a load such as the starter motor. The chemical reaction is reversible, so that when the generator is producing a voltage (electrical pressure) greater than that produced by the battery, electricity is forced into the battery, and the battery is returned to its fully charged state.

The vehicle's generator is driven mechanically, through V belts, by the engine crankshaft. It consists of two coils of fine wire, one stationary (the stator), and one movable (the rotor). The rotor may also be known as the armature and consists of fine wire wrapped around an iron core which is mounted on a shaft. The electricity which flows through the two coils of wire (provided initially by the battery in some cases) creates an intense magnetic field around both rotor and stator, and the interaction between the two fields creates voltage, allowing the generator to power the accessories and charge the battery.

Newer automobiles use alternating current generators or alternators because they are more efficient than the old DC generators, can be rotated at higher speeds, and have fewer brush problems. In an alternator, the field rotates while all the current produced passes only through the stator windings. The brushes bear against continuous slip rings rather than a commutator (which decreases their wear). This causes the current produced to periodically reverse the direction of its flow. Diodes (electrical one-way switches) block the flow of current from traveling in the wrong direction. A series of diodes is wired together to permit the alternating flow of the stator to be converted to a pulsating, but unidirectional flow at the alternator output. The alternator's field is wired in series with the voltage regulator.

The regulator consists of several circuits. Each circuit has a core, or magnetic coil of wire, which operates a switch. Each switch is connected to ground through one or more resistors. The coil of wire responds directly to system voltage. When the voltage reaches the required level, the magnetic field created by the winding of wire closes the switch and inserts a resistance into the generator field circuit, thus reducing the output. The contacts of the switch cycle open and close many times each second to precisely control voltage. Alternators are self-limiting as far as maximum current is concerned.

SAFETY PRECAUTIONS

Observing these precautions will ensure safe handling of the electrical system components, and will avoid damage to the vehicle's electrical system:

• Be absolutely sure of the polarity before making connections. Connect the cables positive to positive, and negative to negative. Connect positive cables first and then make the last connection to a ground on the body of the booster vehicle so that arcing cannot ignite hydrogen gas that may have accumulated near the battery. Even momentary connection of a booster battery with the polarity reserved will damage alternate diodes.

• Disconnect both vehicle battery cables before attempting to charge a battery.

• Never ground the alternator or generator output or battery terminal. Be cautious when using metal tools around a battery to avoid creating a short circuit between the terminals.

• Never ground the field circuit between the alternator and regulator.

• Never run a generator or alternator without load unless the field circuit is disconnected.

• Never attempt to polarize an alternator.

• Keep the regulator in place when taking voltage and current limiter readings.

• Use insulated tools when adjusting the regulator.

Ignition Coil

On all models, the ignition coil is located in the distributor cap, connecting directly to the rotor.

TESTING

Coil-in-Cap

1. Remove the distributor cap and remove the coil from it as described below.

2. Connect an ohmmeter across the primary connections, as shown by the ohmmeter and wiring on the left side. The resistance should be zero or very close to zero. High resistance or infinite resistance indicates a partial or complete open circuit, and the need to replace the coil.

3. Connect the ohmmeter between the primary ground and the coil secondary connector as shown via the ohmmeter and wiring on the right side of the illustration. Set the resistance to the higher scale. Test resistance as shown by the solid wire connections and then repeat the

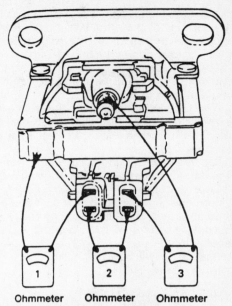

Testing the separately mounted ignition coil

test with the wire connected as shown by the dotted line. If both readings are infinite, the coil is bad. If both or either show continuity, the coil is okay.

Separately Mounted Coil

1. Disconnect the secondary lead and unplug the primary leads. Remove the mounting bolts and remove the coil from the engine.

2. First connect an ohmmeter, set to the high scale, as shown on the left. The resistance should be nearly infinite. If it is not, replace the coil.

3. Connect the ohmmeter as shown in the center picture. Use the low resistance scale. The reading should be very low, nearly zero. Otherwise, replace the coil.

4. Reset the ohmmeter to the high resistance scale and connect it as shown on the right. There should be obvious continuity; the ohmmeter should not read infinite. If it does replace the coil. If all three tests are passed, the coil is satisfactory.

REMOVAL AND INSTALLATION

1. Mark the high tension wires. Then, carefully disconnect each from the distributor cap. Squeeze the latches together and then disconnect the connector that runs from the cap to the distributor base.

2. Use a large, flat bladed screwdriver to first depress and then rotate the wire type latch away from the underside of the distributor on either side. Remove the cap.

3. Turn the cap upside down. Remove the

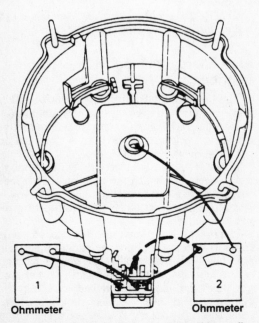

Testing the distributor-cap-mounted ignition coil

four bolts from the four corners of the coil, noting the location of the secondary ground lead. Then, remove the primary wiring from the connector in the cap, noting the routing of positive and negative leads.

4. Remove the coil and wiring. Then, remove the arc seal from underneath.

5. Wipe the mounting area for the coil clean with a soft cloth. Inspect the cap for defects, especially heat or carbon tracks, and replace it if necessary.

6. Install a new coil into position, and carefully route the primary wiring positive and negative leads properly.

7. Position the coil ground wire as it was at removal and then install and snug up the four coil mounting bolts. Install the cap and wiring in reverse order.

Ignition Module

REMOVAL AND INSTALLATION

1. Mark the high tension wires. Then, carefully disconnect each from the distributor cap. Squeeze the latches together and then disconnect the connector that runs from the cap to the distributor base.

2. Use a large, flat bladed screwdriver to first depress and then rotate the wire type latch away from the underside of the distributor on either side. Remove the cap.

3. Carefully note the colors of the two leads. Mark them, if necessary. Then disconnect them.

4. Remove the two module attaching screws and pull the module upward and out, being careful not to disturb the grease, if the module may be re-used.

NOTE: *The module is mounted via a thick layer of grease. This grease is like the coolant in an engine. It carries intense heat away from the module. Make sure to coat the lower surface of the module, as well as the mounting surface in the distributor with the grease included in the packed with the new module if the module is replaced. Make sure not to disturb the old grease layer on the old module if it is to be re-used. Failure to do this will cause the module to fail prematurely!*

5. Remount the module. Connect the leads in the proper order. Reverse the remaining procedures to install.

Distributor

REMOVAL AND INSTALLATION

1. Disconnect the ground cable from the battery.
2. Tag and disconnect the feed and module terminal connectors from the distributor cap.

3. Disconnect the hose at the vacuum advance (1975-80 only).

4. Depress and release the 4 distributor cap-to-housing retainers and lift off the cap assembly.

5. Using crayon or chalk, make locating marks on the rotor and module and on the distributor housing and engine for installation purposes.

6. Loosen and remove the distributor clamp and bolt and clamp, and lift the distributor out of the engine. Noting the relative position of the rotor and module alignment marks, make a second mark on the rotor to align it with the mark on the module.

7. With a new O-ring on the distributor housing and the second mark on the rotor aligned with the mark on the module, install the distributor, taking care to align the mark on the housing with the one on the engine. It may be necessary to lift the distributor and turn the rotor slightly to align the gears and the oil pump driveshaft.

8. With the respective marks aligned, install the clamp and bolt finger-tight.

9. Install and secure the distributor cap.

10. Connect the feed and module connectors to the distributor cap.

11. Connect a timing light to the engine and plug the vacuum hose.

12. Connect the ground cable to the battery.

13. Start the engine and set the timing.

14. Turn the engine off and tighten the distributor clamp bolt. Disconnect the timing light and unplug and connect the hose to the vacuum advance.

NOTE: *To avoid confusion, replace spark plug wires one at a time.*

High Energy Ignition (HEI) Distributor

The Delco-Remy High Energy Ignition (HEI) system is a breakerless (has no ignition points), pulse triggered, transistor controlled, inductive discharge ignition system that is standard on the cars covered in this guide.

There are only nine electrical connections in the system. These are the ignition switch feed wire and the eight spark plug leads. The coil is located in the distributor cap, connecting directly to the rotor.

The magnetic pick up assembly located inside the distributor contains a permanent magnet, a pole piece with internal teeth, and a pick up coil. When the teeth of the rotating timer core and pole piece align, an induced voltage in the pick-up coil signals the electronic module to open the coil primary circuit. As the primary current decreases, a high voltage is induced in the secondary windings of the ignition coil directing a spark through the rotor and high voltage leads to fire the spark plugs. The dwell period is automatically controlled by the electronic module and is increased with increasing engine rpm. The HEI system features, as do most electronic ignition systems, a longer spark duration which is instrumental in firing today's lean and EGR-diluted fuel/air mixtures (a lean mixture requires a much hotter, longer duration spark to ignite it than does a rich mixture). A capacitor, which looks like the condenser in the old points-type ignition systems, is located within the HEI distributor and is used to suppress noise (static) in the car's radio. The capacitor is not a regularly replaced component.

As noted in Chapter 2, 1981 and later models continue to use the HEI distributor, although it now incorporates an Electronic Spark Timing system (for more information on EST, please refer to Chapter 4). With the EST system, all spark timing changes are performed electronically by the Electronic Control Module (ECM) which monitors information from various engine sensors, computes the desired spark timing and then signals the distributor to change the timing accordingly. Because all timing changes are controlled electronically, no vacuum or mechanical advance systems are used.

REMOVAL AND INSTALLATION

Engine Not Disturbed

NOTE: *Do not rotate the engine while the distributor is out in order to make installing it simpler and easier. If the engine is inadvertently disturbed while the distributor is out, use the procedure below.*

1. Disconnect the ground cable from the battery. On 1984 and later models, disconnect the ignition switch battery feed wire and, if the car is equipped with a tach, the tachometer lead from the cap.

2. Tag and disconnect the feed and module terminal connectors from the distributor cap. DO NOT use a screwdriver to release the terminal connectors.

3. On 1975-80 models, disconnect the hose at the vacuum advance unit.

4. Depress and release the 4 distributor cap-to-housing retainers and lift off the cap assembly.

5. Using a magic marker, make locating marks on the rotor and module and on the distributor housing and engine to simplify installation.

NOTE: *The distributor must be installed with the rotor in the correct position.*

6. Loosen and remove the distributor clamp bolt and clamp. Carefully lift the distributor

just until the point where the rotor stops rotating. Be careful not to disturb the position of the rotor. Now, again mark the relative positions of rotor and distributor module. The rotor must be aligned with this position before you engage distributor and camshaft drive gears during installation.

7. With a new O-ring on the distributor housing and the second mark on the rotor aligned with the mark on the module, install the distributor, taking care to align the mark on the housing with the one on the engine. It may be necessary to lift the distributor and turn the rotor slightly to align the gears and the oil pump driveshaft.

8. With the respective marks aligned, install the clamp and the bolt finger-tight.

9. Install and secure the distributor cap.

10. Connect the feed and module connectors to the distributor cap. Reconnect the ignition switch battery feed wire and tach connector where necessary.

11. Connect a timing light to the engine and plug the vacuum hose.

12. Connect the ground cable to the battery.

13. Start the engine and set the timing.

14. Turn the engine off and tighten the distributor clamp bolt. Disconnect the timing light and unplug and disconnect the hose to the vacuum advance.

Engine Disturbed

1. Remove the valve cover on the No. 1 cylinder side or remove the No. 1 cylinder spark plug. Turn the engine over until it reaches Top Dead Center. As the engine approaches Top Center, you will feel air being expelled by the No. 1 cylinder or the valve rockers will both be in the valves closed position. If the crankshaft timing indicator says Top Center has been reached but the other condition is not being met, turn the engine another full turn (360°). Once the engine's position is correct, replace the spark plug or valve cover.

2. Using the firing order illustration if necessary, find No. 1 cylinder on the distributor cap. Turn the rotor until the firing contact is approximately aligned with the wire going to No. 1 cylinder, as if the distributor had just fired No. 1. Install the distributor as described above, turning the rotor slightly to mesh the gear teeth so that the rotor comes out in the proper position.

Alternator

ALTERNATOR PRECAUTIONS

● Always observe proper polarity of the battery connections; be especially careful when jump-starting the car.

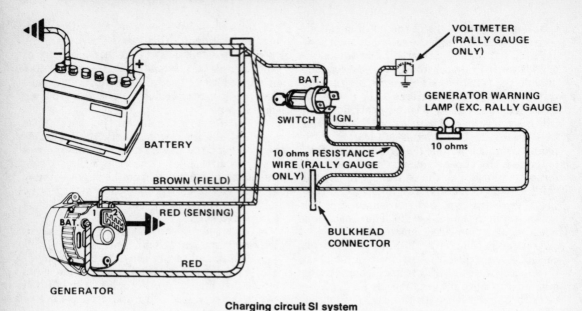

Charging circuit SI system

- Never ground or short out any alternator or alternator regulator terminals.
- Never operate the alternator with any of its or the battery's leads disconnected.
- Always remove the battery or disconnect its output lead while charging it.
- Always disconnect the battery ground cable when replacing any electrical component.
- Never subject the alternator to excessive heat or dampness. If you are steam-cleaning the engine, cover the alternator.
- Never use arc-welding equipment with the alternator connected.

REMOVAL AND INSTALLATION

1. Disconnect the battery ground cable.
2. V8 engines have their alternator mounted high on the right-hand side, unless the car is equipped with power steering and air-conditioning, in which case the alternator is mounted low on the left-hand side. V6 alternators are mounted on the right-hand side.
3. Disconnect all wiring to the alternator, noting the locations of the wires. You may find it helpful to mark the wires.
4. Loosen the alternator over until you can

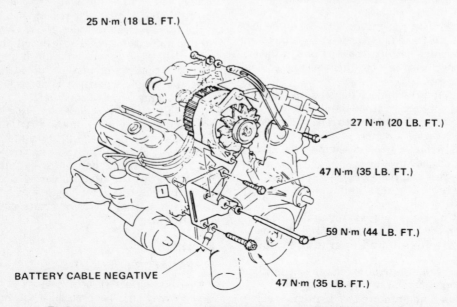

Typical alternator mounting—196, 231, 252, and 350 Buick built engines

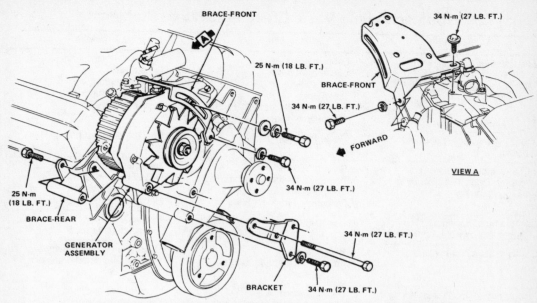

Typical alternator mounting—267, 305 and 350 Chevrolet built engines

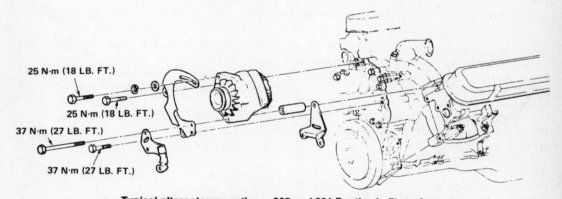

Typical alternator mounting—265 and 301 Pontiac built engines

remove the drive belt. On cars equipped with air-conditioning and/or power steering, it may be necessary to loosen one or the other to gain access to the alternator. In addition, it is sometimes far easier to work from underneath the car.

5. Remove the alternator mounting bolts and remove the alternator.

6. Installation is in the reverse order of removal. When adjusting the belts, make sure you can fairly easily depress the belt ¼-½" at the belt's mid-point with your thumb.

Regulator

A solid state regulator is mounted within the alternator. All regulator components are enclosed in a solid mold. The regulator is non-adjustable and requires no maintenance.

Battery

REMOVAL AND INSTALLATION

WARNING: *When working on the battery, be careful at all times to keep metal wrenches from connecting across the battery terminal posts.*

1. Use a wrench to loosen the through-bolt for the terminal. If necessary, use a screwdriver carefully to spread the terminal halves apart. Disconnect the negative terminal. Then, repeat the process to disconnect the positive terminal.

2. Remove the retainer screw from the retaining block located behind the battery. Remove the retainer.

3. Carefully lift the battery out of the engine compartment.

4. Thoroughly clean the entire battery box area. Use a mild solution of baking soda and wa-

Troubleshooting Basic Charging System Problems

Problem	Cause	Solution
Noisy alternator	• Loose mountings • Loose drive pulley • Worn bearings • Brush noise • Internal circuits shorted (High pitched whine)	• Tighten mounting bolts • Tighten pulley • Replace alternator • Replace alternator • Replace alternator
Squeal when starting engine or accelerating	• Glazed or loose belt	• Replace or adjust belt
Indicator light remains on or ammeter indicates discharge (engine running)	• Broken fan belt • Broken or disconnected wires • Internal alternator problems • Defective voltage regulator	• Install belt • Repair or connect wiring • Replace alternator • Replace voltage regulator
Car light bulbs continually burn out—battery needs water continually	• Alternator/regulator overcharging	• Replace voltage regulator/alternator
Car lights flare on acceleration	• Battery low • Internal alternator/regulator problems	• Charge or replace battery • Replace alternator/regulator
Low voltage output (alternator light flickers continually or ammeter needle wanders)	• Loose or worn belt • Dirty or corroded connections • Internal alternator/regulator problems	• Replace or adjust belt • Clean or replace connections • Replace alternator or regulator

ter to cut through the corrosion. This is done because the battery retains its charge better in a clean environment.

5. Replace the battery with one having an equal or higher rating in amp/hours. Note that the older a car is, the more likely it is to benefit from an increase in battery capacity due to increased resistance in the wiring.

6. Replace the battery in exact reverse order, making sure it is securely mounted before starting to connect the wiring. Make sure the battery terminals are clean, using a special brush designed for that purpose, if necessary.

7. Connect the positive terminal first, and then the negative, tightening them securely. Coat the terminals with petroleum jelly to protect them from corrosion.

WARNING: *Exercise extreme care in handling the battery. Remember it is filled with a highly corrosive acid.*

Starter

REMOVAL AND INSTALLATION

1. Disconnect the negative battery cable at the battery.

2. Raise the car and support it with jack stands.

3. Remove any starter braces or shields that may be in the way.

4. Remove the two starter motor to engine bolts, and allow the starter to drop down, collecting any shims and keeping them in order.

5. Disconnect the solenoid wires and battery cable and remove the starter.

6. Installation is the reverse of removal. Replace any shims that may have been removed.

STARTER SOLENOID REMOVAL AND INSTALLATION

1. Remove the screw and washer from the motor connector strap terminal.

2. Remove the two screws which retain the solenoid housing to the end frame assembly.

3. Twist the solenoid clockwise to remove the flange key from the keyway slot in the housing.

4. Remove the solenoid assembly.

5. With the solenoid return spring installed on the plunger, position the solenoid body on the drive housing and turn it counterclockwise to engage the flange key in the keyway slot.

6. Install the two screws which retain the solenoid housing to the end frame.

OVERHAUL

Drive Replacement

1. Disconnect the field coil straps from the solenoid.

2. Remove the through-bolts (usually 2), and separate the commutator end frame, field frame assembly, drive housing, and armature assembly from each other.

NOTE: *On diesel starters, remove the insulator from the end frame. The armature on the diesel starter remains in the drive end frame.*

Alternator Output Specifications

Year	Part No.	Alternator Field Current @ 12V	Output (amps)	Regulator Volts @ 75°F
1975	1102389	4–4.5	42	13.6–14.2
	1102391	4–4.5	61	13.6–14.2
	1102939	4–4.5	63	13.6–14.2
1976	1102389	4–4.5	42	13.6–14.2
	1102391	4–4.5	61	13.6–14.2
	1102939	4–4.5	63	13.6–14.2
1977	1102485	4–4.5	42	13.6–14.2
	1102486	4–4.5	61	13.6–14.2
	1102854	4–4.5	63	13.6–14.2
1978	1102841	4–4.5	42	13.6–14.2
	1102391	4–4.5	61	13.6–14.2
1979	1102389	4–4.5	42	13.9–14.5
	1102392	4–4.5	63	13.9–14.5
	1102842	4–4.5	63	13.9–14.5
1980	1100110	4–4.5	42	—
	1100111	4–4.5	63	—
	1101038	4–4.5	70	—
	1101044	4–4.5	70	—
	1101071	4–4.5	70	—
	1101060	4–4.5	80	—
1981	1100110	4–5	42	—
	1100167	4–5	63	—
	1103119	4–5	63	—
	1101437	4–5	70	—
	1101082	4–5	70	—
	1101088	4–5	70	—
	1101037	4–5	70	—
	1101084	4–5	85	—
	1101045	4–5	85	—
	1101085	4–5	85	—
1982	1101037	—	70	—
	1101084	—	85	—
	1101088	—	70	—
	1100121	—	60	—
	1101045	—	85	—
	1100110	—	42	—
	1103119	—	63	—
	1101082	—	70	—
	1100190	—	76	—

Alternator Output Specifications

Year	Part No.	Alternator Field Current @ 12V	Output (amps)	Regulator Volts @ 75°F
1982	1100198	—	38	—
	1100165	—	60	—
	1100194	—	70	—
	1101098	—	70	—
	1100156	—	55	—
1983	1101037	—	70	—
	1100121	—	60	—
	1100121	—	63	—
1984	1100206	—	56	—
	1100239	—	56	—
	1100208	—	66	—
	1100243	—	66	—
	1100247	—	66	—
	1105197	—	70	—
	1105250	—	70	—
	1105028	—	78	—
	1105041	—	78	—
	1100200	—	78	—
	1100217	—	78	—
	1105548	—	85	—
	1105552	—	85	—
	1105425	—	94	—
	1105428	—	94	—
	1105444	—	94	—
	1105425	—	94	—
	1105428	—	94	—
	1105441	—	94	—
	1105444	—	94	—
	1105547	—	94	—
	1105561	—	94	—
	1105562	—	94	—
	1105553	—	97	—
	1105509	—	108	—
	1105549	—	108	—
1985	1105441	—	94	13.5–16
	1105443	—	94	13.5–16
	1105444	—	94	13.5–16
	1104446	—	94	13.5–16
	1105447	—	94	13.5–16

Alternator Output Specifications (cont.)

Year	Alternator			Regulator
	Part No.	Field Current @ 12V	Output (amps)	Volts @ 75°F
1985	1105493	—	94	13.5–16
	1105496	—	94	13.5–16
	1105541	—	94	13.5–16
	1105592	—	94	13.5–16
	1105617	—	94	13.5–16
1986	1105197	—	70	13.5–16
	1100200	—	78	13.5–16
	1100239	—	85	13.5–16
	1105444	—	94	13.5–16
	1105546	—	85	13.5–16
	1105565	—	78	13.5–16
	1105685	—	120	13.5–16
1987	1100200	—	78	13.5–16
	1100239	—	56	13.5–16
	1101183	—	120	13.5–16
	1105197	—	70	13.5–16
	1105444	—	94	13.5–16

3. On diesel starters, remove the shift lever pivot bolt. On the diesel 25 MT starter only, remove the center bearing screws and remove the drive gear housing from the armature shaft. The shift lever and plunger assembly will now fall away from the starter clutch.

4. Slide the 2-piece thrust collar off the end of the armature shaft.

5. Slide a ⅝" deep socket, piece of pipe or an old pinion onto the shaft so that the end of the pipe, socket, or pinion butts up against the edge of the pinion retainer.

6. Place the lower end of the armature securely on a soft surface, such as a wooden block or thick piece of foam rubber. Tap the end of the socket, pipe or pinion, driving the retainer toward the armature end of the snapring.

7. Remove the snapring from the groove in the armature shaft with a pair of pliers. If the snapring is distorted, replace it with a new one during reassembly. Slide the retainer and starter drive from the shaft; on diesel starters, remove the fiber washer and the center bearing from the armature shaft. On gasoline engine starters, the shift lever and plunger may be disassembled at this time (if necessary) by removing the roll pin.

8. To reassemble, lubricate the drive end of the armature shaft with silicone lubricant. On diesel starters, install the center bearing with the bearing toward the armature winding, then

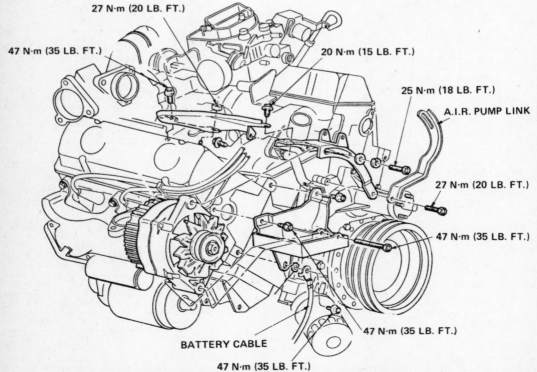

27 N·m (20 LB. FT.)
47 N·m (35 LB. FT.)
20 N·m (15 LB. FT.)
25 N·m (18 LB. FT.)
A.I.R. PUMP LINK
27 N·m (20 LB. FT.)
47 N·m (35 LB. FT.)
47 N·m (35 LB. FT.)
BATTERY CABLE
47 N·m (35 LB. FT.)

Typical alternator mounting—231 (Turbo) Buick built engine

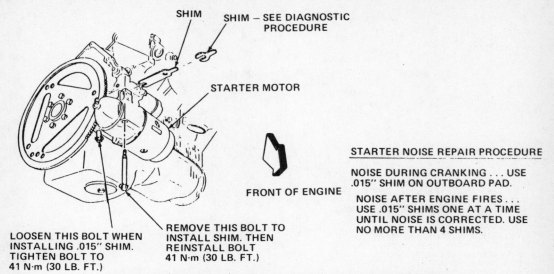

SHIM

SHIM — SEE DIAGNOSTIC PROCEDURE

STARTER MOTOR

FRONT OF ENGINE

LOOSEN THIS BOLT WHEN INSTALLING .015" SHIM. TIGHTEN BOLT TO 41 N·m (30 LB. FT.)

REMOVE THIS BOLT TO INSTALL SHIM. THEN REINSTALL BOLT 41 N·m (30 LB. FT.)

STARTER NOISE REPAIR PROCEDURE

NOISE DURING CRANKING . . . USE .015" SHIM ON OUTBOARD PAD.

NOISE AFTER ENGINE FIRES . . . USE .015" SHIMS ONE AT A TIME UNTIL NOISE IS CORRECTED. USE NO MORE THAN 4 SHIMS.

Typical starter motor mounting—Buick and Chevrolet built engines

install the fiber washer on the armature shaft.

9. Slide the starter drive onto the armature shaft with the pinion facing outward (away from the armature). Slide the retainer onto the shaft with the cupped surface facing outward.

10. Again support the armature on a soft surface, with the pinion on the upper end. Center the snapring on the top of the shaft (use a new ring if the old one was misshapen or damaged).

Gently place a block of wood on top of the snapring so as not to move it from a centered position. Tap the wooden block with a hammer in order to force the snapring around the shaft. Slide the ring down into the snapring groove.

11. Lay the armature down flat on your work surface. Slide the retainer close up onto the shaft and position it and the thrust collar next to the snapring. Using two pairs of pliers on op-

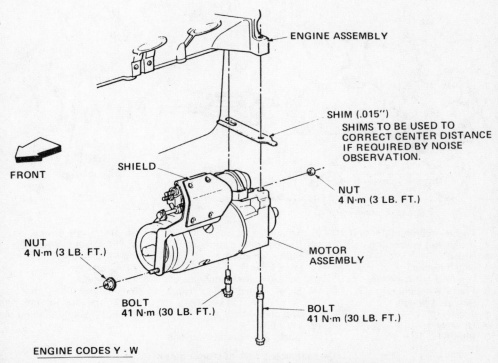

ENGINE ASSEMBLY

SHIM (.015")

SHIMS TO BE USED TO CORRECT CENTER DISTANCE IF REQUIRED BY NOISE OBSERVATION.

FRONT

SHIELD

NUT 4 N·m (3 LB. FT.)

NUT 4 N·m (3 LB. FT.)

MOTOR ASSEMBLY

BOLT 41 N·m (30 LB. FT.)

BOLT 41 N·m (30 LB. FT.)

ENGINE CODES Y - W

Typical starter motor mounting—Pontiac built engines

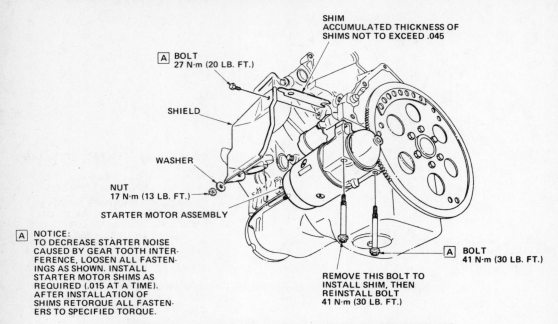

A BOLT
27 N·m (20 LB. FT.)

SHIM
ACCUMULATED THICKNESS OF
SHIMS NOT TO EXCEED .045

SHIELD

WASHER

NUT
17 N·m (13 LB. FT.)

STARTER MOTOR ASSEMBLY

A NOTICE:
TO DECREASE STARTER NOISE
CAUSED BY GEAR TOOTH INTER-
FERENCE, LOOSEN ALL FASTEN-
INGS AS SHOWN. INSTALL
STARTER MOTOR SHIMS AS
REQUIRED (.015 AT A TIME).
AFTER INSTALLATION OF
SHIMS RETORQUE ALL FASTEN-
ERS TO SPECIFIED TORQUE.

REMOVE THIS BOLT TO
INSTALL SHIM, THEN
REINSTALL BOLT
41 N·m (30 LB. FT.)

A BOLT
41 N·m (30 LB. FT.)

Typical starter motor mounting—Oldsmobile built engines (350, 403)

posite ends of the shaft, squeeze the thrust collar and the retainer together until the snapring is forced into the retainer.

12. Lube the drive housing bushing with a silicone lubricant.

13. Engage the shift lever yoke with the clutch. Position the front of the armature shaft into the bushing, then slide the complete drive assembly into the drive gear housing.

NOTE: *On non-diesel starters the shift lever*

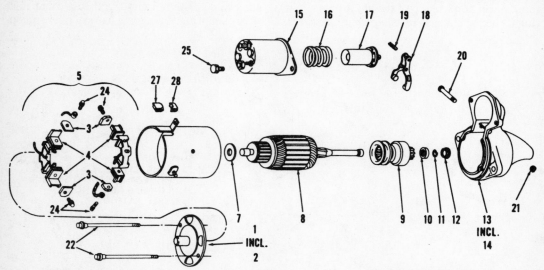

1. Frame—commutator end
2. Brush and holder pkg.
3. Brush
4. Brush holder
5. Housing—drive end
6. Frame and field asm.
7. Solenoid switch
8. Armature
9. Drive asm.
10. Plunger
11. Shift lever
12. Plunger return springer
13. Shift lever shaft
14. Lock washer
15. Screw—brush attaching
16. Screw—field lead to switch
17. Screw—switch attaching
18. Washer—brake
19. Thru bolt
20. Bushing—commutator end
21. Bushing—drive end
22. Pinion stop collar
23. Thrust collar
24. Grommet
25. Grommet
26. Plunger pin
27. Pinion stop retainer ring
28. Lever shaft retaining ring

Disassembled view of starter motor

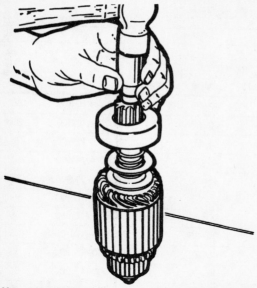

Use a piece of pipe to drive the retainer toward the snap ring

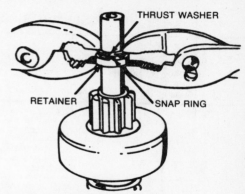

Snap ring installation

may be installed in the drive gear housing first.

14. On the 25 MT diesel starter only, install the center bearing screws and the shift lever pin. Work carefully and slowly to prevent damaging the starter brushes.

15. Apply a sealing compound approved for this application onto the drive housing, to the solenoid flange where the field frame contacts it. Position the field frame around the armature shaft and against the drive housing shaft and into position against the field frame. On diesel starters, install the insulator and then the end frame onto the shaft. Line up the bolt holes, then install and tighten the through-bolts (make sure they pass through the bolt holes in the insulator).

16. Lubricate the bushing in the commutator end frame with a silicone lubricant, place the leather washer onto the armature shaft, and then slide the commutator end frame over the pivot bolt, and tighten securely.

17. Connect the field coil straps to the motor terminal of the solenoid.

NOTE: *If replacement of the starter drive fails to cure improper engagements of the starter pinion to the flywheel, there may be defective parts in the solenoid and/or shift lever. The best procedure is to take the assembly to a shop where a pinion clearance check can be made by energizing the solenoid on a test bench. If the pinion clearance is incorrect, disassemble the solenoid and shift lever, inspect, and replace the worn parts.*

Starter Specifications

Year	Engine No. Cyl Displacement (cu in.)	Engine VIN Code	Starter							Brush String Tension (oz)
			Lock Test			No-Load Test				
			Amps	Volts	Torque (ft. lbs.)	Amps	Volts	RPM		
1978	6-196	C	Not Recommended			60–85	9	6,800–10,300		35
	6-231	A	Not Recommended			60–85	9	6,800–10,300		35
	6-231 ①	G	Not Recommended			60–85	9	6,800–10,300		35
	6-231 ①	3	Not Recommended			60–85	9	6,800–10,300		35
	8-301	Y	Not Recommended			45–70	9	7,000–11,900		35
	8-305	H	Not Recommended			45–70	9	7,000–11,900		35
	8-305	U	Not Recommended			60–85	9	6,800–10,300		35
	8-350	L	Not Recommended			65–95	9	7,500–10,500		35
1979	6-196	C	Not Recommended			60–85	9	6,800–10,300		35
	6-231	A	Not Recommended			60–85	9	6,800–10,300		35

Starter Specifications (cont.)

Year	Engine No. Cyl Displacement (cu in.)	Engine VIN Code	Starter							Brush String Tension (oz)
			Lock Test			No-Load Test				
			Amps	Volts	Torque (ft. lbs.)	Amps	Volts	RPM		
1979	6-231	2	Not Recommended			60–85	9	6,800–10,300		35
	6-231 ①	3	Not Recommended			60–85	9	6,800–10,300		35
	8-301	Y	Not Recommended			45–70	9	7,000–11,900		35
	8-301	W	Not Recommended			45–70	9	7,000–11,900		35
	8-305	A	Not Recommended			45–70	9	7,000–11,900		35
	8-350	L	Not Recommended			65–95	9	7,500–10,500		—
1980	6-231	A	Not Recommended			60–85	9	6,800–10,300		35
	6-231 ①	3	Not Recommended			60–85	9	6,800–10,300		35
	8-301	W	Not Recommended			45–70	9	7,000–11,900		35
	8-305	H	Not Recommended			45–70	9	7,000–11,900		35
1981	6-231	A	Not Recommended			60–85	9	6,800–10,300		35
	6-231 ①	3	Not Recommended			60–85	9	6,800–10,300		35
	6-265	S	Not Recommended			45–70	9	7,000–11,900		35
1982	6-231	A	Not Recommended			60–85	9	6,800–10,300		35
	6-231 ①	3	Not Recommended			60–85	9	6,800–10,300		35
	6-252	4	Not Recommended			65–95	9	7,500–10,500		35
	6-262 ②	V	Not Recommended			65–95	9	7,500–10,500		35
	8-350 ②	N	Not Recommended			160–220	9	4,000–5,500		35
1983	6-231	A	Not Recommended			60–90	10	6,500–11,500		35
	6-231 ①	8	Not Recommended			60–90	10	6,500–11,500		35
	6-252	4	Not Recommended			70–110	10	6,500–10,700		35
	8-350 ②	N	Not Recommended			160–240	10	4,400–6,300 ③		35
	6-260 ②	V	Not Recommended			160–240	10	4,400–6,300 ③		35
1984	6-231	A	Not Recommended			60–90	10	6,500–10,500		—
	6-231 ①	9	Not Recommended			60–90	10	6,500–10,500		—
	6-252	4	Not Recommended			—	10	—		—
	6-260 ② ④	V	Not Recommended			160–240	10	4,400–6,300 ③		—
1985	6-231	A	Not Recommended			60–90	10	6,500–10,500		—
	6-231 ①	9	Not Recommended			60–90	10	6,500–10,500		—
	8-350 ②	N	Not Recommended			125–170	10	3,200–4,100 ③		—
1986	6-231	A	Not Recommended			60–90	10	6,500–10,500		—
	6-231	7	Not Recommended			60–90	10	6,500–10,500		—
	8-307	Y	Not Recommended			50–75	10	6,000–11,900		—
1987	6-231	A	Not Recommended			60–90	10	6,500–10,500		—
	6-231	7	Not Recommended			45–74	10	8,600–12,900		—
	8-307	Y	Not Recommended			50–75	10	6,000–11,900		—

① Turbocharged engine
② Diesel
③ Pinion speed
④ With the aluminum bodied starter, amperage draw is 125–170 at 3,200–4,100 rpm pinion speed

Troubleshooting Basic Starting System Problems

Problem	Cause	Solution
Starter motor rotates engine slowly	• Battery charge low or battery defective	• Charge or replace battery
	• Defective circuit between battery and starter motor	• Clean and tighten, or replace cables
	• Low load current	• Bench-test starter motor. Inspect for worn brushes and weak brush springs.
	• High load current	• Bench-test starter motor. Check engine for friction, drag or coolant in cylinders. Check ring gear-to-pinion gear clearance.
Starter motor will not rotate engine	• Battery charge low or battery defective	• Charge or replace battery
	• Faulty solenoid	• Check solenoid ground. Repair or replace as necessary.
	• Damage drive pinion gear or ring gear	• Replace damaged gear(s)
	• Starter motor engagement weak	• Bench-test starter motor
	• Starter motor rotates slowly with high load current	• Inspect drive yoke pull-down and point gap, check for worn end bushings, check ring gear clearance
	• Engine seized	• Repair engine
Starter motor drive will not engage (solenoid known to be good)	• Defective contact point assembly	• Repair or replace contact point assembly
	• Inadequate contact point assembly ground	• Repair connection at ground screw
	• Defective hold-in coil	• Replace field winding assembly
Starter motor drive will not disengage	• Starter motor loose on flywheel housing	• Tighten mounting bolts
	• Worn drive end busing	• Replace bushing
	• Damaged ring gear teeth	• Replace ring gear or driveplate
	• Drive yoke return spring broken or missing	• Replace spring
Starter motor drive disengages prematurely	• Weak drive assembly thrust spring	• Replace drive mechanism
	• Hold-in coil defective	• Replace field winding assembly
Low load current	• Worn brushes	• Replace brushes
	• Weak brush springs	• Replace springs

Brush Replacement

1. After removing the starter from the engine, disconnect the field coil from the motor solenoid terminal.

2. Remove the starter through bolts and remove the commutator end frame and washer.

3. Remove the field frame and the armature assembly from the drive housing.

4. Remove the brush holder pivot pin which positions one insulated and one grounded brush.

5. Remove the brush springs.

6. Remove the brushes.

7. Installation is in the reverse order of removal.

ENGINE MECHANICAL

Design

All Buick, Olds and Pontiac engines covered in this guide, whether V6 or V8, are water cooled powerplants with pushrod valve actuation. All engines use cast iron cylinder blocks and heads.

The gasoline V8s are all very similar in construction and share common design features such as chain-driven camshafts, hydraulic valve lifters and pressed-steel rocker arms. The Buick engines, including V6s, differ in that they have their rockers mounted on shafts. Because of this similarity between the engines, many removal and installation procedures given here will simultaneously cover all three manufacturers' engines. Likewise, the 231 and 252 V6 engines are nearly identical among themselves and to the Buick V8s.

The 350 diesel is derived from the 350 cu. in. gasoline engine, but virtually all major engine parts were beefed up to withstand the higher compression ratio and combustion pressures. Fairly early in the production run the standard valve lifters were replaced with roller type hydraulic lifters. This was done because the particulates generated in diesel combustion and naturally getting into the oil were causing camshaft and lifter wear problems. Diesel cylinder head design is radically different from gas engine design, especially in that the diesel incorporates a special steel insert that forms a precombustion chamber and must be properly fitted to ensure correct head gasket gas seal.

One especially important difference in the diesel relates to the high compression ratio. The area between the piston top surface and the lower surface of the cylinder head is very small and there is minimal clearance between the piston and valves. For this reason, any engine work related to the valves, lifters and intake manifold requires particular attention to special diesel service procedures. Failure to follow these procedures will often result in bent valves or valve gear.

The diesel fuel system is considerably more complex and precise than the typical gas engine carburetor or injection system. Particular attention must be paid to fuel cleanliness and maintenance of various fuel filters and water separators. Service on this system usually requires extensive specialized tooling and training. It should never be tampered with, as this can even result in personal injury. Make sure you are properly equipped and fully aware of proper service procedures before you begin work on it.

Engine Overhaul Tips

Most engine overhaul procedures are fairly standard. In addition to specific parts replacement procedures and complete specifications for your individual engine, this chapter also is a guide to accepted rebuilding procedures. Examples of standard rebuilding practice are shown and should be used along with specific details concerning your particular engine.

Competent and accurate machine shop services will ensure maximum performance, reliability and engine life.

In most instances it is more profitable for the do-it-yourself mechanic to remove, clean and inspect the component, buy the necessary parts and deliver these to a shop for actual machine work.

On the other hand, much of the rebuilding work (crankshaft, block, bearings, piston rods, and other components) is well within the scope of the do-it-yourself mechanic if he has proper tools and a clean and adequate workshop.

TOOLS

The tools required for an engine overhaul or parts replacement will depend on the depth of your involvement. With a few exceptions, they will be the tools found in a mechanic's tool kit (see Chapter 1). More in-depth work will require any or all of the following:

- a dial indicator (reading in thousandths) mounted on a universal base
- micrometers and telescope gauges
- jaw and screw-type pullers
- scraper
- valve spring compressor
- ring groove cleaner
- piston ring expander and compressor
- ridge reamer
- cylinder hone or glaze breaker
- Plastigage®
- engine stand

Use of most of these tools is illustrated in this chapter. Many can be rented for a one-time use from a local parts jobber or tool supply house specializing in automotive work.

Occasionally, the use of special tools is called for. See the information on Special Tools and Safety Notice in the front of this book before substituting another tool.

INSPECTION TECHNIQUES

Procedures and specifications are given in this chapter for inspecting, cleaning and assessing the wear limits of most major components. Other procedures such as Magnaflux® and Zyglo® can be used to locate material flaws and stress cracks. Magnaflux® is a magnetic process applicable only to ferrous materials (not aluminum). The Zyglo® process coats the material with a fluorescent dye penetrant and can be used on any material. A check for suspected surface cracks can be more readily made using spot check dye. The dye is sprayed onto the suspected area, wiped off and the area sprayed with a developer. Cracks will show up brightly.

OVERHAUL TIPS

Aluminum has become extremely popular for use in engines, due to its low weight. Observe the following precautions when handling aluminum parts:

- Never hot tank aluminum parts (the caustic hot tank solution will eat or chemically destroy the aluminum.

• Remove all aluminum parts (identification tag, etc.) from engine parts prior to the tanking.

• Always coat threads lightly with engine oil or anti-seize compounds before installation, to prevent seizure.

• Never over-torque bolts or spark plugs especially in aluminum threads.

Stripped threads in any component can be repaired using any of several commercial repair kits (Heli-Coil®, Microdot®, Keenserts®, etc.).

When assembling the engine, any parts that will be frictional contact must be prelubed to provide lubrication at initial start-up. Any product specifically formulated for this purpose can be used, but engine oil is **not recommended** as a prelube. It lacks the viscosity necessary to maintain an adequate lubrication film.

When semi-permanent (locked, but removable) installation of bolts or nuts is desired, threads should be cleaned and coated with Loctite® or other similar, commercial non-hardening sealant.

REPAIRING DAMAGED THREADS

Several methods of repairing damaged threads are available. Heli-Coil® (shown here), Keenserts® and Microdot® are among the most widely used. All involve basically the same principle — drilling out stripped threads, tapping the hole and installing a prewound insert — making welding, plugging and oversize fasteners unnecessary.

Two types of thread repair inserts are usually supplied — a standard type for most Inch Coarse, Inch Fine, Metric Course and Metric Fine thread sizes and a spark lug type to fit most spark plug port sizes. Consult the individual manufacturer's catalog to determine exact applications. Typical thread repair kits will contain a selection of prewound threaded inserts, a tap (corresponding to the outside diameter

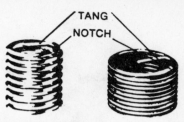

Standard thread repair insert (left) and spark plug thread insert (right)

threads of the insert) and an installation tool. Spark plug inserts usually differ because they require a tap equipped with pilot threads and a combined reamer/tap section. Most manufacturers also supply blister-packed thread repair inserts separately in addition to a master kit containing a variety of taps and inserts plus installation tools.

Before effecting a repair to a threaded hole, remove any snapped, broken or damaged bolts or studs. Penetrating oil can be used to free frozen threads; the offending item can be removed with locking pliers or with a screw or stud extractor. After the hole is clear, the thread can be repaired, as follows:

Drill out the damaged threads with specified drill. Drill completely through the hole or to the bottom of a blind hole

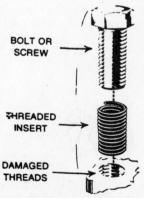

BOLT OR SCREW →

THREADED INSERT →

DAMAGED THREADS →

Damaged bolt holes can be repaired with thread repair inserts

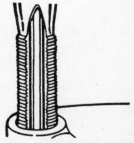

With the tap supplied, tap the hole to receive the thread insert. Keep the tap well oiled and back it out frequently to avoid clogging the threads

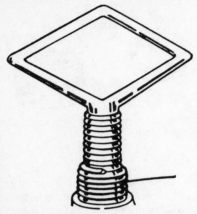

Screw the threaded insert onto the installation tool until the tang engages the slot. Screw the insert into the tapped hole until it is ¼–½ turn below the top surface. After installation, break off the tang with a hammer and punch.

Checking Engine Compression

A noticeable lack of engine power, excessive oil consumption and/or poor fuel mileage measured over an extended period are all indicators of internal engine wear. Worn piston rings, scored or worn cylinder bores, blown head gaskets, sticking or burnt valves and worn valve seats are all possible culprits here. A check of each cylinder's compression will help you locate the problems.

As mentioned in the Tools and Equipment section of Chapter 1, a screw-in type compression gauge is more accurate than the type you simply insert into the spark plug hole and hold, although it takes slightly longer to use. It's worth it to obtain a more accurate reading. Follow the procedures below for gasoline and diesel engined cars.

GASOLINE ENGINES

1. Warm up the engine to normal operating temperature.
2. Remove all spark plugs.
3. Disconnect the high tension lead from the ignition coil.
4. On fully open the throttle either by operating the carburetor throttle linkage by hand or by having an assistant floor the accelerator pedal.
5. Screw the compression gauge into the no.1 spark plug hole until the fitting is snug.
   NOTE: *Be careful not to crossthread the plug hole. On aluminum cylinder heads use extra care, as the threads in these heads are easily ruined.*
6. Ask an assistant to depress the accelerator pedal fully on both carbureted and fuel injected

The screw-in type compression gauge is more accurate

trucks. Then, while you read the compression gauge, ask the assistant to crank the engine two or three times in short bursts using the ignition switch.

7. Read the compression gauge at the end of each series of cranks, and record the highest of these readings. Repeat this procedure for each of the engine's cylinders. Compare the highest reading of each cylinder to the compression pressure specification in the Tune-Up Specifications chart in Chapter 2. The specs in this chart are maximum values.

A cylinder's compression pressure is usually acceptable if it is not less than 80% of maximum. The difference between each cylinder should be no more than 12-14 pounds.

8. If a cylinder is unusually low, pour a tablespoon of clean engine oil into the cylinder through the spark plug hole and repeat the compression test. If the compression comes up after adding the oil, it appears that the cylinder's piston rings or bore are damaged or worn. If the pressure remains low, the valves may not be seating properly (a valve job is needed), or the head gasket may be blown near that cylinder. If compression in any two adjacent cylinders is low, and if the addition of oil doesn't help the compression, there is leakage past the head gasket. Oil and coolant water in the combustion chamber can result from this problem. There

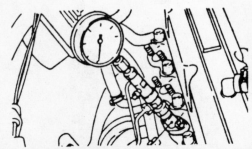

Diesel engines require a special compression gauge adapter

may be evidence of water droplets on the engine dipstick when a head gasket has blown.

Diesel Engines

Checking cylinder compression on diesel engines is basically the same procedure as on gasoline engines except for the following:

1. A special compression gauge adaptor suitable for diesel engines (because these engines have much greater compression pressures) must be used.

2. Remove the injector tubes and remove the injectors from each cylinder.

NOTE: *Don't forget to remove the washer*

General Engine Specifications

Year	Engine V.I.N. Code	Engine Type (No. of cyl- C.I.D.)	Engine Manufac- turer	Fuel Delivery	Horsepower @ rpm ①	Torque @ rpm (ft lbs) ①	Bore x Stroke (in.)	Compression Ratio	Oil Pressure (psi @ rpm)
'75	C	8-350	Buick	2bbl	110 @ 4000	175 @ 2000	3.800 x 3.400	8.0:1	37 @ 2400
	H	8-350	Buick	2bbl	145 @ 3200	270 @ 2000	3.800 x 3.850	8.1:1	37 @ 2400
	J	8-350	Buick	4bbl	165 @ 3800	260 @ 2200	3.800 x 3.850	8.0:1	37 @ 2400
'76	C	6-231	Buick	2bbl	105 @ 3400	185 @ 2000	3.800 x 3.400	8.0:1	37 @ 2600
	H	8-350	Buick	2bbl	140 @ 3400	280 @ 1600	3.800 x 3.850	8.0:1	37 @ 2600
	J	8-350	Buick	4bbl	155 @ 3400	280 @ 1800	3.800 x 3.850	8.0:1	37 @ 2600
'77	C	6-231	Buick	2bbl	105 @ 3200	185 @ 2000	3.800 x 3.400	8.0:1	37 @ 2600
	H	8-350	Buick	2bbl	140 @ 3200	280 @ 1400	4.057 x 3.385	8.0:1	37 @ 2600
	J	8-350	Buick	4bbl	155 @ 3400	275 @ 1800	4.057 x 3.385	8.0:1	37 @ 2600
	R	8-350	Olds.	4bbl	170 @ 3800	275 @ 2400	4.057 x 3.385	8.0:1	40 @ 1500
	L	8-350	Chev.	4bbl	170 @ 3800	270 @ 2400	4.000 x 3.480	8.5:1	35–40 @ 2400
	K	8-403	Olds.	4bbl	185 @ 3600	315 @ 2400	4.351 x 3.385	7.9:1	40 @ 1500
'78	C	6-196	Buick	2bbl	90 @ 3600	165 @ 2000	3.500 x 3.400	8.0:1	37 @ 2600
	A	6-231	Buick	2bbl	105 @ 3400	185 @ 2000	3.800 x 3.400	8.0:1	37 @ 2600
	G	6-231 ②	Buick	2bbl	150 @ 3800	245 @ 2400	3.800 x 3.400	8.0:1	37 @ 2600
	3	6-231 ②	Buick	4bbl	165 @ 4000	285 @ 2800	3.800 x 3.400	8.0:1	37 @ 2600
	Y	8-301	Pont.	2bbl	140 @ 3600	235 @ 2000	4.000 x 3.000	8.2:1	37 @ 2600
	H	8-305	Chev.	2bbl	145 @ 3800	245 @ 2400	3.736 x 3.480	8.5:1	35–40 @ 2400
	U	8-305	Chev.	4bbl	160 @ 4000	285 @ 2400	3.736 x 3.480	8.5:1	35–40 @ 2400
	L	8-350	Chev.	4bbl	170 @ 3800	275 @ 2000	4.000 x 3.480	8.5:1	35–40 @ 2400
'79	C	6-196	Buick	2bbl	105 @ 3800	160 @ 2000	3.500 x 3.400	8.0:1	37 @ 2600
	A	6-231	Buick	2bbl	115 @ 3800	190 @ 2000	3.800 x 3.400	8.0:1	37 @ 2600
	2	6-231	Buick	2bbl	115 @ 3800	190 @ 2000	3.800 x 3.400	8.0:1	37 @ 2600
	3	6-231 ②	Buick	4bbl	165 @ 4000	285 @ 2800	3.800 x 3.400	8.0:1	37 @ 2600
	Y	8-301	Pont.	2bbl	140 @ 3600	235 @ 2000	4.000 x 3.000	8.2:1	40 @ 2000
	W	8-301	Pont.	4bbl	150 @ 3800	255 @ 2400	4.000 x 3.000	8.2:1	40 @ 2600
	H	8-305	Chev.	4bbl	160 @ 4000	235 @ 2400	3.736 x 3.480	8.5:1	35–40 @ 2400
	L	8-350	Chev.	4bbl	160 @ 3800	260 @ 2400	4.000 x 3.480	8.5:1	35–40 @ 2400
'80	A	6-231	Buick	2bbl	115 @ 3800	190 @ 2000	3.800 x 3.400	8.0:1	37 @ 2400
	3	6-231 ②	Buick	4bbl	165 @ 4000	265 @ 2800	3.800 x 3.400	8.0:1	37 @ 2400
	W	8-301	Pont.	4bbl	150 @ 4000	240 @ 2000	4.000 x 3.000	8.2:1	40 @ 2600
	H	8-305	Chev.	4bbl	155 @ 4000	235 @ 2400	3.736 x 3.480	8.5:1	35–40 @ 2400

General Engine Specifications (cont.)

Year	Engine V.I.N. Code	Engine Type (No. of cyl- C.I.D.)	Engine Manufac- turer	Fuel Delivery	Horsepower @ rpm ①	Torque @ rpm (ft lbs) ①	Bore x Stroke (in.)	Compression Ratio	Oil Pressure (psi @ rpm)
'81	A	6-231	Buick	2bbl	110 @ 3800	190 @ 1600	3.800 x 3.400	8.0:1	37 @ 2400
	3	6-231 ②	Buick	4bbl	170 @ 4000	275 @ 2400	3.800 x 3.400	8.0:1	37 @ 2400
	S	8-265	Pont.	2bbl	119 @ 4000	204 @ 2000	3.750 x 3.000	8.0:1	35–40 @ 2600
	W	8-301	Pont.	4bbl	155 @ 4000	240 @ 2000	4.000 x 3.000	8.2:1	40 @ 2600
'82	A	6-231	Buick	2bbl	110 @ 3800	190 @ 1600	3.800 x 3.400	8.0:1	37 @ 2400
	3	6-231 ②	Buick	4bbl	170 @ 3800	275 @ 2600	3.800 x 3.400	8.0:1	37 @ 2400
	4	6-252	Buick	4bbl	125 @ 4000	205 @ 2000	3.965 x 3.400	8.0:1	37 @ 2400
	V	6-263	Olds.	D.F.I.	85 @ 3600	165 @ 1600	4.057 x 3.385	21.6:1	30–45 @ 1500
	J	8-267	Chev.	2bbl	115 @ NA	205 @ NA	3.500 x 3.480	8.3:1	35–40 @ 2600
	H	8-350	Chev.	4bbl	140 @ 3600	240 @ 1600	3.736 x 3.480	8.0:1	35–40 @ 2600
	N	8-350	Olds.	D.F.I.	105 @ 3200	200 @ 1600	4.057 x 3.385	21.6:1	30–45 @ 1500
'83	A	6-231	Buick	2bbl	110 @ 3800	190 @ 1600	3.800 x 3.400	8.0:1	37 @ 2400
	3	6-231 ②	Buick	4bbl	170 @ 3800	275 @ 2600	3.800 x 3.400	8.0:1	37 @ 2400
	4	6-252	Buick	4bbl	125 @ 4000	205 @ 2000	3.965 x 3.400	8.0:1	37 @ 2400
	V	6-263	Olds.	D.F.I.	85 @ 3600	165 @ 1600	4.057 x 3.385	21.6:1	30–45 @ 1500
	N	8-350	Olds.	D.F.I.	150 @ 3200	200 @ 1600	4.057 x 3.385	21.6:1	30–45 @ 1500
'84	A	6-231	Buick	2bbl	110 @ 3800	190 @ 1600	3.800 x 3.400	8.0:1	37 @ 2400
	9	6-231 ②	Buick	SFI	200 @ 4000	300 @ 2400	3.800 x 3.400	8.0:1	37 @ 2400
	4	6-252	Buick	4bbl	125 @ 4000	205 @ 2000	3.965 x 3.400	8.0:1	37 @ 2400
	V	6-263	Olds.	DFI	85 @ 3600	165 @ 1600	4.057 x 3.385	21.6:1	30–45 @ 1500
'85	A	6-231	Buick	2bbl	110 @ 3800	190 @ 1600	3.80 x 3.400	8.0:1	37 @ 2400
	9	6-231 ②	Buick	SFI	200 @ 4000	300 @ 2400	3.800 x 3.400	8.0:1	37 @ 2400
	V	6-263	Olds.	DFI	85 @ 3600	165 @ 1600	4.057 x 3.385	21.6:1	30–45 @ 1500
'86	A	231	Buick	2bbl	110 @ 3800	190 @ 1600	3.800 x 3.400	8.0:1	37 @ 2400
	7	231 ②	Buick	SFI	235 @ 4400	330 @ 2800	3.800 x 3.400	8.0:1	37 @ 2400
	Y	307	Olds.	4bbl	148 @ 3800	250 @ 2400	3.800 x 3.385	8.0:1	40 @ 1500
'87	A	231	Buick	2bbl	110 @ 3800	190 @ 1600	3.800 x 3.400	8.0:1	40 @ 1500
	7	231 ②	Buick	SFI	245 @ 4400	355 @ 2800	3.800 x 3.400	8.9:1	37 @ 2400
	Y	307	Olds.	4bbl	148 @ 3800	250 @ 2400	3.800 x 3.385	8.0:1	40 @ 1500

C.I.D.—Cubic inch displacement   D.F.I.—Diesel fuel injection   NA—Not available at press time.
① Horsepower and torque are SAE net figures. They are measured at the rear of the transmission with all accessories installed and operating. Since the figures vary when a given engine is installed in different models, some are representative rather than exact.
② Turbocharged engine

underneath each injector; otherwise, it may get lost when the engine is cranked.

3. When fitting the compression gauge adaptor to the cylinder head, make sure the bleeder of the gauge (if equipped) is closed.

4. When reinstalling the injector assemblies, install new washers underneath each injector.

Engine
REMOVAL AND INSTALLATION

NOTE: *Refer to the vehicle and engine identification chart at the beginning of Chapter 1 to determine the type and manufacturer of the engine used in your vehicle.*

Valve Specifications

Year	Engine No. Cyl. Displacement (cu in.)	Seat Angle (deg)	Face Angle (deg)	Spring Test Pressure (lbs. @ in.)	Spring Installed Height (in.)	Stem to Guide Clearance (in.) Intake	Stem to Guide Clearance (in.) Exhaust	Stem Diameter (in.) Intake	Stem Diameter (in.) Exhaust
'75–'76	6-231 Buick	45	45	164 @ 1.34 ①	1⁴⁷/₆₄	.0015–.0035	.0015–.0032	.3407	.3407
	8-350 Buick	45	45	180 @ 1.34	1⁴⁷/₆₄	.0015–.0035	.0015–.0032	.3426	.3427
'77	6-231 Buick	45	45	164 @ 1.34	1⁴⁷/₆₄	.0015–.0035	.0015–.0035	.340	.340
	8-350 Olds.	45③	44③	180 @ 1.34	1⁴⁷/₆₄	.0010–.0027	.0015–.0032	.3425	.3420
	8-350 Buick	45	45	180 @ 1.34	1⁴⁷/₆₄	.0015–.0032	.0015–.0032	.3430	.3427
	8-350 Chev.	46	45	206 @ 1.25	1²³/₃₂④	.0010–.0037	.0010–.0037	.3410	.3410
	8-403 Olds.	45③	44③	180 @ 1.34	1⁴⁷/₆₄	.0010–.0027	.0015–.0032	.3425	.3420
'78	6-196 Buick	45	45	168 @ 1.327	1⁴⁷/₆₄	.0015–.0032	.0015–.0032	.3405–.3412	.3405–.3412
	6-231 Buick	45	45	168 @ 1.327	1⁴⁷/₆₄	.0015–.0032	.0015–.0032	.3405–.3412	.3405–.3412
	8-305 Chev.	46	45	200 @ 1.160	1²³/₃₂④	.0010–.0037	.0010–.0037	.3410	.3410
	8-350 Chev.	46	45	200 @ 1.160	1²³/₃₂④	.0010–.0037	.0010–.0037	.3410	.3410
'79–'80	6-196 Buick	45	45	165 @ 1.340	1⁴⁷/₆₄	.0015–.0032	.0015–.0032	.3405–.3412	.3405–.3412
	6-231 Buick	45	45	164 @ 1.340 ①	1⁴⁷/₆₄	.0015–.0032	.0015–.0032	.3401–.3412	.3405–.3412
	8-301 Pont.	46	45	170 @ 1.260	1⁴⁷/₆₄	.0017–.0020	.0017–.0020	.3400	.3400
	8-305 Chev.	46	45	200 @ 1.250	1²³/₃₂	.0010–.0037	.0010–.0047	.3410	.3410
	8-350 Chev.	46	45	200 @ 1.250	1²³/₃₂	.0010–.0037	.0010–.0037	.3410	.3410
'81	6-231 Buick	45	45	164 @ 1.34②	1⁴⁷/₆₄	.0015–.0035	.0015–.0032	.3401–.3412	.3405–.3412
	8-265 Pont.	45	45	170 @ 1.29	1⁴³/₆₄	.0010–.0027	.0010–.0027	.3425	.3425
	8-301 Pont.	46	45	170 @ 1.27	1⁴⁷/₆₄	.0017–.0020	.0017–.0020	.3400	.3400
'82	6-231 Buick	45	45	182 @ 1.34	1⁴⁷/₆₄	.0015–.0035	.0015–.0032	.3407	.3409
	6-252 Buick	45	45	164 @ 1.34	1⁴⁷/₆₄	.0015–.0035	.0015–.0032	.3407	.3409
	6-263 Olds.	⑥	⑥	⑦	⑧	.0010–.0027	.0015–.0032	.3429	.3424
	8-267 Chev.	46	45	180 @ 1.25	1²³/₃₂	.0010–.0027	.0010–.0027	.3414	.3414

Valve Specifications (cont.)

Year	Engine No. Cyl. Displacement (cu in.)	Seat Angle (deg)	Face Angle (deg)	Spring Test Pressure (lbs. @ in.)	Spring Installed Height (in.)	Stem to Guide Clearance (in.)		Stem Diameter (in.)	
						Intake	Exhaust	Intake	Exhaust
'83	8-305 Chev.	46	45	180 @ 1.25	1 23/32	.0010–.0027	.0010–.0027	.3414	.3414
	8-350 Olds.	⑨	⑩	151 @ 1.30	1 43/64	.0010–.0027	.0015–.0032	.3429	.3429
	6-231 Buick	45	45	182 @ 1.34	1 47/64	.0015–.0035	.0015–.0032	.3407	.3407
	6-252 Buick	45	45	164 @ 1.34	1 47/64	.0015–.0035	.0015–.0032	.3407	.3409
	6-263 Olds.	⑥	⑥	⑦	⑧	.0010–.0027	.0015–.0032	.3429	.3424
	8-350 Olds.	⑨	⑩	210 @ 1.23	1 47/64	.0010–.0027	.0015–.0032	.3428	.3428
'84	6-231 Buick	45	45	182 @ 1.34	1 47/64	.0015–.0035	.0015–.0032	.3407	.3407
	6-231 Buick ⑪	45	45	220 @ 1.34	1 47/64	.0015–.0035	.0015–.0032	.3407	.3407
	6-252 Buick	45	45	182 @ 1.34	1 47/64	.0015–.0035	.0015–.0032	.3407	.3407
	6-263 Olds.	⑥	⑥	⑦	⑧	.0010–.0027	.0015–.0032	.3427	.3424
'85	6-231 Buick	45	45	182 @ 1.34	1 47/64	.0015–.0035	.0015–.0032	.3407	.3407
	6-231 Buick ⑪	45	45	220 @ 1.34	1 47/64	.0015–.0035	.0015–.0032	.3407	.3407
	6-263 Olds.	⑥	⑥	⑦	⑧	.0010–.0027	.0015–.0032	.3427	.3424
'86	6-231 Buick	45	45	182 @ 1.34	1 47/64	.0015–.0035	.0015–.0032	.3407	.3409
	6-231 Buick	45	45	185 @ 1.34	1 47/64	.0015–.0035	.0015–.0032	.3407	.3409
	8-307 Olds.	45 ③	45 ③	187 @ 1.27	1 47/64	.0010–.0027	.0015–.0032	.3429	.3424
'87	6-231 Buick	45	45	182 @ 1.34	1 47/64	.0015–.0035	.0015–.0032	.3407	.3409
	6-231 Buick	45	45	185 @ 1.34	1 47/64	.0015–.0035	.0015–.0032	.3407	.3409
	8-307 Olds.	45 ③	45 ③	187 @ 1.27	1 47/64	.0010–.0027	.0015–.0032	.3429	.3424

① Exhaust—182 @ 1.34
② Exhaust—175 @ 1.34
③ Exhaust valve seat angle—31, exhaust valve face angle—30
④ Exhaust—1 19/32
⑤ Intake: 180 @ 1.340
Exhaust: 177 @ 1.450
⑥ Intake—44° face; 45° seat; Exhaust—30° face; 31° seat
⑦ 203–217 @ 1.220 in.
⑧ Not available
⑨ Intake—45°, exhaust—31°
⑩ Intake—46°, exhaust—30°
⑪ Turbocharged Engine

Camshaft Specifications
All measurements in inches

Year	Engine Type/ Disp. L(cu in.)	Journal Diameter					Bearing Clearance	Lobe Lift		Camshaft End Play
		1	2	3	4	5		Intake	Exhaust	
'78–'79	3.2(196) Buick	——————— 1.785–1.786 ———————					①	NA	NA	NA
'75–'87	3.8(231) Buick	——————— 1.785–1.786 ———————					①	NA	NA	NA
'82–'85	4.1(252) Buick	——————— 1.785–1.786 ———————					①	NA	NA	NA
'82–'83	4.3(263) Olds.	NA	2.185–2.224	2.185–2.224	2.185–2.225		.0020–.0059	NA	NA	.0008–.0228
'84–'85	4.3(263) Olds.	NA	2.015–2.016	1.996–1.995	1.976–1.975		.0020–.0043	.252	.279	.0008–.0228
'80–'81	4.3(265) Pont.	——————— 1.900 ———————					NA	NA	NA	NA
'79–'81	4.9(301) Pont.	——————— 1.900 ———————					NA	NA	NA	NA
'78–'81	5.0(305) Chev.	——————— 1.8682–.8692 ———————					NA	.2484	.2667	.004–.012
'86–'87	5.0 (307) Olds.	2.035–2.037	2.015–2.017	1.995–1.997	1.975–1.977	1.955–1.957	.002–.006	.247	.251	.006–.022
'75–'81	5.7(350) Buick	——————— 1.785–1.786 ———————					①	NA	NA	NA
'77–'79	5.7(350) Chev.	——————— 1.8682–1.8692 ———————					NA	.2600	.2733	NA
'77–'83	5.7(350) Olds.	2.0357–2.0365	2.0357–2.0365	1.9957–1.9965	1.9957–1.9965	1.9957–1.9965	.0020–.0058	NA	NA	.011–.077
'77	6.6(403) Olds.	2.0357–2.0365	2.0357–2.0365	1.9957–1.9965	1.9957–1.9965	1.9957–1.9965	.0020–.0058	NA	NA	.011–.077

① #1, .0005–.0025
#2,3,4, and 5, .0005–.0035
NA Not Available

Ring Side Clearance
(All measurements are given in inches)

Year	Engine No. Cyl. Displacement (cu. in.)	Top Compression	Bottom Compression	Oil Control
'75–'87	6-231, 252, 8-350 Buick	.0030–.0050	.0030–.0050	.0035 Max.
'79–'81	8-265, 301 Pont.	.0015–.0035	.0015–.0035	.0015–.0035
'77–'78	8-305, 350 Chev.	.0012–.0042	.0012–.0042	.0020–.0080
'79–'83	8-305, 350 Chev.	.0012–.0032	.0012–.0032	.0020–.0080
'86–'87	8-307 Olds.	.0018–.0038	.0018–.0038	.0010–.0050
'77	8-350 Olds.	.0020–.0040	.0020–.0040	.0010–.0050
'77	8-403 Olds.	.0020–.0040	.0020–.0040	.0150–.0550
'78–'79	6-196 Buick	.0030–.0050	.0030–.0050	.0035 Max.
'81–'83	8-350 Olds Diesel	.005–.007	.0018–.0038	.001–.005
'82–'85	6-263 Olds Diesel	.005–.007	.003–.005	.001–.005

N.A. Not Available

Crankshaft and Connecting Rod Specifications
(All measurements are given in inches)

Year	Engine No. Cyl. Displacement (cu in.)	Crankshaft				Connecting Rod		
		Main Brg. Journal Dia	Main Brg. Oil Clearance	Shaft End-Play	Thrust on No.	Journal Diameter	Oil Clearance	Side Clearance
'75–'76	6-231 Buick	2.4995	.0004–.0015	.004–.008	2	2.0000	.0002–.0023	.006–.014
	8-350 Buick	2.9995	.0004–.0015	.002–.006	3	2.0000	.0005–.0026	.006–.026
'77	6-231 Buick	2.4995	.0004–.0015	.004–.008	2	2.000	.0005–.0026	.006–.027
	8-301 Pont.	3.0000	.0004–.0020	.003–.009	4	2.25	.0005–.0025	.006–.027
	8-305 Chev.	2.4480	.0035 max ②	.002–.006	5	2.200	.0035 max.②	.008–0.014
	8-350 Buick	3.0000	.0004–.0015	.003–.009	3	2.000	.0005–.0026	.006–.027
	8-350 Olds.	2.4995	.0005–.0021①	.003–.013	3	2.125	.0004–.0015	.006–.027
	8-350 Chev.	2.4480	.0035 max.②	.002–.006	5	2.200	.0035 max.②	.008–.014
	8-403 Olds.	2.4995	.0005–.0021①	.003–.013	3	2.125	.0005–.0026	.006–.020
'78–'80	6-196, 231 Buick	2.4995	.0003–.0018	.003–.009	2	2.2487–2.2495	.0005–.0026	.006–.023④
	8-350 Olds Diesel	3.0000	.005–.0021①	.0035–.0135	3	2.1238–2.1248	.005–.0026	.006–.020
	8-265 Pont.	3.000	.0004–.0020	.006–.022	4	2.250	.0005–.0025	.006–.022④
	8-305, 350 Chev.	③	.0035 max.②	.002–.006	5	2.099–2.100	.0035 max.	.006–.014
	8-301 Pont.	3.0000	.0004–.0020	.003–.009	4	2.25	.0005–.0025	.006–.027

Year	Engine							
'81	6-231 Buick	2.4995	.0003-.0018	.003-.011	2	2.2487-2.2495	.0005-.0026	.006-.023 ④
	8-265 Pont.	3.000	.0002-.0018	.0035-.0085	4	2.000	.0005-.0025	.006-.022 ④
	8-301 Pont.	3.0000	.0004-.0020	.003-.009	4	2.25	.0005-.0025	.006-.027
'82-'83	6-231 Buick	2.4995	.0003-.0018	.003-.011	2	2.2487-2.2495	.0005-.0026	.006-.023 ④
	6-252 Buick ⑦	2.4995	.0003-.0018	.011-.003	2	2.2487-2.2495	.0005-.0026	.006-.023
	6-263 Olds Diesel	2.9993-3.0003	.0005-.0021	.0035-.0135	3	2.1238-2.2148	.0005-.0026	.006-.020
'84-'85	8-350 Olds Diesel	3.0000	.0005-.0021 ①	.0035-.0135	3	2.1238-2.1248	.0005-.0026	.006-.020
	6-231 Buick	2.4995	.0003-.0018	.003-.011	2	2.2487-2.2495	.0005-.0026	.006-.023 ④
	6-252 Buick ⑦	2.4995	.0003-.0018	.011-.003	2	2.2487-2.2495	.0005-.0026	.006-.023
	6-263 Olds Diesel	2.9993-3.0003	.0005-.0021 ⑥	.0035-.0135	3	2.2490-2.250	.0005-.0026	.008-.021
1986-87	6-231 Buick	2.4995	.0003-.0018	.003-.011	2	2.2487-2.2495	.0005-.0026	.003-.015
	6-231 Buick ⑦	2.4995	.0003-.0018	.003-.011	2	2.2487-2.2495	.0005-.0026	.003-.015
	8-307 Olds.	2.4985-2.4995 ⑧	.0005-.0021	.0035-.0135	3	2.1238-2.1248	.0004-.0033	.006-.020

① No. 5—.0015-.0031
② No. 1—.002 max.
③ #1:2.4484-2.4493 #2,3,4:2.4481-2.4490 #5:2.4479-2.4488
④ Total for both rods per journal
⑤ Intermediate—.0011-.0023 Rear—.0017-.0033
⑥ #4 Rear: .0020-.0034
⑦ Turbocharged engine
⑧ No 1: 2.4988-2.4998 in.
⑨ No 5: .0016-.0032 in.

Ring Gap
(All measurements are given in inches)

Year	Engine No. Cyl. Displacement (cu. in.)	Top Compression	Bottom Compression	Oil Control
'75–'78	6-231 Buick	.010–.020	.010–.020	.015–.035
'79–'80	6-231 Buick	.013–.023	.013–.023	.015–.035
'79	8-301 Pont.	.010–.020	.010–.020	.035 max.
'77–'81	3-305, 350 Chev.	.010–.030	.010–.035	.015–.065
'77	8-350, 403 Olds.	.010–.023	.010–.023	.015–.055
'78	6-196 Buick	.010–.020	.010–.020	.015–.035
'79	6-196 Buick	.013–.023	.013–.023	.015–.035
'75–'76	8-350 Buick	.013–.023	.013–.023	.015–.035
'77	8-350 Buick	.013–.023	.013–.023	.015–.055
'81	8-350 Buick	.010–.020	.010–.020	.015–.035
'81–'87	6-231, 252 Buick	.010–.020	.010–.020	.015–.055
'80–'81	8-265, 301 Pont.	.010–.028	.010–.028	.015–.055
'81–'83	8-350 Olds Diesel	.015–.025	.015–.025	.015–.055
'82–'83	6-263 Olds Diesel	.015–.025	.015–.025	.015–.055
'84–'85	6-263 Olds Diesel	.019–.027	.013–.021	.015–.055
8-30	8-307 Olds.	.009–.019	.009–.019	.015–.055

N.A. Not Available

Piston Clearance

Year	Engine No. Cyl. Displacement (cu. in.)	Piston to Bore Clearance (in.)
'75–'80	6-231 Buick	.0008–.0020
'79–'81	8-265, 301 Pont.	.0025–.0033
'75–'77	8-350 Buick	.0008–.0020
'81	8-350 Buick	.008–.0020
'77–'81	8-305, 350 Chev.	.0012
'77	8-350, 403 Olds.	.0010–.0020
'78–'79	6-196 Buick	.008–.0020
'81–'87	6-231, 252 Buick	.0008–.0020
'86–'87	8-307 Olds.	.0008–.0018
'81–'83	8-350 Olds Diesel	.005–.006 ①
'82–'85	6-263 Olds Diesel	.003–.004

① At bottom of skirt
N.A. Not available

In the process of removing the engine you will come across a number of steps which call for the removal of a separate component or system, i.e. Disconnect the exhaust system or Re-

move the radiator. In all of these instances, a detailed removal procedure can be found elsewhere in the chapter or, in some cases, in another chapter which deals with the specific component in question.

1. Scribe marks at the hood hinges and the hinge brackets. Remove the hood.

2. Disconnect the battery and drain the coolant.

CAUTION: *When draining the coolant, keep in mind that cats and dogs are attracted by the ethylene glycol antifreeze, and are quite likely to drink any that is left in an uncovered container or in puddles on the ground. This will prove fatal in sufficient quantity. Always drain the coolant into a sealable container. Coolant should be reused unless it is contaminated or several years old.*

3. Remove the air cleaner.

4. On cars with air conditioning (A/C), disconnect the compressor ground wire from the bracket. Remove the electrical connector from the compressor. Remove the compressor and position the compressor out of the way. Do not disconnect any hoses.

WARNING : *If the compressor refrigerant lines do not have enough slack to position the compressor out of the way without disconnecting the refrigerant lines, the air condi-*

Torque Specifications
(All readings in ft. lbs.)

Year	Engine No. Cyl. Displacement (cu in.)	Cylinder Head Bolts	Rod Bearing Bolts	Main Bearing Bolts	Crankshaft Bolt	Flywheel to Crankshaft Bolts	Manifold	
							Intake	Exhaust
'74–'76	6-231 Buick	75	40	115	150 min.	55 ⑤	45	25
	8-350 Buick	80	35 ④	115	140 min.	60	45	28
'77	6-231 Buick	85	42	80 ③	310	60	40	25
	8-350 Buick	80	40	115	175	60	45	25
	8-350 Olds.	130	42	80 ③	310	60 ⑥	40	25
	8-350 Chev.	65	45	70	60	60	30	20
	8-403 Olds.	130	42	80	310	60 ⑥	40	25
'78–'79	6-196, 231 Buick	80	40	100	225	60	45	25
	8-301 Pont.	90	35	60 ①	160	95	40	35
	8-305, 350 Chev.	65	45	70	60	60	30	20
'80–'81	6-231, 8-350 Buick	80	40	100	225	60	45	25
	8-350 Olds Diesel	130 ⑦	42	120	200–310	60	40 ⑦	25
	8-265, 301 Pont.	95	35	⑨	160	95	40	35
	8-305 Chev.	65	45	70	60	60	30	20
'82–'85	6-231, 252 Buick	80	40	100	225	60	45	25
	6-263 Olds Diesel	142 ⑧	42	105	160–350	48	41	29
	8-350 Olds Diesel	130 ⑦	42	120	200–310	60	40 ⑦	25
'86	6-231 Buick	⑩	40	100	200	60	45	20
	8-307 Olds.	126 ⑦	42	80 ⑪	200–310	60	40 ⑦	20
'87	6-231 Buick	⑩	40	100	219	60	45	37
	8-307 Olds	130 ⑦	48	80 ⑪	200–310	60	40 ⑦	25

① 100—rear main
② Center Bolts 25–30; End Bolts 15–20
③ 120—rear main
④ 40 with capscrews
⑤ 60—1976 and later
⑥ Manual transmission—90 ft. lbs.
⑦ Dip bolt in oil before tightening
⑧ No. 5, 6, 11, 12, 13 and 14 (59 ft. lbs.)
⑨ 7/16″ bolt-70 ft. lbs., 1/2″ bolt 100 ft. lbs., rear main bearing 100 ft. lbs.
⑩ Torque cylinder head bolt to 25 ft. lbs. in tightening sequence. Continue to torquing sequence, tightening each bolt 1/4 turn (90°) until 60 ft. lbs. is read on any one cylinder head bolt. Do not continue sequence at this point.
⑪ Rear main cap bolts—120

tioning system will have to be discharged by a trained air conditioning specialist. Under no conditions should an untrained person attempt to disconnect the air conditioning refrigerant lines. These lines contain pressurized refrigerant, which can be extremely dangerous. When the air conditioning lines are disconnected, always unscrew the connections using a backup wrench and then securely seal the openings to prevent the entry of moisture or dirt. The mechanic who dis-

charges the system should also disconnect and cap the hoses.
5. Remove the fan blade, pulley, and belts.
6. Disconnect the radiator and heater hoses. Remove the radiator and shroud assembly.
7. Remove the power steering pump and move it out of the way. Do not disconnect any hoses.
8. Remove the fuel pump hoses and plug them.
9. Disconnect the vapor emission lines from

Troubleshooting Engine Mechanical Problems

Problem	Cause	Solution
External oil leaks	• Fuel pump gasket broken or improperly seated	• Replace gasket
	• Cylinder head cover RTV sealant broken or improperly seated	• Replace sealant; inspect cylinder head cover sealant flange and cylinder head sealant surface for distortion and cracks
	• Oil filler cap leaking or missing	• Replace cap
	• Oil filter gasket broken or improperly seated	• Replace oil filter
	• Oil pan side gasket broken, improperly seated or opening in RTV sealant	• Replace gasket or repair opening in sealant; inspect oil pan gasket flange for distortion
	• Oil pan front oil seal broken or improperly seated	• Replace seal; inspect timing case cover and oil pan seal flange for distortion
	• Oil pan rear oil seal broken or improperly seated	• Replace seal; inspect oil pan rear oil seal flange; inspect rear main bearing cap for cracks, plugged oil return channels, or distortion in seal groove
	• Timing case cover oil seal broken or improperly seated	• Replace seal
	• Excess oil pressure because of restricted PCV valve	• Replace PCV valve
	• Oil pan drain plug loose or has stripped threads	• Repair as necessary and tighten
	• Rear oil gallery plug loose	• Use appropriate sealant on gallery plug and tighten
	• Rear camshaft plug loose or improperly seated	• Seat camshaft plug or replace and seal, as necessary
	• Distributor base gasket damaged	• Replace gasket
Excessive oil consumption	• Oil level too high	• Drain oil to specified level
	• Oil with wrong viscosity being used	• Replace with specified oil
	• PCV valve stuck closed	• Replace PCV valve
	• Valve stem oil deflectors (or seals) are damaged, missing, or incorrect type	• Replace valve stem oil deflectors
	• Valve stems or valve guides worn	• Measure stem-to-guide clearance and repair as necessary
	• Poorly fitted or missing valve cover baffles	• Replace valve cover
	• Piston rings broken or missing	• Replace broken or missing rings
	• Scuffed piston	• Replace piston
	• Incorrect piston ring gap	• Measure ring gap, repair as necessary
	• Piston rings sticking or excessively loose in grooves	• Measure ring side clearance, repair as necessary
	• Compression rings installed upside down	• Repair as necessary
	• Cylinder walls worn, scored, or glazed	• Repair as necessary
	• Piston ring gaps not properly staggered	• Repair as necessary
	• Excessive main or connecting rod bearing clearance	• Measure bearing clearance, repair as necessary
No oil pressure	• Low oil level	• Add oil to correct level
	• Oil pressure gauge, warning lamp or sending unit inaccurate	• Replace oil pressure gauge or warning lamp
	• Oil pump malfunction	• Replace oil pump
	• Oil pressure relief valve sticking	• Remove and inspect oil pressure relief valve assembly
	• Oil passages on pressure side of pump obstructed	• Inspect oil passages for obstruction

Troubleshooting Engine Mechanical Problems (cont.)

Problem	Cause	Solution
No oil pressure (cont.)	• Oil pickup screen or tube obstructed • Loose oil inlet tube	• Inspect oil pickup for obstruction • Tighten or seal inlet tube
Low oil pressure	• Low oil level • Inaccurate gauge, warning lamp or sending unit • Oil excessively thin because of dilution, poor quality, or improper grade • Excessive oil temperature • Oil pressure relief spring weak or sticking • Oil inlet tube and screen assembly has restriction or air leak • Excessive oil pump clearance • Excessive main, rod, or camshaft bearing clearance	• Add oil to correct level • Replace oil pressure gauge or warning lamp • Drain and refill crankcase with recommended oil • Correct cause of overheating engine • Remove and inspect oil pressure relief valve assembly • Remove and inspect oil inlet tube and screen assembly. (Fill inlet tube with lacquer thinner to locate leaks.) • Measure clearances • Measure bearing clearances, repair as necessary
High oil pressure	• Improper oil viscosity • Oil pressure gauge or sending unit inaccurate • Oil pressure relief valve sticking closed	• Drain and refill crankcase with correct viscosity oil • Replace oil pressure gauge • Remove and inspect oil pressure relief valve assembly
Main bearing noise	• Insufficient oil supply • Main bearing clearance excessive • Bearing insert missing • Crankshaft end play excessive • Improperly tightened main bearing cap bolts • Loose flywheel or drive plate • Loose or damaged vibration damper	• Inspect for low oil level and low oil pressure • Measure main bearing clearance, repair as necessary • Replace missing insert • Measure end play, repair as necessary • Tighten bolts with specified torque • Tighten flywheel or drive plate attaching bolts • Repair as necessary
Connecting rod bearing noise	• Insufficient oil supply • Carbon build-up on piston • Bearing clearance excessive or bearing missing • Crankshaft connecting rod journal out-of-round • Misaligned connecting rod or cap • Connecting rod bolts tightened improperly	• Inspect for low oil level and low oil pressure • Remove carbon from piston crown • Measure clearance, repair as necessary • Measure journal dimensions, repair or replace as necessary • Repair as necessary • Tighten bolts with specified torque
Piston noise	• Piston-to-cylinder wall clearance excessive (scuffed piston) • Cylinder walls excessively tapered or out-of-round • Piston ring broken • Loose or seized piston pin • Connecting rods misaligned • Piston ring side clearance excessively loose or tight • Carbon build-up on piston is excessive	• Measure clearance and examine piston • Measure cylinder wall dimensions, rebore cylinder • Replace all rings on piston • Measure piston-to-pin clearance, repair as necessary • Measure rod alignment, straighten or replace • Measure ring side clearance, repair as necessary • Remove carbon from piston

Troubleshooting Engine Mechanical Problems (cont.)

Problem	Cause	Solution
Valve actuating component noise	• Insufficient oil supply	• Check for: (a) Low oil level (b) Low oil pressure (c) Plugged push rods (d) Wrong hydraulic tappets (e) Restricted oil gallery (f) Excessive tappet to bore clearance
	• Push rods worn or bent	• Replace worn or bent push rods
	• Rocker arms or pivots worn	• Replace worn rocker arms or pivots
	• Foreign objects or chips in hydraulic tappets	• Clean tappets
	• Excessive tappet leak-down	• Replace valve tappet
	• Tappet face worn	• Replace tappet; inspect corresponding cam lobe for wear
	• Broken or cocked valve springs	• Properly seat cocked springs; replace broken springs
	• Stem-to-guide clearance excessive	• Measure stem-to-guide clearance, repair as required
	• Valve bent	• Replace valve
	• Loose rocker arms	• Tighten bolts with specified torque
	• Valve seat runout excessive	• Regrind valve seat/valves
	• Missing valve lock	• Install valve lock
	• Push rod rubbing or contacting cylinder head	• Remove cylinder head and remove obstruction in head
	• Excessive engine oil (four-cylinder engine)	• Correct oil level

Troubleshooting the Cooling System

Problem	Cause	Solution
High temperature gauge indication— overheating	• Coolant level low	• Replenish coolant
	• Fan belt loose	• Adjust fan belt tension
	• Radiator hose(s) collapsed	• Replace hose(s)
	• Radiator airflow blocked	• Remove restriction (bug screen, fog lamps, etc.)
	• Faulty radiator cap	• Replace radiator cap
	• Ignition timing incorrect	• Adjust ignition timing
	• Idle speed low	• Adjust idle speed
	• Air trapped in cooling system	• Purge air
	• Heavy traffic driving	• Operate at fast idle in neutral intermittently to cool engine
	• Incorrect cooling system component(s) installed	• Install proper component(s)
	• Faulty thermostat	• Replace thermostat
	• Water pump shaft broken or impeller loose	• Replace water pump
	• Radiator tubes clogged	• Flush radiator
	• Cooling system clogged	• Flush system
	• Casting flash in cooling passages	• Repair or replace as necessary. Flash may be visible by removing cooling system components or removing core plugs.
	• Brakes dragging	• Repair brakes
	• Excessive engine friction	• Repair engine
	• Antifreeze concentration over 68%	• Lower antifreeze concentration percentage
	• Missing air seals	• Replace air seals
	• Faulty gauge or sending unit	• Repair or replace faulty component

Troubleshooting the Cooling System (cont.)

Problem	Cause	Solution
Coolant recovery system inoperative (cont.)	• Loss of coolant flow caused by leakage or foaming • Viscous fan drive failed	• Repair or replace leaking component, replace coolant • Replace unit
Low temperature indication—undercooling	• Thermostat stuck open • Faulty gauge or sending unit	• Replace thermostat • Repair or replace faulty component
Coolant loss—boilover	• Overfilled cooling system • Quick shutdown after hard (hot) run • Air in system resulting in occasional "burping" of coolant • Insufficient antifreeze allowing coolant boiling point to be too low • Antifreeze deteriorated because of age or contamination • Leaks due to loose hose clamps, loose nuts, bolts, drain plugs, faulty hoses, or defective radiator • Faulty head gasket • Cracked head, manifold, or block • Faulty radiator cap	• Reduce coolant level to proper specification • Allow engine to run at fast idle prior to shutdown • Purge system • Add antifreeze to raise boiling point • Replace coolant • Pressure test system to locate source of leak(s) then repair as necessary • Replace head gasket • Replace as necessary • Replace cap
Coolant entry into crankcase or cylinder(s)	• Faulty head gasket • Crack in head, manifold or block	• Replace head gasket • Replace as necessary
Coolant recovery system inoperative	• Coolant level low • Leak in system • Pressure cap not tight or seal missing, or leaking • Pressure cap defective • Overflow tube clogged or leaking • Recovery bottle vent restricted	• Replenish coolant to FULL mark • Pressure test to isolate leak and repair as necessary • Repair as necessary • Replace cap • Repair as necessary • Remove restriction
Noise	• Fan contacting shroud • Loose water pump impeller • Glazed fan belt • Loose fan belt • Rough surface on drive pulley • Water pump bearing worn • Belt alignment	• Reposition shroud and inspect engine mounts • Replace pump • Apply silicone or replace belt • Adjust fan belt tension • Replace pulley • Remove belt to isolate. Replace pump. • Check pulley alignment. Repair as necessary.
No coolant flow through heater core	• Restricted return inlet in water pump • Heater hose collapsed or restricted • Restricted heater core • Restricted outlet in thermostat housing • Intake manifold bypass hole in cylinder head restricted • Faulty heater control valve • Intake manifold coolant passage restricted	• Remove restriction • Remove restriction or replace hose • Remove restriction or replace core • Remove flash or restriction • Remove restriction • Replace valve • Remove restriction or replace intake manifold

NOTE: *Immediately after shutdown, the engine enters a condition known as heat soak. This is caused by the cooling system being inoperative while engine temperature is still high. If coolant temperature rises above boiling point, expansion and pressure may push some coolant out of the radiator overflow tube. If this does not occur frequently it is considered normal.*

Troubleshooting the Serpentine Drive Belt

Problem	Cause	Solution
Tension sheeting fabric failure (woven fabric on outside circumference of belt has cracked or separated from body of belt)	• Grooved or backside idler pulley diameters are less than minimum recommended • Tension sheeting contacting (rubbing) stationary object • Excessive heat causing woven fabric to age • Tension sheeting splice has fractured	• Replace pulley(s) not conforming to specification • Correct rubbing condition • Replace belt • Replace belt
Noise (objectional squeal, squeak, or rumble is heard or felt while drive belt is in operation)	• Belt slippage • Bearing noise • Belt misalignment • Belt-to-pulley mismatch • Driven component inducing vibration • System resonant frequency inducing vibration	• Adjust belt • Locate and repair • Align belt/pulley(s) • Install correct belt • Locate defective driven component and repair • Vary belt tension within specifications. Replace belt.
Rib chunking (one or more ribs has separated from belt body)	• Foreign objects imbedded in pulley grooves • Installation damage • Drive loads in excess of design specifications • Insufficient internal belt adhesion	• Remove foreign objects from pulley grooves • Replace belt • Adjust belt tension • Replace belt
Rib or belt wear (belt ribs contact bottom of pulley grooves)	• Pulley(s) misaligned • Mismatch of belt and pulley groove widths • Abrasive environment • Rusted pulley(s) • Sharp or jagged pulley groove tips • Rubber deteriorated	• Align pulley(s) • Replace belt • Replace belt • Clean rust from pulley(s) • Replace pulley • Replace belt
Longitudinal belt cracking (cracks between two ribs)	• Belt has mistracked from pulley groove • Pulley groove tip has worn away rubber-to-tensile member	• Replace belt • Replace belt
Belt slips	• Belt slipping because of insufficient tension • Belt or pulley subjected to substance (belt dressing, oil, ethylene glycol) that has reduced friction • Driven component bearing failure • Belt glazed and hardened from heat and excessive slippage	• Adjust tension • Replace belt and clean pulleys • Replace faulty component bearing • Replace belt
"Groove jumping" (belt does not maintain correct position on pulley, or turns over and/or runs off pulleys)	• Insufficient belt tension • Pulley(s) not within design tolerance • Foreign object(s) in grooves • Excessive belt speed • Pulley misalignment • Belt-to-pulley profile mismatched • Belt cordline is distorted	• Adjust belt tension • Replace pulley(s) • Remove foreign objects from grooves • Avoid excessive engine acceleration • Align pulley(s) • Install correct belt • Replace belt
Belt broken (Note: identify and correct problem before replacement belt is installed)	• Excessive tension • Tensile members damaged during belt installation • Belt turnover • Severe pulley misalignment • Bracket, pulley, or bearing failure	• Replace belt and adjust tension to specification • Replace belt • Replace belt • Align pulley(s) • Replace defective component and belt

Troubleshooting the Serpentine Drive Belt (cont.)

Problem	Cause	Solution
Cord edge failure (tensile member exposed at edges of belt or separated from belt body)	• Excessive tension • Drive pulley misalignment • Belt contacting stationary object • Pulley irregularities • Improper pulley construction • Insufficient adhesion between tensile member and rubber matrix	• Adjust belt tension • Align pulley • Correct as necessary • Replace pulley • Replace pulley • Replace belt and adjust tension to specifications
Sporadic rib cracking (multiple cracks in belt ribs at random intervals)	• Ribbed pulley(s) diameter less than minimum specification • Backside bend flat pulley(s) diameter less than minimum • Excessive heat condition causing rubber to harden • Excessive belt thickness • Belt overcured • Excessive tension	• Replace pulley(s) • Replace pulley(s) • Correct heat condition as necessary • Replace belt • Replace belt • Adjust belt tension

the carburetor, the vacuum supply hose from the carburetor to the vacuum manifold, and the power brake vacuum hoses, if equipped.

10. Disconnect the throttle linkage at the carburetor.

11. Disconnect the oil pressure and coolant temperature switches.

12. Disconnect the engine-to-body ground strap.

13. Raise the car and disconnect the starter wires.

14. Disconnect the pipes from the exhaust manifold and support the exhaust system. If the car has an AIR pipe going to the catalytic converter, disconnect it at the engine.

15. On Pontiac-built engines:

a. On models with automatic transmission, remove the converter cover, the converter retaining bolts and slide the converter to the rear.

b. On models with manual transmission, disconnect the clutch linkage and remove the clutch cross-shaft, starter motor and the lower flywheel cover.

c. Remove two bell housing bolts from each side.

d. On automatic transmission models, disconnect the transmission filler tube.

e. Remove the two front motor mount nuts.

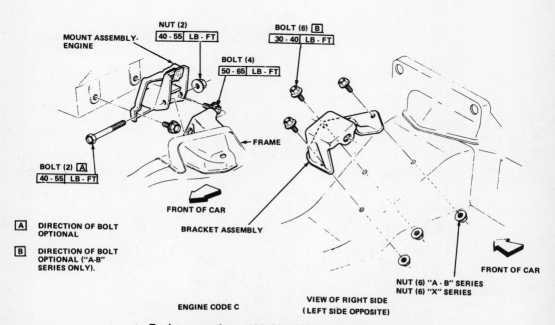

Engine mounting—196, 231, 252 Buick built engines

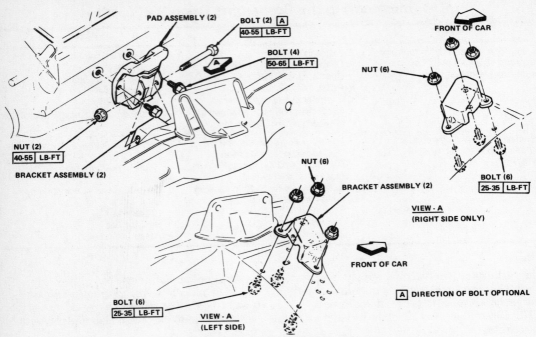

PAD ASSEMBLY (2)

BOLT (2) [A]
40-55 LB-FT

BOLT (4)
50-65 LB-FT

FRONT OF CAR

NUT (6)

NUT (2)
40-55 LB-FT

BRACKET ASSEMBLY (2)

NUT (6)

BRACKET ASSEMBLY (2)

BOLT (6)
25-35 LB-FT

VIEW - A
(RIGHT SIDE ONLY)

FRONT OF CAR

[A] DIRECTION OF BOLT OPTIONAL

BOLT (6)
25-35 LB-FT

VIEW - A
(LEFT SIDE)

Engine mounting—350 Buick built engines

f. Lower the car and support the transmission.

g. Remove the remaining bellhousing bolts and raise the transmission slightly.

h. Remove the engine.

16. On Oldsmobile-built engines:

a. Remove the torque converter cover. Mark the relationship between the converter and the flywheel. Then, remove the converter-to-flywheel retaining bolts.

b. Remove the engine mounting bolts.

c. Remove the three engine-to-transmis-

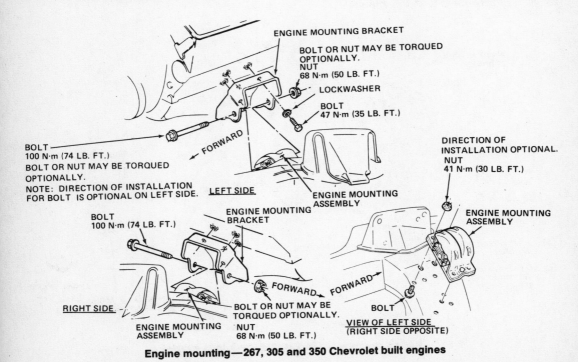

ENGINE MOUNTING BRACKET

BOLT OR NUT MAY BE TORQUED OPTIONALLY.
NUT
68 N·m (50 LB. FT.)

LOCKWASHER

BOLT
47 N·m (35 LB. FT.)

BOLT
100 N·m (74 LB. FT.)
BOLT OR NUT MAY BE TORQUED OPTIONALLY.
NOTE: DIRECTION OF INSTALLATION FOR BOLT IS OPTIONAL ON LEFT SIDE.

FORWARD

LEFT SIDE

ENGINE MOUNTING ASSEMBLY

DIRECTION OF INSTALLATION OPTIONAL.
NUT
41 N·m (30 LB. FT.)

BOLT
100 N·m (74 LB. FT.)

ENGINE MOUNTING BRACKET

FORWARD

FORWARD

ENGINE MOUNTING ASSEMBLY

RIGHT SIDE

ENGINE MOUNTING ASSEMBLY

BOLT OR NUT MAY BE TORQUED OPTIONALLY.
NUT
68 N·m (50 LB. FT.)

BOLT

VIEW OF LEFT SIDE
(RIGHT SIDE OPPOSITE)

Engine mounting—267, 305 and 350 Chevrolet built engines

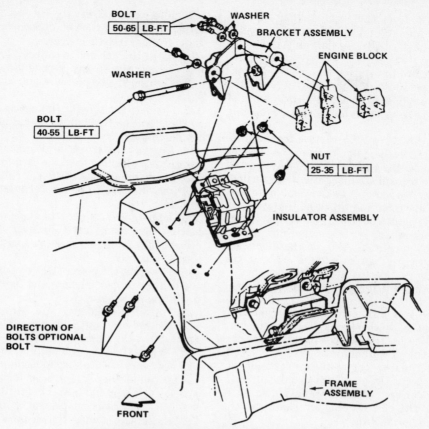

Engine mounting—265, 301 Pontiac built engines

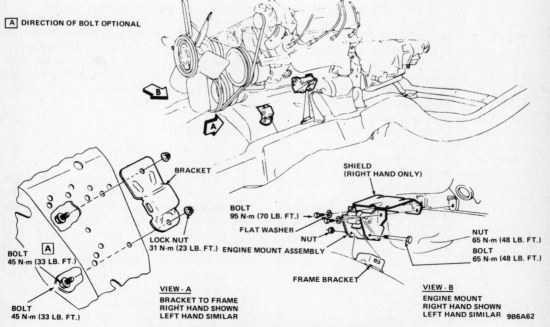

Engine mounting—350, 403 Oldsmobile built engines

sion bolts from the right side on models through 1985. On 1986-87 models, remove five of the six bolts, leaving only the lower left.

d. Remove the starter motor.

e. Lower the car and support the transmission with a floor jack. Use a board on top of the jack to support the pan without damaging it.

f. On cars up to 1985, remove the three engine-to-transmission bolts from the left side and remove the engine. On 1986-87 models, raise the transmission slightly with the floor jack and then remove the one remaining bolt.

17. On Chevrolet and Buick-built engines:

a. On engines built in 1986-87, disconnect the engine wiring harness connector and remove the generator. Also, on these engines, disconnect the battery ground cable at the engine block.

b. Remove the flywheel and converter cover.

c. On cars with automatic transmission, remove the flywheel-to-converter attaching bolts. Matchmark the converter to the flywheel. On all automatic transmission models, remove the engine-to-transmission attaching bolts. On manual transmission models, disconnect the driveshaft, the shift linkage, the clutch equalizer shaft and the transmission mount.

d. Remove the fasteners attaching the engine mounts to the block on cars built in years up to 1985. On 1986-87 models, remove the bolts fastening the engine mounts to the frame bracket. Remove the cruise control bracket, if so equipped.

e. Lower the car and support the transmission, except for models with manual transmissions.

f. Raise the engine slightly so the engine mount through bolts can be removed. On models with manual transmissions, remove the engine and transmission as a unit.

18. Suspend the engine over the engine compartment. Lower it carefully into position, avoiding any contact between the engine and body or transmission parts until the engine is in the right position. Note that there are dowel pins in the block that have matching holes in the bellhousing. These dowel pins must be in almost perfect alignment before the engine will go together with the transmission. See Manual Transmission, Removal and Installation for clutch alignment procedures.

19. Refer to Step 15 for Pontiac built engines, 16 for Olds built engines, and 17 for Buick and Chevrolet built engines. Reverse the procedure there in order to begin fastening the engine in place and installing accessories.

20. If necessary, lower the car. Reconnect the exhaust pipes and, if so-equipped, the AIR line going to the catalytic converter.

21. Raise the car and reconnect starter wiring. Connect the engine-to-body ground strap.

22. Connect the oil pressure and coolant temperature sensors.

23. Connect the throttle linkage and adjust it so there will be freedom of operation without too much play.

24. Connect the power brake vacuum hoses, vacuum hose leading from the carburetor to the vacuum manifold, and the vapor emission control lines leading from the carburetor to the canister.

25. Unplug and connect the fuel pump hoses, placing the clamps carefully over the bulged areas of the pump connectors and tightening clamps securely.

26. Remount the power steering pump, adjust the belt for proper tension, and tighten all the mounting bolts securely.

27. Install the radiator and shroud. Reconnect the radiator and heater hoses and install and tighten the clamps securely.

28. Install the fan blade, pulley, and belts.

29. On cars with air conditioning, remount the air conditioner compressor, install and adjust the belt, and tighten all mounting bolts securely. Connect the compressor ground wire to the bracket and connect the compressor electrical connector. If the system hoses have been disconnected, have them reconnected using new O-rings coated with oil and have the system evacuated and recharged by a professional who is familiar with refrigeration work.

30. Install the air cleaner and all related hoses and heat pipes. Connect the battery. Refill the radiator and engine crankcase (if necessary). Start the engine and run it until it is hot with the radiator cap off. Refill the cooling system. Start the engine and run it, checking for leaks.

Diesel Engine
REMOVAL AND INSTALLATION

1. Drain the cooling system.

CAUTION: *When draining the coolant, keep in mind that cats and dogs are attracted by the ethylene glycol antifreeze, and are quite likely to drink any that is left in an uncovered container or in puddles on the ground. This will prove fatal in sufficient quantity. Always drain the coolant into a sealable container. Coolant should be reused unless it is contaminated or several years old.*

2. Remove the air cleaner.

3. Mark the hood-to-hinge position and remove the hood.

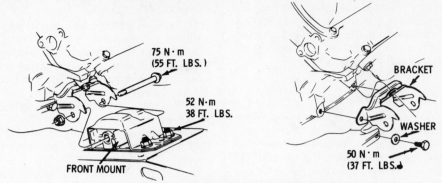

Front engine mounting—263 Oldsmobile built diesel engines

4. Disconnect the ground cables from the batteries.

5. Disconnect the ground wires at the fender panels and the ground strap at the cowl.

6. Disconnect the radiator hoses, cooler lines, heater hoses, vacuum hoses, power steering pump hoses, air conditioning compressor (hose attached), fuel inlet hose and all attached wiring.

7. Remove the bellcrank clip.

8. Disconnect the throttle and transmission cables.

9. Remove the radiator.

10. Raise and support the car.

11. Disconnect the exhaust pipes at the manifold.

12. Remove the torque converter cover. Matchmark the relationship between the torque converter and the flexplate. Remove the three bolts holding the converter to the flywheel.

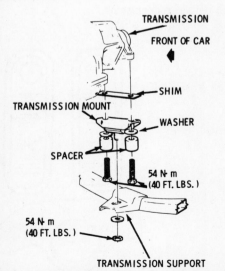

Rear engine (transmission) mount—263 Oldsmobile built diesel engines

13. Remove the engine mount bolts.

14. Remove the three right side transmission-to-engine bolts. Remove the starter.

15. Lower the car and attach a hoist to the engine.

16. Slightly raise the transmission with a jack.

17. Remove the three left side transmission-to-engine bolts and remove the engine.

18. Lower the engine into position carefully in order to avoid hitting any parts of the body or any of the accessories with it. Line the engine up with the transmission and turn the crankshaft as necessary to ensure that the relationship between the torque converter and flex plate is as it was marked.

19. Install the three right side transmission-to-engine bolts. Install the starter. Install the engine mount through bolts.

20. Install the three bolts fastening the torque converter to the flex plate. Install the torque converter cover. Torque the converter cover bolts to 40 ft.lb.

21. Reconnect the exhaust pipes at the bottoms of the two manifolds. Lower the car to the ground in order to work from above the engine.

22. Install the radiator.

23. Connect and then adjust the throttle and transmission cables (see Chapter 5 for adjustment procedures).

24. Install the bellcrank clip.

25. Reconnect the radiator hoses, transmission cooler lines, heater hoses, power steering pump hoses and vacuum lines. Reconnect the wiring harness connectors.

26. Remount the air conditioning compressor and install and tension its drive belt.

27. Reconnect the fender panel ground wires and the ground strap at the cowl.

28. Reconnect the battery cables. Install the hood with the hood hinges positioned according to the marks made during removal. Top off all fluids, adding 50/50 water/antifreeze solution

to the radiator. Start the engine, watching for leaks and running it with the radiator cap off until all air is bled from the cooling system. Add more coolant as necessary. Check and top off the transmission fluid as necessary.

Rocker Arm (Valve) Cover

NOTE: *Some engines are assembled using RTV (room Temperature Vulcanizing) silicone sealant in place of rocker arm cover gasket. If the engine was assembled using RTV, never use a gasket when reassembling. Conversely, if the engine was assembled using a rocker arm gasket, never replace it with RTV. When using RTV, an ⅛" bead is sufficient. Always run the bead on the inside of the bolt holes.*

REMOVAL AND INSTALLATION
Gasoline Engines

1. Remove the air cleaner if necessary.
2. Disconnect the PCV valve from the valve cover.
3. Disconnect the spark plug wires and move away from the valve cover.
4. Remove any accessory mounting brackets as necessary that may be in the way.
5. Remove the valve cover to cylinder head attaching screws and remove the valve cover.
6. Before reinstalling the valve cover, thoroughly clean the cover gasket surface and install a new gasket or RTV (Room Temperature Vulcanizing) sealer.

Diesel Engines

1. Remove the injection pump and lines as outlined in Chapter 5.
2. If removing the right valve cover on the V6 engine, disconnect the crankcase ventilation system pipes, grommets, filter and crankcase depression regulator valve.
3. Remove the valve cover to cylinder head attaching screws.
4. Remove any accessory mounting brackets that may be in the way, then remove the valve cover.
5. Before installing the valve cover make sure the valve cover and head gasket surfaces are thoroughly clean.
6. Apply RTV sealer or equivalent to the valve cover, then install the cover and retaining screws.
7. The remainder of the installation is the reverse of removal.

Rocker Arm and Shaft
REMOVAL AND INSTALLATION
196, 231, 252, and 350 Buick Built Engines

1. Remove the rocker arm covers.
2. Remove the rocker arm shaft assembly bolts.
3. Remove the rocker arm shaft assembly.
4. To remove the rocker arms from the shaft, the nylon arm retainers must be removed. They can be removed with a pair of water pump pliers, or they can be broken by hitting them below the head with a chisel.
5. Remove the rocker arms from the shaft. Make sure you keep them in order. Also note that the external rib on each arm points away from the rocker arm shaft bolt located between each pair of rocker arms.

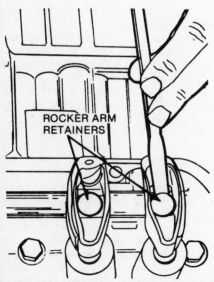

Removing nylon rocker arm retainers—Buick built engines

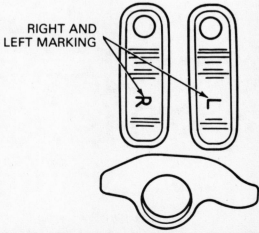

Replacement rocker arm identification—Buick built engines

Position of rocker arms on shaft—Buick built engines

6. If you are installing new rocker arms, note that the replacement rocker arms are marked **R** and **L** for right and left side installation. Do not interchange them.

7. Install the rocker arms on the shaft and lubricate them with oil.

8. Install new nylon retainers using a hammer and a drift of ½" diameter or larger.

9. Install the rocker shaft and torque the mounting bolts to 25 ft.lb.

Rocker Arm

REMOVAL AND INSTALLATION

305, and 350 Chevrolet Built Engines
265 and 301 Pontiac Built Engines

1. Remove the valve covers.

2. Remove the rocker arm nut and rocker arm ball.

3. Lift the rocker arm off the rocker stud. Always keep the rocker arm assemblies together and assemble them on the same stud.

4. Remove the pushrod from its bore. Make

sure the rods are returned to their original bores, with the same end in the block.

5. Reverse the removal procedure to install the rocker arms. Tighten the rocker ball retaining nut to 20 ft.lb. on Pontiac engines. On Chevrolet engines, just start the nut onto the stud and then adjust the valves as follows:

a. Turn the engine over until it reaches Top Dead Center as shown by the timing mark on the vibration damper and both the valves of No. 1 cylinder are closed (pushrods all the way down). In this position, you can adjust Nos. 1, 3, 4, and 8 exhaust valves and Nos. 1, 2, 5, and 7 intakes.

b. To adjust each valve, first feel for looseness in the valve train as demonstrated by play in the rocker or by extremely free rotation of the pushrod. Slowly tighten the nut until rocker play just disappears or the pushrod suddenly can be turned only with noticeable resistance. Then, carefully tighten the nut just one full turn tighter.

c. Turn the engine just one full turn and repeat the adjustment procedure for Nos. 2, 5, 6 and 7 exhausts and Nos. 3, 4, 6, and 8 intakes.

263 (Diesel), 307, 350 (Gas and Diesel), 403 Oldsmobile Engines

NOTE: *If only the rocker arms on the diesels have been removed, Bleed-down, but not dis-*

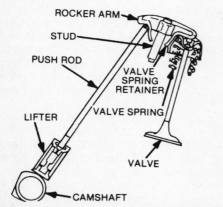

Engine valve system—Chevrolet and Pontiac built engines

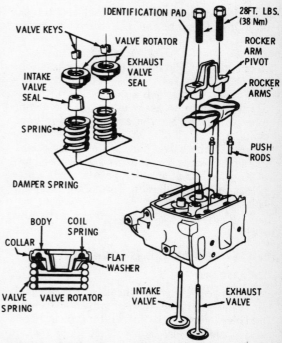

Engine valve system—350, 403 Oldsmobile built engines

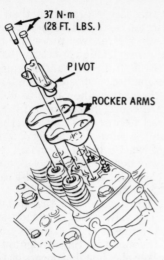

37 N·m
(28 FT. LBS.)

PIVOT

ROCKER ARMS

Rocker arms and pivots—263 Oldsmobile built diesel engine

assembly of the lifters will be necessary. See Diesel Valve Lifter Bleed-Down below before installing the rockers and follow that procedure in tightening the diesel rocker mounting bolts.

1. Remove the valve covers.

2. The rocker arms are removed in pairs for each cylinder. Remove the two bolts that attach the rocker arm pivot to the cylinder head. Remove the two rocker arms.

3. Repeat the procedure for each pair of rocker arms. Keep them in order for proper reassembly.

4. To install the rocker arms, it is necessary to ensure that the lifters are off the cam lobe and that the valves are closed.

5. To do this, attach a remote starter to the engine or have an assistant bump the engine over until the valves are closed for each cylinder.

6. With the valves for each cylinder closed, install the paired rocker arms. Lubricate all pivot and rocker arm wear points with white grease before installation. Torque the retaining bolts to 25 ft.lb.

7. Reinstall the valve covers with new gaskets.

Diesel Valve Lifter Bleed-Down

Olds 350 Diesel

If one or both cylinder heads or the camshaft has been removed, disassembly, reassembly and bleed-down of the valve lifters will be necessary. This will also be necessary if any rockers are removed while the intake manifold is off the engine. This procedure is covered under the

Cylinder Head Removal and Installation procedure. If the rocker arms have been removed or loosened but the intake manifold has been left in place throughout the procedure, the valve lifters must be bled down, although this is accomplished simply by reinstalling and tightening the rockers in a special manner. Proceed as follows:

1. On 1980 and earlier models: The lifters can be bled down for six cylinders at once with the crankshaft in either of the following two positions:

   a. For cylinders numbered 3, 5, 7, 2, 4 and 8, turn the crankshaft so the saw slot on the harmonic balancer is at 0° on the timing indicator.

   b. For cylinders 1, 3, 7, 2, 4 and 6, turn the crankshaft so the saw slot on the harmonic balancer is at 4 o'clock.

2. On these models only, tighten the rocker arm bolts on the numbered cylinders for the position the engine is in only. Torque to 28 ft.lb. It will take 45 minutes to completely bleed down the lifters. If additional lifters must be bled, wait till the 45 minutes has passed, and then turn the engine to the other position. Then tighten the remaining rocker arm pivot bolts and torque them to 28 ft.lb. Make sure you again wait 45 minutes before turning the crankshaft.

On 1981 and later models: Before installing any rockers, turn the crankshaft so No. 1 cylinder is at 32° before Top Dead Center on the compression stroke. 32° BTC is 50mm or 2″ counterclockwise from the 0° pointer. If only the right valve cover was removed for the work you did so that No. 1 cylinder's valves have not been disturbed you can determine that you're on the compression stroke for No. 1 by removing the glow plug for that cylinder and feeling for expulsion of air through that hole as you turn the engine (in the direction of normal rotation) up to the required position. If you have disturbed the rockers for No. 1, the left side valve cover will be off and you can rotate the crankshaft until the No. 5 cylinder intake valve pushrod ball is 7mm or 0.28″ above the No. 5 cylinder exhaust pushrod ball. If this cover is off even if you did not disturb No. 1 cylinder, you may wish to use the pushrod measurement method to save time.

Once the engine is in proper position, install the No. 5 cylinder rockers and rocker nuts, but DO NOT TIGHTEN THEM FULLY. Instead, turn them down by hand cautiously, alternating between intake and exhaust valves and turning both nuts an equal amount just until the intake valve nut begins to be harder to turn, indicating that the intake valve has just begun to crack open. Proceed cautiously so you don't turn too far. You'll see the valve begin to be depressed by the rocker, too.

3. At this point, torque all the remaining rocker nuts except those for cylinder No. 3. For cylinders No. 3 and 5, you'll have to turn the rocker bolts down very cautiously. On these cylinders, the cams are in such a position that installing the rocker nuts fully would open the valves all the way and then bend the pushrods. So, you'll have to feel very carefully for increased resistance as the valve reaches fully open position. Continue to turn the rocker nuts down on these three valves, always proceeding cautiously and stopping just as increased resistance is felt. Alternate, giving some time between tightening operations for the lifters to bleed down somewhat, until you can torque the nuts smoothly (without a sudden increase in resistance) to the required 28 ft.lb. Now, wait a full 45 minutes before the crankshaft is turned for any reason to permit all the lifters to bleed down fully.

Olds 263 Diesel

If one or both cylinder heads or the camshaft has been removed, disassembly, reassembly and bleed-down of the valve lifters will be necessary. This will also be necessary if any rockers are removed while the intake manifold is off the engine. This procedure is covered under Cylinder Head Removal and Installation. If the rocker arms have been removed or loosened but the intake manifold has been left in place throughout the procedure, the valve lifters must be bled down, although this is accomplished simply by reinstalling and tightening the rockers in a special manner. Proceed as follows:

CAUTION: *Use only normal hand wrenches (no air wrenches) in tightening rocker arm pivot nuts. Otherwise, the engine may be damaged.*

1. Before installing any rocker arms, rotate the crankshaft until No.1 cylinder is at 32° BTDC. This point may be determined by measuring 50mm or 2″ counterclockwise from the 0° pointer around the circumference of the vibration damper. It may also be measured (if the left side rocker cover has been removed) by determining that the No. 5 cylinder intake valve pushrod ball is exactly 7mm or 0.28″ above the No. 5 cylinder exhaust valve pushrod ball. If the No. 5 rockers are not in place, make sure both No. 1 rockers are at the same angle (both valves are closed) as you position the engine at the proper point on the damper. If not, turn the engine exactly 360° farther.

If the left side valve cover has not been removed, take out the No. 1 cylinder glow plug before cranking the engine into position. Then, rotating the engine in normal direction of rotation, feel for air being expelled through the glow plug hole as you approach the 32° BTDC position. If no air is expelled, turn the engine another 360° and check that air is expelled on that *revolution of the engine.*

2. If the No. 5 cylinder pivot and rocker arms have been removed, first install them, turning the bolts down *cautiously* and alternately and in equal increments until the intake valve just begins to open. Then, *stop turning immediately!*

3. Install all remaining rocker arms and pivots except No. 3 exhaust valve (if that one has been removed) torquing to 28 ft.lb. on cast iron heads and 11 ft.lb. on aluminum heads.

4. If the No. 3 exhaust valve pivot was removed, install it *but do not torque it past the point where the valve is fully open.* This is the point at which the torque required to turn the pivot retaining nut or bolt suddenly increases. Torque the nut until this occurs and then turn it very, very slowly, maintaining just enough torque to keep the valve fully open. This will gently squeeze the oil out of the lifter as you tighten the nut or bolt. As soon as the nut or bolt begins to tighten, use a torque wrench and torque it gradually to 11 ft.lb. on aluminum heads and 28 ft.lb. on cast iron heads.

5. Finish torquing the No. 5 cylinder rocker arm pivot nuts/bolts *gradually*. Make sure you do not go beyond the point where the valve would be fully open. This is indicated by strong resistance while still turning the pivot retaining nuts or bolts. Turning past the point where resistance starts to increase would bend the pushrod.

6. *Do not* turn the crankshaft for at least 45 minutes.

Thermostat

REMOVAL AND INSTALLATION

To replace the thermostat, drain the cooling system below the level of the thermostat and remove the two bolts holding the water neck in place. Remove the water neck and then lift out the thermostat.

CAUTION: *When draining the coolant, keep in mind that cats and dogs are attracted by the ethylene glycol antifreeze, and are quite likely to drink any that is left in an uncovered container or in puddles on the ground. This will prove fatal in sufficient quantity. Always drain the coolant into a sealable container. Coolant should be reused unless it is contaminated or several years old.*

Clean the mating surfaces of both the intake manifold and the water neck of residual gasket material and/or sealer. Install the thermostat with the wax pellet downward.

Coat both sides of the gasket with sealer and install it on the block.

Intake Manifold

REMOVAL AND INSTALLATION

196, 231, 252, and 350 Buick Built Engines

1. Disconnect the negative battery cable and drain the radiator.

CAUTION: *When draining the coolant, keep in mind that cats and dogs are attracted by the ethylene glycol antifreeze, and are quite likely to drink any that is left in an uncovered container or in puddles on the ground. This will prove fatal in sufficient quantity. Always drain the coolant into a sealable container. Coolant should be reused unless it is contaminated or several years old.*

2. Remove the air cleaner.

3. Disconnect the upper radiator hose and the heater hose at the manifold.

4. Disconnect the accelerator linkage at the carburetor and the linkage bracket at the manifold. Remove the cruise control chain, if so equipped.

5. Remove the fuel line from the carburetor and the booster vacuum pipe from the manifold. Remove the turbocharger, if so equipped.

6. On 1976 models, disconnect the choke pipe at the choke housing.

7. Label and disconnect the transmission vacuum modulator line, idle stop solenoid wire (if so equipped), distributor secondary wires and the temperature sending unit wire.

8. Disconnect and mark the vacuum hoses at the distributor and the carburetor.

9. Disconnect the coolant bypass hose at the manifold. On 1987 and '88 models, disconnect the temperature sending unit and, if it will be in the way, the CCC harness.

10. On six cylinder models, remove the distributor cap and wires to gain access to the Torx® head bolt. Remove the bolt.

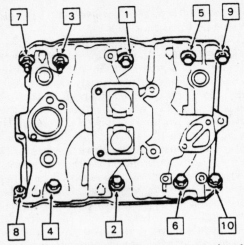

V6 intake manifold torquing pattern for carbureted engines built in 1984 and later years

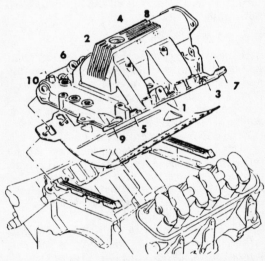

231 V6 Intake manifold torquing pattern for fuel injected engines built in 1984 and later years

11. Remove the throttle linkage springs. On 1976 models, remove the spark plug wires.

12. Remove the A/C compressor top bracket, if so equipped.

13. Remove the manifold.

14. Use a new gasket to install. Use sealer on the ends of the rubber gasket seals. Carefully guide the manifold onto the engine block dowel pin. Observe Turbocharger Precautions given with the previous Turbocharger information. Tighten the bolts in the proper order. On 1987-88 models, make sure the pointed end of the seal fits tight against both the block and heads. Start tightening bolts #1 and #2 first, tightening both gradually and alternately until both are snug. Then, continue through the sequence, using a torque wrench and the figure in

Intake manifold torque sequence—196, 231 through 1983, and 252

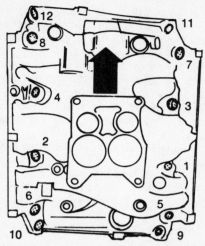

Intake manifold torque sequence—350 Buick built engines

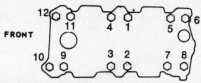

Intake manifold torque sequence—267, 305 and 350 Chevrolet built engines

5. Disconnect all linkage and hoses attached to the manifold and/or carburetor.

6. Remove the distributor, mark the rotor position with chalk on the distributor body, the remove the distributor.

7. Remove the air cleaner bracket, air pump and bracket, accelerator return spring and bracket and accelerator bellcrank.

8. Remove the alternator upper mounting bracket.

9. Unbolt and remove the manifold.

350, 403 Oldsmobile Built Gasoline Engines

1. Remove the carburetor air cleaner. Drain the radiator.

CAUTION: *When draining the coolant, keep in mind that cats and dogs are attracted by the ethylene glycol antifreeze, and are quite likely to drink any that is left in an uncovered container or in puddles on the ground. This will prove fatal in sufficient quantity. Always drain the coolant into a sealable container. Coolant should be reused unless it is contaminated or several years old.*

2. Disconnect the upper radiator hose, by-pass hose, and heater hose from the manifold.

3. Disconnect the throttle linkage, vacuum and gas lines from the carburetor.

4. Remove the generator and air conditioning brackets, as necessary.

WARNING: *Do not disconnect the refrigerant lines. Personal injury could result.*

5. Disconnect the temperature gauge wire.

6. Remove the intake manifold bolts and remove the manifold with the carburetor attached.

7. Install the manifold in reverse order, tightening all bolts in the sequence shown in the illustration first to 15 ft.lb. and then to the figure specified in the torque chart.

307 Oldsmobile Built Gasoline Engines

1. Remove the carburetor air cleaner. Drain the radiator.

CAUTION: *When draining the coolant, keep in mind that cats and dogs are attracted by the ethylene glycol antifreeze, and are quite likely to drink any that is left in an uncovered container or in puddles on the ground. This will prove fatal in sufficient quantity. Always drain the coolant into a sealable container.*

TORX® head bolt

the torque chart for final torquing. The remainder of installation is the reverse of the removal steps.

305 and 350 Chevrolet Built Engines

1. Drain the cooling system.

CAUTION: *When draining the coolant, keep in mind that cats and dogs are attracted by the ethylene glycol antifreeze, and are quite likely to drink any that is left in an uncovered container or in puddles on the ground. This will prove fatal in sufficient quantity. Always drain the coolant into a sealable container. Coolant should be reused unless it is contaminated or several years old.*

2. Remove the air cleaner.

3. Disconnect the battery ground.

4. Disconnect the upper radiator hose and the heater hose at the manifold.

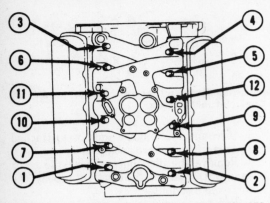

Intake manifold torque seequence—Olds 307, 350, and 403 gasoline V8

Coolant should be reused unless it is contaminated or several years old.

2. Disconnect the upper radiator hose, by-pass hose, and heater hose from the manifold.

3. Disconnect the throttle linkage, vacuum and gas lines from the carburetor. Label the vacuum lines for easy reconnection.

4. Remove the generator and air conditioning compressor rear brackets.

WARNING: *Do not disconnect the A/C lines. Personal injury could result.*

5. Disconnect the temperature gauge wire and any other electrical leads, as necessary.

6. Remove the EGR solenoid assembly and the Idle Load Compensator and bracket or, if so equipped, the TCC vacuum switch.

7. Remove the EGR valve.

8. Remove the intake manifold bolts and remove the manifold with the carburetor attached.

9. Clean all gasket surfaces thoroughly. Apply sealer to both sides of the manifold gasket. Apply RTV sealer to both ends of both of the end seals, top and bottom.

10. Place the end seals in place. Locate the manifold seal in place over the ports in both heads, carefully aligning port holes and boltholes. Then, put the manifold in position.

11. Coat the threads of all the bolts with engine oil. Install the bolts and torque to 15 ft.lb. Then torque, in sequence, to 40 ft.lb.

12. Complete the installation in the reverse order of removal, torquing the EGR mounting bolts to 20 ft.lb.

265 and 301 Pontiac Built Engines

NOTE: *Pontiac doesn't recommend a specific manifold bolt torque sequence for V8 engines.*

1. Remove the EGR valves on all engines except the 301. Drain the radiator and block.

CAUTION: *When draining the coolant, keep in mind that cats and dogs are attracted by*

the ethylene glycol antifreeze, and are quite likely to drink any that is left in an uncovered container or in puddles on the ground. This will prove fatal in sufficient quantity. Always drain the coolant into a sealable container. Coolant should be reused unless it is contaminated or several years old.

NOTE: *You can drain most of the coolant through the radiator drain if you raise the rear of the car 15-18".*

2. Remove the air cleaner and upper radiator hose.

3. Disconnect heater hose.

4. Disconnect temperature gauge wire, then remove two spark plug wire brackets from manifold.

5. Disconnect power brake vacuum and distributor vacuum lines.

NOTE: *Vacuum retard line is located at lower rear of vacuum unit on some exhaust emission distributors.*

6. Disconnect fuel line at carburetor.

7. Disconnect crankcase vent hose and accelerator linkage.

8. Remove bolts that secure accelerator linkage bracket, then remove intake manifold bolts and nuts. If the intake manifold will not clear the distributor, remove the distributor after noting the position of the rotor and the distributor housing.

9. Remove manifold and gasket.

CAUTION: *Make sure the O-ring between the intake manifold and timing chain cover is in place, where used.*

10. If a new manifold is being installed, transfer all parts from the old one.

11. Clean all gasket surfaces. Install new gaskets on the heads and apply a $3/16$" bead of RTV silicone sealer on the front and rear ridges of the block. Extend the sealer $1/2$" up each head to seal the manifold side gaskets. Use sealer at the water passages.

12. Install the manifold and torque the bolts to 30 ft.lb. in the sequence shown.

13. Install all other parts in reverse of the removal sequence.

263 and 350 Oldsmobile Built Diesel Engines

NOTE: *See Diesel Valve Lifter Bleed-down.*

1. Remove the air cleaner.

2. Drain the radiator. Loosen the upper by-pass hose clamp, remove the thermostat housing bolts, and remove the housing and the thermostat from the intake manifold.

CAUTION: *When draining the coolant, keep in mind that cats and dogs are attracted by the ethylene glycol antifreeze, and are quite likely to drink any that is left in an uncovered container or in puddles on the ground. This will prove fatal in sufficient quantity. Always drain the coolant into a sealable container. Coolant should be reused unless it is contaminated or several years old.*

3. Remove the breather pipes from the rocker covers and the air crossover. Remove the air crossover.

4. Disconnect the throttle rod and the return spring. If equipped with cruise control, remove the servo.

5. Remove the hairpin clip at the bellcrank and disconnect the cables. Remove the throttle cable from the bracket on the manifold; position the cable away from the engine. Disconnect and label any wiring as necessary.

6. Remove the alternator bracket if necessary. On the 350 cu. in. engine, if equipped with air conditioning, remove the compressor mounting bolts and remove the compressor aside, without disconnecting any of the hoses. Remove the compressor mounting bracket from the intake manifold.

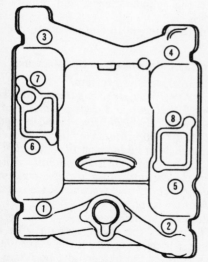

Intake manifold torque sequence—263 diesel engine

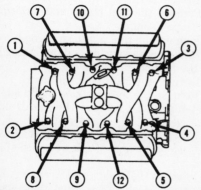

Intake manifold torque sequence—350, 403 Oldsmobile built gasoline and diesel engines

7. Disconnect the fuel line from the pump and the fuel filter. Remove the fuel filter and bracket.

8. Remove the fuel injection pump and lines. See above for procedures.

9. Disconnect and remove the vacuum pump or oil pump drive assembly from the rear of the engine.

10. Remove the intake manifold drain tube.

11. Remove the intake manifold bolts and remove the manifold. Remove the adapter seal. Remove the injection pump adapter.

12. Clean the mating surfaces of the cylinder heads and the intake manifold using a putty knife.

13. Coat both sides of the gasket surface that seal the intake manifold to the cylinder heads with G.M. sealer #1050026 or the equivalent. Position the intake manifold gaskets on the cylinder heads. Install the end seals, making sure that the ends are positioned under the cylinder heads.

14. Carefully lower the intake manifold into place on the engine.

15. Clean the intake manifold bolts thoroughly, then dip them in clean engine oil. Install the bolts and on the 350 V8 tighten to 15 ft.lb. in the sequence shown. Next, tighten all the bolts to 30 ft.lb., in sequence, and finally tighten to 40 ft.lb. in sequence. On the 263 V8 eng. tighten to 15 ft.lb. in the sequence shown, then retorque to 41 ft.lb.

16. Install the intake manifold drain tube and clamp.

17. Install injection pump adapter. See Injection Pump Adapter Seal and New Adapter Timing Mark Removal and Installation in Chapter 5. If a new adapter is not being used, skip steps 4 and 9.

18. Install the fuel injection pump. See Diesel Engine, under Fuel System, above for procedures.

19. Install the vacuum pump or oil pump drive assembly.

CAUTION: *Do not operate the engine without vacuum pump/oil assembly in place as this assembly drives the engine oil pump.*

20. Install the remaining components as they were removed. For throttle rod and transmission cable adjustments, see Diesel Engine, Fuel Injection Pump Removal and Installation, steps 22 and 27, in Chapter 5.

Exhaust Manifold

REMOVAL AND INSTALLATION

196, 231, 252, and 350 Buick Built Engines

1. Jack up the car and support on axle stands.

2. Disconnect the exhaust crossover pipe from the manifolds on both sides of the engine and lower it. On the V6, disconnect the choke pipe and, if necessary, the oxygen sensor lead if you are working on the right side, and the EFE line if you are working on the left.

3. If equipped with manual transmission, remove the equalizer shaft. Disconnect the turbocharger, if so equipped.

4. Remove the exhaust manifold-to-cylinder head bolts.

5. Remove the manifold from beneath the car.

6. Reverse the above to install. Always use the bolt locks.

305 and 350 Chevrolet Built Engines

LEFT SIDE

1. Disconnect the battery ground cable and raise the car. Disconnect the exhaust pipe at the manifold.

2. Remove the front manifold to exhaust pipe flange stud, and then remove the rear spark plug shield; lower the car.

3. Remove the air conditioning compressor and set it aside. DO NOT disconnect any air conditioning lines.

4. Disconnect and label the spark plug wires and their holder, the temperature sending unit lead and the dipstick.

5. Remove the attaching bolts and remove the manifold.

6. To install, reverse the removal procedure.

RIGHT SIDE

1. Disconnect the ground cable, and remove the fan shroud upper bolts and loosen the fan shroud. Remove the air cleaner intake pipe. If equipped with an air pump, remove the air injector manifold assembly.

2. Raise the car and disconnect the exhaust pipe at the manifold.

3. On some models, there will not be enough clearance to remove the manifold. If so, perform the following: Remove the right side engine mounting bracket through bolt. Jack up the right side of the engine, reinstall the right side through bolt, and lower the engine until the through bolt is resting on the mounting bracket.

4. Remove the rear spark plug shield bolt.

5. Lower the car and remove the spark plug wires (label them first), air cleaner heat stove pipe, and the air cleaner intake pipe. Remove the rear spark plug shield.

6. Remove the manifold to engine bolts, the EFE valve and the vacuum can.

7. To install, reverse the removal procedure.

350, 403 Oldsmobile Built Gasoline Engines-- 1975-77

1. Disconnect the negative battery cable and remove the air cleaner.

2. Remove the alternator and the alternator bracket.

3. Raise the car and support it with jackstands.

4. If the car is equipped with a crossover pipe, remove the bolts from the exhaust manifold flanges and remove the crossover pipe.

5. On cars equipped with air-conditioning, it will be necessary to remove the right front wheel to gain access to the right-hand manifold through the opening in the inner fender panel.

6. If the car is equipped with hot air-shrouds, remove them from the manifolds.

7. Unbolt the exhaust pipes from the exhaust manifolds. Spray the manifold studs with a penetrating lubricant first.

8. Remove the bolts which attach the manifolds to the cylinder heads, and remove the manifolds.

9. Installation is in the reverse order of removal.

263 and 350 Oldsmobile Built Diesel Engines

1. Drain the cooling system.
CAUTION: *When draining the coolant, keep in mind that cats and dogs are attracted by the ethylene glycol antifreeze, and are quite likely to drink any that is left in an uncovered container or in puddles on the ground. This will prove fatal in sufficient quantity. Always drain the coolant into a sealable container. Coolant should be reused unless it is contaminated or several years old.*

2. Remove the air cleaner.

3. Disconnect the upper radiator hose and thermostat bypass hose from the water outlet.

4. Disconnect the heater inlet hose and the AC vacuum line from the water valve.

5. Remove the crankcase ventilation pipes from the air crossover (V6) or valve covers (V8).

6. Remove the fuel pump and immediately cap all pipe openings.

7. Remove the fuel injection pump.

8. Disconnect all wiring and remaining hoses from the manifold.

9. Remove the cruise control servo.

10. Remove the intermediate pump adapter.

11. Unbolt and remove the manifold and adapter seal.

12. Clean all gasket surfaces thoroughly.

13. Coat both sides of the new gaskets with sealers.

14. Position the gasket on the engine. Install the end seals making sure that their ends are under the heads.

NOTE: *The seals and their mating surfaces*

must be dry. Apply a bead of RTV silicone sealer at the ends of the seals.

15. Position the intake manifold on the engine and connect the thermostat bypass hose. Dip the bolts in oil and torque them in sequence to 15 ft.lb. Then, retorque them in sequence to 40 ft.lb.

16. Install all other parts in reverse order of removal. Apply Chasiss lube to the seal area of the intake manifold and pump adapter.

265, 301 Pontiac Engines

LEFT SIDE

1. Remove the alternator belt, alternator and mounting bracket as an assembly.

2. Disconnect the exhaust pipes from the manifolds.

3. Straighten the tabs, if used, on the manifold bolt locks and remove the bolts and manifold.

4. Clean the gasket surfaces.

5. Reverse the removal procedures for installation. The notes for the right-side apply here.

RIGHT SIDE

1. Disconnect the exhaust pipes from the manifolds.

2. Straighten the tabs on the manifold bolts, if used, and remove the manifold bolts, manifold, and gasket.

3. Clean the gasket surfaces.

4. Replace the exhaust manifold, using a new gasket; the holes in the end of the gasket are slotted.

NOTE: *The installation of the gasket may be simplified by first installing the manifold using only the front and rear bolts to retain the manifold. Allow clearance of about 1/8-3/16" between the cylinder head and the exhaust manifold. After inserting the gasket between the head and the manifold, the remaining bolts may be installed.*

5. Torque all bolts evenly to specified torque.

6. Bend the tabs against the sides of the bolt heads.

7. Attach thew exhaust pipe, using a new gasket.

1986-87 Olds 307 Engine

LEFT SIDE

1. Remove the air cleaner and then raise and support the car in a secure manner.

2. Pry the attaching bolt locking tabs away from the bolt heads.

3. Unclamp and then disconnect the exhaust pipe at the flange at the bottom of the manifold. Lower the car.

4. Disconnect the intermediate steering shaft as follows:

a. Put the wheels in straight ahead position. Unclip and remove the coupling shield from the intermediate shaft.

b. Unscrew and remove the nut attaching the cross bolt to the steering column; then pull out the cross bolt to remove it. Then, slide the coupling shaft off the steering column.

c. Unscrew and then remove the pinch bolt from the steering gear coupling and then remove the intermediate shaft by sliding it off the splined steering gear shaft.

5. Remove the retaining nuts and bolt and remove the hot air shrouds. Remove the lower generator bracket.

6. Remove the retaining bolts, being careful to retain the washers used on the two upper center bolts. Remove the manifold and gasket.

7. Clean both gasket surfaces and put the manifold in position over a new gasket. Install all bolts and washers, tightening bolts finger tight.

8. Tighten the bolts in several stages and in rotation, starting with the bolt at top center. Torque them to 25 ft.lb.

9. Install the lower generator bracket.

10. Install the hot air shrouds and retaining nuts and bolt. Torque the bolt to 70 ft.lb.

11. Raise and securely support the car. Install the crossover pipe with new gaskets. Bend the lock tabs securely around the exhaust manifold bolts.

12. Lower the car. Reconnect the intermediate steering shaft as follows:

WARNING: *Do not substitute any ordinary bolts or nuts in the following procedure. Failure to use parts specifically designed for this application could cause steering system failure on the road!*

a. Engage the coupling of the intermediate shaft with the splines on the steering gear shaft so that there is 3.0mm or less of spline visible between the coupling and the gear. Install the pinch bolt into the coupling and torque it to 35 ft.lb.

b. With the front wheels and steering column both in the straight ahead position, install the steering shaft female fitting onto the square end of the steering column shaft just far enough to align the crossbolt holes in the two fittings. Then, install the crossbolt, install the nut onto the crossbolt, and torque the nut to 50 ft.lb.

c. Install the coupling shield and latch it so it is seated around the outlet pipe nut. Check to make sure that none of the colored portion of the steering box seal is visible; if it is, recheck the coupling attachment to make sure it is properly assembled (see Step a).

13. Install the air cleaner. Operate the engine

and check for exhaust leaks, making further repairs if necessary.

RIGHT SIDE

1. Disconnect the oxygen sensor lead. Raise the car and support it securely.

2. Remove the crossover pipe. Disconnect the exhaust pipe, lower it, and support the exhaust system from the body.

3. Put a drain pan underneath and then remove the oil filter adapter and gasket.

4. Remove the right front wheel. Flatten the manifold bolt lock tabs.

5. Remove the bolts, and then remove the manifold and gasket.

6. To install, clean both gasket surfaces and then position a new gasket and the manifold onto the block. Install the attaching bolts finger tight.

7. Tighten the bolts, starting with the top center bolt, in rotation in several stages, final torquing to 25 ft.lb.

8. Clean both gasket surfaces and then install the oil filter adapter with a new gasket.

9. Connect the exhaust pipe and install the crossover pipe. Bend up the lock tab.

10. Install the right front wheel. Lower the car to the ground.

11. Connect the oxygen sensor lead. Start the engine and run until oil pressure is restored. Check the oil level and replace oil lost when the filter adapter was removed. Operate the engine and check for oil or exhaust leaks, making further repairs if necessary.

Turbocharger

PRECAUTIONS

There are certain steps to be taken when performing maintenance on a turbocharged engine. When changing the oil and filter, or performing any other operation which results in oil loss or drainage, before restarting the engine, disconnect the pink wire from the distributor, crank the engine several times for short intervals until the oil light goes out.

Any time a main bearing, connecting rod bearing or camshaft bearing is in need of replacement, the oil and filter should be changed as part of the procedure. If the change is the result of sudden damage to the bearing, the turbocharger should be flushed with clean engine oil to reduce the chance of contamination. Any time the center housing or any part of the turbocharger which includes the center housing is replaced, the oil and filter should be changed as part of the procedure.

REMOVAL AND INSTALLATION

1. Disconnect the exhaust inlet and outlet pipes from the turbocharger.

2. Disconnect the oil feed pipe from the center housing.

3. Remove the nut attaching the air intake elbow to the carburetor and remove the elbow and flex tube from the carburetor.

4. Disconnect the accelerator, cruise and detent linkages from the carburetor. Disconnect the plenum linkage bracket.

5. Remove the two bolts attaching the plenum to the side bracket.

6. Disconnect the fuel line and all vacuum lines from the carburetor.

7. Drain the cooling system.

CAUTION: *When draining the coolant, keep in mind that cats and dogs are attracted by the ethylene glycol antifreeze, and are quite likely to drink any that is left in an uncovered container or in puddles on the ground. This will prove fatal in sufficient quantity. Always drain the coolant into a sealable container. Coolant should be reused unless it is contaminated or several years old.*

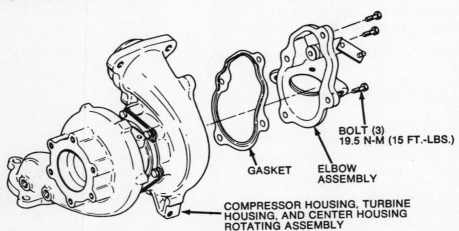

BOLT (3)
19.5 N-M (15 FT.-LBS.)

GASKET   ELBOW
          ASSEMBLY

COMPRESSOR HOUSING, TURBINE
HOUSING, AND CENTER HOUSING
ROTATING ASSEMBLY

Elbow assembly

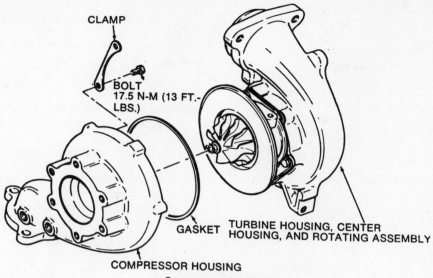

CLAMP

BOLT
17.5 N-M (13 FT.-
LBS.)

GASKET

TURBINE HOUSING, CENTER
HOUSING, AND ROTATING ASSEMBLY

COMPRESSOR HOUSING

Compressor housing

8. Disconnect the coolant lines from the front and rear of the plenum.

9. Disconnect the power brake vacuum line from the plenum.

10. Remove the two bolts attaching the turbine housing to the intake manifold bracket.

11. Remove the two bolts attaching the EGR valve manifold to the plenum. Loosen the two bolts attaching the EGR valve to the intake manifold.

12. Remove the AIR bypass hose from the check valve.

13. Remove the three bolts attaching the compressor housing to the intake manifold.

14. Remove the turbocharger, actuator, carburetor and plenum from the engine.

15. Remove the six bolts attaching the carburetor and plenum to the turbocharger and actuator.

16. Remove the oil drain from the center housing.

To install:

1. Install the oil drain on the center housing. Torque to 15 ft.lb.

2. Install the six turbocharger/actuator-to-carburetor/plenum bolts.

3. Place the assembly on the engine and connect all vacuum hoses.

4. Install the three bolts attaching the compressor housing to the intake manifold. Torque to 35 ft.lb.

5. Install the AIR bypass hose.

6. Loosely install the two bolts attaching the EGR valve manifold to the plenum. Tighten the two bolts attaching the EGR valve to 15 ft.lb. Tighten the EGR manifold-to-plenum bolts to 15 ft.lb.

7. Install the two bolts attaching the turbine housing to the intake manifold bracket. Torque to 20 ft.lb.

8. Connect the power brake vacuum line at the plenum. Torque to 10 ft.lb.

9. Connect the plenum front bracket and install one bolt attaching the bracket to the manifold. Torque to 20 ft.lb.

10. Connect the coolant hoses to the plenum.

11. Refill the cooling system.

12. Connect the carburetor fuel line and remaining vacuum hoses.

13. Install the two bolts attaching the plenum to the side bracket. Torque to 20 ft.lb.

14. Connect the linkage bracket to the plenum. Torque to 20 ft.lb.

15. Connect the accelerator, detent and cruise linkages to the carburetor.

16. Install the nut attaching to the carburetor.

17. Install the nut attaching the air intake elbow to the carburetor. Torque to 15 ft.lb.

18. Connect the oil feed pipe to the center housing. Torque to 7 ft.lb.

19. Connect the inlet and outlet pipes to the turbocharger. Torque to 14 ft.lb

TURBOCHARGING SYSTEM COMPONENT REMOVAL AND INSTALLATION

NOTE: *In the course of servicing the engine, component parts of the turbocharger assembly, including the unit itself, piping, hoses and lines, and electrical connections may have to be removed or disconnected. If removal and installation of turbocharger components becomes necessary, refer to the proper service procedure below.*

CAUTION: *If the turbocharger unit has to be removed, first clean around the unit thoroughly with a non-caustic solution. When removing the turbocharger, take great care to avoid bending, nicking or in ANY WAY damaging the compressor or turbine blades. Any damage to the blades will result in imbalance, failure of the center housing bearing, damage to the unit and possible personal injury or damage to other engine parts. This happens because of the extremely high rpm at which turbochargers turn.*

ESC Detonation Sensor

1. Squeeze the side of the connector and carefully pull it straight up.

2. Using a deep socket, unscrew the sensor.

3. To install, reverse the removal procedure. Torque the sensor to 14 ft.lb. Do not over-torque the sensor or apply a side load when installing.

Wastegate Actuator Assembly

1. Disconnect the two hoses from the actuator.

2. Remove the wastegate linkage-to-actuator rod clip.

3. Remove the two bolts attaching the actuator to the compressor housing.

4. Installation is the reverse of removal.

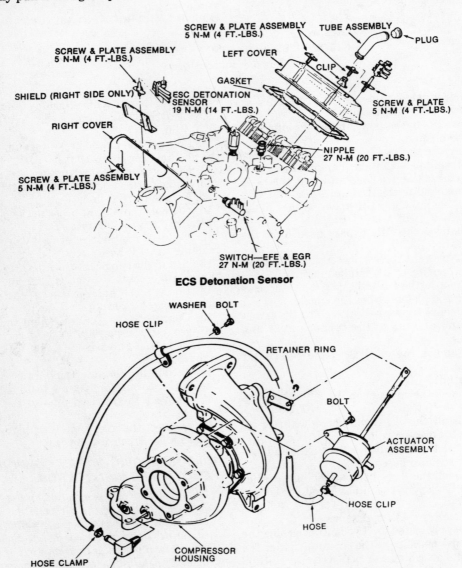

ECS Detonation Sensor

Wastegate actuator

Center Housing

1. Disconnect the exhaust outlet pipe from the elbow assembly.
2. Raise and support the car.
3. Disconnect the exhaust outlet pipe from the catalytic converter.
4. Lower the car.
5. Disconnect the exhaust inlet pipe from the turbine housing.
6. Disconnect the exhaust inlet pipe from the right exhaust manifold.
7. Remove the two turbine housing-to-intake manifold bolts.
8. Disconnect the oil feed pipe from the center housing rotating assembly.
9. Remove the oil drain hose from the oil drain pipe.
10. Remove the wastegate linkage-to-actuator rod clip.
11. Remove the six bolts and three clamps attaching the center housing to the compressor housing.
12. Installation is the reverse of removal.

Plenum

1. Remove the turbocharger and actuator assembly.
2. Remove the four bolts attaching the carburetor to the plenum.
3. Installation is the reverse of removal. Torque the bolts to 20 ft.lb.

Air Conditioner Compressor

REMOVAL AND INSTALLATION

WARNING: *The air conditioning system contains highly pressurized refrigerant gas which is capable of freezing any part of the body it comes in contact with. The system's refrigerant must be discharged in a safe manner before any attempt is made to disconnect the hoses. Since this type of work is most often done by professionals and is most safely done with specialized equipment and training, refer to the material under Air Conditioning System in Chapter 1 and either have a professional discharge the system or, if you have satisfied yourself that you can handle the job safely, do this yourself, carefully observing the procedures and precautions provided there.*

NOTE: *You will need caps or tape for sealing open fittings, as well as new O-rings and refrigerant oil to securely reseal them.*

1. Once the system's refrigerant has been discharged, remove items that may make access to the unit for removal of either attaching bolts or the compressor itself difficult. These may include the fan and shroud, the generator or power steering pump, or various hoses or belts.
2. Trace back both the suction and discharge lines until you have reached a coupling at which these lines may be disconnected. On some compressors, both lines connect to the back of the compressor through a common fitting. If there is room, you may want to disconnect these lines there.
3. Thoroughly clean the areas around the fittings you'll be disconnecting with rags and a safe solvent. This is necessary to help prevent dirt from getting into the system. Then, using a backup wrench except where a hose connects directly to the compressor, disconnect and cap or tape over all open ends of the fittings.
4. If the mounting system for the compressor is complex, take a moment and draw a de-

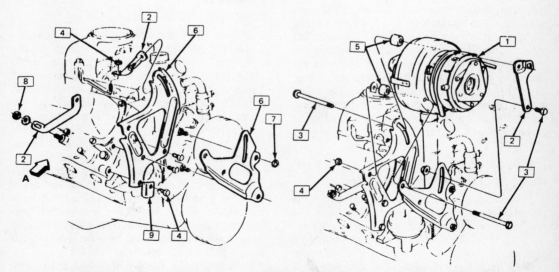

Air conditioner compressor mounting arrangement typical of late model Regals with the 307 V8

tailed diagram, being especially sure to reflect the locations of spacers and the relative lengths of bolts. Loosen the bolt or bolts that pass(es) through the slotted portion of the compressor mounting system, rotate the compressor toward the engine, and remove its drive belt. If necessary, remove other drive belts that may block access to the compressor drive belt. Then, being careful to catch any spacers or other brackets that will be disassembled, remove that bolt or those bolts from the compressor.

5. Then, one by one, remove the remaining mounting bolts, nuts, and spacers. Observe each bolt carefully before removal and make sure to catch all the hardware that may be involved, especially if you have not already checked out the system to make a drawing. Make sure to support the compressor adequately throughout this procedure as it can be damaged not only by dropping a short distance but by being supported unevenly. When all supports have been disconnected and all related parts, including brackets, have been removed, remove the compressor.

6. Carefully orient the compressor and, if necessary, brackets that have been removed. You may want to support it with a wooden block or lever of some sort as you work. Position the brackets and bolts on which the unit hinges during adjustment, along with the related hardware such as spacers. Install attaching nuts and tighten nuts/bolts just slightly.

7. Install the bolts, spacers and other hardware which permit the compressor belt tension to be adjusted. Tighten them loosely with the compressor as close to the engine as the adjusting slots permit. Install the belt, tension it so there is about ¾" play at the center of a long span and tighten all bolts.

8. Coat the O-rings with oil, remove the tape or covers from the fittings, and then remove old O-rings. Install the new O-rings. Connect the fittings and tighten with backup wrenches.

9. Install any other underhood items removed to gain access to the compressor. Then, have the air conditioning system evacuated with a good vacuum pump and have it recharged or recharge it yourself, according to the procedures in Chapter 1.

Radiator

REMOVAL AND INSTALLATION

1. Drain the radiator and disconnect the upper and lower radiator hoses. Disconnect the transmission fluid cooler lines, if so equipped.

CAUTION: *When draining the coolant, keep in mind that cats and dogs are attracted by the ethylene glycol antifreeze, and are quite likely to drink any that is left in an uncovered*

container or in puddles on the ground. This will prove fatal in sufficient quantity. Always drain the coolant into a sealable container. Coolant should be reused unless it is contaminated or several years old.

2. Disconnect the coolant recovery hose.

3. Remove the fan shroud-to-radiator screws. Lift the shrouds out of the clips and hang the shroud over the fan.

4. Remove the radiator upper mounting panel.

5. Remove the radiator. Reverse to install.

1977 and later

1. Refer to steps 1-2 of the above procedure.

2. On 1978 and later models, remove the fan blade and the fan clutch.

3. Remove the fan housing attaching screws and lift out the shroud. On models which have the fan shroud stapled together, remove the staples, then remove the upper shroud half. During assembly, the shroud halves must be drilled and bolted together.

NOTE: *Some air conditioned models have a high-pressure A/C line which runs across the top of the upper radiator shroud. It is not necessary to remove the line in order to remove the shroud. If the A/C line is clamped to the shroud, disconnect the clamp. Carefully slide the upper shroud half out from under the A/C line, toward the passenger side of the vehicle (fan removed).*

4. Remove the radiator. Reverse the removal procedure to install. Make sure to fill the system with coolant, operate the engine until hot, refill the system, and then cap it off, running the engine for a few more minutes to check for leaks.

Condenser

REMOVAL AND INSTALLATION

NOTE: *To perform this procedure, you will need refrigerant oil and new O-rings for the fittings by which the condenser is attached to the rest of the system, as well as tape or caps to seal off the openings. Make sure you also have enough wrenches so you can always use a backup wrench when you disconnect or connect fittings.*

Make sure you do not disconnect any system part without first discharging the system, or severe personal injury could result.

1. Refer to the Air Conditioning section of Chapter 1 and discharge the refrigerant from the system. If you do not feel comfortable performing these procedures, have this potentially dangerous job performed by a professional air conditioning mechanic.

2. Remove the bolts which fasten the condenser retainers to the radiator/condenser sup-

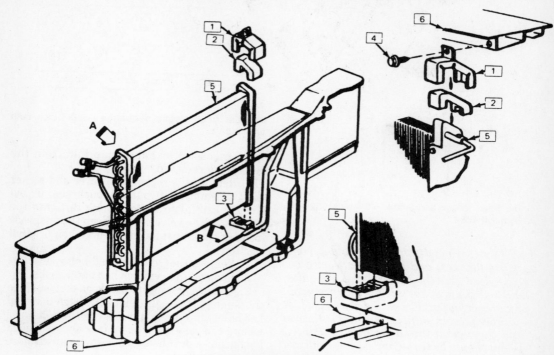

Typical condenser mounting

port. This will permit the condenser to be rocked forward slightly during the next step.

3. Using a backup wrench, disconnect the two refrigerant line connectors and then seal the openings. Lift the retainers and upper insulators off the top of the condenser.

4. Lift the condenser straight up and out of the area between the support and the front bumper.

5. Install the condenser in reverse order, being careful to locate the bottom squarely into the lower insulators, and making sure that the upper insulators are in place in the brackets. Install new O-rings coated with refrigerant oil and screw together the high and low pressure connections. Using a back-up wrench, torque each to 18 ft.lb.

6. Install the mounting bolts and torque them to 7 ft.lb. When the assembly is complete, have the system evacuated and then recharge it according to the procedure given in Chapter 1.

Water Pump
REMOVAL AND INSTALLATION
All Engines

1. Drain the cooling system. Remove the fan shroud, if necessary for clearance.

CAUTION: *When draining the coolant, keep in mind that cats and dogs are attracted by the ethylene glycol antifreeze, and are quite likely to drink any that is left in an uncovered container or in puddles on the ground. This will prove fatal in sufficient quantity. Always drain the coolant into a sealable container. Coolant should be reused unless it is contaminated or several years old.*

2. Loosen the belt or belts, then remove the fan blades and pulley or pulleys from the hub on the water pump shaft. Remove the belt or belts.

3. Disconnect the hose from the water pump inlet and the heater hose from the nipple. Remove the bolts, then remove the pump and gasket from the timing case cover or engine block.

To install the pump:

1. Install the pump assembly with a new gasket. Bolts and lock washers must be torqued evenly.

2. Connect the radiator hose to the pump inlet and the heater hose to the nipple. Fill the cooling system and check all points of possible coolant leaks.

3. Install the fan pulley or pulleys and the fan blade. install the belt or belts and adjust for correct tension.

Cylinder Head
REMOVAL AND INSTALLATION
196, 231, 252, and 350 Buick Built Engines

1. Disconnect the battery.
2. Drain the coolant.

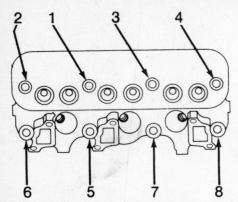

Cylinder head torque sequence—V6 Buick engines built through 1984

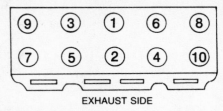

EXHAUST SIDE

Cylinder head torque sequence—350 Buick built engines

CAUTION: *When draining the coolant, keep in mind that cats and dogs are attracted by the ethylene glycol antifreeze, and are quite likely to drink any that is left in an uncovered container or in puddles on the ground. This will prove fatal in sufficient quantity. Always drain the coolant into a sealable container. Coolant should be reused unless it is contaminated or several years old.*

3. Remove the air cleaner.

4. Remove the air conditioning compressor, but do not disconnect any lines. Disconnect the AIR hose at the check valve. Remove the turbocharger assembly, if so equipped.

5. Remove the intake manifold.

6. When removing the right cylinder head, loosen the alternator belt, disconnect the wiring and remove the alternator. If equipped with A/C, remove the compressor from the mounting bracket and position it out of the way *without disconnecting any of the hoses.*

7. When removing the left cylinder head, remove the dipstick, power steering pump and air pump if so equipped.

8. Disconnect and label the plug wires.

9. Disconnect exhaust manifold from the head being removed.

10. Remove the rocker arm cover and rocker shaft assembly. Lift out the pushrods. Be extremely careful to avoid getting dirt into the area under the valve covers. Keep the pushrods in order; they must be returned to their original positions.

11. Remove the cylinder head bolts.

12. Remove the cylinder head and gasket.

13. Clean the engine block gasket surface thoroughly. Make sure that no foreign material has fallen into the cylinder bores, the bolt holes or into the valve lifter area. It is always a good idea to clean out the bolt holes with an air hose if one is available.

14. Install a new head gasket with the bead facing down toward the cylinder block. The dowels in the block will hold the gasket in place.

15. Clean the gasket surface of the cylinder head and carefully set it into place on the dowels in the cylinder block.

16. Use a heavy body thread sealer on all of the head bolts since the bolt holes go all the way through into the coolant.

17. Install the head bolts. Tighten the bolts a little at a time about three times around in the sequence shown in the illustration. Tighten the bolts to a final torque equal to that given in the Torque Specifications chart.

18. Installation of the remaining components is in the reverse order of removal.

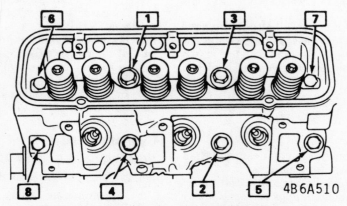

Cylinder head torque sequence for the 1985–87 231 V6

305 and 350 Chevrolet Built Engines

NOTE: *The engine should be overnight cold before the cylinder head is removed to prevent warpage.*

CAUTION: *Do not discharge the compressor or disconnect the A/C lines. Personal injury could result.*

1. Drain coolant. Remove the air cleaner.

CAUTION: *When draining the coolant, keep in mind that cats and dogs are attracted by the ethylene glycol antifreeze, and are quite likely to drink any that is left in an uncovered container or in puddles on the ground. This will prove fatal in sufficient quantity. Always drain the coolant into a sealable container. Coolant should be reused unless it is contaminated or several years old.*

2. Disconnect:
    a. battery
    b. Radiator and heater hose from manifold
    c. Throttle linkage
    d. Fuel line
    e. Coil wires
    f. Temperature sending unit
    g. Power brake hose, distributor vacuum hose, and crankcase vent hoses.

3. Remove:
    a. Distributor marking position
    b. Alternator bracket
    c. Coil and bracket
    d. Manifold attaching bolts
    e. Intake manifold and carburetor.

4. Remove:
    a. rocker arm covers
    b. Rocker arm nuts, balls, rocker arms, and pushrods. These items must be replaced in their original locations.

5. Remove cylinder head bolts, cylinder head, and gasket.

6. Reverse procedure to install. Tighten head bolts evenly to the specified torque. On engines having a steel gasket, use sealer on both sides. No sealer should be used on steel-asbestos gaskets. Adjust the valve lash.

7. Install in the reverse order of removal. It is recommended that the head gasket be coated on both sides with sealer. Dip head bolts in oil before installing. Tighten all head bolts in the correct sequence to the specified torque, then again in sequence to the specified torque. See Specifications at the beginning of this section for correct head bolt torque. Retorque the bolts after engine is warmed up.

265, 301 Pontiac Built Engines

1. Drain the cooling system including the block. Remove the intake manifold, valley cover, and rocker arm cover.

CAUTION: *When draining the coolant, keep in mind that cats and dogs are attracted by the ethylene glycol antifreeze, and are quite likely to drink any that is left in an uncovered container or in puddles on the ground. This will prove fatal in sufficient quantity. Always drain the coolant into a sealable container. Coolant should be reused unless it is contaminated or several years old.*

2. Loosen all rocker arm retaining nuts and pivot rockers off the pushrods.

3. Remove the pushrods and place in order. The pushrods must be replaced in the same position with the same end in the block.

4. Remove the battery ground strap and engine ground strap on the left head; engine ground strap and automatic transmission filler tube bracket on the right head.

5. Remove the cylinder head bolts and head, with the exhaust manifold attached.

NOTE: *Left head must be maneuvered to*

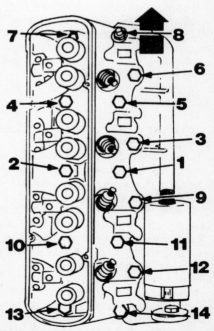

Cylinder head torque sequence—265 and 301 Pontiac built engines

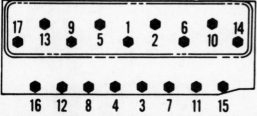

Cylinder head torque sequence—267, 305 and 350 Chevrolet built engines

clear the power steering and power brake units.

6. Check the head surface for straightness, then place a new head gasket on the block.

NOTE: *Bolts are of three different lengths. When they are properly installed, they will project an equal distance from the head, before tightening.*

7. Install all the bolts and tighten evenly to the specified torque. Tighten to specifications in three stages.

NOTE: *On the 265 and 301 V8 engine, coat all rocker stud lower threads, the cylinder head bolt threads, and the underside of the bolt head with thread sealer.*

8. Install each pushrod in its original position.

9. Position the rocker arms over the push-rods. Tighten the rocker arm ball retaining nut to 20 ft.lb.

10. Install the rocker arm cover.

11. Install the valley cover.

12. Install the ground straps, oil filler tube bracket, and intake manifold.

NOTE: *When installing the intake manifold remember to use new gaskets and O-ring seals, if so equipped.*

13. Install the exhaust pipe flange nuts.

307, 350, and 403 Oldsmobile Built Engines

1. Drain the cooling system.

CAUTION: *When draining the coolant, keep in mind that cats and dogs are attracted by the ethylene glycol antifreeze, and are quite likely to drink any that is left in an uncovered container or in puddles on the ground. This will prove fatal in sufficient quantity. Always drain the coolant into a sealable container. Coolant should be reused unless it is contaminated or several years old.*

2. Remove the intake manifold and carburetor as an assembly.

3. Remove exhaust manifolds.

4. Loosen or remove any accessory brackets which interfere.

5. Remove the valve cover. Loosen any accessories which are in the way.

6. Remove the battery ground strap from the cylinder head.

7. Remove rocker arm bolts, pivots, rocker arms and pushrods. Scribe the pivots and identify the rocker arms and pushrods so that they may be installed in their original locations.

8. Remove cylinder head bolts and cylinder head(s).

9. Install in the reverse order of removal. It is recommended that the head gasket be coated on both sides with sealer. Dip head bolts in oil before installing. Tighten all head bolts in the correct sequence to 60-70 ft.lb., then again in sequence to the specified torque. See Specifica-

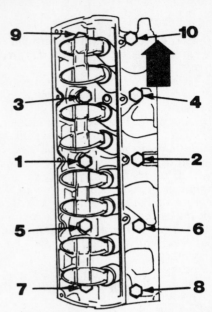

Cylinder head torque sequence—307, 350, 403 Oldsmobile built engines

tions at the beginning of this section for correct head bolt torque. Retorque the bolts after engine is warmed up.

263 and 350 Oldsmobile Built Diesel Engines

NOTE: *See diesel valve lifter bleed down procedure.*

1. Remove the intake manifold, using the procedure outlined above.

2. Remove the rocker arm cover(s), after removing any accessory brackets which interfere with cover removal.

3. Disconnect and label the glow plug wiring.

4. If the right cylinder head is being removed, remove the ground strap from the head.

5. Remove the rocker arm bolts, the bridged pivots, the rocker arms, and the pushrods, keeping all the parts in order so that they can be returned to their original positions. It is a good practice to number or mark the parts to avoid interchanging them.

6. Remove the fuel return lines from the nozzles.

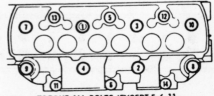

TORQUE ALL BOLTS (EXCEPT 5, 6, 11, 12, 13 & 14) TO 193 N·m (142 FT. LBS.). NUMBERS 5, 6, 11, 12, 13 & 14 TORQUE TO 80 N·m (59 FT. LBS.).

Cylinder head torque sequence—263 Diesel engine (V6)

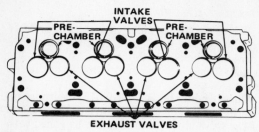

Valve location—350, 403 Oldsmobile built engines

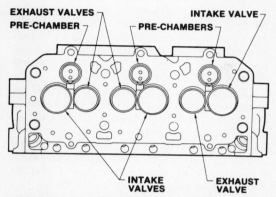

Valve location—263 Oldsmobile built diesel engine

VALVE SEAL IDENTIFICATION

Intake:
Std. to 0.005″ O.S.: Gray Colored
0.010-0.013″ O.S.: Orange Colored
Exhaust:
Std. to 0.005″ O.S.: Ivory Colored
0.010-0.013″ O.S.: Blue Colored

INSPECTING VALVES

• Inspect the valve stem tip for wear. This portion of the valve may be reconditioned on a grinder. Check the wear pattern on the valve tip to verify that the rotator is working properly. There should be a circular pattern. A pattern running directly across the tip of the valve like an ordinary screw slot, or an **X** or asterisk pattern indicates the rotator functions only sporadically and should be replaced.

• Inspect the keeper and oil seal grooves for chipped or worn lands and replace the valve if these conditions appear.

• Inspect the valve face for burning or cracking. If pieces are broken off, inspect the piston for that cylinder and the appropriate area of the cylinder head for damage.

• Inspect the valve stem for burrs or scratches. Burrs and minor scratches may be removed with an oil stone.

• Inspect the stem for straightness and the head for bends or distortion by placing the valve on V blocks. Replace the valve for either condition.

• Inspect the valve face for grooving. If the groove is so deep that removing the groove through refacing would bring the margin to less than specification, the valve must be replaced. If necessary, machine the valve to specification and then measure the margin, discarding the valve if necessary.

• Measure the inside diameter of the valve guide with a hole gauge and then measure the valve stem with a micrometer. Subtract the stem diameter from the i.d. of the guide to determine the clearance and compare it with specifications. If the clearance exceeds spec's, the valve guide will have to be reamed to a standard oversize and a new valve of the corresponding oversize will have to be installed.

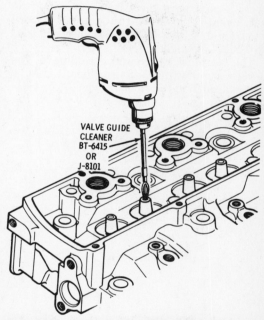

Cleaning valve guide bores—263 diesel shown

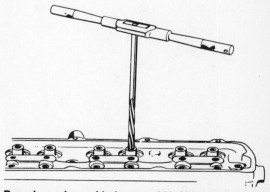

Reaming valve guide bores—350 Oldsmobile built engine shown

RECONDITIONING VALVES

When reconditioning valves and valve seats, clean carbon from cylinder heads and valves, using care not to gouge or scratch machined surfaces. A soft wire brush is suitable for this purpose. Whenever valves are replaced, or new valves installed, the valve seats must be reconditioned.

Narrow the valve seats to the specified width. This operation is done by grinding the portside with a 30° stone to lower the seat and a 60° stone to raise the seat. See chart for valve seat width.

Intake valve seats are induction hardened and must be ground, not cut. If valve guide bores are worn excessively, they can be reamed oversize. This will require replacement of the valves with oversize valves (stems). The guide bores should be reamed before grinding the valve seats. Valve clearance in guide bore should be 0.0015″ to 0.0032″ (exhaust) or 0.001″ to 0.0027″ for intake valve.

The tip must be ground according to the grinder manufacturer's instructions; it must be perpendicular to the stem.

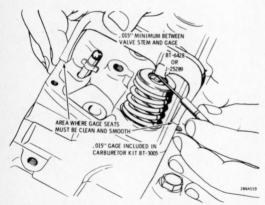

Measuring valve stem height—Oldsmobile built engines

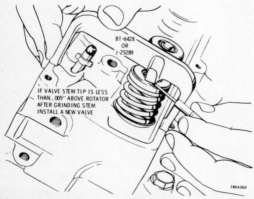

Measuring rotor height—Oldsmobile built engines

MEASURING VALVE STEM HEIGHT

Whenever a new valve is installed, or after grinding valves, it will be necessary to measure valve stem height as follows:

Install gage J-25289 across the top of the cylinder head.

There should be at least 0.015″ clearance on all valves between the gage surface and the end of the valve stem. The valve can be gaged with or without the valve rotator on the valve. If clearance is less than 0.015″, remove valve and grind the tip of the stems as required on a valve refacing machine, using the Vee block attachment to insure a smooth 90° end. Also be certain to break any sharp edge on ground valve tip. Observe an original valve to determine chamfer.

After all valve keys have been installed on valves, tap each valve stem end with a mallet to seat valve rotators and keys. Using gage J-25289, re-gage all valves between valve stem and gage (.015″ minimum) and valve rotator and gauge (.030″ minimum). If any valve stem is less than 0.005″ above rotator, the valve is too short and a new valve must be installed.

REAMING VALVE GUIDES

If stem-to-guide clearance is excessive, the normal procedure is to ream the valve guide to a standard oversize and install a new valve of the equivalent oversize. If the valve is badly worn and the guide can be reamed to a standard oversize without removing the spiraling which helps ensure adequate oil supply, this is the best procedure (if reaming the guide to a sufficient oversize will remove the spiraling, the head will have to be replaced).

There is another way of repairing this problem known as knurling. Knurling raises metal in the bore of the guide to create an uneven surface out of that remaining metal. This uneven surface ensures adequate oil flow to the valve. If the valve is in very good condition and the guide is not severely worn so that the clearance is only slightly beyond specification, you may want to knurl the guide. Consult the manufacturer of knurling tools to determine the clearances that are suitable for such a process and to get the proper tools.

If the normal procedure is to be followed, first, procure the proper tools and oversize valves. Engines built in years up to 1983 offer various oversizes while those built in 1984 and later years offer only the 0.003″ oversize. Consult the tool manufacturer for specifics.

Clean the guide with a tool such as J-8101, driven by an electric drill. Then, ream the guide to the appropriate oversize. The reamer must not be forced down into the guide. Instead, allow it to choose its own path down through the

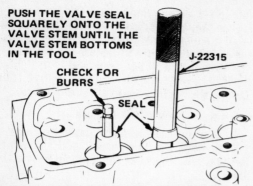

PUSH THE VALVE SEAL SQUARELY ONTO THE VALVE STEM UNTIL THE VALVE STEM BOTTOMS IN THE TOOL

J-22315

CHECK FOR BURRS

SEAL

Valve seal installation—Oldsmobile built engines

Have the valve spring test pressure checked professionally

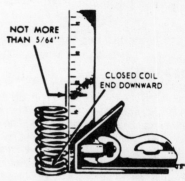

NOT MORE THAN 5/64"

CLOSED COIL END DOWNWARD

Check the valve spring free length and squareness

guide by merely turning it. Be careful to keep excessive amounts of chips and/or carbon out of the guide, if necessary, by occasionally backing the reamer out and removing chips from the flutes.

INSTALLATION

1. Install valves in their respective guides.
2. Install new oil seals over valve stems, using Tool J-22315 (350), J-26251 (307) or Tool J-2651 (263). Position seals down as far as possible on valve stem except on the 307. On the 307, install the seal into the tool, and then install the tool over the valve stem so the seal goes on squarely and gently force the tool downward until the stem bottoms in the tool. The seals will correctly position themselves when the engine is started. Inspect seal for cracks after installation.
3. Position valve springs over valve stems.
4. Install valve rotators, then compress springs with a tool such as J-22891, and install valve stem keys.
5. Check valve springs and keys to be sure they are properly seated.
6. Measure the valve spring installed height. This can be excessive, even though stem height has been corrected by machining, if the seat and valve face have been machined considerably. If spring installed height is greater than specification, place shims under the spring to bring height within limits. Failure to do this may cause poor valve performance at high rpm.

Valve Springs

HEIGHT AND PRESSURE CHECK

1. Place the valve spring on a flat, clean surface next to a square.
2. Measure the height of the spring, and rotate it against the edge of the square to measure distortion (out-of-roundness). If spring height varies between springs by more than $1/16''$ (1.6mm) or if the distortion exceeds $1/16''$ (1.6mm), replace the spring.

A valve spring tester is needed to test spring test pressure, so the valve springs must usually be taken to a professional machine shop for this test. Spring pressure at the installed and compressed heights is checked, and a tolerance of plus or minus 5 lbs. ($\pm$ 1 lb. on the 231V6) is permissible on the springs covered in this guide.

Oil Pan

REMOVAL AND INSTALLATION

350 Buick Built Engines

1. Disconnect the battery ground cable.
2. Remove the fan shroud-to-radiator screws.
3. Remove the air cleaner and disconnect the throttle linkage.
4. Raise the front end and support it on jackstands.
5. Drain the oil.
6. Disconnect the exhaust crossover pipe at the engine.
7. Remove the lower flywheel housing cover.
8. Remove the shift linkage bolt and swing it out of the way.
9. Remove the front engine mount bolts.
10. Raise the front of the engine, either by placing a block of wood and a jack under the

crankshaft pulley mounting or by lifting it with a hoist.

WARNING: *On air conditioned cars, place a support under the right side of the transmission before raising the engine. If you don't do this, the engine and transmission will flip to the right due to the weight of the air conditioning equipment.*

11. Unbolt and remove the pan. It may be necessary to turn the crankshaft so that it doesn't interfere with the front of the pan.

12. Reverse the procedure for installation. Coat the new gasket with sealer. Torque the oil pan bolts in rotation and in several stages to 7-10 ft.lb. Torque the engine mount bolts to 50 ft.lb.

231 and 252 Buick Built Engines

1. Raise the car, support it securely, and drain the oil.

2. Remove the flywheel cover.

3. Remove the exhaust crossover pipe.

4. On 1982 and later models, remove the bolts fastening the engine mounts to the frame brackets. Then, install a suitable hoist and raise the engine to provide clearance between the bottom of the pan and the crossmember.

5. Remove the oil pan attaching bolts and remove the oil pan.

6. Clean the mating surfaces of both the pan and the block. If no gasket is used, coat the surface of the oil pan flange with RTV sealer. If a cork gasket is used, coat both sides with a sealer. If a rubber type gasket is used, do not use sealer but make sure to replace the gasket.

7. Install the oil pan bolts and then tighten them in several stages, torquing to 7-10 ft.lb. Torque the engine mount bolts to 50 ft.lb.

305 and 350 Chevrolet Built Engines

1. Disconnect battery ground cable.

2. Remove distributor cap.

3. Remove radiator upper mounting panel or fan shroud.

4. Remove fan.

5. Drain engine oil.

6. Disconnect exhaust or crossover pipes.

7. Remove converter housing underpan and splash shield. On cars with manual transmission, remove the starter, then remove the flywheel cover.

8. Rotate crankshaft until timing mark on torsional damper is at 6:00 o'clock position.

9. Remove front engine mount through-bolts.

10. Raise engine and insert blocks under engine mounts.

11. Remove oil pan.

12. Clean the mating surfaces of both the pan and the block. If no gasket is used, coat the sur-

face of the oil pan flange with RTV sealer. If a cork gasket is used, coat both sides with a sealer. If a rubber type gasket is used, do not use sealer but make sure to replace the gasket.

13. Install the oil pan bolts and then tighten them in several stages, torquing to 7-10 ft.lb. Torque the engine mount bolts to 50 ft.lb.

265 and 301 Pontiac Built Engines

1. Disconnect the negative battery terminal.

2. Remove the fan shroud and the power steering belt, then push the pump in toward the block.

3. Remove the fan and pulley.

4. Disconnect the engine shroud straps. Drain the radiator.

CAUTION: *When draining the coolant, keep in mind that cats and dogs are attracted by the ethylene glycol antifreeze, and are quite likely to drink any that is left in an uncovered container or in puddles on the ground. This will prove fatal in sufficient quantity. Always drain the coolant into a sealable container. Coolant should be reused unless it is contaminated or several years old.*

5. On A/C cars, remove the compressor from the brackets and swing it aside without disconnecting hoses.

6. Check all wiring, fuel line and hoses for clearance, and disconnect the thermal feed switch from the left rear cylinder head, as the engine must be raised. Disconnect the bottom radiator hose at the water pump.

7. Jack up the car and drain the engine oil.

8. Rotate crankshaft until number one cylinder is at bottom dead center.

9. Remove the exhaust crossover pipe.

10. Remove the flywheel housing cover, starter motor and motor bracket.

11. Attach a hoist to the front of the engine.

12. Support the engine on a hoist and remove the front motor mount bolts and mounts.

13. Loosen the rear motor mount at transmission or, remove it entirely and allow the extension housing to rest on the crossmember.

14. Remove the oil pan bolts, then raise the engine straight up about 4½" until the top of the transmission is touching the floor pan. On some models, it also helps to move the engine forward about 1½". Place wood blocks between the engine and motor mount brackets for safety.

15. Rotate the oil pan forward to clear the oil pump, then remove the oil pan.

16. Clean the mating surfaces of both the pan and the block. If no gasket is used, coat the surface of the oil pan flange with RTV sealer. If a cork gasket is used, coat both sides with a sealer. If a rubber type gasket is used, do not use sealer but make sure to replace the gasket.

17. Install the oil pan bolts and then tighten them in several stages, torquing to 7-10 ft.lb. Torque the engine mount bolts to 50 ft.lb.

307, 350, 403 Oldsmobile Built Gasoline Engines

WARNING: *Be careful when handling the oil pan gasket. Some gaskets contain a hard metal core that can be sharp!*

NOTE: *To perform this procedure, you will need a safe and reliable means to raise the front of the engine. You can use any of several support bar systems (GM Tools BT-7109, BT-7203 and BT-6501 or equivalent) that hang from the frame and support the engine via the bottom of the crankshaft damper. Or you may be able to use a hoist to raise the engine by its lifting hooks or rig a floor jack to raise the engine by the damper. Plan very carefully and be sure the means you use will support the engine safely while you work!*

1. On the 350 and 403 engines only, remove the distributor cap. On 1975-77 models, align the rotor to No. 1 firing position. On 1978 and later models, align the timing marks so No. 1 is at top dead center. Doing this aligns the crankshaft counterweights for more clearance.

2. Disconnect the battery ground cable and remove the dipstick.

3. Remove the upper radiator support and the fan shroud attaching screws.

4. Raise the car and drain the oil.

5. Remove the flywheel cover.

6. Remove the starter motor assembly.

7. Disconnect the exhaust pipes and support the exhaust system. Disconnect the crossover pipe.

8. Unbolt the engine mounts at the block and raise the front of the engine as far as possible.

9. Remove the oil pan attaching bolts and remove the pan.

10. Coat both sides of the new side, front, and rear gaskets with sealer when installing. On 1983-87 307 V8s, run a $3/32''$ bead of RTV sealer in the groove of the front cover, as shown in the illustration. Installation is the reverse of removal. Torque the attaching bolts to 10 ft.lb.

263 and 350 Oldsmobile Built Diesel Engines

1. On V8s, remove the vacuum pump and drive (with A/C) or the oil pump drive (without A/C). On V6s, remove the oil pump drive and vacuum pump.

2. Disconnect the batteries and remove the dipstick.

3. Remove the upper radiator support and fan shroud.

4. Raise and support the car. Drain the oil.

5. Remove the flywheel cover.

6. Disconnect the exhaust and crossover pipes.

7. Remove the oil cooler lines at the filter base.

8. Remove the starter assembly. Support the engine with a jack.

9. Remove the engine mounts from the block.

10. Raise the front of the engine mounts from the block.

11. Raise the front of the engine and remove the oil pan.

12. Clean the mating surfaces of both the pan and the block. If no gasket is used, coat the surface of the oil pan flange with RTV sealer. If a cork gasket is used, coat both sides with a sealer. If a rubber type gasket is used, do not use sealer but make sure to replace the gasket.

13. Install the oil pan bolts and then tighten them in several stages, torquing to 7-10 ft.lb. Torque the engine mount bolts to 50 ft.lb.

Oil Pump

REMOVAL AND INSTALLATION

231, 252 and 350 Buick Built Engines

The oil pump is located in the timing chain cover and is connected by a drilled passage to

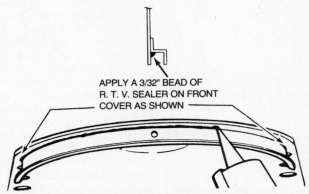

APPLY A 3/32" BEAD OF
R. T. V. SEALER ON FRONT
COVER AS SHOWN

On 1983–88 307 V8s, apply RTV sealer to the bottom sealing surface of the front cover, as shown

the oil screen housing and pipe assembly in the oil pan. All oil is discharged from the pump to the oil pump cover assembly, on which the oil filter is mounted.

1. To remove the oil pump cover and gears, first remove the oil filter.

2. Remove the screws which attach the oil pump cover assembly to the timing chain cover.

3. Remove the cover assembly and slide out the oil pump gears. Clean the gears and inspect them for any obvious defects such as chipping or scoring.

NOTE: *This step applies only to 1981-87 engines, for which oil pump wear specifications are supplied. For earlier engines, skip to Step 5.*

4. Run a straightedge across the oil pump housing face and then measure the clearance between the straightedge and the sides of the oil pump drive and driven gears. If the dimension is less than shown, replace the gears or gears and housing to bring the wear dimension to within specification:

- 1987: 0.001-0.0035″
- 1986 231 V6: 0.005-0.015″
- 1986 307 V8: 0.063-0.165″
- 1985 231 V6: 0.002-0.006″
- 1985 307 V8: 0.0025-0.0065″
- 1984: 0.002-0.006″
- 1983: 0.002-0.006″
- 1982: 0.002-0.006″
- 1981: 0.002-0.006″

Measure gear tip wear by passing a narrow feeler gauge between the oil pump housing wall and the tips of the gear teeth. On the gerotor type pump, measure this clearance between the tips of several teeth of the inner gear where they are passing across the center of one of the lobes in the outer gear. Rotate the gear as necessary to produce this alignment and check several of the teeth and lobes. Clearances are:

- 1987: 0.006
- 1986 231 V6: 0.003-0.005″
- 1986 307 V8: 0.040-0.120″
- 1985 231 V6: 0.0015-0.0140″
- 1985 307 V8: 0.040-0.0120″
- 1984: 0.003-0.005″
- 1983: 0.003-0.005″
- 1982: 0.002-0.005″
- 1981: 0.002-0.005″

In addition, on the gerotor type pump, measure the clearance between the outer diameter of the outer gear and the housing. The limit is 0.008-0.015″.

5. Remove the oil pressure relief valve cap, spring and valve. Clean them and inspect for wear or scoring. Check the relief valve spring to see that it is not worn on its side or collapsed. Replace the spring if it seems questionable.

6. Check the relief valve for a correct fit in its bore. It should be an easy slip fit and no tighter. If any perceptible binding can be felt, the valve piston and/or the cover should be replaced.

7. To install, lubricate the pressure relief valve and spring with clean engine oil and place them in the cover. Install the cap and the gasket. Torque the cap to 20 ft.lb.

8. Pack the oil pump gear cavity full of petroleum jelly. Do not use gear lube. Reinstall the oil pump gears so that the petroleum jelly is forced into every cavity of the gear pocket, and between the gear teeth. *There must be no air spaces* .

CAUTION: *This step is very important. Unless the pump is packed, it may not begin to pump oil as soon as the engine is started. This, of course, could severely damage the engine mechanically.*

9. Install the cover assembly using a new gasket and a sealer. Tighten the screws to 10 ft.lb.

10. Install the oil filter.

All Except Buick Built Engines

1. Remove the oil pan.

2. Remove the attaching bolts, and then remove the pump and drive shaft extension.

3. To install, insert the drive shaft extension through the opening in the main bearing cap until the shaft mates with the distributor drive gear. You nay have to turn the drive shaft extension one way or the other to get the two to mesh.

4. Position the pump on the cap and install the attaching bolts. Torque the bolts to 35 ft.lb.

5. Reinstall the oil pan.

Timing Chain, Cover Oil Seal and Cover

REMOVAL AND INSTALLATION
Buick Built Engines

1. Drain the cooling system.

CAUTION: *When draining the coolant, keep in mind that cats and dogs are attracted by the ethylene glycol antifreeze, and are quite likely to drink any that is left in an uncovered container or in puddles on the ground. This will prove fatal in sufficient quantity. Always drain the coolant into a sealable container. Coolant should be reused unless it is contaminated or several years old.*

2. Remove the radiator, fan, pulley and belt.

3. Remove the fuel pump and alternator, if necessary, to remove cover.

4. Remove the distributor. If the timing chain and sprockets will not be disturbed, note the position of the distributor for installation in the same position.

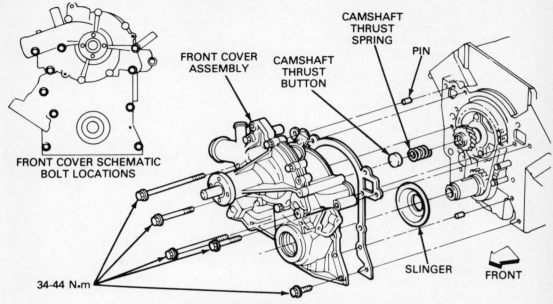

CAMSHAFT
THRUST
SPRING

PIN

FRONT COVER
ASSEMBLY

CAMSHAFT
THRUST
BUTTON

FRONT COVER SCHEMATIC
BOLT LOCATIONS

34-44 N·m

SLINGER

FRONT

Timing chain cover—196, 231, 252 Buick built V6 engines

5. Remove the thermostat bypass hose.

6. Remove the harmonic balancer.

7. Remove the timing chain-to-crankcase bolts.

8. Remove the oil pan-to-timing chain cover bolts and remove the timing chain cover.

9. Using a punch, drive out the old seal and the shedder toward the rear of the seal.

10. Coil the new packing around the opening so the ends are at the top. Drive in the shedder using a punch. Properly size the packing by rotating a hammer handle around the packing until the balancer hub can be inserted through the opening.

11. Align the timing marks on the sprockets.

12. Remove the camshaft sprocket bolt without changing the position of the sprocket. On the V6, remove the oil pan.

13. Remove the front crankshaft oil slinger.

14. On the 350, remove the crankshaft distributor drive gear and the fuel pump eccentric.

On the V6, remove the camshaft sprocket bolts.

15. Using the two large screwdrivers, carefully pry the camshaft sprocket and the crankshaft sprocket forward until they are free. Remove the sprockets and the chain.

To install:

1. Make sure, with sprockets temporarily installed, that No. 1 piston is at top dead center and the camshaft sprocket O-mark is straight down and on the centerline of both shafts.

2. Remove the camshaft sprocket and assem-

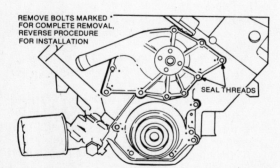

REMOVE BOLTS MARKED
FOR COMPLETE REMOVAL,
REVERSE PROCEDURE
FOR INSTALLATION

SEAL THREADS

Timing chain cover—350 Buick built V8 engines

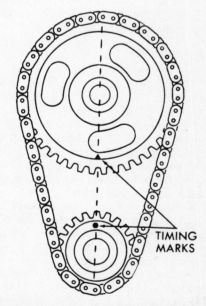

TIMING
MARKS

Valve timing marks—Buick built engines

ble the timing chain on both sprockets. then slide the sprockets-and-chain assembly on the shafts with the O-marks in their closest together position and on a centerline with the sprocket hubs.

3. Assemble the slinger on the crankshaft with I.D. against the sprocket, (concave side toward the front of engine). Install the oil pan, if removed.

4. On the 350, slide the fuel pump eccentric on the camshaft and the Woodruff key with the oil groove forward. On the V6, install the camshaft sprocket bolts.

5. Install the distributor drive gear.

6. Install the drive gear and eccentric bolt and retaining washer. Torque to 40-55 ft.lb.

7. Install the timing case cover. Install a new seal by lightly tapping it in place. The lip of the seal faces inward. Pay particular attention to the following points:

   a. Remove the oil pump cover and pack the space around the oil pump gears completely full of petroleum jelly. There must be no air space left inside the pump. Reinstall the pump cover using a new gasket.

   b. The gasket surface of the block and timing chain cover must be clean and smooth. Use a new gasket correctly positioned.

   c. Install the chain cover being certain the dowel pins engage the dowel pin holes before starting the attaching bolts.

   d. Lube the bolt threads and then install them.

   e. If the car has power steering the front pump bracket should be installed at this time.

   f. Lube the O.D. of the harmonic balancer hub before installation to prevent damage to the seal when starting the engine.

265, 301 Pontiac Built Engines

1. Drain the cooling system.
CAUTION: *When draining the coolant, keep in mind that cats and dogs are attracted by the ethylene glycol antifreeze, and are quite likely to drink any that is left in an uncovered container or in puddles on the ground. This will prove fatal in sufficient quantity. Always drain the coolant into a sealable container. Coolant should be reused unless it is contaminated or several years old.*

2. Disconnect all water hoses, vacuum lines and spark plug wires. remove the radiator.

3. Disconnect accelerator linkage, temperature gauge wire, and fuel lines.

4. Remove hood latch brace.

5. Remove PCV valve hose, then remove rocker covers.
NOTE: *On air conditioned models, remove alternator and bracket.*

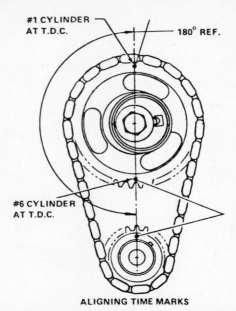

#1 CYLINDER AT T.D.C.   180° REF.

#6 CYLINDER AT T.D.C.

ALIGNING TIME MARKS

V8 engine timing mark alignment—Pontiac built engines

6. Remove distributor, then remove intake manifold.

7. Remove valley cover.

8. Loosen rocker arm nuts and pivot rockers out of the way.

9. Remove pushrods and lifters (keep them in proper order).

10. Remove harmonic balancer, fuel pump, and four oil pan-to-timing cover bolts.

11. Remove timing cover and gasket, then remove fuel pump eccentric and bushing.

12. Align timing marks, then remove timing chain and sprockets.
NOTE: *To set crankshaft and camshaft gear marks for timing chain installation, position the engine with the No. 6 piston at top dead center. Slowly rotate the crankshaft one revolution until the camshaft gear mark is at 12 o'clock. No. 1 piston will now be at TDC on the compression stroke.*

13. Remove camshaft thrust plate.

14. Remove camshaft by pulling straight forward, being careful not to damage cam bearings in the process.
NOTE: *It may be necessary to jack up the car slightly to gain clearance, especially if motor mounts are worn.*

15. Install new camshaft, with lobes and journals coated with heavy (SAE 50-60) oil, into the engine, being careful not to damage cam bearings.

16. Install camshaft thrust plate and tighten bolts to 20 ft.lb.

17. To install timing chain and camshaft, re-

verse Steps 1-12, tightening camshaft timing sprocket bolt to 40 ft.lb., timing cover bolts and nuts to 30 ft.lb., and oil pan bolts to 12 ft.lb.

305 and 350 Chevrolet Built Engines

NOTE: *If the timing chain is to be replaced, position the engine to align the timing marks at TDC (**O** on the scale) with the No. 1 cylinder on its compression stroke (valves closed.)* DO NOT rotate the cam or crankshaft while the chain is removed.

1. Drain and remove the radiator.

CAUTION: *When draining the coolant, keep in mind that cats and dogs are attracted by the ethylene glycol antifreeze, and are quite*

Cutting the oil pan front seal—Chevrolet built engines

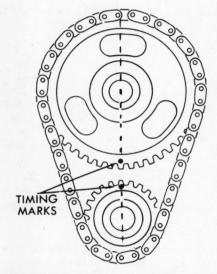

TIMING MARKS

Valve timing marks—Chevrolet built engines

likely to drink any that is left in an uncovered container or in puddles on the ground. This will prove fatal in sufficient quantity. Always drain the coolant into a sealable container. Coolant should be reused unless it is contaminated or several years old.

2. Remove the fan belt and accessory drive belts. Remove the crankshaft pulley.

3. Remove harmonic balancer, using a puller.

NOTE: *The outer ring (weight) of the harmonic balancer is bonded to the hub with rubber. The balancer must be removed with a puller which acts on the inner hub only. Pulling on the outer portion of the balancer will break the rubber bond or destroy the timing of the torsional damper.*

4. Remove the water pump. If the oil pan

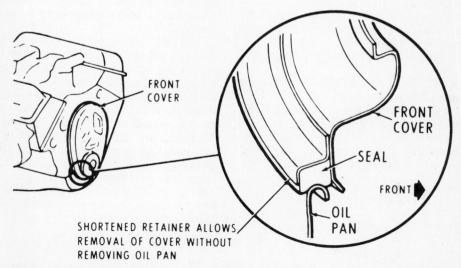

FRONT COVER

FRONT COVER

SEAL

FRONT ▶

OIL PAN

SHORTENED RETAINER ALLOWS REMOVAL OF COVER WITHOUT REMOVING OIL PAN

It is not necessary on the Chevrolet built engines to remove or lower the pan to remove the timing cover. The seal retainer is shortened enough to clear the pan

isn't to be removed cut the pan seal off flush with the block.

5. Remove timing gear cover attaching screws, and cover and bracket.

6. Clean all the gasket mounting surfaces.

7. Apply a bead of silicone sealer to the oil pan-to-cylinder block joint.

8. Install a centering tool in the crankshaft snout hole in the front cover and install the cover.

9. Install the front cover bolts finger tight, remove the centering tool and tighten the cover bolts. Install the harmonic balancer, pulley, water pump, belts, radiator, and all other parts.

CAUTION: *The engines use a harmonic balancer. Breakage may occur if the balancer is hammered back onto the crankshaft. A special installation tool is necessary.*

NOTE: *When replacing the crankshaft damper, it has been found that lightly polishing the crankshaft damper with crocus cloth will greatly ease replacement. this procedure will also assist in any future removals, as it is sometimes difficult to pull a damper even with a puller. Be sure that the pulling is not overdone, or the damper will wobble on the crankshaft.*

307, 350, and 403 Oldsmobile Built Gasoline Engines

1. Drain the coolant. Disconnect the radiator hose and the bypass hose. Remove the fan, belts and pulley.

CAUTION: *When draining the coolant, keep in mind that cats and dogs are attracted by the ethylene glycol antifreeze, and are quite likely to drink any that is left in an uncovered container or in puddles on the ground. This will prove fatal in sufficient quantity. Always drain the coolant into a sealable container. Coolant should be reused unless it is contaminated or several years old.*

2. Remove the vibration damper and crankshaft pulley.

3. On 1975-76 models only (which have no dowel pins), remove the oil pan.

4. Remove the front cover attaching bolts and remove the cover, timing indicator and water pump from the front of the engine. This requires removing all the bolts (four) that hold the cover on at the bottom, and four larger wa-

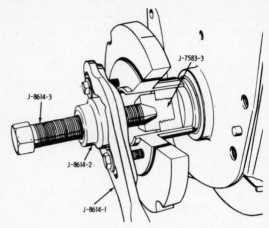

Removing the balancer—Oldsmobile built V8 engines

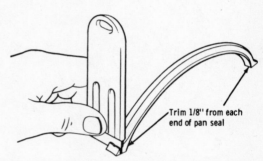

Trim 1/8'' from each end of pan seal

Trimming the oil pan seals—Oldsmobile built engines

ter pump mounting bolts that go right through the cover into the block. The two top center water pump mounting bolts and the two bottom such bolts remain in place and retain the water pump and gasket to the front of the cover. The other four water pump mounting bolts are removed.

On 1977 and later models, remove the two dowel pins from the block. You may have to grind a flat on each pin to get a good grip.

5. On 1977 and later models, grind a chamfer on the end of each dowel pin as illustrated. When installing the dowel pins, they must be inserted chamfered end first. Trim about 1/8'' (3.1mm) from each end of the new front pan seal and trim any excess material from the front edge of the oil pan gasket. Be sure all mating surfaces are clean.

6. On 1975-76 models apply a sealer around water holes on the new cover gasket before applying it to the block.

On 1977 and later models

a. Clean all seal mating surfaces with solvent.

b. When installing the new front cover gasket, first apply sealer to the water pump

CHAMFER

Chamfer the alignment pin—Oldsmobile built engines

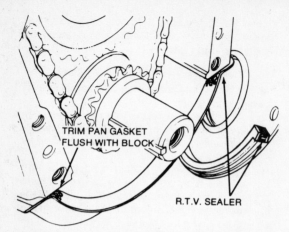

Applying sealer and trimming the pan gasket—Oldsmobile built engines

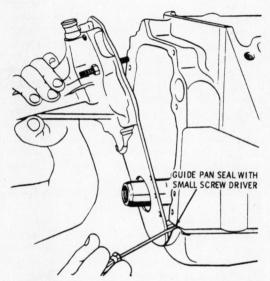

Installing the front cover—Oldsmobile built engines

bolt hole areas of the seal and then position the gasket to the block.

c. Apply RTV sealer to the junction of block, pan, and front cover.

d. In positioning the front cover onto the block and gasket, press it downward to compress the seal. Then, rotate the cover left and right while you guide the pan seal into the cavity with a small screwdriver, as shown. Now, apply oil to the threads and install two of the bolts finger tight to hold the cover in place. Install the two dowel pins, chamfered end first.

7. Complete the installation in reverse of removal, noting these points:

a. When installing cover bolts, first coat them with engine oil. Tighten evenly, torqu-

ing the four lower bolts to 35 ft.lb. and the four bolts passing through the water pump to 22 ft.lb.

b. Apply a high quality lubricant (an example is GM 1050169) to the sealing surface of the balancer.

c. When installing the balancer bolt, torque to 200-300 ft.lb. Crankshaft pulley attaching bolts are torqued to 10 ft.lb.; fan pulley attaching bolts are torqued to 20 ft.lb.

263 and 350 Oldsmobile Built Diesel Engines

1. Drain the cooling system and disconnect the radiator hoses.

CAUTION: *When draining the coolant, keep in mind that cats and dogs are attracted by the ethylene glycol antifreeze, and are quite likely to drink any that is left in an uncovered container or in puddles on the ground. This will prove fatal in sufficient quantity. Always drain the coolant into a sealable container. Coolant should be reused unless it is contaminated or several years old.*

2. Remove all belts, fan and pulley, crankshaft pulley and balancer, using a balancer puller.

WARNING: *The use of any other type of puller, such as a universal claw type which pulls on the outside of the hub, can destroy the balancer. The outside ring of the balancer is bonded in rubber to the hub. Pulling on the outside will break the bond. The timing mark is on the outside ring. If it is suspected that the bond is broken, check that the center of the keyway is 16° from the center of the timing slot. In addition, there are chiseled alignment marks between the weight and the hub.*

3. Unbolt and remove the cover, timing indicator and water pump.

4. It may be necessary to grind a flat on the cover for gripping purposes.

5. Grinds a chamfer on one end of each dowel pin.

6. Cut the excess material from the front end of the oil pan gasket on each side of the block.

7. Clean the block, oil pan and front and front cover mating surfaces with solvent.

8. Trim about ⅛" off each end of a new front pan seal.

9. Install a new front cover gasket on the block and a new seal in the front cover.

10. Apply sealer to the gasket around the coolant holes.

11. Apply sealer to the block at the junction of the pan and front cover. On V6, apply R.T.V. sealer on the front cover oil pan seal retainer.

12. Place the cover on the block and press down to compress the seal. Rotate the cover left and right to guide the pan seal into the cavity using a small screwdriver. Oil bolt threads and

heads, install two to hold the cover in place, then install both dowel pins (chamfered end first). Install remaining front cover bolts.

13. Apply lubricant, compatible with rubber, on the balancer seal surface.

14. Install the balancer and bolt. Torque the bolt to 200-300 ft.lb. on V8, 160-350 ft.lb. on V6.

15. Install all other parts in reverse of removal.

Timing Chain
REMOVAL AND INSTALLATION
305 and 350 Chevrolet Built Engines

All Chevrolet V8 engines are equipped with a timing chain. To replace the chain, remove the crankcase front cover. This will allow access to the timing chain. Crank the engine until the marks punched on both sprockets are closest to one another and in line between the shaft centers. Take out the three bolts that hold the camshaft sprocket to the camshaft. This sprocket is a light press fit on the camshaft and will come off readily. It is located by a dowel. The chain comes off with the camshaft sprocket. A gear puller will be required to remove the crankshaft sprocket.

Without disturbing the position of the engine, mount the new crank sprocket on the shaft, then mount the chain over the camshaft sprocket. Arrange the camshaft sprocket in such a way that the timing marks will line up between the shaft centers and the camshaft locating dowel will enter the dowel hole in the cam sprocket.

Place the cam sprocket, with its chain mounted over it, in position on the front of the camshaft and pull up with the three bolts that hold it to the camshaft.

After the sprockets are in place, turn the engine two full revolutions to make certain that the timing marks are in correct alignment between the shaft centers.

307, 350, and 403 Oldsmobile Built Engines

1. Remove the timing case cover and take off the camshaft gear.

NOTE: *The fuel pump operating cam is bolted to the front of the camshaft sprocket and the sprocket is located on the camshaft by means of a dowel.*

2. Remove the oil slinger, timing chain, and the camshaft sprocket. If the crankshaft sprocket is to be replaced, remove it also at this time. Remove the crankshaft key before using the puller. If the key cannot be removed, align the puller so it does not overlap the end of the key, as the keyway is only machined part of the way into the crankshaft gear.

3. Reinstall the crankshaft sprocket, being careful to start it with the keyway in perfect alignment since it is rather difficult to correct for misalignment after the gear has been started on the shaft. Turn the timing mark on the crankshaft gear until it points directly toward the center of the camshaft. Mount the timing gear over the camshaft gear and start the camshaft gear up on to its shaft with the timing marks as close as possible to each other and in line between the shaft centers. Rotate the camshaft to align the shaft with the new gear.

4. Install the fuel pump eccentric with the flat side toward the rear.

5. Drive the key in with a hammer until it bottoms.

6. Install the oil slinger.

NOTE: *Any time the timing chain and gears are replaced on the diesel engine it will be necessary to retime the engine's injection pump. Refer to the paragraph on Diesel Engine Injection Timing.*

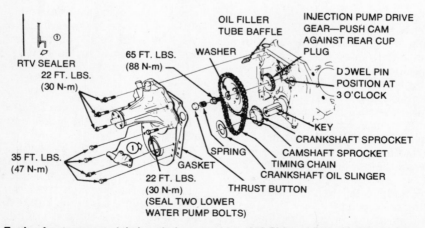

Engine front cover and timing chain assembly—350 Oldsmobile built diesel engine

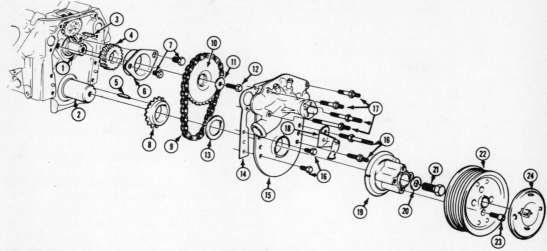

1. Camshaft	9. Timing chain	17. 28 N·m (21 ft. lbs.)
2. Crankshaft	10. Camshaft sprocket	18. Probe holder (rpm counter)
3. Camshaft sprocket key	11. Washer	19. Crankshaft balancer
4. Injection pump drive gear	12. 87 N·m (65 ft. lbs.)	20. Washer
5. Crankshaft sprocket key	13. Slinger	21. 217−475 N·m (160−350 ft. lbs.)
6. Front camshaft bearing retainer	14. Gasket	22. Pulley assembly
7. 65 N·m (48 ft. lbs.)	15. Front cover	23. 40 N·m (30 ft. lbs.)
8. Crankshaft sprocket	16. 55 N·m (41 ft. lbs.)	24. Cover

Engine front cover and timing chain assembly—263 Oldsmobile built diesel engine

263 Oldsmobile Built Diesel Engines

1. Remove the front cover. See above for procedure. Remove the valve covers.

2. Loosen all rocker arm pivot bolts evenly so that lash exists between the rocker arms and valves. It is not necessary to completely remove the rocker arms unless related service is being performed.

3. Remove the crankshaft oil slinger and the camshaft sprocket bolt washer.

4. Remove the timing chain, camshaft and crankshaft sprockets. If the crankshaft sprocket is a tight fit on the crankshaft use an appropriate puller to remove it.

5. If the camshaft sprocket-to-cam key comes out with the camshaft sprocket, proceed with this step and Step 6. If it has remained in position, proceed to Step 7. Remove the front camshaft bearing retainer and install the key into the camshaft and injection pump drive gear. Install the bearing retainer, but do not tighten the bolts--just run them in until they lightly pin the retainer against the block.

6. Rotate the camshaft at least 4 full turns (this will center the retainer over the camshaft on the surface of the block.) Now, torque the retainer retaining bolts alternately and in several stages to 48 ft.lb.

7. Install the key in the crankshaft, if removed.

8. Assemble the camshaft and crankshaft

sprockets and the timing chain on a flat work table. Turn the sprockets so the timing mark of the camshaft gear is facing the crankshaft sprocket (is at the bottom) and the mark on the crankshaft sprocket is facing the camshaft sprocket (is straight up). Engage the sprocket teeth with the teeth on the chain so that the timing marks stay in proper alignment (are directly across from each other). Then, install the camshaft sprocket, crankshaft sprocket, and

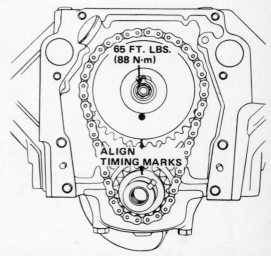

Timing mark alignment—Oldsmobile built engines

the timing chain together, keeping the timing marks on the camshaft and the crankshaft properly aligned. Tighten the camshaft sprocket bolt to 64 ft.lb. on 1983-84 models and 70 ft.lb. on 1985 models.

9. Install the oil slinger and the remaining parts of the front cover assembly.

10. After installing the front cover, bleed down the valve lifters as instructed in Diesel Engine, Rocker Arm Replacement, above.

11. The remaining steps of the installation are performed in the reverse of removal. Sealant is used in place of valve cover gaskets. Check injection timing as described in Chapter 5.

Camshaft and Bearings

196, 231, 252, AND 350 BUICK BUILT ENGINES

Removal

1. Complete steps 1 through 8 under Timing Chain, Cover Oil Seal, & Cover Removal and Installation, above. Skip steps 9 and 10 and complete steps 11 through 15.
NOTE: *If equipped with air conditioning, you will have to unbolt the condenser and position it out of the way before removing the radiator. This requires discharging the refrigerant as described in Chapter 1. If you do not feel safe doing this work, have a mechanic discharge the system.*
2. Remove the hydraulic lifters, keeping them in order for installation.
3. Slide the camshaft forward, out of the bearing bores. Do this carefully to avoid damage to the bearing surfaces and bearings.
NOTE: *Slightly scored camshaft bearings will be satisfactory if the surfaces of camshaft journals are polished and bearings are cleaned up to remove burrs, and the fit of*

shaft in bearings is free and within the specification. Should the bearing be galled beyond repair, the bearing will have to be replaced. Replacement camshaft bearings may be installed with Tool OTC 817, or equivalent. Care must be exercised during removal and installation not to damage bearings that are not being replaced.
4. Remove the camshaft.
5. Assemble the puller screw to the required length.
6. Select the proper size expanding collet and back-up nut.
7. Install the expanding collet on the expanding mandrel. Install the back-up nut.
8. Insert this assembly into the camshaft bearing to be removed. Tighten the back-up nut to expand the collet to fit the I.D. of bearing.
9. Thread the end of the puller screw assembly into the end of the expanding mandrel and collet assembly.
10. Install the pulling plate, thrust bearing, and pulling nut on threaded end of puller screw.
11. Remove the bearing by turning the pulling nut.
WARNING: *Make certain to grip the ⅝" hex end of the puller screw with a wrench to keep it from rotating when the pulling nut is turned. Failure to do this will result in the locking up of all threads in the pulling assembly and possible over expansion of the collet.*
12. Repeat the above procedure to remove any other bearings, except the front bearing, which may be pulled from the rear of the engine.
NOTE: *If you must remove the rear cam bearing, it is necessary to first remove the welch plug at the back of cam bore. However, if only the front three bearings are being replaced, it is not necessary to remove the welch*

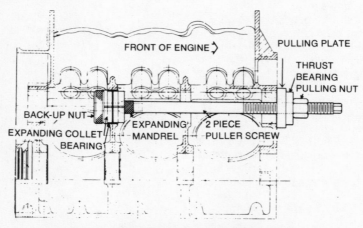

Removal and installation of camshaft bearings

plug. The front bearing can be removed by using a spacer between the pulling plate and the cylinder block to enable the tool to work in spite of the fact that only the front half is threaded.

Installation

1. Assemble puller screw to required length.
2. Select proper size expanding collet and back-up nut.
3. Install expanding collet on expanding mandrel.
4. Install back-up nut.

NOTE: *Any camshaft bearings that have been removed require replacement even though inspection reveals that their surfaces are in usable condition. This is because the bearing is damaged as it is pulled out of the block.*

5. Place new camshaft bearing on the collet and GENTLY hand tighten back-up nut to expand collet to fit bearing. Do not over tighten back-up nut. A loose sliding fit between collet and bearing surface is adequate. This will provide just enough clearance to allow for the slight collapse which will occur when the new bearing is pulled into the engine block.
6. Slide the mandrel assembly and bearing into the bearing bore as far as it will go without force.
7. Thread end of puller screw onto the end of the mandrel. Make certain to align oil holes in bearing and block properly. One of the collet separation lines may be used as a reference point.
8. Install pulling plate, thrust bearing and pulling nut on threaded end of the puller screw.
9. Install bearing in the same manner as described in Steps 11 and 12.

NOTE: *When installing rear cam bearing, install new welch plug at back of cam bore. Coat O.D. of plug with non-hardening sealer before installation.*

10. The remainder of the installation is the reverse of removal. Clean all gasket surfaces thoroughly and use new gaskets. Lubricate the camshaft lobes with heavy oil before installation, and be careful not to contact any of the bearings with the cam lobes. Make sure that the camshaft timing marks are aligned with the crankshaft marks. See installation steps under Timing Chain, Cover Oil Seal, & Cover Removal and Installation.

305 and 350 CHEVROLET BUILT ENGINES

Measuring Lobe Lift

1. With the rocker arms removed, position indicator with ball socket adapter (Tool J-8520) on pushrod. Make sure rod is in the lifter socket.

2. Rotate the crankshaft slowly in the direction of rotation until the lifter is on the heel of the cam lobe. At this point, the pushrod will be in its lowest position.
3. Set dial indicator on zero, then rotate the crankshaft slowly, or attach the auxiliary starter switch and bump the engine over, until the pushrod is in fully raised position.

CAUTION: *Whenever the engine is cranked remotely at the starter, with a special jumper cable or other means, the distributor primary lead must be disconnected from the coil.*

4. Compare the total lift recorded from the dial indicator with specifications.
5. If camshaft readings for all lobes are within specifications, remove dial indicator assembly.
6. Install and adjust valve mechanism as outlined.

Removal

1. Remove valve lifters as previously outlined.
2. Remove crankcase front cover as previously outlined.
3. Remove grille.
4. Remove fuel pump pushrod.
5. Complete camshaft removal as follows: The sprocket is a light fit on camshaft. If the sprocket does not come off easily a light blow on the lower edge of the sprocket (with a plastic mallet) should dislodge the sprocket.
6. Install two $5/16$"-18 x 4" bolts in camshaft bolt holes then remove camshaft.

NOTE: *All camshaft journals are the same diameter and care must be used in removing camshaft to avoid damage to bearings. Note also that camshaft bearing journals should be checked with a micrometer for an out-of-round condition. If the journals exceed 0.001" out-of-round, the camshaft should be replaced. Camshaft bearings can be replaced while the engine is disassembled for overhaul, or without complete disassembly of the engine. To replace bearings without complete disassembly remove the camshaft and crankshaft leaving cylinder heads attached and pistons in place. Before removing crankshaft, tape threads of connecting rod bolts to prevent damage to crankshaft. Fasten connecting rods against sides of engine so they will not be in the way while replacing camshaft bearings.*

7. With camshaft and crankshaft removed, drive camshaft rear plug from cylinder block.
8. Using Tool J-6098 or equivalent with nut and thrust washer installed to end of threads, index pilot in camshaft front bearing and install puller screw through pilot.
9. Install remover and install tool with

shoulder toward bearing, making sure a sufficient amount of threads are engaged.

10. Using two wrenches, hold puller screw while turning nut. When bearing has been pulled from bore, remove remover and installer tool and bearing from puller screw.

11. Remove remaining bearings (except front and rear) in the same manner. It will be necessary to index pilot in camshaft rear bearing to remove the rear intermediate bearing.

12. Assemble remover and installer tool on driver handle and remove camshaft front and rear bearings by driving towards center on cylinder block.

Installation

NOTE: *The camshaft front and rear bearings should be installed first. These bearings will act as guides for the pilot and center the remaining bearings being pulled into place.*

1. Assemble remover and installer tool on driver handle and install camshaft front and rear bearings by driving towards center of cylinder block.

2. Using Tool set J-6098, with nut then thrust washer installed to end of threads, index pilot in camshaft front bearing and install puller screw through pilot.

3. Index camshaft bearing in bore (with oil hole aligned as outlined below), then install remover and installer tool on puller screw with shoulder toward bearing.

NOTE: *Number one cam bearing oil hole must be positioned so that oil holes are equidistant from 6 o'clock position. Number two through number four bearing oil holes must be positioned at 5 o'clock position (toward left side of engine and at a position even with bottom of cylinder bore). Number five bearing oil hole must be in 12 o'clock position.*

4. Install the front and rear bearings first. Using two wrenches, hold the puller screw while turning nut. After bearing has been pulled into bore, remove the remover and installer tool from outer screw and check alignment of oil hole in camshaft bearing.

5. Install the remaining bearings in the same manner. It will be necessary to index the pilot in the camshaft rear bearing to install the rear intermediate bearing.

6. Install a new camshaft rear plug. The plug should be installed flush to $\frac{1}{32}$" deep and be parallel with rear surface of cylinder block.

NOTE: *Whenever a new camshaft is installed coat camshaft lobes with Molykote® or its equivalent. Also, whenever a new camshaft is installed, replacement of all valve lifters is recommended to insure durability of the camshaft lobes and lifter feet.*

7. Lubricate camshaft journals with engine oil and install camshaft.

8. Install timing chain on camshaft sprocket. Hold the sprocket vertically with the chain hanging down, and align marks on camshaft and crankshaft sprockets.

9. Align dowel in camshaft with dowel hole in camshaft sprocket then install sprocket on camshaft.

10. Draw the camshaft sprocket onto camshaft using the mounting bolts. Torque to specifications.

11. Lubricate the timing chain with engine oil.

12. Install fuel pump pushrod.

13. Install grille.

14. Install the crankcase front cover.

15. Install the valve lifters.

265 and 301 PONTIAC BUILT ENGINES
Removal

The camshaft and camshaft bearings can be replaced with engine installed in car or with overhaul; however, to replace the rear camshaft bearing without removing and completely disassembling engine, the transmission and flywheel must first be removed. To replace the camshaft and/or the rear center, center, front center or front camshaft bearing without removing and completely disassembling the engine, proceed as follows.

NOTE: *If the car is equipped with air conditioning, you will have to unbolt the condenser and position it out of the way before removing the radiator. Do not disconnect any of the air conditioning lines. Note also that the equivalents of the special tools mentioned in the following procedures may be used.*

1. Drain cooling system and remove air cleaner.

CAUTION: *When draining the coolant, keep in mind that cats and dogs are attracted by the ethylene glycol antifreeze, and are quite likely to drink any that is left in an uncovered container or in puddles on the ground. This will prove fatal in sufficient quantity. Always drain the coolant into a sealable container. Coolant should be reused unless it is contaminated or several years old.*

2. Disconnect all water hoses, vacuum lines and spark plug wires. Remove the radiator.

3. Disconnect accelerator linkage, temperature gauge wire, and fuel lines.

4. Remove the hood latch brace.

5. Remove the PCV hose, then remove the rocker covers.

NOTE: *On air-conditioned models, remove alternator and bracket.*

6. Remove distributor, then remove intake manifold.

7. Remove valley cover.

8. Loosen rocker arm nuts and pivot rockers out of the way.

9. Remove pushrods and lifters (keep them in proper order).

10. Remove harmonic balancer, fuel pump, and four oil pan to timing cover bolts.

11. Remove timing cover and gasket, then remove fuel pump eccentric and bushing.

12. Align timing marks, then remove timing chain and sprockets.

13. Remove camshaft thrust plate.

14. Remove camshaft by pulling straight forward, being careful not to damage cam bearings in the process.

NOTE: *It may be necessary to jack up the engine slightly to gain clearance, especially if motor mounts are worn.*

15. Insert remover adapter J-6173-4 into front bearing to act as a support for shaft J-6173-1. If the front bearing is to be replaced, insert installer adapter J-6173-3 into rear of bearing to be removed so that shoulder on remover bears against rear edge of bearing.

16. Place indexing collar J-6173-6 on the threaded end of the shaft with the open side toward the unthreaded end. Start the thrust washer and nut on the shaft.

17. Insert shaft and indexing collar through remover and replacer adapters and position lug on indexing collar in ventilator hole in front of block. This indexes shaft so that it cannot rotate.

18. Slip key J-6173-5 into notches in shaft behind bearing to be removed.

19. Turn nut on front of shaft to pull key against remover adapter J-6173-4, them continue to turn nut until bearing is pulled out of its hole.

Installation

1. Place a clean rag against each side of transverse member just below bearing hole to catch any shavings and carefully clean up hole. All scratches or nicks in cast iron should be smoothed with a scraper or file. Slightly chamfer the edge of the hole in which bearing is being installed to reduce possibility of scoring the outer diameter of the bearing when it is installed.

2. Insert remover adapter J-6173-4 into front bearing to act as a support for the shaft.

NOTE: *If the front bearing is being replaced, insert remover adapter in center bearing to act as a support for the shaft.*

3. Insert pilot J-6173-7 into hole in which bearing is to be installed.

4. Coat outside of new bearing with oil and place it over replacer adapter J-6173-3, index-ing notch in edge of bearing with pin on replacer adapter.

WARNING: *The notch in the edge of the bearing is used to properly position the bearing with respect to oil holes when it is installed. When bearings are installed in production, notches all face front except the one in the rear bearing. In service it is necessary to install the bearings with notches facing the rear. Position replacer adapter J-6173-3, with bearing in position against shoulder, against rear of hole in which bearing is to be installed. Index mark on shoulder of replacer must point down (toward crankshaft side) to properly position the bearing.*

6. Insert shaft with indexing collar, thrust washer, and nut through the remover, pilot and replacer adapters. Index lug on collar with ventilation hole in front of block.

7. Slip the key J-6173-5 into notches in shaft behind replacer adapter J-6173-3 and tighten nut to start bearing into hole. Continue to tighten nut until bearing has been pulled completely into its hole. When properly positioned, it will be approximately flush with both sides of the transverse member. The rear bearing should be pulled in until front edge is flush with the block. This will leave shoulder at end of counter bore for camshaft rear plug visible behind bearing.

8. Remove the remover and replacer set J-6173.

9. Visually observe that holes in bearing line up with drillings in block.

10. Carefully remove all metal particles from block surfaces and oil drillings.

11. Install new camshaft, with lobes and journals coated with heavy (SAE 50-60) oil, into the engine, being careful not to damage cam bearing.

NOTE: *Most specialty cams come with a special break-in lubricant for the lobes and journals; if such lubricant is available, use it instead of heavy oil.*

12. Install camshaft thrust plate and tighten bolts to 20 ft.lb.

13. Align timing marks, then install the sprocket and timing chain. Torque the sprocket bolt to 40 ft.lb.

14. Install the fuel pump eccentric and bushing.

15. Install the timing cover and gasket. Torque the bolts to 30 ft.lb.

16. Install the harmonic balancer, fuel pump, and four oil pan to timing cover bolts. Torque the bolts to 12 ft.lb.

17. Install the pushrods and lifters (keep them in proper order).

18. Position the rocker arms and torque the nuts at described earlier in this section.

19. Install the valley cover.
20. Install the distributor.
21. Install the intake manifold.
   NOTE: *On air-conditioned models, install the alternator and bracket.*
22. Install the rocker covers.
23. Install the hood latch brace.
24. Connect accelerator linkage, temperature gauge wire, and fuel lines.
25. Connect all water hoses, vacuum lines and spark plug wires.
26. Install the radiator.
27. Fill cooling system.
28. Install the air cleaner.

307, 350, and 403 OLDSMOBILE BUILT GASOLINE ENGINES

CAUTION: *All Oldsmobile V8s require discharging of the air conditioning system for camshaft removal. This requires discharging the refrigerant as described in Chapter 1. If you do not feel safe doing this work, have a mechanic discharge the system.*

Removal

1. Disconnect the battery.
2. Drain and remove the radiator as described above.
   CAUTION: *When draining the coolant, keep in mind that cats and dogs are attracted by the ethylene glycol antifreeze, and are quite likely to drink any that is left in an uncovered container or in puddles on the ground. This will prove fatal in sufficient quantity. Always drain the coolant into a sealable container. Coolant should be reused unless it is contaminated or several years old.*
3. Disconnect the fuel line at the fuel pump. Remove the pump on 1978 and later models.
4. Disconnect the throttle cable and the air cleaner.
5. Remove the alternator belt, loosen the alternator bolts, and move the alternator to one side. On 1986-87 models with the 307 V8, remove the generator bracket too.
6. Remove the power steering pump from its brackets and move it out of the way.
7. Remove the air conditioning compressor from its brackets and move it out of the way without disconnecting the lines.
8. Disconnect the hoses from the water pump. On 1986-87 models with the 307 V8, remove the bypass hose.
9. Disconnect the electrical and vacuum connections.
10. Mark the distributor as to location in the block. Remove the distributor.
   On 1977 and later models: Remove the

crankshaft pulley and the hub attaching bolt. Remove the crankshaft hub with a puller. Then, to continue, skip to step 19.
   On all other models, proceed with the next step:
11. Raise the car and drain the oil pan.
12. Remove the exhaust crossover pipe and starter motor.
13. Disconnect the exhaust pipe at the manifold.
14. Remove the harmonic balancer and pulley.
15. Support the engine and remove the front motor mounts.
16. Remove the flywheel inspection cover.
17. Remove the engine oil pan.
18. Support the engine by placing wooden blocks between the exhaust manifolds and the front crossmember.
19. Remove the engine front cover.
20. Remove the valve covers.
21. Remove the intake manifold, oil filler pipe, and temperature sending switch.
22. Mark the lifters, pushrods, and rocker arms as to location so that they may be installed in the same position. Remove these parts.
23. If the car is equipped with air conditioning, discharge the A/C system and remove the condenser. See CAUTION above.
24. Remove the fuel pump eccentric, camshaft gear, oil slinger, and timing chain.
25. Carefully remove the camshaft from the engine.
   NOTE: *The camshaft bearings must be replaced in complete sets. All bearings must be removed before any can be installed. No. 1 bearing must be removed first, then No. 2, then 3, 4, and 5. When installing the bearings, No. 5 must be installed first, then 4, 3, 2 and 1. Note also that the Camshaft Bearing Remover and Installer Set BT-6409 is an available tool. This set can be used to remove cam bearings with the engine either in or out of the car. To replace bearings with the engine in the car, proceed as follows:*
26. Install No. 1 Cam Bearing Remover and Installer BT-6409-1 on Handle J-8092 and drive out front cam bearing.
27. Place Pilot BT-6409-6 on Driver BT-6409-7 and install No. 2 Cam Bearing BT-6409-2 on driver and drive out No. 2 bearing.
28. Remove No. 3 and 4 bearings in the same manner, using BT-6409-3 and BT-6409-4 removers.
   NOTE: *Each cam bearing is a different diameter and the correct sequence must be used for both removal and installation.*
29. To remove No. 5 bearing with engine in chassis, use puller BT-6409-8.

Installation

NOTE: *To aid in aligning bearings with oil passages, place each bearing in the front bore with the tapered edge toward the block and align the oil hole in the bearing with the center of the oil slot in the bore. Mark top of bearing. When installing the bearings the mark will act as a guide.*

1. Place new No. 5 bearing on BT-6409-5 and drive bearing in until the last white line on the driver is flush with the front face of the pilot.

2. Use BT-6409-9 to check oil hole opening.

3. Remove BT-6409-5 Installer and install BT-6409-4. Place No. 4 bearing on installer and drive in until the next to the last white line on driver is flush with pilot.

4. Follow the same procedure to install No. 3 and No. 2.

5. Install Tool BT-6409-1 on Handle J-8092 and place No. 1 bearing on installer. Drive bearing until white line on Installer BT-6409 is flush with the front face of block.

6. Use BT-6409-9 to check all oil hole openings. Wire must enter hole or the bearing will not receive sufficient lubrication.

7. Inspect the shaft for signs of excessive wear or damage.

8. Liberally coat camshaft and bearings with engine assembly lubricant and insert the cam into the engine.

9. Align the timing marks on the camshaft and crankshaft gears. See timing Chain Replacement and Valve Timing for details.

10. Install the distributor using the locating marks made during removal. If any problems are encountered, see Distributor Installation.

11. To complete the installation, reverse the removal procedure but pay attention to the following points:

a. Install the timing indicator before installing the power steering pump bracket.

b. Install the flywheel inspection cover after installing the starter.

c. Replace the engine oil, radiator coolant, and transmission fluid. Charge the air conditioning system as described in Chapter 1 or have it charged by a mechanic.

263 AND 350 OLDSMOBILE BUILT DIESEL ENGINES

Removal of the camshaft requires removal of the injection pump drive and driven gears, removal of the intake manifold, disassembly of the valve lifters, and re-timing of the injection pump.

NOTE: *The air conditioning system, if the car is so-equipped, must be discharged according to the procedure in Chapter 1 or by a* professional technician and the condenser removed.

1. Disconnect the negative battery cables. Drain the coolant. Remove the radiator.

CAUTION: *When draining the coolant, keep in mind that cats and dogs are attracted by the ethylene glycol antifreeze, and are quite likely to drink any that is left in an uncovered container or in puddles on the ground. This will prove fatal in sufficient quantity. Always drain the coolant into a sealable container. Coolant should be reused unless it is contaminated or several years old.*

2. Remove the intake manifold and gasket and the front and rear intake manifold seals. Refer to the intake manifold removal and installation procedure. Remove the oil pump drive assembly on the V6.

3. Remove the balancer pulley and the balancer. See Caution under V8 diesel engine front cover removal and installation, above, for V8 engine. Remove the engine front cover using the appropriate procedure. Rotate the engine so that the timing marks align on V6s.

4. Remove the valve covers. Remove the rocker arms, pushrods and valve lifters; see the procedure earlier in this section. Be sure to keep the parts in order so that they may be returned to their original positions.

5. On V8s, if equipped with air conditioning, the condenser must be discharged and removed from the car. See the note above.

WARNING: *Compressed refrigerant expands (boils) into the atmosphere at a temperature of –21°F or less. It will freeze any surface it contacts, including your skin or eyes.*

6. Remove the camshaft sprocket retaining bolt, and remove the timing chain and sprockets, using the procedure outlined earlier.

7. On V6s, remove the front camshaft bearing retainer bolt and the retainer, then remove the camshaft sprocket key and the injection pump drive gear.

8. Position the camshaft dowel pin at the 3 o'clock position on the V8.

9. On V8s, push the camshaft rearward and hold it there, being careful not to dislodge the oil gallery plug at the rear of the engine. Remove the fuel injection pump drive gear by sliding it from the camshaft while rocking the pump driven gear.

10. To remove the fuel injection pump driven gear, remove the injection pump intermediate pump adapter (V6s only) and the pump adapter (either type of engine), remove the snap ring, and remove the selective washer. Remove the driven gear and spring.

11. Remove the camshaft by sliding it out the front of the engine. Be extremely careful not to

allow the cam lobes to contact any of the bearings, or the journals to dislodge the bearings during camshaft removal. Do not force the camshaft, or bearing damage will result.

Camshaft Bearing Removal and Installation

263 V6 DIESEL

The front camshaft bearing may be replaced separately but numbers 2, 3 and 4 must be replaced as a complete set. This is because it is necessary to remove the forward bearings to gain access to the rearward bearings.

Camshaft Bearing Remover and Installer Set BT-6409 and camshaft pilot spacer BT-7817 are available tools. This set or its equivalent can be used to remove cam bearings with the engine either in or out of the car. To replace bearings with the engine in the car, proceed as follows:

1. To remove the front (No. 1) camshaft bearing, support the retainer in a vise and drive the bearing out using BT-6409-2 with driver BT-6409-7.

2. To install the bearing use the same tools but make certain that the oil hole in the bearing is in alignment with the oil hole in the retainer.

3. Install tool BT-6409-2 on handle BT-6409-7 and drive out No.2 cam bearing.

4. Remove the No. 3 bearing in the same manner using BT-6409-3 on handle BT-6409-7.

5. Remove the No. 4 bearing using puller BT-6408-8.

NOTE: *To aid in aligning the bearings with the oil passages, place each bearing in the front of the bore with tapered edge toward the block and align the oil hole in the bearing with the center of the oil slot in the bore. Mark bottom of bearing. When installing the bearings, the mark will act as a guide.*

Using pilot BT-6409-1 will aid in installing the No. 4 and 3 bearings by preventing cocking of the bearings.

6. Install No. 4 bearing using tool BT-6409-4.

NOTE: *Drive the bearing in carefully, stopping to make certain that the oil holes are in alignment. Otherwise, it is possible to drive the bearing in beyond the oil passage opening. Use a piece of $3/32''$ brass rod with a 90° bend at the end to check the oil hole opening.*

7. Install the No. 3 bearing using tool BT-6409-3 carefully until the holes are in alignment.

8. Install the No. 2 bearing using tool BT-6409-2 carefully until the holes are in alignment.

9. Use a piece of $3/32''$ brass rod with a 90° bend at the end to check all oil hole openings. The wire must enter the hole or the bearing will not receive sufficient lubrication.

350 DIESEL ENGINE

CAUTION: *The camshaft bearings must be replaced in complete sets. All bearings must be removed before any can be installed. Each cam bearing has a different diameter and the correct sequence must be used both for removal and installation. No. 1 bearing must be removed first, then No. 2, then 3, 4, and 5. When installing the bearings, No. 5 must be installed first, then 4, 3, 2 and 1. Camshaft Bearing Remover and Installer Set J-25262 is an available tool. This set or an equivalent can be used to remove cam bearings with the engine either in or out of the car. To replace bearings with the engine in the car, proceed as follows:*

1. Remove the camshaft and oil pan.

2. Install No. 1 Cam Bearing remover and Installer J-25262-1 on handle J-25262-7 and drive out front cam bearing.

3. Place pilot J-25262-6 on driver J-25262-7 and install No. 2 Cam Bearing Tool J-25262-2 on driver and drive out No. 2 bearing.

4. Remove No. 3 and 4 bearings in the same manner, using J-25262-3 and J-25262-4 removers.

5. To remove No. 5 bearing with the engine in the car, use puller 25262-8.

6. To remove the injection pump driven gear bushings, drive both bushings at the same time from the rear to the front of the block using tool J-28439-2 and driver handle J-25262-7.

NOTE: *To aid in aligning the bearings with the oil passages, place each bearing in the front bore with the tapered edge toward block and align the oil hole in the bearing with the center of the oil slot in the bore. Mark the bottom of the bearing. When installing the bearings, the mark will act as a guide. Failure to align the oil hole could result in engine damage.*

7. Slide the bearing pilot spacer onto the bearing pilot J-25262-6. For bearings 5, 4, 3 and 2 put the driver J-25262-7 through the pilot J-25262-6, then screw the installer on the driver. Install the bearings as follows:

a. Place the new No. 5 bearing on J-25262-5 and drive the bearing in until the last white line on the driver is flush with the front face of the pilot.

b. Use a piece of $3/32''$ brass rod with a 90° bend at the end to check the oil hole opening.

c. Remove J-25262-5 Installer and install J-25262-4. Place No. 4 bearing on the installer and drive it in until the next to last white line on the driver is flush with the pilot.

8. Follow the same procedure to install No. 3 and No. 2.

9. Install Tool J-25262-1 on Handle J-25262-7 and place No. 1 bearing on installer. Drive the

bearing in until it is flush with the front face of block.

10. To install the injection pump bushings, align the holes in the bushings with the holes in the block. Install both bushings from the front, driving the rear bushing first, using the long end of tool J-28439-1 and driver handle J-8092. Drive the front bushing with the short end of J-28439-1.

11. Use a piece of $\frac{3}{32}''$ brass rod with a 90° bend at the end to check all oil hole openings. Wire must enter hole or the bearing will not receive sufficient lubrication.

Camshaft Installation

1. If either the injection pump drive or driven gears are to be replaced, replace both gears. Make certain the marks (○) are in alignment on both gears before inserting the cam gear key on the V6.

2. Coat the camshaft and the cam bearings with GM lubricant #1052365 or the equivalent--a heavy lubricant designed to protect new parts during engine start-up and break in.

3. Carefully slide the camshaft into position in the engine.

4. Fit the crankshaft and camshaft sprockets, aligning the timing marks as shown in the timing chain removal and installation procedure, above. Remove the sprockets without disturbing the timing.

5. Install the injection pump driven gear, spring, shim, and snap ring. Check the gear end play. If the end play is not within 0.002-0.006″ on V8s through 1979 and V6s, and 0.002-0.015″ on 1980 and later V8s, replace the shim to obtain the specified clearance. Shims are available in 0.003″ increments, from 0.080-0.115″.

6. On V8s position the camshaft dowel pin at the 3 o'clock position. Align the zero marks on the pump drive gear and pump driven gear. Hold the camshaft in the rearward position and slide the pump drive gear onto the camshaft. On the V6, align the zero marks on the injection pump drive and driven gears, then install the camshaft sprocket key. Install the camshaft bearing retainer.

7. Install the timing chain and sprockets, making sure the timing marks are aligned.

8. Install the lifters, pushrods and rocker arms. See Rocker Arm Replacement, Diesel Engine for lifter bleed down procedures. Failure to bleed down the lifters could bend valves when the engine is turned over.

9. Install the injection pump adapter and injection pump. See the appropriate sections under Fuel System in Chapter 5 for procedures.

10. Install the remaining components in the reverse order of removal.

Pistons And Connecting Rods
REMOVAL AND INSTALLATION
All Engines

Before removing the pistons, the top of the cylinder bore must be examined for a ridge. A ridge at the top of the bore is the result of normal cylinder wear, caused by the fact that the piston rings are mounted below the top of the piston and so only travel part way up the bore in the course of the piston stroke. The ridge can be felt by hand; it must be removed before the pistons are removed or the surfaces of the parts will be damaged in the process of disassembly.

A ridge reamer is necessary for this operation. Place the piston at the botttom of its stroke, and cover it with a rag. Cut the ridge away with the ridge reamer, using extreme care to avoid cutting too deeply. Remove the rag, and remove the cuttings that remain on the piston with a magnet and a rag soaked in clean oil. Make sure the piston top and cylinder bore are absolutely clean before moving the piston to avoid damage to the parts during the removal process.

1. Remove intake manifold and cylinder head or heads.

2. Remove oil pan.

3. Remove oil pump assembly, if it is located under or near the crankshaft so that it would interfere with the removal of the connecting rod caps.

4. Matchmark the connecting rod cap to the connecting rod with a scribe; each cap must be reinstalled on its proper rod in the proper direction. Remove the connecting rod bearing cap and the rod bearing. Number the top of each piston with silver paint or a felt-tip pen for later assembly.

5. Cut lenghts of ⅜″ diameter hose to use as rod bolt guides. Install the hose over the threads of the rods, to prevent the bolt threads from damaging the crankshaft journals and cylinder walls when the piston is removed.

6. Squirt some clean engine oil onto the cylinder wall from above, until the wall is coated. Carefully push the piston and rod assembly up and out of the cylinder by tapping on the bottom of the connecting rod with a wooden hammer and handle.

7. Place the rod bearing and cap back on the connecting rod, and install the nuts temporarily. Using a number stamp or punch, stamp the cylinder number on the side of the connecting rod and cap; this will help keep the proper piston and rod assembly on the proper cylinder.

NOTE: *On V6 engines, starting at the front the cylinders are numbered 2-4-6 on the right bank and 1-3-5 on the left. On all V8s, starting at the front the right (passenger side)*

RIDGE CAUSED BY CYLINDER WEAR

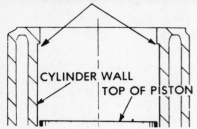

CYLINDER WALL

TOP OF PISTON

Cylinder bore ridge

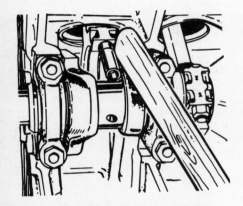

Push the piston out with a hammer handle

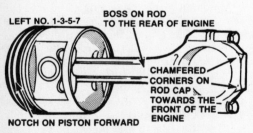

LEFT NO. 1-3-5-7

BOSS ON ROD TO THE REAR OF ENGINE

CHAMFERED CORNERS ON ROD CAP TOWARDS THE FRONT OF THE ENGINE

NOTCH ON PISTON FORWARD

Piston and connecting rod assembly—(left bank)—350 Buick built engine

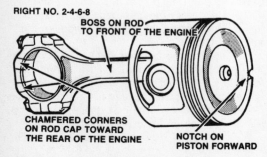

RIGHT NO. 2-4-6-8

BOSS ON ROD TO FRONT OF THE ENGINE

CHAMFERED CORNERS ON ROD CAP TOWARD THE REAR OF THE ENGINE

NOTCH ON PISTON FORWARD

Piston and connecting rod assembly—(right bank)—350 Buick built engine

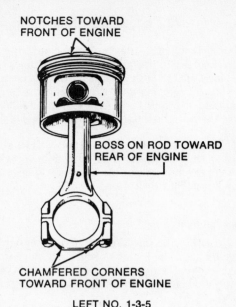

NOTCHES TOWARD FRONT OF ENGINE

BOSS ON ROD TOWARD REAR OF ENGINE

CHAMFERED CORNERS TOWARD FRONT OF ENGINE

LEFT NO. 1-3-5

Piston and connecting rod assembly—(left bank)—V6 Buick built engines

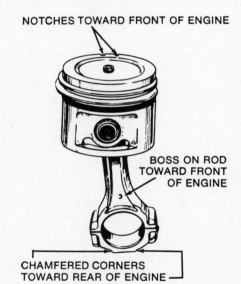

NOTCHES TOWARD FRONT OF ENGINE

BOSS ON ROD TOWARD FRONT OF ENGINE

CHAMFERED CORNERS TOWARD REAR OF ENGINE

RIGHT NO. 2-4-6

Piston and connecting rod assembly—(right bank)—V6 Buick built engines

bank cylinders are 2-4-6-8 and the left bank 1-3-5-7.

8. Remove the remaining pistons in a similar manner.

On all engines, the notch on the piston will face the front of the engine for assembly. The chamfered corners of the bearing caps should face toward the front of the left bank and toward the rear of the right bank. The boss on the

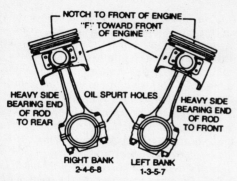

Piston and connecting rod assembly—V8 Chevrolet and Pontiac built engines

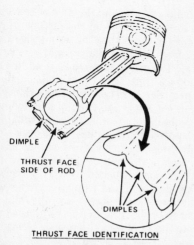

The dimples identify the connecting rod thrust faces on Pontiac built V8 engines

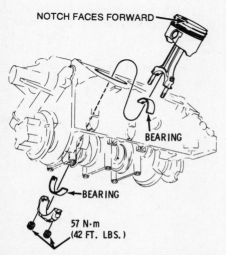

Piston and connecting rod assembly—Oldsmobile built engines

connecting rod should face toward the front of the engine for the right bank and to the rear of the engine on the left bank. On some Pontiac-built engines, the rods have three dimples on one side of the rod and a single dimple on the rod cap. The dimples must face to the rear on the right bank and forward on the left.

On various engines, the piston compression rings are marked with a dimple, a letter **T**, a letter **O**, **GM** or the word **TOP** to identify the side of the ring which must face toward the top of the piston. Whatever the mark, *it must face upward*.

CLEANING

Scrub both the bore of each cylinder and the pistons with soap and water to remove all gum and varnish. Dry the parts thoroughly and then rub in clean engine oil to preserve the metal surfaces from corrosion during inspection.

PISTON RING AND WRIST PIN REMOVAL

Some of the engines covered in this guide utilize pistons with pressed-in wrist pins; these must be removed by a special press designed for this purpose and a toolset J-240856 or equivalent. Other pistons have their wrist pins secured by snap rings, which are easily removed with a small, flat bladed screwdriver *and must then be discarded*. Separate the piston from the connecting rod.

A piston ring expander is necessary for removing piston rings without damaging them; any other method (screwdriver blades, pliers, etc.) usually results in the rings being bent, scratched or distorted, or the piston itself being damaged. When the rings are removed, clean the ring grooves using an appropriate ring groove cleaning tool, using care not to cut too deeply. Thoroughly clean all carbon and varnish from the piston with solvent.

CAUTION: *Do not use a wire brush or caustic solvent (acids, etc.) on pistons.*

Inspect the pistons for scuffing, scoring, cracks, pitting, or excessive ring groove wear. If these are evident, the piston must be replaced.

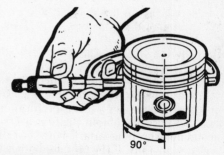

Measuring the piston

The piston should also be checked in relation to the cylinder diameter. Using a telescopic gauge and micrometer, or a dial gauge, measure the cylinder bore diameter perpendicular (90°) to the piston pin, 2½" below the cylinder block deck (the surface where the block mates with the heads). Then, with the micrometer, measure the piston perpendicular to its wrist pin on the skirt on engines built in years through 1984; on 1985 and later engines, measure the piston ¾" below the centerline of the wristpin hole. The difference between the two measurements is the piston clearance.

On 1983-85 engines, check piston clearance by inverting the piston and fitting it into the cylinder bore with its arrow pointing toward the front of the block (the way it would normally be oriented in terms of rotation). Insert a feeler gauge 0.015" thick into the clearance between piston and cylinder bore 90° from the piston pin axis and attach a spring scale to the top of the gauge material (you can loop the material around the gauge to do this). Pull the gauge out slowly, noting the reading on the spring scale. The tension required to pull the gauge must be 6-12 lbs. Of course, if the tension is too great, the piston fits too tight and more honing is required. If the tension is less than 6 lbs., you will need to find a slightly larger piston.

On earlier models, determine piston-to-bore clearance by first inverting the piston/rod assembly and inserting it into a clean, dry cylinder bore. The piston/rod assembly must drop into the cylinder when it is released with the bottom of the piston skirt is ½-1" from the block deck.

CAUTION: *When performing this procedure, be carefully to prevent damage to the piston, rod, or deck by somehow stopping the assembly before it falls too far!*

After determining, as in the paragraph above, that the piston is not too tight, make sure it is not too loose by repeating the last step with a 0.0025" strip of feeler gauge, not over ½" wide, inserted between the piston and the cylinder bore at a position 90° from the pin. If the piston can be released without falling with this gauge in position, it is snug enough; if it falls when released, then it is too small. Repeat the process until the piston passes both of these tests.

If the piston is within specifications or slightly below (after the cylinders have been bored or honed), finish honing is all that is necessary. If the clearance is excessive, try to obtain a larger piston to bring clearance within specifications. If this is not possible, obtain the first oversize piston and hone or, if necessary, bore the cylinder to size. Generally, if the cylinder bore is tapered to 0.005" or more, or cut out of round

0.003" or more, it is advisable to rebore for the smallest possible oversize piston and ring.

After measuring, mark the pistons with a felt tip pen for reference and assembly.

NOTE: *Cylinder honing and/or boring should be performed by a reputable, professional mechanic with proper equipment. In some cases, clean-up honing can be done with the cylinder block in the car but most substantial honing and all cylinder boring must be done with the block removed from the car. All main bearing caps must be in place when boring/honing are done so that the block will be under normal tension; otherwise, the bores will end up being distorted.*

PISTON RING END GAP

Piston ring end gap should be checked while the rings are removed from the pistons. Incorrect end gaps indicate that the wrong size rings are being used; ring breakage could occur.

Compress the piston rings to be used in a cylinder, one at a time, into the cylinder, using a ring compressor. Squirt clean oil into the cylinder, so that the rings and the top 2" of cylinder wall are coated. Using an inverted piston, press the rings approximately 1" below the deck of the block (on diesels, measure ring gap clearance with the ring positioned at the bottom of ring travel in the bore). Measure the ring end gap with a feeler gauge, and compare to the Ring Gap chart in this chapter. Carefully pull the ring out of the cylinder and file the ends square with a fine file to obtain the proper clearance.

PISTON PIN REPLACEMENT

NOTE: *To perform this operation on engines with press-fitted piston pins, you will need a large, powerful press and tool set J-240856 or equivalent, or you will have to take the piston/rod assemblies to a well equipped machine shop. If the engine has circlips to retain free-floating pins and is a diesel, you will need a BT-8346-1 or J-34594-1 or equivalent installer and a J-34594-2 or equivalent pilot.*

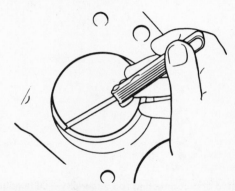

Checking the piston ring end gap

Free floating piston pins are used in some engines (V6 and V8 diesels and the 307 gasoline engines, for example) and utilize circlips to retain the pin. To check the fit of the pin, first clean the parts thoroughly of not only varnish and carbon but of oil. The correct fit in the piston is 0.0003-0.0005"; the correct fit in the rod is 0.0003-0.0013", which is a loose fit. High limits are 0.0005" in the piston and 0.0013" in the rod. At the high limit, the pin can be inserted into the piston easily and will fall through the piston if it is positioned with the pin in a perfectly vertical position. At the minimum clearance, the pin will be supported by friction if the piston is positioned with the pin in a perfectly vertical position. Always use new circlips, and install them with appropriate tools where required, so as to avoid distortion.

If you're rebuilding a diesel, you'll need a special installer and pilot. The GM tool numbers are BT-8346-1 or J-34594-1 for the installer and J-34594-2 for the pilot--you may be able to purchase these tools from other sources, using these numbers to find the appropriate number through cross reference.

Remove the retainers as follows:

1. Locate the installer into the inside diameter of the piston pin and hold it in a secure position there.

WARNING: *Place a heavy rag or towel over the installer for your protection. If the retainer should fly out of the piston, this, along with holding the installer securely in position, will protect you.*

2. Locate the blade of a regular, thin-bladed screwdriver into the notch and *slowly and carefully* pry the retainer out of the piston.

3. Repeat the procedure on the other side.

To install the retainers:

1. Insert one end of a new retainer into the piston pin retainer bore, orienting the retainer so that its gap is downward (toward the rod).

2. Position the installer into the end of the pin; then, rotate the installer so its pin rides around the retainer and works it into the groove in the outside of the piston. Remove the installer.

3. Inspect the retainer to determine whether or not is seated all the way around the groove and to make sure the gap is facing downward.

4. Turn the retainer as necessary. If the retainer is not fully seated in the groove, install the pilot into the end of the piston pin and push downward (inward) until it has seated fully.

5. Repeat these steps to install the retainer on the other side.

To install the piston pin on those assemblies using a press fit:

1. Assemble the piston and rod according to the markings and then orient the assembly so

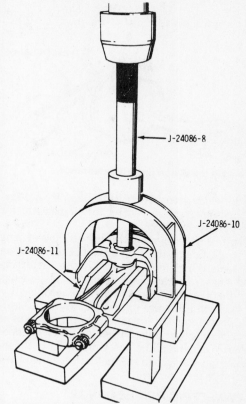

Jig, frame, and pintle set used to press piston pins to the proper position in the pistons of some engines

one pin hole is upward, locating it on the J-24086-11 jig. Install the J-24086-10 frame, which limits the travel of the press to center the pin in the piston.

2. Install the J-24086-8 pintle through the hole in the frame and underneath the piston of the press. Press the pin into the piston until the collar on the pintle rests against the frame and then release press pressure.

PISTON RING SIDE CLEARANCE CHECK AND INSTALLATION

Check the pistons to see that the ring grooves and oil return holes have been properly cleaned. Slide a piston ring into its groove, and check the side clearance with a feeler gauge. On gasoline engines, make sure you insert the gauge between the ring and its lower land (lower edge of the groove), because any wear that occurs forms a step at the inner portion of the lower land. On diesels, insert the gauge between the ring and the upper land. If the piston grooves have worn to the extent that relatively high steps exist on the lower land, the piston should be replaced, because these will interfere with the operation of the new rings and ring clear-

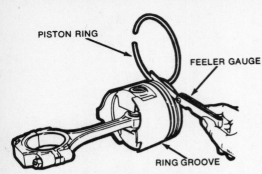

PISTON RING

FEELER GAUGE

RING GROOVE

Checking the piston ring side clearance

ances will be excessive. Piston rings are not furnished in oversize widths to compensate for ring groove wear.

Install the rings on the piston, lowest ring first, using a piston ring expander. There is an extremely high risk of breaking or distorting the rings, or scratching the piston, if the rings are installed by hand or other means.

Position the rings on the piston as illustrated; spacing of the various piston ring gaps is crucial to proper oil retention and even cylinder wear. When installing new rings, refer to the installation diagram in the instructions furnished with the new parts.

CONNECTING ROD BEARINGS

Connecting rod bearings for the engines covered in this guide consist of two halves or shells which are interchangeable in the rod and cap. When the shells are placed in position, the end extends slightly beyond the rod and cap surfaces so that when the rod bolts are torqued the shells will be clamped tightly in place to insure positive seating and to prevent turning. A tang holds the shells in place.

NOTE: *Under no circumstances should the rod end or cap be filed to adjust the bearing clearance, nor should shims of any kind be used. The ends of the bearing shells must never be filed flush with the mating surface of the rod and cap.*

If a rod bearing becomes noisy or or is worn so that its clearance on the crank journal is sloppy, a new bearing of the correct undersize must be selected and installed, since there is no provision for adjustment.

Inspect the rod bearings while the rod assemblies are out of the engine. If the shells are scored or show flaking, they should be replaced. If they are in good shape, check for proper clearance on the crank journal (see below). Any scoring or ridges on the crank journal mean the crankshaft must be replaced, or reground and fitted with undersized bearings.

NOTE: *If turbo V6 crank journals are scored or ridged the crankshaft must be replaced, as*

regrinding will reduce the durability of the crankshaft.

Checking Bearing Clearance and Replacing Bearings

Replacement bearings are available in standard size, and in undersizes for reground crankshafts. Connecting rod-to-crankshaft bearing clearance is checked using Plastigage® at either the top or bottom of each crank journal. The Plastigage® has a range of 0.001-0.003".

NOTE: *Make sure the connecting rods and their caps are kept together, and that the caps are installed in the proper (original) direction. On some engines like the Buick-built 350 V8, the caps can be only be installed one way.*

1. Remove the rod cap with the bearing shell. Completely clean the bearing shell and the crank journal, and blow any oil from the oil hole in the crankshaft. Note that Plastigage® is soluble in water; thus, the bearing surfaces must also be free of any water that may have been used in cleaning the surfaces.

2. Place a piece of Plastigage® lengthwise along the bottom/center of the lower bearing shell, then install the cap with shell and torque the bolts or nuts to specification. DO NOT turn the crankshaft with Plastigage® in the bearing.

3. Remove the bearing cap with the shell. The flattened Plastigage® will be found sticking to either the bearing shell or crank journal. Do not remove it yet.

4. Use the scale printed on the Plastigage® envelope to measure the flattened material at its widest point. The number within the scale which most closely corresponds to the width of the Plasitgage® indicates bearing clearance in thousandths of an inch.

5. Check the specifications chart in this chapter for the desired clearance. It is advisable to install a new bearing if clearance exceeds 0.003 in; however, if the bearing is in good condition and is not being checked because of bearing noise, bearing replacement is not necessary.

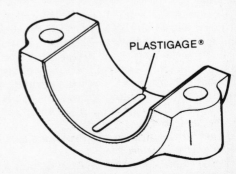

PLASTIGAGE®

Plastigage® installed on the lower bearing shell

6. If you are installing new bearings, try a standard size, then each undersize in order until one is found that is within the specified limits when checked for clearance with Plastigage®. Each undersize shell has its size stamped on it.

7. When the proper size shell is found, clean off the Plastigage®, oil the bearing thoroughly, reinstall the cap with its shell and torque the rod bolt nuts to specification.

NOTE: *With the proper bearing selected and the nuts torqued, it should be possible to move the connecting rod back and forth freely on the crank journal as allowed by the specified connecting rod end clearance. If the rod cannot be moved, either the rod bearing is too far undersize or the rod is misaligned.*

PISTON AND CONNECTING ROD ASSEMBLY AND INSTALLATION

Install the connecting rod to the piston, making sure piston installation notches and any marks on the rod are in proper relation to one another. Lubricate the wrist pin with clean engine oil, and install the pin into the rod and piston assembly, either by hand or by using a wrist pin press as required. Install snap rings if equipped, and rotate them in their grooves to make sure they are seated. To install the piston and connecting rod assembly:

1. Make sure connecting rod big-end bearings (including end cap) are of the correct size and properly installed.

2. Fit rubber hoses over the connecting rod bolts to protect the crankshaft journals, as in the Piston Removal procedure. Coat the rod bearings with clean oil.

3. Using the proper ring compressor, insert the piston assembly into the cylinder so that the notch in the top of the piston faces the front of the engine (this assumes that the dimple(s) or other markings on the connecting rods are in correct relation to the piston notch(es).

4. From beneath the engine, coat each crank journal with clean oil. Pull the connecting rod, with the bearing shell in place, into position again against the crank journal.

5. Remove the rubber hoses. Install the bearing cap nuts and torque to specification.

NOTE: *When more than one rod and piston assembly is being assembled, the connecting rod cap attaching nuts should only be tightened enough to keep each rod in position until*

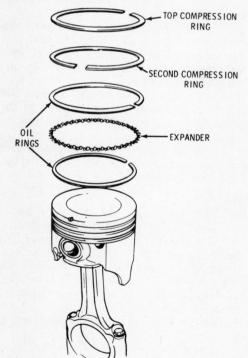

For detailed instructions and specifications for installation of the piston rings refer to the instructions furnished with the parts package

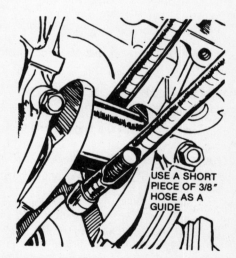

Use lengths of vacuum hose or rubber tubing to protect the crankshaft journals and cylinder walls during piston installation

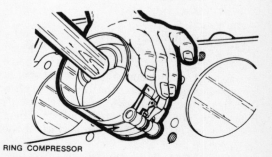

RING COMPRESSOR

Install the piston using a ring compressor

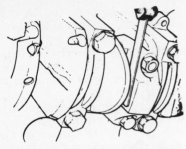

Check the connecting rod side clearance with a feeler gauge

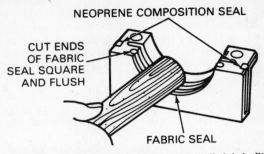

Installing rear bearing cap oil seals—Buick built engines

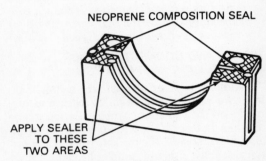

Apply a small amount of sealer to split line—Buick built engines

all have been installed. This will ease the installation of the remaining piston assemblies.

6. Check the clearance between the sides of the connecting rods and the crankshaft using a feeler gauge. Spread the rods slightly with a screwdriver to insert the gauge. If clearance is below the minimum tolerance, the rod may be machined to provide adequate clearance. If clearance is excessive, substitute an unworn rod, and recheck. If clearance is still outside specifications, the crankshaft must be welded and reground, or replaced.

7. Replace the oil pump if removed and the oil pan.

8. Install the cylinder head(s) and intake manifold.

Rear Main Seal

REMOVAL AND INSTALLATION

231, 252, and 350 Buick Built Engines and Olds 307

LOWER HALF

1. Remove the oil pan and rear main bearing cap.

2. Remove the oil seal from the bearing cap. Apply a sealer such as GM 1052621 sealer or Loctite® 414 or an equivalent to the seal groove. Work quickly, as less than one minute must elapse before you complete the next step; Roll a new seal into the groove with both ends projecting above the parting surface of the cap. You can use a wooden dowel or a special, semi-circular seal installer such as GM BT-23-18, J-28693 or equivalent.

3. Apply a thin film of chassis grease to the working surface of the rope seal. Force the seal into the groove by rubbing down with a hammer handle or other smooth tool or the special tool specified above. Force the seal inward until it projects above the groove not more than $1/16$". Rotate the tool back and forth slightly. Then, cut the ends off flush with the surface of the cap, using a razor blade.

4. On the 231, 252, and 350, soak new neoprene side seals in kerosene for five minutes;

then place the new seals in the grooves in the sides of the bearing cap.

NOTE: *The neoprene composition seals will swell up once exposed to the oil and heat. It is normal for the seals to leak for a short time, until they become properly seated. These seals must not be cut to fit.*

5. Apply a *thin* film of a sealer such as GM 1052756 or equivalent to the surface of the bearing cap that mates with the block, around the seal groove.

6. To install, reverse the above. The engine must be operated at low rpm when first started, after a new seal is installed.

UPPER HALF

NOTE: *Although the manufacturer recommends removing the crankshaft to replace the top half of the oil seal, the following procedure can be used without removing the crankshaft. The ideal method of seal replacement is to remove the crankshaft and replace the seal exactly as described above, in Steps 2 and 3.*

1. Remove the oil pan and rear main bearing cap.

2. Loosen the rest of the crankshaft main bearings and allow the crankshaft to drop about $1/16$".

3. Remove the old upper half of the seal.

4. Wrap some soft copper wire around the

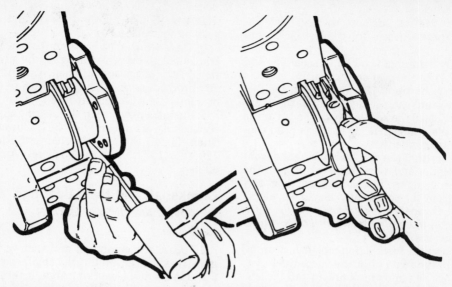

Removing the upper half of the oil seal—Chevrolet, Pontiac and Oldsmobile built engines

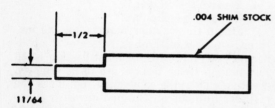

Fabricate an oil seal tool—Chevrolet, Pontiac and Oldsmobile built engines

end of the new seal and leave about 12″ on the end. Generously lubricate the new seal with oil on cars built in years up to 1984; on later years, cover the seal with a light coating of chassis grease.

5. Slip the free end of the copper wire into the oil seal groove and around the crankshaft. Pull the wire until the seal protrudes an equal amount on each side, rotating the crankshaft in synchronization with the seal as it is pulled into place.

6. Remove the wire. Push any excess seal that may be protruding back into the groove.

7. Before tightening the crankshaft bearing caps, visually check the bearings to make sure they are in place. Torque the bearing cap bolts to specifications in several stages. Make sure there is no oil on the mating surfaces.

8. Replace the oil pan. Run the engine slowly for the first few minutes of operation to break in the new seal.

305 and 350 Chevrolet Built Engines

The rear main bearing seal may be replaced without removing the crankshaft. Seals should only be replaced as a pair. The seal lips should face the front of the engine when properly installed.

1. Remove the oil pan, and pump as previously outlined, and remove the rear main bearing cap.

2. Pry the lower seal out of the bearing cap with a screwdriver, being careful not to gouge the cap surface.

3. Remove the upper seal by lightly tapping on one end with a brass pin punch until the other end can be grasped and pulled out with pliers.

4. Clean the bearing cap, cylinder block, and

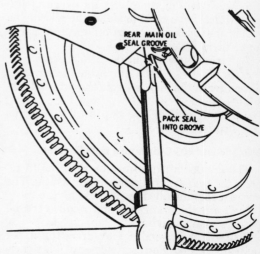

Pack the old seal into the groove—Chevrolet, Pontiac and Oldsmobile built engines

crankshaft mating surfaces with solvent. Inspect all these surfaces for gouges, nicks, and burrs.

5. Apply light engine oil on the seal lips and bead, but keep the seal ends clean.

6. Insert the tip of the installation tool between the crankshaft and the seal of the cylinder block. Place the seal between the tip of the tool and the crankshaft, so that the bead contacts the tip of the tool.

7. Be sure that the seal lip is facing the front of the engine, and work the seal around the crankshaft using the installation tool to protect the seal from the corner of the cylinder block.

NOTE: *Do not remove the tool until the opposite end of the seal is flush with the cylinder block surface.*

8. Remove the installation tool, being careful not to pull the seal out at the same time.

9. Using the same procedure, install the lower seal into the bearing cap. Use your finger and thumb to lever the seal into the cap.

10. Apply sealer to the cylinder block only where the cap mates to the surface. do not apply sealer to the seal ends.

11. Install the rear cap and torque the bolts to specifications. Install the oil pan and pump as previously described.

265 and 301 Pontiac Built Engines

1. Remove the oil pan and baffle.

2. Remove the rear main bearing cap.

3. Make a seal tool as illustrated.

4. Insert the tool against one end of the oil seal in the block and drive the seal gently into the groove until it bottoms. Repeat on the other end of the seal.

5. Form a new seal in the cap. Cut four 3/8" long pieces from this seal.

6. Work two of the pieces into each of the gaps which have been made at the end of the seal in the block. do not cut off any material to make them fit.

7. Form a new seal in the bearing cap.

8. Apply a 1/16" bead of silicone sealer from the center of the seal across to the external gasket groove.

9. Reassemble the cap and torque to specification.

263, 350 and 403 Oldsmobile Built Engines

The crankshaft need not be removed to replace the rear main bearing upper oil seal. The lower seal is installed in the bearing cap.

1. Drain the crankcase and remove the oil pan and rear main bearing cap.

2. Using a flat-ended tool, drive the upper seal into its groove on each side until it is tightly packed. This is usually 1/4-3/4".

3. Cut the pieces of the new seal 1/16" longer

than required to fill the grooves and install, packing into place.

4. Place shim stock between the seal and the crankshaft to prevent damaging the surface of the crankshaft journal. Then, carefully trim any protruding seal, being sure not to scratch or damage the bearing surface.

5. Install a new seal in the bearing cap as described above, under Olds 307, Lower Half. Then, install the cap, tightening the bolts to 120 ft.lb. (107 ft.lb. on the V6 diesel). Install the oil pan.

Crankshaft and Main Bearings
REMOVAL AND INSTALLATION
All Engines

1. Drain the engine oil and remove the engine from the car. Mount the engine on a work stand in a suitable working area. Invert the engine, so the oil pan is facing up.

2. Remove the engine front (timing) cover.

3. Remove the timing chain and gears.

4. Remove the oil pan.

5. Remove the oil pump.

6. Stamp the cylinder number on the machined surfaces of the bolt bosses of the connecting rods and caps for identification when reinstalling. If the pistons are to be removed eventually from the connecting rod, mark the cylinder number on the pistons with silver paint or felt-tip pen for proper cylinder identification and cap-to-rod location.

7. Remove the connecting rod caps. Install lengths of rubber hose to each of the connecting rod bolts, to protect the crank journals when the crank is removed.

8. Mark the main bearing caps with a number punch or center punch (using different numbers of dots) so that they can be reinstalled in their original positions.

9. Remove all main bearing caps.

10. Note the position of the keyway in the crankshaft so it can be installed in the same position.

11. Install rubber bands between a bolt on each connecting rod and an adjacent oil pan bolt that has been reinstalled in the block. This will keep the rods from banging on the block after the crank has been removed.

12. Carefully lift the crankshaft out of the block. The rods will pivot to the center of the engine when the crank is removed.

CLEANING AND INSPECTION

Like connecting rod big-end bearings, the crankshaft main bearings are shell-type inserts that do not utilize shims and cannot be adjusted. The bearings are available in various standard and undersizes; if main bearing clearance is found to be too sloppy, a new bearing (both upper and lower halves) is required.

NOTE: *Factory-undersize crankshafts are marked, sometimes with a **9** and/or a large spot of light green paint; the bearing caps also will have the paint on each side of the undersized journal.*

Generally, the lower half of the bearing shell (except No.1 bearing) shows greater wear and fatigue. If the lower half only shows the effect of normal wear (no heavy scoring or discoloration), it can usually be assumed that the upper half is also in good shape; conversely, if the lower half is heavily worn or damaged, both halves should be replaced. Never replace one bearing half without replacing the other.

CHECKING CLEARANCE

Main bearing clearance can be checked either with the crankshaft in the car or with the engine out of the car. If the engine block is still in the car, the crankshaft should be supported both front and rear (in front by the damper) to remove clearance from the upper bearing. If the engine is out of the car, the clearance should be checked with the engine upside down. The crank will then rest on the upper bearings. Total clearance can then be measured between the lower bearing and journal. Main bearing clearance is checked in the same manner as that of the connecting rod bearings, with Plastigage®.

NOTE: *Crankshaft bearing caps and bearing shells should NEVER be filed flush with the cap-to-block mating surface to adjust for wear in the old bearings. Always install new bearings. Also, do not touch the wear surfaces of the bearings with your fingers as the oils and acids in your skin will etch the surfaces and result in uneven wear.*

1. If the crankshaft has been removed, install it (block removed from the car). If the block is still in the car, remove the oil pan and oil pump. Also, if the block is in the car, loosen the accessory drive belts when checking the No.1 main bearing. Otherwise, the crankshaft will be very slightly bent and you will get a tapered reading. Starting with the rear bearing cap, remove the cap and wipe all oil from the crank journal and bearing cap.

2. Place a strip of Plastigage® the full width of the bearing, (parallel to the crankshaft), on the journal.

WARNING: *Do not rotate the crankshaft while the gauging material is between the bearing and journal.*

3. Install the bearing cap and evenly torque the cap bolts to specification.

4. Remove the bearing cap. The flattened Plastigage® will be sticking to either the bearing shell or the crank journal.

5. Use the graduated scale on the Plastigage® envelope to measure the material at its widest point.

NOTE: *If the flattened Plastigage® tapers towards the middle or ends, there is a difference in clearance indicating the bearing or journal has a taper, low spot or other irregularity. If this is indicated, measure the crank journal with a micrometer.*

6. If bearing clearance is within specifications, the bearing insert is in good shape. Replace the insert if the clearance is not within specifications. Always replace both upper and lower inserts as a unit.

7. Standard 0.001″ or 0.002″ undersize bearings should produce the proper clearance. If these sizes still produce too sloppy a fit, the crankshaft must be reground for use with the next undersize bearing. Always recheck all clearances after installing new bearings.

NOTE: *Any regrinding of crankshaft journals should be performed by a competent machine shop.*

8. Replace the rest of the bearings in the same manner. After all bearings have been checked, rotate the crankshaft to make sure it turns freely. If there is excessive drag, this indicates inadequate clearance of one or more bearings.

BEARING REPLACEMENT

Engine Out of Car

1. After the bearings have been properly fitted, as described above, coat the bearing surfaces of the new, correct size main bearings with clean engine oil and install them in the bearing saddles in the block and in the main bearing caps.

2. Install the crankshaft. See Crankshaft End Play and Installation below.

Engine in Car

NOTE: *See also Crankshaft End Play and Installation just below for thrust bearing service and other relevant information.*

1. With the oil pan, oil pump and spark plugs removed, remove the cap from the main bearing needing replacement and remove the bearing from the cap.

2. Make a bearing roll-out pin, using a bent cotter pin as shown in the illustration. Install the end of the pin in the oil hole in the crankshaft journal.

3. Rotate the crankshaft clockwise as viewed from the front of the engine. This will roll the upper bearing out of the block.

4. Lube the new upper bearing with clean engine oil and insert the plain (unnotched) end between the crankshaft and the indented or notched side of the block. Roll the bearings into

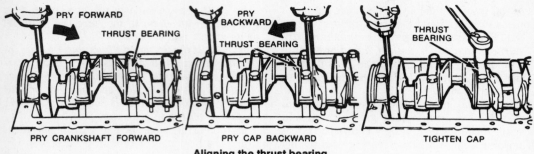

Aligning the thrust bearing

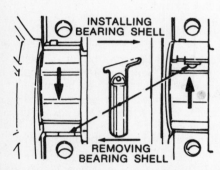

Remove or install the upper bearing insert using a roll-out pin

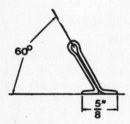

Home-made bearing roll-out pin

oil and torque all main bearing caps, excluding the thrust bearing cap, to specifications (see the Crankshaft and Connecting Rod chart in this chapter to determine which bearing is the thrust bearing). Tighten the thrust bearing bolts finger tight. To align the thrust bearing, pry the crankshaft the extent of its axial travel several times, holding the last movement toward the front of the engine. Add thrust washers if required for proper alignment. Torque the thrust bearing cap to specifications.

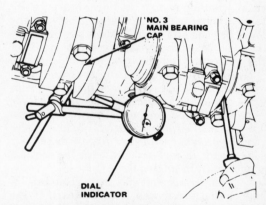

Check the crankshaft end-play with a dial indicator

place, making sure that the oil holes are aligned. Remove the roll pin from the oil hole.

5. Lube each new lower bearing and install the associated main bearing cap. Install the main bearing cap, making sure it is positioned in the proper direction with the matchmarks in alignment.

6. Torque the main bearing cap bolts to specification.

CRANKSHAFT END PLAY AND INSTALLATION

When main bearing clearance has been checked, bearings examined and/or replaced, the crankshaft can be installed. Thoroughly clean the upper and lower bearing surfaces, and lube them with clean engine oil. Install the crankshaft and main bearing caps.

Dip all main bearing cap bolts in clean engine

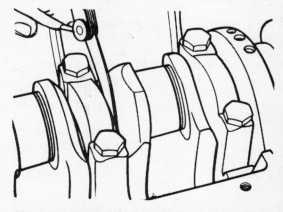

Checking the crankshaft end-play using a feeler gauge

To check crankshaft end-play, pry the crankshaft to the extreme rear of its axial travel, then to the extreme front of its travel. Using a feeler gauge, measure the end-play at the front of the rear main bearing. End play must also be measured at the thrust bearing. Install a new rear main bearing oil seal in the cylinder block and main bearing cap. Continue to reassemble the engine.

Flywheel and Ring Gear
REMOVAL AND INSTALLATION
Manual Transmission

1. Remove transmission and clutch assembly, being careful to mark clutch cover and flywheel so clutch may be reinstalled in original position. (See Chapter 7 for transmission removal.)

2. Remove flywheel. Flywheel is attached by unevenly spaced bolts.

3. If the ring gear is to be replaced, drill a hole between the two teeth and split the gear with a cold chisel.

4. Heat and shrink a new gear into place as follows:

   a. Polish several spots on ring with emery cloth.

   b. Use a hot plate or slowly moving torch to heat the ring until the polished spots turn blue - approximately 600°F (316°C) Heating the ring in excess of 800°F (427°C) will destroy the heat treatment.

   c. Quickly place the ring in position against the shoulder of the flywheel with the chamfered inner edge of the ring gear toward flywheel shoulder. Allow the ring to cool slowly until it contracts and is firmly held in place.

5. Make certain the flywheel and crankshaft flange are free from burrs that would cause run-out. Install flywheel.

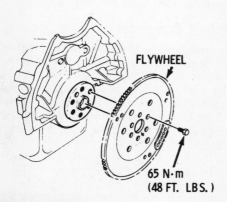

FLYWHEEL

65 N·m
(48 FT. LBS.)

Flywheel installation

Automatic Transmission

1. Remove the transmission (refer to Chapter 7).

2. Remove the six bolts attaching the flywheel to the crankshaft flange.

3. Inspect the flywheel; if it is cracked, badly worn or it has broken teeth, replace it.

4. Inspect the crankshaft flange and flywheel for burrs. Remove any burrs with a mill file.

5. Install the flywheel. The bolt holes are unevenly spaced so all the flywheel bolts can be installed with the flywheel in correct position. Install the bolts and torque to specifications.

6. Mount a dial indicator on the engine block and check flywheel run-out at three attaching bosses. Run-out should not exceed 0.015". The crankshaft end play must be held in one direction during this check.

7. If run-out exceeds 0.015", attempt to correct it by tapping the high side with a mallet. If this does not correct the problem, remove the flywheel and check for burrs between it and the crankshaft mounting flange.

EXHAUST SYSTEM

Safety Precautions

For a number of reasons, exhaust system work can be the most dangerous type of work you can do on your car. Always observe the following precautions:

- Support the car extra securely. Not only will you often be working directly under it, but you'll frequently be using a lot of force, say, heavy hammer blows, to dislodge rusted parts. This can cause a car that's improperly supported to shift and possibly fall.

- Wear goggles. Exhaust system parts are always rusty. Metal chips can be dislodged, even when you're only turning rusted bolts. Attempting to pry pipes apart with a chisel makes the chips fly even more frequently.

- If you're using a cutting torch, keep it a great distance from either the fuel tank or lines. Stop what you're doing and feel the temperature of the fuel bearing pipes on the tank frequently. Even slight heat can expand and/or vaporize fuel, resulting in accumulated vapor, or even a liquid leak, near your torch.

- Watch where your hammer blows fall and make sure you hit squarely. You could easily tap a brake or fuel line when you hit an exhaust system part with a glancing blow. Inspect all lines and hoses in the area where you've been working.

Special Tools

A number of special exhaust system tools can be rented from auto supply houses or local stores that rent special equipment. A common one is a tail pipe expander, designed to enable you to join pipes of identical diameter.

It may also be quite helpful to use solvents designed to loosen rusted bolts or flanges. Soaking rusted parts the night before you do the job can speed the work of freeing rusted parts considerably. Remember that these solvents are often flammable. Apply only to parts after they are cool!

Exhaust Manifold
REMOVAL AND INSTALLATION

Exhaust manifolds rarely rust, but they may crack due to road damage or thermal shock. The first step is to disconnect the exhaust pipe or crossover pipe by removing the nuts from the manifold studs. Then slide the collar or pull the flanged portion of the exhaust pipe or crossover away. In some cases, you may have to loosen the crossover pipe on the other side in order to gain clearance for easy manifold removal. Make sure you remove and replace seals. If the Early Fuel Evaporation valve is involved remove it and install it later with all new seals.

Remove parts that are in the way. These may include the hot air shroud, or various accessory brackets on the engine. You may have to disconnect the steering shaft on certain vehicles. Disconnect the oxygen sensor, if it's on the manifold.

You'll have to bend back locking tabs that ensure that mounting nuts remain tight. Then,

after the mounting nuts are soaked with solvent, loosen and remove them. Finally, remove the manifold and seal. Clean the surface of the block.

Install in reverse order, being careful to ensure that seals are installed facing in the proper direction so all exhaust ports are fully open and all bolt or stud holes or slots are in proper position. Install nuts loosely and then tighten in several stages, going around the manifold, until you reach the specified torque. Take your time here as even and proper torquing helps prevent leaks. If necessary, torque nuts further to align a flat with the locking tab. Then, make sure to bend all tabs over to prevent loosened nuts and leaks.

If the manifold has an oxygen sensor installed in it, you'll have to remove it and install it into the new manifold, using a high temperature sealer on the threads. Make sure you don't forget to reconnect the sensor when the manifold is in place.

Crossover Pipe Replacement

The crossover pipe (used on V-type engines only) is typically connected to the manifolds by flanged connections or collars. In some cases, bolts that are unthreaded for part of their length are used in conjunction with springs. Make sure you install the springs and that they are in good mechanical condition (no broken coils) when installing the new pipe. Replace ring type seals, also.

Headpipe Replacement

The headpipe is typically attached to the rear of one exhaust manifold with a flange or collar type connector and flagged to the front of the catalytic converter. Remove nuts and bolts and, if springs are used to maintain the seal, the springs. The pipe may then be separated from the rest of the system at both flanges.

Replace ring seals; inspect springs and replace them if any coils are broken.

Catalytic Converter

Remove bolts at the flange at the rear end. Then, loosen nuts and remove U-clamp to remove the catalyst. Slide the catalyst out of the outlet pipe. Replace all ring seals. In some cases, you'll have to disconnect an air line coming from the engine compartment before catalyst removal. In some cases, a hanger supports the converter via one of the flange bolts. Make sure the hanger gets properly reconnected. Also, be careful to retain all parts used to heat shield the converter and reinstall them.

Make sure the converter is replaced for proper direction of flow and air supply connections.

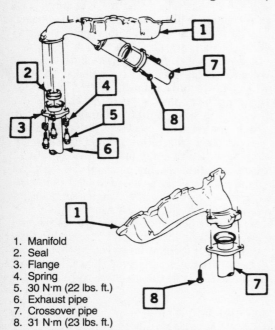

1. Manifold
2. Seal
3. Flange
4. Spring
5. 30 N·m (22 lbs. ft.)
6. Exhaust pipe
7. Crossover pipe
8. 31 N·m (23 lbs. ft.)

Disconnecting the crossover and exhaust pipes on the Olds 350 diesel

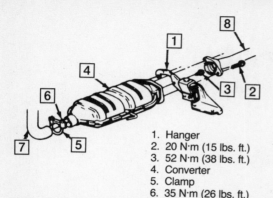

1. Hanger
2. 20 N·m (15 lbs. ft.)
3. 52 N·m (38 lbs. ft.)
4. Converter
5. Clamp
6. 35 N·m (26 lbs. ft.)
7. Outlet pipe
8. Intermediate pipe

Disconnecting the catalytic converter—1984 turbo V6 engine

Mufflers and Tailpipes

These units are typically connected by flanges at the rear of the converter and at either end of mufflers either by an original weld or by U-clamps working over a pipe connection in which one side of the connection is slightly larger than the other. You may have to cut the original connection and use the pipe expander to allow the original equipment exhaust pipe to be fitted over the new muffler. In this case, you'll have to purchase new U-clamps to fasten the joints. GM recommends that whenever you replace a muffler, all parts to the rear of the muffler in the exhaust system must be replaced. Also, all slip joints rearward of the converter should be coated with sealer before they are assembled.

Be careful to connect all U-clamps or other hanger arrangements so the exhaust system will not flex. Assemble all parts loosely and rotate parts inside one another or clamps on the pipes to ensure proper routing of all exhaust system parts to avoid excessive heating of the floorpan, fuel lines and tank, etc. Also, make sure there is clearance to prevent the system from rattling against spring shackles, the differential, etc. You may be able to bend long pipes slightly by hand to help get enough clearance, if necessary.

While disassembling the system, keep your eye open for any leaks or for excessively close clearance to any brake system parts. Inspect the brake system for any sort of heat damage and repair as necessary.

Emission Controls

GASOLINE ENGINE EMISSION CONTROLS

Positive Crankcase Ventilation System

OPERATION

All Centurys and Regals are equipped with a positive crankcase ventilation (PCV) system to control crankcase blow-by vapors. The system functions as follows:

When the engine is running, a small portion of the gases which are formed in the combustion chamber leak by the piston rings and enter the crankcase. Since these gases are under pressure, they tend to escape from the crankcase and enter the atmosphere. If these gases are allowed to remain in the crankcase for any period of time, they contaminate the engine oil and cause sludge to build up in the crankcase. If these gases are allowed to escape into the atmosphere, they pollute the air with hydrocarbons. The job of the crankcase emission control equipment is to recycle these gases back into the engine combustion chamber where they are reburned.

The crankcase (blow-by) gases are recycled in the following way: as the engine is running, clean, filtered air is drawn through the air filter and into the crankcase. As the air passes through the crankcase, it picks up the combustion gases and carries them out of the crankcase, through the oil separator, through the PCV valve, and into the induction system. As they enter the intake manifold, they are drawn into the combustion chamber where they are reburned.

The most critical component in the system is the PCV valve. This valve controls the amount of gases which are recycled into the combustion chamber. At low engine speeds and with the throttle partly closed, the valve is also partially closed, limiting the flow of the gases into the in-take manifold. As engine speed increases and the throttle approaches the wide open position, the valve opens to admit greater quantities of the gases into the intake manifold. If the valve should become blocked or plugged, the gases will be prevented from escaping from the crankcase by the normal route. Since these gases are under pressure, they will find their own way out of the crankcase. This alternate route is usually a weak oil seal or gasket in the engine. As the gas escapes by the gasket, it also creates an oil leak. Besides causing oil leaks, a clogged PCV valve allows these gases to remain in the crankcase for an extended period of time, promoting the formation of sludge in the engine. See the Maintenace Chart in Chapter 1 for PCV valve replacement intervals.

SERVICE

1. Remove the PCV valve system components, filler cap, PCV valve, hoses, fittings, etc. from the engine.

2. Clean all the hoses with solvent and a brush if necessary. Wash the breather cap in solvent, and shake it dry. Do not blow it dry with compressed air. Damage may result.

3. PCV valves cannot be cleaned. Install a new PCV valve, and reinstall all the hoses and fittings removed earlier.

Evaporative Emission Control System

OPERATION

This system reduces the amount of escaping gasoline vapors. Float bowl emissions are controlled by internal carburetor modifications. Redesigned bowl vents, reduced bowl capacity, heat shields, and improved intake manifold-to-carburetor insulation reduce vapor loss into the atmosphere. The venting of fuel tank vapors into the air has been stopped by means of the carbon canister storage method. This method transfers fuel vapors to an activated carbon storage device which absorbs and stores the vapor that is emitted from the engine's induction system while the engine is not running. When the engine is running, the stored vapor is purged from the carbon storage device by the intake air flow and then consumed in the normal combustion process. As the manifold vacuum reaches a certain point, it opens a purge control valve atop the charcoal storage canister. This allows air to be drawn into the canister, thus forcing the existing fuel vapors back into the engine to be burned normally.

Beginning in 1981, the purge function on the 231 V6 engine is electronically controlled by a purge solenoid in the line which is itself controlled by the Electronic Control Module (ECM). When the system is in the Open Loop mode, the solenoid valve is energized, blocking all vacuum to the purge valve. When the system is in the Closed Loop mode, the solenoid is de-energized, thus allowing existing vacuum to operate the purge valve. This releases the trapped fuel vapor and it is forced into the induction system.

Most carbon canisters used are of the Open design, meaning that air is drawn in through the bottom (filter) of the canister. Some (1981 and later 231 V6) canisters are of the Closed design which means that the incoming air is drawn directly from the air cleaner.

SERVICE

The only service required is the periodic replacement of the canister filter (if so equipped). If the fuel tank cap on your car ever requires re-placement, make sure that it is one of the same type as the original.

Thermostatic Air Cleaner (THERMAC)
OPERATION

All the carbureted engines covered in this guide utilize the THERMAC system (in 1975-1978 it was called TAC, but worked the same way). This system is designed to warm the air entering the carburetor as much as possible when underhood temperatures are low, and to stabilize the temperature of the air passing into the carburetor at all other times. By allowing only air preheated to a controlled temperature to enter the carburetor, the metering of fuel is practically unaffected by outside temperature. This permits a leaner calibration than with a system that takes in unheated air. Also, the amount of time the choke is on and engine warm-up time are reduced. These facts result in better fuel economy and lower emissions. Because of the way the system works, if the engine runs well in warm weather but poorly as it gets colder, and the engine's thermostat is working properly, suspect this system. It can also cause very poor running part way through the warmup process.

The Thermac system is composed of the air cleaner body, a filter, temperature sensor unit, vacuum diaphragm, damper door, and associated hoses and connections. Some of the air entering the carburetor is drawn through a heat stove which surrounds the exhaust manifold and is ducted to the air cleaner to supply heated

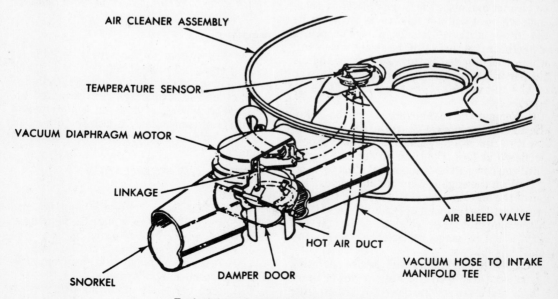

Typical thermostatic air cleaner assembly

air to the carburetor. A moveable door in the air cleaner case snorkel allows air to be drawn in from the heat stove (cold operation), from underhood air (hot engine, hot weather operation), or from both in an appropriate mixture (most driving conditions). The door position is controlled by the vacuum motor, which receives intake manifold vacuum as modulated by the temperature sensor and balances it against an internal spring.

SYSTEM CHECKS

1. Check the vacuum hoses for leaks, kinks, breaks, clogging, or improper connections and correct any defects.

2. With the engine off, check the position of the damper door within the snorkel. A mirror can be used to make this job easier. The damper door should be open to admit outside air. If not, there is a mechanical problem causing binding and the mechanism must either be freed-up or replaced.

3. Apply at least 7 in.Hg of vacuum to the damper diaphragm unit. The door should close. If it doesn't, check the diaphragm linkage for binding and correct hookup.

4. With vacuum still applied and the door closed, clamp the tube to trap the vacuum. If the door doesn't remain closed, there is a leak in the diaphragm assembly.

5. Once it is proven that the door operates properly, and that all hoses are intact, test the performance of the temperature sensor. Start with the engine overnight cold. Use a small thermometer such as the thin, metal duct thermometers used in air conditioning work (do not use a glass thermometer!). Take the top off the air cleaner and place the thermometer in a safe spot, where it will not tend to be drawn in by the intake airflow. Usually, it can be placed along the inside surface of the air filter element, where the rounded bottom surface of the air cleaner will keep it in position. Replace the top of the air cleaner, making sure it seals effectively.

6. Remove the cold air hose from the end of the air cleaner snorkel. Start the engine and allow it to run at a fast idle. The air door should be closed at first. Continue to run the engine until you can see the air door just start to open.

7. With the engine still running, remove the top of the air cleaner and quickly read the thermometer. The temperature should be 80-100°F. If the temperature at which the door starts to open is out of range, replace the temperature sensor as follows:

a. With the engine well below operating temperature, open the radiator lower drain cock and drain several quarts of coolant from the system.

b. Disconnect the vacuum hoses from the temperature sensor. Remove the unit from the manifold with a wrench.

c. Coat the threads of the new sensor with a light coating of a sealer designed to work with engine coolant and prevent corrosion. The sensor need not be very tight--just make it slightly snug, as the sealer will prevent leakage.

d. Reconnect vacuum lines.

Air Injection Reactor System (A.I.R.)
OPERATION

The AIR system, used on 1975-80 models, injects compressed air into the exhaust system, near enough to the exhaust valves to continue the burning of the normally unburned segment of the exhaust gases. To do this, it employs an air injection pump and a system of hoses, valves, tubes, etc. necessary to carry the compressed air from the pump to the exhaust manifolds. Carburetors and distributors for AIR engines have specific modifications to adapt them to the air injection system; those components should not be interchanged with those intended for use on engines that do not have the system.

A diverter valve is used to prevent backfiring. The valve senses sudden increases in manifold vacuum and stops the injection of air during fuel-rich periods to prevent backfire. During coasting, this valve diverts the entire airflow through the pump muffler and, during periods of high engine speed, expels it through a relief valve. Check valves in the system prevent exhaust gases from entering the pump.

NOTE: *The AIR system on the 231 V6 engine is slightly different, but its purpose remains the same.*

SERVICE

The AIR system's effectiveness depends on correct engine idle speed, ignition timing, and dwell. These settings should be strictly adhered to and checked frequently. All hoses and fittings should be inspected for condition and tightness of connections. Check the drive belt for wear and tension every 12 months or 12,000 miles.

REMOVAL AND INSTALLATION
Air Pump

WARNING: *Do not pry on the pump housing or clamp the pump in a vise: the housing is soft and may become distorted.*

1. Disconnect the air hoses at the pump.

2. Hold the pump pulley to keep it from turning and loosen the pulley bolts.

3. Loosen the pump mounting bolt and adjustment bracket bolt. Remove the drive belt.

4. Remove the mounting bolts, and then remove the pump.

5. Install the pump by reversing the removal procedure.

Diverter (Anti-afterburn) Valve

1. Detach the vacuum sensing line from the valve.

2. Remove the other hose(s) from the valve.

3. Unfasten the diverter valve from the elbow or the pump body.

4. Installation is performed in the reverse order of removal. Always use a new gasket. Tighten the valve securing bolts to 85 in.lb.

Air Management System - 1981 and Later

OPERATION

The Air Management System is used to provide additional oxygen to continue the combustion process after the exhaust gases leave the combustion chamber; it is very similar to the AIR system described just above. Air is injected into either the exhaust port(s), the exhaust manifold(s) or the catalytic converter by an engine driven air pump. The system is in operation at all times and will bypass air momentarily during deceleration and at high speeds. The bypass function is performed by the Air Management Valve, while the check valve protects the air pump by preventing any backflow of exhaust gases.

The AIR system helps to reduce HC and CO content in the exhaust gases by injecting air into the exhaust ports during cold engine operation. This air injection also helps the catalytic converter to reach the proper temperature more quickly during warm-up. When the engine is warm (closed loop), the Air system injects air into the beds of a three-way converter to lower the HC and CO content of the exhaust.

The Air Management System utilizes the following components:

- An engine-driven air pump
- Air management valves (Air Control and Air Switching).
- Air flow and control hoses.
- Check valves.
- A dual-bed, three-way catalytic converter.

The belt driven, vane-type air pump is located at the front of the engine and supplies clean air to the system for the purposes already stated. When the engine is cold, the Electronic Control Module (ECM) energizes an air control solenoid. This allows air to flow to the air switching valve. The air switching valve is then energized to direct air into the exhaust ports.

When the engine is warm, the ECM de-energizes the air switching valve, thus directing the air between the beds of the catalytic converter. This then provides additional oxygen for the oxidizing catalyst in the second bed to decrease HC and CO levels, while at the same time keeping oxygen levels low in the first bed, enabling the reducing catalyst to effectively decrease the levels of NOx.

If the air control valve detects a rapid increase in manifold vacuum (deceleration), certain operating modes (wide open throttle, etc.) or if the ECM self-diagnostic system detects any problems in the system, air is diverted to the air cleaner or directly into the atmosphere.

The primary purpose of the ECM's divert mode is to prevent backfiring. Throttle closure at the beginning of deceleration will temporarily create air/fuel mixtures in the exhaust manifold which are too rich to burn. These mixtures will become burnable when they reach the exhaust if they are combined with injection air. The next firing of the engine will ignite the mixture causing an exhaust backfire. Momentarily diverting the injection air from the exhaust prevents this.

The Air Management System check valves and hoses should be checked periodically for any leaks, cracks or deterioration.

REMOVAL AND INSTALLATION

Air Pump

1. Remove the valves and/or adapter at the air pump.

2. Loosen the air pump adjustment bolt and remove the drive belt.

3. Unscrew the three mounting bolts and then remove the pump pulley.

4. Unscrew the pump mounting bolts and then remove the pump.

5. Installation is in the reverse order of removal. Be sure to adjust the drive belt tension after installing it.

Check Valve

1. Release the clamp and disconnect the air hose from the valve.

2. Unscrew the check valve from the air injection pipe.

3. Installation is in the reverse order of removal.

Air Management Valve

1. Disconnect the negative battery cable.

2. Remove the air cleaner.

3. Tag and disconnect the vacuum hose from the valve.

4. Tag and disconnect the air outlet hoses from the valve.

5. Bend back the lock tabs and then remove the bolts holding the elbow to the valve.

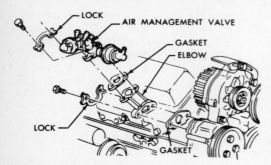

Typical Air Management Valve

6. Tag and disconnect any electrical connections at the valve and then remove the valve from the elbow.

7. Installation is in the reverse order of removal.

Early Fuel Evaporation System
OPERATION

1975 and later models are equipped with this system to reduce engine warm-up time, improve driveability, and reduce engine emissions. On start-up, a vacuum motor acts to close a heat valve in the exhaust manifold which causes exhaust gases to enter the intake manifold heat riser passages. This provides evaporation of incoming fuel during warm-up.

The system consists of a Thermal Vacuum Switch and an Exhaust Heat Valve and actuator. The Thermal Vacuum Switch is located on the coolant outlet housing on V8s, and on the block on in-line six cylinder engines. When the engine is cold, the TVS conducts manifold vacuum to the actuator to close the valve. When engine coolant or, on 6 cylinder engines, oil warms up, vacuum is interrupted and the actuator should open the valve.

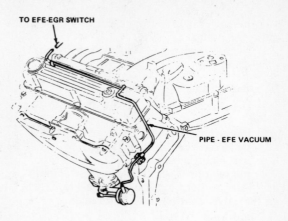

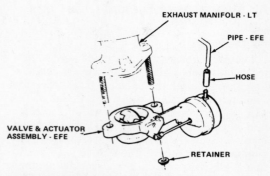

Typical EFE Valve—Buick built V8 engines

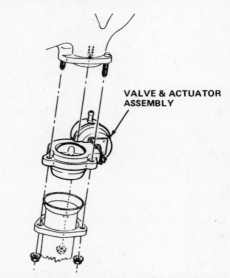

Typical EFE Valve—Pontiac built V8 engines

NOTE: *On 1981 and later models with the 231 V6 engine, the EFE system is controlled by the ECM.*

As of 1981, the 231 V6 Turbo utilizes a slightly different system. Although the function of this system remains the same--to reduce engine warm-up time, improve driveability and to reduce emissions--the operation is entirely differ-

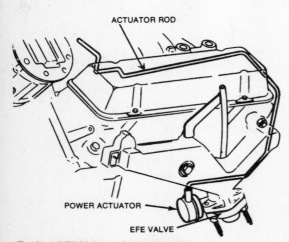

Typical EFE Valve—Buick built V6 engines

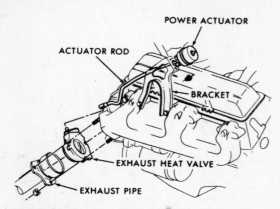

Typical EFE Valve—Chevrolet built V8 engines

ent. The new system is electric and uses a ceramic heater grid located underneath the primary bore of the carburetor insulator/gasket. When the engine coolant temperature is below the specific calibration value, electrical current is supplied to the heater through an ECM controlled relay.

CHECKING THE EFE SYSTEM

1. With the engine overnight cold, have someone start the engine while you observe the Exhaust Heat Valve. On some cars, the valve and arm are covered by a two-piece cover which must be removed for access. The valve should snap to the closed position.

2. Watch the valve as the engine warms up. By the time the coolant starts circulating through the radiator the valve should snap open.

3. If the valve does not close, immediately disconnect the hose at the actuator, and check for vacuum by placing your finger over the end of the hose, or use a vacuum gauge. If there is vacuum, replace the actuator. If there is no vacuum, immediately disconnect the hose leading to the TVS from the manifold at the TVS. If there is vacuum here, but not at the actuator, replace the TVS. If vacuum does not exist at the hose going to the TVS, check that the vacuum hose is free of cracks or breaks and tightly connected at the manifold, and that the manifold port is clear.

4. If the valve does not open when the engine coolant warms up, disconnect the hose at the actuator, and check for vacuum by placing your finger over the end of the hose or by using a vacuum gauge. If there is vacuum, replace the TVS. If there is no vacuum, the valve could also be seized; lubricate it with spray type manifold heat valve lube. If the valve does not close when vacuum is applied and when it is lubricated, replace the valve. replace the actuator.

TVS REMOVAL AND INSTALLATION

Drain coolant until the level is below the coolant outlet housing. Apply sealer to threads. Note that the valve must be installed until just snug (120 in.lb.) and then turned by hand just far enough to line up the fittings for hose connection.

EFE VALVE REMOVAL AND INSTALLATION

NOTE: *If the car is equipped with an oxygen sensor, it is located near the EFE valve. Use care when removing the EFE valve so as not to damage the oxygen sensor.*

1. Disconnect the vacuum hose at the EFE valve.

2. Remove the exhaust pipe-to-manifold nuts, and the washers and tension springs if used.

3. Lower the exhaust cross-over pipe. On some models, complete removal of the pipe is not necessary.

4. Remove the EFE valve.

5. To install, reverse the removal procedure. Always install new seals and gaskets.

EFE SOLENOID REMOVAL AND INSTALLATION

1. Disconnect the battery ground.

2. Remove the air cleaner assembly if necessary.

3. Disconnect and tag all electrical and vacuum hoses as required.

4. Remove the screw securing the solenoid to the valve cover bracket and remove the solenoid.

5. Installation is reverse of removal.

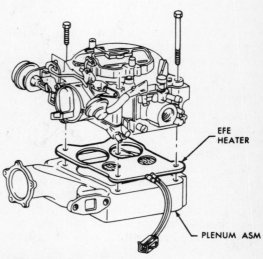

EFE heater on the 231 Turbo

HEATER GRID REMOVAL AND INSTALLA-TION (1981 AND LATER CARBURETED TURBO ONLY)

1. Remove the air cleaner.
2. Tag and disconnect all electrical, vacuum and fuel connections from the carburetor.
3. Disconnect the EFE heater electrical connection.
4. Remove the carburetor as detailed later in this chapter.
5. Lift off the EFE heater and insulator plate assembly.
6. Installation is performed in the reverse order of removal.
7. Start the engine and check for any leaks.

Exhaust Gas Recirculation (EGR)

All engines are equipped with exhaust gas recirculation (EGR). This system consists of a metering valve, a vacuum line to the carburetor, and cast-in exhaust gas passages in the intake manifold. The EGR valve is controlled by carburetor vacuum, and accordingly opens and closes to admit exhaust gases into the fuel/air mixture. It maintains the proportions of recirculated exhaust to fresh mixture under conditions of vacuum and exhaust pressure that vary widely. This is done because excessive exhaust recirculation causes misfire while too little will cause ping at part throttle, especially on late-model engines. The exhaust gases lower the combustion temperature, and reduce the amount of oxides and nitrogen (NOx) produced. The valve is closed at idle and at full throttle.

In most installations, vacuum to the EGR valve is controlled by a thermal vacuum switch (TVS); the switch, which is installed into the engine block, shuts off vacuum to the EGR valve until the engine is hot. This prevents the stalling and lumpy idle which result if EGR occurs when the engine is cold. At idle, the valve is closed because there is a lot of exhaust in the mixture under these conditions even without EGR. As the car accelerates, the carburetor throttle plate uncovers the vacuum port for the EGR valve and at 3-5 in.Hg, the EGR valve opens and then some of the exhaust gases are allowed to flow into the air/fuel mixture to lower the combustion temperature. At full throttle the valve closes again to provide the best possible full throttle performance.

Some California engines are equipped with a dual diaphragm EGR valve. This valve further limits the exhaust gas opening (compared to the single diaphragm EGR valve) during high intake manifold vacuum periods, such as a high speed cruising, and provides more exhaust gas recirculation during acceleration when manifold vacuum is low. In addition to the hose running to the thermal vacuum switch, a second hose is connected directly to the intake manifold.

For 1977 and later years, all California models and cars delivered in areas above 4,000 ft. are equipped with back pressure EGR valves. This type of valve is also used on 1986-87 5.0 liter V8s. The EGR valve receives exhaust back pressure through its hollow shaft. This exerts a force on the bottom of the control valve diaphragm, opposed by a light spring. Under low exhaust pressure (low engine load and partial throttle), the EGR signal is reduced by an air bleed. Under conditions of high exhaust pressure (high engine load and large throttle opening), the air bleed is closed and the EGR valve responds to an unmodified vacuum signal. At wide open throttle, the EGR flow is reduced in proportion to the amount of vacuum signal available.

1979 and later models have a ported signal vacuum EGR valve. The valve opening is controlled by the amount of vacuum obtained from a ported vacuum source on the carburetor.

If you still are not sure about the type of valve in use, you can check the part number stamped on the top side of the valve. Positive backpressure valves will show a **P**.

1986-87 cars with the 3.8L engine use a pulse width modulated signal from the Electronic Control Module to block or control vacuum to the EGR valve under operating conditions which require elimination of or less EGR than would normally be provided. At cold engine temperatures, at idle, and at wide-open throttle, the EGR solenoid is energized with a pulse width modulated signal, partially or completely blocking vacuum to the valve. These cars also use a diagnostic switch, which monitors the vacuum that is being fed to the EGR valve. If the vacuum circuit fails, the switch will trigger the Service Engine Soon light and set a Code 53.

On the 5.0L V8, the vacuum to the EGR valve passes through a normally-open solenoid valve which closes when the Electronic Control Module completes the solenoid's ground circuit. This permits the Electronic Control Module to eliminate EGR when the engine is cold and when other types of operating conditions require that EGR be cut off.

The 3.8L Turbo engine also uses pulse width modulation. An EVRV (Electronic Vacuum Regulator Valve) converts a pulse from the ECM to a vacuum signal. Two part of the EVRV accomplish this. The first is a normally closed, EGR Solenoid, which blocks vacuum to the EGR valve until it is energized. The second is a normally open EGR vacuum switch. When the ECM completes the ground circuit of the EGR

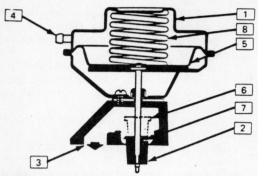

Cross section of a standard port type EGR valve. This one is used on 1986–87 3.8L V6 engines.

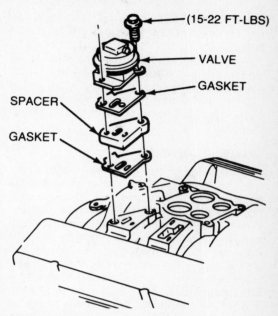

Typical EGR valve mounting location

Solenoid thousands of times a second, in a modulated pattern, it actuates the EGR valve through controlled vacuum. The longer the length of time the pulses last (the solenoid is energized), the greater the vacuum. The vacuum switch permits the ECM to monitor the amount of EGR. It also limits the vacuum going to the EGR valve. The switch includes an orifice which, once vacuum reaches a preset level, restricts the flow of vacuum to the EGR valve. The switch itself also incorporates the function which measures vacuum and actuates the switch when it reaches the preset level. You can tell if this switch has failed (is closed at idle or open under load) by the setting of a Code 32 to the ECM.

TESTING AND TROUBLESHOOTING

Too much EGR will cause poor combustion-- that is, surge at part throttle, or extremely rough running or stalling at idle. Stalling after a cold start may indicate that EGR is occurring when it shouldn't be on at all.

Too little EGR will create excessive combustion temperatures--ping at part throttle and, as a consequence, possible overheating of the engine.

Check out the system as follows:

1. Make sure that the ignition switch is off and that the ECM has not stored a code 53.

2. Inspect the EGR vacuum hose for kinks, cracks, restrictions, or brittle ends which do not seal properly and replace sections of hose that are worn or damaged.

3. Push the bottom of the EGR diaphragm upward and then release it. Watch it carefully to make sure the valve closes firmly. If the valve sticks, remove it for cleaning or replacement. Otherwise, proceed with the tests below.

4. Start the engine and allow it to idle. Disconnect the EGR valve vacuum line and apply 10″ vacuum to the open end of the line with a pump or with engine vacuum, using a gauge teed into the line. If you are using engine vacu-

um, just make sure there are no vacuum leaks when you observe the valve's response.

5. When the valve receives the vacuum, the engine should suddenly idle much more roughly. If it responds this way, the valve is okay. If not, clean the EGR passages in the intake manifold or replace the valve, as necessary.

EGR VALVE REMOVAL AND INSTALLATION

1. If the routing of the vacuum lines is not obvious, mark them. Then, detach them from the EGR valve.

2. Unfasten the two bolts or bolt and clamp which attach the valve to the manifold. Withdraw the valve.

3. Installation is the reverse of removal. Always use a new gasket between the valve and the manifold and clean both gasket sealing surfaces, if necessary. On dual diaphragm valves, attach the carburetor vacuum line to the tube at the top of the valve, and the manifold vacuum line to the tube at the center of the valve.

TVS SWITCH REMOVAL AND INSTALLATION

1. Drain the radiator.

CAUTION: *When draining the coolant, keep in mind that cats and dogs are attracted by the ethylene glycol antifreeze, and are quite likely to drink any that is left in an uncovered container or in puddles on the ground. This will prove fatal in sufficient quantity. Always drain the coolant into a sealable container. Coolant should be reused unless it is contaminated or several years old.*

2. Disconnect the vacuum lines from the switch noting their locations. Remove the switch.

3. Apply sealer to the threaded portion of the new switch, and install it, torquing to 15 ft.lb.

4. Rotate the head of the switch to a position that will permit easy hookup of vacuum hoses. Then install the vacuum hoses to the proper connectors.

Catalytic Converter

All 1975 and later models are equipped with a catalytic converter. The converter is located midway in the exhaust system. Stainless steel pipes are used ahead of the converter. The converter is stainless steel with an aluminized steel cover and a ceramic felt blanket to insulate the converter from the floor-pan. The catalyst pellet bed inside the converter consists of noble metals which cause a reaction that converts hydrocarbons and carbon monoxide into water and carbon dioxide. No adjustments or repairs are possible.

On these models, lead-free fuel must be used exclusively in order to prevent the converter pellets from being coated with lead particles, rendering it ineffective. There are many other precautions which should be taken to prevent a large amount of unburned hydrocarbons from reaching the converter, as more than minimal concentrations will cause it to overheat. There could also be damage to nearby mechanical components or even a fire hazard. Therefore,

when working on/operating your car, the following conditions should be avoided:

• The use of fuel system cleaning agents and additives.

• Operating the car with an inoperative (closed) choke, or submerged carburetor float.

• Extended periods of engine run-on (dieseling).

• Turning off the ignition with the car in motion.

• Ignition or charging system failures.

• Misfiring of one or more spark plugs.

• Disconnecting a spark plug wire while testing for bad wire, plug, or poor compression in one cylinder.

• Pushing or jump starting the car, especially when hot.

• Pumping the gas pedal when attempting to start a hot engine.

General Motors Computer Controlled Catalytic Converter (C-4) System, and Computer Command Control (CCC) System

OPERATION

The GM designed Computer Controlled Catalytic Converter System (C-4 System), introduced in 1979 and used on GM cars through 1980, is a revised version of the 1978-79 Electronic Fuel Control System (although parts are not interchangeable between the systems). The

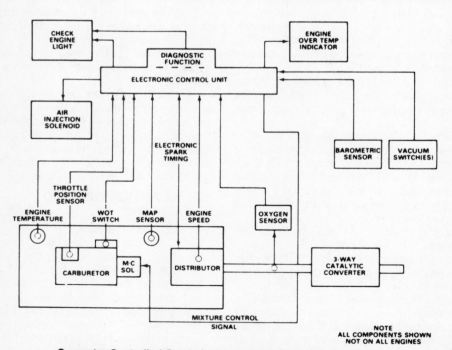

Computer Controlled Catalytic Converter (C-4) system schematic

C-4 system primarily maintains the ideal air/fuel ratio at which the catalytic converter is most effective. Some versions of the system also control the ignition timing.

The Computer Command Control System (CCC System), introduced on some 1980 California models and used on all 1981 and later carbureted car lines, is an expansion of the C-4 System. The CCC System monitors up to fifteen engine/vehicle operating conditions which it uses to control up to nine engine and emission control systems. In addition to maintaining the ideal air/fuel ratio for the catalytic converter and adjusting ignition timing, the CCC System also controls the Air Management System so that the catalytic converter can operate at the highest efficiency possible. The system also controls the lockup on the transmission torque clutch (certain automatic transmission models only), adjusts idle speed over a wide range of conditions, purges the evaporative emissions charcoal canister, controls the EGR valve operation and operates the early fuel evaporative (EFE) system. Not all engines use all the above systems.

There are two operation modes for both the C-4 System and the CCC System: closed loop and open loop fuel control. Closed loop fuel control means the oxygen sensor is controlling the carburetor's air/fuel mixture ratio. Under open loop fuel control operating conditions (wide open throttle, or engine and/or oxygen sensor cold), the oxygen sensor has no effect on the air/fuel mixture.

NOTE: *On some engines, the oxygen sensor will cool off while the engine is idling, putting the system into open loop operation. To restore closed loop operation, run the engine at part throttle and accelerate from idle to part throttle a few times.*

Computer Controlled Catalytic Converter (C-4) System
OPERATION

Major components of the system include an Electronic Control Module (ECM), an oxygen sensor, an electronically controlled variable-mixture carburetor, and a three-way oxidation-reduction catalytic converter.

The oxygen sensor generates a voltage which varies with exhaust gas content. Lean mixtures (more oxygen) reduce voltage; rich mixtures (less oxygen) increase voltage. Voltage output is sent to the ECM.

An engine temperature sensor installed in the engine coolant outlet monitors coolant temperatures. Vacuum control switches and throttle position sensors also monitor engine conditions and supply signals to the ECM.

The Electronic Control Module (ECM) monitors the voltage input of the oxygen sensor along with information from other input signals. It processes these signals and generates a control signal sent to the carburetor. The control signal cycles between ON (lean command) and OFF (rich command). The amount of ON and OFF time is a function of the input voltage sent to the ECM by the oxygen sensor. The ECM has a calibration unit called a PROM (Programmable Read Only Memory) which contains the specific instructions for a given engine application. In other words, the PROM

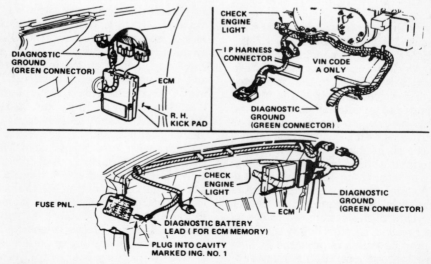

Typical C-4 system harness layouts. The location of the test lead will depend on the position of the ECM computer

unit is specifically programmed or tailor made for the system in which it is installed. The PROM assembly is a replaceable component which plugs into a socket on the ECM and requires a special tool for removal and installation.

On some 231 cu. in. V6 engines, the ECM controls the Electronic Spark Timing System (EST), AIR control system, and on the Turbocharged 231 cu. in. C-4 System it controls the early fuel evaporative system (EFE) and the EGR valve control (on some models). On some 350 V8 engines, the ECM controls the electronic module retard (EMR) system, which retards the engine timing 10° during certain engine operations to reduce the exhaust emissions.

NOTE: *Electronic Spark Timing (EST) allows continuous spark timing adjustments to be made by the ECM. Engines with EST can easily be identified by the absence of vacuum and mechanical spark advance mechanisms on the distributor. Engines with EMR systems may be recognized by the presence of five connectors, instead of the HEI module's usual four.*

To maintain good idle and driveability under all conditions, other input signals are used to modify the ECM output signal. Besides the sensors and switches already mentioned, these input signals include the manifold absolute pressure (MAP) or vacuum sensors and the barometric pressure (BARO) sensor. The MAP or vacuum sensors sense changes in the manifold vacuum, while the BARO sensor senses changes in barometric pressure. One important function of the BARO sensor is the maintenance of good engine performance at various altitudes. These sensors act as throttle position sensors on some engines. See the following paragraph for a description.

A Rochester Dualjet carburetor is used with the C-4 System. It may be an E2SE, E2ME, E4MC or E4ME model, depending on engine application. An electronically operated mixture control solenoid is installed in the carburetor float bowl. The solenoid controls the air/fuel mixture metered to the idle and main metering systems. Air metering to the idle systems is controlled by an idle air bleed valve. It follows the movement of the mixture solenoid to control the amount of air bled into the idle system, enrichening or leaning out the mixture as appropriate. Air/fuel mixture enrichment occurs when the fuel valve is open and the air bleed is closed. All cycling of this system, which occurs ten times per second, is controlled by the ECM. A throttle position switch informs the ECM of open or closed throttle operation. A number of different switches are used, varying with application. The V6 engines use two pressure sensors -- MAP (Manifold Absolute Pressure) and BARO (Barometric Pressure) -- as well as a throttle-actuated wide open throttle switch mounted in a bracket on the side of the float bowl. The 231 cu. in. turbo V6 and V8 engines use a throttle position sensor mounted in the carburetor bowl cover under the accelerator pump arm. When the ECM receives a signal from the throttle switch, indicating a change of position, it immediately searches its memory for the last set of operating conditions that resulted in an ideal air/fuel ratio, and shifts to that set of conditions. The memory is continually updated during normal operation.

Many C-4 equipped engines with AIR systems (Air Injection Reaction systems) have an AIR system diverted solenoid controlled by the ECM. These systems are similar in function to the AIR Management system used in the CCC System. See below for information. Most C-4 Systems include a maintenance reminder flag connected to the odometer which becomes visible in the instrument cluster at regular intervals, signaling the need for oxygen sensor replacement.

Computer Command Control (CCC) System
OPERATION

The CCC has many components in common with the C-4 system (although they should probably not be interchanged between systems). These include: the Electronic Control Module (ECM), which is capable of monitoring and adjusting more sensors and components than the ECM used on the C-4 System; an oxygen sensor; an electronically controlled variable-mixture carburetor; a three way catalytic converter; throttle position and coolant sensors; a barometric pressure (BARO) sensor; a manifold absolute pressure (MAP) sensor; a check engine light on the instrument cluster; and an Electronic Spark Timing (EST) distributor. On turbocharged engines, this distributor is equipped with an Electronic Spark Control (ESC) which retards ignition spark if the engine begins to knock.

Components used almost exclusively by the CCC System include: the AIR Injection Reaction (AIR) Management System; a charcoal canister purge solenoid; an EGR valve and associated controls; a vehicle speed sensor (located in the instrument cluster); a transmission torque converter clutch solenoid (automatic transmission models only); an idle speed control; and an early fuel evaporative (EFE) system.

See the operation descriptions under C-4 Sys-

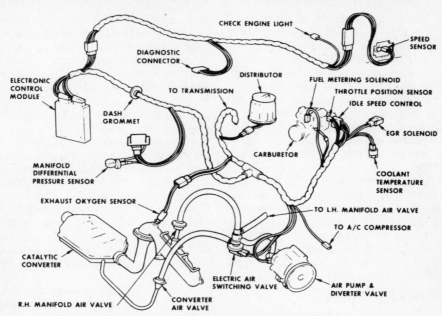

Computer Command Control (CCC) system schematic

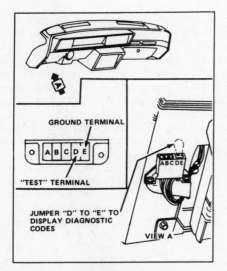

Typical 1981 and later CCC test terminal

tem for those components (except the ECM) the CCC System shares with the C-4 System.

The CCC System ECM, in addition to monitoring sensors and sending a control signal to the carburetor, controls the following components or sub-systems: charcoal canister purge, AIR Management System, idle speed control, automatic transmission converter lockup, distributor ignition timing, EGR valve control, EFE control, and the air conditioner compressor clutch operation. The CCC ECM is equipped with a Prom assembly similar to the one used with the C-4 ECM. See above for description.

The AIR Management System is an emission control which provides additional oxygen to the catalyst, the cylinder head exhaust ports, or to the exhaust manifold. An AIR Management System, composed of an air switching valve and/or an air control valve, controls the air pump flow and is itself controlled by the ECM. A complete description of the AIR system is given elsewhere in this unit repair section. The major difference between the CCC AIR System and the systems used on other cars is that the flow of air from the air pump is controlled electrically by the ECM, rather than by vacuum signal.

The charcoal canister purge control is an electronically operated solenoid controlled by the ECM. When energized, the purge control solenoid blocks vacuum from reaching the canister purge valve, When the ECM de-energizes the purge control solenoid, vacuum is allowed to reach the canister and operate the purge valve. This releases the fuel vapors collected in the canister into the induction system.

The EGR valve control solenoid is activated by the ECM in similar fashion to the canister purge solenoid. When the engine is cold, the ECM energizes the solenoid, which blocks the vacuum signal to the EGR valve. When the engine is warm, the ECM de-energizes the solenoid and the vacuum signal is allowed to reach and activate the EGR valve.

The Transmission Converter Clutch (TCC) lock is controlled by the ECM through an electrical solenoid in the automatic transmission.

When the vehicle speed sensor in the instrument panel signals the ECM that the vehicle has reached the correct speed, the ECM energizes the solenoid which allows the torque converter to mechanically couple the engine to the transmission. When the brake pedal is pushed or during deceleration, passing, etc., the ECM returns the transmission to fluid drive.

The idle speed control adjusts the idle speed to load conditions, and will lower the idle speed under no-load or low-load conditions to conserve gasoline.

The Early Fuel Evaporative (EFE) system is used on some engines to provide rapid heat to the engine induction system to promote smooth start-up and operation. There are two types of systems: vacuum servo and electrically heated. They used different means to achieve the same end, which is to preheat the incoming air/fuel mixture. They are controlled by the ECM.

BASIC TROUBLESHOOTING

NOTE: *The following explains how to activate the Trouble Code signal light in the instrument cluster and gives an explanation of what each code means. This is not a full C-4 or CCC System troubleshooting and isolation procedure.*

Before suspecting the C-4 or the CCC system or any of its components as faulty, check the ignition system including distributor, timing, spark plugs and wires. Check the engine compression, air cleaner, and emission control components not controlled by the ECM. Also check the intake manifold, vacuum hoses and hose connectors for leaks and the carburetor blots for tightness.

The following symptoms could indicate a possible problem with the C-4 or CCC System.

- Detonation
- Stalls or rough idle - cold
- Stalls or rough idle - hot
- Missing
- Hesition
- Surges
- Poor gasoline mileage
- Sluggish or spongy performance
- Hard starting - cold
- Hard staring - hot
- Objectionable exhaust odors
- Cuts out
- Improper idle speed (CCC System)

As a bulb and system check, the Check Engine light will come on when the ignition switch is turned to the ON position but the engine is not started.

The Check Engine light will also produce the trouble code or codes by a series of flashes which translate as follows. When the diagnostic test lead (C-4) or terminal (CCC) under the dash is grounded, with the ignition in the ON position and the engine not running, the Check Engine light will flash once, pause, then flash twice in rapid succession. This is a code 12, which indicates that the diagnostic system is working. After a longer pause, the code 12 will repeat itself two more times. The cycle will then repeat itself until the engine is started or the ignition is turned off.

When the engine is started, if the Check Engine light remains on, the self-diagnostic system has detected a problem. If the test lead (C-4) or test terminal (CCC) is then grounded, the trouble code will the flash three times. If more than one problem is found, each trouble code that applies will flash three times. Trouble codes will flash in numerical order (lowest code number to highest). The trouble code series will repeat as long as the test lead or terminal is grounded.

A trouble code indicates a problem with a given circuit. For example, trouble code 14 indicates a problem in the cooling sensor circuit. This includes the coolant sensor, its electrical harness, and the Electronic Control Module (ECM).

Since the self-diagnostic system cannot diagnose every possible fault in the system, the absence of a trouble code does not mean the system is trouble-free. To determine problems within the system which do not activate a trouble code, a system performance check must be made. This job should be left to a qualified technician.

In the case of an intermittent fault in the system, the Check Engine light will go out when the fault goes away, but the trouble code will remain in the memory of the ECM. Therefore, if a trouble code can be obtained even though the Check Engine light is not on, the trouble code must be evaluated. It must be determined if the fault is intermittent or if the engine must be at a certain operating conditions (under load, etc.) before the Check Engine light will come on. Some trouble codes will not be recorded in the ECM until the engine has been operated at part throttle for about 5 to 19 minutes.

On the C-4 System, the ECM erases all trouble codes every time the ignition is turned off. In the case of intermittent faults, a long term memory is desirable. This can be produced by connecting the orange connector/lead from terminal **S** of the ECM directly to the battery (or to a hot fuse panel terminal). This terminal must be disconnected after diagnosis is complete or it will drain the battery.

On the CCC System, a trouble code will be stored until terminal **R** of the ECM has been disconnected from the battery for 10 seconds. An easy way to erase the computer memory

Explanation of Trouble Codes
GM C-4 and CCC Systems

Ground test lead or terminal AFTER engine is running.

Trouble Code	Applicable System	Notes	Possible Problem Area
12	C-4, CCC		No tachometer or reference signal to computer (ECM). This code will only be present while a fault exists, and will not be stored if the problem is intermittent.
13	C-4, CCC		Oxygen sensor circuit. The engine must run for about five minutes (eighteen on C-4 equipped 231 cu in. V6) at part throttle (and under road load—CCC equipped cars) before this code will show.
13 & 14 (at same time)	C-4		See code 43.
14	C-4, CCC		Shorted coolant sensor circuit. The engine has to run 2 minutes before this code will show.
15	C-4, CCC		Open coolant sensor circuit. The engine has to operate for about five minutes (18 minutes for C-4 equipped 231 cu in. V6) at part throttle (some models) before this code will show.
21	C-4		Shorted wide open throttle switch and/or open closed-throttle switch circuit (when used).
	C-4, CCC		Throttle position sensor circuit. The engine must be run up to 10 seconds (25 seconds—CCC System) below 800 rpm before this code will show.
21 & 22 (at same time)	C-4		Grounded wide open throttle switch circuit (231 cu in. V6).
22	C-4		Grounded closed throttle or wide open throttle switch circuit (231 cu in. V6).
23	C-4, CCC		Open or grounded carburetor mixture control (M/C) solenoid circuit.
24	CCC		Vehicle speed sensor (VSS) circuit. The car must operate up to five minutes at road speed before this code will show.
32	C-4, CCC		Barometric pressure sensor (BARO) circuit output low.
32 & 55 (at same time)	C-4		Grounded +8V terminal or V(REF) terminal for barometric pressure sensor (BARO), or faulty ECM computer.
34	C-4		Manifold absolute pressure (MAP) sensor output high (after ten seconds and below 800 rpm).

on the CCC System is to disconnect the battery terminals from the battery. If this method is used, don't forget to reset clocks and electronic pre-programmable radios. Another method is to remove the fuse marked ECM in the fuse panel. However, not all models have such a fuse.

ACTIVATING THE TROUBLE CODE

On the C-4 System, activate the trouble code by grounding the trouble code test lead. Use the illustrations to locate the test lead under the instrument panel (usually a white and black wire or a wire with a green connector). Run a wire from the test lead to ground.

On the CCC System, locate the test terminal under the instrument panel. Use a jumper wire and ground only the lead. Jumper **B** to **A** on all models where letters run from **F** to **A** going from right to left. Ground the test lead. On many systems, the test lead is situated side by side with a ground terminal. In addition, on

Explanation of Trouble Codes
GM C-4 and CCC Systems (cont.)

Ground test lead or terminal AFTER engine is running.

Trouble Code	Applicable System	Notes	Possible Problem Area
34	CCC		Manifold absolute pressure (MAP) sensor circuit or vacuum sensor circuit. The engine must run up to five minutes below 800 RPM before this code will set.
35	CCC		Idle speed control (ISC) switch circuit shorted (over ½ throttle for over two seconds).
41	CCC		No distributor reference pulses to the ECM at specified engine vacuum. This code will store in memory.
42	CCC		Electronic spark timing (EST) bypass circuit grounded.
43	C-4		Throttle position sensor adjustment (on some models, engine must run at part throttle up to ten seconds before this code will set).
44	C-4, CCC		Lean oxygen sensor indication. The engine must run up to five minutes in closed loop (oxygen sensor adjusting carburetor mixture), as part throttle and under road load (drive car) before this code will set.
44 & 55 (at same time)	C-4, CCC		Faulty oxygen sensor circuit.
45	C-4, CCC	Restricted air cleaner can cause code 45	Rich oxygen sensor system indication. The engine must run up to five minutes in closed loop (oxygen sensor adjusting carburetor mixture), at part throttle under road load before this code will set.
51	C-4, CCC		Faulty calibration unit (PROM) or improper PROM installation in electronic control module (ECM). It takes up to thirty seconds for this code to set.
52 & 53	C-4		"Check Engine" light off: Intermittent ECM computer problem. "Check Engine" light on: Faulty ECM computer (replace).
52	C-4, CCC		Faulty ECM computer.
53	CCC		Faulty ECM computer.
54	C-4, CCC		Faulty mixture control solenoid circuit and/or faulty ECM computer.
55	C-4		Faulty oxygen sensor, open manifold absolute pressure sensor or faulty ECM computer (231 cu in. V6).
55			Faulty throttle position sensor or ECM computer (except 231 cu in. V6).
55	CCC	Including 1980 260 cu in.	Grounded +8 volt supply (terminal 19 of ECM computer connector), grounded 5 volt reference (terminal 21 of ECM computer connector), faulty oxygen sensor circuit or faulty ECM computer.

some models, the partition between the test terminal and the ground terminal has a cut section so that a spade terminal can be used to connect the two terminals.

NOTE: *Ground the test lead/terminal according to the instructions given previously in the Basic Troubleshooting section.*

Oxygen Sensor
REMOVAL AND INSTALLATION

NOTE: *The oxygen sensor uses a permanently attached pigtail and connector. This pigtail should not be removed from the oxygen sensor. Damage or removal of the pigtail or connector could affect proper operation of the oxygen sensor. The oxygen sensor is installed in the exhaust manifold and is removed in the same manner as a spark plug. The sensor may be difficult to remove when the engine temperature is below 120°F (48°C) and excessive force may damage threads in the exhaust manifold or exhaust pipe. Before trying to remove the sensor, run the engine until it is warm. Then allow it to cool for 10-15 minutes so that the manifold and sensor are at about engine temperature so that it will be safe to work around the sensor. Exercise care when handling the oxygen sensor; the electrical connector and louvered end must be kept free of grease, dirt, or other contaminants. Avoid using cleaning solvents of any kind and don't*

drop or handle the sensor roughly. A special anti-seize compound is present on the threads of new oxygen sensors. If you should have to remove a sensor and then reuse it, coat the threads with an anti-seize compound such as GM Part No. 5613695 or equivalent. Care should be used NOT to get the compound on the sensor itself. You should disconnect the negative battery cable when servicing the oxygen sensor and torque it to 30 ft.lb. when installing.

DIESEL ENGINE EMISSION CONTROLS

Exhaust Gas Recirculation (EGR)

To lower the formation of nitrogen oxides (NOx), it is necessary to reduce combustion temperatures. This is done by introducing exhaust gases into the cylinders.

FUNCTIONAL TESTS OF COMPONENTS
Vacuum Regulator Valve (VRV)

The Vacuum Regulator Valve is attached to the side of the injection pump and regulates vacuum in proportion to throttle angle. Vacuum from the vacuum pump is supplied to port **A** and vacuum at port **B** is reduced as the throttle is opened. At closed throttle, the vacuum is 15

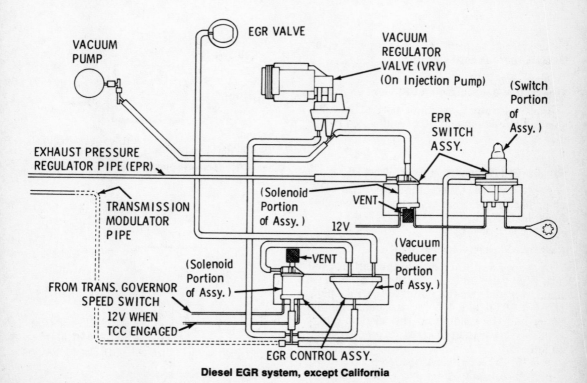

Diesel EGR system, except California

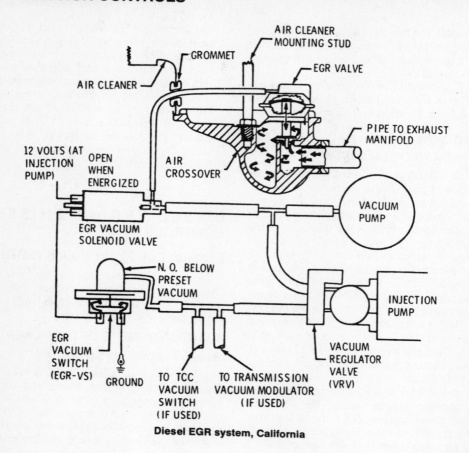

Diesel EGR system, California

inches; at half throttle - 6 inches; at wide open throttle there is zero vacuum.

Exhaust Gas Recirculation (EGR) Valve V8

Apply vacuum to vacuum port. The valve should be fully open at 10.5″ and closed below 6″.

Exhaust Gas Recirculation (EGR) Valve V6

Apply vacuum to vacuum port. The valve should be fully open at 12 inches and closed below 6 inches.

Response Vacuum Reducer (RVR)

Connect a vacuum gauge to the port marked "To EGR valve or T.C.C. solenoid". Connect a hand operated vacuum pump to the VRV port. Draw a 50.66 kPa (15 inch) vacuum on the pump and the reading on the vacuum gauge should be lower than the vacuum pump reading as follows:

- 0.75″ Except High Altitude V8
- High Altitude V8

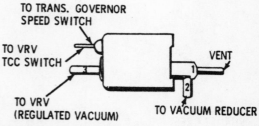

Diesel EGR vacuum solenoid

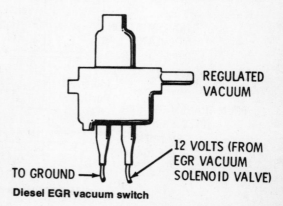

Diesel EGR vacuum switch

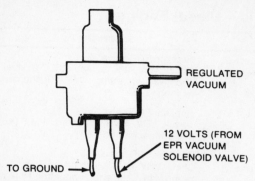

Diesel exhaust pressure regulator, except California

(Labels: REGULATED VACUUM; 12 VOLTS (FROM EPR VACUUM SOLENOID VALVE); TO GROUND)

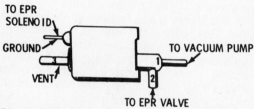

Diesel exhaust pressure regulator, California

(Labels: TO EPR SOLENOID; GROUND; VENT; TO VACUUM PUMP; TO EPR VALVE)

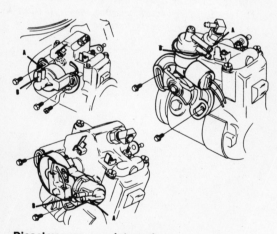

Diesel vacuum regulator valve

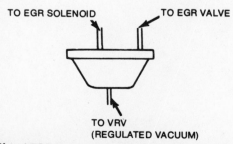

Diesel EGR vacuum reducer, except California

(Labels: TO EGR SOLENOID; TO EGR VALVE; TO VRV (REGULATED VACUUM))

Torque Converter Clutch Operated Solenoid

When the Torque converter clutch is engaged, an electrical signal energizes the solenoid allowing ports 1 and 2 to be interconnected. When the solenoid is not energized, port 1 is closed and ports 2 and 3 are are interconnected.

Solenoid Energized

- Ports 1 and 3 are connected.

Solenoid De-Energized

- Ports 2 and 3 are connected.

Vacuum Modulator Valve (VMV) V6

To test the VMV, block the drive wheels, apply the parking brake with the shift lever in Park, start the engine and run at low idle. Connect a vacuum gauge to the hose that connects to the port marked **MAN**. There should be at least 14" of vacuum. If not, check the Vacuum pump, VRV, RVR, solenoid and connecting hoses. Reconnect the hose to the **Man** port. Connect a vacuum gauge to the **DIST** port on VMV. The vacuum reading should be as follows":

- 12" Except High Altitude
- 9" High Altitude

Engine Temperature Sensor (ETS)
OPERATION

The engine temperature sensor has two terminals. Twelve volts are applied to one terminal and the wire from the other terminal leads to the fast idle solenoid and Housing Pressure Cold Advance solenoid that is part of the injection pump.

The switch contacts are closed below 125°F. At the calibration point, the contacts are open which turns off the solenoids.

Above Calibration

- Closed circuit.

Below Calibration

- Closed circuit.

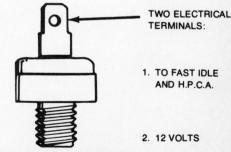

Diesel Engine Temperature Sensor

(Labels: TWO ELECTRICAL TERMINALS: 1. TO FAST IDLE AND H.P.C.A.; 2. 12 VOLTS)

EGR System Diagnosis—Diesel Engine

Condition	Possible Causes	Correction
EGR valve will not open.	Binding or stuck EGR valve. No vacuum to EGR valve.	Replace EGR valve. Check VRV,RVR, solenoid, T.C.C. operation, vacuum pump, VMV (V6) and connecting hoses.
EGR valve will not close. (Heavy smoke on acceleration).	Binding or stuck EGR valve. Constant high vacuum to EGR valve.	Replace EGR valve. Check VRV, RVR, solenoid, VMV (V6) and connecting hoses.
EGR valve opens partially.	Binding EGR valve. Low vacuum at EGR valve.	Replace EGR valve. Check VRV, RVR, solenoid, vacuum pump, VMV (V6) and connecting hoses.

Crankcase Ventilation

A Crankcase Depression Regulator Valve is used to regulate (meter) the flow of crankcase gases back into the engine. The Crankcase Depression Regulator Valve (C.D.R.V.) is designed to limit vacuum in the crankcase as the gases are drawn from the valve cover(s) through the C.D.R.V. and into the intake manifold (air crossover).

Fresh air enters the engine through the combination fitler, check valve and oil fill cap. The fresh air mixes with blow-by gases and enters both (V8), or one (V6) valve cover. The gases pass through a filter installed on the valve cover(s) and are drawn into connecting tubing.

Intake manifold vacuum acts against a spring loaded diaphragm to control the flow of crankcase gases. Higher intake vacuum levels pull the diaphragm closer to the top of the outlet tube. This reduces the amount of gases being drawn from the crankcase and decreases the vacuum level in the crankcase. As the intake vacuum decreases, the spring pushes the diaphragm away from the top of the outlet tube allowing more gases to flow to the intake manifold.

NOTE: *Do not allow any solvent to come in contact with the diaphragm of the Crankcase Depression Regulator because this will damage the diaphragm and cause it to fail.*

GASOLINE ENGINE FUEL SYSTEM

Fuel Pump

Fuel pumps used on all carbureted engines are of the single-action mechanical type. The fuel pump rocker arm is held in constant engagement with the eccentric on the camshaft by the rocker arm spring. As the end of the rocker arm which is in contact with the eccentric moves upward, the fuel link pulls the fuel diaphragm downward. The action of the diaphragm enlarges the fuel chamber, drawing fuel from the tank. Fuel flows to the carburetor only when the pressure in the outlet line is less than the pressure maintained by the diaphragm spring.

All the fuel pumps on Century//Regal models are sealed units and cannot be repaired. All must be replaced if defective.

REMOVAL AND INSTALLATION

Mechanical Fuel Pumps

1. Locate the fuel pump and disconnect the fuel lines.
2. Remove the two pump mounting bolts.
3. Remove the pump and the gasket.
4. Use a new gasket when installing the pump.
5. Install the fuel lines, start the engine and check for leaks.

TESTING

The fuel line from the tank to the pump is the suction side of the system and the line from the pump to the carburetor is the pressure side of the system. A leak on the pressure side, therefore, would be made apparent by dripping fuel, but a leak on the suction side would not be apparent while the car is running except for the reduction of the volume of fuel on the pressure side. Suction side leaks may appear when the engine is off, however, depending on how the car is parked.

1. Tighten any loose line connections and look for bends or kinks.
2. Disconnect the fuel pump at the carburetor. Disconnect the distributor-to-coil primary wire so that the engine can be cranked without firing. Place a container at the end of the pipe and crank the engine a few revolutions. If little or no gasoline flows from the open end of the pipe, the fuel pipe is clogged or the pump is defective.
3. If fuel flows in good volume from the pipe at the carburetor, check fuel pressure to be certain that the pump is operating within specified limits as follows:

   a. Attach a fuel pump pressure test gauge to the disconnected end of the pipe.

   b. Run the engine at approximately 450 to 1,000 rpm (on gasoline in the carburetor bowl) and note the reading on the pressure gauge.

   c. If the pump is operating properly the pressure will be within the specifications listed in the Tune-Up Specifications chart found in Chapter 2. The pressure will remain constant between speeds of 450 and 1,000 rpm. If the pressure is too low or too high at different speeds, the pump should be replaced.

Carburetor

IDENTIFICATION

General Motors Rochester carburetors are identified by their model code. The first number indicates the number of barrels, while one of the last letters indicates the type of choke used. These are **V** for the manifold mounted choke coil, **C** for the choke coil mounted in the carburetor body, and **E** for electric choke, also mounted on the carburetor. Model codes ending in **A** indicate an altitude compensating carburetor.

Troubleshooting Basic Fuel System Problems

Problem	Cause	Solution
Engine cranks, but won't start (or is hard to start) when cold	• Empty fuel tank • Incorrect starting procedure • Defective fuel pump • No fuel in carburetor • Clogged fuel filter • Engine flooded • Defective choke	• Check for fuel in tank • Follow correct procedure • Check pump output • Check for fuel in the carburetor • Replace fuel filter • Wait 15 minutes; try again • Check choke plate
Engine cranks, but is hard to start (or does not start) when hot— (presence of fuel is assumed)	• Defective choke	• Check choke plate
Rough idle or engine runs rough	• Dirt or moisture in fuel • Clogged air filter • Faulty fuel pump	• Replace fuel filter • Replace air filter • Check fuel pump output
Engine stalls or hesitates on acceleration	• Dirt or moisture in the fuel • Dirty carburetor • Defective fuel pump • Incorrect float level, defective accelerator pump	• Replace fuel filter • Clean the carburetor • Check fuel pump output • Check carburetor
Poor gas mileage	• Clogged air filter • Dirty carburetor • Defective choke, faulty carburetor adjustment	• Replace air filter • Clean carburetor • Check carburetor
Engine is flooded (won't start accompanied by smell of raw fuel)	• Improperly adjusted choke or carburetor	• Wait 15 minutes and try again, without pumping gas pedal • If it won't start, check carburetor

ADJUSTMENTS

Preliminary Checks (All Carburetors)

The following should be observed before attempting any adjustments.

1. Thoroughly warm up the engine. If the engine is cold, be sure that it reaches operating temperature. This has occurred when hot water suddenly flows through the upper radiator hose (be careful checking for this hot water, as you could easily be burned).

2. Check the torque of all carburetor mounting nuts and assembly screws. Also check the intake manifold-to-cylinder head bolts. If air is leaking at any of these points, any attempts at adjustment will inevitably lead to frustration.

3. Check the manifold heat valve (if used) to be sure that it is free.

4. Check and adjust the choke as necessary.

5. Adjust the idle speed and mixture. If the mixture screws are capped, don't adjust them unless all other causes of rough idle have been eliminated. If any adjustments are performed that might possibly change the idle speed or mixture, adjust both again when you are finished.

6. Before you make any carburetor adjustment make sure that the engine is in tune. Many problems which are thought to be carburetor related can be traced to an engine which is simply out-of-tune. Any troubles in these areas will have symptoms like those of carburetor problems.

Model 2GC, 2GV, 2GE Carburetor

FAST IDLE SPEED ADJUSTMENT

The fast idle is set automatically when the curb idle and mixture are set.

CHOKE ROD (FAST IDLE CAM)

1. Turn in the idle cam stop screw, if any, until it just contacts the bottom step of the fast idle cam. Then turn the screw one full turn.

2. Place the idle screw on the second step of the fast idle cam against the shoulder of the high step.

3. Hold the choke valve closed and check the clearance between the upper edge of the choke valve and the air horn wall.

4. Adjust the clearance by bending the tang on the choke lever.

2GC, 2GE INTERMEDIATE CHOKE ROD (CHOKE COIL LEVER) ADJUSTMENT

1. Remove the thermostatic cover coil, gasket, and inside baffle plate assembly.

2. Place the idle speed screw on the highest step of the fast idle cam.

3. Close the choke valve by pushing up on the intermediate choke lever.

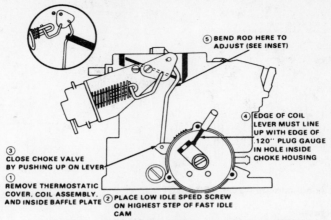

Intermediate choke rod adjustment—2GV, 2GC, 2GE

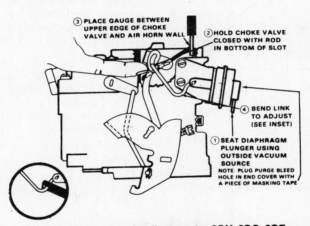

Primary vacuum break adjustment—2GV, 2GC, 2GE

4. The edge of the coil lever inside the choke housing must line up with the edge of a 0.120" drill bit inserted into the hole inside the choke housing.

5. Adjust by bending the intermediate choke rod at the first bend from the bottom of the rod.

VACUUM BREAK ADJUSTMENT

1. Remove the air cleaner. Vehicles with a Therm AC air cleaner should have the sensor's vacuum take-off plugged.

2. Using an external vacuum source, apply vacuum to the vacuum break diaphragm until the plunger is fully seated. If the diaphragm has a bleed hole, tape it over.

3. When the plunger is seated, push the choke valve toward the closed position. For 1976 models, place the idle speed screw on the high step of the fast idle cam.

4. Holding the choke valve in the closed position, place the specified size gauge between the upper edge of the choke valve and the air horn wall.

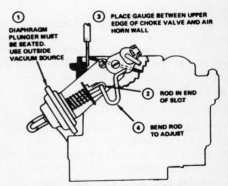

Vacuum break adjustment—2GV, 2GC, 2GE

5. If the measurement is not correct, bend the vacuum break rod.

AUXILIARY VACUUM BREAK

1. Seat the auxiliary vacuum diaphragm by applying an outside source of vacuum. Tape over the vacuum bleed hole so the vacuum will not bleed down.

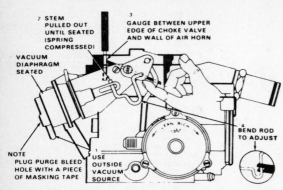

Auxillary vacuum break adjustment—2GV, 2GE, 2GC

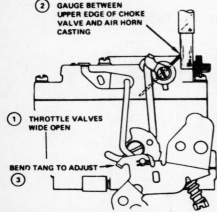

Choke unloader adjustment—2GV, 2GC, 2GE

2. Place the idle speed screw on the high step of the fast idle cam.

3. Hold the choke toward the closed choke position.

4. Measure the distance between the upper edge of the choke valve and the air horn wall.

5. Adjust by bending the auxiliary vacuum break rod at the bottom of the U-shaped bend. Remove the piece of tape from the auxiliary vacuum diaphragm.

CHOKE UNLOADER ADJUSTMENT

1. Hold the throttle valves wide open.
2. Close the choke valve.
3. Bend the unloader tang to obtain the proper clearance between the upper edge of the choke valve and air horn wall.

2GV CHOKE COIL ROD ADJUSTMENT

1. Hold the choke valve completely open.
2. Disconnect the coil rod from the upper lever and push down on the rod to the end of its travel.
3. When the rod is all the way down, the top of the rod should line up with the bottom of the slotted hole on the choke valve linkage.
4. Adjust by bending the lever.

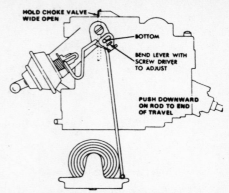

Choke coil rod adjustment—2GV, 2GC, 2GE

FLOAT LEVEL

With the air horn assembly upside down, measure the distance from the air horn gasket to the lip at the toe of the float. Bend the float arm to adjust to specifications.

FLOAT DROP

Holding the air horn assembly upright, measure the distance from the gasket to the lip or notch at the toe of the float. If correction is necessary, bend the float tang at the rear, next to the needle and seat.

ACCELERATOR PUMP ROD

1. Back out the idle speed screw and completely close the throttle valves.
2. Place the pump gauge across the air horn ring.

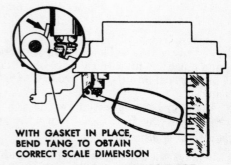

Float drop (metal float)—2GV, 2GC, 2GE

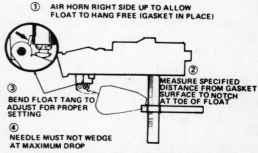

Float drop (plastic float)—2GV, 2GC, 2GE

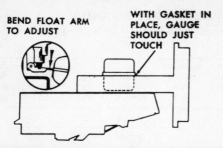

BEND FLOAT ARM TO ADJUST

WITH GASKET IN PLACE, GAUGE SHOULD JUST TOUCH

Float level measurement (metal float)—2GV, 2GC, 2GE

3. With the T-scale set to the specified height, the lower leg of the gauge should just touch the top of the accelerator pump rod.

4. Bend the pump rod to adjust.

BOWL VENT ADJUSTMENT

NOTE: *Check and adjust, if necessary, the pump rod clearance and curb idle speed before adjusting the bowl vent valve.*

1. Remove the two bowl vent valve cover attaching screws in the top of the air horn and remove the cover and gasket. Remove the bowel vent valve spring.

2GC, 2GV, 2GE Carburetor Specifications

NOTE: New model year carburetor specifications are not released by the manufacturers until well after the press date for this book.

Year	Carburetor Identification ①	Float Level (in.)	Float Drop (in.)	Pump Rod (in.)	Idle Vent (in.)	Primary Vacuum Break (in.)	Secondary Vacuum Break (in.)	Automatic Choke (notches)	Choke Rod (in.)	Choke Unloader (in.)	Fast Idle Speed (rpm)
1975	7045145	$15/32$	$19/32$	$1^{15}/32$	—	0.120	0.120	Index	0.080	0.120	—
	7045146	$15/32$	$19/32$	$1^{15}/32$	—	0.120	0.120	—	0.080	0.120	—
	7045147	$15/32$	$19/32$	$1^{15}/32$	—	0.120	0.120	1 Lean	0.080	0.120	—
	7045148	$15/32$	$19/32$	$1^{15}/32$	—	0.120	0.120	1 Rich	0.080	0.120	—
	7045149	$15/32$	$19/32$	$1^{15}/32$	—	0.120	0.120	1 Rich	0.080	0.120	—
	7045446	$15/32$	$19/32$	$1^{15}/32$	—	0.120	0.120	—	0.080	0.120	—
	7045448	$15/32$	$19/32$	$1^{15}/32$	—	0.120	0.120	Index	0.080	0.120	—
	7045449	$15/32$	$19/32$	$1^{15}/32$	—	0.120	0.120	1 Lean	0.080	0.120	—
	7045143	$15/32$	$19/32$	$1^{15}/32$	—	0.140	0.120	1 Rich	0.080	0.140	—
	7045140	$15/32$	$19/32$	$1^{15}/32$	—	0.140	0.120	1 Rich	0.080	0.140	—
1976	17056447	$7/16$	$19/32$	$19/32$	—	0.130	0.100	1 Rich	0.080	0.140	—
	17056145	$13/32$	$19/32$	$1^{19}/32$	—	0.110	0.100	1 Rich	0.080	0.140	—
	17056148	$7/16$	$19/32$	$1^{19}/32$	—	0.120	0.100	1 Rich	0.080	0.140	—
	17056149	$7/16$	$19/32$	$1^{19}/32$	—	0.120	0.100	1 Rich	0.800	0.140	—
	17056448	$7/16$	$19/32$	$1^{19}/32$	—	0.130	0.110	1 Rich	0.080	0.140	—
	17056449	$7/16$	$19/32$	$1^{19}/32$	—	0.130	0.110	1 Rich	0.080	0.140	—
	17056143	$15/32$	$19/32$	$1^{19}/32$	—	0.140	0.100	1 Rich	0.080	0.180	—
	17056140	$15/32$	$19/32$	$1^{19}/32$	—	0.140	0.100	1 Rich	0.080	0.180	—
1977	17057140	$15/32$	$15/32$	$19/16$	—	0.140	0.100	1 Rich	0.080	0.180	—
	17057141, 17057145, 17057147	$7/16$	$15/32$	$1^{1}/2$	—	0.110	0.040	1 Rich	0.080	0.140	—
	17057143, 17075144	$7/16$	$15/32$	$1^{17}/32$	—	0.130	0.100	1 Rich	0.080	0.140	—
	17057146, 17057148	$7/16$	$15/32$	$1^{17}/32$	—	0.110	0.040	1 Rich	0.080	0.140	—
	17057445	$7/16$	$15/32$	$1^{1}/2$	—	0.140	0.100	1 Rich	0.080	0.140	—
	17057446, 17057448	$7/16$	$15/32$	$1^{1}/2$	—	0.130	0.110	1 Rich	0.080	0.140	—
	17057447	$7/16$	$15/32$	$1^{1}/2$	—	0.130	0.100	1 Rich	0.080	0.140	—

2GC, 2GV, 2GE Carburetor Specifications (cont.)

NOTE: New model year carburetor specifications are not released by the manufacturers until well after the press date for this book.

Year	Carburetor Identification ①	Float Level (in.)	Float Drop (in.)	Pump Rod (in.)	Idle Vent (in.)	Primary Vacuum Break (in.)	Secondary Vacuum Break (in.)	Automatic Choke (notches)	Choke Rod (in.)	Choke Unloader (in.)	Fast Idle Speed (rpm)
1978	17058104	$^{15}/_{32}$	$1^9/_{32}$	$1^{21}/_{32}$	—	0.160	—	Index	0.260	0.325	—
	17058105	$^{15}/_{32}$	$1^9/_{32}$	$1^{21}/_{32}$	—	0.160	—	Index	0.260	0.325	—
	17058108	$^{19}/_{32}$	$1^9/_{32}$	$1^{21}/_{32}$	—	0.160	—	Index	0.260	0.325	—
	17058110	$^{19}/_{32}$	$1^9/_{32}$	$1^{21}/_{32}$	—	0.160	—	Index	0.260	0.325	—
	17058112	$^{19}/_{32}$	$1^9/_{32}$	$1^{21}/_{32}$	—	0.160	—	Index	0.260	0.325	—
	17058114	$^{19}/_{32}$	$1^9/_{32}$	$1^{21}/_{32}$	—	0.160	—	Index	0.260	0.325	—
	17058126	$^{19}/_{32}$	$1^9/_{32}$	$1^{17}/_{32}$	—	0.150	—	Index	0.260	0.325	—
	17058128	$^{19}/_{32}$	$1^9/_{32}$	$1^{17}/_{32}$	—	0.150	—	Index	0.260	0.325	—
	17058404	$^1/_2$	$1^9/_{32}$	$1^{21}/_{32}$	—	0.160	—	$^1/_2$ Lean	0.260	0.325	—
	17058405	$^1/_2$	$1^9/_{32}$	$1^{21}/_{32}$	—	0.160	—	$^1/_2$ Lean	0.260	0.325	—
	17058408	$^{21}/_{32}$	$1^9/_{32}$	$1^{21}/_{32}$	—	0.160	—	$^1/_2$ Lean	0.260	0.325	—
	17058410	$^{21}/_{32}$	$1^9/_{32}$	$1^{21}/_{32}$	—	0.160	—	$^1/_2$ Lean	0.260	0.325	—
	17058412	$^{21}/_{32}$	$1^9/_{32}$	$1^{21}/_{32}$	—	0.160	—	$^1/_2$ Lean	0.260	0.325	—
	17058414	$^{21}/_{32}$	$1^9/_{32}$	$1^{21}/_{32}$	—	0.160	—	$^1/_2$ Lean	0.260	0.325	—
	17058140	$^7/_{16}$	$1^5/_{32}$	$1^{19}/_{32}$	—	0.070	0.110	1 Rich	0.080	0.140	—
	17058143	$^7/_{16}$	$1^5/_{32}$	$1^9/_{16}$	—	0.080	0.110	1 Rich	0.080	0.140	—
	17058144	$^7/_{16}$	$1^5/_{32}$	$1^5/_8$	—	0.060	0.110	1 Rich	0.080	0.140	—
	17058145	$^7/_{16}$	$1^5/_{32}$	$1^{19}/_{32}$	—	0.060	0.110	1 Rich	0.080	0.160	—
	17058148	$^7/_{16}$	$1^5/_{32}$	$1^{19}/_{32}$	—	0.080	0.110	1 Rich	0.080	0.150	—
	17058149	$^7/_{16}$	$1^5/_{32}$	$1^{19}/_{32}$	—	0.080	0.110	1 Rich	0.080	0.150	—
	17058141	$^7/_{16}$	$1^5/_{32}$	$1^{19}/_{32}$	—	0.100	0.140	1 Rich	0.080	0.140	—
	17058147	$^7/_{16}$	$1^5/_{32}$	$1^{19}/_{32}$	—	0.100	0.140	1 Rich	0.080	0.140	—
	17058182	$^7/_{16}$	$1^5/_{32}$	$1^{19}/_{32}$	—	0.080	0.110	1 Rich	0.080	0.140	—
	17058183	$^7/_{16}$	$1^5/_{32}$	$1^{19}/_{32}$	—	0.080	0.110	1 Rich	0.080	0.140	—
	17058444	$^7/_{16}$	$1^5/_{32}$	$1^{19}/_{32}$	—	0.100	0.140	1 Rich	0.080	0.140	—
	17058446	$^7/_{16}$	$1^5/_{32}$	$1^{19}/_{32}$	—	0.110	0.130	1 Rich	0.080	0.140	—
	17058447	$^7/_{16}$	$1^5/_{32}$	$1^{19}/_{32}$	—	0.110	0.150	1 Rich	0.080	0.140	—
	17058448	$^7/_{16}$	$1^5/_{32}$	$1^9/_{16}$	—	0.100	0.140	1 Rich	0.080	0.140	—
	17058185	$^7/_{16}$	$1^5/_{32}$	$1^{19}/_{32}$	—	0.050	0.110	1 Rich	0.080	0.140	—
	17058187	$^7/_{16}$	$1^5/_{32}$	$1^{19}/_{32}$	—	0.050	0.110	1 Rich	0.080	0.140	—
	17058189	$^7/_{16}$	$1^5/_{32}$	$1^{19}/_{32}$	—	0.080	0.110	1 Rich	0.080	0.140	—
	17058188	$^7/_{16}$	$1^5/_{32}$	$1^5/_8$	—	0.050	0.120	1 Rich	0.080	0.140	—

① The carburetor identification number is stamped on the float bowl, next to the fuel inlet nut.

2. Place the idle speed screw on the second step of the fast idle cam next to the highest step. In this position, the bowl vent valve should just be closed.

3. If the vent valve is just closed with the idle the fast idle cam, rotate the fast idle cam so that the idle speed screw is on the next lower step. In this position, the vent valve should just begin to open.

4. If it is necessary to adjusat the bowl vent

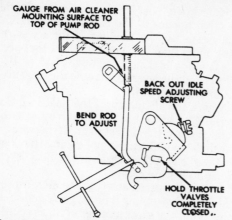

Accelerator pump rod—2GV, 2GC, 2GE

GAUGE FROM AIR CLEANER MOUNTING SURFACE TO TOP OF PUMP ROD

BACK OUT IDLE SPEED ADJUSTING SCREW

BEND ROD TO ADJUST

HOLD THROTTLE VALVES COMPLETELY CLOSED

valve, turn the adjustment screw in the top of the valve, to obtain the conditions mentioned in Steps 2 and 3.

Model 2MC, M2MC, M2ME, M2ME, E2ME Carburetor Adjustments

FLOAT LEVEL ADJUSTMENT

NOTE: *You will need several small special tools to accomplish this adjustment on the E2ME. See the text below and order them from your dealer or any alternate source using the GM part numbers shown for reference.*

See the illustration for float level adjustment for all carburetors. The E2ME procedure is the same except for adjustment (see the text below and the appropriate figure). For the E2ME only, if the float level is too high, hold the retainer firmly in place and push down on the center of the float to adjust.

1. If the float level is too low or too high on the E2ME, first remove the solenoid plunger as follows:

● Remove the solenoid connector attaching screw.

● Using a special tool such as J-28696-10 or BT-7928 or equivalent, turn the solenoid adjusting screw down (clockwise)*very cautiously* precisely counting the number of turns and fractional turn required to bottom it *very lightly*. Record the number.

● Turn the screw outward and remove it.

● Lift out the solenoid plunger.

2. Lift out the metering rods and float bowl insert (if the carburetor has one).

3. Mount a jig J-34817-1 or BT-8227A-1 or equivalent onto the float bowl. Then, mount a weighted positioner J-34817-3 or BT-8227 A or equivalent on the carburetor with its contact pin resting on the outer edge of the float lever.

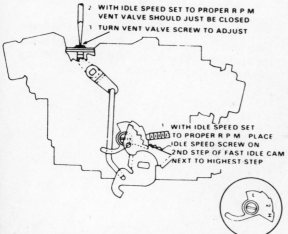

2 WITH IDLE SPEED SET TO PROPER R P M VENT VALVE SHOULD JUST BE CLOSED

3 TURN VENT VALVE SCREW TO ADJUST

1 WITH IDLE SPEED SET TO PROPER R P M PLACE IDLE SPEED SCREW ON 2ND STEP OF FAST IDLE CAM NEXT TO HIGHEST STEP

Bowel vent valve adjustment—2GV, 2GC, 2GE

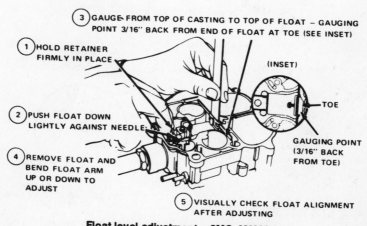

3 GAUGE FROM TOP OF CASTING TO TOP OF FLOAT – GAUGING POINT 3/16" BACK FROM END OF FLOAT AT TOE (SEE INSET)

1 HOLD RETAINER FIRMLY IN PLACE

2 PUSH FLOAT DOWN LIGHTLY AGAINST NEEDLE

4 REMOVE FLOAT AND BEND FLOAT ARM UP OR DOWN TO ADJUST

5 VISUALLY CHECK FLOAT ALIGNMENT AFTER ADJUSTING

(INSET)

TOE

GAUGING POINT (3/16" BACK FROM TOE)

Float level adjustment—2MC, M2MC

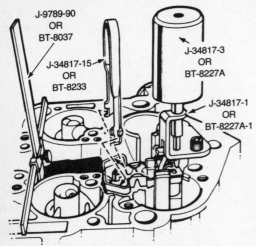

Float level adjustment—E2ME, E4ME

4. Use J-9780-90, BT-8037 or any other, similar arrangement of ruler and mounting system, or use a small ruler and simply measure carefully by eye. Measure the distance between the top surface of the carburetor casting and the top of the float $3/16''$ from the larger end of the float.

5. Check the float level specification in the chart that applies to the E2ME. Compare the specification to your reading. If the measurement is more than $2/32''$ above or below the spec', use a bending tool such as J-34817-15 or BT-8037 to bend the lever to increase the measurement or to decrease it.

6. Check the alignment of the float to make sure the float hinge has not been bent side-to-side in making the adjustment. If necessary, make slight modifications by bending the float arm straight and then recheck the float level, readjusting it if necessary.

7. Install the parts, starting the mixture solenoid screw, bottoming it *very lightly* and then turning it out the exact number of turns counted earlier.

FAST IDLE SPEED

1. Place the fast idle lever on the high step of the fast idle cam.
2. Turn the fast idle screw out until the throttle valves are closed.
3. Turn the screw in to contact the lever, then turn it in the number of turns listed in the specifications. Check this preliminary setting against the sticker figure.

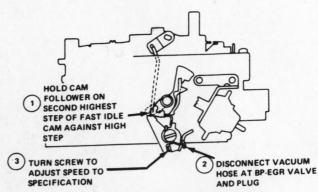

Fast idle speed adjustment—2MC, M2MC

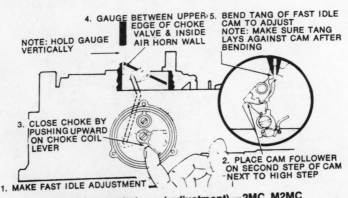

Fast idle cam (choke rod adjustment)—2MC, M2MC

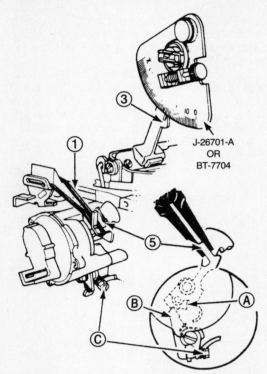

Adjusting the fast idle cam on 1986–87 E2ME carburetors

FAST IDLE CAM (CHOKE ROD) ADJUSTMENT (THROUGH 1985)

1. Adjust the fast idle speed.

2. Place the cam follower lever on the second step of the fast idle cam, holding it firmly against the rise of the high step.

3. Close the choke valve by pushing upward on the choke coil lever inside the choke housing, or by pushing up on the vacuum break lever tang.

4. Gauge between the upper edge of the choke valve and the inside of the air horn wall.

5. Bend the tang on the fast idle cam to adjust.

FAST IDLE CAM (CHOKE ROD) ADJUSTMENT (1986-87)

NOTE: *This is an easy procedure to perform, but you will need a special gauge which reads the opening angle of the choke butterfly such as GM Part No. J-26701-A or BT-7704 or equivalent. You may wish to try and use a common protractor to do this, but it may be difficult to use and the results may be somewhat uncertain.*

1. Open the throttle to close the choke. Run a rubber band from the vacuum break lever of the intermediate choke shaft to an anchor point so it will tend to pull the choke closed. Then, situate the angle gauge via its magnet onto a wide area of the choke butterfly.

2. Rotate the degree scale until the zero is opposite the pointer. Center the bubble in the level indicator. If you're using a protractor, mount it somehow on the carburetor so its zero axis is precisely parallel with the choke blade and when the choke opens you will get a positive angle reading.

3. Now, rotate the scale to 18°. Then, open the throttle slightly and carefully turn the fast idle cam and choke back until the cam follower lever will just touch the rise (bottom edge) of the highest step of the cam. If the lever does not touch the cam with the choke in this position, tighten the fast idle adjusting screw until it does.

4. Note the position of the bubble. If it is not centered, (or if the protractor does not show 18°), bend the fast idle kick lever with pliers to change the angle of the choke blade appropriately until it does.

5. Remove the rubber band.

PUMP ADJUSTMENT

This adjustment is not required on E2ME carburetors used in conjuction with the computer controlled systems.

1. With the fast idle cam follower off the

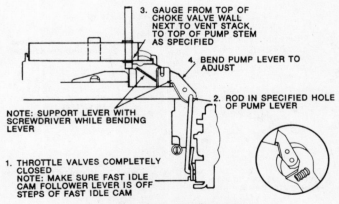

3. GAUGE FROM TOP OF CHOKE VALVE WALL NEXT TO VENT STACK, TO TOP OF PUMP STEM AS SPECIFIED

4. BEND PUMP LEVER TO ADJUST

2. ROD IN SPECIFIED HOLE OF PUMP LEVER

NOTE: SUPPORT LEVER WITH SCREWDRIVER WHILE BENDING LEVER

1. THROTTLE VALVES COMPLETELY CLOSED
NOTE: MAKE SURE FAST IDLE CAM FOLLOWER LEVER IS OFF STEPS OF FAST IDLE CAM

Pump adjustment—2MC, M2MC

steps of the fast idle cam, back out the idle speed screw until the throttle valves are completely closed.

2. Place the pump rod in the proper hole of the lever.

3. Measure from the top of the choke valve wall, next to the vent stack, to the top of the pump stem.

4. Bend the pump lever to adjust.

CHOKE COIL LEVER ADJUSTMENT

NOTE: *Before performing this procedure, note that a thermostatic coil cover kit will be required for assembly.*

1. Remove the choke cover and thermostatic coil from the choke housing. On models with a fixed choke cover, drill out the rivets and remove the cover.

2. Push up on the coil tang (counterclockwise) until the choke valve is closed. The top of the choke rod should be at the bottom of the slot in the choke valve lever. Place the fast idle cam follower on the high step of the cam.

3. Insert a 0.120″ plug gauge in the hole in the choke housing.

4. The lower edge of the choke coil lever should just contact the side of the plug gauge.

5. Bend the choke rod to adjust.

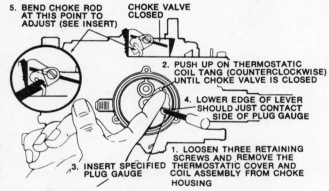

Choke coil lever adjustment—2MC, M2MC

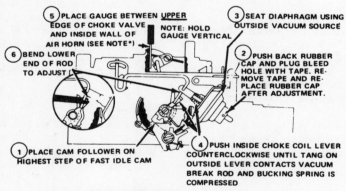

2MC rich vacuum break setting

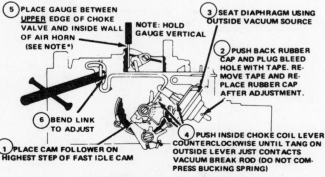

2MC lean vacuum break setting

2MC, M2MC, M2ME, E2ME E2MC Carburetor Specifications

Year	Carburetor Identification ①	Float Level (in.)	Choke Rod (in.)	Choke Unloader (in.)	Vacuum Break Lean or Front (in.)	Vacuum Break Rich or Rear (in.)	Pump Rod (in.)	Choke Coil Lever (in.)	Automatic Choke (notches)
1975	7045156	5/32	0.130	0.285	0.235	0.150	9/32 ②	0.120	1 Rich
	7045248	5/32	0.130	0.285	0.235	0.150	9/32 ②	0.120	1 Rich
	7045358	3/16	0.130	0.285	0.300	0.150	5/16 ③	0.120	1 Rich
	7045354	3/16	0.130	0.285	0.300	0.150	5/16 ③	0.120	1 Rich
1976	17056156	1/8	0.105	0.210	0.175	0.110	9/32 ②	0.120	1 Rich
	17056158	1/8	0.105	0.210	0.175	0.110	9/32 ②	0.120	1 Rich
	17056458	1/8	0.105	0.210	0.175	0.110	3/16 ③	0.120	1 Rich
	17056454	1/8	0.105	0.210	0.175	0.110	3/16 ③	0.120	1 Rich
1977	17057172	11/32	0.075	0.240	0.135	0.240	3/8 ③	0.120	2 Rich
	17057173	11/32	0.075	0.240	0.165	0.240	3/8 ③	0.120	2 Rich
1978	17058160	11/32	0.133	0.220	0.149	0.227	1/4 ③	0.120	2 Lean
	17058192	1/4	0.074	0.350	0.117	0.103	9/32 ②	0.120	1 Rich
	17058496	1/4	0.077	0.243	0.136	0.211	3/8 ③	0.120	1 Rich
1979	17059134	15/32	0.243	0.243	0.157	—	1/4	0.120	1 Lean
	17059136	15/32	0.243	0.243	0.157	—	1/4	0.120	1 Lean
	17059193	13/32	0.139	0.220	0.103	0.090	1/4 ②	0.120	2 Rich
	17059194	11/32	0.139	0.220	0.103	0.090	1/4 ②	0.120	2 Rich
	17059190	11/32	0.139	0.243	0.103	0.090	1/4 ②	0.120	2 Rich
	17059191	11/32	0.139	0.243	0.103	0.090	9/32 ②	0.120	2 Rich
	17059491	11/32	0.139	0.277	0.129	0.117	9/32 ②	0.120	1 Rich
	17059492	11/32	0.139	0.277	0.129	0.117	9/32 ②	0.120	1 Rich
	17059196	11/32	0.139	0.277	0.129	0.117	1/4 ②	0.120	1 Rich
	17059498	11/32	0.139	0.277	0.129	0.117	9/32 ②	0.120	2 Rich
	17059180	11/32	0.139	0.243	0.103	0.090	1/4 ②	0.120	2 Rich
	17059184	11/32	0.139	0.220	0.103	0.090	1/4 ②	0.120	2 Rich
	17059496	5/16	0.139	0.243	0.117	0.179	3/8 ②	0.120	2 Rich
1980	17080496	5/16	0.139	0.243	0.117	0.203	3/8	0.120	Fixed
	17080498	5/16	0.139	0.243	0.117	0.203	3/8	0.120	Fixed
	17080490	5/16	0.139	0.243	0.117	0.203	3/8	0.120	Fixed
	17080492	5/16	0.139	0.243	0.117	0.203	3/8	0.120	Fixed
	17080491	5/16	0.139	0.243	0.117	0.220	3/8	0.120	Fixed
	17080190	9/32	0.139	0.243	0.123	0.110	1/4 ②	0.120	Fixed
	17080191	11/32	0.139	0.243	0.096	0.096	1/4 ②	0.120	Fixed
	17080195	9/32	0.139	0.243	0.103	0.071	1/4 ②	0.120	Fixed
	17080197	9/32	0.139	0.243	0.103	0.071	1/4 ②	0.120	Fixed
	17080192	9/32	0.139	0.243	0.123	0.110	1/4 ②	0.120	Fixed
	17080160	5/16	0.074	0.239	0.168	0.207	1/4 ②	0.120	Fixed
1981	17080491	5/16	0.139	0.243	0.117	0.220	Fixed	0.120	Fixed
	17080496	5/16	0.139	0.243	0.117	0.203	Fixed	0.120	Fixed

2MC, M2MC, M2ME, E2ME E2MC Carburetor Specifications (cont.)

Year	Carburetor Identification ①	Float Level (in.)	Choke Rod (in.)	Choke Unloader (in.)	Vacuum Break Lean or Front (in.)	Vacuum Break Rich or Rear (in.)	Pump Rod (in.)	Choke Coil Lever (in.)	Automatic Choke (notches)
1981	17080498	5/16	0.139	0.243	0.117	0.203	Fixed	0.120	Fixed
	17081130	11/32	0.110	0.243	0.142	—	Fixed	0.120	Fixed
	17081131	11/32	0.110	0.243	0.142	—	Fixed	0.120	Fixed
	17081132	11/32	0.110	0.243	0.142	—	Fixed	0.120	Fixed
	17081133	11/32	0.110	0.243	0.142	—	Fixed	0.120	Fixed
	17081138	11/32	0.110	0.260	0.142	—	Fixed	0.120	Fixed
	17081140	11/32	0.110	0.260	0.142	—	Fixed	0.120	Fixed
	17081160	11/32	0.074	0.220	0.136	0.234	Fixed	0.120	Fixed
	17081190	5/16	0.139	0.243	0.117	0.187	Fixed	0.120	Fixed
	17081191	5/16	0.139	0.243	0.164	0.136	Fixed	0.120	Fixed
	17081192	3/8	0.139	0.243	0.164	0.136	Fixed	0.120	Fixed
	17081193	5/16	0.139	0.243	0.117	0.187	Fixed	0.120	Fixed
	17081194	5/16	0.139	0.243	0.117	0.179	Fixed	0.120	Fixed
	17081196	5/16	0.139	0.243	0.164	0.136	Fixed	0.120	Fixed
	17081197	3/8	0.096	0.243	0.164	0.136	Fixed	0.120	Fixed
	17081198	3/8	0.139	0.243	0.164	0.136	Fixed	0.120	Fixed
	17081150	13/32	0.071	0.220	0.136	0.227	Fixed	0.120	Fixed
	17081152	13/32	0.071	0.220	0.136	0.227	Fixed	0.120	Fixed
1982	17082130	3/8	0.110	0.164	0.157	—	④	④	Fixed
	17082132	3/8	0.110	0.164	0.157	—	④	④	Fixed
	17082136	3/8	0.110	0.164	0.157	—	④	④	Fixed
	17082138	3/8	0.110	0.164	0.157	—	④	④	Fixed
	17082140	3/8	0.110	0.243	0.157	—	④	④	Fixed
	17082150	13/32	0.071	0.220	0.136	0.243 ⑤	④	④	Fixed
	17082182	5/16	0.096	0.195	0.164	0.136	④	④	Fixed
	17082184	5/16	0.096	0.195	0.164	0.136	④	④	Fixed
	17082186	5/16	0.096	0.157	0.117	0.103	④	④	Fixed
	17082192	5/16	0.096	0.195	0.164	0.136	④	④	Fixed
	17082194	5/16	0.096	0.195	0.164	0.136	④	④	Fixed
	17082196	5/16	0.096	0.157	0.117	0.103	④	④	Fixed
1983	17082130, 132	3/8	0.110	0.243	0.157	—	④	.120	Fixed
	17083190, 192	5/16	0.096	0.195	0.164	0.136	④	.120	Fixed
	17083193	5/16	0.090	0.157	0.129	0.164	④	.120	Fixed
	17083194	5/16	0.090	0.220	0.157	0.142	④	.120	Fixed
1984	17082130	3/8	0.110	0.243	0.157	None	④	.120	Fixed
	17082132	3/8	0.110	0.243	0.157	None	④	.120	Fixed
	17084191	5/16	0.096	0.195	0.164	0.136	④	0.120	Fixed
	17084193	5/16	0.090	0.220	0.157	0.142	④	0.120	Fixed
	17084194	5/16	0.090	0.220	0.157	0.142	④	0.120	Fixed
	17084195	5/16	0.090	0.220	0.157	0.142	④	.120	Fixed

2MC, M2MC, M2ME, E2ME E2MC Carburetor Specifications (cont.)

Year	Carburetor Identification ①	Float Level (in.)	Choke Rod (in.)	Choke Unloader (in.)	Vacuum Break Lean or Front (in.)	Vacuum Break Rich or Rear (in.)	Pump Rod (in.)	Choke Coil Lever (in.)	Automatic Choke (notches)
				CANADIAN SPECIFICATIONS					
1981	17080191	¹¹⁄₃₂	0.139	0.243	0.096	0.096	¼ ②	0.120	Fixed
	17081492	⁹⁄₃₂	0.139	0.243	0.090	0.103	¼ ②	0.120	Fixed
	17081493	⁹⁄₃₂	0.139	0.243	0.090	0.103	¼ ②	0.120	Fixed
	17081170	¹³⁄₃₂	0.110	0.243	0.142	—	¼ ②	0.120	Fixed
	17081171	¹³⁄₃₂	0.110	0.243	0.142	—	¼ ②	0.120	Fixed
	17081174	⁹⁄₃₂	0.110	0.243	0.142	—	¼ ②	0.120	Fixed
	17081175	⁹⁄₃₂	0.110	0.243	0.142	—	¼ ②	0.120	Fixed
1982	17082174	⁹⁄₃₂	0.110	0.243	0.142	—	⁵⁄₁₆ ②	0.120	Fixed
	17082175	⁹⁄₃₂	0.110	0.243	0.142	—	⁵⁄₁₆ ②	0.120	Fixed
	17082492	⁹⁄₃₂	0.139	0.243	0.090	0.103	¼ ②	0.120	Fixed
	17082172	⁹⁄₃₂	0.110	0.243	0.142	—	⁵⁄₁₆ ②	0.120	Fixed
	17082173	⁹⁄₃₂	0.110	0.243	0.142	—	⁵⁄₁₆ ②	0.120	Fixed
1983–1984	17083172	⁹⁄₃₂	0.139	0.243	0.090	0.103	¼ ②	0.120	Fixed
1985	17085190	⁵⁄₁₆	—	32°	28°	24°	—	.120	—
	17085192	¹¹⁄₃₂	—	35°	27°	25°	—	.120	—
	17085194	¹¹⁄₃₂	—	35°	27°	25°	—	.120	—
1986	17086190	¹⁰⁄₃₂	—	32°	28°	24°	—	.120	—
1987	17086190	¹⁰⁄₃₂	—	32°	28°	24°	—	.120	—

① The carburetor identification number is stamped on the float bowl, next to the fuel inlet nut.
② Inner hole
③ Outer hole
④ Not Adjustable
⑤ High altitude—0.206.

2MC LEAN/RICH VACUUM BREAK ADJUSTMENT

1. Place the cam follower on the highest step of the fast idle cam.
2. Seat the vacuum break diaphragm by using an outside vacuum source. Tape over the bleed hole, if any, under the rubber cover on the diaphragm.
3. Remove the choke cover and thermostatic coil and push up on the coil lever inside the choke housing until the tang on the vacuum break lever contacts the tang on the vacuum break plunger stem. Do not compress the bucking spring for the rich adjustment.
4. With the choke rod in the bottom of the slot in the choke lever, gauge between the upper edge of the choke valve and the inside wall of the air horn.
5. Bend the link rod at the vacuum plunger stem to adjust the rich setting. Bend the link rod at the opposite end from the diaphragm to adjust the lean setting.

FRONT/REAR VACUUM BREAK ADJUSTMENT (MODELS THROUGH 1980)

1. Seat the front diaphragm, using an outside vacuum source. If there is an air bleed hole on the diaphragm, tape it over.
2. Remove the choke cover and coil. Rotate the inside coil lever counterclockwise. On models with a fixed choke cover (riveted), push up on the vacuum break lever tang and hold it in position with a rubber band.
3. Check that the specified gap is present between the top of the choke valve and the air horn wall.
4. Turn the front vacuum break adjusting screw to adjust.
5. To adjust the rear vacuum break diaphragm, perform Steps 1-3 on the rear diaphragm, but make sure that the plunger bucking spring is compressed and seated in Step 2. Adjust by bending the link at the bend nearest the diaphragm.

FRONT/REAR VACUUM BREAK ADJUSTMENT (1981 AND LATER)

NOTE: *On these models a choke valve measuring gauge J-26701-A or equivalent is used to measure angle (degrees instead of inches). You will also need a source of vacuum of at least 15". The best source is a vacuum pump.*

1. Open the throttle to close the choke. Run a rubber band from the vacuum break lever of the intermediate choke shaft to an anchor point so it will tend to pull the choke closed. Then, situate the angle gauge via its magnet onto a wide area of the choke butterfly.

2. Rotate the degree scale until the zero is opposite the pointer. Center the bubble in the level indicator. If you're using a protractor, mount it somehow on the carburetor so its zero axis is precisely parallel with the choke blade and when the choke opens you will get a positive angle reading.

3. Now, rotate the scale to the figure specified for the year and the particular (front or rear) vacuum break unit you are adjusting. If you're using a protractor, just note the degree reading you should be looking for.

4. Plug any bleed holes in evidence on the vacuum break unit you are adjusting. Then, apply 15" vacuum to fully seat the vacuum break plunger. If the (front) vacuum break has a bucking spring, verify that it is seated by noting that the adjustable tang seats against the stop. If the (rear) vacuum break has a bucking spring, note that it has seated by noting that the spring plunger stem has extended.

5. Turn the adjusting screw of the front vacuum break or the hex head screw of the rear vacuum break, or bend the rear vacuum break link if there is no adjusting screw, to adjust the angle of the choke blade to specification.

6. Unplug or uncap any bleed holes you have covered and then restore all vacuum hoses to their normal connections.

UNLOADER ADJUSTMENT (MODELS THROUGH 1980)

1. Hold the throttle valves wide open with the choke valve resting against the unloader mechanism.

2. Measure between the upper edge of the choke valve and air horn wall with a drill of appropriate diameter.

3. Bend the tang on the fast idle lever to obtain the proper measurement.

UNLOADER ADJUSTMENT (1981 AND LATER)

1. Open the throttle to close the choke. Run a rubber band from the vacuum break lever of the intermediate choke shaft to an anchor point

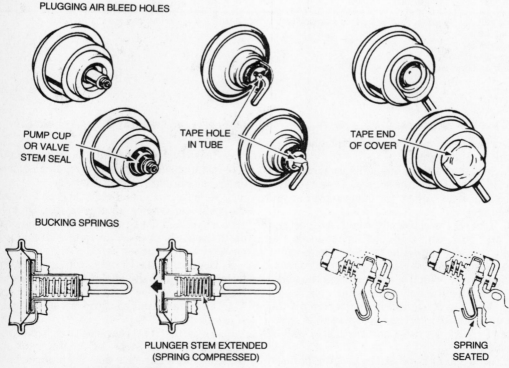

PLUGGING AIR BLEED HOLES

PUMP CUP OR VALVE STEM SEAL

TAPE HOLE IN TUBE

TAPE END OF COVER

BUCKING SPRINGS

PLUNGER STEM EXTENDED (SPRING COMPRESSED)

PLUNGER BUCKING SPRING

SPRING SEATED

LEAF TYPE BUCKING SPRING

How to ensure that the vacuum breaks are fully seated for effective adjustment

so it will tend to pull the choke closed. Then, situate the angle gauge via its magnet onto a wide area of the choke butterfly.

2. Rotate the degree scale until the zero is opposite the pointer. Center the bubble in the level indicator. If you're using a protractor, mount it somehow on the carburetor so its zero axis is precisely parallel with the choke blade and when the choke opens you will get a positive angle reading.

3. Now, rotate the scale to the figure specified for the unloader on the year car and the particular carburetor you are adjusting. If you're using a protractor, just note the degree reading you should be looking for.

4. Hold the throttle lever in the wide-open position. If the choke does not open to the required angle, bend the appropriate portion of the fast idle lever with a pair of needlenose pliers or a special tool such as J-9789-111 or BT-3006M so that it does.

AIR CONDITIONING IDLE SPEED-UP SOLENOID ADJUSTMENT

NOTE: *Do not adjust if carburetor is computer controlled.*

1. With the engine at normal operating temperature and the air conditioning turned on but

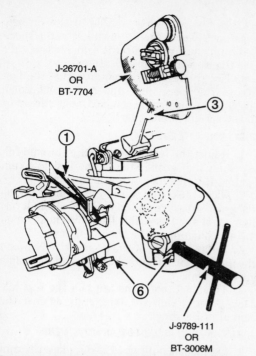

Bend the fast idle lever as shown to adjust the unloader on 1981 and later E2ME carburetors

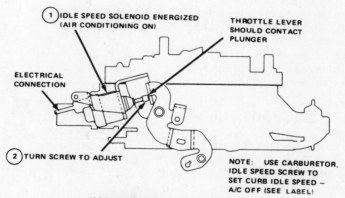

2MC, M2MC unloader adjustment

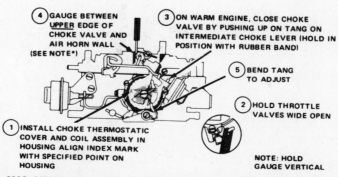

2MC, M2MC air conditioning idle speed-up solenoid adjustment

the compressor clutch lead disconnected, the solenoid should be electrically energized (plunger stem extended). Open the throttle slightly to allow the solenoid plunger to fully extend.

2. Adjust the plunger screw to obtain the specified idle speed.

3. Turn off the air conditioner. The solenoid plunger should move away from the tang on the throttle lever.

4. Adjust the curb idle speed with the idle speed screw, if necessary.

1975-80 Rochester Quadrajet Carburetor Adjustments

The Rochester Quadrajet carburetor is a two stage, 4-barrel downdraft carburetor. It has been built in many variations designated as 4MC, 4MV, M4MC, M4MCA, M4ME, M4MEA, E4MC, and E4ME. See the beginning of the Rochester section for an explanation of these designations.

The primary side of the carburetor is equipped with two primary bores and a triple venturi with plain tube nozzles. During off-idle and part throttle operation, the fuel is metered through tapered metering rods operating in specially designed jets and positioned by a piston that responds to manifold vacuum.

The secondary side of the carburetor contains two secondary bores. An air valve is used on the secondary side for metering control and supplements the primary bore.

The secondary air valve operates tapered metering rods which constantly regulate the fuel in proportion to the air being supplied.

FAST IDLE SPEED

1. Position the fast idle lever on the high step of the fast idle cam.

2. Be sure that the choke is wide open and the engine warm. Plug the EGR vacuum hose. Disconnect the vacuum hose to the front vacuum break unit, if there are two.

3. Make a preliminary adjustment by turn-

ing the fast idle screw out until the throttle valves are closed, then screwing it in the specified number of turns after it contacts the lever (see the carburetor specifications).

4. Use the fast idle screw to adjust the fast idle to the speed, and under the conditions, specified in the engine compartment sticker or in the specifications chart.

CHOKE ROD (FAST IDLE CAM)

1. Adjust the fast idle and place the cam follower on the second step of the fast idle cam against the shoulder of the high step.

2. Close the choke valve by exerting counterclockwise pressure on the external choke lever. Remove the coil assembly from the choke housing and push upon the choke coil lever.

3. Insert a gauge of the proper size between the upper edge of the choke valve and the inside air horn wall.

4. To adjust, bend the tang on the fast idle cam. Be sure that the tang rests against the cam after bending.

PRIMARY (FRONT) VACUUM BREAK ADJUSTMENT

1. On models built in 1975-77, place the cam follower lever on the highest step of the fast idle cam.

2. On models built in 1978-79, loosen the three retaining screws and remove the thermo-

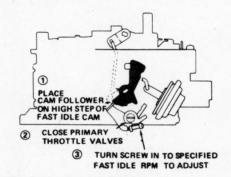

Fast idle adjustment—Quadrajet

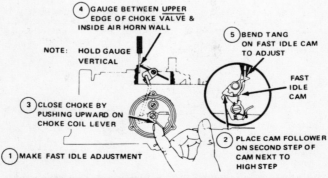

Choke rod (fast idle cam) adjustment—Quadrajet

static cover and coil assembly from the choke housing.

3. Seat the front vacuum diaphragm using an outside vacuum source. If there is a diaphragm unit bleed hole, tape it over.

4. Push up on the inside choke coil lever until the tang on the vacuum break lever contacts the tang on the vacuum break plunger. On models with a fixed choke coil cover, push up on the vacuum break lever tang.

5. Place the proper size gauge between the upper edge of the choke valve and the inside of the air horn wall.

6. To adjust, turn the adjustment screw on the vacuum break plunger lever.

7. Install the vacuum hose to the vacuum break unit.

SECONDARY (REAR) VACUUM BREAK ADJUSTMENT (1975-80 MODELS)

1. On all models built in years through 1979, remove the thermostatic cover and coil assembly from the choke housing

2. On all models built in years through 1977, place the cam follower on the highest step of the fast idle cam.

3. Tape over the bleed hole in the rear vacuum break diaphragm and then seat the diaphragm using an outside vacuum source. Make sure the diaphragm plunger bucking spring, if any, is fully compressed. On models with a delay type diaphragm (1980), plug the end cover with a pump plunger cup or equivalent during the adjustment procedure and then remove it after the adjustment is complete.

4. Close the choke by pushing up on the choke coil lever inside the choke housing. On models with a fixed choke coil cover, push up on the vacuum break lever tang and use a rubber band to hold it in place.

5. With the choke rod in the bottom of the slot in the choke lever, measure between the upper edge of the choke valve and the air horn wall with a wire type gauge.

6. To adjust, bend the vacuum break rod at the first bend near the diaphragm except on 1980 models with a screw at the rear of the diaphragm; on those models, turn the screw to adjust.

7. Remove the tape covering the bleed hole of the diaphragm and connect the vacuum hose.

1981-87 Rochester Quadrajet Carburetor Adjustments

NOTE: *On these models a choke valve measuring gauge J-26701 or equivalent is used to measure angle (degrees instead of inches). See the appropriate illustration for the applicable procedure. You may be able to use a protractor in place of the angle gauge, but it may be difficult to accomplish an accurate adjustment in this way.*

CHOKE UNLOADER

1. Open the throttle to close the choke. Run a rubber band from the vacuum break lever of the intermediate choke shaft to an anchor point so it will tend to pull the choke closed. Then, situate the angle gauge via its magnet onto a wide area of the choke butterfly.

2. Rotate the degree scale until the zero is opposite the pointer. Center the bubble in the level indicator. If you're using a protractor, mount it somehow on the carburetor so its zero axis is precisely parallel with the choke blade and when the choke opens you will get a positive angle reading.

3. Now, rotate the scale to the figure specified for the unloader on the year car and the particular carburetor you are adjusting. If

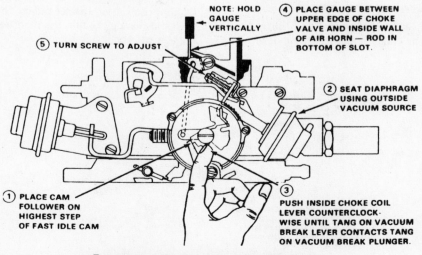

Front vacuum break adjustment—Quadrajet

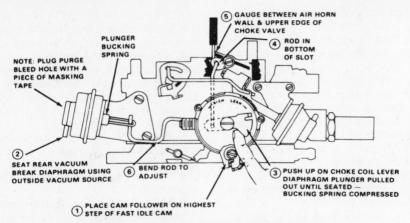

Rear vacuum break adjustment—Quadrajet

you're using a protractor, just note the degree reading you should be looking for.

4. Holding the secondary lockout lever away from the pin, open the throttle lever to the wide-open position and hold it there. If the choke does not open to the required angle, bend the appropriate portion of the fast idle lever with a pair of needlenose pliers or a special tool such as J-9789-111 or BT-3006M so that it does.

4MV CHOKE COIL ROD

1. Close the choke valve by rotating the choke coil lever counterclockwise.
2. Disconnect the thermostatic coil rod from the upper lever.
3. Push down on the rod until it contacts the bracket of the coil.
4. The rod must fit in the notch of the upper lever. If it does not, bend it on the curved portion just below the upper lever to create the proper fit.

MC, ME CHOKE COIL LEVER ADJUSTMENT

1. Remove the choke cover and thermostatic coil from the choke housing. On models with a fixed (riveted) choke cover, the rivets must be drilled out. A choke stat kit is necessary for assembly. Place the fast idle cam follower on the high step of the fast idle cam.

2. Push up on the coil tang (counterclockwise) until the choke valve is closed.
3. Insert a 0.120″ drill bit in the hole in the choke housing.
4. The lower edge of the choke coil lever should just contact the side of the plug gauge.
5. Bend the choke rod at the top angle to adjust.

SECONDARY CLOSING ADJUSTMENT

This adjustment assures proper closing of the secondary throttle plates.

1. Set the slow idle as per instructions in the appropriate car section. Make sure that the fast idle cam follower is not resting on the fast idle cam and the choke valve is wide open.
2. There should be 0.020″ clearance between the secondary throttle actuating rod and the front of the slot on the secondary throttle lever with the closing tang on the throttle lever resting against the lever.

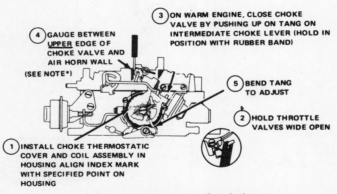

Unloader adjustment—Quadrajet

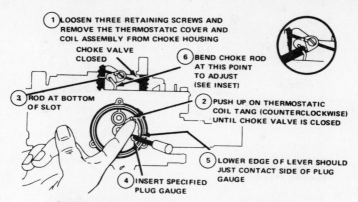

Choke coil lever adjustment—Quadrajet (MC, ME)

3. Bend the secondary closing tang on the primary throttle actuating rod or lever to adjust.

SECONDARY OPENING ADJUSTMENT

1. Open the primary throttle valves until the actuating link contacts the upper tang on the secondary lever.

2. With two point linkage, the bottom of the link should be in the center of the secondary lever slot.

3. With three point linkage, there should be 0.070″ clearance between the link and the middle tang.

4. Bend the upper tang on the secondary lever to adjust as necessary.

FLOAT LEVEL

With the air horn assembly removed, measure the distance from the air horn gasket surface (gasket removed) to the top of the float at the toe ($\frac{1}{16}$″ back from the toe on 1975 models; $\frac{3}{16}$″ back on 1976 and later models).

NOTE: *Make sure the retaining pin is firmly held in place and that the tang of the float is slightly held against the needle and seat assembly.*

Remove the float and bend the float arm to

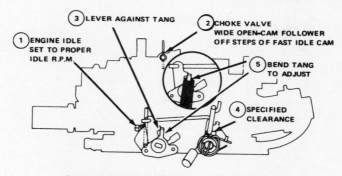

Secondary closing adjustment—Quadrajet

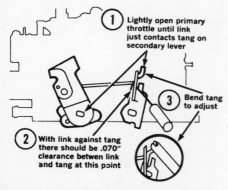

Secondary opening adjustment—Quadrajet

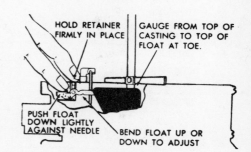

Float level adjustment—Quadrajet

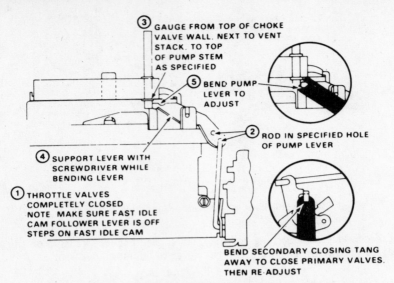

Accelerator pump rod adjustment—Quadrajet

Quadrajet Carburetor Specifications

Year	Carburetor Identification ①	Float Level (in.)	Air Valve Spring (turn)	Pump Rod (in.)	Primary Vacuum Break (in.)	Secondary Vacuum Break (in.)	Secondary Opening (in.)	Choke Rod (in.)	Choke Unloader (in.)	Fast Idle Speed ④ (rpm)
1975	7045240	7/16	7/16	9/32	0.135	0.120	②	0.095	0.240	1800
	7045548	7/16	7/16	9/32	0.135	0.120	②	0.095	0.240	1800
	7045244	5/16	3/4	15/32	0.130	0.115	②	0.095	0.240	1800
	7045246	5/16	3/4	15/32	0.130	0.115	②	0.095	0.240	1800
	7045544	5/16	3/4	15/32	0.145	0.130	②	0.095	0.240	1800
	7045546	5/16	3/4	15/32	0.145	0.130	②	0.095	0.240	1800
1976	17056240	5/16	7/16	3/8	0.135	0.120	②	0.095	0.250	1800
	17056540	15/32	7/16	3/8	0.135	0.120	②	0.095	0.250	1800
	17056244	5/16	3/4	3/8	0.130	0.120	②	0.095	0.250	1800
	17056246	5/16	3/4	3/8	0.130	0.120	②	0.095	0.250	1800
	17056544	5/16	3/4	3/8	0.130	0.130	②	0.095	0.250	1800
	17056546	5/16	3/4	3/8	0.130	0.130	②	0.095	0.250	1800
1977	17057241	5/16	3/4	3/8	0.120	0.105	②	0.095	0.240	⑤
	17057250, 17057253, 17057255, 17057256	13/32	1/2	9/32	0.120	0.170	②	0.095	0.205	⑤
	17057258	13/32	1/2	9/32	0.125	0.215	②	0.095	0.205	⑤
	17057550, 17057553	13/32	1/2	9/32	0.125	0.215	②	0.095	0.200	⑤
1978	17058240	1/32	3/4	9/32	0.117	0.117	②	0.074	0.243	⑤
	17058241	5/16	3/4	3/8	0.120	0.103	②	0.096	0.243	⑤
	17058250	13/32	1/2	9/32	0.129	0.183	②	0.096	0.220	⑤
	17058253	13/32	1/2	9/32	0.129	0.183	②	0.096	0.220	⑤

Quadrajet Carburetor Specifications (cont.)

Year	Carburetor Identification ①	Float Level (in.)	Air Valve Spring (turn)	Pump Rod (in.)	Primary Vacuum Break (in.)	Secondary Vacuum Break (in.)	Secondary Opening (in.)	Choke Rod (in.)	Choke Unloader (in.)	Fast Idle Speed ④ (rpm)
1978	17058254	15/32	1/2	9/32	0.136	—	②	0.103	0.220	⑤
	17058257	13/32	1/2	9/32	0.136	0.231	②	0.103	0.220	⑤
	17058258	13/32	1/2	9/32	0.136	0.231	②	0.103	0.220	⑤
	17058259	13/32	1/2	9/32	0.136	0.231	②	0.103	0.220	⑤
	17058582	15/32	7/8	9/32	0.179	—	②	0.314	0.277	⑤
	17058584	15/32	7/8	9/32	0.179	—	②	0.314	0.277	⑤
	17058282	15/32	7/8	9/32	0.157	—	②	0.314	0.277	⑤
	17058284	15/32	7/8	9/32	0.157	—	②	0.314	0.277	⑤
	17058228	15/32	1	9/32	0.179	—	②	0.314	0.277	⑤
	17058502	15/32	7/8	9/32	0.164	—	②	0.314	0.277	⑤
	17058504	15/32	7/8	9/32	0.164	—	②	0.314	0.277	⑤
	17058202	15/32	7/8	9/32	0.157	—	②	0.314	0.277	⑤
	17058204	15/32	7/8	9/32	0.157	—	②	0.314	0.277	⑤
	17058540	7/32	3/4	9/32	0.117	0.117	②	0.074	0.243	⑤
	17058550	13/32	1/2	9/32	0.136	0.231	②	0.103	0.220	⑤
	17058553	15/32	1/2	9/32	0.129	0.231	②	0.096	0.220	⑤
	17058559	15/32	1/2	9/32	0.136	—	②	0.096	0.231	⑤
1979	17059240	7/32	3/4	9/32	0.117	0.117	②	0.074	0.179	⑥
	17059243	7/32	3/4	9/32	0.117	0.117	②	0.074	0.179	⑥
	17059540	7/32	3/4	9/32	0.117	0.129	②	0.074	0.243	⑥
	17059543	7/32	3/4	9/32	0.117	0.129	②	0.074	0.243	⑥
	17059242	7/32	3/4	9/32	0.066	0.066	②	0.074	0.179	⑥
	17059553	13/32	1/2	9/32	0.136	0.230	②	0.103	0.220	⑥
	17059555	13/32	1/2	9/32	0.149	0.230	②	0.103	0.220	⑥
	17059250	13/32	1/2	9/32	0.129	0.182	②	0.096	0.220	⑥
	17059253	13/32	1/2	9/32	0.129	0.182	②	0.096	0.220	⑥
	17059208	15/32	7/8	9/32	—	0.129	②	0.314	0.277	⑥
	17059209	15/32	7/8	9/32	—	0.129	②	0.314	0.277	⑥
	17059210	15/32	1	9/32	0.157	—	②	0.243	0.243	⑥
	17059211	15/32	1	9/32	0.157	—	②	0.243	0.243	⑥
	17059228	15/32	1	9/32	0.157	—	②	0.243	0.243	⑥
	17059241	5/16	3/4	3/8	0.120	0.113	②	0.096	0.243	⑥
	17059247	5/16	3/4	3/8	0.110	0.103	②	0.096	0.243	⑥
	17059272	15/32	5/8	3/8	0.136	0.195	②	0.074	0.220	⑥
1980	17080240	3/16	9/16	9/32 ③	0.083	0.083	②	0.074	0.179	⑥
	17080241	7/16	3/4	9/32 ③	0.129	0.114	②	0.096	0.243	⑥
	17080242	13/32	9/16	9/32 ③	0.077	0.096	②	0.074	0.220	⑥
	17080243	3/16	9/16	9/32 ③	0.083	0.083	②	0.074	0.179	⑥
	17080244	5/16	5/8	9/32 ③	0.096	0.071	②	0.139	0.243	⑥

Quadrajet Carburetor Specifications (cont.)

Year	Carburetor Identification ①	Float Level (in.)	Air Valve Spring (turn)	Pump Rod (in.)	Primary Vacuum Break (in.)	Secondary Vacuum Break (in.)	Secondary Opening (in.)	Choke Rod (in.)	Choke Unloader (in.)	Fast Idle Speed ④ (rpm)
1980	17080249	7/16	3/4	9/32 ③	0.129	0.114	②	0.096	0.243	⑥
	17080253	13/32	1/2	9/32 ③	0.149	0.211	②	0.090	0.220	⑥
	17080259	13/32	1/2	9/32 ③	0.149	0.211	②	0.090	0.220	⑥
	17080270	15/32	5/8	3/8 ⑦	0.149	0.211	②	0.074	0.220	⑥
	17080271	15/32	5/8	3/8 ⑦	0.142	0.211	②	0.110	0.203	⑥
	17080272	15/32	5/8	3/8 ⑦	0.129	0.175	②	0.074	0.203	⑥
	17080502	1/2	7/8	Fixed	0.136	0.179	②	0.110	0.243	⑥
	17080504	1/2	7/8	Fixed	0.136	0.179	②	0.110	0.243	⑥
	17080540	3/8	9/16	Fixed	0.103	0.129	②	0.074	0.243	⑥
	17080542	3/8	9/16	Fixed	0.103	0.066	②	0.074	0.243	⑥
	17080543	3/8	9/16	Fixed	0.103	0.129	②	0.074	0.243	⑥
	17080553	15/32	1/2	Fixed	0.142	0.220	②	0.090	0.220	⑥
	17080554	15/32	1/2	Fixed	0.142	0.211	②	0.090	0.220	⑥
1981	17081202 204	11/32	7/8	Fixed	0.157 ⑧	—	②	0.110	0.243	⑩
	17081203 207	11/32	7/8	Fixed	0.157 ⑧	—	②	0.110	0.243	⑩
	17081216 218	11/32	7/8	Fixed	0.157 ⑧	—	②	0.110	0.243	⑩
	17081242	3/8	9/16	Fixed	0.090 ⑧	0.077 ⑨	②	0.139	0.243	⑩
	17081243	5/16	9/16	Fixed	0.103 ⑧	0.090 ⑨	②	0.139	0.243	⑩
	17081245	3/8	5/8	Fixed	0.164 ⑧	0.136 ⑨	②	0.139	0.243	⑩
	17081247	3/8	5/8	Fixed	0.164 ⑧	0.136 ⑨	②	0.139	0.243	⑩
	17081248 249	3/8	5/8	Fixed	0.164 ⑧	0.136 ⑨	②	0.139	0.243	⑩
	17081253 254	15/32	1/2	Fixed	0.142 ⑧	0.227 ⑨	②	0.071	0.220	⑩
	17081270	7/16	5/8	Fixed	0.136 ⑧	0.211 ⑨	②	0.074	0.220	⑩
	17081272	5/8	5/8	Fixed	0.136 ⑧	0.260 ⑨	②	0.074	0.220	⑩
	17081274	5/8	5/8	Fixed	0.136 ⑧	0.220 ⑨	②	0.083	0.220	⑩
	17081289	5/8	5/8	Fixed	0.164 ⑧	0.136 ⑨	②	0.139	0.243	⑩
1982	17082202	11/32	7/8	Fixed	0.110/20	—	②	0.110	0.243	⑤
	17082204	11/32	3/8	Fixed	0.110/20	—	②	0.110	0.243	⑤
	17082244	7/16	9/16	Fixed	0.117/21	0.083/16	②	0.139	0.195	⑤
	17082245	3/8	5/8	Fixed	0.149/26	0.149/26	②	0.139	0.195	⑤
	17082246	3/8	5/8	Fixed	0.149/26	0.149/26	②	0.139	0.195	⑤
	17082247	13/32	5/8	Fixed	0.164/28	0.136/24	②	0.139	0.243	⑤
	17082248	13/32	5/8	Fixed	0.164/28	0.136/24	②	0.139	0.243	⑤
	17082251	15/32	1/2	Fixed	0.142/25	0.304/45	②	0.071	0.220	⑤
	17082253	15/32	1/2	Fixed	0.142/25	0.227/36	②	0.071	0.220	⑤
	17082264	7/16	9/16	Fixed	0.117/20	0.083/16	②	0.139	0.195	⑤

Quadrajet Carburetor Specifications (cont.)

Year	Carburetor Identification ①	Float Level (in.)	Air Valve Spring (turn)	Pump Rod (in.)	Primary Vacuum Break (in.)	Secondary Vacuum Break (in.)	Secondary Opening (in.)	Choke Rod (in.)	Choke Unloader (in.)	Fast Idle Speed ④ (rpm)
1982	17082265	3/8	5/8	Fixed	0.149/26	0.149/26	②	0.139	0.195	⑤
	17082266	3/8	5/8	Fixed	0.149/26	0.149/26	②	0.139	0.195	⑤
	17082267	3/8	5/8	fixed	0.164/28	0.136/24	②	0.139	0.243	⑤
	17082268	13/32	5/8	Fixed	0.164/28	0.136/24	②	0.139	0.243	⑤
1983	17082265	3/8	5/8	Fixed	0.149/26	0.149/26	—	0.139	0.195	⑪
	17082266	3/8	5/8	Fixed	0.149/26	0.149/26	—	0.139	0.195	⑪
	17082267	3/8	5/8	Fixed	0.149/26	0.149/26	—	0.096	0.195	⑪
	17082268	3/8	5/8	Fixed	0.149/26	0.149/26	—	0.096	0.195	⑪
	17083242	9/32	9/16	Fixed	0.110/20	—	—	0.139	0.243	⑪
	17083244	1/4	9/16	Fixed	0.117/21	0.083/16	—	0.139	0.195	⑪
	17083248	3/8	5/8	Fixed	0.149/26	0.149/26	—	0.139	0.195	⑪
	17083250	7/16	1/2	Fixed	0.157/27	0.271/42	—	0.071	0.220	⑪
	17083253	7/16	1/2	Fixed	0.151/27	0.269/41	—	0.071	0.220	⑪
	17083553	7/16	1/2	Fixed	0.157/27	0.269/41	—	0.071	0.220	⑪
1984	17084201	11/32	7/8	Fixed	0.157	—	—	0.110	0.243	⑪
	17084205	11/32	7/8	Fixed	0.157	—	—	0.243	0.243	⑪
	17084208	11/32	7/8	Fixed	0.157	—	—	0.110	0.243	⑪
	17084209	11/32	7/8	Fixed	0.157	—	—	0.243	0.243	⑪
	17084210	11/32	7/8	Fixed	0.157	—	—	0.110	0.243	⑪
	17084240	5/16	1	Fixed	0.136	—	—	—	0.195	⑪
	17084244	5/16	1	Fixed	0.136	—	—	—	0.195	⑪
	17084246	5/16	1	Fixed	0.123	0.136	—	—	0.195	⑪
	17084248	5/16	1	Fixed	0.136	—	—	—	0.195	⑪
	17084252	7/16	1/2	Fixed	0.157	0.269	—	—	0.220	⑪
	17084254	7/16	1/2	Fixed	0.157	0.269	—	—	0.220	⑪
1985	17085202	11/32	7/8	—	27° ⑫	—	—	20° ⑬	38°	⑪
	17085203	11/32	7/8	—	27° ⑫	—	—	20° ⑬	38°	⑪
	17085204	11/32	7/8	—	27° ⑫	—	—	20° ⑬	38°	⑪
	17085207	11/32	7/8	—	27° ⑫	—	—	38° ⑬	38°	⑪
	17085218	11/32	7/8	—	27° ⑫	—	—	20° ⑬	38°	⑪
	17085282	11/32	1/2	—	25° ⑫	—	—	14° ⑬	35°	⑪
	17085502	14/32	7/8	—	26° ⑫	43 ⑫	—	20° ⑬	39°	⑪
	17085503	14/32	7/8	—	26° ⑫	36° ⑫	—	20° ⑫	39°	⑪
	17085506	14/32	1	—	27° ⑫	36° ⑫	—	20° ⑬	36°	⑪
	17085508	14/32	1	—	27° ⑫	36° ⑫	—	20° ⑬	36°	⑪
	17085524	14/32	1	—	25° ⑫	36° ⑫	—	20° ⑬	36°	⑪
	17085526	14/32	1	—	25° ⑫	36° ⑫	—	20° ⑬	36°	⑪
	17085554	14/32	1/2	—	27° ⑫	41° ⑫	—	14° ⑬	35°	⑪
1986	17086008	11/32	1/2	—	25° ⑫	43° ⑫	—	14° ⑬	35°	⑪

Quadrajet Carburetor Specifications (cont.)

Year	Carburetor Identification ①	Float Level (in.)	Air Valve Spring (turn)	Pump Rod (in.)	Primary Vacuum Break (in.)	Secondary Vacuum Break (in.)	Secondary Opening (in.)	Choke Rod (in.)	Choke Unloader (in.)	Fast Idle Speed ④ (rpm)
1986	17086077	11/32	1/2	—	25° ⑫	43° ⑫	—	14° ⑬	35°	⑪
1987	17086190	10/32	—	—	28° ⑫	24 ⑫	—	18° ⑬	32°	2,200 ④

① The carburetor identification number is stamped on the float bowl, near the secondary throttle lever.
② No measurement necessary on two point linkage; see text
③ Inner hole
④ On high step of cam, automatic in Park
⑤ 3 turns after contacting lever for preliminary setting
⑥ 2 turns after contacting lever for preliminary setting
⑦ Outer hole
⑧ Front
⑨ Rear
⑩ 4½ turns after contacting lever for preliminary setting
⑪ See underhood decal
⑫ Choke blade opening angle. See text.
⑬ Choke link cam angle. See text.

adjust except on carburetors used with the C-4 system (E4MC and E4ME). For those carburetors not used with C-4, if the float level is too high, hold the retainer firmly in place and push down on the the center of the float to adjust. If the float level is too low on C-4 models, lift out the metering rods and then remove the solenoid connector screw. Turn the lean mixture solenoid screw in clockwise, counting and recording the exact number of turns until the screw is lightly bottomed in the bowl. Then turn the screw out clockwise and remove. Lift out the solenoid and connector. Remove the float and bend the arm up to adjust. Install the parts, turning the mixture solenoid screw in until it is lightly bottomed, then unscrewing it the exact number of turns counted earlier.

ACCELERATOR PUMP

The accelerator pump is not adjustable on C-4 carburetors (E4MC and E4ME).
1. Close the primary throttle valves by backing out the slow idle screw and making sure that the fast idle cam follower is off the steps of the fast idle cam.
2. Bend the secondary throttle closing tang

Quadrajet Carburetor Specifications
All Canadian Models

NOTE: New model year carburetor specifications are not released by the manufacturers until well after the press date for this book.

Year	Carburetor Identification ①	Float Level (in.)	Air Valve Spring (turn)	Pump Rod (in.)	Primary Vacuum Break (deg./in.)	Secondary Vacuum Break (deg./in.)	Secondary Opening (in.)	Choke Rod (in.)	Choke Unloader (in.)	Fast Idle Speed (rpm)
1981	17080201	15/32	7/8	9/32 ②	—	23/0.129	④	0.314	0.277	⑤
	17080205	15/32	7/8	9/32 ②	—	23/0.129	④	0.314	0.277	⑤
	17080206	15/32	7/8	9/32 ②	—	23/0.129	④	0.314	0.277	⑤
	17080290	15/32	7/8	9/32 ②	—	26/0.149	④	0.314	0.277	⑤
	17080291	15/32	7/8	9/32 ②	—	26/0.149	④	0.314	0.277	⑤
	17080292	15/32	7/8	9/32 ②	—	26/0.149	④	0.314	0.277	⑤
	17080213	3/8	1	9/32 ②	23/0.129	30/0.179	④	0.234	0.260	⑤
	17080215	3/8	1	9/32 ②	23/0.129	30/0.179	④	0.234	0.260	⑤
	17080298	3/8	1	9/32 ②	23/0.129	30/0.179	④	0.234	0.260	⑤
	17080507	3/8	1	9/32 ②	23/0.129	30/0.179	④	0.234	0.260	⑤
	17080513	3/8	1	9/32 ②	23/0.129	30/0.179	④	0.234	0.260	⑤

Quadrajet Carburetor Specifications
All Canadian Models (cont.)

NOTE: New model year carburetor specifications are not released by the manufacturers until well after the press date for this book.

Year	Carburetor Identification ①	Float Level (in.)	Air Valve Spring (turn)	Pump Rod (in.)	Primary Vacuum Break (deg./in.)	Secondary Vacuum Break (deg./in.)	Secondary Opening (in.)	Choke Rod (in.)	Choke Unloader (in.)	Fast Idle Speed (rpm)
1981	17081250	13/32	1/2	9/32 ②	26/0.149	34/0.211	④	0.090	0.220	⑤
	17080260	13/32	1/2	9/32 ②	26/0.149	34/0.211	④	0.090	0.220	⑤
	17081276	15/32	5/8	5/16 ②	20/0.110	28/0.164	④	0.083	0.203	⑤
	17081286	13/32	1/2	9/32 ②	18/0.096	34/0.211	④	0.077	0.220	⑤
	17081287	13/32	1/2	9/32 ②	18/0.096	34/0.211	④	0.077	0.220	⑤
	17081282	3/8	5/8	9/32 ②	20/0.110	—	④	0.110	0.243	⑤
	17081283	3/8	7/8	9/32 ②	20/0.110	—	④	0.110	0.243	⑤
	17081284	1/2	7/8	9/32 ③	20/0.110	—	④	0.110	0.243	⑤
	17081285	1/2	7/8	9/32 ③	20/0.110	—	④	0.110	0.243	⑤
	17080243	3/16	9/16	9/32 ②	14.5/0.075	16/0.083	④	0.075	0.179	⑤
	17081295	13/32	9/16	9/32 ②	14.5/0.075	13/0.066	④	0.075	0.220	⑤
	17081294	5/16	5/8	9/32 ②	24.5/0.139	14/0.071	④	0.139	0.243	⑤
	17081290	13/32	7/8	9/32 ②	46/0.314	24/0.136	④	0.314	0.277	⑤
	17081291	13/32	7/8	9/32 ②	46/0.314	24/0.136	④	0.314	0.277	⑤
	17081292	13/32	7/8	9/32 ②	46/0.314	24/0.136	④	0.314	0.277	⑤
	17081506	13/32	7/8	9/32 ②	46/0.314	36/0.227	④	0.314	0.227	⑤
	17081508	13/32	7/8	9/32 ②	46/0.314	36/0.227	④	0.314	0.227	⑤
	17080202	7/16	7/8	1/4 ②	20/0.110	—	④	0.110	0.243	⑤
	17080204	7/16	7/8	1/4 ②	20/0.110	—	④	0.110	0.243	⑤
	17080207	7/16	7/8	1/4 ②	20/0.110	—	④	0.110	0.243	⑤
1982	17082280	3/8	7/8	9/32 ②	25/0.142	—	④	0.110	0.243	⑤
	17082281	3/8	7/8	9/32 ②	25/0.142	—	④	0.110	0.243	⑤
	17082282	3/8	7/8	9/32 ②	25/0.142	—	④	0.110	0.243	⑤
	17082283	3/8	7/8	9/32 ②	25/0.142	—	④	0.110	0.243	⑤
	17082286	13/32	1/2	9/32 ②	22/0.123	34/0.211	④	0.077	0.243	⑤
	17082287	13/32	1/2	9/32 ②	22/0.123	34/0.211	④	0.077	0.243	⑤
	17082288	3/8	7/8	9/32 ②	25/0.142	—	④	0.110	0.243	⑤
	17082289	3/8	7/8	9/32 ②	25/0.142	—	④	0.110	0.243	⑤
	17082296	1/2	7/8	9/32 ②	25/0.142	—	④	0.110	0.243	⑤
	17082297	1/2	7/8	9/32 ②	25/0.142	—	④	0.110	0.243	⑤
1983	17080213	3/8	1	9/32	23/.129	30/.179	④	0.234	0.260	⑤
	17082213	9/32	1	9/32	23/.129	30/.179	④	0.234	0.260	⑤
	17082282	3/8	7/8	9/32	25/.142	—	④	0.110	0.243	⑤
	17082283	3/8	7/8	9/32	25/.142	—	④	0.110	0.243	⑤
	17082286	13/32	1/2	9/32	23/.129	34/.211	④	0.107	0.220	⑤
	17082287	13/32	1/2	9/32	23/.129	34/.211	④	0.107	0.220	⑤
	17082296	1/2	7/8	9/32	25/.142	—	④	0.110	0.243	⑤

Quadrajet Carburetor Specifications
All Canadian Models (cont.)

NOTE: New model year carburetor specifications are not released by the manufacturers until well after the press date for this book.

Year	Carburetor Identification ①	Float Level (in.)	Air Valve Spring (turn)	Pump Rod (in.)	Primary Vacuum Break (deg./in.)	Secondary Vacuum Break (deg./in.)	Secondary Opening (in.)	Choke Rod (in.)	Choke Unloader (in.)	Fast Idle Speed (rpm)
1983	17082297	½	⅞	9/32	25/.142	—	④	0.110	0.243	⑤
	17083280	⅜	⅞	9/32	25/.142	—	④	0.110	0.243	⑤
	17083281	⅜	⅞	9/32	25/.142	—	④	0.110	0.243	⑤
	17083282	⅜	⅞	9/32	25/.142	—	④	0.110	0.243	⑤
	17083283	⅜	⅞	9/32	25/.142	—	④	0.110	0.243	⑤
	17083290	13/32	⅞	9/32	—	24/.136	④	0.314	0.251	⑤
	17083292	13/32	⅞	9/32	—	24/.136	④	0.314	0.251	⑤
	17083298	⅜	1	9/32	23/.129	30/.179	④	0.234	0.260	⑤
1984	17084280	⅜	⅞	9/32 ②	23/.129	—	④	0.110	0.243	⑤
	17084281	⅜	⅞	9/32 ②	23/.129	—	④	0.110	0.243	⑤
	17084282	⅜	⅞	9/32 ②	23/.129	—	④	0.110	0.243	⑤
	17084283	⅜	⅞	9/32 ②	23/.129	—	④	0.110	0.243	⑤
	17084284	⅜	⅞	9/32 ②	23/.129	—	④	0.110	0.243	⑤
	17084285	⅜	⅞	9/32 ②	23/.129	—	④	0.110	0.243	⑤
	17084286	13/32	½	9/32 ②	23/.129	34/.211	④	0.107	0.220	⑤
	17084287	13/32	½	9/32 ②	23/.129	34/.211	④	0.107	0.220	⑤
	17084288	⅜	⅞	9/32 ②	23/.129	—	④	0.110	0.243	⑤
	17084289	⅜	⅞	9/32 ②	23/.129	—	④	0.110	0.243	⑤
	17084296	½	⅞	9/32 ②	23/.129	—	④	0.110	0.243	⑤
	17084297	½	⅞	9/32 ②	23/.129	—	④	0.110	0.243	⑤

① The carburetor identification number is stamped on the float bowl, near the secondary throttle lever.
② Inner hole
③ Outer hole
④ No measurement necessary on two point linkage; see text.
⑤ See underhood decal.

away from the primary throttle lever, if necessary, to insure that the primary throttle valves are fully closed.

3. With the pump link in the appropriate hole in the pump lever, measure from the top of the choke valve wall to the top of the pump stem.

4. To adjust, bend the pump lever.

5. After adjusting, readjust the secondary throttle tang and the slow idle screw.

AIR VALVE SPRING ADJUSTMENT

To adjust the air valve spring windup, loosen the Allen head lockscrew and turn the adjustment screw counterclockwise to remove all spring tension. With the air valve closed, turn the adjusting screw clockwise the specified number of turns after the torsion spring con-

tacts the pin on the shaft. Hold the adjusting screw in this position and tighten the lockscrew.

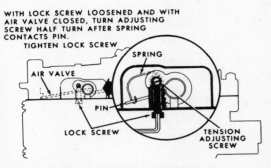

WITH LOCK SCREW LOOSENED AND WITH AIR VALVE CLOSED, TURN ADJUSTING SCREW HALF TURN AFTER SPRING CONTACTS PIN.
TIGHTEN LOCK SCREW   SPRING
AIR VALVE
PIN
LOCK SCREW   TENSION ADJUSTING SCREW

Air valve spring adjustment—Quadrajet

REMOVAL AND INSTALLATION

1. Remove the air cleaner and its gasket.
2. Disconnect the fuel and vacuum lines from the carburetor.
3. Disconnect the choke coil rod, heated air line tube, or electrical connector.
4. Disconnect the throttle linkage.
5. On automatic transmission cars, disconnect the throttle valve and downshift linkages if so equipped.
6. If CEC equipped, remove the CEC valve vacuum hose and electrical connector. Disconnect the EGR line, if so equipped.
7. If the car is equipped with an idle stop solenoid, disconnect the wiring. Then, remove the solenoid.
8. Remove the carburetor attaching nuts and/or bolts, gasket or insulator, and remove the carburetor.
9. Install the carburetor by reversing the removal procedure. Before installing the top of the carburetor, fill the float bowl with gasoline to ease the starting of the engine. Use a new gasket.

OVERHAUL

All Types

Efficient carburetion depends greatly on careful cleaning and inspection during overhaul, since dirt, gum, water, or varnish in or on the carburetor parts are often responsible for poor performance.

Overhaul your carburetor in a clean, dust-free area. Carefully disassemble the carburetor, refering often to the exploded views and directions packaged with the rebuilding kit. Keep all similar and look-alike parts segregated during assembly and cleaning to avoid accidental interchange during assembly. Make a note of all jet sizes.

When the carbuetor id disassembled, wash all parts (except diaphragms, electric choke units, pump lunger, and any other plastic, leather, fiber, or rubber parts) in clean carburetor solvent. Do not leave parts in the solvent any longer than is necessary to sufficiently loosen the deposits. Excessive cleaning may remove the special finish from the float bowl and choke valve bodies, leaving these parts unfit for service. Rinse all parts in clean solvent and blow them dry with compressed air or allow them to air dry. Wipe clean all cork, plastic, leather, and fiber parts with a clean, lint-free cloth.

Blow out all passages and jets with compressed air and be sure that there are no restrictions or blockages. Never use wire or similar tools to clean jets, fuel passages, or air blleds. Clean all jets and valves separsately to avoid accidental interchange.

Check all parts for wear or damage. If wear or damage is found, replace the defective parts. Especially check the following:

1. Check the float needle and seat for wear. If wear is found, replace the complete assembly.
2. Check the float hinge pin for wear and the float(s) for dents or distortion. Replace the float if fuel has leaked into it.
3. Check the throttle and choke shaft bores for wear or an out-of-round condition. Damage or wear to the throttle arm, shaft, or shaft bore will often require replacement of the throttle body. These parts require a close tolerance of fit; wear will allow leakage, which will then affect starting and idling.

NOTE: *Throttle shafts and bushings are not included in overhaul kits. They can be purchased separately.*

4. Inspect the idle mixture adjusting needles for burrs or grooves. Any such conditions requires replacement of the needle, since you will not be able to obtain a satisfactory idle.
5. Test the accelerator pump check valves. they should pass air one way but not the other. test for proper seating by blowing and sucking on the valve. Replace the valve check ball and spring as necessary. If the valve is satisfactory, wash the valve parts again to remove breath moisture.
6. Check the bowl cover for warped surfaces with a straightedge.
7. Closely inspect the accelerator pump plunger wear and damage, replascing as necessary.
8. After the carbuetor is assembled, check the choke valve for freedom of operation.

Carburetor overhaul kits are recommended for each overhaul. These kits contain all gaskets and new parts to replace those which deteriorate most rapidly. Failure to replace all parts supplied with the kit (especially gaskets) can result in poor performance later.

Some carburetor manufacturers supply overhaul kits of three basic types: minor repair; major repair; and gasket kits. Basically, they contain the following:

Minor Repair Kits:
- All gaskets
- Float needle valve
- All diagrams
- Spring for the pump diagram

Major Repai Kits
- All jets and gaskets
- All diaphragms
- Float needle valve
- Pump ball valve
- Float
- Complete intermediate rod
- Intermediate pump lever
- Some cover holddown screws and washers

Gasket Kits
● All gaskets

After cleaning and checking all components, reassemble the carburetor, using new parts and referring to the exploded view. When reassembling, make sure that all screws and jets are tight in their seats, nut do not overtighten as the tips will be distorted. Tighten all screws gradually, in rotation. Do not tighten needle valves into their seats; uneven jeting will result. Always use new gaskets. Be sure to adjust the float level when reassembling.

GENERAL MOTORS SEQUENTIAL (SFI) FUEL INJECTION SYSTEMS

NOTE: *This book contains simple testing and service procedures for your car's fuel injection system. More comprehensive testing and diagnosis procedures may be found in* CHILTON'S GUIDE TO FUEL INJECTION AND FEEDBACK CARBURETORS, *book N. 7488, available at your local retailer.*

General Information

On 1984 and later turbocharged models, a sequential port fuel injection system (SFI) is used for precise fuel control. With SFI, metered fuel is timed and injected sequentially through six Bosch injectors into individual cylinder ports. Each cylinder receives one injection per working cycle (every two revolutions), just prior to the opening of its intake valve. By injecting the fuel into a moving airstream, atomization is preserved, rather than being lost when fuel lays in the manifold. This enhances both performance and economy. The SFI system incorporates a new Computer Controlled Coil Ignition system that uses an electronic coil module that replaces the conventional distributor and coil used on most engines. An electronic spark control (ESC) is used to adjust the spark timing.

The SFI system uses Bosch injectors, one at each intake port, rather than the single injector found on the earlier throttle body system. The injectors are mounted on a fuel rail and are activated individually by a signal from the electronic control module. The injector is a solenoid-operated valve which remains open depending on the width of the electronic pulses (length of the signal) from the ECM; the longer the open time, the more fuel is injected. in this manner, the air/fuel mixture can be precisely controlled for maximum performance with minimum emissions.

Fuel is pumped from the tank by a high pressure fuel pump, located inside the fuel tank. It is a positive displacement roller vane pump.

The impeller serves as a vapor separator and precharges the high pressure assembly. A pressure regulator maintains 28-50 psi in the fuel line to the injectors by feeding the excess fuel is fed back to the tank. This also keeps the fuel cool whenever the engine is running.

The Mass Air Flow Sensor is used to measure the mass of air that is drawn into the engine cylinders. It is located just ahead of the air throttle in the intake system and consists of a heated film which measures the mass of air, rather than just the volume. A resistor is used to measure the temperature of the incoming air and the air mass sensor maintains the temperature of the film at 75° above ambient temperature. As the ambient (outside) air temperature rises, less energy is required to maintain the heated film 75° above ambient because the density of the air (mass) decreases. The control unit then uses this difference in required energy to calculate the actual mass of the incoming air. It, in turn, uses this information to determine the duration of the fuel injection pulse, to adjust ignition timing and to help determine EGR flow.

The throttle body incorporates an idle air control (IAC) that provides for a bypass channel through which air can flow. It consists of an orifice and pintle which is controlled by the ECM through a stepper motor. The IAC provides air flow for idle and allows additional air during cold start until the engine reaches operating temperature. As the engine temperature rises, the opening through which air passes is gradually closed.

The throttle position sensor (TPS) provides the control unit with information on throttle position, in order to determine injector pulse width and hence correct mixture. The TPS is connected to the throttle shaft on the throttle body and consists, basically, of a potentiometer. One end of this potentiometer is connected to a 5 volt source from the ECM. The other end is connected to the ECM, permitting it to measure the voltage output from the TPS. This output changes as the throttle valve angle is changed (accelerator pedal moves). At the closed throttle position, the output is low (approximately 0.4 volts); as the throttle valve opens, the output increases to a maximum of five volts at wide open throttle (WOT). The TPS can be misadjusted, open, shorted, or loose. If it is out of adjustment, either the idle quality or the WOT performance may be poor. A loose TPS can cause intermittent bursts of fuel from the injectors and an unstable idle because the ECM thinks the throttle is moving. This should cause a trouble code to be set. Once a trouble code is set, the ECM will use a preset value for TPS and some vehicle performance may return. A small amount of engine coolant is routed through the throttle assembly to prevent freezing inside the throttle bore during cold operation.

CHECK ENGINE LIGHTS

The check engine light on the instrument panel is used as a warning lamp to tell the driver that a problem has occurred in the electronic engine control system. When the self-diagnosis mode is activated by grounding the test terminal of the diagnostic connector, the check engine light will flash stored trouble codes to help isolate system problems. The electronic control module (ECM) has a memory that knows approximately what certain engine sensors should read out under certain conditions. If the sensor reading is not what the ECM thinks it should be, the control unit will illuminate the check engine light and store a trouble code in its memory. The trouble code indicates what circuit the problem is in, each circuit consisting of a sensor, the wiring harness and connectors to it, and the ECM.

The Assembly Line Communications Link (ALCL) is a diagnostic connector located in the passenger compartment, usually under the left side of the instrument panel. It has terminals which are used in the assembly plant to check that the engine is operating properly before shipment. Terminal **B** is the diagnostic test terminal and Terminal **A** is the ground. By connecting the two terminals together with a jumper wire, the diagnostic mode is activated and the control unit will begin to flash trouble codes using the check engine light.

NOTE: *Some models have a Service Engine Soon light instead of a Check Engine display.*

When the test terminal is grounded with the key ON and the engine stopped, the ECM will display Code 12 to show that the system is working. The ECM will usually display Code 12 three times, then start to display any stored trouble codes. If no trouble codes are stored, the ECM will continue to display Code 12 until the test terminal is disconnected. Each trouble code will be flashed three times, then Code 12 will display again. The ECM will also energize all controlled relays and solenoids when in the diagnostic mode to check function.

When the test terminal is grounded with the engine running, it will cause the ECM to enter the Field Service Mode. In this mode, the service engine soon will indicate whether the system is in Open or Closed Loop operation. In Open Loop, the light will flash 2½ times per second; in Closed Loop, the light will stay out most of the time if the system is too rich.

NOTE: *The vehicle may be driven in the Field Service mode and system evaluated at*

GM Port Injection Trouble Codes

Trouble Codes	Circuit
12	Normal operation
13	Oxygen sensor
14	Coolant sensor (low voltage)
15	Coolant sensor (high voltage)
21	Throttle position sensor (high voltage)
22	Throttle position sensor (low voltage)
24	Speed sensor
32	EGR vacuum control
33	Mass air flow sensor
34	Mass air flow sensor
42	Electronic spark timing
43	Electronic spark control
44	Lean exhaust
45	Rich exhaust
51	PROM failure

any steady road speed. This mode is useful in diagnosing driveability problems where the system is too rich or lean too long.

Trouble codes should be cleared after the service is completed. To clear the trouble code memory, disconnect the battery for at least 10 seconds. This may be accomplished by disconnecting the ECM harness from the positive battery pigtail or by removing the ECM fuse.

CAUTION: *The ignition switch must be OFF when disconnecting or reconnecting power to the ECM. The vehicle should be driven at part throttle under moderate acceleration with the engine at normal operating temperature. A change in performance should be noted initially, but normal performance should return quickly.*

Electric Fuel Pump

The port injected turbocharged V6 engines with which 1986-87 models are equipped use an electric fuel pump. This pump is located directly in the fuel tank; thus, the tank must be removed to replace the pump.

REMOVAL AND INSTALLATION

WARNING: *Do not disconnect the fuel lines at the fuel filter until the system has been* *depressurized. The fuel system retains full operating pressure after the engine is shut off due to the action of check valves. All pressure must be cleared from the system to avoid a high pressure spray. Failure to heed this warning could produce a dangerous, high pressure spray of fuel that is highly combustible. Keep all sources of ignition, including smoking, away from the area, as fuel can drain from open lines even after the system is depressurized. Keep a CO_2 type fire extinguisher nearby. You will need a pump or siphon system and a safe, closed container so that you can drain all fuel from the tank and store it safely while you work.*

1. Disconnect the power supply to the fuel pump by disconnecting the fuel tank electrical harness connector.

Now, start the engine and allow it to run until it stalls. Then, engage the starter again for at least three seconds to make sure all fuel pressure has been removed from the system. It must be possible to crank the engine for three seconds without it firing.

2. Disconnect the negative battery cable. Drain all fuel from the tank through the filler tube with a pump or siphon.

3. Raise and support the car in a secure manner (for example, on axle stands) so that there will be enough room to remove the fuel tank from underneath.

4. Support the tank from underneath (with a floorjack, if you have one), and then remove the bolts and spacers at the ends of the two supporting straps.

5. Note the location of the fuel gauge sending unit wire and carefully lower the tank without stretching that wire, just until you can reach the connection. Disconnect the wire at the sending unit. Then lower the tank and remove it.

6. Turn the cam locking ring counterclockwise to unlock it. Once it is unlocked, remove the fuel gauge sending unit/pump assembly by lifting the assembly straight upward and out of the tank.

7. Remove the pump assembly from the sending unit. Then, pull it upward and into the attaching hose as you pull it outward and and away from the bottom support; watch the rubber insulator and the strainer as you do this to keep them from being damaged.

8. When the pump is clear of the bottom support, pull it out of the rubber connector and remove it.

9. Inspect the attaching hose and rubber sound insulator for cracking or brittleness. Replace either or both if they are damaged.

10. Slide the pump assembly into the attaching hose. Then, install a new O-ring. Install the fuel gauge sending unit and pump assembly into the fuel tank.

11. Install the cam lock over the sending unit/pump assembly and turn it clockwise to lock it.

12. Install the fuel tank in reverse order of removal.

FUEL SYSTEM PRESSURE TEST

When the ignition switch is turned ON, the intank fuel pump is energized for as long as the engine is cranking or running and the control unit is receiving signals from the HEI distributor. If there are no reference pulses, the control unit will shut off the fuel pump within two seconds. The pump will deliver fuel to the fuel rail and injectors, then the pressure regulator where the system pressure is controlled to maintain 24-46 psi. The pressure is regulated down in direct relation to the manifold vacuum so that fuel metering will be directly proportional to time under all operating conditions. Thus, reading fuel pressure under various engine operating conditions can help find the source of fuel system problems.

1984-85 Models

1. Wrap a rag around the pressure tap to absorb any leakage that may occur when installing the gauge and then connect pressure gauge J-34730-1, or equivalent, to the fuel pressure test point on the fuel rail.

2. Turn the ignition ON and check that pump pressure is 34-40 psi. This pressure is controlled by spring pressure within the regulator assembly.

3. Start the engine and allow it to idle. The fuel pressure should drop to 28-32 psi due to the lower manifold pressure.

NOTE: *The fuel pressure at idle will vary*

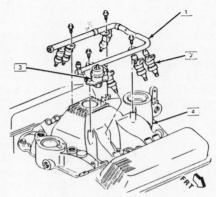

1. Fuel rail assembly
2. Injector
3. Pressure regulator
4. Intake manifold

Fuel rail and injector assembly on 3.8L V6 turbo engine

somewhat depending on barometric pressure. Check for a drop in pressure indicating regulator control, rather than specific values.

4. Use a low pressure air pump to apply air pressure to the regulator to simulate turbocharger boost pressure. Boost pressure should increase fuel pressure one pound for every pound of boost. Again, look for consistent changes rather than specific pressures. The maximum fuel pressure should not exceed 46 psi.

5. If the fuel pressure drops, check the operation of the check valve, the pump coupling connection, fuel pressure regulator valve and the injectors. A restricted fuel line or filter may also cause a pressure drop. To check the fuel pump output, restrict the fuel return line and run 12 volts to the pump. The fuel pressure should rise to approximately 75 psi with the return line restricted.

1986-87 Models

WARNING: *In many of the steps in the procedure below, it is necessary for you to disconnect fuel lines. Note that you must always depressurize the system as described above, before disconnecting these lines. Failure to do this will result in a high pressure spray of fuel which could ignite and cause a fire.*

To perform all of the steps of this test, it will be necessary to supply a source of 12-14 in.Hg of vacuum to the fuel pressure regula-

tor. A hand vacuum pump of some sort is useful in doing this; an accurate gauge and fittings needed to tee it into the vacuum line are required. You may be able to rig a vacuum line from an alternate tap on the intake manifold in place of using the vacuum pump. You will also need a length of $5/16''$ inside diameter flexible hose.

Note that fuel flows through this system as follows: It first leaves the tank and flows through the filter, then through a flexible hose and into the injector rail. It flows around the rail past all six injectors, moving past the pressure gauge test fitting and toward the fuel pressure regulator. It finally flows through the regulator and returns to the tank through the fuel return line. When the word "downstream" is used, it, of course, refers to the fuel return line side of the system.

1. Wrap a rag around the pressure tap to absorb any leakage that may occur when installing the gauge and then connect pressure gauge J-34730-1, or equivalent, to the fuel pressure test point on the fuel rail. This is located between the No. 6 injector and the pressure regulator on the injector fuel rail.

2. Make sure the ignition switch has been off for at least 10 seconds and that the air conditioning is off, if the car has it. Then, turn the ignition switch on, noting the sound of the fuel pump.

3. Verify that the pump runs for about two

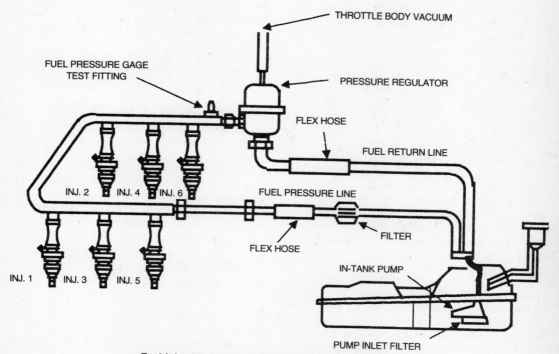

Fuel injection system circuit for 1986–87 turbo models

seconds. Then, check fuel pressure. It should be 25-35 psi. If there is some pressure but it is outside of specification, go to Step 6. If there is no pressure at all, see the procedure below for checking the fuel system wiring. Turn off the ignition switch. Note whether or not the pressure holds by watching the gauge for more than 10 seconds. If it does, proceed with the next step; if the pressure is correct but does not hold, proceed with the rest of this step:

a. Pinch the fuel supply hose closed tightly at the flex hose on the downstream (pressure regulator) side of the fuel pressure gauge test fitting.

b. Turn on (or have an assistant turn on) the ignition switch *just* until the pressure rises to specification. Then, turn it back off. Watch the pressure to see if it holds. If it drops off, check for a leaking flex coupling at the pump. Otherwise, check and, if necessary, replace the in-tank fuel pump. If the pressure does not hold, proceed with Step c.

c. Move the pinching device (or your fingers) to the flex hose on the downstream side of the fuel pressure regulator. Then, repeat the application of power to the fuel pump by turning on the ignition switch for a few seconds, and then turning it back off after the pump stops.

d. If the pressure holds now, replace the pressure regulator assembly. If not, remove the spark plugs to check for a flooded cylinder. If the cylinder is flooding, the plugs will show evidence of dry, soft, black soot in most cases. If the engine has been cranked a great deal recently, there may actually be a smell of raw fuel on the plug. If the cylinder has been flooding, this will be due to a leaking injector. Replace that cylinder's injector unit.

e. If the problem is not due to a leaking injector, check for small but visible leaks in the injector pipe, connections, or flexible hoses and repair as necessary.

4. Start the engine and allow it to idle. If necessary, run it until it warms up; this test must be done with the engine at normal operating temperature. With the engine idling and at operating temperature (so that warm coolant is flowing through the radiator), read the fuel pressure. It should be 25-35 psi. If the system meets this specification, search for trouble in areas other than fuel pump and pressure regulator performance.

5. If the pressure is outside this range, continue running the test and disconnect the vacuum hose from the fuel pressure regulator. Supply a vacuum of 12-14 in.Hg to the vacuum connection on the regulator. The fuel pressure should be 24-35 psi. If it is now within the specified range, locate and correct the cause of insufficient vacuum to the regulator. This might be a broken connection, cracked or soft line that pinches closed under high vacuum, or a clogged line or connection. If the fuel pressure is still incorrect, replace the pressure regulator.

6. This Step is for fuel pressure that is too low; if pressure is too high, go to Step 8. Depressurize the system, remove the fuel filter and tilt it to drain the intake (tank) side into a metal container. Check for the presence of water and dirt. If there is evidence of more than a minimal amount of either, install a new filter and recheck the pressures.

7. Pinch the fuel return line downstream of the pressure regulator to close it off tightly. Then, turn on the ignition switch until the pressure stabilizes and read the pressure gauge. Pressure should be above 75 psi. If it is, check for a restricted pressure line or flexible hose in the line somewhere between the tank and the test gauge. If all the lines are okay, replace the pressure regulator. If the pressure is below 75 psi, check the hose coupling the tank to the pressure line and, if that's okay, replace the pump, which must be faulty or of incorrect specification.

8. Depressurize the system and then disconnect the flexible hose from the return line. Attach the $5/16''$ inside diameter flexible hose to the return line connection on the pressure regulator. Insert the downstream end into a metal container. Turn the ignition switch on for just two seconds and read the fuel pressure. It should be 37-43 psi. If it is, you will have to clean or repair the return line to the tank to remove an obstruction. If it is not, replace the fuel pressure regulator.

CAUTION: *Before attempting to remove or service any fuel system component, it is necessary to relieve the fuel system pressure.*

RELIEVING FUEL SYSTEM PRESSURE

1. Remove the fuel pump fuse from the fuse block or disconnect the harness connector at the tank.

2. Start the engine. It should run and then stall when the fuel in the lines is exhausted. When the engine stops, crank the starter for about three seconds to make sure all pressure in the fuel lines is released.

3. Replace the fuel pump fuse.

Throttle Body
REMOVAL AND INSTALLATION

1. Disconnect the air inlet duct. Disconnect the electrical connectors for the Idle Air Control valve and the Throttle Position Sensor.

2. Label and then disconnect the vacuum lines.

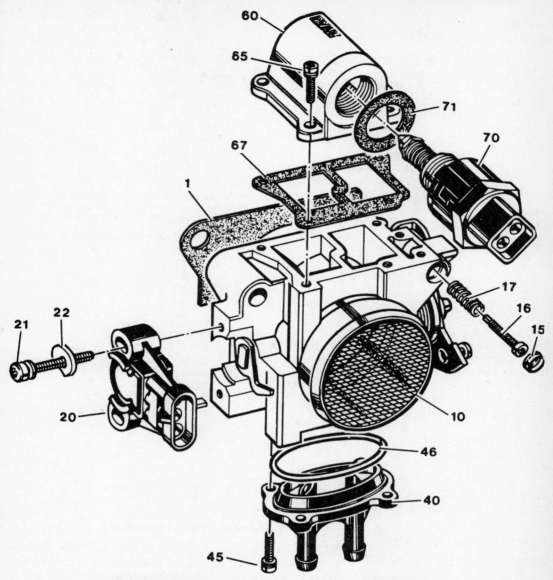

The throttle body used with the Multi-port system on the 3.8L Turbo

3. With the engine cool, drain coolant from the bottom of the radiator until the level is below the bottom of the top tank. Then, unclamp and disconnect the coolant hoses at the throttle body.

4. Disconnect the throttle, automatic transmission Throttle Valve, and Cruise Control cables at the throttle body, depending upon the car's equipment.

5. Remove the bolts fastening the throttle body assembly to the intake manifold flange and remove the throttle body.

6. Remove the flange gasket and clean both surfaces with a dull tool.

7. Install a new flange gasket, put the throt-

tle body into position, and install the retaining bolts. Torque them evenly to 11 ft.lb.

8. Connect the throttle, transmission TV and cruise control cables.

9. Reconnect and securely clamp the two coolant hoses.

10. Reconnect the vacuum lines according to the markings. Reconnect the air inlet duct so as to avoid leakage.

11. Refill the radiator with fresh coolant. Start the engine and check for vacuum or water leaks. After coolant begins to circulate through the radiator, shut the engine off, allow it to cool, and then check the coolant level again, replenishing as necessary.

Fuel Injectors
REMOVAL AND INSTALLATION

Use care in removing the fuel injectors to prevent damage to the electrical connector pins on the injector and the nozzle. The fuel injector is serviced as a complete assembly only and should never be immersed in any kind of cleaner. The injectors are sealed at either end by interchangeable O-rings. Replace these whenever injectors are remove and replaced.

CAUTION: *Work with the engine cool, avoiding any sources of ignition, to prevent any chance of fire because small amounts of fuel may be spilled when pressure regulator and injector connections are broken. Make sure not to start the engine until an spilled fuel has been safely removed or has thoroughly evaporated.*

1. Relieve fuel system pressure as described above.

2. Disconnect the injector electrical connections. Disconnect the pressure line to the fuel rail. Disconnect the vacuum and fuel return line connections to the fuel pressure regulator.

3. Remove the fuel rail mounting bolts. Remove the fuel rail by carefully pulling it straight upward so the injectors will be pulled out of the manifold as straight as possible. Drain fuel from the rail and into a metal container.

4. Remove the injector clips, if they are used. Separate each injector from the fuel rail by carefully pulling it straight out of the rail connection.

5. Installation is the reverse of removal. Replace all the O-rings, coating each with engine oil first to ensure damage-free installation.

Fuel Pressure Regulator
REMOVAL AND INSTALLATION

1. Relieve fuel system pressure.

2. Unclamp and disconnect the fuel connectors and vacuum line. Remove the presure regulator from the fuel rail. Place a rag around the base of the regulator to catch any spilled fuel.

3. Installation is the reverse of removal.

Idle Air Control Valve
REMOVAL AND INSTALLATION

1. Remove electrical connector from the idle air control valve.

2. Remove the idle air control valve using a suitable wrench. The wrench must be 32mm or 1¼" in size.

3. Installation is the reverse of removal. Before installing the idle air control valve, measure the distance that the valve is extended. Measurement should be made from the motor

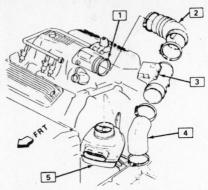

1. Throttle body assembly
2. Rear air intake duct
3. Mass air flow sensor
4. Intake air duct
5. Air cleaner assembly

Mass air flow (MAF) sensor assembly—V6 3.8L

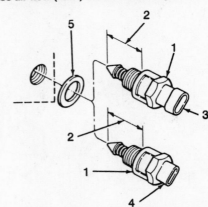

1. Idle air control valve
2. Less than 1⅛ inch (28 mm)
3. Type 1 (with collar)
4. Type 2 (without collar)
5. Gasket

Idle air control valve installation

housing to the end of the cone. The distance should not exceed 1⅛", or damage to the valve may occur when it is installed. Use a new gasket and turn the ignition on then off again to allow the ECM to reset the idle air control valve.

NOTE: *Identify replacement IAC valve as being either Type 1 (with collar at electric terminal end) or Type 2 (without collar). If measuring distance is greater than specified above, proceed as follows:*
Type 1: Press on valve firmly to retract it.
Type 2: Compress retaining spring from valve while turning valve in with a clockwise motion. Return spring to original position of spring end aligned with flat surface of valve.

Throttle Position Sensor
REMOVAL AND INSTALLATION

1. Disconnect the electrical connector from the sensor.

2. Remove the attaching screws, lockwashers and retainers.

3. Remove the throttle position sensor. If necessary, remove the screw holding the actuator to the end of the throttle shaft.

4. With the throttle valve in the normal closed idle position, install the throttle position sensor on the throttle body assembly, making sure the sensor pickup lever is located above the tang on the throttle actuator lever.

5. Install the retainers, screws and lockwashers using a thread locking compound. DO NOT tighten the screws until the throttle position switch is adjusted.

6. Install three jumper wires between the throttle position switch and the harness connector.

7. With the ignition switch ON, use a digital voltmeter connected to terminals **B** and **C** and adjust the switch to obtain 0.35-0.45volts.

8. Tighten the mounting screws, then recheck the reading to insure that the adjustment hasn't changed.

9. Turn ignition OFF, remove jumper wires, then reconnect harness to throttle position switch.

Electronic Control Module (ECM)
REMOVAL AND INSTALLATION

The electronic control module (ECM) is located under the instrument panel. To allow one basic type of ECM to be used on different car models, a device called a calibrator or PROM (Programmable Read Only Memory) is installed inside the ECM. The PROM contains information on the vehicle weight, engine, transmission, axle ratio, etc. The PROM is specific to the exact model and replacement part numbers must be checked carefully to make sure the correct PROM is being installed during service. Replacement ECM units (called Controllers) are supplied WITHOUT a PROM. The PROM from the old ECM must be carefully removed and installed in the replacement unit during service. Another device called a CALPAK is used to allow fuel delivery if other parts of the ECM are damaged (the "limp home" mode). The CALPAK is similar in appearance to the PROM and is located in the same place in the ECM, under the access cover. Like the PROM, the CALPAK must be removed and transferred to the new ECM unit being installed.
NOTE: *If the diagnosis indicates a faulty ECM unit, the PROM should be checked to see if they are the correct parts. Trouble code 51 indicates that the PROM is installed incorrectly. When the replacing the production ECM with a new part, it is important to transfer the Broadcast code and production ECM*

number to the new part label. Do not record on the ECM cover.
CAUTION: *The ignition must be OFF whenever disconnecting or connecting the ECM electrical harness. It is possible to install a PROM backwards during service. Exercise care when replacing the PROM that it is installed correctly, or the PROM will be destroyed when the ignition is switched ON.*
To remove the ECM, first disconnect the battery. Remove the wiring harness and mounting hardware, then remove the ECM from the passenger compartment. The PROM and CALPAK are located under the access cover on the top of the control unit. Using the rocker type PROM removal tool, or equivalent, engage one end of the PROM carrier with the hook end of the tool. Press on the vertical bar end of the tool and rock the engaged end of the PROM carrier up as far as possible. Engage the opposite end of the PROM carrier in the same manner and rock this end up as far as possible. Repeat this process until the PROM carrier and PROM are free of the socket. The PROM carrier should only be removed with the removal tool or damage to the PROM or PROM socket may occur.

DIESEL ENGINE FUEL SYSTEM

Fuel Supply Pump
REMOVAL AND INSTALLATION

The fuel supply pump is serviced in the same manner as the fuel pump on the gasoline engine.

Fuel Filter
REMOVAL AND INSTALLATION

The fuel filter is a square assembly located at the back of the engine above the intake manifold. Disconnect the fuel lines and remove the filter. Install the lines to the new filter. Start the engine and check for leaks.

Fuel Injection Pump
REMOVAL AND INSTALLATION

NOTE: *Diesel injection pump repair or overhaul work requires extremely expensive test equipment, and clean room work conditions, and is a highly specialized field. You may find that you can remove the injection pump from your diesel and have it repaired or overhauled and tested by a diesel specialist, or you may find it worthwhile to exchange it for a quality rebuilt injection pump.*
1. Remove the air cleaner.
2. Remove the filters and pipes from the valve covers and air crossover.

3. Remove the air crossover and cap and intake manifold with screened covers (tool J-26996-1).

4. Disconnect the throttle rod and return spring.

5. Remove the bellcrank.

6. Remove the throttle and transmission cables from the intake manifold brackets.

7. Disconnect the fuel line from the filter and remove the filter.

8. Disconnect the fuel inlet line at the pump.

9. Remove the rear A/C compressor brace and remove the fuel line.

10. Disconnect the fuel return line from the injection pump.

11. Remove the clamps and pull the fuel return lines from each injection nozzle.

12. Using two wrenches, disconnect the high pressure lines at the nozzles.

13. Remove the three injection pump retaining nuts with tool J-26987 or its equivalent.

14. Remove the pump and cap all lines and nozzles.

To install:

15. Remove the protective caps.

16. Line up the offset tang on the pump driveshaft with the pump driven gear and install the pump.

17. Install, but do not tighten the pump retaining nuts.

18. Connect the high pressure lines at the nozzles.

19. Using two wrenches, torque the high pressure line nuts to 25 ft.lb.

20. Connect the fuel return lines to the nozzles and pump.

21. Align the timing mark on the injection pump with the line on the timing mark adaptor and torque the mounting nuts to 35 ft.lb.

NOTE: *A ¾" open end wrench on the boss at the front of the injection pump will aid in rotating the pump to align the marks.*

22. Adjust the throttle rod as follows:

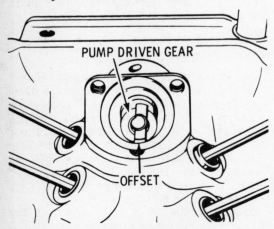

Offset on the pump driven gear

PUMP DRIVEN GEAR

OFFSET

a. Remove the clip from the cruise control rod and remove the rod from the bellcrank.

b. Loosen the locknut on the throttle rod a few turns, then shorten the rod several.

c. Rotate the bellcrank to the full throttle stop, then lengthen the throttle rod until the injection pump lever contacts the injection pump full throttle stop, the release the bellcrank.

d. Tighten the throttle rod locknut.

23. Install the fuel inlet line between the transfer pump and the filter.

24. Install the rear A/C compressor brace.

25. Install the bellcrank and clip.

26. Connect the throttle rod and return spring.

27. Adjust the transmission cable as follows:

a. Push the snap-lock to the disengaged position.

b. Rotate the injection pump lever to the full throttle stop and hold it there.

c. Push in the snap-lock until it is flush.

d. Release the injection pump lever.

28. Start the engine and check for fuel leaks.

29. Remove the screened covers and install the air crossover.

30. Install the tubes in the air flow control valve in the air crossover and install the ventilation filters in the valve covers.

31. Install the air cleaner.

32. Start the engine and allow it to run for two minutes. Stop the engine, let it stand for two minutes, then restart. This permits the air to bleed off within the pump.

SLOW IDLE SPEED ADJUSTMENT

NOTE: *To make this adjustment, you will need a special magnetic pickup type tachometer to measure the rpm. Since the diesel has no ignition system, a magnetic signal generator is incorporated in the injection pump drive; the special tachometer reads rpm off this.*

1. Run the engine until it reaches normal operating temperature.

2. Insert the probe of a magnetic pickup tachometer into the timing indicator hole.

3. Set the parking brake and block the drive wheels.

4. Place the transmission in Drive and turn the A/C Off.

5. Turn the slow idle screw on the injection pump to obtain the idle specification on the emission control label.

Fast Idle Solenoid

ADJUSTMENT

1978-79

1. Set the parking brake and block the drive wheels.

CHILTON'S
FUEL ECONOMY
& TUNE-UP TIPS

Tune-up • Spark Plug Diagnosis • Emission Controls

Fuel System • Cooling System • Tires and Wheels

General Maintenance

55 WAYS TO IMPROVE FUEL ECONOMY

CHILTON'S FUEL ECONOMY & TUNE-UP TIPS

Fuel economy is important to everyone, no matter what kind of vehicle you drive. The maintenance-minded motorist can save both money and fuel using these tips and the periodic maintenance and tune-up procedures in this Repair and Tune-Up Guide.

There are more than 130,000,000 cars and trucks registered for private use in the United States. Each travels an average of 10-12,000 miles per year, and, and in total they consume close to 70 billion gallons of fuel each year. This represents nearly ⅔ of the oil imported by the United States each year. The Federal government's goal is to reduce consumption 10% by 1985. A variety of methods are either already in use or under serious consideration, and they all affect you driving and the cars you will drive. In addition to "down-sizing", the auto industry is using or investigating the use of electronic fuel

delivery, electronic engine controls and alternative engines for use in smaller and lighter vehicles, among other alternatives to meet the federally mandated Corporate Average Fuel Economy (CAFE) of 27.5 mpg by 1985. The government, for its part, is considering rationing, mandatory driving curtailments and tax increases on motor vehicle fuel in an effort to reduce consumption. The government's goal of a 10% reduction could be realized — and further government regulation avoided — if every private vehicle could use just 1 less gallon of fuel per week.

How Much Can You Save?

Tests have proven that almost anyone can make at least a 10% reduction in fuel consumption through regular maintenance and tune-ups. When a major manufacturer of spark plugs sur-

TUNE-UP

1. Check the cylinder compression to be sure the engine will really benefit from a tune-up and that it is capable of producing good fuel economy. A tune-up will be wasted on an engine in poor mechanical condition.

2. Replace spark plugs regularly. New spark plugs alone can increase fuel economy 3%.

3. Be sure the spark plugs are the correct type (heat range) for your vehicle. See the Tune-Up Specifications.

Heat range refers to the spark plug's ability to conduct heat away from the firing end. It must conduct the heat away in an even pattern to avoid becoming a source of pre-ignition, yet it must also operate hot enough to burn off conductive deposits that could cause misfiring.

The heat range is usually indicated by a number on the spark plug, part of the manufacturer's designation for each individual spark plug. The numbers in bold-face indicate the heat range in each manufacturer's identification system.

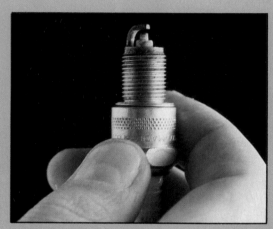

Periodically, check the spark plugs to be sure they are firing efficiently. They are excellent indicators of the internal condition of your engine.

On AC, Bosch (new), Champion, Fram/Autolite, Mopar, Motorcraft and Prestolite, a higher number indicates a hotter plug. On Bosch (old), NGK and Nippondenso, a higher number indicates a colder plug.

4. Make sure the spark plugs are properly gapped. See the Tune-Up Specifications in this book.

5. Be sure the spark plugs are firing efficiently. The illustrations on the next 2 pages show you how to "read" the firing end of the spark plug.

6. Check the ignition timing and set it to specifications. Tests show that almost all cars have incorrect ignition timing by more than 2°.

Manufacturer	Typical Designation
AC	R **45** TS
Bosch (old)	WA **145** T30
Bosch (new)	HR **8** Y
Champion	RBL **15** Y
Fram/Autolite	4**15**
Mopar	P-**62** PR
Motorcraft	BRF-**42**
NGK	BP **5** ES-15
Nippondenso	W **16** EP
Prestolite	14GR **5** 2A

veyed over 6,000 cars nationwide, they found that a tune-up, on cars that needed one, increased fuel economy over 11%. Replacing worn plugs alone, accounted for a 3% increase. The same test also revealed that 8 out of every 10 vehicles will have some maintenance deficiency that will directly affect fuel economy, emissions or performance. Most of this mileage-robbing neglect could be prevented with regular maintenance.

Modern engines require that all of the functioning systems operate properly for maximum efficiency. A malfunction anywhere wastes fuel. You can keep your vehicle running as efficiently and economically as possible, by being aware of your vehicle's operating and performance characteristics. If your vehicle suddenly develops performance or fuel economy problems it could be due to one or more of the following:

PROBLEM	POSSIBLE CAUSE
Engine Idles Rough	Ignition timing, idle mixture, vacuum leak or something amiss in the emission control system.
Hesitates on Acceleration	Dirty carburetor or fuel filter, improper accelerator pump setting, ignition timing or fouled spark plugs.
Starts Hard or Fails to Start	Worn spark plugs, improperly set automatic choke, ice (or water) in fuel system.
Stalls Frequently	Automatic choke improperly adjusted and possible dirty air filter or fuel filter.
Performs Sluggishly	Worn spark plugs, dirty fuel or air filter, ignition timing or automatic choke out of adjustment.

Check spark plug wires on conventional point type ignition for cracks by bending them in a loop around your finger.

Be sure that spark plug wires leading to adjacent cylinders do not run too close together. (Photo courtesy Champion Spark Plug Co.)

7. If your vehicle does not have electronic ignition, check the points, rotor and cap as specified.

8. Check the spark plug wires (used with conventional point-type ignitions) for cracks and burned or broken insulation by bending them in a loop around your finger. Cracked wires decrease fuel efficiency by failing to deliver full voltage to the spark plugs. One misfiring spark plug can cost you as much as 2 mpg.

9. Check the routing of the plug wires. Misfiring can be the result of spark plug leads to adjacent cylinders running parallel to each other and too close together. One wire tends to pick up voltage from the other causing it to fire "out of time".

10. Check all electrical and ignition circuits for voltage drop and resistance.

11. Check the distributor mechanical and/or vacuum advance mechanisms for proper functioning. The vacuum advance can be checked by twisting the distributor plate in the opposite direction of rotation. It should spring back when released.

12. Check and adjust the valve clearance on engines with mechanical lifters. The clearance should be slightly loose rather than too tight.

SPARK PLUG DIAGNOSIS

Normal

APPEARANCE: This plug is typical of one operating normally. The insulator nose varies from a light tan to grayish color with slight electrode wear. The presence of slight deposits is normal on used plugs and will have no adverse effect on engine performance. The spark plug heat range is correct for the engine and the engine is running normally.

CAUSE: Properly running engine.

RECOMMENDATION: Before reinstalling this plug, the electrodes should be cleaned and filed square. Set the gap to specifications. If the plug has been in service for more than 10-12,000 miles, the entire set should probably be replaced with a fresh set of the same heat range.

Oil Deposits

APPEARANCE: The firing end of the plug is covered with a wet, oily coating.

CAUSE: The problem is poor oil control. On high mileage engines, oil is leaking past the rings or valve guides into the combustion chamber. A common cause is also a plugged PCV valve, and a ruptured fuel pump diaphragm can also cause this condition. Oil fouled plugs such as these are often found in new or recently overhauled engines, before normal oil control is achieved, and can be cleaned and reinstalled.

RECOMMENDATION: A hotter spark plug may temporarily relieve the problem, but the engine is probably in need of work.

Incorrect Heat Range

APPEARANCE: The effects of high temperature on a spark plug are indicated by clean white, often blistered insulator. This can also be accompanied by excessive wear of the electrode, and the absence of deposits.

CAUSE: Check for the correct spark plug heat range. A plug which is too hot for the engine can result in overheating. A car operated mostly at high speeds can require a colder plug. Also check ignition timing, cooling system level, fuel mixture and leaking intake manifold.

RECOMMENDATION: If all ignition and engine adjustments are known to be correct, and no other malfunction exists, install spark plugs one heat range colder.

Photos Courtesy Fram Corporation

Carbon Deposits

APPEARANCE: Carbon fouling is easily identified by the presence of dry, soft, black, sooty deposits.

CAUSE: Changing the heat range can often lead to carbon fouling, as can prolonged slow, stop-and-start driving. If the heat range is correct, carbon fouling can be attributed to a rich fuel mixture, sticking choke, clogged air cleaner, worn breaker points, retarded timing or low compression. If only one or two plugs are carbon fouled, check for corroded or cracked wires on the affected plugs. Also look for cracks in the distributor cap between the towers of affected cylinders.

RECOMMENDATION: After the problem is corrected, these plugs can be cleaned and reinstalled if not worn severely.

MMT Fouled

APPEARANCE: Spark plugs fouled by MMT (Methycyclopentadienyl Maganese Tricarbonyl) have reddish, rusty appearance on the insulator and side electrode.

CAUSE: MMT is an anti-knock additive in gasoline used to replace lead. During the combustion process, the MMT leaves a reddish deposit on the insulator and side electrode.

RECOMMENDATION: No engine malfunction is indicated and the deposits will not affect plug performance any more than lead deposits (see Ash Deposits). MMT fouled plugs can be cleaned, regapped and reinstalled.

High Speed Glazing

APPEARANCE: Glazing appears as shiny coating on the plug, either yellow or tan in color.

CAUSE: During hard, fast acceleration, plug temperatures rise suddenly. Deposits from normal combustion have no chance to fluff-off; instead, they melt on the insulator forming an electrically conductive coating which causes misfiring.

RECOMMENDATION: Glazed plugs are not easily cleaned. They should be replaced with a fresh set of plugs of the correct heat range. If the condition recurs, using plugs with a heat range one step colder may cure the problem.

Ash (Lead) Deposits

APPEARANCE: Ash deposits are characterized by light brown or white colored deposits crusted on the side or center electrodes. In some cases it may give the plug a rusty appearance.

CAUSE: Ash deposits are normally derived from oil or fuel additives burned during normal combustion. Normally they are harmless, though excessive amounts can cause misfiring. If deposits are excessive in short mileage, the valve guides may be worn.

RECOMMENDATION: Ash-fouled plugs can be cleaned, gapped and reinstalled.

Detonation

APPEARANCE: Detonation is usually characterized by a broken plug insulator.

CAUSE: A portion of the fuel charge will begin to burn spontaneously, from the increased heat following ignition. The explosion that results applies extreme pressure to engine components, frequently damaging spark plugs and pistons.

Detonation can result by over-advanced ignition timing, inferior gasoline (low octane) lean air/fuel mixture, poor carburetion, engine lugging or an increase in compression ratio due to combustion chamber deposits or engine modification.

RECOMMENDATION: Replace the plugs after correcting the problem.

Photos Courtesy Champion Spark Plug Co.

EMISSION CONTROLS

13. Be aware of the general condition of the emission control system. It contributes to reduced pollution and should be serviced regularly to maintain efficient engine operation.

14. Check all vacuum lines for dried, cracked or brittle conditions. Something as simple as a leaking vacuum hose can cause poor performance and loss of economy.

15. Avoid tampering with the emission control system. Attempting to improve fuel econ-

FUEL SYSTEM

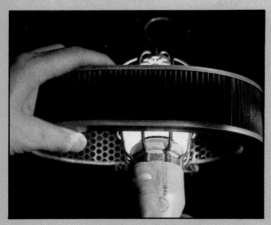

Check the air filter with a light behind it. If you can see light through the filter it can be reused.

Extremely clogged filters should be discarded and replaced with a new one.

18. Replace the air filter regularly. A dirty air filter richens the air/fuel mixture and can increase fuel consumption as much as 10%. Tests show that ⅓ of all vehicles have air filters in need of replacement.

19. Replace the fuel filter at least as often as recommended.

20. Set the idle speed and carburetor mixture to specifications.

21. Check the automatic choke. A sticking or malfunctioning choke wastes gas.

22. During the summer months, adjust the automatic choke for a leaner mixture which will produce faster engine warm-ups.

COOLING SYSTEM

29. Be sure all accessory drive belts are in good condition. Check for cracks or wear.

30. Adjust all accessory drive belts to proper tension.

31. Check all hoses for swollen areas, worn spots, or loose clamps.

32. Check coolant level in the radiator or expansion tank.

33. Be sure the thermostat is operating properly. A stuck thermostat delays engine warm-up and a cold engine uses nearly twice as much fuel as a warm engine.

34. Drain and replace the engine coolant at least as often as recommended. Rust and scale

TIRES & WHEELS

38. Check the tire pressure often with a pencil type gauge. Tests by a major tire manufacturer show that 90% of all vehicles have at least 1 tire improperly inflated. Better mileage can be achieved by over-inflating tires, but never exceed the maximum inflation pressure on the side of the tire.

39. If possible, install radial tires. Radial tires deliver as much as ½ mpg more than bias belted tires.

40. Avoid installing super-wide tires. They only create extra rolling resistance and decrease fuel mileage. Stick to the manufacturer's recommendations.

41. Have the wheels properly balanced.

omy by tampering with emission controls is more likely to worsen fuel economy than improve it. Emission control changes on modern engines are not readily reversible.

16. Clean (or replace) the EGR valve and lines as recommended.

17. Be sure that all vacuum lines and hoses are reconnected properly after working under the hood. An unconnected or misrouted vacuum line can wreak havoc with engine performance.

23. Check for fuel leaks at the carburetor, fuel pump, fuel lines and fuel tank. Be sure all lines and connections are tight.

24. Periodically check the tightness of the carburetor and intake manifold attaching nuts and bolts. These are a common place for vacuum leaks to occur.

25. Clean the carburetor periodically and lubricate the linkage.

26. The condition of the tailpipe can be an excellent indicator of proper engine combustion. After a long drive at highway speeds, the inside of the tailpipe should be a light grey in color. Black or soot on the insides indicates an overly rich mixture.

27. Check the fuel pump pressure. The fuel pump may be supplying more fuel than the engine needs.

28. Use the proper grade of gasoline for your engine. Don't try to compensate for knocking or "pinging" by advancing the ignition timing. This practice will only increase plug temperature and the chances of detonation or pre-ignition with relatively little performance gain.

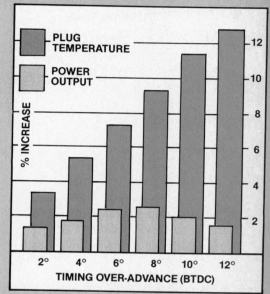

Increasing ignition timing past the specified setting results in a drastic increase in spark plug temperature with increased chance of detonation or preignition. Performance increase is considerably less. (Photo courtesy Champion Spark Plug Co.)

that form in the engine should be flushed out to allow the engine to operate at peak efficiency.

35. Clean the radiator of debris that can decrease cooling efficiency.

36. Install a flex-type or electric cooling fan, if you don't have a clutch type fan. Flex fans use curved plastic blades to push more air at low speeds when more cooling is needed; at high speeds the blades flatten out for less resistance. Electric fans only run when the engine temperature reaches a predetermined level.

37. Check the radiator cap for a worn or cracked gasket. If the cap does not seal properly, the cooling system will not function properly.

42. Be sure the front end is correctly aligned. A misaligned front end actually has wheels going in differed directions. The increased drag can reduce fuel economy by .3 mpg.

43. Correctly adjust the wheel bearings. Wheel bearings that are adjusted too tight increase rolling resistance.

Check tire pressures regularly with a reliable pocket type gauge. Be sure to check the pressure on a cold tire.

GENERAL MAINTENANCE

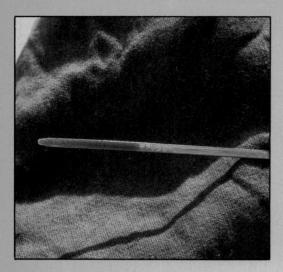

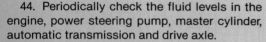

Check the fluid levels (particularly engine oil) on a regular basis. Be sure to check the oil for grit, water or other contamination.

A vacuum gauge is another excellent indicator of internal engine condition and can also be installed in the dash as a mileage indicator.

44. Periodically check the fluid levels in the engine, power steering pump, master cylinder, automatic transmission and drive axle.

45. Change the oil at the recommended interval and change the filter at every oil change. Dirty oil is thick and causes extra friction between moving parts, cutting efficiency and increasing wear. A worn engine requires more frequent tune-ups and gets progressively worse fuel economy. In general, use the lightest viscosity oil for the driving conditions you will encounter.

46. Use the recommended viscosity fluids in the transmission and axle.

47. Be sure the battery is fully charged for fast starts. A slow starting engine wastes fuel.

48. Be sure battery terminals are clean and tight.

49. Check the battery electrolyte level and add distilled water if necessary.

50. Check the exhaust system for crushed pipes, blockages and leaks.

51. Adjust the brakes. Dragging brakes or brakes that are not releasing create increased drag on the engine.

52. Install a vacuum gauge or miles-per-gallon gauge. These gauges visually indicate engine vacuum in the intake manifold. High vacuum = good mileage and low vacuum = poorer mileage. The gauge can also be an excellent indicator of internal engine conditions.

53. Be sure the clutch is properly adjusted. A slipping clutch wastes fuel.

54. Check and periodically lubricate the heat control valve in the exhaust manifold. A sticking or inoperative valve prevents engine warm-up and wastes gas.

55. Keep accurate records to check fuel economy over a period of time. A sudden drop in fuel economy may signal a need for tune-up or other maintenance.

2. Run the engine to normal operating temperature.

3. Place the transmission in Drive and disconnect the compressor clutch wire. Turn the A/C On. On cars without A/C, disconnect the solenoid wire, and connect jumper wires to the solenoid terminals. Ground one of the wires and connect the other to a 12 volt battery to activate the solenoid.

4. Adjust the fast idle solenoid plunger to obtain 650 rpm.

1980 AND LATER

1. With the ignition off, disconnect the single green wire from the fast idle relay located on the front of the firewall.

2. Set the parking brake and block the drive wheels.

3. Start the engine and adjust the solenoid (energized) to the specifications on the underhood emission control label.

4. Turn off the engine and reconnect the green wire.

Cruise Control Servo Relay Rod
ADJUSTMENT

1. Turn the engine Off.

2. Adjust the rod to minimum slack then put the clip in the first free hole closest to the bellcrank, but within the servo ball.

Injection Timing
ADJUSTMENT

For the engine to be properly timed, the lines on the top of the injection pump adapter and the flange of the injection pump must be aligned.

1. The engine must be off for resetting the timing.

2. Loosen the three pump retaining nuts with J-26987 on V8's or J-25304 on V6's, an injection pump intake manifold wrench, or its equivalent.

3. Align the timing marks and torque the pump retaining nuts to 35 ft.lb.

NOTE: *The use of a ¾" open end wrench on the boss at the front of the pump will aid in rotating the pump to align the marks.*

4. Adjust the throttle rod. (See Fuel Injection Pump Removal and Installation, Step 22.)

Injection Nozzle
REMOVAL AND INSTALLATION
1978-79

1. Remove the fuel return line from the nozzle.

2. Remove the nozzle holddown clamp and spacer using tool J-26952.

3. Cap the high pressure line and nozzle tip.

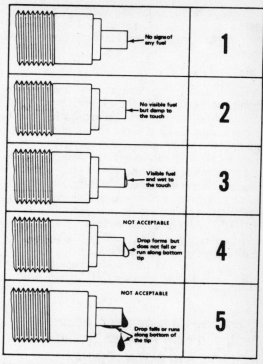

Injection nozzle seat tightness check

NOTE: *The nozzle tip is highly susceptible to damage and must be protected at all times.*

4. If an old nozzle is to be reinstalled, a new compression seal and carbon stop seal must be installed after removal of the used seals.

**INLET FITTING TO BODY TORQUE
DIESEL EQUIPMENT — 45 FT. LBS. (60 N·m)
C.A.V. LUCAS — 25 FT. LBS. (34 N·m)**

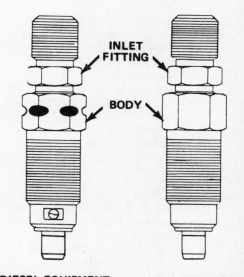

DIESEL EQUIPMENT   C.A.V. LUCAS

Injection nozzles

5. Remove the caps and install the nozzle, spacer and clamp. Torque to 25 ft.lb.

6. Replace return line, start the engine and check for leaks.

1980 and Later

The injection nozzles on these engines are simply screwed out of the cylinder head, after the fuel lines are removed, in similar fashion to a spark plug. Be careful not to damage the nozzle end and make sure you remove the copper nozzle gasket from the cylinder head if it does not come off with the nozzle.

Clean the carbon off the tip of the nozzle with a soft brass wire brush and install the nozzles, with new copper gaskets.

NOTE: *1981 and later models use two different types of injectors, CAV Lucas and Diesel Equipment. When installing the inlet fittings, torque the Diesel Equipment injector fitting to 45 ft.lb. and the CAV Lucas fitting to 25 ft.lb.*

Injection Pump Adapter, Adapter Seal, and New Adapter Timing Mark
REMOVAL AND INSTALLATION

NOTE: *Skip steps 4 and 9 if a new adapter is not being installed.*

1. Remove injection pump and lines as described earlier.

2. Remove the injection pump adapter.

3. Remove the seal from the adapter.

4. File the timing mark from the adapter. Do not file the mark off the pump.

5. Position the engine at TDC of No. 1 cylinder. Align the mark on the balancer with the zero mark on the indicator. The index is offset to the right when No. 1 is at TDC.

6. Apply chassis lube to the seal areas. Install, but do not tighten the injection pump.

7. Install the new seal on the adapter using tool J-28425, or its equivalent.

8. Torque the adapter bolts to 25 ft.lb.

9. Install timing tool J-26896 into the injection pump adapter. Torque the tool, toward No. 1 cylinder, to 50 ft.lb. Mark the injection pump adapter. Remove the tool.

10. Install the injection pump.

Glow Plugs

There are two types of glow plugs used on General Motors Corp. diesels; the fast glow type and the slow glow type. The fast glow type use pulsing current applied to 6 volt glow plugs while the slow glow type use continuous current applied to 12 volt glow plugs.

An easy way to tell the plugs apart is that the fast glow (6 volt) plugs have a $\frac{5}{16}$" wide electri-

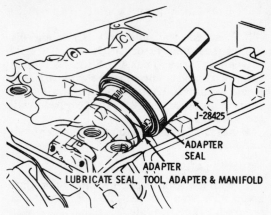

Installing the adapter seal

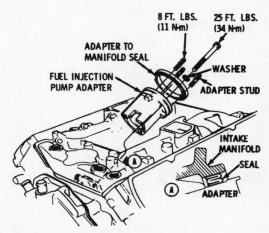

Injection pump adapter bolts

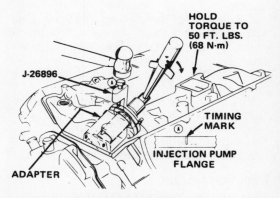

Marking the injection pump adapter

cal connector plug while the slow glow (12 volt) connector plug is ¼" wide. Do not attempt to interchange any parts of these two glow plug systems.

FUEL TANK

DRAINING

1. Remove the fuel tank cap.

2. Connect a siphon pump to the ¼" fuel return hose (the smaller of the two hoses) above the rear axle, or under the hood near the fuel pump on the passenger's side of the engine, near the front.

3. Operate the siphon pump until all fuel is removed from the fuel tank. Be sure to reinstall the fuel return hose and the fuel cap.

REMOVAL AND INSTALLATION

1975-77

1. Siphon the fuel from the tank as there is no drain plug.

2. Disconnect the fuel gauge sending unit wire from the rear wiring harness connector. On sedans, push the grommet out and work the gauge wire through the trunk floor hole.

3. Raise the car to a convenient working height.

4. Remove the fuel gauge wire screw from the underbody.

5. Disconnect the fuel line at the sending unit pickup line.

6. Remove the vent hoses.

7. Remove the strap retaining bolts, lower the support straps, and carefully drop the tank out of the car.

8. Reverse the removal steps to install the fuel tank.

1978 and Later

1. Siphon the fuel from the tank, as there is no drain plug.

2. Disconnect the fuel gauge sending unit wire from the rear wiring harness connector. Push the grommet out and work the gauge wire through the trunk floor hole.

3. Raise the car to a convenient working height.

4. Remove the fuel gauge ground wire screw from the underbody.

5. Disconnect the fuel line at the sending unit pickup line.

6. Remove the vent hoses.

7. Remove the strap retaining bolts, lower the support straps, and carefully lower the tank out of the car.

8. Reverse the removal steps to install the fuel tank.

Chassis Electrical

UNDERSTANDING AND TROUBLESHOOTING ELECTRICAL SYSTEMS

At the rate which both import and domestic manufacturers are incorporating electronic control systems into their production lines, it won't be long before every new vehicle is equipped with one or more on-board computer, like the EEC-IV unit installed on the truck. These electronic components (with no moving parts) should theoretically last the life of the vehicle, provided nothing external happens to damage the circuits or memory chips.

While it is true that electronic components should never wear out, in the real world malfunctions do occur. It is also true that any computer-based system is extremely sensitive to electrical voltages and cannot tolerate careless or haphazard testing or service procedures. An inexperienced individual can literally do major damage looking for a minor problem by using the wrong kind of test equipment or connecting test leads or connectors with the ignition switch ON. When selecting test equipment, make sure the manufacturers instructions state that the tester is compatible with whatever type of electronic control system is being serviced. Read all instructions carefully and double check all test points before installing probes or making any test connections.

The following section outlines basic diagnosis techniques for dealing with computerized automotive control systems. Along with a general explanation of the various types of test equipment available to aid in servicing modern electronic automotive systems, basic repair techniques for wiring harnesses and connectors is given. Read the basic information before attempting any repairs or testing on any computerized system, to provide the background of information necessary to avoid the most common and obvious mistakes that can cost both time and money. Although the replacement and testing procedures are simple in themselves, the systems are not, and unless one has a thorough understanding of all components and their function within a particular computerized control system, the logical test sequence these systems demand cannot be followed. Minor malfunctions can make a big difference, so it is important to know how each component affects the operation of the overall electronic system to find the ultimate cause of a problem without replacing good components unnecessarily. It is not enough to use the correct test equipment; the test equipment must be used correctly.

Safety Precautions

CAUTION: *Whenever working on or around any computer based microprocessor control system, always observe these general precautions to prevent the possibility of personal injury or damage to electronic components.*

● Never install or remove battery cables with the key ON or the engine running. Jumper cables should be connected with the key OFF to avoid power surges that can damage electronic control units. Engines equipped with computer controlled systems should avoid both giving and getting jump starts due to the possibility of serious damage to components from arcing in the engine compartment when connections are made with the ignition ON.

● Always remove the battery cables before charging the battery. Never use a high output charger on an installed battery or attempt to use any type of "hot shot" (24 volt) starting aid.

● Exercise care when inserting test probes into connectors to insure good connections without damaging the connector or spreading the pins. Always probe connectors from the rear (wire) side, NOT the pin side, to avoid accidental shorting of terminals during test procedures.

• Never remove or attach wiring harness connectors with the ignition switch ON, especially to an electronic control unit.

• Do not drop any components during service procedures and never apply 12 volts directly to any component (like a solenoid or relay) unless instructed specifically to do so. Some component electrical windings are designed to safely handle only 4 or 5 volts and can be destroyed in seconds if 12 volts are applied directly to the connector.

• Remove the electronic control unit if the vehicle is to be placed in an environment where temperatures exceed approximately 176°F (80°C), such as a paint spray booth or when arc or gas welding near the control unit location in the car.

ORGANIZED TROUBLESHOOTING

When diagnosing a specific problem, organized troubleshooting is a must. The complexity of a modern automobile demands that you approach any problem in a logical, organized manner. There are certain troubleshooting techniques that are standard:

1. Establish when the problem occurs. Does the problem appear only under certain conditions? Were there any noises, odors, or other unusual symptoms?

2. Isolate the problem area. To do this, make some simple tests and observations; then eliminate the systems that are working properly. Check for obvious problems such as broken wires, dirty connections or split or disconnected vacuum hoses. Always check the obvious before assuming something complicated is the cause.

3. Test for problems systematically to determine the cause once the problem area is isolated. Are all the components functioning properly? Is there power going to electrical switches and motors? Is there vacuum at vacuum switches and/or actuators? Is there a mechanical problem such as bent linkage or loose mounting screws? Doing careful, systematic checks will often turn up most causes on the first inspection without wasting time checking components that have little or no relationship to the problem.

4. Test all repairs after the work is done to make sure that the problem is fixed. Some causes can be traced to more than one component, so a careful verification of repair work is important to pick up additional malfunctions that may cause a problem to reappear or a different problem to arise. A blown fuse, for example, is a simple problem that may require more than another fuse to repair. If you don't look for a problem that caused a fuse to blow, for example, a shorted wire may go undetected.

Experience has shown that most problems tend to be the result of a fairly simple and obvious cause, such as loose or corroded connectors or air leaks in the intake system; making careful inspection of components during testing essential to quick and accurate troubleshooting. Special, hand held computerized testers designed specifically for diagnosing the EEC-IV system are available from a variety of aftermarket sources, as well as from the vehicle manufacturer, but care should be taken that any test equipment being used is designed to diagnose that particular computer controlled system accurately without damaging the control unit (ECU) or components being tested.

NOTE: *Pinpointing the exact cause of trouble in an electrical system can sometimes only be accomplished by the use of special test equipment. The following describes commonly used test equipment and explains how to put it to best use in diagnosis. In addition to the information covered below, the manufacturer's instructions booklet provided with the tester should be read and clearly understood before attempting any test procedures.*

TEST EQUIPMENT

Jumper Wires

Jumper wires are simple, yet extremely valuable, pieces of test equipment. Jumper wires are merely wires that are used to bypass sections of a circuit. The simplest type of jumper wire is merely a length of multistrand wire with an alligator clip at each end. Jumper wires are usually fabricated from lengths of standard automotive wire and whatever type of connector (alligator clip, spade connector or pin connector) that is required for the particular vehicle being tested. The well equipped tool box will have several different styles of jumper wires in several different lengths. Some jumper wires are made with three or more terminals coming from a common splice for special purpose testing. In cramped, hard-to-reach areas it is advisable to have insulated boots over the jumper wire terminals in order to prevent accidental grounding, sparks, and possible fire, especially when testing fuel system components.

Jumper wires are used primarily to locate open electrical circuits, on either the ground (–) side of the circuit or on the hot (+) side. If an electrical component fails to operate, connect the jumper wire between the component and a good ground. If the component operates only with the jumper installed, the ground circuit is open. If the ground circuit is good, but the component does not operate, the circuit between the power feed and component is open. You can sometimes connect the jumper wire directly from the battery to the hot terminal of the component, but first make sure the component uses 12 volts in operation. Some electrical components, such as fuel injectors, are designed to operate on about 4 volts and running 12 volts directly to the injector terminals can burn out the wiring. By inserting an inline fuseholder between a set of test leads, a fused jumper wire can be used for bypassing open circuits. Use a 5 amp fuse to provide protection against voltage spikes. When in doubt, use a voltmeter to check the voltage input to the component and measure how much voltage is being applied normally. By moving the jumper wire successively back from the lamp toward the power source, you can isolate the area of the circuit where the open is located. When the component stops functioning, or the power is cut off, the open is in the segment of wire between the jumper and the point previously tested.

CAUTION: *Never use jumpers made from wire that is of lighter gauge than used in the circuit under test. If the jumper wire is of too small gauge, it may overheat and possibly melt. Never use jumpers to bypass high resistance loads (such as motors) in a circuit. Bypassing resistances, in effect, creates a short circuit which may, in turn, cause damage and fire. Never use a jumper for anything other than temporary bypassing of components in a circuit.*

12 Volt Test Light

The 12 volt test light is used to check circuits and components while electrical current is flowing through them. It is used for voltage and ground tests. Twelve volt test lights come in different styles but all have three main parts; a ground clip, a probe, and a light. The most commonly used 12 volt test lights have pick-type probes. To use a 12 volt test light, connect the ground clip to a good ground and probe wherever necessary with the pick. The pick should be sharp so that it can penetrate wire insulation to make contact with the wire, without making a large hole in the insulation. The wrap-around light is handy in hard to reach areas or where it is difficult to support a wire to push a probe pick into it. To use the wrap around light, hook the wire to probed with the hook and pull the trigger. A small pick will be forced through the wire insulation into the wire core.

CAUTION: *Do not use a test light to probe electronic ignition spark plug or coil wires. Never use a pick-type test light to probe wiring on computer controlled systems unless specifically instructed to do so. Any wire insulation that is pierced by the test light probe*

should be taped and sealed with silicone after testing.

Like the jumper wire, the 12 volt test light is used to isolate opens in circuits. But, whereas the jumper wire is used to bypass the open to operate the load, the 12 volt test light is used to locate the presence of voltage in a circuit. If the test light glows, you know that there is power up to that point; if the 12 volt test light does not glow when its probe is inserted into the wire or connector, you know that there is an open circuit (no power). Move the test light in successive steps back toward the power source until the light in the handle does glow. When it does glow, the open is between the probe and point previously probed.

NOTE: *The test light does not detect that 12 volts (or any particular amount of voltage) is present; it only detects that some voltage is present. It is advisable before using the test light to touch its terminals across the battery posts to make sure the light is operating properly.*

Self-Powered Test Light

The self-powered test light usually contains a 1.5 volt penlight battery. One type of self-powered test light is similar in design to the 12 volt test light. This type has both the battery and the light in the handle and pick-type probe tip. The second type has the light toward the open tip, so that the light illuminates the contact point. The self-powered test light is dual purpose piece of test equipment. It can be used to test for either open or short circuits when power is isolated from the circuit (continuity test). A powered test light should not be used on any computer controlled system or component unless specifically instructed to do so. Many engine sensors can be destroyed by even this small amount of voltage applied directly to the terminals.

Open Circuit Testing

To use the self-powered test light to check for open circuits, first isolate the circuit from the vehicle's 12 volt power source by disconnecting the battery or wiring harness connector. Connect the test light ground clip to a good ground and probe sections of the circuit sequentially with the test light. (start from either end of the circuit). If the light is out, the open is between the probe and the circuit ground. If the light is on, the open is between the probe and end of the circuit toward the power source.

Short Circuit Testing

By isolating the circuit both from power and from ground, and using a self-powered test light, you can check for shorts to ground in the circuit. Isolate the circuit from power and ground. Connect the test light ground clip to a good ground and probe any easy-to-reach test point in the circuit. If the light comes on, there is a short somewhere in the circuit. To isolate the short, probe a test point at either end of the isolated circuit (the light should be on). Leave the test light probe connected and open connectors, switches, remove parts, etc., sequentially, until the light goes out. When the light goes out, the short is between the last circuit component opened and the previous circuit opened.

NOTE: *The 1.5 volt battery in the test light does not provide much current. A weak battery may not provide enough power to illuminate the test light even when a complete circuit is made (especially if there are high resistances in the circuit). Always make sure that the test battery is strong. To check the battery, briefly touch the ground clip to the probe; if the light glows brightly the battery is strong enough for testing. Never use a self-powered test light to perform checks for opens or shorts when power is applied to the electrical system under test. The 12 volt vehicle power will quickly burn out the 1.5 volt light bulb in the test light.*

Voltmeter

A voltmeter is used to measure voltage at any point in a circuit, or to measure the voltage drop across any part of a circuit. It can also be used to check continuity in a wire or circuit by indicating current flow from one end to the other. Voltmeters usually have various scales on the meter dial and a selector switch to allow the selection of different voltages. The voltmeter has a positive and a negative lead. To avoid damage to the meter, always connect the negative lead to the negative (–) side of circuit (to ground or nearest the ground side of the circuit) and connect the positive lead to the positive (+) side of the circuit (to the power source or the nearest power source). Note that the negative voltmeter lead will always be black and that the positive voltmeter will always be some color other than black (usually red). Depending on how the voltmeter is connected into the circuit, it has several uses.

A voltmeter can be connected either in parallel or in series with a circuit and it has a very high resistance to current flow. When connected in parallel, only a small amount of current will flow through the voltmeter current path; the rest will flow through the normal circuit current path and the circuit will work normally. When the voltmeter is connected in series with a circuit, only a small amount of current can flow through the circuit. The circuit will not

work properly, but the voltmeter reading will show if the circuit is complete or not.

Available Voltage Measurement

Set the voltmeter selector switch to the 20V position and connect the meter negative lead to the negative post of the battery. Connect the positive meter lead to the positive post of the battery and turn the ignition switch ON to provide a load. Read the voltage on the meter or digital display. A well charged battery should register over 12 volts. If the meter reads below 11.5 volts, the battery power may be insufficient to operate the electrical system properly. This test determines voltage available from the battery and should be the first step in any electrical trouble diagnosis procedure. Many electrical problems, especially on computer controlled systems, can be caused by a low state of charge in the battery. Excessive corrosion at the battery cable terminals can cause a poor contact that will prevent proper charging and full battery current flow.

Normal battery voltage is 12 volts when fully charged. When the battery is supplying current to one or more circuits it is said to be "under load". When everything is off the electrical system is under a "no-load" condition. A fully charged battery may show about 12.5 volts at no load; will drop to 12 volts under medium load; and will drop even lower under heavy load. If the battery is partially discharged the voltage decrease under heavy load may be excessive, even though the battery shows 12 volts or more at no load. When allowed to discharge further, the battery's available voltage under load will decrease more severely. For this reason, it is important that the battery be fully charged during all testing procedures to avoid errors in diagnosis and incorrect test results.

Voltage Drop

When current flows through a resistance, the voltage beyond the resistance is reduced (the larger the current, the greater the reduction in voltage). When no current is flowing, there is no voltage drop because there is no current flow. All points in the circuit which are connected to the power source are at the same voltage as the power source. The total voltage drop always equals the total source voltage. In a long circuit with many connectors, a series of small, unwanted voltage drops due to corrosion at the connectors can add up to a total loss of voltage which impairs the operation of the normal loads in the circuit.

INDIRECT COMPUTATION OF VOLTAGE DROPS

1. Set the voltmeter selector switch to the 20 volt position.

2. Connect the meter negative lead to a good ground.

3. Probe all resistances in the circuit with the positive meter lead.

4. Operate the circuit in all modes and observe the voltage readings.

DIRECT MEASUREMENT OF VOLTAGE DROPS

1. Set the voltmeter switch to the 20 volt position.

2. Connect the voltmeter negative lead to the ground side of the resistance load to be measured.

3. Connect the positive lead to the positive side of the resistance or load to be measured.

4. Read the voltage drop directly on the 20 volt scale.

Too high a voltage indicates too high a resistance. If, for example, a blower motor runs too slowly, you can determine if there is too high a resistance in the resistor pack. By taking voltage drop readings in all parts of the circuit, you can isolate the problem. Too low a voltage drop indicates too low a resistance. If, for example, a blower motor runs too fast in the MED and/or LOW position, the problem can be isolated in the resistor pack by taking voltage drop readings in all parts of the circuit to locate a possibly shorted resistor. The maximum allowable voltage drop under load is critical, especially if there is more than one high resistance problem in a circuit because all voltage drops are cumulative. A small drop is normal due to the resistance of the conductors.

HIGH RESISTANCE TESTING

1. Set the voltmeter selector switch to the 4 volt position.

2. Connect the voltmeter positive lead to the positive post of the battery.

3. Turn on the headlights and heater blower to provide a load.

4. Probe various points in the circuit with the negative voltmeter lead.

5. Read the voltage drop on the 4 volt scale. Some average maximum allowable voltage drops are:

FUSE PANEL — 7 volts
IGNITION SWITCH — 5volts
HEADLIGHT SWITCH — 7 volts
IGNITION COIL (+) — 5 volts
ANY OTHER LOAD — 1.3 volts

NOTE: *Voltage drops are all measured while a load is operating; without current flow, there will be no voltage drop.*

Ohmmeter

The ohmmeter is designed to read resistance (ohms) in a circuit or component. Although there are several different styles of ohmmeters,

all will usually have a selector switch which permits the measurement of different ranges of resistance (usually the selector switch allows the multiplication of the meter reading by 10, 100, 1000, and 10,000). A calibration knob allows the meter to be set at zero for accurate measurement. Since all ohmmeters are powered by an internal battery (usually 9 volts), the ohmmeter can be used as a self-powered test light. When the ohmmeter is connected, current from the ohmmeter flows through the circuit or component being tested. Since the ohmmeter's internal resistance and voltage are known values, the amount of current flow through the meter depends on the resistance of the circuit or component being tested.

The ohmmeter can be used to perform continuity test for opens or shorts (either by observation of the meter needle or as a self-powered test light), and to read actual resistance in a circuit. It should be noted that the ohmmeter is used to check the resistance of a component or wire while there is no voltage applied to the circuit. Current flow from an outside voltage source (such as the vehicle battery) can damage the ohmmeter, so the circuit or component should be isolated from the vehicle electrical system before any testing is done. Since the ohmmeter uses its own voltage source, either lead can be connected to any test point.

NOTE: *When checking diodes or other solid state components, the ohmmeter leads can only be connected one way in order to measure current flow in a single direction. Make sure the positive (+) and negative (–) terminal connections are as described in the test procedures to verify the one-way diode operation.*

In using the meter for making continuity checks, do not be concerned with the actual resistance readings. Zero resistance, or any resistance readings, indicate continuity in the circuit. Infinite resistance indicates an open in the circuit. A high resistance reading where there should be none indicates a problem in the circuit. Checks for short circuits are made in the same manner as checks for open circuits except that the circuit must be isolated from both power and normal ground. Infinite resistance indicates no continuity to ground, while zero resistance indicates a dead short to ground.

RESISTANCE MEASUREMENT

The batteries in an ohmmeter will weaken with age and temperature, so the ohmmeter must be calibrated or "zeroed" before taking measurements. To zero the meter, place the selector switch in its lowest range and touch the two ohmmeter leads together. Turn the calibration knob until the meter needle is exactly on zero.

NOTE: *All analog (needle) type ohmmeters must be zeroed before use, but some digital ohmmeter models are automatically calibrated when the switch is turned on. Self-calibrating digital ohmmeters do not have an adjusting knob, but its a good idea to check for a zero readout before use by touching the leads together. All computer controlled systems require the use of a digital ohmmeter with at least 10 meagohms impedance for testing. Before any test procedures are attempted, make sure the ohmmeter used is compatible with the electrical system or damage to the onboard computer could result.*

To measure resistance, first isolate the circuit from the vehicle power source by disconnecting the battery cables or the harness connector. Make sure the key is OFF when disconnecting any components or the battery. Where necessary, also isolate at least one side of the circuit to be checked to avoid reading parallel resistances. Parallel circuit resistances will always give a lower reading than the actual resistance of either of the branches. When measuring the resistance of parallel circuits, the total resistance will always be lower than the smallest resistance in the circuit. Connect the meter leads to both sides of the circuit (wire or component) and read the actual measured ohms on the meter scale. Make sure the selector switch is set to the proper ohm scale for the circuit being tested to avoid misreading the ohmmeter test value.

CAUTION: *Never use an ohmmeter with power applied to the circuit. Like the self-powered test light, the ohmmeter is designed to operate on its own power supply. The normal 12 volt automotive electrical system current could damage the meter.*

Ammeters

An ammeter measures the amount of current flowing through a circuit in units called amperes or amps. Amperes are units of electron flow which indicate how fast the electrons are flowing through the circuit. Since Ohms Law dictates that current flow in a circuit is equal to the circuit voltage divided by the total circuit resistance, increasing voltage also increases the current level (amps). Likewise, any decrease in resistance will increase the amount of amps in a circuit. At normal operating voltage, most circuits have a characteristic amount of amperes, called "current draw" which can be measured using an ammeter. By referring to a specified current draw rating, measuring the amperes, and comparing the two values, one can determine what is happening within the circuit to aid

in diagnosis. An open circuit, for example, will not allow any current to flow so the ammeter reading will be zero. More current flows through a heavily loaded circuit or when the charging system is operating.

An ammeter is always connected in series with the circuit being tested. All of the current that normally flows through the circuit must also flow through the ammeter; if there is any other path for the current to follow, the ammeter reading will not be accurate. The ammeter itself has very little resistance to current flow and therefore will not affect the circuit, but it will measure current draw only when the circuit is closed and electricity is flowing. Excessive current draw can blow fuses and drain the battery, while a reduced current draw can cause motors to run slowly, lights to dim and other components to not operate properly. The ammeter can help diagnose these conditions by locating the cause of the high or low reading.

Multimeters

Different combinations of test meters can be built into a single unit designed for specific tests. Some of the more common combination test devices are known as Volt/Amp testers, Tach/Dwell meters, or Digital Multimeters. The Volt/Amp tester is used for charging system, starting system or battery tests and consists of a voltmeter, an ammeter and a variable resistance carbon pile. The voltmeter will usually have at least two ranges for use with 6, 12 and 24 volt systems. The ammeter also has more than one range for testing various levels of battery loads and starter current draw and the carbon pile can be adjusted to offer different amounts of resistance. The Volt/Amp tester has heavy leads to carry large amounts of current and many later models have an inductive ammeter pickup that clamps around the wire to simplify test connections. On some models, the ammeter also has a zero-center scale to allow testing of charging and starting systems without switching leads or polarity. A digital multimeter is a voltmeter, ammeter and ohmmeter combined in an instrument which gives a digital readout. These are often used when testing solid state circuits because of their high input impedance (usually 10 megohms or more).

The tach/dwell meter combines a tachometer and a dwell (cam angle) meter and is a specialized kind of voltmeter. The tachometer scale is marked to show engine speed in rpm and the dwell scale is marked to show degrees of distributor shaft rotation. In most electronic ignition systems, dwell is determined by the control unit, but the dwell meter can also be used to check the duty cycle (operation) of some electronic engine control systems. Some tach/dwell meters are powered by an internal battery, while others take their power from the car battery in use. The battery powered testers usually require calibration much like an ohmmeter before testing.

Special Test Equipment

A variety of diagnostic tools are available to help troubleshoot and repair computerized engine control systems. The most sophisticated of these devices are the console type engine analyzers that usually occupy a garage service bay, but there are several types of aftermarket electronic testers available that will allow quick circuit tests of the engine control system by plugging directly into a special connector located in the engine compartment or under the dashboard. Several tool and equipment manufacturers offer simple, hand held testers that measure various circuit voltage levels on command to check all system components for proper operation. Although these testers usually cost about $300-$500, consider that the average computer control unit (or ECM) can cost just as much and the money saved by not replacing perfectly good sensors or components in an attempt to correct a problem could justify the purchase price of a special diagnostic tester the first time it's used.

These computerized testers can allow quick and easy test measurements while the engine is operating or while the car is being driven. In addition, the on-board computer memory can be read to access any stored trouble codes; in effect allowing the computer to tell you where it hurts and aid trouble diagnosis by pinpointing exactly which circuit or component is malfunctioning. In the same manner, repairs can be tested to make sure the problem has been corrected. The biggest advantage these special testers have is their relatively easy hookups that minimize or eliminate the chances of making the wrong connections and getting false voltage readings or damaging the computer accidentally.

NOTE: *It should be remembered that these testers check voltage levels in circuits; they don't detect mechanical problems or failed components if the circuit voltage falls within the preprogrammed limits stored in the tester PROM unit. Also, most of the hand-held testers are designed to work only on one or two systems made by a specific manufacturer.*

A variety of aftermarket testers are available to help diagnose different computerized control systems. Owatonna Tool Company (OTC), for example, markets a device called the OTC Monitor which plugs directly into the assembly line diagnostic link (ALDL). The OTC tester makes diagnosis a simple matter of pressing the correct buttons and, by changing the internal PROM or inserting a different diagnosis cartridge, it will work on any model from full size to subcompact, over a wide range of years. An adapter is supplied with the tester to allow connection to all types of ALDL links, regardless of the number of pin terminals used. By inserting an updated PROM into the OTC tester, it can be easily updated to diagnose any new modifications of computerized control systems.

Wiring Harnesses

The average automobile contains about ½ mile of wiring, with hundreds of individual connections. To protect the many wires from damage and to keep them from becoming a confusing tangle, they are organized into bundles, enclosed in plastic or taped together and called wire harnesses. Different wiring harnesses serve different parts of the vehicle. Individual wires are color coded to help trace them through a harness where sections are hidden from view.

A loose or corroded connection or a replacement wire that is too small for the circuit will add extra resistance and an additional voltage drop to the circuit. A ten percent voltage drop can result in slow or erratic motor operation, for example, even though the circuit is complete. Automotive wiring or circuit conductors can be in any one of three forms:

1. Single strand wire
2. Multistrand wire
3. Printed circuitry

Single strand wire has a solid metal core and is usually used inside such components as alternators, motors, relays and other devices. Multistrand wire has a core made of many small strands of wire twisted together into a single conductor. Most of the wiring in an automotive electrical system is made up of multistrand wire, either as a single conductor or grouped together in a harness. All wiring is color coded on the insulator, either as a solid color or as a colored wire with an identification stripe. A printed circuit is a thin film of copper or other conductor that is printed on an insulator backing. Occasionally, a printed circuit is sandwiched between two sheets of plastic for more protection and flexibility. A complete printed circuit, consisting of conductors, insulating material and connectors for lamps or other components is called a printed circuit board. Printed circuitry is used in place of individual wires or harnesses in places where space is limited, such as behind instrument panels.

Wire Gauge

Since computer controlled automotive electrical systems are very sensitive to changes in resistance, the selection of properly sized wires is critical when systems are repaired. The wire gauge number is an expression of the cross section area of the conductor. The most common system for expressing wire size is the American Wire Gauge (AWG) system.

Wire cross section area is measured in circular mils. A mil is $\frac{1}{1000}''$ (0.001"); a circular mil is the area of a circle one mil in diameter. For example, a conductor $\frac{1}{4}''$ in diameter is 0.250", or 250 mils. The circular mil cross section area of the wire is 250 squared (250^2) or 62,500 circular mils. Imported car models usually use metric wire gauge designations, which is simply the cross section area of the conductor in square millimeters (mm^2).

Gauge numbers are assigned to conductors of various cross section areas. As gauge number increases, area decreases and the conductor becomes smaller. A 5 gauge conductor is smaller than a 1 gauge conductor and a 10 gauge is smaller than a 5 gauge. As the cross section area of a conductor decreases, resistance increases and so does the gauge number. A conductor with a higher gauge number will carry less current than a conductor with a lower gauge number.

NOTE: *Gauge wire size refers to the size of the conductor, not the size of the complete wire. It is possible to have two wires of the same gauge with different diameters because one may have thicker insulation than the other.*

12 volt automotive electrical systems generally use 10, 12, 14, 16 and 18 gauge wire. Main power distribution circuits and larger accessories usually use 10 and 12 gauge wire. Battery cables are usually 4 or 6 gauge, although 1 and 2 gauge wires are occasionally used. Wire length must also be considered when making repairs to a circuit. As conductor length increases, so does resistance. An 18 gauge wire, for example, can carry a 10 amp load for 10 feet without excessive voltage drop; however if a 15 foot wire is required for the same 10 amp load, it must be a 16 gauge wire.

An electrical schematic shows the electrical current paths when a circuit is operating properly. It is essential to understand how a circuit works before trying to figure out why it doesn't. Schematics break the entire electrical system down into individual circuits and show only one particular circuit. In a schematic, no attempt is made to represent wiring and components as they physically appear on the vehicle; switches and other components are shown as simply as possible. Face views of harness connectors show the cavity or terminal locations in all multi-pin connectors to help locate test points.

If you need to backprobe a connector while it is on the component, the order of the terminals must be mentally reversed. The wire color code can help in this situation, as well as a keyway, lock tab or other reference mark.

NOTE: *Wiring diagrams are not included in this book. As trucks have become more complex and available with longer option lists, wiring diagrams have grown in size and complexity. It has become almost impossible to provide a readable reproduction of a wiring diagram in a book this size. Information on ordering wiring diagrams from the vehicle manufacturer can be found in the owner's manual.*

WIRING REPAIR

Soldering is a quick, efficient method of joining metals permanently. Everyone who has the occasion to make wiring repairs should know how to solder. Electrical connections that are soldered are far less likely to come apart and will conduct electricity much better than connections that are only "pig-tailed" together. The most popular (and preferred) method of soldering is with an electrical soldering gun. Soldering irons are available in many sizes and wattage ratings. Irons with higher wattage ratings deliver higher temperatures and recover lost heat faster. A small soldering iron rated for no more than 50 watts is recommended, especially on electrical systems where excess heat can damage the components being soldered.

There are three ingredients necessary for successful soldering; proper flux, good solder and sufficient heat. A soldering flux is necessary to clean the metal of tarnish, prepare it for soldering and to enable the solder to spread into tiny crevices. When soldering, always use a resin flux or resin core solder which is non-corrosive and will not attract moisture once the job is finished. Other types of flux (acid core) will leave a residue that will attract moisture and cause the wires to corrode. Tin is a unique metal with a low melting point. In a molten state, it dissolves and alloys easily with many metals. Solder is made by mixing tin with lead. The most common proportions are 40/60, 50/50 and 60/40, with the percentage of tin listed first. Low priced solders usually contain less tin, making them very difficult for a beginner to use because more heat is required to melt the solder. A common solder is 40/60 which is well suited for all-around general use, but 60/40 melts easier, has more tin for a better joint and is preferred for electrical work.

Soldering Techniques

Successful soldering requires that the metals to be joined be heated to a temperature that will melt the solder—usually 360-460°F (182-238°C). Contrary to popular belief, the purpose of the soldering iron is not to melt the solder itself, but to heat the parts being soldered to a temperature high enough to melt the solder when it is touched to the work. Melting flux-cored solder on the soldering iron will usually destroy the effectiveness of the flux.

NOTE: *Soldering tips are made of copper for good heat conductivity, but must be "tinned" regularly for quick transference of heat to the project and to prevent the solder from sticking to the iron. To "tin" the iron, simply heat it and touch the flux-cored solder to the tip; the solder will flow over the hot tip. Wipe the excess off with a clean rag, but be careful as the iron will be hot.*

After some use, the tip may become pitted. If so, simply dress the tip smooth with a smooth file and "tin" the tip again. An old saying holds that "metals well cleaned are half soldered." Flux-cored solder will remove oxides but rust, bits of insulation and oil or grease must be removed with a wire brush or emery cloth. For maximum strength in soldered parts, the joint must start off clean and tight. Weak joints will result in gaps too wide for the solder to bridge.

If a separate soldering flux is used, it should be brushed or swabbed on only those areas that are to be soldered. Most solders contain a core of flux and separate fluxing is unnecessary. Hold the work to be soldered firmly. It is best to solder on a wooden board, because a metal vise will only rob the piece to be soldered of heat and make it difficult to melt the solder. Hold the soldering tip with the broadest face against the work to be soldered. Apply solder under the tip close to the work, using enough solder to give a heavy film between the iron and the piece being soldered, while moving slowly and making sure the solder melts properly. Keep the work level or the solder will run to the lowest part and favor the thicker parts, because these require more heat to melt the solder. If the soldering tip overheats (the solder coating on the face of the tip burns up), it should be retinned. Once the soldering is completed, let the soldered joint stand until cool. Tape and seal all soldered wire splices after the repair has cooled.

Wire Harness and Connectors

The on-board computer (ECM) wire harness electrically connects the control unit to the various solenoids, switches and sensors used by the control system. Most connectors in the engine compartment or otherwise exposed to the elements are protected against moisture and dirt which could create oxidation and deposits on the terminals. This protection is important because of the very low voltage and current levels used by the computer and sensors. All connectors have a lock which secures the male and female terminals together, with a secondary lock holding the seal and terminal into the connector. Both terminal locks must be released when disconnecting ECM connectors.

These special connectors are weather-proof and all repairs require the use of a special terminal and the tool required to service it. This tool is used to remove the pin and sleeve terminals. If removal is attempted with an ordinary pick, there is a good chance that the terminal will be bent or deformed. Unlike standard blade type terminals, these terminals cannot be straightened once they are bent. Make certain that the connectors are properly seated and all of the sealing rings in place when connecting leads. On some models, a hinge-type flap provides a backup or secondary locking feature for the terminals. Most secondary locks are used to improve the connector reliability by retaining the terminals if the small terminal lock tangs are not positioned properly.

Molded-on connectors require complete replacement of the connection. This means splicing a new connector assembly into the harness. All splices in on-board computer systems should be soldered to insure proper contact. Use care when probing the connections or replacing terminals in them as it is possible to short between opposite terminals. If this happens to the wrong terminal pair, it is possible to damage certain components. Always use jumper wires between connectors for circuit checking and never probe through weather-proof seals.

Open circuits are often difficult to locate by sight because corrosion or terminal misalignment are hidden by the connectors. Merely wiggling a connector on a sensor or in the wiring harness may correct the open circuit condition. This should always be considered when an open circuit or a failed sensor is indicated. Intermittent problems may also be caused by oxidized or loose connections. When using a circuit tester for diagnosis, always probe connections from the wire side. Be careful not to damage sealed connectors with test probes.

All wiring harnesses should be replaced with identical parts, using the same gauge wire and connectors. When signal wires are spliced into a harness, use wire with high temperature insulation only. With the low voltage and current levels found in the system, it is important that the best possible connection at all wire splices be made by soldering the splices together. It is seldom necessary to replace a complete harness. If replacement is necessary, pay close attention to insure proper harness routing. Secure the harness with suitable plastic wire clamps to prevent vibrations from causing the harness to wear in spots or contact any hot components.

NOTE: *Weatherproof connectors cannot be*

replaced with standard connectors. Instructions are provided with replacement connector and terminal packages. Some wire harnesses have mounting indicators (usually pieces of colored tape) to mark where the harness is to be secured.

In making wiring repairs, it's important that you always replace damaged wires with wires that are the same gauge as the wire being replaced. The heavier the wire, the smaller the gauge number. Wires are color-coded to aid in identification and whenever possible the same color coded wire should be used for replacement. A wire stripping and crimping tool is necessary to install solderless terminal connectors. Test all crimps by pulling on the wires; it should not be possible to pull the wires out of a good crimp.

Wires which are open, exposed or otherwise damaged are repaired by simple splicing. Where possible, if the wiring harness is accessible and the damaged place in the wire can be located, it is best to open the harness and check for all possible damage. In an inaccessible harness, the wire must be bypassed with a new insert, usually taped to the outside of the old harness.

When replacing fusible links, be sure to use fusible link wire, NOT ordinary automotive wire. Make sure the fusible segment is of the same gauge and construction as the one being replaced and double the stripped end when crimping the terminal connector for a good contact. The melted (open) fusible link segment of the wiring harness should be cut off as close to the harness as possible, then a new segment spliced in as described. In the case of a damaged fusible link that feeds two harness wires, the harness connections should be replaced with two fusible link wires so that each circuit will have its own separate protection.

NOTE: *Most of the problems caused in the wiring harness are due to bad ground connections. Always check all vehicle ground connections for corrosion or looseness before performing any power feed checks to eliminate the chance of a bad ground affecting the circuit.*

Repairing Hard Shell Connectors

Unlike molded connectors, the terminal contacts in hard shell connectors can be replaced. Weatherproof hard-shell connectors with the leads molded into the shell have non-replaceable terminal ends. Replacement usually involves the use of a special terminal removal tool that depress the locking tangs (barbs) on the connector terminal and allow the connector to be removed from the rear of the shell. The connector shell should be replaced if it shows any evidence of burning, melting, cracks, or breaks.

Replace individual terminals that are burnt, corroded, distorted or loose.

NOTE: *The insulation crimp must be tight to prevent the insulation from sliding back on the wire when the wire is pulled. The insulation must be visibly compressed under the crimp tabs, and the ends of the crimp should be turned in for a firm grip on the insulation.*

The wire crimp must be made with all wire strands inside the crimp. The terminal must be fully compressed on the wire strands with the ends of the crimp tabs turned in to make a firm grip on the wire. Check all connections with an ohmmeter to insure a good contact. There should be no measurable resistance between the wire and the terminal when connected.

Mechanical Test Equipment

Vacuum Gauge

Most gauges are graduated in inches of mercury (in.Hg), although a device called a manometer reads vacuum in inches of water (in.H_2O). The normal vacuum reading usually varies between 18 and 22 in.Hg at sea level. To test engine vacuum, the vacuum gauge must be connected to a source of manifold vacuum. Many engines have a plug in the intake manifold which can be removed and replaced with an adapter fitting. Connect the vacuum gauge to the fitting with a suitable rubber hose or, if no manifold plug is available, connect the vacuum gauge to any device using manifold vacuum, such as EGR valves, etc. The vacuum gauge can be used to determine if enough vacuum is reaching a component to allow its actuation.

Hand Vacuum Pump

Small, hand-held vacuum pumps come in a variety of designs. Most have a built-in vacuum gauge and allow the component to be tested without removing it from the vehicle. Operate the pump lever or plunger to apply the correct amount of vacuum required for the test specified in the diagnosis routines. The level of vacuum in inches of Mercury (in.Hg) is indicated on the pump gauge. For some testing, an additional vacuum gauge may be necessary.

Intake manifold vacuum is used to operate various systems and devices on late model vehicles. To correctly diagnose and solve problems in vacuum control systems, a vacuum source is necessary for testing. In some cases, vacuum can be taken from the intake manifold when the engine is running, but vacuum is normally provided by a hand vacuum pump. These hand vacuum pumps have a built-in vacuum gauge that allow testing while the device is still attached to the component. For some tests, an additional vacuum gauge may be necessary.

Troubleshooting Basic Turn Signal and Flasher Problems

Most problems in the turn signals or flasher system, can be reduced to defective flashers or bulbs, which are easily replaced. Occasionally, problems in the turn signals are traced to the switch in the steering column, which will require professional service.

F = Front   R = Rear   ● = Lights off   ○ = Lights on

Problem		Solution
Turn signals light, but do not flash		• Replace the flasher
No turn signals light on either side		• Check the fuse. Replace if defective. • Check the flasher by substitution • Check for open circuit, short circuit or poor ground
Both turn signals on one side don't work		• Check for bad bulbs • Check for bad ground in both housings
One turn signal light on one side doesn't work		• Check and/or replace bulb • Check for corrosion in socket. Clean contacts. • Check for poor ground at socket
Turn signal flashes too fast or too slow		• Check any bulb on the side flashing too fast. A heavy-duty bulb is probably installed in place of a regular bulb. • Check the bulb flashing too slow. A standard bulb was probably installed in place of a heavy-duty bulb. • Check for loose connections or corrosion at the bulb socket
Indicator lights don't work in either direction		• Check if the turn signals are working • Check the dash indicator lights • Check the flasher by substitution
One indicator light doesn't light		• On systems with 1 dash indicator: See if the lights work on the same side. Often the filaments have been reversed in systems combining stoplights with taillights and turn signals. Check the flasher by substitution • On systems with 2 indicators: Check the bulbs on the same side Check the indicator light bulb Check the flasher by substitution

Troubleshooting Basic Lighting Problems

Problem	Cause	Solution
Lights		
One or more lights don't work, but others do	• Defective bulb(s) • Blown fuse(s) • Dirty fuse clips or light sockets • Poor ground circuit	• Replace bulb(s) • Replace fuse(s) • Clean connections • Run ground wire from light socket housing to car frame
Lights burn out quickly	• Incorrect voltage regulator setting or defective regulator • Poor battery/alternator connections	• Replace voltage regulator • Check battery/alternator connections
Lights go dim	• Low/discharged battery • Alternator not charging • Corroded sockets or connections • Low voltage output	• Check battery • Check drive belt tension; repair or replace alternator • Clean bulb and socket contacts and connections • Replace voltage regulator
Lights flicker	• Loose connection • Poor ground • Circuit breaker operating (short circuit)	• Tighten all connections • Run ground wire from light housing to car frame • Check connections and look for bare wires
Lights "flare"—Some flare is normal on acceleration—if excessive, see "Lights Burn Out Quickly"	• High voltage setting	• Replace voltage regulator
Lights glare—approaching drivers are blinded	• Lights adjusted too high • Rear springs or shocks sagging • Rear tires soft	• Have headlights aimed • Check rear springs/shocks • Check/correct rear tire pressure
Turn Signals		
Turn signals don't work in either direction	• Blown fuse • Defective flasher • Loose connection	• Replace fuse • Replace flasher • Check/tighten all connections
Right (or left) turn signal only won't work	• Bulb burned out • Right (or left) indicator bulb burned out • Short circuit	• Replace bulb • Check/replace indicator bulb • Check/repair wiring
Flasher rate too slow or too fast	• Incorrect wattage bulb • Incorrect flasher	• Flasher bulb • Replace flasher (use a variable load flasher if you pull a trailer)
Indicator lights do not flash (burn steadily)	• Burned out bulb • Defective flasher	• Replace bulb • Replace flasher
Indicator lights do not light at all	• Burned out indicator bulb • Defective flasher	• Replace indicator bulb • Replace flasher

HEATING AND AIR CONDITIONING

CAUTION: *These procedures for heating and air conditioning repairs do not apply to models with the A.C.R.S. (air bag) system. For those cars with air bags, it is advisable to take the car to a dealer for proper servicing.*
NOTE: *Vacuum hose routing clips, electrical wires and relays, weather seals, and other items, may be attached to the heater housing, and will have to be re-located during removal and replacement of the heater core and/or the* blower motor. *Always tag any disconnected hoses or wires for installation. Note also that you should replace any damaged seal or sealer during reassembly to prevent water and air leaks.*

Heater or Heater A/C Blower motor
REMOVAL AND INSTALLATION

1. Disconnect negative battery cable.
2. Tag and disconnect the electrical connections from the blower motor.

Troubleshooting Basic Dash Gauge Problems

Problem	Cause	Solution
Coolant Temperature Gauge		
Gauge reads erratically or not at all	• Loose or dirty connections • Defective sending unit • Defective gauge	• Clean/tighten connections • Bi-metal gauge: remove the wire from the sending unit. Ground the wire for an instant. If the gauge registers, replace the sending unit. • Magnetic gauge: disconnect the wire at the sending unit. With ignition ON gauge should register COLD. Ground the wire; gauge should register HOT.
Ammeter Gauge—Turn Headlights ON (do not start engine). Note reaction		
Ammeter shows charge Ammeter shows discharge Ammeter does not move	• Connections reversed on gauge • Ammeter is OK • Loose connections or faulty wiring • Defective gauge	• Reinstall connections • Nothing • Check/correct wiring • Replace gauge
Oil Pressure Gauge		
Gauge does not register or is inaccurate	• On mechanical gauge, Bourdon tube may be bent or kinked • Low oil pressure • Defective gauge • Defective wiring • Defective sending unit	• Check tube for kinks or bends preventing oil from reaching the gauge • Remove sending unit. Idle the engine briefly. If no oil flows from sending unit hole, problem is in engine. • Remove the wire from the sending unit and ground it for an instant with the ignition ON. A good gauge will go to the top of the scale. • Check the wiring to the gauge. If it's OK and the gauge doesn't register when grounded, replace the gauge. • If the wiring is OK and the gauge functions when grounded, replace the sending unit
All Gauges		
All gauges do not operate All gauges read low or erratically All gauges pegged	• Blown fuse • Defective instrument regulator • Defective or dirty instrument voltage regulator • Loss of ground between instrument voltage regulator and car • Defective instrument regulator	• Replace fuse • Replace instrument voltage regulator • Clean contacts or replace • Check ground • Replace regulator
Warning Lights		
Light(s) do not come on when ignition is ON, but engine is not started Light comes on with engine running	• Defective bulb • Defective wire • Defective sending unit • Problem in individual system • Defective sending unit	• Replace bulb • Check wire from light to sending unit • Disconnect the wire from the sending unit and ground it. Replace the sending unit if the light comes on with the ignition ON. • Check system • Check sending unit (see above)

Troubleshooting the Heater

Problem	Cause	Solution
Blower motor will not turn at any speed	• Blown fuse • Loose connection • Defective ground • Faulty switch • Faulty motor • Faulty resistor	• Replace fuse • Inspect and tighten • Clean and tighten • Replace switch • Replace motor • Replace resistor
Blower motor turns at one speed only	• Faulty switch • Faulty resistor	• Replace switch • Replace resistor
Blower motor turns but does not circulate air	• Intake blocked • Fan not secured to the motor shaft	• Clean intake • Tighten security
Heater will not heat	• Coolant does not reach proper temperature • Heater core blocked internally • Heater core air-bound • Blend-air door not in proper position	• Check and replace thermostat if necessary • Flush or replace core if necessary • Purge air from core • Adjust cable
Heater will not defrost	• Control cable adjustment incorrect • Defroster hose damaged	• Adjust control cable • Replace defroster hose

Troubleshooting Basic Windshield Wiper Problems

Problem	Cause	Solution
Electric Wipers		
Wipers do not operate— Wiper motor heats up or hums	• Internal motor defect • Bent or damaged linkage • Arms improperly installed on linking pivots	• Replace motor • Repair or replace linkage • Position linkage in park and reinstall wiper arms
Wipers do not operate— No current to motor	• Fuse or circuit breaker blown • Loose, open or broken wiring • Defective switch • Defective or corroded terminals • No ground circuit for motor or switch	• Replace fuse or circuit breaker • Repair wiring and connections • Replace switch • Replace or clean terminals • Repair ground circuits
Wipers do not operate— Motor runs	• Linkage disconnected or broken	• Connect wiper linkage or replace broken linkage
Vacuum Wipers		
Wipers do not operate	• Control switch or cable inoperative • Loss of engine vacuum to wiper motor (broken hoses, low engine vacuum, defective vacuum/fuel pump) • Linkage broken or disconnected • Defective wiper motor	• Repair or replace switch or cable • Check vacuum lines, engine vacuum and fuel pump • Repair linkage • Replace wiper motor
Wipers stop on engine acceleration	• Leaking vacuum hoses • Dry windshield • Oversize wiper blades • Defective vacuum/fuel pump	• Repair or replace hoses • Wet windshield with washers • Replace with proper size wiper blades • Replace pump

3. If the vehicle is equipped with a plastic splash shield, remove it from the right side of the cowl. Remove the blower motor attaching screws and the motor.

4. Installation is the reverse of removal.

Heater Core

REMOVAL AND INSTALLATION

1975-77 Models Without A/C

1. Disconnect Negative battery cable.
2. Drain the radiator and disconnect the

heater inlet and outlet hoses at the dash. Remove the blower inlet to firewall screws, remove the blower inlet, motor and wheel as an assembly.

CAUTION: *When draining the coolant, keep in mind that cats and dogs are attracted by the ethylene glycol antifreeze, and are quite likely to drink any that is left in an uncovered container or in puddles on the ground. This will prove fatal in sufficient quantity. Always drain the coolant into a sealable container. Coolant should be reused unless it is contaminated or several years old.*

3. Disconnect the control wires from the defroster door and vacuum hose diverter door actuator diaphragm and control cable from the temperature door lever. (Mark or tag for correct installation).

4. Remove the four nuts securing the heater assembly to the dash.

5. Remove the screw securing the defroster outlet tab to the heater assembly.

6. Remove the heater assembly from the car.

7. Remove the heater core from the heater assembly.

8. Reverse the above steps for installation, refill cooling system, start engine check for leaks.

1978 And Later

1. Disconnect the negative battery cable.

2. Drain the radiator and disconnect the heater hoses at the core tubes.

CAUTION: *When draining the coolant, keep in mind that cats and dogs are attracted by the ethylene glycol antifreeze, and are quite likely to drink any that is left in an uncovered container or in puddles on the ground. This will prove fatal in sufficient quantity. Always drain the coolant into a sealable container. Coolant should be reused unless it is contaminated or several years old.*

3. Disconnect all electrical connections and wires at the module cover.

4. Remove the front module cover screws and front module cover.

5. Remove the core. On later models, remove core bracket and screws to gain access to heater core.

6. Reverse the above for installation. Refill cooling system, start engine and check for leaks.

1975-79 Models With A/C

NOTE: *This procedure includes removal of the heater assembly.*

1. Disconnect Negative battery cable.

2. Drain the radiator and disconnect the heater hoses.

CAUTION: *When draining the coolant, keep in mind that cats and dogs are attracted by the ethylene glycol antifreeze, and are quite likely to drink any that is left in an uncovered container or in puddles on the ground. This will prove fatal in sufficient quantity. Always drain the coolant into a sealable container. Coolant should be reused unless it is contaminated or several years old.*

3. Disconnect the temperature control cable

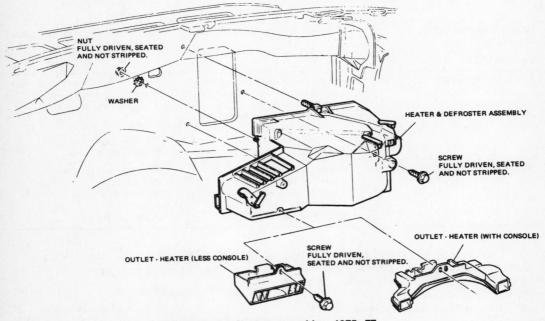

Heater and defroster assembly—1975–77

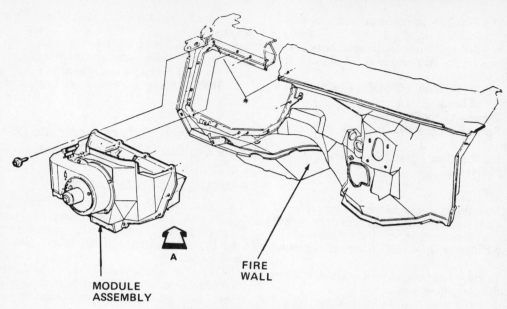

MODULE
ASSEMBLY

FIRE
WALL

Heater module assembly—1978 and later

and the vacuum hoses (mark or tag for correct installation).

4. Remove the resistor assembly. Reach through the opening and remove the attaching nut. Remove the attaching nut directly over the transmission and the two attaching nuts to the upper and lower inboard evaporator case.

5. From inside the car, remove the screw in the lower right corner of the passenger side of the heater assembly.

6. Remove the lower attaching outlets. Carefully work the assembly to the rear until the studs clear. Remove the heater assembly from car.

7. Remove the heater core from the heater assembly.

8. Reverse the above on installation, adjust the control cable to get about a ⅛″ springback in the hot position. Check adjustment of cable.

9. Refill the cooling system, start the engine and check for leaks.

1980-1983

1. Engage the right wiper arm so it is in the **UP** position.

2. Drain the radiator enough so you can disconnect the heater core hoses, then plug them. Disconnect the battery ground cable.

CAUTION: *When draining the coolant, keep in mind that cats and dogs are attracted by the ethylene glycol antifreeze, and are quite likely to drink any that is left in an uncovered container or in puddles on the ground. This will prove fatal in sufficient quantity. Always drain the coolant into a sealable container.*

Coolant should be reused unless it is contaminated or several years old.

3. Pull off the trim seal and remove the screens from the assembly. Mark and remove any electrical connections in the way.

4. Loosen and move up the lower windshield trim. Remove the windshield molding cowl brackets.

5. Tape a strip of wood below the lower edge of the windshield glass near the module for protection. Remove all module cover screws.

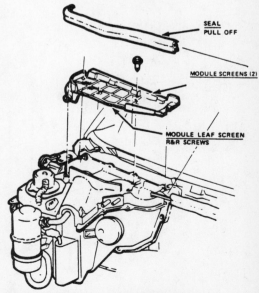

SEAL
PULL OFF

MODULE SCREENS (2)

MODULE LEAF SCREEN
R&R SCREWS

Heater / A/C exterior service procedures

6. Cut through the sealing material along the cowl with a knife.

7. Pry the module cover off from the side, not from the top, to insure you don't damage the windshield.

8. Lift the cover off and away from the flange/cowl brace.

9. Remove the core.

10. Reverse to install. Use new strip caulk sealer.

11. Refill cooling system, start the engine and check for leaks.

1984-1987

1. Disconnect the negative battery cable.

2. Disconnect electrical harness from blower motor,resistor,pressure cycling switch and HI-BLOWER relay.Disconnect heater core ground strap.

3. Remove right end of hood seal and remove air inlet screens screws.

4. Remove case to dash bolts along top,and upper to lower case screws around flange,and upper to lower case screws inside air intake plenum.

5. Remove upper case by lifting straight up and off.

6. To remove heater core,disconnect hoses and prop up to prevent loss of coolant.Lift heater core straight up.

NOTE: *Replace sealer during reassembly to prevent air and water leaks.*

7. Install heater core and heater hoses.

8. Install upper case and tighten.

9. Connect right end of hood seal and air inlet screens.

10. Attach all electrical connections.

11. Connect heater core ground strap.

12. Connect Negative battery cable.

13. Refill cooling system, start engine and check for leaks.

Control Head (Except Automatic Climate Control Or Touch Climate Control)

REMOVAL AND INSTALLATION

1. Disconnect the negative battery cable.

2. Remove the center instrument panel trim. On some models, screws for this panel are covered by left and right panel trims. Remove these panels first.

NOTE: *On earlier model years, the instrument trim plate is removed by pulling rearward and unsnapping from the instrument panel (note location of clips on trim plate.)*

3. Remove screws from control face.

4. Gently pull control outward until you can gain acccess to the electrical and/or vacuum connectors. On some models, unscrew cable clip attaching screws from the heater case until the cable housing can be freed and the cable can be unhooked.

NOTE: *Slide controls all the way to the left. Note the routing of each cable to each damper lever.*

5. Disconnect all electrical, vacuum

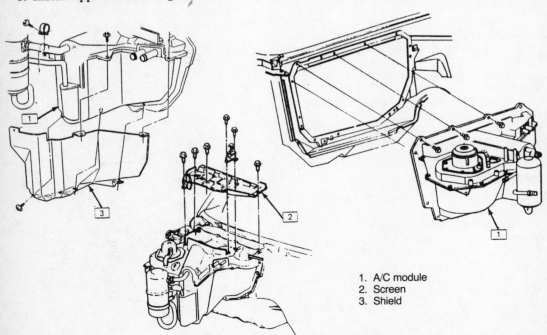

1. A/C module
2. Screen
3. Shield

Heater / A/C module for 1980–87 models

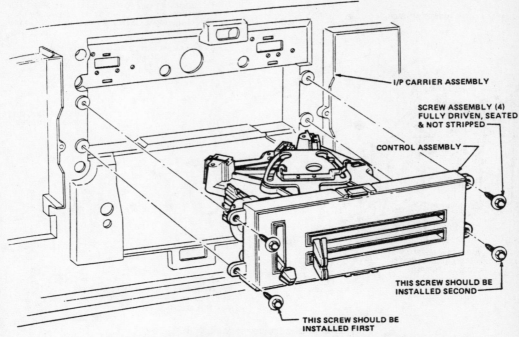

Removal and installation of the heater or A/C control head—typical

connections, and control cables. Remove the control head, pulling the cables and vacuum and electrical connections out through the hole in the dash.

6. Feed the cables, vacuum lines, and electrical connections through the hole in the dash and locate the head so the vacuum and electrical connections can be made. Connect vacuum and/or electrical connectors.

7. Connect the cables and adjust each so that its damper is forced all the way closed or open, depending on lever position on the control face.

8. Install the mounting screws for the control head.

9. Install the trim panels (or panel) in reverse order of their removal.

Evaporator Core

REMOVAL AND INSTALLATION

WARNING: *Do not attempt to CHARGE or DISCHARGE the refrigerant system unless you are thoroughly familiar with its operation and all the hazards involved. Refer to chapter 1 before starting A/C repairs.*

1975-1979

1. Discharge the refrigerant from system (see Discharge The System in Chapter 1).

2. Disconnect the Negative battery cable.

3. Disconnect all evaporator/blower case at-

taching wiring including the blower motor ground wire to dash.

4. Remove accumulator.

5. Tape closed all refrigerant line openings.

6. Remove all the attaching screws and stamped nuts from the evaporator/blower case.

7. Remove the evaporator/blower assembly from the engine compartment.

8. Remove the screws that secure the evaporator blower assembly halves together and remove the evaporator core.

9. Reverse the removal procedures to install using new O rings on line fittings (coated with refrigerant oil).

10. Evacuate, charge and leak test system.

1980-1987

1. Disconnect the negative battery cable.

2. Disconnect electrical harness from blower motor, resistor, pressure cycling switch and HI-BLOWER relay. Disconnect heater core ground strap.

3. Discharge refrigerant system (see Discharge The System in Chapter 1).

4. Disconnect refrigerant line at evaporator inlet pipe.

5. Disconnect compressor suction hose at accumulator outlet pipe.

NOTE: *Tape all open lines to prevent moisture from entering A/C system.*

6. Remove right end of hood seal and remove air inlet screens screws.

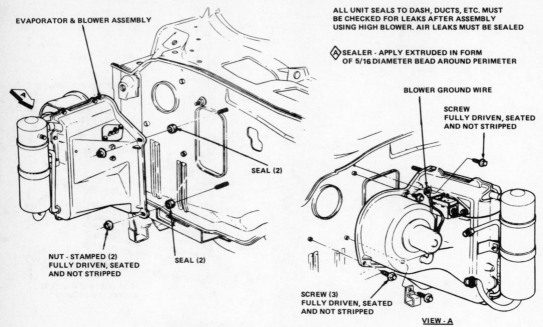

EVAPORATOR & BLOWER ASSEMBLY

ALL UNIT SEALS TO DASH, DUCTS, ETC. MUST
BE CHECKED FOR LEAKS AFTER ASSEMBLY
USING HIGH BLOWER. AIR LEAKS MUST BE SEALED

SEALER - APPLY EXTRUDED IN FORM
OF 5/16 DIAMETER BEAD AROUND PERIMETER

BLOWER GROUND WIRE

SCREW
FULLY DRIVEN, SEATED
AND NOT STRIPPED

SEAL (2)

NUT - STAMPED (2)
FULLY DRIVEN, SEATED
AND NOT STRIPPED

SEAL (2)

SCREW (3)
FULLY DRIVEN, SEATED
AND NOT STRIPPED

VIEW - A

Evaporator and blower assembly 1975–79

7. Remove case to dash bolts along top, upper-to-lower case screws around flange, and upper to lower case screws inside air intake plenum.

8. Remove upper case by lifting straight up and off.

9. Remove accumulator pipe bracket to case screws.

10. Remove evaporator core by lifting core straight up and out of case.

NOTE: *Replace sealer during reassembly to prevent air and water leaks.*

11. Install evaporator core.

12. Attach accumulator pipe bracket to case.

13. Install upper case and tighten.

14. Connect right end of hood seal and air inlet screens.

NOTE: *Use new O-Rings coated with refrigerant oil at all line connections.*

15. Connect compressor suction hose to accumulator outlet pipe.

16. Connect refrigerant line to evaporator inlet pipe.

17. Attach all electrical connections.

18. Connect heater core ground strap.

19. Connect Negative battery cable.

20. Evacuate and charge A/C system and leak test system.

RADIO

The antenna trim must be adjusted on AM radios, or the AM part of AM/FM radios, when major repair has been done to the unit or antenna changed. The trimmer screw is located behind the right side knob on most radios. Raise the antenna to its full height and tune to a weak station around 1400 AM and turn the volume down until barely audible. Turn the trimmer screw with a small scewdriver until the maximum volume is achieved.

WARNING: *Don't turn on the radio without first connecting the speaker as the output transistors may be damaged. Also, these procedures for radio removal and installation do not apply to models with the A.C.R.S. (air bag) system. For those models with air bags, it is advisable to take the car to a dealer for proper servicing because the airbag may accidentally deploy when you are servicing the car.*

REMOVAL AND INSTALLATION

1975-1977

1. Disconnect the negative battery cable.

2. Remove the radio knobs.

3. Disconnect the center air duct assembly control, if so equipped, by removing the two retaining screws.

4. Disconnect the left side air conditioning hose, if so equipped.

5. Disconnect the radio wiring.

6. Loosen the radio supporting nut.

7. Remove the two front attaching nuts at the radio face and slide the radio toward the front of the car.

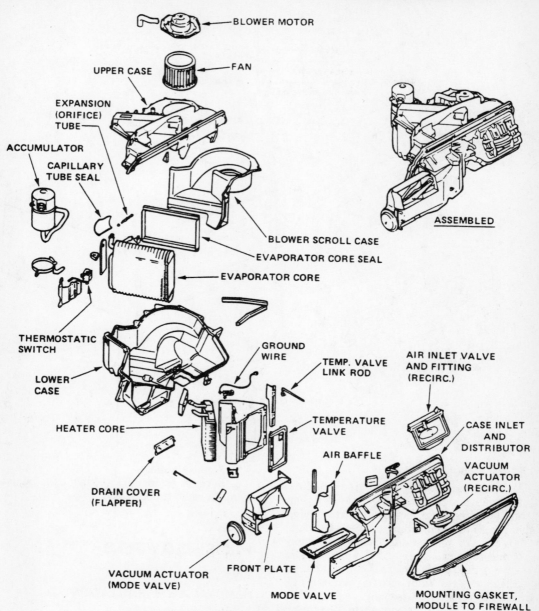

Exploded view of a typical A/C / heater module—1980–87

8. Reverse to install, trimming radio before installing right radio knob.

1978-1984

1. Disconnect the negative battery cable.
2. Remove cigar lighter knob, radio knobs and escutcheons by pulling straight out.
3. Remove center instrument panel trim plate by grasping plate firmly and pulling straight out. To ease the removal process, a flat blade screwdriver may be used to gently pry up the edge of the center I/P trim plate. Note location of retaining clips on panel trim plate.

4. Remove (4) 7mm screws retaining radio bracket to center I/P assembly.
5. Reach inside glove box and loosen (1) 10mm nut on holding bracket at right rear side of radio chassis.
6. Remove antenna lead-in at right rear of radio.
7. Grasp radio and gently remove from center I/P support.
8. Remove radio harness wiring by pinching connectors and pulling straight out.
9. Remove radio bracket.
10. Install in reverse of removal procedure make trim adjustment on radio if necessary.

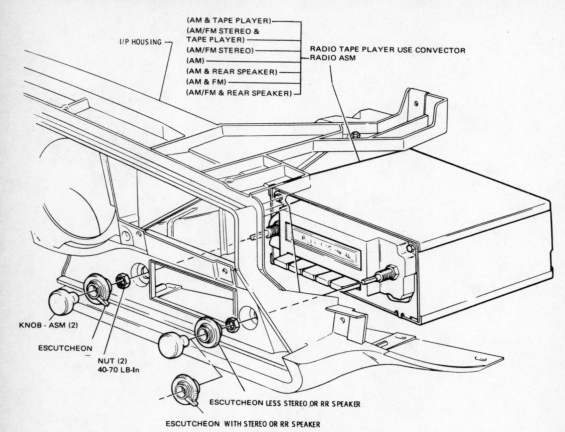

(AM & TAPE PLAYER)
(AM/FM STEREO & TAPE PLAYER)
(AM/FM STEREO)
(AM)
(AM & REAR SPEAKER)
(AM & FM)
(AM/FM & REAR SPEAKER)

I/P HOUSING

RADIO TAPE PLAYER USE CONVECTOR
RADIO ASM

KNOB - ASM (2)

ESCUTCHEON

NUT (2)
40-70 LB-In

ESCUTCHEON LESS STEREO OR RR SPEAKER

ESCUTCHEON WITH STEREO OR RR SPEAKER

Radio installation—1975-77

1984 and Later

1. Disconnect the negative battery cable.
2. Remove screws that hold the left hand trim cover and right side switch trim plate,to gain access to radio retaining bracket screws.
NOTE: *On some model years only center trim cover has to be removed. To remove this cover grasp firmly and pull straight out.*
3. Remove (4) 7mm screws retaining radio bracket to center I/P assembly.
4. Pull radio out far enough to disconnect 3 electrical connectors,antenna lead,clock connector if so equipped.

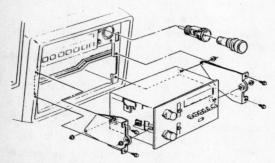

Typical late model radio mounting

5. Remove radio.
6. Reverse to install, making trim adjustment on radio if necessary.

WINDSHIELD WIPERS

Arm

REMOVAL AND INSTALLATION

Removal of the wiper arms requires the use of a special tool, G.M. J8966 or its equivalent. Versions of this tool are generally available in auto parts stores.

1. Insert the tool or a screwdriver under the wiper arm and pry the arm off the shaft. Be careful not to scratch the paint.
NOTE: *Raising the hood on most later models will facilitate easier wiper arm removal.*
2. Disconnect the washer hose from the arm (if so equipped). Remove the arm.
3. To install, position the arm over the shaft and press down.Make sure you install the arms in the same position on the windshield as they were when they were removed.
WARNING: *On some model years when in-*

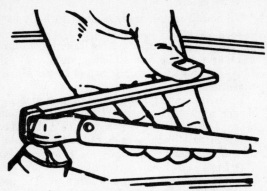

Remove the wiper arm with the special tool

stalling arm on spindle shaft note location of key-way on spindle shaft and arm inproper alignment of key-way on arm to spindle shaft could cause damage to spindle shaft on transmission housing.

Blade

REMOVAL AND INSTALLATION

Three methods are used to retain wiper blades to wiper arms.

1. The first type blade uses an internal spring. To remove wiper blade, press down on blade, release spring and remove blade from arm.

2. The second type blade uses a press-type release lever.When release lever is depressed, the blade assembly can be slid off the wiper arm pin.

3. The third type blade uses an exterior spring.To remove wiper blade,insert a scewdriver under spring and then push downward on screwdriver to raise spring. Blade can then be removed from arm.

To install blades to the arm, insert blade over pin at top of arm and press until spring retainer engages groove in pin.

Windshield Wiper Motor

REMOVAL AND INSTALLATION

1. Raise hood and remove cowl screen to gain access to wiper motor it may be necessary to remove wiper arms(see section on wiper arm removal) on some model years wiper motor is mounted on the driver's side of the cowl panel, accessible from engine compartment.

2. Reach through opening in cowl panel loosen(do not remove)transmission drive link(s) to motor crank arm attaching nuts.Then detach drive link(s) from motor crank arm.

NOTE: *On early model years transmission drive links have adjustment slots where crank arm and drive links connect,when loosing drive links to motor crank arm attaching nuts note location of these nuts.*

3. Disconnect electrical connector and washer hoses if so equipped.

4. Remove the attaching bolts being careful that the rubber bushing remain in the slots of the motor base. Guide the crank arm out of the hole in the cowl and remove the motor.

5. Install in exact reverse order. Motor must

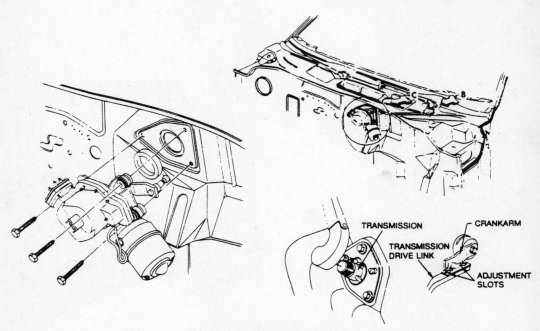

TRANSMISSION

CRANKARM

TRANSMISSION
DRIVE LINK

ADJUSTMENT
SLOTS

Wiper motor installation—typical

be in PARK position when assembling crank arm to tranmission drive link(s).

6. Check operation of wiper/washer system.

Wiper Linkage
REMOVAL AND INSTALLATION

1. Raise hood and remove cowl vent screen.

2. Remove right and left wiper arm and blade assemblies.(see section on wiper arm removal).

3. Loosen (do not remove) attaching nuts securing transmission drive link(s) to motor crank arm.On early model years transmission drive links have adjustment slots where crank arm and drive links connect,when loosing drive links to motor crank arm attaching nuts note location of these nuts.

4. Disengage drive link(s) from crank arm.

5. Remove the right and left transmission to body attaching screws.Remove transmission(s) and linkage assembly by guiding it through plenum chamber opening.

6. To install transmission(s) and linkage assemblies, position assembly in plenum chamber through the openings.

7. Loosely install transmission to body attaching screws.

8. Install transmission drive link(s) to motor crank arm and tighten attaching nuts.

NOTE : *Wiper motor must be in park position.*

9. Align transmission(s) and tighten attaching screws to body.

10. Install wiper arm and blade assemblies.Check wiper operation,wiper pattern,and park position.

11. Install cowl vent screen.

12. Check washer nozzle alignment if so equipped.

INSTRUMENTS AND SWITCHES

Instrument Cluster
REMOVAL AND INSTALLATION

WARNING: *These procedures for instrument cluster removal and installation do not apply to models with the A.C.R.S. (air bag) system. For these models with air bags, it is*

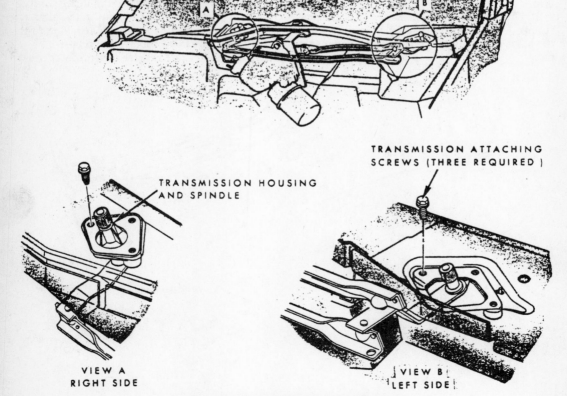

TRANSMISSION HOUSING AND SPINDLE

TRANSMISSION ATTACHING SCREWS (THREE REQUIRED)

VIEW A
RIGHT SIDE

VIEW B
LEFT SIDE

Typical wiper transmission installation

advisable to take the car to a dealer for proper servicing. When removing or installing any electrical gauges,disconnect the negative battery cable to prevent short circuit damage. All procedures, when possible, are done from the front or driver's side of the instrument panel. All fasteners should be fully driven, seated and not stripped.

1975-1983

NOTE: *The instrument cluster on these models is not removed as a unit. Instead, each square gauge is removed.*

1. Disconnect negative battery cable.
2. Remove headlight switch knob and escutcheon.
3. Carefully pry out and remove instrument trim plate.
4. Remove (5) screws and cluster lens.
5. Remove screws and gage.
6. Install in reverse of removal procedure.

1984 and Later Standard Instrument Cluster

1. Disconnect negative battery cable.
2. Remove left hand I/P trim cover.On some model years grasp trim cover on both sides and pull straight out.
3. Remove (4) screws holding cluster carrier to instrument panel.
4. Disconnect the speedometer cable at the transmission or in the engine compartment if 2 piece cable is used in order to gain slack for latter work.

NOTE: *May be necessary to loosen retaining clips that attach cable to the body on 1 piece cable to gain slack for latter work*

5. Remove steering column trim cover.
6. Disconnect the shift indicator clip.
7. Lower the steering column by removing the two bolts that fasten the column to dash panel and positon onto front seat.

8. Pull the cluster forward far enough to disconnect the speedometer cable and bulbs at rear of the cluster.To disconnect speedometer cable from cluster push down on the spring tab to release.
9. Securely apply the handbrake or block the wheels.Pull the gear selector lever down into low gear.Pull the instrument cluster out far enough to remove the single screw which fastens the Speed Sensor optic head to the speedometer and then remove the cluster.
10. Installation is the reverse of removal.

1984 and Later Digital Instrument Cluster

1. Disconnect the negative battery cable.
2. Remove the cluster the same way as in Standard Instrument Cluster removal procedure only remember to disconnect cluster harness connector.
3. Disconnect the ground strap from the back side cluster carrier.
4. Pull whole cluster assembly out.
5. Unscrew knob from trip set lever.
6. Remove (4) screws from clear cluster lens cover to cluster carrier.
7. Remove clear lens and black filler.
8. Remove spring and needle assembly from shift indicator.
9. Remove (5) screws holding tube and circuit board assembly to cluster carrier.Lift tube and circuit board assembly out of cluster carrier noting the position of the gaskets covering the indicator lights.
10. Hold the speedometer frame against the tube and circuit board face plate and remove the two standard head screws from the face plate.
11. Remove mechanical speedometer assembly.
12. Installation is the reverse of removal.

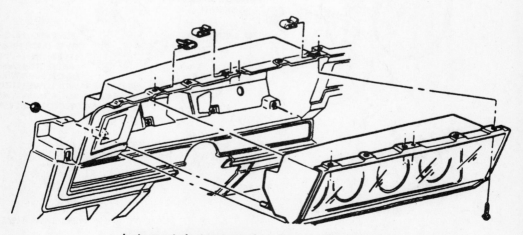

Instrument cluster removal—typical of 1984–87 models

Wiper Switch
REMOVAL AND INSTALLATION
1975-77

1. If the wiper switch is found to be defective, insert one or two narrow bladed screw drivers into each of the two slots within the switch face immediately above the knobs and bend the retaining clips downward or break them off, then rotate the top of the switch outward to remove.

NOTE: Be sure to take notice how wire(s) are connect to switch before removing switch.

2. Disconnect the wire connector from the back of the switch.

3. After connecting the wire to the back of the new switch, simply align and press the switch into place.

1978-81

1. Remove the headlight switch knob and escutcheon. See the section on headlight switch removal later in this chapter.

2. Remove the left I/P trim plate.On some model years grasp trim cover on both sides and pull straight out.

3. Remove the two retaining screws and remove the switch.

4. Installation is the reverse of removal.

1982 and Later

NOTE: *Special tool or equivalent needed for this repair.*

All 1982 and later models use the multi-function lever on the steering column.

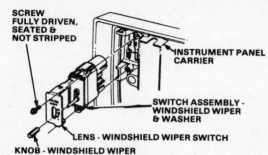

Washer and wiper switch—1978–81

1. Disconnect the negative battery cable.

2. Disconnect the turn signal electrical connector at the base of the steering column jacket.

3. Remove the wiring protector on the bottom of the column to ease the wiring harness removal.

4. Grasp lever assembly firmly and pull straight out.

5. See illustration to install.

Headlight Switch
REMOVAL AND INSTALLATION
1975-1983

1. Disconnect the negative battery cable.

NOTE: *On 1975-79 models with air conditioning, remove the left A/C duct or tube.*

2. Pull the switch knob to the last notch and depress the spring loaded latch button on top of the switch while pulling the knob and rod out of the switch. On 1978 and later models, depress

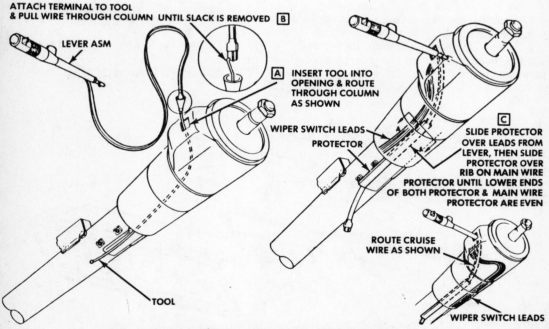

Windshield wiper switch removal and installation—1982 and later

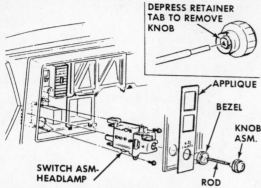

Headlight switch mounting—typical of 1975–83 models

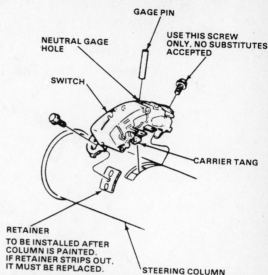

Automatic transmission neutral safety/backup lamp switch typical of 1975–81 column shift cars without automatic doorlocks

the retainer tab behind the knob and remove the knob.

3. Remove left I/P trim plate by grasping plate and careful pull straight out note location of clips on trim plate when installing.

4. Remove screws securing headlight switch.

5. Disconnect the multiple electrical connector from the switch and remove switch.

6. Install in the reverse of the above.

1984-1987

1. Disconnect the negative battery cable.

2. Remove left hand I/P trim cover. On some model years grasp trim cover on both sides and pull straight out.

3. Remove 3 (7mm) screws.

4. Pull switch straight out. This will also disconnect electrical connection.

5. To install new switch push switch straight in being careful not to damage prongs on new switch.

6. Tighten screws, connect battery cable and check operation.

Back-up Light Switch

REMOVAL AND INSTALLATION

On all column shift automatic transmission cars the backup light switch is combined with the starter neutral safety switch. It is mounted on the steering column under the instrument panel. The backup lamp switch is controlled by a carrier tang actuated by transmission shift tube in the steering column.

1975-1981 (Automatic Transmission w/Column Shift; wo/Automatic Door Locks)

1. Disconnect wiring connectors from switch.

2. Remove (2) attaching screws and lift switch off column.(Do not lose screws use these screws only for installation), NO SUBSTITUTES ACCEPTED.

3. To install position gear shift lever in NEUTRAL.

4. Install switch to column by inserting switch carrier tang into shift tube slot and tighten retaining screws.

5. Move gear shift lever out of NEUTRAL to extreme postion (LOW) to shear switch pin. Switch is pinned in NEUTRAL with plastic shear pin (no additional pinning required for installation).

6. Check operation of switch, after switch installation verify that engine will only start in PARK or NEUTRAL. If engine will start in any other position, readjust switch.

7. To readjust switch, position gear shift lever in NEUTRAL, loosen (2) retaining screws, rotate switch slighty on column until NEUTRAL gage hole in back of switch freely admits a No.41 ($^3/_{32}$") size drill bite to the depth of $^3/_8$" then tighten retaining nuts.

8. Check operation of switch, verify that engine will only start in PARK or NEUTRAL.

1975-1981 Automatic Transmission w/Console Shift

1. Disconnect wiring connectors from switch.

2. Remove (2) attaching screws and lift switch off column.(Do not lose screws use these screws only for installation), NO SUBSTITUTES ACCEPTED.

3. To install position steering column in LOCK position and floor shifter in PARK position.

4. Rotate shift bowl clockwise (as viewed from upper end of column) to remove free play and lightly hold against lock stop.

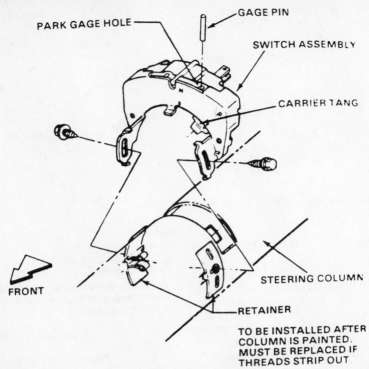

PARK GAGE HOLE

GAGE PIN

SWITCH ASSEMBLY

CARRIER TANG

FRONT

STEERING COLUMN

RETAINER

TO BE INSTALLED AFTER
COLUMN IS PAINTED.
MUST BE REPLACED IF
THREADS STRIP OUT.

Typical automatic transmission neutral safety switch for 1975–81 models with console mounted shift levers

5. Install switch to column by inserting switch carrier tang into shift tube slot and tighten retaining screws.

6. Unlock steering column and move floor shift lever out of PARK to extreme postion (LOW) to shear switch pin. Switch is pinned in PARK with plastic shear pin (no additional pinning required for installation).

7. Check operation of switch, after switch installation verify that engine will only start in PARK or NEUTRAL. If engine will start in any other position, readjust switch.

8. To readjust switch, position floor shift lever in PARK and LOCK steering column loosen (2) retaining screws, rotate switch slighty on column until PARK gage hole in back of switch freely admits a No.41 ($3/32$″) size drill bite to depth of $3/8$″.

9. Rotate shift bowl clockwise (as viewed from upper end of column) to remove free play and lightly hold against lock stop then tighten retaining screws on switch.

10. Check operation of switch, verify that engine will only start in PARK or NEUTRAL.

1982 and Later Automatic Transmission w/Console And Column Shift

1. Disconnect wiring at switch.

2. Carefully pry switch from steering column using small blade screwdriver.

3. To install switch set gear shift lever in NEUTRAL position.

4. Align acuator on switch with hole in shift tube.

5. Position rearward portion of switch (connector side) to fit into cut out of lower jacket.

6. Push down on front of switch:The (2) tangs on housing back will snap into place in rectangular holes in steering column jacket.

7. Adjust switch by moving gear selector to park.The main housing and the housing back should ratchet, providing proper switch adjustment.

8. Check operation of switch, verify that engine will only start in PARK or NEUTRAL. If engine will start in any other position, readjust switch.

9. To readjust switch rotate the housing of switch all the way toward LOW gear position (rotate clockwise as viewed from upper end of column.) Move gear selector to PARK switch should ratchet providing proper switch adjustment.

10. Check operation of switch.

Early Model Years w/Manual Transmission

On cars with manual transmission, the back-up light switch will be mounted on the transmission.

Late Model Years w/Manual Transmission

On cars equipped with manual transmission, the backup light switch is usually on the gear shifter assembly.

Speedometer Cable

WARNING: *These procedures for speedometer cable and housing removal and installation do not apply to models with the A.C.R.S.(air bag) system.For these models with air bags,it is advisable to take the car to a dealer for proper servicing.*

Note that the speedometer cable can be replaced without replacing the cable housing.

REMOVAL AND INSTALLATION (CABLE ONLY)

1. Reach up underneath the instrument panel and disconnect the cable housing from the cluster housing. To disconnect the speedometer cable housing push down on the spring tab to release. On some model years you might first have to remove the left air conditioning duct or trim plate remove as necessary to gain access to speedometer cable housing release tab.

2. Carefully pull the cable housing down and pull out the cable.

3. Hold the cable vertically and turn it slowly between your fingers. If it is kinked, you will notice it flopping around. Replace any kinked cable.

4. If the cable is broken, raise and support the car. Disconnect the cable housing from the transmission tailshaft. Large pliers or a similar tool will loosen retaining nut and pull out the other piece of broken cable from the cable housing.

5. Before installing a new inner cable thoroughly lubricate it with approved speedometer cable lubricant. Do not over-lubricate cable. Note that it is important that all lube be kept away from the speedometer head.

6. Install greased cable at top end of speedometer cable housing first then feed cable through until it comes out at lower end. Connect the lower end of speedometer cable housing to the tailshaft. Connect upper end of cable to speedometer head. Install any ductwork or trim plates that you had to remove to gain access.

NOTE: *Tighten retaining nut on lower end of speedometer cable housing no more than 24-60 in.lb.*

7. Road test car check for proper operation of speedometer.

REMOVAL AND INSTALLATION (CABLE AND CABLE HOUSING)

1. Remove instrument cluster bezel and lens.

2. Remove speedometer head assembly out of the cluster housing.

3. Disconnect cable from speedometer head by pushing down on spring tab to release.

4. Disconnect the lower cable housing from the transmission tailshaft, using a large pliers or similar tool to loosen retaining nut.

5. Remove any retaining clips or grommets that attach the cable housing to the body and carefully pull the cable housing out of the car. If the cable housing will not pull out easily, it is still clipped to the car at some point, or it is stuck on other wires or components.

6. Reverse the procedure for installation. Before installing,grease both ends of the cable with an approved speedometer cable lubricant. Be careful to route the cable housing properly. Any bends in the cable housing must not have a radius of less than 6" (152mm) unless there is a pre-formed bend in the cable housing. Make sure the cable housing is not routed where it could be pinched or chafed by moving parts or overheated by an exhaust pipe or the catalytic converter.

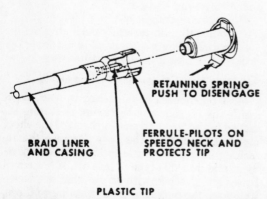

Speedometer cable attachment at the instrument cluster end

RETAINING SPRING PUSH TO DISENGAGE

BRAID LINER AND CASING

FERRULE-PILOTS ON SPEEDO NECK AND PROTECTS TIP

PLASTIC TIP

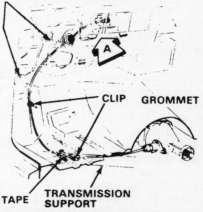

CRUISE CONTROL CABLE ROUTING TO TRANSDUCER

CLIP   GROMMET

TAPE   TRANSMISSION SUPPORT

Typical speedometer cable routing

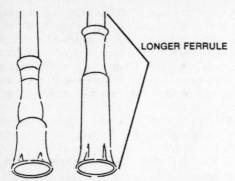

The replacement speedometer cable on 1981–82 models has a longer ferrule

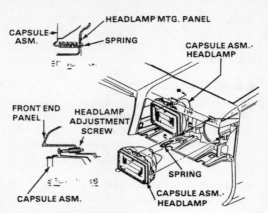

Typical headlight mounting

NOTE: *Tighten retaining nut on lower end of speedometer cable housing to no more than 24-60 in.lb.*

7. Road test car and check for proper operation of speedometer.

NOTE: *A new upper speedometer cable and housing was released during the 1982 model year for vehicles equipped with cruise control. This cable offers improved lubrication, grease retention, and noise suppression however, this cable and housing should not be used on other than 1981-1982 models. This cable can be identified by a longer ferrule at the speedometer end.*

LIGHTING

Headlights

REMOVAL AND INSTALLATION (SEAL BEAM TYPE BULB)

CAUTION: *If car is equipped with Composite Headlamps, it is advisable to take it to a dealer or a professional mechanic for headlamp replacement.*

1. Remove the headlight bezel (outer trim around seal beam).

2. Remove the headlight bulb retaining ring. To remove ring on some model years you must remove retaining screws and a spring use a suitable tool with a hook on it.

NOTE: *Do not touch the two headlight aiming screws, at the top and the side of the retaining ring (these screws will have different heads), or the headlight aim will have to be re-adjusted.*

3. Pull the seal beam forward and unplug the electrical connector from the rear of the bulb.

4. Plug the new seal beam into the electrical connector. Check operation of bulb (low and high beam). Hold the seal beam in place and install retaining ring. Install the headlight bezel.

5. Check headlight aim.It is advisable to take

the car to professional mechanic for headlight aiming.

Signal And Marker Lights

REMOVAL AND INSTALLATION

Front Turn Signal and Parking Lights

1. To replace the bulbs, reach up behind the front bumper and carefully twist the bulb socket conterclockwise until it can be pulled backward and out.

2. Slighty depress the bulb and turn it counterclockwise to release it.

3. To install bulb carefully push down and turn bulb clockwise at the same time.

4. Install the bulb socket and turn the socket clockwise to lock it in the light housing.

NOTE: *When replacing the bulbs make sure to install correct bulb size as some bulbs are single and others are double contact.*

Side Marker Lights

1. To replace the bulb, reach up behind the housing (front or rear) and carefully twist the bulb socket counterclockwise until it can be pulled backward and out.

2. Pull bulb straight out.

3. To install bulb carefully push straight in.

4. Install the bulb socket and turn the socket clockwise to lock it in the light housing.

Rear Turn Signal, Brake and Parking Lights

Most rear lenses are fastened in place from inside the luggage compartment. A stud is attached to the lens and passes through the sheet metal at the rear of the body. Remove the attaching nuts from inside the luggage compartment and pull this type of lens off. A few small lenses are attached with screws that are accessible from the outside the car. To remove these, simply remove the screws and remove the lens. Once the lens is removed:

1. Slighty depress the bulb and turn it counterclockwise to release it.

2. To install bulb carefully push down and turn bulb clockwise at the same time.

3. Install the bulb socket and turn the socket clockwise to lock it in the light housing. (Some model years just push right in).

NOTE: *When replacing the bulbs make sure to install correct bulb size as some bulbs are single and others are double contact.*

CIRCUIT PROTECTION

Fuses

The fuse block on a Century and Regal is located underneath the far left side of the instrument panel. On some model years a kick-panel or access cover may have to be removed to service fuses. Two types of fuses have been used; the conventional type (cylindrical) fuse and the new mini fuses, found on later models. The conventional type (cylindrical) fuses are held in the fuse block by small tangs, and are best removed with a small blade screwdriver.

NOTE: *Some early models use an in-line 30 amp. fuse for the air conditioning blower High speed, located at the cowl relay and an in-line 10 amp. fuse for power antenna.*

The mini fuses, with blade terminal design, allow fingertip removal and replacement. To determine whether either type of fuse is blown, remove the suspected fuse and examine the element in the fuse for a break. If the element (the strip of silver metal inside) is broken, replace the fuse with one of equal amperage. Some fuses have their amperage value molded into the fuse end, and others (and all of the miniaturized fuses) have a color coding system.

Vehicles built in years up to and including 1985:

- 3 amps-Violet
- 5 amps-Tan
- 7.5 amps-Brown
- 10 amps-Red
- 20 amps-Clear
- 25 amps-White

GOOD FUSE   BLOWN FUSE

Mini-fuses used on 1978 and later models

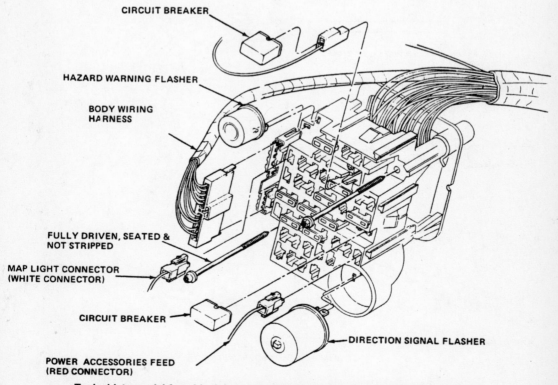

CIRCUIT BREAKER

HAZARD WARNING FLASHER

BODY WIRING HARNESS

FULLY DRIVEN, SEATED & NOT STRIPPED

MAP LIGHT CONNECTOR (WHITE CONNECTOR)

CIRCUIT BREAKER

DIRECTION SIGNAL FLASHER

POWER ACCESSORIES FEED (RED CONNECTOR)

Typical late model fuse block incorporating both mini-fuses and circuit breakers

REMOVE EXISTING VINYL TUBE SHIELDING
REINSTALL OVER FUSE LINK BEFORE CRIMPING
FUSE LINK TO WIRE ENDS

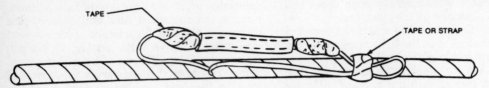

TYPICAL REPAIR USING THE SPECIAL #17 GA. (9.00" LONG-YELLOW) FUSE LINK REQUIRED FOR THE AIR/COND.
CIRCUITS (2) #687E and #261A LOCATED IN THE ENGINE COMPARTMENT

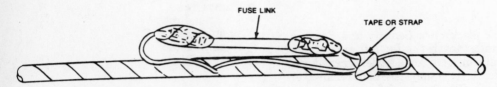

TYPICAL REPAIR FOR ANY IN-LINE FUSE LINK USING THE SPECIFIED GAUGE FUSE LINK FOR THE SPECIFIC CIRCUIT

TYPICAL REPAIR USING THE EYELET TERMINAL FUSE LINK OF THE SPECIFIED GAUGE FOR ATTACHMENT TO A CIRCUIT WIRE END

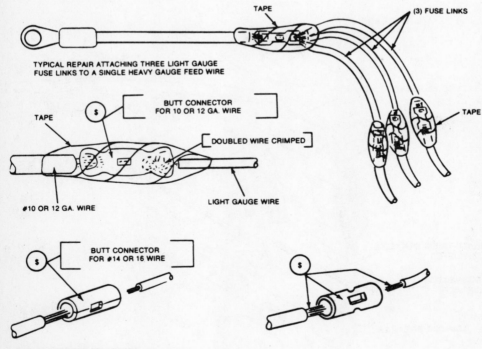

TYPICAL REPAIR ATTACHING THREE LIGHT GAUGE
FUSE LINKS TO A SINGLE HEAVY GAUGE FEED WIRE

FUSIBLE LINK REPAIR PROCEDURE

General fuse link repair procedure

Vehicles built in 1986 and later years:
- 3 amps-Purple
- 5 amps-Tan
- 10 amps-Red
- 20 amps-Yellow
- 25 amps-Brown or White
- 30 amps-Green

Fusible Links

NOTE: *A physical check can be made to determine whether or not a fusible link is burned out. To perform this check, simply feel and, or gently pull on each link. A good link will be or remain in tact.*

All Buick Century and Regal models are equipped with fusible links. These links are attached to the lower ends of the main supply wires and connect to the starter solenoid. One of the main wires is a No. 12 red wire which supplies the headlight circuit and the other is a No. 10 red wire which supplies all electrical units except the headlights. On latter models there are many more fusible links. The links consist of wire which is several gages smaller than the supply wires they are connected to and function as additional protection to the wiring in the event of an overloaded or short circuited condition in that they will melt before the wir-

ing insulation is damaged elsewhere in the circuit. A burned out fusible link would be indicated by the following condition: All the electrical accessories dead except the headlights or, headlights dead but all other electrical units operative.

REPLACEMENT

1. Disconnect the battery grounded cable.
2. Disconnect the fusible link from the junction block or starter solenoid.
3. Cut the harness directly behind the connector to remove the damaged fusible link.
4. Strip the harness wire approximately ½".
5. Connect the new fusible link to the harness wire using a crimp-on connector. Solder the connection using resin core solder.
6. Tape all exposed wires with plastic electrical tape.
7. Connect the fusible link to the junction block or starter solenoid and reconnect the battery ground cable.

Circuit Breakers

Circuit breakers are also located in the fuse block. A circuit breaker is an electrical switch which breaks the circuit during an electrical

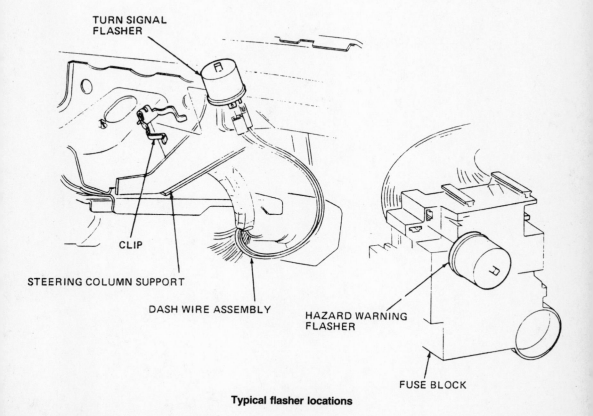

TURN SIGNAL FLASHER

CLIP

STEERING COLUMN SUPPORT

DASH WIRE ASSEMBLY

HAZARD WARNING FLASHER

FUSE BLOCK

Typical flasher locations

overload. The circuit breaker will remain open until the short or overload condition in the circuit is corrected.

Flashers

On early model years turn signal flasher is located under the dash to the right of the steering column, usually clip to the steering column support. The hazzard flasher is under the dash, to the left of the steering column or in the upper top corner of the fuse block. On later model years both the turn signal and hazzard flashers are located in the fuse block. When replacing a flasher be sure to locate the proper flasher and carefully remove from the electrical connector or fuse block.

Drive Train

7

MANUAL TRANSMISSION

Understanding the Manual Transmission and Clutch

Because of the way the gasoline engine breathes, it can produce torque, or twisting force, only within a narrow speed range. Most modern engines must turn at about 2,500 rpm to produce their peak torque. By 4,500 rpm they are producing so little torque that continued increases in engine speed produce no power increases.

The transmission and clutch are employed to vary the relationship between engine speed and the speed of the wheels so that adequate engine power can be produced under all circumstances. The clutch allows engine torque to be applied to the transmission input shaft gradually, due to mechanical slippage. The car can, consequently, be started smoothly from a full stop.

The transmission changes the ratio between the rotating speeds of the engine and the wheels by the use of gears. 3-speed or 4-speed transmissions are most common. The lower gears allow full engine power to be applied to the rear wheels during acceleration at low speeds.

The clutch driven plate is a thin disc, the center of which is splined to the transmission input shaft. Both sides of the disc are covered with a layer of material which is similar to brake lining and which is capable of allowing slippage without roughness or excessive noise.

The clutch cover is bolted to the engine flywheel and incorporates a diaphragm spring which provides the pressure to engage the clutch. The cover also houses the pressure plate. The driven disc is sandwiched between the pressure plate and the smooth surface of the flywheel when the clutch pedal is released, thus forcing it to turn at the same speed as the engine crankshaft.

The transmission contains a mainshaft which passes all the way through the transmission, from the clutch to the driveshaft. This shaft is separated at one point, so that front and rear portions can turn at different speeds.

Power is transmitted by a countershaft in the lower gears and reverse. The gears of the countershaft mesh with gears on the mainshaft, allowing power to be carried from one to the other. All the countershaft gears are integral with that shaft, while several of the mainshaft gears can either rotate independently of the shaft or be locked to it. Shifting from one gear to the next causes one of the gears to be freed from rotating with the shaft, and locks another to it. Gears are locked and unlocked by internal dog clutches which slide between the center of the gear and the shaft. The forward gears usually employ synchronizers: friction members which smoothly bring gear and shaft to the same speed before the toothed dog clutches are engaged.

The clutch is operating properly if:

1. It will stall the engine when released with the vehicle held stationary.

2. The shift lever can be moved freely between 1st and reverse gears when the vehicle is stationary and the clutch disengaged.

A clutch pedal free-play adjustment is incorporated in the linkage. If there is about 1-2" of motion before the pedal begins to release the clutch, it is adjusted properly. Inadequate free-play wears all parts of the clutch releasing mechanisms and may cause slippage. Excessive free-play may cuase inadequate release and hard shifting of gears.

Some clutches use a hydraulic system in place of mechanical linkage. If the clutch fails to release, fill the clutch master cylinder with fluid to the proper level and pump the clutch pedal to fill the system with fluid. Bleed the system in the same way as a brake system. If leaks are lo-

Troubleshooting the Manual Transmission

Problem	Cause	Solution
Transmission shifts hard	• Clutch adjustment incorrect • Clutch linkage or cable binding • Shift rail binding	• Adjust clutch • Lubricate or repair as necessary • Check for mispositioned selector arm roll pin, loose cover bolts, worn shift rail bores, worn shift rail, distorted oil seal, or extension housing not aligned with case. Repair as necessary.
	• Internal bind in transmission caused by shift forks, selector plates, or synchronizer assemblies • Clutch housing misalignment • Incorrect lubricant • Block rings and/or cone seats worn	• Remove, dissemble and inspect transmission. Replace worn or damaged components as necessary. • Check runout at rear face of clutch housing • Drain and refill transmission • Blocking ring to gear clutch tooth face clearance must be 0.030 inch or greater. If clearance is correct it may still be necessary to inspect blocking rings and cone seats for excessive wear. Repair as necessary.
Gear clash when shifting from one gear to another	• Clutch adjustment incorrect • Clutch linkage or cable binding • Clutch housing misalignment • Lubricant level low or incorrect lubricant • Gearshift components, or synchronizer assemblies worn or damaged	• Adjust clutch • Lubricate or repair as necessary • Check runout at rear of clutch housing • Drain and refill transmission and check for lubricant leaks if level was low. Repair as necessary. • Remove, disassemble and inspect transmission. Replace worn or damaged components as necessary.
Transmission noisy	• Lubricant level low or incorrect lubricant • Clutch housing-to-engine, or transmission-to-clutch housing bolts loose • Dirt, chips, foreign material in transmission • Gearshift mechanism, transmission gears, or bearing components worn or damaged • Clutch housing misalignment	• Drain and refill transmission. If lubricant level was low, check for leaks and repair as necessary. • Check and correct bolt torque as necessary • Drain, flush, and refill transmission • Remove, disassemble and inspect transmission. Replace worn or damaged components as necessary. • Check runout at rear face of clutch housing
Jumps out of gear	• Clutch housing misalignment • Gearshift lever loose • Offset lever nylon insert worn or lever attaching nut loose • Gearshift mechanism, shift forks, selector plates, interlock plate, selector arm, shift rail, detent plugs, springs or shift cover worn or damaged • Clutch shaft or roller bearings worn or damaged	• Check runout at rear face of clutch housing • Check lever for worn fork. Tighten loose attaching bolts. • Remove gearshift lever and check for loose offset lever nut or worn insert. Repair or replace as necessary. • Remove, disassemble and inspect transmission cover assembly. Replace worn or damaged components as necessary. • Replace clutch shaft or roller bearings as necessary

Troubleshooting the Manual Transmission (cont.)

Problem	Cause	Solution
Jumps out of gear (cont.)	• Gear teeth worn or tapered, synchronizer assemblies worn or damaged, excessive end play caused by worn thrust washers or output shaft gears	• Remove, disassemble, and inspect transmission. Replace worn or damaged components as necessary.
	• Pilot bushing worn	• Replace pilot bushing
Will not shift into one gear	• Gearshift selector plates, interlock plate, or selector arm, worn, damaged, or incorrectly assembled	• Remove, disassemble, and inspect transmission cover assembly. Repair or replace components as necessary.
	• Shift rail detent plunger worn, spring broken, or plug loose	• Tighten plug or replace worn or damaged components as necessary
	• Gearshift lever worn or damaged	• Replace gearshift lever
	• Synchronizer sleeves or hubs, damaged or worn	• Remove, disassemble and inspect transmission. Replace worn or damaged components.
Locked in one gear—cannot be shifted out	• Shift rail(s) worn or broken, shifter fork bent, setscrew loose, center detent plug missing or worn	• Inspect and replace worn or damaged parts
	• Broken gear teeth on countershaft gear, clutch shaft, or reverse idler gear	• Inspect and replace damaged part
	Gearshift lever broken or worn, shift mechanism in cover incorrectly assembled or broken, worn damaged gear train components	• Disassemble transmission. Replace damaged parts or assemble correctly.
Lubricant leaking from output shaft seals or from vent	• Output shaft seals damaged or installed incorrectly	• Replace seals. Be sure seal lip faces interior of case when installed. Also be sure yoke seal surfaces are not scored or nicked. Remove scores, nicks with fine sandpaper or replace yoke(s) if necessary.
Abnormal tire wear	• Extended operation on dry hard surface (paved) roads in 4H range	• Operate in 2H on hard surface (paved) roads

cated, tighten loose connections or overhaul the master or slave cylinder as necessary.

Identification

See Chapter 1, which lists the basic types of manual transmissions and the various locations of their serial numbers. By finding the serial number on your transmission and comparing its location with the information there, you can readily determine the type of gearbox used.

MANUAL TRANSMISSION

Identification

A fully synchronized Saginaw 3-speed transmission has been available in these cars. It can be identified by the single bolt at the top of the side cover. The production code and transmis-

sion serial number are on the right side of the transmission case.

The only 4-speed used is a Saginaw unit.

Adjustments
LINKAGE ADJUSTMENT
Column Shift

1. Place the column shift lever in Reverse. Turn the ignition lock to the LOCK position.
2. Loosen 1st-reverse clamp bolt.
3. Place the transmission 1st-reverse lever (the rear one) into the reverse (forward) position. Pull down on the shift rod and tighten the clamp bolt.
4. Unlock the ignition lock and shift the transmission levers into their neutral (center) positions.
5. Loosen 2nd-3rd clamp bolt.
6. Install $^3/_{16}$" diameter rod through the 2nd-

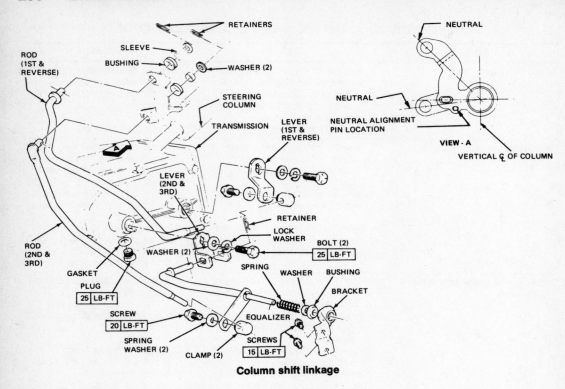

Column shift linkage

3rd lever, selector plate, 1st-reverse lever, and alignment plate at the bottom of the column.

7. Tighten 2nd-3rd clamp bolt.

8. With the shift lever in Reverse, the key must move freely to the LOCK position. You should not be able to get into the LOCK position in any gear position other than Reverse.

3-Speed Floorshift

1. Place the transmission levers into neutral.

2. Loosen the shift rod adjusting clamp bolts.

3. Place a rod ($^{11}/_{64}$" diameter 1975-77; $^1/_4$" diameter 1978-83) in the notch in the rear portion of the shift bracket assembly.

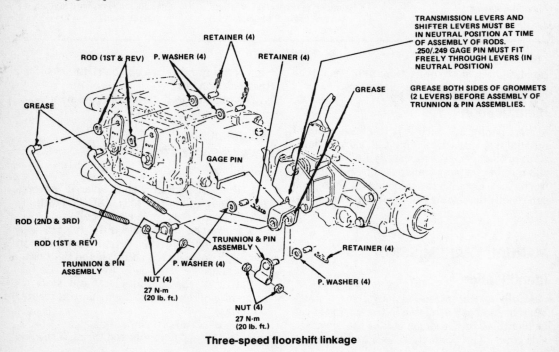

Three-speed floorshift linkage

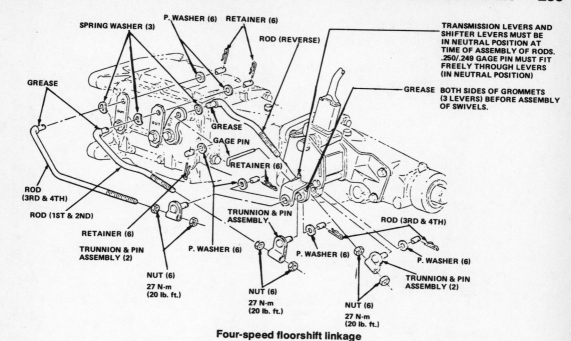

SPRING WASHER (3) P. WASHER (6) RETAINER (6)

ROD (REVERSE)

GREASE

TRANSMISSION LEVERS AND SHIFTER LEVERS MUST BE IN NEUTRAL POSITION AT TIME OF ASSEMBLY OF RODS. .250/.249 GAGE PIN MUST FIT FREELY THROUGH LEVERS (IN NEUTRAL POSITION)

GREASE BOTH SIDES OF GROMMETS (3 LEVERS) BEFORE ASSEMBLY OF SWIVELS.

GREASE
GAGE PIN
RETAINER (6)

ROD (3RD & 4TH)
ROD (1ST & 2ND)
RETAINER (6)
TRUNNION & PIN ASSEMBLY (2)
P. WASHER (6)
TRUNNION & PIN ASSEMBLY
ROD (3RD & 4TH)
P. WASHER (6)
P. WASHER (6)
P. WASHER (6)
TRUNNION & PIN ASSEMBLY (2)
NUT (6) 27 N·m (20 lb. ft.)
NUT (6) 27 N·m (20 lb. ft.)
NUT (6) 27 N·m (20 lb. ft.)

Four-speed floorshift linkage

4. Move both shift levers back against the rod.

5. Tighten the shift rod adjusting bolts.

4-Speed Floorshift

1. Place the transmission levers in neutral positions.

2. Place ¼" diameter rod in the rear lower portion of the shift bracket assembly.

3. Adjust all three shift levers back against the rod.

4. Tighten the adjusting clamp bolts.

Transmission

REMOVAL AND INSTALLATION

1. Raise the vehicle on a hoist and drain the transmission fluid.

2. Mark the universal joint and transmission shaft companion flange to aid proper alignment at the time of installation. Remove the two U-bolts and disconnect the driveshaft at the rear joint. Slide the driveshaft rearward as far as possible and remove it.

3. Disconnect the shift linkage from the transmission.

4. Disconnect the speedometer cable and the back-up light switch at the transmission.

5. On 1978 and later 3-speeds and 1976 and later 4-speeds, remove the crossmember-to-transmission mounting bolts, the catalytic converter-to-transmission bracket (if equipped) and remove the crossmember-to-frame bolts. Raise the transmission slightly and remove the crossmember.

6. Remove the two upper transmission-to-flywheel housing bolts and insert guide pins.

7. Remove the lower transmission-to-flywheel housing bolts.

NOTE: *If guide pins are not used, damage to the clutch driven plate can result.*

8. Slide the transmission back until the drive gear shaft disengages the clutch disc and clears the flywheel housing. Lower the transmission.

9. On installation, install the guide pins in the upper and lower right side bolt holes for alignment. If the guide pins aren't used, the clutch plate might be damaged.

TRANSMISSION OVERHAUL

Saginaw 3-Speed

TRANSMISSION CASE DISASSEMBLY

1. Remove the side cover assembly and the shift forks.

2. Remove the clutch gear bearing retainer.

3. Remove the clutch gear bearing-to-gear stem snapring. Pull the clutch gear outward until a screwdriver can be inserted between the bearing and the case. Remove the clutch gear bearing.

4. Remove the speedometer driven gear and the extension bolts.

5. Remove the Reverse idler shaft snapring.

6. Remove the mainshaft and the extension assembly through the rear of the case.

7. Remove the clutch gear and the 3rd speed blocking ring from inside the case. Remove the 14 roller bearings from the clutch gear.

8. Expand the snapring which retains the

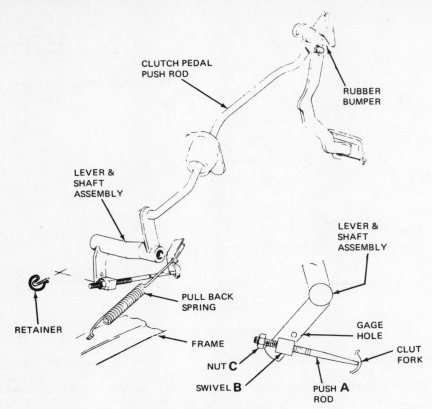

CLUTCH PEDAL
PUSH ROD

RUBBER
BUMPER

LEVER &
SHAFT
ASSEMBLY

LEVER &
SHAFT
ASSEMBLY

RETAINER

PULL BACK
SPRING

GAGE
HOLE

CLUT
FORK

FRAME

NUT **C**

SWIVEL **B**

PUSH **A**
ROD

Clutch linkage adjustment

mainshaft rear bearing and remove the extension.

9. Using a dummy shaft, drive the countershaft and the key out through the rear of the case. Remove the gear, the two tanged thrust washers and the dummy shaft. Remove the bearing washer and the 27 roller bearings from each end of the countergear.

10. Using a long drift, drive the Reverse idler shaft and key through the rear of the case.

11. Remove the Reverse idler gear and the tanged steel thrust washer.

TRANSMISSION CASE ASSEMBLY

1. Using a dummy shaft, grease and load a row of 27 roller bearings and a thrust washer at each end of countergear.

2. Place the countergear assembly into the case from the rear. Place a tanged thrust washer (tang away from the gear) at each end. Install the countershaft and the key, making sure that the tangs align with the notches in the case.

3. Install the Reverse idler gear thrust washer, the gear and the shaft with a key from the rear of the case.

NOTE: *Be sure the thrust washer is between the gear and the rear of the case with the tang toward the notch in the case.*

4. Expand the snapring in the extension housing. Assemble the extension over the rear of the mainshaft and onto the rear bearing. Seat the snapring in the rear bearing groove.

5. Install the 14 mainshaft pilot bearings into the clutch gear cavity. Assemble the 3rd speed blocking ring onto the clutch gear clutching surface with the teeth toward the gear.

6. Place the clutch gear, the pilot bearings and the 3rd speed blocking ring assembly over the front of the mainshaft assembly; be sure the blocking rings align with the keys in the 2nd-3rd synchronizer assembly.

7. Stick the extension gasket to the case with grease. Install the clutch gear, the mainshaft and the extension together; be sure the clutch gear engages the teeth of the countergear anti lash plate. Torque the extension bolts to 45 ft.lb.

8. Place the bearing over the stem of the clutch gear and into the front case bore. Install the front bearing to the clutch gear snapring.

9. Install the clutch gear bearing retainer and the gasket. The retainer oil return hole must be at the bottom. Torque the retainer bolts to 10 ft.lb.

10. Install the Reverse idler gear shaft E-ring.

11. Shift the synchronizer sleeves to the Neu-

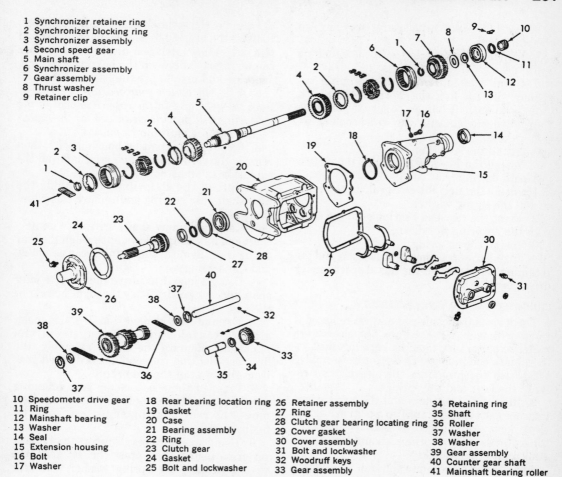

1 Synchronizer retainer ring
2 Synchronizer blocking ring
3 Synchronizer assembly
4 Second speed gear
5 Main shaft
6 Synchronizer assembly
7 Gear assembly
8 Thrust washer
9 Retainer clip

10 Speedometer drive gear	18 Rear bearing location ring	26 Retainer assembly
11 Ring	19 Gasket	27 Ring
12 Mainshaft bearing	20 Case	28 Clutch gear bearing locating ring
13 Washer	21 Bearing assembly	29 Cover gasket
14 Seal	22 Ring	30 Cover assembly
15 Extension housing	23 Clutch gear	31 Bolt and lockwasher
16 Bolt	24 Gasket	32 Woodruff keys
17 Washer	25 Bolt and lockwasher	33 Gear assembly

34 Retaining ring
35 Shaft
36 Roller
37 Washer
38 Washer
39 Gear assembly
40 Counter gear shaft
41 Mainshaft bearing roller

Exploded view of Saginaw 3-speed transmission

tral positions. Install the cover, the gasket and the forks; aligning the forks with the synchronizer sleeve grooves. Torque the side cover bolts to 10 ft.lb.

12. Install the speedometer driven gear.

MAINSHAFT DISASSEMBLY

1. Remove the 2nd-3rd speed sliding clutch hub snapring from the mainshaft. Remove the clutch assembly, the 2nd speed blocking ring and the 2nd gear from front of the mainshaft.

2. Depress the speedometer drive gear retaining clip and remove the gear. Some units have a metal speedometer driver gear which must be pulled off.

3. Remove the rear bearing snapring.

4. Support the Reverse gear and press on the rear of the mainshaft. Remove the Reverse gear, the thrust washer, the spring washer, the rear bearing and the snapring.

NOTE: *When pressing off the rear bearing, be careful not to cock the bearing on the shaft.*

5. Remove the 1st and Reverse sliding clutch

hub snapring. Remove the clutch assembly, 1st speed blocking ring and the 1st gear; sometimes the synchronizer hub and gear must be pressed off.

MAINSHAFT ASSEMBLY

1. Turn the front of the mainshaft up.

2. Install the 2nd gear with the clutching teeth up; the rear face of the gear butts against the flange on the mainshaft.

3. Install a blocking ring with the clutching teeth down. The three blocking rings are the same.

4. Install the 2nd/3rd speed synchronizer assembly with the fork slot down; press it onto the mainshaft splines.

NOTE: *Both synchronizer assemblies are the same. Be sure that the blocking ring notches align with the synchronizer assembly keys.*

5. Install the synchronizer snapring; both synchronizer snaprings are the same.

6. Turn the rear of the shaft up, then install the 1st gear with the clutching teeth up; the

front face of the gear butts against the flange on the mainshaft.

7. Install a blocking ring with the clutching teeth down.

8. Install the 1st/Reverse synchronizer assembly with the fork slot down, then press it onto the mainshaft splines; be sure the blocking ring notches align with the synchronizer assembly keys.

9. Install the snapring.

10. Install the Reverse gear with the clutching teeth down.

11. Install the steel Reverse gear thrust washer and the spring washer.

12. Press the rear ball bearing onto the shaft with the snapring slot down.

13. Install the snapring.

14. Install the speedometer drive gear and the retaining clip; press on the metal speedometer drive gear.

CLUTCH KEYS AND SPRINGS REPLACEMENT

The keys and the springs may be replaced if worn or broken, but the hubs and sleeves are matched pairs, they must be kept together.

1. Mark the hub and sleeve for reassembly.

2. Push the hub from the sleeve, then remove the keys and the springs.

3. Place the three keys and the two springs (one on each side of hub) in position, so the three keys are engaged by both springs; the tanged ends of the springs should not be installed into the same key.

4. Slide the sleeve onto the hub by aligning the marks.

NOTE: *A groove around the outside of the synchronizer hub marks the end that must be opposite the fork slot in the sleeve when assembled.*

EXTENSION OIL SEAL AND BUSHING REPLACEMENT

1. Remove the seal.

2. Using the bushing removal and installation tool, drive the bushing into the extension housing.

3. Drive the new bushing in from the rear. Lubricate the inside of the bushing and the seal. Install a new oil seal with the extension seal installation tool or other suitable tool.

CLUTCH BEARING RETAINER OIL SEAL REPLACEMENT

1. Pry the old seal out.

2. Install the new seal using the seal installer. Seat the seal in the bore.

Saginaw 4-Speed

TRANSMISSION CASE DISASSEMBLY

1. Drain the lubricant. Remove the side cover and the shift forks.

2. Remove the clutch gear bearing retainer. Remove the bearing-to-gear stem snapring and pull out on the clutch gear until a small pry bar can be inserted between the bearing, the large snapring and case to pry the bearing off.

NOTE: *The clutch gear bearing is a slip fit on the gear and in the case. Removal of the bearing will provide clearance for the clutch gear and the mainshaft removal.*

3. Remove the extension housing bolts, then remove the clutch gear, the mainshaft and the extension as an assembly.

4. Spread the snapring which holds the mainshaft rear bearing and remove the extension case.

5. Using a dummy shaft, drive the countershaft and its woodruff key out through the rear of the case. Remove the countergear assembly and the bearings.

6. Using a long drift, drive the Reverse idler shaft and the woodruff key through the rear of the case.

7. Expand and remove the 3rd/4th speed sliding clutch hub snapring from the mainshaft. Remove the clutch assembly, the 3rd gear blocking ring and the 3rd speed gear from the front of the mainshaft.

8. Press in the speedometer gear retaining clip and slide the gear off the mainshaft. Remove the rear bearing snapring from the mainshaft.

9. Using an arbor press, support the 1st gear on press plates, then press the 1st gear, the thrust washer, the spring washer, the rear bearing and snapring from the rear of the mainshaft.

CAUTION: *Be sure to center the gear, the washers, the bearings and the snapring when pressing the rear bearing.*

10. Expand and remove the 1st/2nd sliding clutch hub snapring from the mainshaft, then remove the clutch assembly, the 2nd speed blocking ring and the 2nd speed gear from rear of the mainshaft.

NOTE: *After thoroughly cleaning the parts and the transmission case, inspect and replace the damaged or worn parts. When checking the bearings, do not spin them at high speeds. Clean and rotate the bearings by hand to detect the roughness or unevenness. Spinning can damage the balls and the races.*

TRANSMISSION CASE ASSEMBLY

1. Grease both inside ends of the countergear. Install a dummy shaft into the countergear, then load a row of roller bearings (27) and thrust washers at each end of the countergear.

2. Position the countergear assembly into the case through the rear opening. Place a

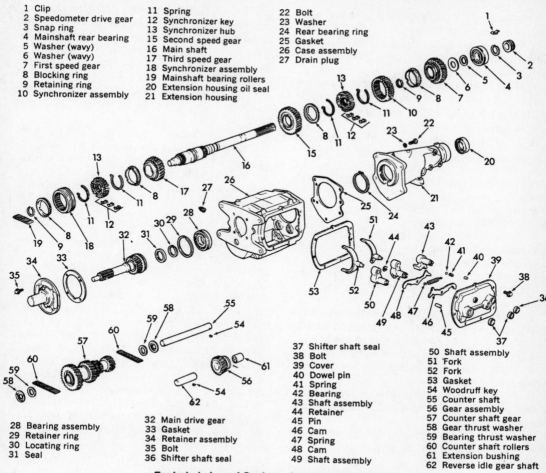

1 Clip
2 Speedometer drive gear
3 Snap ring
4 Mainshaft rear bearing
5 Washer (wavy)
6 Washer (wavy)
7 First speed gear
8 Blocking ring
9 Retaining ring
10 Synchronizer assembly
11 Spring
12 Synchronizer key
13 Synchronizer hub
15 Second speed gear
16 Main shaft
17 Third speed gear
18 Synchronizer assembly
19 Mainshaft bearing rollers
20 Extension housing oil seal
21 Extension housing
22 Bolt
23 Washer
24 Rear bearing ring
25 Gasket
26 Case assembly
27 Drain plug

37 Shifter shaft seal
38 Bolt
39 Cover
40 Dowel pin
41 Spring
42 Bearing
43 Shaft assembly
44 Retainer
45 Pin
46 Cam
47 Spring
48 Cam
49 Shaft assembly

50 Shaft assembly
51 'Fork
52 Fork
53 Gasket
54 Woodruff key
55 Counter shaft
56 Gear assembly
57 Counter shaft gear
58 Gear thrust washer
59 Bearing thrust washer
60 Counter shaft rollers
61 Extension bushing
62 Reverse idle gear shaft

28 Bearing assembly
29 Retainer ring
30 Locating ring
31 Seal
32 Main drive gear
33 Gasket
34 Retainer assembly
35 Bolt
36 Shifter shaft seal

Exploded view of Saginaw 4-speed transmission

tanged thrust washer at each end of the countergear.

3. Install the countergear shaft and woodruff key from the rear of the case.

NOTE: *Make sure that the shaft engages both thrust washers and that the tangs align with their notches in the case.*

4. Install the Reverse idler gear, the shaft and the woodruff key. Install the extension-to-rear bearing snapring. Assemble the extension housing over the rear of the mainshaft and onto the rear bearing.

5. Install the 14 mainshaft pilot bearings into the clutch opening and the 4th speed blocking ring onto the clutching surface of the clutch gear (with the clutching teeth facing the gear).

6. Assemble the clutch gear, the pilot bearings and the 4th speed blocking ring unit over the front of the mainshaft. Do not assemble the bearing to the gear at this point.

CAUTION: *Be sure that the blocking ring notches align with the 3rd-4th synchronizer assembly keys.*

7. Install the extension-to-case gasket and secure it with grease. Install the clutch gear, the mainshaft and the extension housing as an assembly. Install the extension-to-case bolts (apply sealer to the bottom bolt) and torque to 45 ft.lb.

8. Install the outer snapring on the front bearing and place the bearing over the stem of the clutch gear and into the case bore.

9. Install the snapring to the clutch gear stem. Install the clutch gear bearing retainer and the gasket, with the retainer oil return hole at the bottom.

10. Place the synchronizer sleeves into the Neutral positions and install the cover, the gasket and the fork assemblies to the case; be sure the forks align with the synchronizer sleeve grooves. Torque the cover bolts to 22 ft.lb.

MAINSHAFT ASSEMBLY

Install the following parts with the front of the mainshaft facing up:

1. Install the 3rd speed gear with the clutch-

ing teeth up; the rear face of the gear will abut with the mainshaft flange.

2. Install a blocking ring (with the clutching teeth down) over the 3rd speed gear synchronizing surface.

NOTE: *The four blocking rings are the same.*

3. Press the 3rd-4th synchronizer assembly (with the fork slot down) onto the mainshaft splines until it bottoms.

CAUTION: *The blocking ring notches must align with the synchronizer assembly keys.*

4. Install the synchronizer hub-to-mainshaft snapring; both synchronizer snaprings are the same.

Install the following parts with the rear of the mainshaft facing up:

5. Install the 2nd speed gear with the clutching teeth up; the front face of the gear will abut with the flange on the mainshaft.

6. Install a blocking ring (with the clutching teeth down) over the 2nd speed gear synchronizing surface.

7. Press the 1st-2nd synchronizer assembly (with the fork slot down) onto the mainshaft.

CAUTION: *The blocking ring notches must align with the synchronizer assembly keys.*

8. Install the synchronizer hub-to-mainshaft snapring.

9. Install a blocking ring with the notches down so they align with the 1st-2nd synchronizer assembly keys.

10. Install the 1st gear with the clutching teeth down. Install the 1st gear thrust washer and the spring washer.

11. Press the rear ball bearing (with the slot down) onto the mainshaft. Install the snapring. Install the speedometer gear and clip.

CLUTCH

Understanding the Clutch

The purpose of the clutch is to disconnect and connect engine power from the transmission. A car at rest requires a lot of engine torque to get all that weight moving. An internal combustion engine does not develop a high starting torque (unlike steam engines), so it must be allowed to operate without any load until it builds up enough torque to move the car. Torque increases with engine rpm. The clutch allows the engine to build up torque by physically disconnecting the engine from the transmission, relieving the engine of any load or resistance. The transfer of engine power to the transmission (the load) must be smooth and gradual; if it weren't, drive line components would wear out or break quickly. This gradual power transfer is made possible by gradually releasing the clutch pedal. The clutch disc and pressure plate are the connecting link between the engine and transmission. When the clutch pedal is released, the disc and plate contact each other (clutch engagement), physically joining the engine and transmission. When the pedal is pushed in, the disc and plate separate (the clutch is disengaged), disconnecting the engine from the transmission.

The clutch assembly consists of the flywheel, the clutch disc, the clutch pressure plate, the throwout bearing and fork, the actuating linkage and the pedal. The flywheel and clutch pressure plate (driving members) are connected to the engine crankshaft and rotate with it. The clutch disc is located between the flywheel and pressure plate, and splined to the transmission shaft. A driving member is one that is attached to the engine and transfers engine power to a driven member (clutch disc) on the transmission shaft. A driving member (pressure plate) rotates (drives) a driven member (clutch disc) on contact and, in so doing, turns the transmission shaft. There is a circular diaphragm spring within the pressure plate cover (transmission side). In a relaxed state (when the clutch pedal is fully released), this spring is convex; that it, it is dished outward toward the transmission. Pushing in the clutch pedal actuates an attached linkage rod. Connected to the other end of this rod is the throwout bearing fork. The throwout bearing is attached to the fork. When the clutch pedal is depressed, the clutch linkage pushes the fork and bearing forward to contact the diaphragm spring of the pressure plate. The outer edges of the spring are secured to the pressure plate and are pivoted on rings so that when the center of the spring is compressed by the throwout bearing, the outer edges bow outward and, by so doing, pull the pressure plate in the same direction - away from the clutch disc. This action separates the disc from the plate, disengaging the clutch and allowing the transmission to be shifted into another gear. A coil type clutch return spring attached to the clutch pedal arm permits full release of the pedal. Releasing the pedal pulls the throwout bearing away from the diaphragm spring resulting in a reversal of spring position. As bearing pressure is gradually released from the spring center, the outer edges of the spring bow outward, pushing the pressure plate into closer contact with the clutch disc. As the disc and plate move closer together, friction between the two increases and slippage is reduced until, when full spring pressure is applied (by fully releasing the pedal), The speed of the disc and plate are the same. This stops all slipping, creating a direct connection between the plate and disc which results in the transfer of power from the engine to the

Troubleshooting Basic Clutch Problems

Problem	Cause
Excessive clutch noise	Throwout bearing noises are more audible at the lower end of pedal travel. The usual causes are: • Riding the clutch • Too little pedal free-play • Lack of bearing lubrication A bad clutch shaft pilot bearing will make a high pitched squeal, when the clutch is disengaged and the transmission is in gear or within the first 2″ of pedal travel. The bearing must be replaced. Noise from the clutch linkage is a clicking or snapping that can be heard or felt as the pedal is moved completely up or down. This usually requires lubrication. Transmitted engine noises are amplified by the clutch housing and heard in the passenger compartment. They are usually the result of insufficient pedal free-play and can be changed by manipulating the clutch pedal.
Clutch slips (the car does not move as it should when the clutch is engaged)	This is usually most noticeable when pulling away from a standing start. A severe test is to start the engine, apply the brakes, shift into high gear and SLOWLY release the clutch pedal. A healthy clutch will stall the engine. If it slips it may be due to: • A worn pressure plate or clutch plate • Oil soaked clutch plate • Insufficient pedal free-play
Clutch drags or fails to release	The clutch disc and some transmission gears spin briefly after clutch disengagement. Under normal conditions in average temperatures, 3 seconds is maximum spin-time. Failure to release properly can be caused by: • Too light transmission lubricant or low lubricant level • Improperly adjusted clutch linkage
Low clutch life	Low clutch life is usually a result of poor driving habits or heavy duty use. Riding the clutch, pulling heavy loads, holding the car on a grade with the clutch instead of the brakes and rapid clutch engagement all contribute to low clutch life.

transmission. The clutch disc is now rotating with the pressure plate at engine speed and, because it is splined to the transmission shaft, the shaft now turns at the same engine speed. Understanding clutch operation can be rather difficult at first; if you're still confused after reading this, consider the following analogy. The action of the diaphragm spring can be compared to that of an oil can bottom. The bottom of an oil can is shaped very much like the clutch diaphragm spring and pushing in on the can bottom and then releasing it produces a similar effect. As mentioned earlier, the clutch pedal return spring permits full release of the pedal and reduces linkage slack due to wear. As the linkage wears, clutch free-pedal travel will increase and free-travel will decrease as the clutch wears. Free-travel is actually throwout bearing lash.

The diaphragm spring type clutches used are available in two different designs: flat diaphragm springs or bent spring. The bent fingers are bent back to create a centrifugal boost ensuring quick re-engagement at higher engine speeds. This design enables pressure plate load to increase as the clutch disc wears and makes low pedal effort possible even with a heavy-duty clutch. The throwout bearing used with the bent finger design is 1¼″ long and is shorter than the bearing used with the flat finger design. These bearings are not interchangeable. If the longer bearing is used with the bent finger clutch, free-pedal travel will not exist. This results in clutch slippage and rapid wear.

The transmission varies the gear ratio between the engine and rear wheels. It can be shifted to change engine speed as driving conditions and loads change. The transmission allows disengaging and reversing power from the engine to the wheels.

Adjustments
LINKAGE

1. Remove the return spring.
2. Turn the clutch lever and shaft assembly until the pedal is firmly against the stop.
3. Push the outer end of the clutch fork to the rear until the throwout bearing touches the spring fingers.

4. Install the lower pushrod in the fork and the swivel in the gauge hole. Turn the rod clockwise as viewed from the front to remove all play from the linkage.

5. Remove the swivel from the gauge hole and install it in the hole furthest from the centerline of the lever and shaft assembly. Install the washers and retainer.

6. Tighten the locknut against the swivel, being careful not to change the rod length.

7. Install the clutch retainer spring. The above procedure should produce ⅔-1⅓" of free play when measured at the pedal pad center.

REMOVAL AND INSTALLATION

WARNING: *The clutch driven disc contains asbestos, which has been determined to be a cancer causing agent. Never clean clutch surfaces with compressed air, as this will cause particles containing asbestos to concentrate in the air, making them readily inhaled! Avoid inhaling even the dust created when wiping the clutch surfaces. When cleaning these surfaces, use a commercially available, safe brake cleaning fluid.*

The only service adjustment necessary on the clutch is to maintain the correct pedal free-play (see Linkage Adjustment directly above).

1. Remove the pedal return spring from the clutch fork. Remove the transmission as outlined under Manual Transmission.

2. Remove the flywheel housing.

3. Remove the throw-out bearing from the clutch fork.

4. Disconnect the clutch fork from the ball stud.

5. Mark the clutch cover and the flywheel to assure proper balance on reassembly.

6. Loosen the clutch cover and the flywheel bolts one turn at a time until the spring pressure is released.

7. Support the pressure plate and cover assembly while removing the last bolts, then remove the cover assembly and the driven plate.

8. Inspect the flywheel for scoring, grooves, or signs of overheating (discoloration). Reface or replace the flywheel as necessary.

9. Install the clutch by reversing the removal procedure. Use a clutch aligning pilot or a spare transmission input shaft through the hub of the driven plate and into the pilot bushing. Be sure to align the clutch cover-to-flywheel index marks.

AUTOMATIC TRANSMISSION

Understanding Automatic Transmissions

The automatic transmission allows engine torque and power to be transmitted to the rear wheels within a narrow range of engine operating speeds. The transmission will allow the engine to turn fast enough to produce plenty of power and torque at very low speeds, while keeping it at a sensible rpm at high vehicle speeds. The transmission performs this job entirely without driver assistance. The transmission uses a light fluid as the medium for the transmission of power. This fluid also works in the operation of various hydraulic control circuits and as a lubricant. Because the transmission fluid performs all of these three functions, trouble within the unit can easily travel from one part to another. For this reason, and because of the complexity and unusual operating principles of the transmission, a very sound understanding of the basic principles of operation will simplify troubleshooting.

THE TORQUE CONVERTER

The torque converter replaces the conventional clutch. It has three functions:

1. It allows the engine to idle with the vehicle at a standstill, even with the transmission in gear.

2. It allows the transmission to shift from range to range smoothly, without requiring that the driver close the throttle during the shift.

3. It multiplies engine torque to an increasing extent as vehicle speed drops and throttle opening is increased. This has the effect of making the transmission more responsive and reduces the amount of shifting required.

The torque converter is a metal case which is shaped like a sphere that has been flattened on opposite sides. It is bolted to the rear end of the engine's crankshaft. Generally, the entire metal case rotates at engine speed and serves as the engine's flywheel.

The case contains three sets of blades. One set is attached directly to the case. This set forms the torus or pump. Another set is directly connected to the output shaft, and forms the turbine. The third set is mounted on a hub which, in turn, is mounted on a stationary shaft through a one-way clutch. This third set is known as the stator.

A pump, which is driven by the converter hub at engine speed, keeps the torque converter full of transmission fluid at all times. Fluid flows continuously through the unit to provide cooling.

Under low speed acceleration, the torque converter functions as follows:

The torus is turning faster than the turbine. It picks up fluid at the center of the converter and, through centrifugal force, slings it outward. Since the outer edge of the converter moves faster than the portions at the center, the fluid picks up speed.

The fluid then enters the outer edge of the turbine blades. It then travels back toward the center of the converter case along the turbine blades. In impinging upon the turbine blades, the fluid loses the energy picked up in the torus.

If the fluid were now to immediately be returned directly into the torus, both halves of the converter would have to turn at approximately the same speed at all times, and torque input and output would both be the same.

In flowing through the torus and turbine, the fluid picks up two types of flow, or flow in two separate directions. It flows through the turbine blades, and it spins with the engine. The stator, whose blades are stationary when the vehicle is being accelerated at low speeds, converts one type of flow into another. Instead of allowing the fluid to flow straight back into the torus, the stator's curved blades turn the fluid almost 90° toward the direction of rotation of the engine. Thus the fluid does not flow as fast toward the torus, but is already spinning when the torus picks it up. This has the effect of allowing the torus to turn much faster than the turbine. This difference in speed may be compared to the difference in speed between the smaller and larger gears in any gear train. The result is that engine power output is higher, and engine torque is multiplied.

As the speed of the turbine increases, the fluid spins faster and faster in the direction of engine rotation. As a result, the ability of the stator to redirect the fluid flow is reduced. Under cruising conditions, the stator is eventually forced to rotate on its one-way clutch in the direction of engine rotation. Under these conditions, the torque converter begins to behave almost like a solid shaft, with the torus and turbine speeds being almost equal.

THE PLANETARY GEARBOX

The ability of the torque converter to multiply engine torque is limited. Also, the unit tends to be more efficient when the turbine is rotating at relatively high speeds. Therefore, a planetary gearbox is used to carry the power output of the turbine to the driveshaft.

Planetary gears function very similarly to conventional transmission gears. However, their construction is different in that three elements make up one gear system, and, in that all three elements are different from one another. The three elements are: an outer gear that is shaped like a hoop, with teeth cut into the inner surface; a sun gear, mounted on a shaft and located at the very center of the outer gear; and a set of three planet gears, held by pins in a ring-like planet carrier, meshing with both the sun gear and the outer gear. Either the outer gear or the sun gear may be held stationary, providing more than one possible torque multiplication factor for each set of gears. Also, if all three gears are forced to rotate at the same speed, the gearset forms, in effect, a solid shaft.

Most modern automatics use the planetary gears to provide either a single reduction ratio of about 1.8:1, or two reduction gears: a low of about 2.5:1, and an intermediate of about 1.5:1. Bands and clutches are used to hold various portions of the gearsets to the transmission case or to the shaft on which they are mounted. Shifting is accomplished, then, by changing the portion of each planetary gearset which is held to the transmission case or to the shaft.

THE SERVOS AND ACCUMULATORS

The servos are hydraulic pistons and cylinders. They resemble the hydraulic actuators used on many familiar machines, such as bulldozers. Hydraulic fluid enters the cylinder, under pressure, and forces the piston to move to engage the band or clutches.

The accumulators are used to cushion the engagement of the servos. The transmission fluid must pass through the accumulator on the way to the servo. The accumulator housing contains a thin piston which is sprung away from the discharge passage of the accumulator. When fluid passes through the accumulator on the way to the servo, it must move the piston against spring pressure, and this action smooths out the action of the servo.

THE HYDRAULIC CONTROL SYSTEM

The hydraulic pressure used to operate the servos comes from the main transmission oil pump. This fluid is channeled to the various servos through the shift valves. There is generally a manual shift valve which is operated by the transmission selector lever and an automatic shift valve for each automatic upshift the transmission provides: i.e., 2-speed automatics have a low/high shift valve, while 3-speeds have a 1-2 valve, and a 2-3 valve.

There are two pressures which effect the operation of these valves. One is the governor pressure which is affected by vehicle speed. The other is the modulator pressure which is affected by intake manifold vacuum or throttle position. Governor pressure rises with an increase in vehicle speed, and modulator pressure rises as the throttle is opened wider. By responding to these two pressures, the shift valves cause the upshift points to be delayed with increased throttle opening to make the best use of the engine's power output.

Most transmissions also make use of an auxiliary circuit for downshifting. This circuit may be actuated by the throttle linkage or the vacuum line which actuates the modulator, or by a cable or solenoid. It applies pressure to a special downshift surface on the shift valve or valves.

The transmission modulator also governs the line pressure, used to actuate the servos. In this way, the clutches and bands will be actuated with a force matching the torque output of the engine.

Identification

Many different automatic transmissions have been used in rear wheel drive Buick models since 1975. Basically, all of the transmissions used fall into 3 basic groups, as follows:

THM-200 GROUP
THM-200: 3-Speed standard duty
THM-200-C: 3-Speed LTC
THM-200-4R: 4-Speed LTC

THM-350 GROUP
THM-250: 3-Speed light duty
THM-350: 3-Speed standard duty

THM-350-C: 3-Speed LTC
THM-375-B: 3-Speed heavy duty

THM-400 GROUP
THM-400: 3-Speed heavy duty

PAN REMOVAL, FLUID AND FILTER CHANGE

The fluid should be changed with the engine and transmission at normal operating temperature. If the car is raised, the transmission should be level. Be careful when draining because the fluid will be hot.

1. Raise and safely support the vehicle.

2. On some models, it may be necessary to remove the transmission supporting crossmember in order to gain access to all of the pan bolts.

WARNING :*Support the transmission with a jack before removing the crossmember! Also, anticipate the flow of hot fluid out of the pan because you could easily be burned!*

3. Place a large pan underneath the transmission to catch the fluid. Loosen all the pan screws, then pull down one corner to drain

Troubleshooting Basic Automatic Transmission Problems

Problem	Cause	Solution
Fluid leakage	• Defective pan gasket	• Replace gasket or tighten pan bolts
	• Loose filler tube	• Tighten tube nut
	• Loose extension housing to transmission case	• Tighten bolts
	• Converter housing area leakage	• Have transmission checked professionally
Fluid flows out the oil filler tube	• High fluid level	• Check and correct fluid level
	• Breather vent clogged	• Open breather vent
	• Clogged oil filter or screen	• Replace filter or clean screen (change fluid also)
	• Internal fluid leakage	• Have transmission checked professionally
Transmission overheats (this is usually accompanied by a strong burned odor to the fluid)	• Low fluid level	• Check and correct fluid level
	• Fluid cooler lines clogged	• Drain and refill transmission. If this doesn't cure the problem, have cooler lines cleared or replaced.
	• Heavy pulling or hauling with insufficient cooling	• Install a transmission oil cooler
	• Faulty oil pump, internal slippage	• Have transmission checked professionally
Buzzing or whining noise	• Low fluid level	• Check and correct fluid level
	• Defective torque converter, scored gears	• Have transmission checked professionally
No forward or reverse gears or slippage in one or more gears	• Low fluid level	• Check and correct fluid level
	• Defective vacuum or linkage controls, internal clutch or band failure	• Have unit checked professionally
Delayed or erratic shift	• Low fluid level	• Check and correct fluid level
	• Broken vacuum lines	• Repair or replace lines
	• Internal malfunction	• Have transmission checked professionally

Lockup Torque Converter Service Diagnosis

Problem	Cause	Solution

No lockup	• Faulty oil pump
	• Sticking governor valve
	• Valve body malfunction
	  (a) Stuck switch valve
	  (b) Stuck lockup valve
	  (c) Stuck fail-safe valve
	• Failed locking clutch
	• Leaking turbine hub seal
	• Faulty input shaft or seal ring
		• Replace oil pump
		• Repair or replace as necessary
		• Repair or replace valve body or its internal components as necessary
		
		• Replace torque converter
		• Replace torque converter
		• Repair or replace as necessary

Will not unlock	• Sticking governor valve
	• Valve body malfunction
	  (a) Stuck switch valve
	  (b) Stuck lockup valve
	  (c) Stuck fail-safe valve
		• Repair or replace as necessary
		• Repair or replace valve body or its internal components as necessary

Stays locked up at too low a speed in direct	• Sticking governor valve
	• Valve body malfunction
	  (a) Stuck switch valve
	  (b) Stuck lockup valve
	  (c) Stuck fail-safe valve
		• Repair or replace as necessary
		• Repair or replace valve body or its internal components as necessary

Locks up or drags in low or second	• Faulty oil pump
	• Valve body malfunction
	  (a) Stuck switch valve
	  (b) Stuck fail-safe valve
		• Replace oil pump
		• Repair or replace valve body or its internal components as necessary

Sluggish or stalls in reverse	• Faulty oil pump
	• Plugged cooler, cooler lines or fittings
	• Valve body malfunction
	  (a) Stuck switch valve
	  (b) Faulty input shaft or seal ring
		• Replace oil pump as necessary
		• Flush or replace cooler and flush lines and fittings
		• Repair or replace valve body or its internal components as necessary

Loud chatter during lockup engagement (cold)	• Faulty torque converter • Failed locking clutch • Leaking turbine hub seal	• Replace torque converter • Replace torque converter • Replace torque converter
Vibration or shudder during lockup engagement	• Faulty oil pump • Valve body malfunction • Faulty torque converter • Engine needs tune-up	• Repair or replace oil pump as necessary • Repair or replace valve body or its internal components as necessary • Replace torque converter • Tune engine
Vibration after lockup engagement	• Faulty torque converter • Exhaust system strikes underbody • Engine needs tune-up • Throttle linkage misadjusted	• Replace torque converter • Align exhaust system • Tune engine • Adjust throttle linkage
Vibration when revved in neutral Overheating: oil blows out of dip stick tube or pump seal	• Torque converter out of balance • Plugged cooler, cooler lines or fittings • Stuck switch valve	• Replace torque converter • Flush or replace cooler and flush lines and fittings • Repair switch valve in valve body or replace valve body
Shudder after lockup engagement	• Faulty oil pump • Plugged cooler, cooler lines or fittings • Valve body malfunction • Faulty torque converter • Fail locking clutch • Exhaust system strikes underbody • Engine needs tune-up • Throttle linkage misadjusted	• Replace oil pump • Flush or replace cooler and flush lines and fittings • Repair or replace valve body or its internal components as necessary • Replace torque converter • Replace torque converter • Align exhaust system • Tune engine • Adjust throttle linkage

Transmission Fluid Indications

The appearance and odor of the transmission fluid can give valuable clues to the overall condition of the transmission. Always note the appearance of the fluid when you check the fluid level or change the fluid. Rub a small amount of fluid between your fingers to feel for grit and smell the fluid on the dipstick.

If the fluid appears:	It indicates:
Clear and red colored	• Normal operation
Discolored (extremely dark red or brownish) or smells burned	• Band or clutch pack failure, usually caused by an overheated transmission. Hauling very heavy loads with insufficient power or failure to change the fluid, often result in overheating. Do not confuse this appearance with newer fluids that have a darker red color and a strong odor (though not a burned odor).
Foamy or aerated (light in color and full of bubbles)	• The level is too high (gear train is churning oil) • An internal air leak (air is mixing with the fluid). Have the transmission checked professionally.
Solid residue in the fluid	• Defective bands, clutch pack or bearings. Bits of band material or metal abrasives are clinging to the dipstick. Have the transmission checked professionally.
Varnish coating on the dipstick	• The transmission fluid is overheating

most of the fluid. Be careful; the fluid will be hot! Do not pry between the pan and the transmission with a screwdriver or the like to remove the pan, as this will damage the mating surfaces. The pan can be tapped with a rubber mallet to loosen its grip.

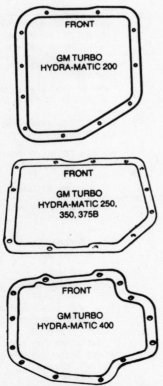

Identifying automatic transmission by pan gasket

4. Remove the pan screws and empty out the pan. The pan can be cleaned with solvent but it must be air dried thoroughly before replacement. Be very careful not to leave any lint or threads from rags in the pan.

NOTE: *It is normal to find a SMALL amount of metal shaving in the pan. An excessive amount of metal shavings indicates transmission damage which must be professionally investigated.*

5. Remove the filter or strainer retaining bolt (two on the Turbo Hydra-Matic 200, 250 and 350). A re-useable strainer is used on the Turbo Hydra-Matic 200 and 250. The strainer may be cleaned in solvent and thoroughly air dried. Filters are to be replaced. On the 400, Turbo Hydra-Matic, remove the filter retaining bolt(s), filter, and intake pipe O-ring (or gasket).

6. Install the new filter or cleaned strainer with a new gasket (or O-ring). Tighten the screws to 12 ft.lb. On the 400 install a new intake pipe O-ring and a new filter, tightening the retaining bolts to 10 ft.lb.

7. Install the pan with a new gasket. Tighten the bolts evenly in a crisscross pattern to 12 ft.lb.

8. Replace the crossmember if removed.

9. Lower the car. Add DEXRON®II fluid through the dipstick tube.

10. Start the engine and let it idle. Do not race the engine. Shift into each lever position, holding the brakes. Check the fluid level with the engine idling in Park. The level should be between the two dimples on the dipstick, about 1/4" below the ADD mark. Add fluid as necessary.

11. Check the fluid level after the car has been

driven enough to thoroughly warm up the transmission. The level should be at the FULL mark on the dipstick. If the transmission is overfilled, the excess must be drained off. Over-filling causes aerated fluid, resulting in trans-mission slippage and probable damage.

Gasoline Engine Automatic Trans-mission Adjustments

INTERMEDIATE BAND ADJUSTMENT

Only the THM-250 has an externally adjust-able band. Band adjustments are not externally possible on other transmissions. The interme-diate band must be adjusted with every re-quired fluid change or whenever there is slippage.

1. Position the shift lever in Neutral.
2. Loosen the locknut on the right side of the transmission. Tighten the adjusting screw to 30 in.lb.
3. Back the screw out three turns and then tighten the locknut to 15 ft.lb.

NEUTRAL SAFETY SWITCH ADJUSTMENT

The neutral safety switch prevents the en-gine from being started in any transmission po-sition except Neutral or Park. The switch is lo-cated on the upper side of the steering column under the instrument panel on column shift cars and inside the shift console on floor shift models.

Column Mounted Switch

1. Place the shifter in Neutral.
2. Loosen the screws which secure the switch.
3. Fit a 0.090″ gauge pin into the outer hole on the switch cover.
4. Move the switch until the gauge pin drops into the alignment hole on the inner slide.

Tighten the switch securing screws. Remove the gauge pin.

Console Mounted Switch

1. Place the shifter in Park.
2. Remove the center console.
3. Loosen the switch securing screws.
4. Fit a 0.090″ gauge pin into the outer hole on the switch cover.
5. Move the switch until the gauge pin drops into the alignment hole on the inner slide. Tighten the switch securing screws.
6. Remove the gauge pin. Check to make sure the car will only start in Neutral or Park.

SHIFT LINKAGE ADJUSTMENT

Column Shift

1. Place the shift lever in Neutral.
2. Loosen the shift rod clamp screw and

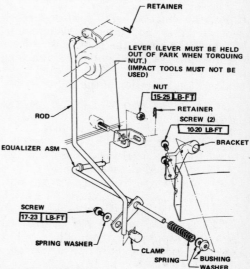

Column shift linkage

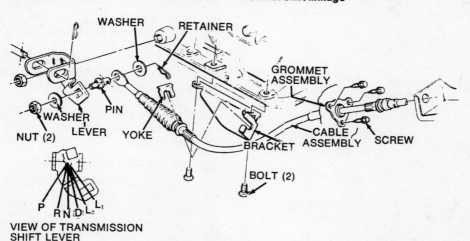

Console shift linkage

make sure the lever on the transmission is in the Neutral position. Have someone move the shift lever through the gears while you watch the lever on the transmission, if you are unsure as to which position is the Neutral position.

3. With the lever on the transmission in the Neutral position and the shift lever on the column being held against the Neutral stop (do not raise the lever), tighten the shift rod clamp screw to 23 ft.lb.

4. Check the operation of the shifter.

Console Shift

1. Place the shift lever in the Park position.
2. Put the ignition key in the Lock position.
3. Make sure the lever on the transmission is in the Park position.
4. Loosen the shift rod clamp screw. See the illustration.
5. Loosen the pin in the lever on the transmission.
6. Pull the shift rod lightly against the lock stop at the shifter and tighten the clamp screw.
7. Adjust the pin at the transmission lever for a "free pin" fit, and tighten the attaching nut.
8. Check the operation of the shifter.

THROTTLE VALVE (TV) OR DETENT CABLE ADJUSTMENT

Gas Engine Models Only

On all transmissions except the THM-250, THM-350 and THM-400 models, a TV cable is used to control hydraulic pressures, shift points, shift feel, and downshifting. The THM-250 and THM-350 use a detent cable.

NOTE: *THM-400 models use an electrical detent (downshift) switch. Adjustment of this switch is covered separately, after cable adjustment.*

Though the detent cable is virtually identical in appearance to the TV cable, the detent cable

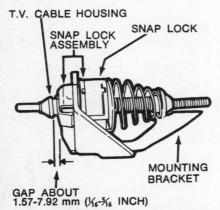

T.V. CABLE HOUSING

SNAP LOCK
ASSEMBLY

SNAP LOCK

MOUNTING
BRACKET

GAP ABOUT
1.57-7.92 mm (1/16-5/16 INCH)

Turbo Hydra-Matic 200 throttle valve adjustment

controls only the downshift functions of the transmission. The difference in terminology (TV vs. detent) is due to the function of the cable, not the design of the cable itself.

Before attempting adjustment, identify the style of the cable which is used in your vehicle (Type One or Type Two). The Type One Cable uses a snap-lock assembly which is integral with the cable. The snap-lock is located next to the cable mounting bracket at the engine. In its normal position, the snap-lock is pushed fully downward (locked) so that it is flush with the snap-lock assembly. Adjustment is made with the snap lock in the raised (unlocked) position, as outlined in the Type One adjustment procedure.

The Type Two cable uses a different type of locking mechanism. Though it is located in the same position as the Type One snaplock, the Type Two lock tab is set when released (upward) and adjusted when pushed downward (unlocked). On 1981 and earlier models, the Type Two cable can be easily identified by the presence of a spring, visible beneath the lock tab. The spring is not exposed on 1982 and later cable assemblies. Refer to the Type Two adjusting procedure to adjust the cable.

TYPE ONE

1. Remove the engine air cleaner assembly.
2. Push up on the bottom of the snaplock at the cable bracket. Make sure that the cable is free to slide through the snaplock.
3. Move the carburetor lever to the wide open throttle position and hold it there.
4. Push the snap-lock flush and then let the lever return to the closed position.
5. If the adjustment does not correct late shifting or no part throttle downshift, a transmission fluid pressure test should by made by a qualified mechanic.

TYPE TWO

1. Depress and hold the metal lock tab on the TV cable.
2. Move the slider back through the fitting in the direction away from the throttle body until the slider stops against the fitting.
3. Release the metal lock tab.
4. Open the throttle lever to "full throttle stop" position. This will automatically adjust the slider on the cable to correct the setting.

DETENT SWITCH ADJUSTMENT

Turbo Hydra-Matic 400 transmissions are equipped with an electrical detent, or downshift switch operated by the throttle linkage.

1. Pull the detent switch driver rearward until the hole in the switch body aligns with the hole in the driver. Insert a 0.092" diameter pin

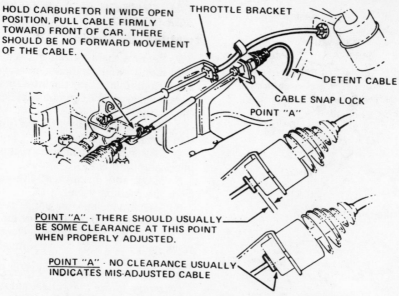

HOLD CARBURETOR IN WIDE OPEN
POSITION, PULL CABLE FIRMLY
TOWARD FRONT OF CAR. THERE
SHOULD BE NO FORWARD MOVEMENT
OF THE CABLE.

THROTTLE BRACKET

DETENT CABLE

CABLE SNAP LOCK

POINT "A"

POINT "A" - THERE SHOULD USUALLY
BE SOME CLEARANCE AT THIS POINT
WHEN PROPERLY ADJUSTED.

POINT "A" - NO CLEARANCE USUALLY
INDICATES MIS-ADJUSTED CABLE

Typical downshift cable adjustment—Turbo Hydra-Matic 200

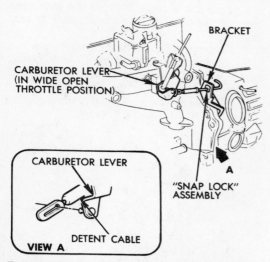

BRACKET

CARBURETOR LEVER
(IN WIDE OPEN
THROTTLE POSITION)

A

"SNAP LOCK"
ASSEMBLY

CARBURETOR LEVER

DETENT CABLE

VIEW A

Typical detent cable adjustment—Turbo Hydra-Matic 200, 250, and 350

ing characteristics. Also note that these adjustments should be performed together. The vacuum valve adjustment (THM-350s only) on 1979 and later models requires the use of several special tools. If you do not have these tools at your disposal, refer the adjustment to a qualified, professional mechanic.

THROTTLE ROD ADJUSTMENT

1. If equipped with cruise control, remove the clip from the control rod, then remove the rod from the bellcrank.
2. Remove the throttle valve cable (THM-

through the aligned holes to hold the driver in position.

2. Loosen the switch plunger as far forward as possible. This will preset the switch for adjustment, which will occur on the 1st application of wide open throttle.

Diesel Engine Automatic Transmission Adjustments

NOTE: Before making any linkage adjustments, check the injection timing, and adjust if necessary. This must be done because engine performance affects transmission shift-

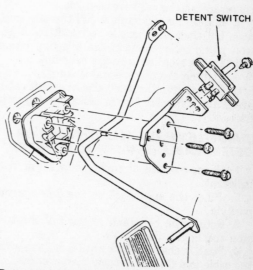

DETENT SWITCH

Detent switch—Turbo Hydra-Matic 400

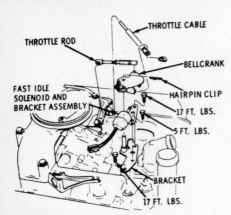

Diesel throttle linkage adjustment

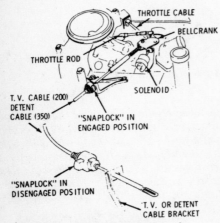

Diesel throttle valve cable adjustment

200) or detent cable (THM-350) from the bellcrank.

3. Loosen the locknut on the throttle rod, then shorten the rod several turns.

4. Rotate the bellcrank to full throttle stop, then lengthen the throttle rod until the injection pump lever contacts the injection pump full throttle stop. Release the bellcrank.

5. Tighten the throttle rod locknut.

6. Connect the throttle valve or detent cable and cruise control rod to the bellcrank. Adjust if necessary.

THROTTLE VALVE CABLE (THM-200) OR DETENT CABLE (THM-350) ADJUSTMENT

1. Remove the throttle rod from the bellcrank.

2. Push the snap lock to the disengaged position.

3. Rotate the bellcrank to the full throttle stop and hold it there.

4. Push in the snap lock until it is flush with the cable end fitting. Release the bellcrank.

5. Reconnect the throttle.

TRANSMISSION VACUUM VALVE ADJUSTMENT

1981 And Later Models

1. Remove the air cleaner assembly.

2. Remove the air intake crossover from the intake manifold. Cover the intake manifold passages to prevent foreign material from entering the engine.

3. Disconnect the throttle rod from the injection pump throttle lever.

4. Loosen the transmission vacuum valve-to-injection pump bolts.

5. Mark and disconnect the vacuum line from the vacuum valve.

6. Attach a carburetor angle gauge adaptor (Kent-Moore tool J-26701-15 or its equivalent) to the injection pump throttle lever. Attach an angle gauge (J-26701 or its equivalent) to the gauge adaptor.

NOTE: *To service the V6 diesel, it may be necessary to file the gauge adapter in order for it to fit the thicker throttle lever of the V6 injection pump.*

7. Turn the throttle lever to the wide open throttle position. Set the angle gauge to zero degrees.

8. Center the bubble in the gauge level.

9. Set the angle gauge to one of the following settings, according to the year and type of engine:

10. Tighten the vacuum valve retaining bolts.

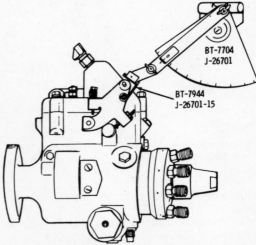

Vacuum regulator valve with an angle gauge attached and set to zero degrees

Year	Engine	Setting
1981	V8—Calif.	49–50°
1981	V8—non-Calif.	58°
1982–83	V8	58°
All	V6	49°

11. Reconnect the original vacuum lines to the vacuum valve.

12. Remove the angle gauge and adaptor.

13. Connect the throttle rod to the throttle lever.

14. Install the air intake crossover, using new gaskets.

15. Install the air cleaner assembly.

Neutral Safety Switch

REMOVAL AND INSTALLATION

1. Apply the parking brake securely, block the wheels, and put the transmission selector in Neutral. Disconnect the shift linkage at the transmission.

2. Unplug the electrical connector at the switch.

3. Remove the switch mounting bolts and remove the switch.

4. Align the flats of the new switch with the flats on the shift shaft. Then, fit the new switch over the shift shaft and onto the transmission. *If the boltholes do not line up, don't turn the switch because this will break an internal pin designed to ensure proper adjustment. Instead, turn the shift shaft, as it is not in neutral* until they do. Then, install the mounting bolts for the switch and torque to 22 ft.lb. and connect the electrical connector. If you *should* turn the switch and break the pin, align it as follows:

   a. Turn the shift shaft two positions from Park to place the transmission in Neutral.

   b. Insert a $^3/_{32}$″ drill bit into the service adjustment hole in the side of the switch. Turn the switch back and forth slowly until the drill drops into the switch to a depth of $^9/_{64}$″. Then, install the switch mounting bolts and torque them. Remove the drill bit.

Transmission

REMOVAL AND INSTALLATION

1. Disconnect the negative battery cable at the battery.

2. If so equipped, disconnect the detent/ downshift cable at its upper end (accelerator pedal or carburetor).

3. Raise the vehicle and support it safely with jackstands. Preferably, the front AND rear of the vehicle should be raised to provide adequate clearance for transmission removal.

4. Disconnect the exhaust crossover pipe at the manifolds, if exhaust system-to-transmission interference is obvious. It may be necessary to remove the catalytic converter, exhaust pipe, or just brackets in order to clear the transmission.

WARNING: *Exhaust system services must be performed while all components are COLD.*

5. Remove the transmission inspection cover.

6. Mark the torque converter-to-flywheel bolts. The relationship between the flywheel and converter must be marked so that proper balance is maintained after installation. Remove the torque converter-to-flywheel bolts.

7. Matchmark the propeller shaft and the rear yoke (for reinstallation purposes). On 1986-87 models, there is a floor pan reinforcement that may interfere with driveshaft removal. If it seems that it will interfere, remove it. With a drain pan positioned under the front yoke, unbolt and remove the propeller shaft.

8. Mark and disconnect the vacuum lines, wiring, and speedometer cable from the transmission, as required.

9. Place a transmission jack (carefully) up against the transmission oil pan. Then, secure the transmission to the jack. On 1986-87 models, remove the catalytic converter support bracket, if you haven't done so in Step 4.

10. Remove the transmission mounting pad bolt(s), then carefully raise the transmission just enough to take the weight of the transmission off of the supporting crossmember.

CAUTION: *Exercise extreme care to avoid damage to underhood components while raising or lowering the transmission.*

11. Unbolt and remove the transmission crossmember, complete with the mount. It may be necessary to raise or lower the transmission a small amount to remove the crossmember. Slide the crossmember rearward and out. Then, lower the transmission slightly for access to items to be removed or disconnected in the next two steps.

12. Remove the transmission dipstick, then unbolt and remove the filler tube.

13. Disconnect the shift linkage (or cable on floor shift equipped models) and oil cooler lines from the transmission. Cap the open ends.

14. Support the engine using a jackstand placed beneath the engine oil pan. Be sure to put a block of wood between the jackstand and the oil pan, to prevent damage to the pan.

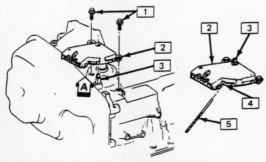

Installing and adjusting the Park/Neutral and Backup Lamp switch on manual transmission cars

15. Securely wire the torque converter to the transmission case.

16. Remove the transmission-to-engine mounting bolts, then carefully move the transmission rearward, downward, and out from beneath the vehicle.

CAUTION: *If interference is encountered with the cable(s), cooler lines, etc., remove the component(s), before finally lowering the transmission.*

17. Installation is basically the reverse of the previous steps. Note the following points during and after installation:

a. Torque the transmission-to-engine mounting bolts to 30-40 ft.lb.

b. Align the matchmarks of the propeller shaft with the marks of the rear yoke before installing the joint straps and bolts.

c. Align the converter and flywheel markings before installing the converter bolts. Make sure the weld nuts on the converter are flush with the flexplate. Test the converter for freedom of rotation. Tighten the bolts finger tight and then torque them to 46 ft.lb. Retorque the 1st bolt torqued.

d. Add the proper type and quantity of transmission fluid. If the converter was replaced, an additional 4 pints (approx.) should be added. NEVER overfill the transmission.

e. Adjust the shift linkage (or cable) and the detent/downshift cable.

f. Make sure that all vacuum lines, electrical connections, and oil cooler line connections are secure before driving the vehicle.

g. Check for fluid leakage, then after the transmission is hot, recheck the fluid level.

DRIVELINE

Driveshaft and U-Joints

REMOVAL AND INSTALLATION

1. Raise the vehicle in the air and support it with jackstands.

2. Mark the relationship of the driveshaft to the differential flange so that they can be reassembled in the same position.

3. Disconnect the rear U-joint by removing the U-bolts or retaining straps.

4. To prevent the loss of the needle bearings, tape the bearing caps in place. If you are replacing the U-joint, this is not necessary.

5. Remove the driveshaft from the transmission by sliding it rearward. There will be some oil leakage from the rear of the transmission. It can be contained by placing a small plastic bag over the rear of the transmission and holding it in place with a rubber band.

6. To install the driveshaft, insert the front yoke into the transmission so that the driveshaft splines mesh with the transmission splines.

7. Using the reference marks made earlier, align the driveshaft with the differential flange and secure it with the U-bolts or retaining straps.

U-JOINT OVERHAUL

1. Remove the driveshaft as explained above and remove the snaprings from the ends of the bearing cup.

2. After removing the snaprings, place the driveshaft on the floor and place a large diame-

Troubleshooting Basic Driveshaft and Rear Axle Problems

When abnormal vibrations or noises are detected in the driveshaft area, this chart can be used to help diagnose possible causes. Remember that other components such as wheels, tires, rear axle and suspension can also produce similar conditions.

Basic Driveshaft Problems

Problem	Cause	Solution
Shudder as car accelerates from stop or low speed	• Loose U-joint • Defective center bearing	• Replace U-joint • Replace center bearing
Loud clunk in driveshaft when shifting gears	• Worn U-joints	• Replace U-joints
Roughness or vibration at any speed	• Out-of-balance, bent or dented driveshaft • Worn U-joints • U-joint clamp bolts loose	• Balance or replace driveshaft • Replace U-joints • Tighten U-joint clamp bolts
Squeaking noise at low speeds	• Lack of U-joint lubrication	• Lubricate U-joint; if problem persists, replace U-joint
Knock or clicking noise	• U-joint or driveshaft hitting frame tunnel • Worn CV joint	• Correct overloaded condition • Replace CV joint

BASIC REAR AXLE PROBLEMS

First, determine when the noise is most noticeable.

Drive Noise: Produced under vehicle acceleration.

Coast Noise: Produced while the car coasts with a closed throttle.

Float Noise: Occurs while maintaining constant car speed (just enough to keep speed constant) on a level road.

Road Noise

Brick or rough surfaced concrete roads produce noises that seem to come from the rear axle. Road noise is usually identical in Drive or Coast and driving on a different type of road will tell whether the road is the problem.

Tire Noise

Tire noises are often mistaken for rear axle problems. Snow treads or unevenly worn tires produce vibrations seeming to originate elsewhere. **Temporarily** inflating the tires to 40 lbs will significantly alter tire noise, but will have no effect on rear axle noises (which normally cease below about 30 mph).

Engine/Transmission Noise

Determine at what speed the noise is most pronounced, then stop the car in a quiet place. With the transmission in Neutral, run the engine through speeds corresponding to road speeds where the noise was noticed. Noises produced with the car standing still are coming from the engine or transmission.

Front Wheel Bearings

While holding the car speed steady, lightly apply the footbrake; this will often decease bearing noise, as some of the load is taken from the bearing.

Rear Axle Noises

Eliminating other possible sources can narrow the cause to the rear axle, which normally produces noise from worn gears or bearings. Gear noises tend to peak in a narrow speed range, while bearing noises will usually vary in pitch with engine speeds.

Noise Diagnosis

The Noise Is	Most Probably Produced By
• Identical under Drive or Coast	• Road surface, tires or front wheel bearings
• Different depending on road surface	• Road surface or tires
• Lower as the car speed is lowered	• Tires
• Similar with car standing or moving	• Engine or transmission
• A vibration	• Unbalanced tires, rear wheel bearing, unbalanced driveshaft or worn U-joint
• A knock or click about every 2 tire revolutions	• Rear wheel bearing
• Most pronounced on turns	• Damaged differential gears
• A steady low-pitched whirring or scraping, starting at low speeds	• Damaged or worn pinion bearing
• A chattering vibration on turns	• Wrong differential lubricant or worn clutch plates (limited slip rear axle)
• Noticed only in Drive, Coast or Float conditions	• Worn ring gear and/or pinion gear

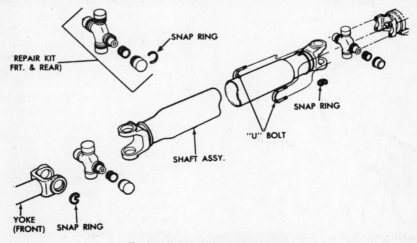

Typical driveshaft and U-Joints

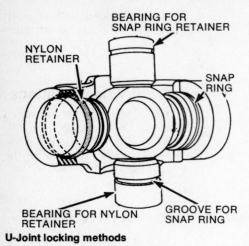

BEARING FOR
SNAP RING RETAINER

NYLON
RETAINER

SNAP
RING

BEARING FOR NYLON
RETAINER

GROOVE FOR
SNAP RING

U-Joint locking methods

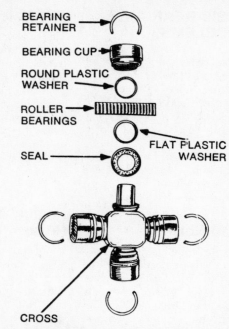

BEARING
RETAINER

BEARING CUP

ROUND PLASTIC
WASHER

ROLLER
BEARINGS

SEAL

FLAT PLASTIC
WASHER

CROSS

Plastic retainer U-Joint repair kit components

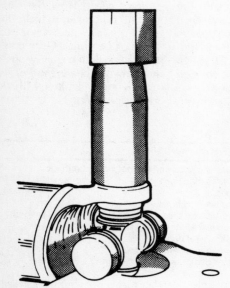

Bearing removal

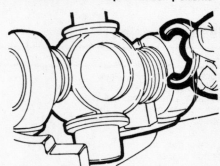

Service snap rings are installed inside the yoke

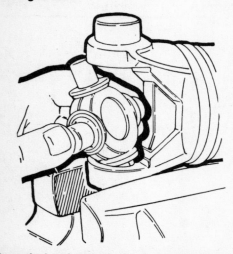

Press the bearing cup into the yoke, then install the cross

ter socket under one of the bearing cups. Using a hammer and a drift, tap on the bearing opposite this one. This will push the trunnion through the yoke enough to force the bearing cup out of the yoke and into the socket. Repeat this procedure for the other bearing cups. If a hammer doesn't loosen the cups, they will have to be pressed out.

NOTE: *A Saginaw design driveshaft secures its U-joints in a different manner from the conventional snaprings of the Dana and Cleveland designs. Nylon material is injected through a small hole in the yoke and flows along a circular groove between the U-joint and the yoke, thus creating a nylon snapring. Disassembly of this Saginaw type U-joint requires that the joint be pressed from the yoke. If a press is not available, it may be carefully hammered out using the same procedure (Step 2) as the Dana design although it may* require more force to break the nylon rings. Either method, press or hammer, will damage the bearing cups and destroy the nylon rings. Replacement kits include new bearing cups and conventional metal snaprings to replace the original nylon type rings.

3. Using solvent, thoroughly clean the entire U-joint assembly. Inspect for excessive wear in the yoke bores and on the four ends of the trunnion. The needle bearings could be scored, broken, or loose in their cups. Bearing cups may suffer slight distortion during removal and should be replaced.

4. Pack the bearings with chassis lube (lithium base) and completely fill each trunnion end with the same lubricant.

5. Place new dust seals on trunnions with cavity of seal toward end of trunnion. Care must be taken to avoid distortion of the seal. A suitable size socket and a vise can be used to press on the seal.

6. Insert one bearing cup about ¼ of the way into the yoke and place the trunnion into yoke and bearing cup. Install another bearing cup and press both cups in and install the snaprings. Snaprings on the Dana and Cleveland shafts must go on the outside of the yoke while the Saginaw shaft requires that the rings go on the inside of the yoke. The gap in the Saginaw ring must face in toward the yoke. Once installed, the trunnion must move freely in the yoke.

NOTE: *The Saginaw shaft uses two different size bearing cups (the ones with the groove fit into the driveshaft yoke).*

REAR AXLE

Identification

The rear axle number is located in the right or left axle tube adjacent to the axle carrier (differential). Antislip differentials are identified by a tag attached to the lower right section of the axle cover.

Determining Axle Ratio

The rear axle is said to have a certain ratio, say 4:11. An axle with this ratio is called a 4.11 even though this number actually means 4.11:1. This means that the driveshaft will turn 4.11 times for every turn of the rear wheels. The number 4.11 is determined by dividing the number of teeth on the pinion gear into the number of teeth on the ring gear. In the case of a 4.11 rear axle, there could be 9 teeth on the pinion and 37 teeth on the ring gear. This provides a sure way, although troublesome, of determining your rear axle's ratio. To do this, you

must drain the fluid from the axle, remove the rear cover, and then count the teeth.

A much easier method of determining the ratio begins with jacking up the car and supporting it safely with jackstands so BOTH rear wheels are off the ground. You will need two assistants. Next, block the front wheels, set the parking brake, and put the transmission into Neutral. Make a chalk mark on each of the rear wheels and another on the driveshaft. Turn both rear wheels exactly one turn as one of you counts the turns of the driveshaft. The number of turns the driveshaft turns in one complete revolution of the rear wheel is the axle ratio. Even if your count is approximate, this should enable you to determine which axle you have.

Axle Shaft, Bearing and Seal
REMOVAL AND INSTALLATION

These cars use two different types of drive axle, the C-lock and the non C-lock type. Axle shafts in the C-lock type are retained by C-shaped locks, which fit grooves at the inner end of the shaft. Axle shafts in the non C-lock type are retained by the bracket backing plate, which is bolted to the axle housing. Bearings in the C-lock type axle consist of an outer race, bearing rollers and a roller cage, retained by snaprings. The non C-lock axle uses a unit roller bearing (inner race, rollers and outer race), which is pressed onto the shaft up to a shoulder. It is imperative to determine the axle type before attempting any service.

The axle identification number is stamped on the front of the passenger side axle tube next to the differential carrier on all models except those with an 8½" ring gear. These models have the I.D. on a tag under one of the differential rear cover bolts.

Non C-Lock Type

CAUTION: *Before attempting any service to the drive axle or axle shafts, remove the differential carrier cover and visually determine if the axle shafts are retained by C-shaped locks at the inner end, or by the brake backing plate at the outer end. If the shafts are not retained by C-locks, proceed as follows.*

Design allows for maximum axle shaft endplay of 0.022", which can be measured with a dial indicator. If endplay is found to be excessive, the bearing should be replaced. Shimming the bearing is not recommended as this ignores endplay of the bearing itself and could result in improper seating of the bearing.

1. Remove the wheel, tire and brake drum.
2. Remove the nuts holding the retainer

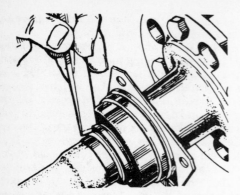

Breaking the bearing retainer with a chisel

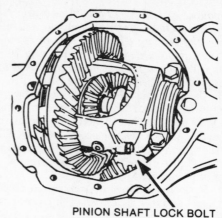

PINION SHAFT LOCK BOLT

Removing the pinion shaft lock bolt from the differential

plate to the backing plate. Disconnect the brake line.

3. Remove the retainer and install the two lower nuts fingertight, to prevent the brake backing plate from being dislodged.

4. Pull out the axle shaft and bearing assembly, using a slide hammer.

5. Using a chisel, nick the bearing retainer in three or four places. The retainer does not have to be cut, merely collapsed sufficiently to allow the bearing retainer to be slid from the shaft.

6. Press off the bearing and install the new one by pressing it into position.

NOTE: *Do not attempt to press the bearing and the retainer on at the same time.*

7. Assemble the shaft and bearing in the housing, being sure that the bearing is seated properly in the housing.

8. Install the retainer, drum , wheel and tire. Bleed the brakes.

C-Lock Type

CAUTION: *Before attempting any service to the drive axle or axle shafts, remove the carrier cover and visually determine if the axle shaft(s) are retained by C-shaped locks at the inner end or by a brake backing plate at the outer end. If they are retained by C-shaped locks, proceed as follows.*

1. Raise the vehicle and remove the wheels.

2. The differential cover has already been removed (see Caution note above). Remove the differential pinion shaft lockscrew and the differential pinion shaft.

3. Push the flanged end of the axle shaft toward the center of the vehicle and remove the C-lock from the end of the shaft.

4. Remove the axle shaft from the housing, being careful not to damage the oil seal.

5. Remove the oil seal by inserting the button end of the axle shaft behind the steel case of the oil seal. Pry the seal loose from the bore.

6. Seat the legs of a bearing puller behind the bearing. Seat the washer against the bearing

AXLE SHAFT "C" LOCK

Removing the axle shaft C lock

and hold it in place with a nut. Use a slide hammer to pull the bearing.

7. Pack the cavity between the seal lips with wheel bearing lubricant and lubricate a new wheel bearing with same.

8. Use a suitable driver and install the bearing until it bottoms against a tube. Install the oil seal.

9. Slide the axle shaft into place. Be sure that the splines on the shaft do not damage the oil seal. Make sure that the splines engage the differential side gear.

10. Install the axle shaft C-lock on the inner end of the axle shaft and push the shaft outward so that the C-lock seats in the differential side gear counterbore.

11. Position the differential pinion shaft through the case and pinions, aligning the hole in the case with the hole for the lockscrew.

12. Install the pinion shaft lockscrew.

13. Use a new gasket and install the carrier cover. Be sure that the gasket surfaces are clean before installing the gasket and cover.

14. Fill the axle with lubricant to the bottom of the filler hole.

15. Install the brake drum and wheels and lower the car. Check for leaks and road test the car.

Pinion Seal

REMOVAL AND INSTALLATION

1. Mark the driveshaft and the pinion companion flange so that they can be reassembled in the same position.

2. Disconnect the driveshaft from the pinion companion flange and support the propeller shaft up in the body tunnel by wiring it to the exhaust pipe.

NOTE: *If the joint bearing caps are not retained by a retainer strap, use a piece of tape to hold the bearing caps on their trunnions.*

3. Mark the position of the companion flange, pinion shaft and nut, so that the proper pinion bearing preload can be maintained upon reassembly.

4. Using Tool J-8614-10 to hold the pinion companion flange, remove the companion flange nut and washer.

5. With a suitable container in place to hold any fluid that may drain from thee rear axle, remove the pinion companion flange with Tool J-8614-10.

6. Remove the seal by driving it out with a blunt chisel.

WARNING: *Be careful not to damage the carrier.*

7. Examine the pinion companion flange for any nicks or damage. If so, replace it.

8. Examine the pinion seal bore in the carrier and remove any burrs.

9. Using Tool J-23911, install a new seal.

10. Apply Special Seal Lubricant, No. 1050169 or equivalent to the O.D. of the pinion flange and sealing lip of the new seal.

11. Install the pinion companion flange and nut and tighten the nut $1/16''$ beyond the alignment marks.

Axle Housing

REMOVAL AND INSTALLATION

1. Break the torque on the lugnuts. Raise the car and support the frame securely at four points. Put a floor jack or other secure support under the rear axle. Remove the rear wheels and tires.

WARNING: *Because the springs will be pushing downward on the axle with the kind of force required to support the car, make sure that the means by which you are supporting the axle is secure and will keep it from moving for and aft and from tilting. Failure to support the axle properly is very dangerous!*

2. Unbolt the shock absorbers where they attach to the rear axle.

3. Mark the relationship between the driveshaft U-joint and the companion flange on the axle housing (this must be done to preserve balance). Then, remove the four bolts and associated nuts and disconnect the driveshaft at the companion flange. Lower the driveshaft carefully and wire it up and out of the way.

4. Disconnect the brake lines going to the junction block at the rear axle where they connect with the wheel cylinders and drain the fluid. Disconnect the lines from the clips on the axle. Then, unbolt the junction block from the axle and remove it. Store it and the lines in a clean, dry location.

5. Remove the nuts and bolts to disconnect the upper control arms at the axle.

6. Lower the rear axle slowly until all spring tension is removed, *note their orientation*, and then remove the springs.

7. Unbolt and disconnect the lower control arms at the axle housing.

8. Lower and remove the axle assembly.

9. To install the axle, 1st orient it under the car so the companion flange faces forward, and support it securely.

10. Raise the axle so the lower control arms can be fitted to their locations on the axle and install bolts and nuts. Torque bolts to 110 ft.lb. and nuts to 95 ft.lb.

11. Orient the springs properly against the body and then slowly raise the axle, guiding the lower ends of the springs into the pads on the axle. Raise the axle past the point where springs begin to compress to hold them in place.

12. Install the brake lines into their clips, make connections at the wheel cylinders, and position the junction block and install its mounting bolt.

13. Raise the axle until the upper control arms can be connected. Then, line up the holes in the axle fittings and control arms. Install the bolts, torquing to 110 ft.lb. and install the nuts, torquing to 95 ft.lb.

14. Connect the driveshaft, lining up matchmarks if you're using the same axle. Torque the bolts to 16 ft.lb.

15. Put the shocks in proper position and install the bolts.

16. Install the wheels and tighten lugnuts as much as possible. Refill the axle to the level of the fller plug with the recommended fluid.

17. Lower the car, and torque the lugnuts. Fill the master cylinder with fresh brake fluid of proper specification and bleed the system thoroughly.

Suspension and Steering

FRONT SUSPENSION

The front suspension is designed to allow each wheel to compensate for changes in the read surface level without appreciably affecting the opposite wheel. Each wheel is independently connected to the frame by a steering knuckle, ball joint assemblies, and upper and lower control arms. The control arms are specifically designed and positioned to allow the steering knuckles to move in a prescribed three dimensional arc. The front wheels are held in proper relationship to each other by two tie rods which are connected to steering arms on the knuckles and to an intermediate rod.

Coil chassis springs are mounted between the spring housings on the frame or front end sheet metal and the lower control arms. Ride control is provided by double, direct acting, shock absorbers mounted inside the coil springs and attached to the lower control arms by bolts and nuts. The upper portion of each shock absorber extends through the upper control arms frame bracket and is secured with two grommets, two grommet retainers, and a nut.

Side role of the front suspension is controlled by a spring steel stabilizer shaft. It is mounted in rubber bushings which are held to the frame side rails by brackets. The ends of the stabilizer are connected to the lower control arms by link bolts isolated by rubber grommets.

The upper control arm is attached to a cross shaft through isolating rubber bushing. The cross shaft, in turn, is bolted to frame brackets.

A ball joint assembly is riveted to the outer end of the upper arm. It is pre-loaded by a rubber spring to insure proper seating of the ball in the socket. The upper ball joint is attached to the steering knuckle by a torque prevailing nut.

The inner end of the lower control arm have pressed-in bushings. Bolts, passing through the bushings, attach the arm to the frame. The lower ball joint assembly is a press fit in the arm and attaches to the steering knuckle with a torque prevailing nut.

Rubber grease seals are provided at ball socket assemblies to keep dirt and moisture from entering the joint and damaging the bearing surfaces.

Coil Springs

REMOVAL AND INSTALLATION

1. Raise the front of the car and remove the wheel.
2. Disconnect and remove the shock absorber.
3. Remove the front stabilizer rod link from the lower control arm.
4. Disconnect the brake reaction rod from the lower control arm.
5. As a safety precaution and to gain maximum leverage, place a jack about ½" below the lower ball joint stud. Now, remove the ball stud cotter pin and loosen the nut about ⅛". Do not remove the nut.

CAUTION: *If the nut is removed, the full force of the coil spring could be released.*

6. Rap the steering knuckle in the area of the stud or use a ball joint removal tool to separate the stud from the knuckle.
7. After the stud has broken loose from the knuckle, raise the jack against the control arm. Remove the nut and separate the steering knuckle from the tapered stud.
8. Carefully lower the jack under the control arm and release the spring. With the jack entirely lowered, it may be necessary to pry the spring off its seat on the lower control arm with a pry bar.
9. When installing the spring on 1984-87 models, note that there are two holes drilled where it fits into the lower control arm. Turn the spring so its bottom end covers one of the holes but the second hole is uncovered. Also, note that the flat surface goes to the top, while the straight helical coils face the bottom. Re-

Troubleshooting Basic Steering and Suspension Problems

Problem	Cause	Solution
Hard steering (steering wheel is hard to turn)	• Low or uneven tire pressure • Loose power steering pump drive belt • Low or incorrect power steering fluid • Incorrect front end alignment • Defective power steering pump • Bent or poorly lubricated front end parts	• Inflate tires to correct pressure • Adjust belt • Add fluid as necessary • Have front end alignment checked/adjusted • Check pump • Lubricate and/or replace defective parts
Loose steering (too much play in the steering wheel)	• Loose wheel bearings • Loose or worn steering linkage • Faulty shocks • Worn ball joints	• Adjust wheel bearings • Replace worn parts • Replace shocks • Replace ball joints
Car veers or wanders (car pulls to one side with hands off the steering wheel)	• Incorrect tire pressure • Improper front end alignment • Loose wheel bearings • Loose or bent front end components • Faulty shocks	• Inflate tires to correct pressure • Have front end alignment checked/adjusted • Adjust wheel bearings • Replace worn components • Replace shocks
Wheel oscillation or vibration transmitted through steering wheel	• Improper tire pressures • Tires out of balance • Loose wheel bearings • Improper front end alignment • Worn or bent front end components	• Inflate tires to correct pressure • Have tires balanced • Adjust wheel bearings • Have front end alignment checked/adjusted • Replace worn parts
Uneven tire wear	• Incorrect tire pressure • Front end out of alignment • Tires out of balance	• Inflate tires to correct pressure • Have front end alignment checked/adjusted • Have tires balanced

verse the remaining portions of the procedure to install. Torque the control arm frame bolts, with the car on the ground, to the following settings:

- 1975-76: 9 ft.lb.
- 1977: 125 ft.lb.
- 1978-87: 95 ft.lb.

Shock Absorbers

REMOVAL AND INSTALLATION

1. Remove the upper shock absorber attaching nut, grommet retainer, and grommet.
2. Remove the lower retaining screws. Lower the shock through the hole in the lower control arm.

NOTE: *Purge new shocks of air by repeatedly extending them in their normal position and compressing them while inverted.*

3. Reverse the above steps to install. Tighten the upper nut to 8 ft.lb.; the lower bolts to 20 ft.lb.

TESTING

Visually inspect the shock absorber. If there is evidence of leakage and the shock absorber is covered with oil, the shock is defective and should be replaced.

If there is no sign of excessive leakage (a small amount of weeping is normal) bounce the car at one corner by pressing down on the fender or bumper and releasing. When you have the car bouncing as much as you can, release the fender or bumper. The car should stop bouncing after the first rebound. If the bouncing continues past the center point of the bounce more than once, the shock absorbers are worn and should be replaced.

Upper Ball Joint

INSPECTION

1. Place a jack under each lower control arm between the suspension spring pocket and the ball joint and raise the car.
2. Grasp the wheel at the 6 and 12 o'clock position and shake the top of the wheel in and out. Observe the steering knuckle for any movement relative to the control arm. If the ball joint is loose, it must be replaced.

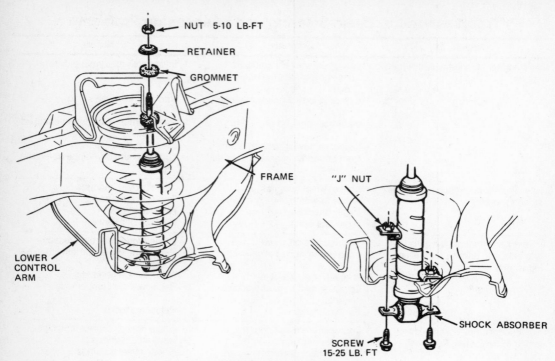

NUT 5-10 LB-FT

RETAINER

GROMMET

FRAME

LOWER
CONTROL
ARM

"J" NUT

SHOCK ABSORBER

SCREW
15-25 LB. FT

Front shock absorber installation

REMOVAL AND INSTALLATION

NOTE: *On cars built in 1986-87, you'll need a special installer, GM tool J-29193 or equivalent.*

1. Turn the lug nuts counterclockwise just far enough to break the torque. Raise the car and place a floorjack or axle stand under the frame. Remove the wheel and tire.

2. With another jack, support the outer edge of the lower control arm to handle the downforce of the spring. Then, raise the jack just far enough so that you will be able to free the upper control arm from the upper ballstud.

WARNING: *If the upper ball joint stud nut is removed, rather than being loosened just slightly, in the next step, the full force of the spring could be released, causing severe injury!*

3. Remove the cotter pin from the upper ball joint stud. Then, loosen but *do not remove* the nut. Install a ball joint removal tool and press the ball joint downward just far enough to free the tapered portion of it from the steering knuckle.

4. Wire the knuckle and associated parts in place to prevent damage to the brake hose. Turn the nut off the end of the ball stud and remove it and any washers that may be used. Then, lift the upper arm to free the ballstud from the knuckle.

5. Center punch and drill out the four rivets

that attach the ball joint to the control arm. Use a hammer and chisel to cut off the rivet heads. Remove the ball joint from the control arm.

6. Install the new joint into the control arm, and install the bolts and nuts provided with replacement joints (nut on top). Torque to 8 ft.lb.

7. On cars built in 1975-85: Maneuver the ballstud through the upper control arm and install the washer (if used) and the nut. Torque the ball joint stud nut to 60-65 ft.lb. Then, turn the nut *tighter* as necessary to align one of the castellations with the cotter pin hole in the stud. When the hole is lined up, install a *new* cotter pin and bend the ends over fully. On cars built in 1986-87, you'll need a special installer, GM tool J-29193 or equivalent. Position the ball joint stud in the steering knuckle and install the tool. Torque this tool's operating nut to 30 ft.lb. Remove the tool and install and torque the ball joint stud nut to 65 ft.lb. Then, turn the nut *tighter* as necessary to align one of the castellations with the cotter pin hole in the stud. When the hole is lined up, install a *new* cotter pin and bend the ends over fully.

8. Reverse the remaining steps of the removal procedure to complete the installation.

Lower Ball Joint
REMOVAL AND INSTALLATION

All 1975 and later cars have visual wear indicators on the lower ball joints. The lower ball

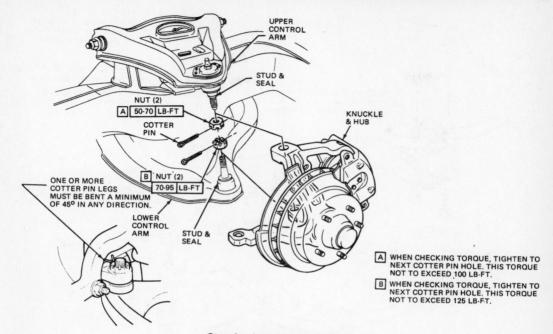

Steering knuckle assembly

joint grease plus screws into the wear indicator which protrudes from the bottom of the ball joint housing. As long as the wear indicator extends out of the ball joint housing, the ball joint is not worn. If the tip of the wear indicator is parallel with, or recessed into the ball joint housing, the ball joint is defective.

REMOVAL AND INSTALLATION

NOTE: *On 1986-87 cars, you'll need a special ball joint installer GM tool No. J-29194 or equivalent.*

1. Refer to steps 1-7 of the lower control arm procedure, below.
2. Install a ball joint remover and tighten the tool to force the ball joint out of the lower control arm.

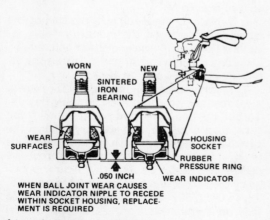

Lower ball joint wear indicator

3. Reverse the above to install. On 1975-85 cars: Torque the castellated nut to 85-90 ft.lb. Always tighten the castellated nut to the next slot if necessary to align the castellation (slot) in the nut with the hole in the ball joint stud. Then, install a new cotter pin. On 1986-87 cars, you'll need a special ball joint installer GM tool No. J-29194 or equivalent. Position the ball joint stud in the steering knuckle and install the tool. Torque the operating nut on the tool to 40 ft.lb. Remove the tool and torque the nut to 81 ft.lb. Always tighten the castellated nut to the next slot if necessary to align the castellation (slot) in the nut with the hole in the ball joint stud. Then, install a new cotter pin.

Stabilizer Bar

REMOVAL AND INSTALLATION

1. Raise the car and support it securely on axle stands.
2. Note the order of assembly of all nuts, washers, spacers, and bushings. Remove the nut from the top of the connecting link; then remove the washers and rubber bushings, keeping them in order. Repeat for the other side.
3. Remove the two bolts on each side attaching the stabilizer bar bracket to the frame. Then, remove each bracket and the stabilizer bar. Note that the brackets are two-piece assemblies and retain all parts.
4. Inspect both the bushings that separate the bolt parts and those separating the stabilizer bar from the frame mounts. Replace bush-

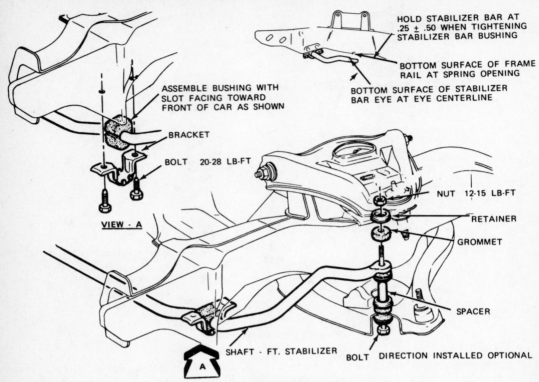

ASSEMBLE BUSHING WITH
SLOT FACING TOWARD
FRONT OF CAR AS SHOWN

BRACKET

BOLT   20-28 LB-FT

VIEW - A

HOLD STABILIZER BAR AT
.25 ± .50 WHEN TIGHTENING
STABILIZER BAR BUSHING

BOTTOM SURFACE OF FRAME
RAIL AT SPRING OPENING

BOTTOM SURFACE OF STABILIZER
BAR EYE AT EYE CENTERLINE

NUT   12-15 LB-FT

RETAINER

GROMMET

SPACER

SHAFT - FT. STABILIZER   BOLT   DIRECTION INSTALLED OPTIONAL

Front stabilizer shaft installation

ings that are cracked, torn, or hard and brittle. Inspect washers and spacers for cracks, breaks, or deformation and replace as necessary.

5. If the stabilizer link bolt or the bushings separating it from the frame are damaged, remove the bolt by unscrewing the mounting nut from underneath, using a socket and angle drive. Replace parts as necessary.

6. Assemble the stabilizer bar and associated parts in reverse order. Make sure the bushings are position squarely in the frame brackets with the slits facing the front of the car. Torque the stabilizer bar link nut to 13 ft.lb. and the the bracket bolts to 25 ft.lb.

Upper Control Arm
REMOVAL AND INSTALLATION

1. Perform Steps 1-4 of the Upper Ball Joint Removal and Installation procedure above.
NOTE: *You'll have to perform the next step-- removal of the control arm--so as to retain all shim packs in order and restore proper front end alignment. Plan ahead so you won't drop any of the shims and end up assembling them in a different way.*
2. Remove the upper control arm shaft-to-

bracket nuts and lock washers. Pull the control arm and shaft and the shim packs off the bolts. You might want to wire shim packs together to avoid losing any of them.

3. If you need to replace the control arm bushings, use a special tool designed for this purpose to press them out. Assemble the new bushings into the arm and over the shaft from the outer ends and install the washers and nuts, tightening the nuts just firmly (final torque them with weight on the car as described in Step 5).

4. Replace the control arm by positioning the outer shim packs on the mounting bolts, installing the control arm and shafts and, finally, installing the outer shim packs. Install the attaching nuts, torquing to 46 ft.lb.

5. Reverse the remaining steps of the removal procedure to complete the installation. Torque the ball joint stud nut to 60-65 ft.lb.; then, turn it tighter, as necessary to align the castellation in the nut with the cotter pin hole in the stud. Install a new cotter pin. Torque the control arm bushing nuts with the car supported by the suspension to: 55 rear, 90 front 1975-78; 45 front, 55 rear on 1979-85 models; and 85 ft.lb. on later models. Torque the upper control arm-to-frame nuts to 48 ft.lb.

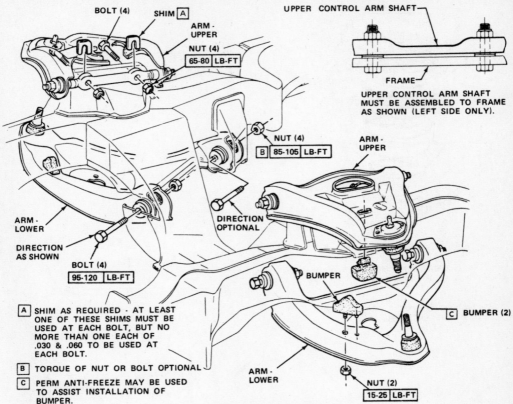

Upper and lower control arm installation

Lower Control Arm (Or Spring)
REMOVAL AND INSTALLATION

1. Raise the front of the car and remove the wheel.

2. Disconnect and remove the shock absorber.

3. Remove the front stabilizer rod link from the lower control arm.

4. Disconnect the brake reaction rod from the lower control arm.

5. As a safety precaution and to gain maximum leverage, place a jack about ½" below the lower ball joint stud. Now, remove the ball stud cotter pin and loosen the nut about ⅛". Do not remove the nut.

CAUTION: *If the nut is removed, the full force of the coil spring could be released.*

6. Rap the steering knuckle in the area of the stud or use a ball joint removal tool to separate the stud from the knuckle.

7. After the stud has broken loose from the knuckle, raise the jack against the control arm. Remove the nut and separate the steering knuckle from the tapered stud.

8. Carefully lower the jack under the control arm and release the spring. With the jack entirely lowered, it may be necessary to pry the

spring off its seat on the lower control arm with a pry bar.

9. After the spring is removed, the lower control arm may be removed by removing the locknut which attaches the control arm to the frame.

10. When installing the spring on 1984-87 models, note that there are two holes drilled where it fits into the lower control arm. Turn the spring so its bottom end covers one of the holes but the second hole is uncovered. Also, note that the flat surface goes to the top, while the straight helical coils face the bottom. Reverse the remaining portions of the procedure to install. Torque the control arm frame bolts, with the car on the ground, to the following settings:

- 1975-76: 9 ft.lb.
- 1977: 125 ft.lb.
- 1978-87: 95 ft.lb.

Knuckle and Spindle
REMOVAL AND INSTALLATION

1. Turn the lug nuts counterclockwise just far enough to break the torque. Raise the car and place a floorjack or axle stand under the frame. Remove the wheel and tire.

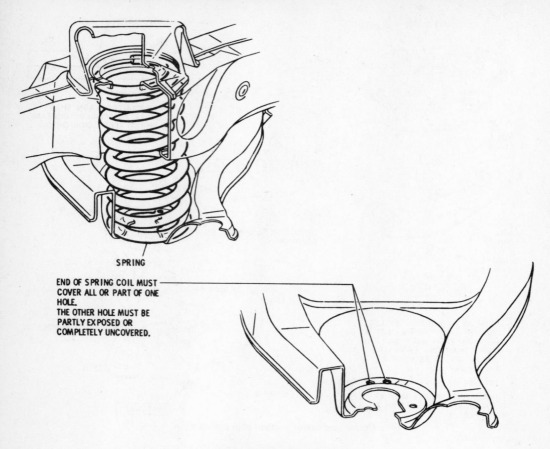

SPRING

END OF SPRING COIL MUST
COVER ALL OR PART OF ONE
HOLE.
THE OTHER HOLE MUST BE
PARTLY EXPOSED OR
COMPLETELY UNCOVERED.

Front spring installation

2. Refer to Chapter 9 and remove the brake caliper without disconnecting the brake hose, leaving it suspended where it will not put stress on the hose.

3. Again refer to Chapter 9 and remove the brake disc/hub from the knuckle.

4. Remove the three bolts attaching the brake disc splash shield to the steering knuckle and remove the shield.

5. Remove the cotter pin and then remove the nut which retains the tie rod end in the steering knuckle. Use a tool designed to remove ball joints to press the tapered tie rod end out of the knuckle.

6. Remove the cotter pins from the upper and lower ball joint retaining nuts and then clean the threads of both ball joint studs.

7. Loosen both the upper and the lower ball joint stud retaining nuts just two turns.

CAUTION: *Make sure there is clearance between the nut and the knuckle but that there are threads showing so spring force will not be released.*

8. Press both the upper and lower ball joint tapered studs out of the steering knuckle.

WARNING: *Place a floorjack in a secure position under the lower control arm spring seat. The jack must be capable of securely supporting the downforce of the spring. If spring force is released in an uncontrolled manner, personal injury could result.*

9. Remove the upper and lower ball joint retaining nuts. Then, raise the upper control arm and separate the ballstud from the arm. Pull the steering knuckle upward to separate the ballstud from the lower control arm and remove the assembly.

10. Insert the lower ball joint stud into the lower control arm. Lift the upper control arm and insert the upper ball joint stud into the upper control arm. See the Upper and Lower Ball Joint Removal And Installation procedures above and use the appropriate procedure to connect the ball joints studs to the control arms and install the retaining nuts.

11. Install the tie rod end into the knuckle. Install the retaining nut and torque it to 35 ft.lb. If the castellations on the nut do not line up with the cotter pin hole in the stud, tighten the nut just a little bit further to align them. In-

stall the cotter pin and bend it over the nut securely.

12. Install the splash shield-to-knuckle seal and shield, install the attaching bolts, and torque them to 10 ft.lb.

13. Install the hub and disc as described in Chapter 9. Also refer to Chapter 9 and install the brake caliper.

14. Install the wheel and tire and adjust the wheel bearings as described just below.

Front Wheel Bearings

REPLACEMENT

1. Raise and support the vehicle safely. Remove the wheel assembly. Remove the caliper.

2. Pry off the dust cap. Tap out and discard the cotter pin. Remove the locknut.

3. Being careful not to drop the outer bearing, pull off the brake disc and wheel hub.

4. Remove the grease inside the wheel hub.

5. Using a brass drift, carefully drive the outer bearing race out of the hub.

6. Remove the inner grease seal and bearing.

7. Check the bearings for wear or damage and replace them if necessary.

8. Coat the inner surface of the hub with grease.

9. Grease the outer surface of the bearing race and drift it into place in the hub.

10. Pack the inner and outer wheel bearings with grease. If the brake disc has been removed and/or replaced, tighten the retaining bolts to specification.

11. Install the inner bearing in the hub. Being careful not to distort it, install the oil seal with its lip facing the bearing. Drive the seal on until its outer edge is even with the edge of the hub.

12. Install the hub/disc assembly on the spindle, being careful not to damage the oil seal.

13. Install the outer bearing, washer and spindle nut. Adjust the bearing.

Adjustment

1. Remove the wheel and dust cover. Remove the cotter pin and lock cap from the nut.

2. Torque the wheel bearing nut to 14.5 ft.lb. and loosen the nut. Retorque the nut to 3.6 ft.lb.

3. Install the lock cap and cotter pin.

4. Install the dust cover and wheel assembly.

Front End Alignment

NOTE: *Do-it-yourselfers typically cannot perform front end alignment operations. The reason is that alignment is difficult to measure precisely and cannot be performed in a reasonably precise manner without a permanent and extremely expensive front end alignment machine. These machines are used exclusively by professional mechanics and speciality front end shops. Since improper alignment not only causes severe tire wear but will have a drastic effect on operating safety, we strongly recommend you avoid any attempt to set alignment for any reason. We provide a complete explanation here of what alignment is and how it is adjusted so you can intelligently discuss alignment problems with your mechanic and can appreciate the cost of performing this precision type of front end work.*

Wheel Alignment Specifications

Year	Model	Caster Range (deg)	Caster Pref Setting (deg)	Camber Range (deg)	Camber Pref Setting (deg)	Toe-in (in.)	Steering Axis Inclin. (deg)	Wheel Pivot Ratio (deg) Inner Wheel	Wheel Pivot Ratio (deg) Outer Wheel
'76–'77	Century, Regal	1½P to 2½ ②	2P	0 to 1P RH ½P to 1½P LH	½P RH 1P LH	0 to ⅛	8	20	①
'78–'81	Century, Regal manual steer.	½P to 1½P	1P	0 to 1P	½P	1/16 to 3/16	③	③	③
	Century, Regal power steer.	2½P to 3½P	3P	0 to 1P	½P	1/16 to 3/16	③	③	③
'82–'85	Regal	2½P to 3½P	3P	0 to 1P	½P	⅛ ± 1/16	③	③	③
'86–'87	Regal	2P–4P	3P	0–1⅝P	13/16P	⅛	③	③	③

① Manual steering and station wagon: RH—19 3/16, LH—18 13/16; Power steering, except station wagon: RH—19, LH—18 11/16
② 1977 Caster with radial tires, 1½P to 2½P—2P preferred; Caster with bias tires, ½P to 1½P—1P preferred
③ Not available
RH Right-hand side
LH Left-hand side
—Not specified
N Negative
P Positive

CASTER AND CAMBER ADJUSTMENT

Caster and camber are controlled by shims between the frame bracket and the upper suspension arm pivot shaft. To adjust caster, shims are removed from the front bolt and replaced at the rear bolt, or vice versa. To adjust camber, the procedure is to add or remove the same number of shims from each bolt.

TOE-IN ADJUSTMENT

Adjust toe-in by loosening the clamps on the sleeves at the outer end of the tie rod, and turning the sleeves an equal amount in the opposite direction, to maintain steering wheel spoke alignment while adjusting toe-in.

REAR SUSPENSION

Coil Spring

REMOVAL AND INSTALLATION

1. Jack up the back of the car and support both sides on jack stands on the frame, in front of the rear axle. Support the rear axle with an adjustable lifting device. Disconnect the shock absorber.

2. Detach the upper control arm at the differential.

3. Disconnect the stabilizer bar, if so equipped.

4. Remove any brake hose supports but disconnect the brake hose, only if necessary.

5. Carefully lower the axle until the tension is released from the coil spring. Be careful not to stretch the brake hose. Remove the spring. Note the direction in which the end of the last coil is pointing. Install the spring in the same position.

6. When starting a new coil spring, make certain that the bottom of the coil is properly inserted into the socket in the frame and into the form plate on the trailing arm.

7. Jack the axle into place and reinstall the control arm bolt. Tighten the bolts with the car's weight on the springs.

Shock Absorber

REMOVAL AND INSTALLATION

NOTE: *Purge new shocks of air by repeatedly extending them in their normal position and compressing them while inverted.*

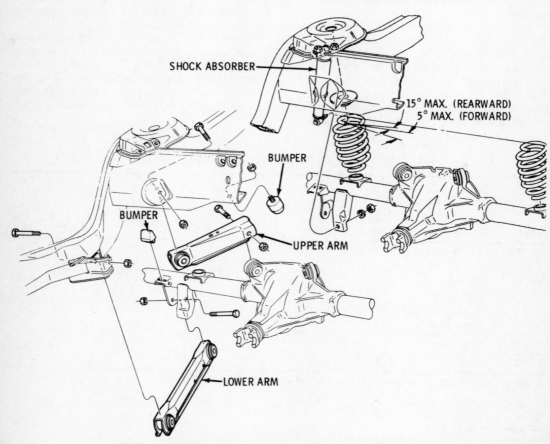

SHOCK ABSORBER

15° MAX. (REARWARD)
5° MAX. (FORWARD)

BUMPER

BUMPER

UPPER ARM

LOWER ARM

Rear suspension—1978 and later shown, earlier years similar

1. Raise the car and axle housing.

2. Remove the nut, retainer, and grommet, or nut and lockwasher, as equipped, which attaches the lower end of the shock absorber to its mounting.

3. Remove the two shock absorber upper attaching screws and remove the shock absorber.

4. Reverse the removal procedures to install. Tighten the upper bolts to 18-20 ft.lb. for all models. The nuts that lock the upper bolts on some 1977 and later models are torqued to 12 ft.lb. Tighten the lower nut to 65 ft.lb.

Sway Bar
REMOVAL AND INSTALLATION

A simple stabilizer bar is an available option on late model Regals. The unit bolts to the lower control arm on either side. To remove the unit:

1. Raise the rear of the car and support it in a secure manner. Remove the two nuts from the inner side of the lower control arm on either side.

2. Be prepared to support the bar and catch the shims used between the bar and the control arm. Hold the bar up with one hand or a suitable prop. Pull the mounting bolts out from the outside and remove the bolts and shims on one side; then repeat this procedure on the other side and remove the bar.

3. Locate the bar in position with bolt holes lined up. Put the bolts through the control arms and holes in the sway bar from outside. Then, slip the shims with the cuts facing downward in between the bar and trailing arm on either side. Install the nuts, torquing them and the bolts to 35 ft.lb.

STEERING

Steering Wheel
REMOVAL AND INSTALLATION
Except Tilt and Telescope Column

1. Disconnect the battery ground and unplug the horn wire connector from the steering column.

2. On cars with a standard wheel or optional wood-rim wheel, pull off the cap, remove the three screws and the contact, insulator, and spring. On cars with the bar type horn actuator, remove the screws securing the actuator from the underside of the steering wheel, unhook the lead connector plug, and remove the actuator assembly.

3. Loosen the steering wheel nut.

4. Apply the steering wheel puller and pull

the wheel up to the nut. Now remove the puller, nut and steering wheel.

WARNING: *Don't pound on the steering wheel in either direction or the collapsible steering column will collapse, requiring replacement.*

On installation:

NOTE: *Location marks are provided on the steering wheel and shaft to simplify proper indexing at the time of installation.*

1. Install wheel with the location mark aligned with that of the shaft.

2. Install the wheel nut and torque to 30 ft.lb.

3. Re-install horn button or actuator assembly.

Tilt and Telescope Column

1. Disconnect the battery ground.

2. Remove the attaching screws and lift the pad from the column.

3. Disconnect the horn wire by pushing the connector and turning it counterclockwise.

4. Push the locking lever counterclockwise until full release is obtained.

5. Mark the lock plate-to-locking lever position and remove the plate and lever.

6. Remove the steering wheel retaining nut and remove the wheel with a puller.

7. Install a $5/16$" × 18 set screw into the upper shaft at the fully extended position and lock it.

8. Install the steering wheel, observing the aligning mark on the hub and the slash mark

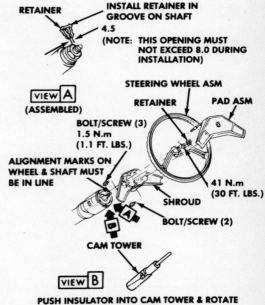

Typical standard steering wheel installation

Troubleshooting the Steering Column

Problem	Cause	Solution
Will not lock	• Lockbolt spring broken or defective	• Replace lock bolt spring
High effort (required to turn ignition key and lock cylinder)	• Lock cylinder defective	• Replace lock cylinder
	• Ignition switch defective	• Replace ignition switch
	• Rack preload spring broken or deformed	• Replace preload spring
	• Burr on lock sector, lock rack, housing, support or remote rod coupling	• Remove burr
	• Bent sector shaft	• Replace shaft
	• Defective lock rack	• Replace lock rack
	• Remote rod bent, deformed	• Replace rod
	• Ignition switch mounting bracket bent	• Straighten or replace
	• Distorted coupling slot in lock rack (tilt column)	• Replace lock rack
Will stick in "start"	• Remote rod deformed	• Straighten or replace
	• Ignition switch mounting bracket bent	• Straighten or replace
Key cannot be removed in "off-lock"	• Ignition switch is not adjusted correctly	• Adjust switch
	• Defective lock cylinder	• Replace lock cylinder
Lock cylinder can be removed without depressing retainer	• Lock cylinder with defective retainer	• Replace lock cylinder
	• Burr over retainer slot in housing cover or on cylinder retainer	• Remove burr
High effort on lock cylinder between "off" and "off-lock"	• Distorted lock rack	• Replace lock rack
	• Burr on tang of shift gate (automatic column)	• Remove burr
	• Gearshift linkage not adjusted	• Adjust linkage
Noise in column	• One click when in "off-lock" position and the steering wheel is moved (all except automatic column)	• Normal—lock bolt is seating
	• Coupling bolts not tightened	• Tighten pinch bolts
	• Lack of grease on bearings or bearing surfaces	• Lubricate with chassis grease
	• Upper shaft bearing worn or broken	• Replace bearing assembly
	• Lower shaft bearing worn or broken	• Replace bearing. Check shaft and replace if scored.
	• Column not correctly aligned	• Align column
	• Coupling pulled apart	• Replace coupling
	• Broken coupling lower joint	• Repair or replace joint and align column
	• Steering shaft snap ring not seated	• Replace ring. Check for proper seating in groove.
	• Shroud loose on shift bowl. Housing loose on jacket—will be noticed with ignition in "off-lock" and when torque is applied to steering wheel.	• Position shroud over lugs on shift bowl. Tighten mounting screws.
High steering shaft effort	• Column misaligned	• Align column
	• Defective upper or lower bearing	• Replace as required
	• Tight steering shaft universal joint	• Repair or replace
	• Flash on I.D. of shift tube at plastic joint (tilt column only)	• Replace shift tube
	• Upper or lower bearing seized	• Replace bearings
Lash in mounted column assembly	• Column mounting bracket bolts loose	• Tighten bolts
	• Broken weld nuts on column jacket	• Replace column jacket
	• Column capsule bracket sheared	• Replace bracket assembly

Troubleshooting the Steering Column (cont.)

Problem	Cause	Solution
Lash in mounted column assembly (cont.)	• Column bracket to column jacket mounting bolts loose • Loose lock shoes in housing (tilt column only) • Loose pivot pins (tilt column only) • Loose lock shoe pin (tilt column only) • Loose support screws (tilt column only)	• Tighten to specified torque • Replace shoes • Replace pivot pins and support • Replace pin and housing • Tighten screws
Housing loose (tilt column only)	• Excessive clearance between holes in support or housing and pivot pin diameters • Housing support-screws loose	• Replace pivot pins and support • Tighten screws
Steering wheel loose—every other tilt position (tilt column only)	• Loose fit between lock shoe and lock shoe pivot pin	• Replace lock shoes and pivot pin
Steering column not locking in any tilt position (tilt column only)	• Lock shoe seized on pivot pin • Lock shoe grooves have burrs or are filled with foreign material • Lock shoe springs weak or broken	• Replace lock shoes and pin • Clean or replace lock shoes • Replace springs
Noise when tilting column (tilt column only)	• Upper tilt bumpers worn • Tilt spring rubbing in housing	• Replace tilt bumper • Lubricate with chassis grease
One click when in "off-lock" position and the steering wheel is moved	• Seating of lock bolt	• None. Click is normal characteristic sound produced by lock bolt as it seats.
High shift effort (automatic and tilt column only)	• Column not correctly aligned • Lower bearing not aligned correctly • Lack of grease on seal or lower bearing areas	• Align column • Assemble correctly • Lubricate with chassis grease
Improper transmission shifting—automatic and tilt column only	• Sheared shift tube joint • Improper transmission gearshift linkage adjustment • Loose lower shift lever	• Replace shift tube • Adjust linkage • Replace shift tube

Troubleshooting the Ignition Switch

Problem	Cause	Solution
Ignition switch electrically inoperative	• Loose or defective switch connector • Feed wire open (fusible link) • Defective ignition switch	• Tighten or replace connector • Repair or replace • Replace ignition switch
Engine will not crank	• Ignition switch not adjusted properly	• Adjust switch
Ignition switch wil not actuate mechanically	• Defective ignition switch • Defective lock sector • Defective remote rod	• Replace switch • Replace lock sector • Replace remote rod
Ignition switch cannot be adjusted correctly	• Remote rod deformed	• Repair, straighten or replace

Troubleshooting the Turn Signal Switch

Problem	Cause	Solution
Turn signal will not cancel	• Loose switch mounting screws • Switch or anchor bosses broken • Broken, missing or out of position detent, or cancelling spring	• Tighten screws • Replace switch • Reposition springs or replace switch as required

Troubleshooting the Turn Signal Switch (cont.)

Problem	Cause	Solution
Turn signal difficult to operate	• Turn signal lever loose • Switch yoke broken or distorted • Loose or misplaced springs • Foreign parts and/or materials in switch • Switch mounted loosely	• Tighten mounting screws • Replace switch • Reposition springs or replace switch • Remove foreign parts and/or material • Tighten mounting screws
Turn signal will not indicate lane change	• Broken lane change pressure pad or spring hanger • Broken, missing or misplaced lane change spring • Jammed wires	• Replace switch • Replace or reposition as required • Loosen mounting screws, reposition wires and retighten screws
Turn signal will not stay in turn position	• Foreign material or loose parts impeding movement of switch yoke • Defective switch	• Remove material and/or parts • Replace switch
Hazard switch cannot be pulled out	• Foreign material between hazard support cancelling leg and yoke	• Remove foreign material. No foreign material impeding function of hazard switch—replace turn signal switch.
No turn signal lights	• Inoperative turn signal flasher • Defective or blown fuse • Loose chassis to column harness connector • Disconnect column to chassis connector. Connect new switch to chassis and operate switch by hand. If vehicle lights now operate normally, signal switch is inoperative • If vehicle lights do not operate, check chassis wiring for opens, grounds, etc.	• Replace turn signal flasher • Replace fuse • Connect securely • Replace signal switch • Repair chassis wiring as required
Instrument panel turn indicator lights on but not flashing	• Burned out or damaged front or rear turn signal bulb • If vehicle lights do not operate, check light sockets for high resistance connections, the chassis wiring for opens, grounds, etc. • Inoperative flasher • Loose chassis to column harness connection • Inoperative turn signal switch • To determine if turn signal switch is defective, substitute new switch into circuit and operate switch by hand. If the vehicle's lights operate normally, signal switch is inoperative.	• Replace bulb • Repair chassis wiring as required • Replace flasher • Connect securely • Replace turn signal switch • Replace turn signal switch
Stop light not on when turn indicated	• Loose column to chassis connection • Disconnect column to chassis connector. Connect new switch into system without removing old. Operate switch by hand. If brake lights work with switch in the turn position, signal switch is defective.	• Connect securely • Replace signal switch

Troubleshooting the Turn Signal Switch (cont.)

Problem	Cause	Solution
Stop light not on when turn indicated (cont.)	· If brake lights do not work, check connector to stop light sockets for grounds, opens, etc.	· Repair connector to stop light circuits using service manual as guide
Turn indicator panel lights not flashing	· Burned out bulbs · High resistance to ground at bulb socket · Opens, ground in wiring harness from front turn signal bulb socket to indicator lights	· Replace bulbs · Replace socket · Locate and repair as required
Turn signal lights flash very slowly	· High resistance ground at light sockets · Incorrect capacity turn signal flasher or bulb · If flashing rate is still extremely slow, check chassis wiring harness from the connector to light sockets for high resistance · Loose chassis to column harness connection · Disconnect column to chassis connector. Connect new switch into system without removing old. Operate switch by hand. If flashing occurs at normal rate, the signal switch is defective.	· Repair high resistance grounds at light sockets · Replace turn signal flasher or bulb · Locate and repair as required · Connect securely · Replace turn signal switch
Hazard signal lights will not flash—turn signal functions normally	· Blow fuse · Inoperative hazard warning flasher · Loose chassis-to-column harness connection · Disconnect column to chassis connector. Connect new switch into system without removing old. Depress the hazard warning lights. If they now work normally, turn signal switch is defective. · If lights do not flash, check wiring harness "K" lead for open between hazard flasher and connector. If open, fuse block is defective	· Replace fuse · Replace hazard warning flasher in fuse panel · Conect securely · Replace turn signal switch · Repair or replace brown wire or connector as required

Troubleshooting the Manual Steering Gear

Problem	Cause	Solution
Hard or erratic steering	· Incorrect tire pressure · Insufficient or incorrect lubrication · Suspension, or steering linkage parts damaged or misaligned · Improper front wheel alignment · Incorrect steering gear adjustment · Sagging springs	· Inflate tires to recommended pressures · Lubricate as required (refer to Maintenance Section) · Repair or replace parts as necessary · Adjust incorrect wheel alignment angles · Adjust steering gear · Replace springs
Play or looseness in steering	· Steering wheel loose · Steering linkage or attaching parts loose or worn	· Inspect shaft spines and repair as necessary. Tighten attaching nut and stake in place. · Tighten, adjust, or replace faulty components

Troubleshooting the Power Steering Gear

Problem	Cause	Solution
Play or looseness in steering (cont.)	• Pitman arm loose	• Inspect shaft splines and repair as necessary. Tighten attaching nut and stake in place
	• Steering gear attaching bolts loose	• Tighten bolts
	• Loose or worn wheel bearings	• Adjust or replace bearings
	• Steering gear adjustment incorrect or parts badly worn	• Adjust gear or replace defective parts
Wheel shimmy or tramp	• Improper tire pressure	• Inflate tires to recommended pressures
	• Wheels, tires, or brake rotors out-of-balance or out-of-round	• Inspect and replace or balance parts
	• Inoperative, worn, or loose shock absorbers or mounting parts	• Repair or replace shocks or mountings
	• Loose or worn steering or suspension parts	• Tighten or replace as necessary
	• Loose or worn wheel bearings	• Adjust or replace bearings
	• Incorrect steering gear adjustments	• Adjust steering gear
	• Incorrect front wheel alignment	• Correct front wheel alignment
Tire wear	• Improper tire pressure	• Inflate tires to recommended pressures
	• Failure to rotate tires	• Rotate tires
	• Brakes grabbing	• Adjust or repair brakes
	• Incorrect front wheel alignment	• Align incorrect angles
	• Broken or damaged steering and suspension parts	• Repair or replace defective parts
	• Wheel runout	• Replace faulty wheel
	• Excessive speed on turns	• Make driver aware of conditions
Vehicle leads to one side	• Improper tire pressures	• Inflate tires to recommended pressures
	• Front tires with uneven tread depth, wear pattern, or different cord design (i.e., one bias ply and one belted or radial tire on front wheels)	• Install tires of same cord construction and reasonably even tread depth, design, and wear pattern
	• Incorrect front wheel alignment	• Align incorrect angles
	• Brakes dragging	• Adjust or repair brakes
	• Pulling due to uneven tire construction	• Replace faulty tire

Troubleshooting the Power Steering Gear

Problem	Cause	Solution
Hissing noise in steering gear	• There is some noise in all power steering systems. One of the most common is a hissing sound most evident at standstill parking. There is no relationship between this noise and performance of the steering. Hiss may be expected when steering wheel is at end of travel or when slowly turning at standstill.	• Slight hiss is normal and in no way affects steering. Do not replace valve unless hiss is extremely objectionable. A replacement valve will also exhibit slight noise and is not always a cure. Investigate clearance around flexible coupling rivets. Be sure steering shaft and gear are aligned so flexible coupling rotates in a flat plane and is not distorted as shaft rotates. Any metal-to-metal contacts through flexible coupling will transmit valve hiss into passenger compartment through the steering column.
Rattle or chuckle noise in steering gear	• Gear loose on frame	• Check gear-to-frame mounting screws. Tighten screws to 88 N·m (65 foot pounds) torque.

Troubleshooting the Power Steering Gear

Problem	Cause	Solution
Rattle or chuckle noise in steering gear (cont.)	• Steering linkage looseness	• Check linkage pivot points for wear. Replace if necessary.
	• Pressure hose touching other parts of car	• Adjust hose position. Do not bend tubing by hand.
	• Loose pitman shaft over center adjustment	• Adjust to specifications
	NOTE: A slight rattle may occur on turns because of increased clearance off the "high point." This is normal and clearance must not be reduced below specified limits to eliminate this slight rattle.	
	• Loose pitman arm	• Tighten pitman arm nut to specifications
Squawk noise in steering gear when turning or recovering from a turn	• Damper O-ring on valve spool cut	• Replace damper O-ring
Poor return of steering wheel to center	• Tires not properly inflated	• Inflate to specified pressure
	• Lack of lubrication in linkage and ball joints	• Lube linkage and ball joints
	• Lower coupling flange rubbing against steering gear adjuster plug	• Loosen pinch bolt and assemble properly
	• Steering gear to column misalignment	• Align steering column
	• Improper front wheel alignment	• Check and adjust as necessary
	• Steering linkage binding	• Replace pivots
	• Ball joints binding	• Replace ball joints
	• Steering wheel rubbing against housing	• Align housing
	• Tight or frozen steering shaft bearings	• Replace bearings
	• Sticking or plugged valve spool	• Remove and clean or replace valve
	• Steering gear adjustments over specifications	• Check adjustment with gear out of car. Adjust as required.
	• Kink in return hose	• Replace hose
Car leads to one side or the other (keep in mind road condition and wind. Test car in both directions on flat road)	• Front end misaligned	• Adjust to specifications
	• Unbalanced steering gear valve	• Replace valve
	NOTE: If this is cause, steering effort will be very light in direction of lead and normal or heavier in opposite direction.	
Momentary increase in effort when turning wheel fast to right or left	• Low oil level	• Add power steering fluid as required
	• Pump belt slipping	• Tighten or replace belt
	• High internal leakage	• Check pump pressure. (See pressure test)
Steering wheel surges or jerks when turning with engine running especially during parking	• Low oil level	• Fill as required
	• Loose pump belt	• Adjust tension to specification
	• Steering linkage hitting engine oil pan at full turn	• Correct clearance
	• Insufficient pump pressure	• Check pump pressure. (See pressure test). Replace relief valve if defective.
	• Pump flow control valve sticking	• Inspect for varnish or damage, replace if necessary
Excessive wheel kickback or loose steering	• Air in system	• Add oil to pump reservoir and bleed by operating steering. Check hose connectors for proper torque and adjust as required.
	• Steering gear loose on frame	• Tighten attaching screws to specified torque

Troubleshooting the Power Steering Gear (cont.)

Problem	Cause	Solution
Excessive wheel kickback or loose steering (cont.)	• Steering linkage joints worn enough to be loose • Worn poppet valve • Loose thrust bearing preload adjustment • Excessive overcenter lash	• Replace loose pivots • Replace poppet valve • Adjust to specification with gear out of vehicle • Adjust to specification with gear out of car
Hard steering or lack of assist	• Loose pump belt • Low oil level **NOTE:** Low oil level will also result in excessive pump noise • Steering gear to column misalignment • Lower coupling flange rubbing against steering gear adjuster plug • Tires not properly inflated	• Adjust belt tension to specification • Fill to proper level. If excessively low, check all lines and joints for evidence of external leakage. Tighten loose connectors. • Align steering column • Loosen pinch bolt and assemble properly • Inflate to recommended pressure
Foamy milky power steering fluid, low fluid level and possible low pressure	• Air in the fluid, and loss of fluid due to internal pump leakage causing overflow	• Check for leak and correct. Bleed system. Extremely cold temperatures will cause system aeration should the oil level be low. If oil level is correct and pump still foams, remove pump from vehicle and separate reservoir from housing. Check welsh plug and housing for cracks. If plug is loose or housing is cracked, replace housing.
Low pressure due to steering pump	• Flow control valve stuck or inoperative • Pressure plate not flat against cam ring	• Remove burrs or dirt or replace. Flush system. • Correct
Low pressure due to steering gear	• Pressure loss in cylinder due to worn piston ring or badly worn housing bore • Leakage at valve rings, valve body-to-worm seal	• Remove gear from car for disassembly and inspection of ring and housing bore • Remove gear from car for disassembly and replace seals

Troubleshooting the Power Steering Pump

Problem	Cause	Solution
Chirp noise in steering pump	• Loose belt	• Adjust belt tension to specification
Belt squeal (particularly noticeable at full wheel travel and stand still parking)	• Loose belt	• Adjust belt tension to specification
Growl noise in steering pump	• Excessive back pressure in hoses or steering gear caused by restriction	• Locate restriction and correct. Replace part if necessary.
Growl noise in steering pump (particularly noticeable at stand still parking)	• Scored pressure plates, thrust plate or rotor • Extreme wear of cam ring	• Replace parts and flush system • Replace parts
Groan noise in steering pump	• Low oil level • Air in the oil. Poor pressure hose connection.	• Fill reservoir to proper level • Tighten connector to specified torque. Bleed system by operating steering from right to left—full turn.
Rattle noise in steering pump	• Vanes not installed properly • Vanes sticking in rotor slots	• Install properly • Free up by removing burrs, varnish, or dirt

Troubleshooting the Power Steering Pump (cont.)

Problem	Cause	Solution
Swish noise in steering pump	• Defective flow control valve	• Replace part
Whine noise in steering pump	• Pump shaft bearing scored	• Replace housing and shaft. Flush system.
Hard steering or lack of assist	• Loose pump belt • Low oil level in reservoir **NOTE:** Low oil level will also result in excessive pump noise • Steering gear to column misalignment • Lower coupling flange rubbing against steering gear adjuster plug • Tires not properly inflated	• Adjust belt tension to specification • Fill to proper level. If excessively low, check all lines and joints for evidence of external leakage. Tighten loose connectors. • Align steering column • Loosen pinch bolt and assemble properly • Inflate to recommended pressure
Foaming milky power steering fluid, low fluid level and possible low pressure	• Air in the fluid, and loss of fluid due to internal pump leakage causing overflow	• Check for leaks and correct. Bleed system. Extremely cold temperatures will cause system aeriation should the oil level be low. If oil level is correct and pump still foams, remove pump from vehicle and separate reservoir from body. Check welsh plug and body for cracks. If plug is loose or body is cracked, replace body.
Low pump pressure	• Flow control valve stuck or inoperative • Pressure plate not flat against cam ring	• Remove burrs or dirt or replace. Flush system. • Correct
Momentary increase in effort when turning wheel fast to right or left	• Low oil level in pump • Pump belt slipping • High internal leakage	• Add power steering fluid as required • Tighten or replace belt • Check pump pressure. (See pressure test)
Steering wheel surges or jerks when turning with engine running especially during parking	• Low oil level • Loose pump belt • Steering linkage hitting engine oil pan at full turn • Insufficient pump pressure	• Fill as required • Adjust tension to specification • Correct clearance • Check pump pressure. (See pressure test). Replace flow control valve if defective.
Steering wheel surges or jerks when turning with engine running especially during parking (cont.)	• Sticking flow control valve	• Inspect for varnish or damage, replace if necessary
Excessive wheel kickback or loose steering	• Air in system	• Add oil to pump reservoir and bleed by operating steering. Check hose connectors for proper torque and adjust as required.
Low pump pressure	• Extreme wear of cam ring • Scored pressure plate, thrust plate, or rotor • Vanes not installed properly • Vanes sticking in rotor slots • Cracked or broken thrust or pressure plate	• Replace parts. Flush system. • Replace parts. Flush system. • Install properly • Freeup by removing burrs, varnish, or dirt • Replace part

on the end of the shaft. Make certain that the unattached end of the horn upper contact assembly is seated flush against the top of the horn contact carrier button.

9. Install the nut on the upper steering shaft and torque to 30 ft.lb.

10. Remove the set screw installed in Step 7.

11. Install the plate assembly finger tight.

12. Position the locking lever in the vertical position and move it counterclockwise until the holes in the plate align with the holes in the lever. Install the attaching screws.

13. Align the pad assembly with the holes in the steering wheel and install the retaining screws.

14. Connect the battery.

15. Make certain that the locking lever securely locks the wheel travel and that the wheel travel is free in the unlocked position.

Special Procedure for Cars with A.C.R.S. (Air Bags)

Some 1976 models have an air cushion, or air bag, restraint system. One of the elements of this complex system is an air cushion module in the top of the steering wheel. The steering wheel can be removed in the manner described above after the module has been removed. Note that you will need one special tool to remove the four module-to-steering wheel screws and another to disconnect the module wire connector.

WARNING: *This is a procedure that could be dangerous if the air bag should deploy as you are working on it. The steps are designed to make it impossible for the system to deploy accidentally by disarming the system before you start. Follow all procedures with particular care to ensure that you are proceeding in proper order and not accidentally skipping any steps. You should satisfy yourself that you can perform this without making any mistakes before proceeding to protect yourself from injury.*

To remove the module:

1. Turn the ignition lock to the LOCK position.

2. Disconnect the battery ground cable and tape the end to prevent any possibility of a complete circuit.

3. Remove the 4 module-to-steering wheel screws. A special tool is available to do this.

4. Lift up the module and disconnect the horn wire.

5. Disconnect the module wire connector. A special tool is available to do this, too.

WARNING: *The driver air cushion module should always be carried with the vinyl cover away from all parts of one's body and should always be laid on a flat surface with the vinyl side up. This is necessary so that a free space*

is provided to allow the air cushion to expand in the case of accidental deployment.

Do not attempt to repair any portion of the module. The module must be serviced as a unit. Attempting repairs such as soldering wires, changing covers, etc. may cause accidental inflation or impair operation of the driver module and cause serious injury.

Do not dispose of the module in any way. The highly inflammable material in the module can cause serious burns if ignited. Modules must be exchanged at an authorized dealer's parts department.

To install the module:

6. Hold the module with the emblem in the lower right corner.

7. Loop the air cushion harness clockwise from the 11 o'clock position to the 6 o'clock position.

8. Install the module connector by pushing it onto the column circuit firmly. Check that it is fully seated.

9. Install the horn wire.

10. Position the module, making sure that the wiring is still in place, and install the 4 screws. Torque them to 40 in.lb.

11. Reconnect the battery ground cable.

12. Turn the ignition lock to any position other than LOCK and check that the restraint indicator light operates correctly.

Turn Signal Switch
REMOVAL AND INSTALLATION
Except Tilt and Telescope Column; Except A.C.R.S.

NOTE: *The steering wheel must always be supported. Use extreme care not to bend the steering column.*

1. Remove the steering wheel.

2. Remove the three cover screws and the cover. All 1976 and later steering columns have a redesigned lock plate which is removed by inserting a screwdriver in the cover slot and prying out. This must be done in at least two of the slots to avoid breaking the plate.

3. Depress the lock plate and remove the snapring. Remove the lock plate.

4. Remove the spring and horn contact signal cancelling cam.

5. Place the turn signal lever in the right turn position, remove the attaching screw and remove the turn signal lever. On models with the dimmer switch mounted on the column, remove the actuator arm screw and the actuator arm. Pull the turn signal lever straight out to remove. Depress the hazard warning knob, and remove the knob. Some models have a screw in the end of the knob which must be removed.

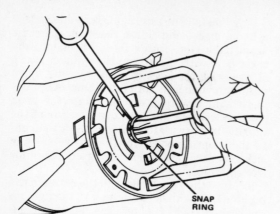

Using the special steering wheel lockplate compressing tool and removing the snap-ring

6. Remove the three turn signal switch mounting screws.

7. Remove the instrument panel lower trim panel and disconnect the turn signal connector from the harness.

8. Remove the four bracket attaching screws and remove the bracket.

9. On 1977 and later models with automatic transmissions, loosen the shift indicator needle attaching screw and remove the needle.

10. On 1977 and later models, remove the two steering column supporting bolts while supporting the column. Do not allow the column to drop suddenly.

11. Remove the bracket and wiring from the column. Loosely reinstall the column supporting bolts, if removed.

12. Pull the switch straight up with the wire protector and wire harness.

13. Reverse the above steps to install.

Tilt and Telescope Column; Except A.C.R.S.

1. Disconnect the battery ground.

2. Remove the steering wheel and lock plate as previously described.

3. Remove the upper bearing preload spring.

4. Position the turn signal lever in the right turn position and remove the lever and screw.

5. With column mounted dimmer switches, remove the actuator arm and screw, then remove the turn signal arm by pulling it straight out.

6. Push in on the warning hazard knob, then remove the retaining screw and knob.

7. Position the column in the center position and remove the three turn signal switch attaching screws.

8. Remove the instrument panel lower trim pad and disconnect the turn signal harness connector. Lift the connector from the mounting bracket on the right side of the jacket.

9. Remove the toe pan bolts.

10. Remove the four bolts attaching the bracket assembly to the jacket.

11. Remove the shift indicator retaining clip.

12. Support the column and remove the bracket assembly. Remove the wire protector from the turn signal wiring. Pull the turn signal switch and wiring from the column.

13. Prior to installation, coat all moving parts with lithium based grease.

14. Insert switch wiring into the column.

15. Place the switch in the right turn position and push it straight down until seated.

CAUTION: *Angling or cocking of the switch can cause damage to the buzzer terminal or tangs.*

16. Install the switch attaching screws and torque them to 25 ft.lb.

17. Position the turn signal in the center.

18. Connect the wiring to the harness.

19. Install the hazard warning knob and turn signal lever.

20. Install the lock plate and carrier and the steering wheel.

21. Install the wiring protector and bracket. Torque the bracket bolts to 18 ft.lb. and the nuts to 24 ft.lb.

22. Install the shift indicator needle or clip.

23. Position the harness connector in the bracket on the right side of the jacket.

24. Install the instrument panel lower trim pad and connect the battery ground.

1976 With A.C.R.S. (Air Bags)

Follow the procedure for removing the steering wheel and air cushion module which appears previously under "Steering Wheel Removal and Installation, Special Procedure for Cars with A.C.R.S."

1. Remove the 3 screws from the retainer and cover. Carefully lift the cover and retainer from the column.

2. Carefully insert a screwdriver blade into the locking tab at the side and lift the slip ring from the column.

3. Proceed with the Turn Signal Switch Replacement procedure, beginning at Step 3.

4. To replace the slip ring, align the slip ring locating tab with the slot in the bowl and push the slip ring into position. Make sure that all 3 locking tabs are securely positioned.

5. Install the cover and retainer, aligning the cover over the locating tab. Torque the screws to 15 in.lb.

Ignition Switch and Lock Cylinder
REMOVAL AND INSTALLATION

1. Refer to the Turn Signal Switch Replacement procedure, Steps 1-6.

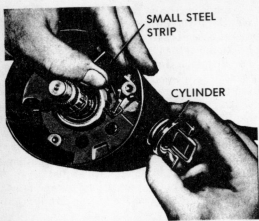

SMALL STEEL STRIP

CYLINDER

Depress the spring latch to remove the lock cylinder on models through 1978

2. Disconnect the turn signal connector from the harness and pull out the turn signal switch. Allow it to hang.

3. With the lock cylinder in the RUN position, insert a small screwdriver or steel strip into the slot next to the turn signal switch mounting screw boss (right hand slot), depress the spring latch and remove the key lock. On 1979 and later models remove the retaining screw and lock cylinder.

4. Pull the buzzer switch straight out, depressing the switch clip with pliers.

5. Place the ignition switch in the OFF-UNLOCKED position by pulling up on the connecting rod until there is a definite stop or detent felt.

6. Remove the two attaching screws and the ignition switch.

7. Assembly is the reverse of the above. However, note the following steps before proceeding with reassembly.

8. To install the steering lock, hold the lock cylinder sleeve and rotate the knob clockwise against the stop. Insert the cylinder into the cover bore with the key on the cylinder sleeve aligned with the keyway in the housing. Then push the cylinder in until it bottoms. Maintaining a light inward pressure, rotate the knob counterclockwise until the drive section of the cylinder mates with the drive shaft. Push in until the snapring pops into the groove and the lock cylinder is secured in the cover. Check for free rotation.

9. Move the switch slider to the extreme left position (ACC), then two detents to the right, to the OFF-UNLOCKED position. Fit the actuator rod into the hole and attach the switch to the column.

10. The neutral start switch is adjusted with the shift lever in the Drive position.

Tilt Column

1. Refer to the Turn Signal Switch Replacement procedure for tilt and telescopic columns, Steps 1-6.

2. Position the tilt column in the center position and remove the three turn signal switch screws. Tape the wires to the wire shift bowl in Low. Pull the switch straight up and out, allowing it to hang.

3. Insert a small screwdriver or steel strip into the slot next to the turn signal switch mounting screw boss (right hand slot), depress the spring latch and remove the key lock. On 1979 and later models, remove the retaining screw and the lock cylinder.

4. Remove the buzzer switch straight out, depressing the switch clip with pliers.

5. Remove the three housing cover screws and cover.

6. Install the tilt release lever and place column in full UP position.

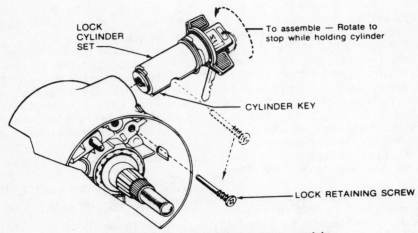

LOCK CYLINDER SET

To assemble — Rotate to stop while holding cylinder

CYLINDER KEY

LOCK RETAINING SCREW

Ignition lock removal—1979 and later models

7. Place a screwdriver in the slot of the tilt spring retainer, press in about $3/16"$ and turn counterclockwise. Remove the spring and guide.

CAUTION: *Be careful! The spring is very strong.*

8. Push the column in neutral position, push in on the upper steering shaft, remove the inner race seat and race.

9. Remove the upper flange pinch bolt, place the ignition switch in the accessory position, remove the two switch mounting screws and switch.

NOTE: *The neutral start switch can be removed at this time, if necessary.*

10. Assembly is the reverse of the above. However, note the following steps before proceeding with the reassembly.

11. To install the steering lock, hold the lock cylinder sleeve and rotate the knob clockwise against the stop. Insert the cylinder into the cover bore with the key on the cylinder sleeve aligned with the keyway in the housing. Push the cylinder in until it bottoms. Maintaining a light inward pressure, rotate the knob counterclockwise until the drive section of the cylinder mates with the driveshaft. Push in until the snapring pops into the groove and the lock cylinder is secured in the cover. Check for free rotation.

12. When installing the ignition switch, be sure the lock cylinder is in the LOCK position. Put the shift bowl or shroud in the PARK position. Make sure the ignition switch is in the LOCK position. Insert the actuator rod into the switch and assemble the switch to the column.

13. The neutral start switch is adjusted with the shift lever in the drive position.

Steering Column

NOTE: *Because the steering column is collapsible in an accident, it is necessary that it be handled with care in order to avoid distortion of major parts. It must not be dropped, hammered on or even leaned on, or vitally important parts may deform.*

1. Disconnect the negative battery cable. Remove the clamp bolt from the steering coupling at the lower end of the steering column shaft (located near the steering box, under the hood).

2. Disconnect the shift linkage from the shift tube lever at the lower end of the column.

3. Remove the steering wheel with a puller, as described above.

4. Remove the left sound insulator and lower column cover.

5. Remove the trim cap or lower trim panel from the instrument panel, depending on equipment.

6. Remove the steering column cover and toe pan attaching screws. Remove the shift indicator needle from the shift bowl.

7. Securely support the column in position and remove the two nuts attaching the column to the to the underside of the instrument panel.

8. Lower the column carefully, being careful to retain any spacers that may have been used in order. Disconnect the wiring. Then, carefully remove the column from inside the car.

9. Reinstall the column into the car. Make sure, when assembling the upper and lower dash covers that they can slide on the column.

10. If the bracket which mounts the column to the dash has been removed, install the bolts in this order:

   a. Left rear.
   b. Left front.
   c. Right front.
   d. Right rear.

11. Tighten the bolts just snug to avoid distorting the column.

12. Install the switch connector to the ignition switch. Then, position the column in the body and support it there. Install the lockwashers and nuts for the coupling and then tighten them. Then, loosely assemble the nuts fastening the mounting bracket for the column to the lower side of the instrument panel.

13. Position the lower cover to the firewall and ensure that the cover is lined up by starting the left lower screw. Then, install and tighten the right lower screw. Then tighten the left lower screw. Finally, install and tighten the two screws that fit into the top of the cover.

14. Tighten first the screw for the left side of the cover clamp; then tighten the screw for the right side of the cover clamp. Finally, install and tighten the remaining cover screws.

15. Finally, tighten the nuts fastening the column to the underside of the dash. Reinstall the steering wheel as described above. Reinstall the bolt for the steering coupling clamp.

Steering Linkage

REMOVAL AND INSTALLATION

Tie Rod End

1. Raise and support the car. Loosen the tie rod adjuster sleeve clamp nuts.

2. Remove the tie rod stud nut cotter pin and nut.

3. Remove the tie rod stud from the steering arm or intermediate rod. This is a taper fit. Removal is accomplished using a ball joint removal tool or by hitting the steering arm sharply with a hammer as a backup. If the joint is to be reused, the removal joint must be used.

4. Unthread the tie rod from the adjusted sleeve. Outer tie rods have right hand threads and inner tie rods have left hand threads.

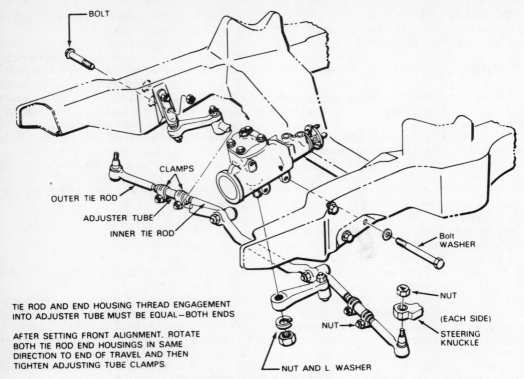

TIE ROD AND END HOUSING THREAD ENGAGEMENT INTO ADJUSTER TUBE MUST BE EQUAL—BOTH ENDS

AFTER SETTING FRONT ALIGNMENT. ROTATE BOTH TIE ROD END HOUSINGS IN SAME DIRECTION TO END OF TRAVEL AND THEN TIGHTEN ADJUSTING TUBE CLAMPS.

Steering linkage—typical

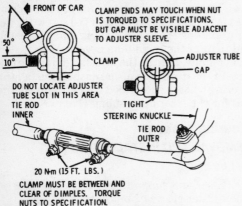

BOLTS MUST BE INSTALLED IN DIRECTION SHOWN, ROTATE BOTH INNER AND OUTER TIE ROD HOUSINGS REARWARD TO THE LIMIT OF BALL JOINT TRAVEL BEFORE TIGHTENING CLAMPS. WITH THIS SAME REARWARD ROTATION ALL BOLT CENTERLINES MUST BE BETWEEN ANGLES SHOWN AFTER TIGHTENING CLAMPS.

CLAMP ENDS MAY TOUCH WHEN NUT IS TORQUED TO SPECIFICATIONS. BUT GAP MUST BE VISIBLE ADJACENT TO ADJUSTER SLEEVE.

DO NOT LOCATE ADJUSTER TUBE SLOT IN THIS AREA

20 N·m (15 FT. LBS.)

CLAMP MUST BE BETWEEN AND CLEAR OF DIMPLES. TORQUE NUTS TO SPECIFICATION.

Tie rod clamp and sleeve positioning

Count the number of turns the tie rod must be rotated to remove it from the adjusting sleeve. This will allow a reasonably accurate realignment upon reassembly.

NOTE: *If a turning force of more than 7 ft.lb. is needed for end removal, after break-away, the nuts and bolts should be replaced.*

5. Reverse the removal procedures to install. Clean rust and dirt from the threads. Observe the following torque specifications: steering arm-to-tie rod end nut, 35 ft.lb.; tie rod clamp nuts, 11-14 ft.lb.; tie rod-to-intermediate nut, 40 ft.lb. Check the alignment and adjust if necessary.

Pitman Arm

NOTE: *To perform this procedure, you will need special pullers to pull the center link out of the Pitman arm and to pull the Pitman arm off the steering box shaft without stressing the bearings in the steering box.*

1. Raise the car and support it securely by the frame rails. Remove the nut from the Pitman arm ballstud.

2. Disconnect the center link at the Pitman arm with a puller. Then, pull down on the intermediate rod to remove the stud.

3. Remove the Pitman arm nut and lockwasher from the Pitman shaft. Provide replacement parts and discard both.

4. Mark the relationship between the Pitman arm and the steering box shaft. Then, pull the arm off the shaft. Mark the new arm at the same place as the old one was marked.

5. Install the new arm on the shaft, aligning the marks. Install the new nut and lockwasher and torque the nut to 185 ft.lb.

6. Put the center link into position on the Pitman arm, install the attaching nut, and torque it to 40 ft.lb. Lower the car.

Idler Arm

NOTE: *You will need a puller suitable for removing the tapered stud on the idler arm from the center link.*

1. Raise the car and support it securely by the frame rails. Remove the nuts, bolts, and washers that attach the idler arm to the frame.
2. Remove the nut that attaches the idler arm to the center link ballstud.
3. Pull the idler arm out of the center link with the puller and remove it.
4. Note that the idler arm has a threaded support. The threaded bushing must be loosened and the support turned in the arm to adjust the distance between lower bolt hole and the top surface of the arm to $2^{11}/_{32}$" (59.5mm). This ensures that, when installed, the idler arm socket will be level with the Pitman arm ball socket. Retighten the threaded bushing. Make sure all idler supports will still be fully free to rotate at least 90°.
5. Position the idler arm support against the frame, lining up the two sets of holes. Install the bolts, washers and nuts, and torque to 60 ft.lb.
6. Install the center link to the idler arm by inserting the tapered section of the arm into the link. Make sure the seal is on the stud. Install the nut and torque it to 40 ft.lb. On some models, this nut uses a cotter pin. If so, tighten the nut just enough farther to line up holes and then install and secure a new cotter pin. Lower the car.

Center Link

NOTE: *You will need pullers that are suitable for separating the tie rod ends, idler arm, and Pitman arm from the center link. It is ideal to have a tool J-29193 or equivalent to seat the idler arm into the center link.*

1. Raise the car and support it securely by the frame rails. Remove the cotter pins, remove the nuts, and then disconnect the tie rod inner ends at the center link with pullers.
2. Remove the nut from the ballstud on the center link where it attaches to the Pitman arm. Then, use a puller to remove the arm from the ballstud. Shift the linkage to eliminate torque and pull the link away from the Pitman arm.
3. Remove the nut attaching the center link to the idler arm from the idler arm. Use a puller to separate the center link from the idler arm.
4. Inspect all seals and replace any that are damaged. Make sure all seals that are satisfactory are in place.

5. Install the center link onto the idler arm. If it is available, install the special tool and torque its nut to 15 ft.lb. Remove the tool and install the attaching nut. Torque it to 40 ft.lb.
6. Raise the end of the center link and install it into the Pitman arm. Install the nut and torque it to 40 ft.lb.
7. Install the inner tie rod ends into the center link. Install the nuts and torque them to 30 ft.lb. Tighten them just enough farther to line up the holes and then install new cotter pins.
8. Have the toe-in set at an alignment shop.

Manual Steering Gear
ADJUSTMENTS

Steering gear adjustments consist of difficult preload adjustments that must be made with the gear off the car. These adjustments are only made at time of rebuild. Once correct, they are not repeated to compensate for wear; rather, steering box problems must be corrected by rebuild.

REMOVAL AND INSTALLATION

1. Disconnect the steering shaft coupling.
2. Remove the Pitman arm with a puller after marking the arm-to-shaft relationship.
3. Remove the steering gear-to-frame mounting bolts and remove the steering gear.
4. Reverse the removal steps to install the steering gear. Tighten the frame mounting bolts to 70 ft.lb. Tighten the Pitman shaft nut to 180 ft.lb. and the steering coupling nuts to 20 ft.lb.

Power Steering Gear
REMOVAL AND INSTALLATION

Installation and removal of power steering gears is the same as that described for manual steering gears above, with the addition of disconnecting and reconnecting the hydraulic lines. Cap both hoses and steering gear outlets to prevent foreign material from entering the system.

ADJUSTMENTS

Steering gear adjustments consist of difficult preload adjustments that must be made with the gear off the car. These adjustments are only made at time of rebuild. Once correct, they are not repeated to compensate for wear; rather, steering box problems must be corrected by rebuild.

Power Steering Pump
REMOVAL AND INSTALLATION

1. Remove the hoses at the pump and tape the openings shut to prevent contamination.

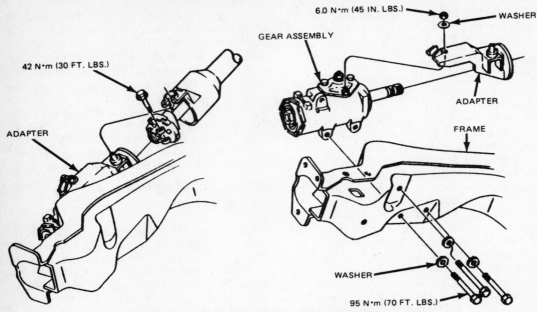

Manual steering gear installation, power steering gear similar

Position the disconnected lines in a raised position to prevent leakage.

2. Remove the pump belt.

3. Loosen the retaining bolts and any braces, and remove the pump.

4. Install the pump on the engine with the retaining bolts hand-tight.

5. Connect and tighten the hose fittings.

6. Refill the pump with fluid and bleed by turning the pulley counterclockwise (viewed from the front). Stop the bleeding when air bubbles no longer appear.

7. Install the pump belt on the pulley and adjust the tension.

BLEEDING

1. Fill the pump reservoir to the proper level. See the steering index page for fluid recommendations. Operate the engine and turn the steering wheel fully to the left and right without hitting the stops until the power steering fluid reaches normal operating temperature (165-175°F), then stop the engine.

2. Raise the front of the vehicle off the ground and support on jack stands. Failure to raise the front end off the ground could cause flat spots to be worn into the tires during bleeding procedure.

3. Turn the wheels to full left turn position and add power steering fluid to the COLD mark on the dipstick, if necessary.

4. Bleed the system by turning the wheels, with the engine running, from side to side without hitting hard against the stops. Maintain the fluid level at the COLD mark on the dipstick. Fluid with air in it will have a milky appearance. Air must be eliminated from the fluid before normal steering action can be obtained. Continue turning the wheels back and forth until all of the air is bled from the system.

5. Return the wheels to center position and operate the engine for an additional 2-3 minutes, then stop the engine.

6. Road test the car to make sure the steering functions normally and is free of noise. Check the fluid level. Add fluid to the HOT mark.

PRELIMINARY TESTS

NOTE: *The following tests are generally applicable to most power steering systems.*

Turning Effort

Check the effort required to turn the steering wheel after aligning the front wheels and inflating the tires to proper pressure.

1. With the vehicle on dry pavement and the front wheels straight ahead, set the parking brake and turn the engine on.

2. After a short warm-up period turn the steering wheel back and forth several times to warm the steering fluid.

3. Attach a spring scale to the steering wheel rim and measure the pull required to turn the steering wheel one complete revolution in each direction.

NOTE: *This test may be done with torque wrench on the steering wheel nut. See the sec-*

tion on Manual Steering for a discussion of this test.

Checking the Fluid Flow and Pressure Relief Valve in the Pump Assembly

When the wheels are turned hard right or hard left, against the stops, the fluid flow and pressure relief valves come into action. If these valves are working, there should be a slight buzzing noise. Do not hold the wheels in the extreme position for over three or four seconds because, if the pressure relief valve is not working, the pressure could get high enough to damage the system.

Brakes

BASIC OPERATING PRINCIPLES

Hydraulic systems are used to actuate the brakes of all automobiles. The system transports the power required to force the frictional surfaces of the braking system together from the pedal to the individual brake units at each wheel. A hydraulic system is used for two reasons.

First, fluid under pressure can be carried to all parts of an automobile by small pipes and flexible hoses without taking up a significant amount of room or posing routing problems.

Second, a great mechanical advantage can be given to the brake pedal end of the system, and the foot pressure required to actuate the brakes can be reduced by making the surface area of the master cylinder pistons smaller than that of any of the pistons in the wheel cylinders or calipers.

The master cylinder consists of a fluid reservoir and a double cylinder and piston assembly. Double type master cylinders are designed to separate the front and rear braking systems hydraulically in case of a leak.

Steel lines carry the brake fluid to a point on the vehicle's frame near each of the vehicle's wheels. The fluid is then carried to the calipers and wheel cylinders by flexible tubes in order to allow for suspension and steering movements.

In drum brake systems, each wheel cylinder contains two pistons, one at either end, which push outward in opposite directions.

In disc brake systems, the cylinders are part of the calipers. One cylinder in each caliper is used to force the brake pads against the disc.

All pistons employ some type of seal, usually made of rubber, to minimize fluid leakage. A rubber dust boot seals the outer end of the cylinder against dust and dirt. The boot fits around the outer end of the piston on disc brake calipers, and around the brake actuating rod on wheel cylinders.

The hydraulic system operates as follows: When at rest, the entire system, from the piston(s) in the master cylinder to those in the wheel cylinders or calipers, is full of brake fluid. Upon application of the brake pedal, fluid trapped in front of the master cylinder piston(s) is forced through the lines to the wheel cylinders. Here, it forces the pistons outward, in the case of drum brakes, and inward toward the disc, in the case of disc brakes. The motion of the pistons is opposed by return springs mounted outside the cylinders in drum brakes, and by spring seals, in disc brakes.

Upon release of the brake pedal, a spring located inside the master cylinder immediately returns the master cylinder pistons to the normal position. The pistons contain check valves and the master cylinder has compensating ports drilled in it. These are uncovered as the pistons reach their normal position. The piston check valves allow fluid to flow toward the wheel cylinders or calipers as the pistons withdraw. Then, as the return springs force the brake pads or shoes into the released position, the excess fluid reservoir through the compensating ports. It is during the time the pedal is in the released position that any fluid that has leaked out of the system will be replaced through the compensating ports.

Dual circuit master cylinders employ two pistons, located one behind the other, in the same cylinder. The primary piston is actuated directly by mechanical linkage from the brake pedal through the power booster. The secondary piston is actuated by fluid trapped between the two pistons. If a leak develops in front of the secondary piston, it moves forward until it bottoms against the front of the master cylinder, and the fluid trapped between the pistons will operate the rear brakes. If the rear brakes develop a leak, the primary piston will move forward until direct contact with the secondary piston takes place, and it will force the secondary piston to actuate the front brakes. In either case, the brake pedal moves farther when the brakes are applied, and less braking power is available.

All dual circuit systems use a switch to warn the driver when only half of the brake system is operational. This switch is located in a valve body which is mounted on the firewall or the frame below the master cylinder. A hydraulic piston receives pressure from both circuits, each circuit's pressure being applied to one end of the piston. When the pressures are in balance, the piston remains stationary. When one circuit has a leak, however, the greater pressure in that circuit during application of the brakes will push the piston to one side, closing the switch and activating the brake warning light.

In disc brake systems, this valve body also contains a metering valve and, in some cases, a proportioning valve. The metering valve keeps pressure from traveling to the disc brakes on the front wheels until the brake shoes on the rear wheels have contacted the drums, ensuring that the front brakes will never be used alone. The proportioning valve controls the pressure to the rear brakes to lessen the chance of rear wheel lock-up during very hard braking.

Warning lights may be tested by depressing the brake pedal and holding it while opening one of the wheel cylinder bleeder screws. If this does not cause the light to go on, substitute a new lamp, make continuity checks, and, finally, replace the switch as necessary.

The hydraulic system may be checked for leaks by applying pressure to the pedal gradually and steadily. If the pedal sinks very slowly to the floor, the system has a leak. This is not to be confused with a springy or spongy feel due to the compression of air within the lines. If the system leaks, there will be a gradual change in the position of the pedal with a constant pressure.

Check for leaks along all lines and at wheel cylinders. If no external leaks are apparent, the problem is inside the master cylinder.

Disc Brakes
BASIC OPERATING PRINCIPLES

Instead of the traditional expanding brakes that press outward against a circular drum, disc brake systems utilize a disc (rotor) with brake pads positioned on either side of it. Braking effect is achieved in a manner similar to the way you would squeeze a spinning phonograph record between your fingers. The disc (rotor) is a casting with cooling fins between the two braking surfaces. This enables air to circulate between the braking surfaces making them less

sensitive to heat buildup and more resistant to fade. Dirt and water do not affect braking action since contaminants are thrown off by the centrifugal action of the rotor or scraped off the by the pads. Also, the equal clamping action of the two brake pads tends to ensure uniform, straight line stops. Disc brakes are inherently self-adjusting.

There are three general types of disc brake:
1. A fixed caliper.
2. A floating caliper.
3. A sliding caliper.

The fixed caliper design uses two pistons mounted on either side of the rotor (in each side of the caliper). The caliper is mounted rigidly and does not move.

The sliding and floating designs are quite similar. In fact, these two types are often lumped together. In both designs, the pad on the inside of the rotor is moved into contact with the rotor by hydraulic force. The caliper, which is not held in a fixed position, moves slightly, bringing the outside pad into contact with the rotor. There are various methods of attaching floating calipers. Some pivot at the bottom or top, and some slide on mounting bolts. In any event, the end result is the same.

All the cars covered in this book employ the sliding caliper design.

Drum Brakes
BASIC OPERATING PRINCIPLES

Drum brakes employ two brake shoes mounted on a stationary backing plate. These shoes are positioned inside a circular drum which rotates with the wheel assembly. The shoes are held in place by springs. This allows them to slide toward the drums (when they are applied) while keeping the linings and drums in alignment. The shoes are actuated by a wheel cylinder which is mounted at the top of the backing plate. When the brakes are applied, hydraulic pressure forces the wheel cylinder's actuating links outward. Since these links bear directly against the top of the brake shoes, the tops of the shoes are then forced against the inner side of the drum. This action forces the bottoms of the two shoes to contact the brake drum by rotating the entire assembly slightly (known as servo action). When pressure within the wheel cylinder is relaxed, return springs pull the shoes back away from the drum.

Most modern drum brakes are designed to self-adjust themselves during application when the vehicle is moving in reverse. This motion causes both shoes to rotate very slightly with the drum, rocking an adjusting lever, thereby causing rotation of the adjusting screw.

Power Boosters

Power brakes operate just as non-power brake systems except in the actuation of the master cylinder pistons. A vacuum diaphragm is located on the front of the master cylinder and assists the driver in applying the brakes, reducing both the effort and travel he must put into moving the brake pedal.

The vacuum diaphragm housing is connected to the intake manifold by a vacuum hose. A check valve is placed at the point where the hose enters the diaphragm housing, so that during periods of low manifold vacuum brake assist vacuum will not be lost.

Depressing the brake pedal closes off the vacuum source and allows atmospheric pressure to enter on one side of the diaphragm. This causes the master cylinder pistons to move and apply the brakes. When the brake pedal is released, vacuum is applied to both sides of the diaphragm, and return springs return the diaphragm and master cylinder pistons to the released position. If the vacuum fails, the brake pedal rod will butt against the end of the master cylinder actuating rod, and direct mechanical application will occur as the pedal is depressed.

The hydraulic and mechanical problems that apply to conventional brake systems also apply to power brakes, and should be checked for if the tests below do not reveal the problem.

Test for a system vacuum leak as described below:

1. Operate the engine at idle without touching the brake pedal for at least one minute.
2. Turn off the engine, and wait one minute.
3. Test for the presence of assist vacuum by depressing the brake pedal and releasing it several times. Light application will produce less and less pedal travel, if vacuum was present. If there is no vacuum, air is leaking into the system somewhere.

Test for system operation as follows:

1. Pump the brake pedal (with engine off) until the supply vacuum is entirely gone.
2. Put a light, steady pressure on the pedal.
3. Start the engine, and operate it at idle. If the system is operating, the brake pedal should fall toward the floor if constant pressure is maintained on the pedal.

Power brake systems may be tested for hydraulic leaks just as ordinary systems are tested.

BRAKE SYSTEM

Front disc brakes are standard equipment on all models.

The standard drum brakes are of the conventional, internal-expanding type which have been in use on American cars for decades. Unless they have been replaced, the brake shoe lining will be of the bonded type. Replacement linings may either be bonded or riveted. Front disc brakes are of the single piston floating caliper type.

Dual reservoir master cylinders are used on all models.

Drum Brakes
ADJUSTMENT

Adjustment procedures are given here for drum brakes only. No adjustment is possible on disc brakes since they are inherently self-adjusting. All Century/Regal drum brakes are of the self-adjusting type, also. All that is normally required to adjust the brakes is to stop the car moderately hard several times whiles backing up. If more adjustment is required, however, or if the brakes have been replaced, use the following procedure:

1. Raise the car and support it safely with stands.
2. Remove the rubber plug from the adjusting slot on the backing plate.
3. Insert a brake adjusting spoon into the slot and engage to lowest possible tooth on the starwheel. Move the end of the brake spoon downward to move the starwheel upward and expand the adjusting screw. Repeat this operation until the brakes lock the wheel.
4. Insert a small screwdriver or piece of firm wire (coat hanger wire) into the adjusting slot and push the automatic adjuster lever out and free of the starwheel on the adjusting screw.
5. Holding the adjusting lever out of the way, engage the topmost tooth possible on the

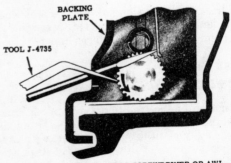

BACKING PLATE

TOOL J-4735

INSERT SMALL SCREWDRIVER OR AWL THROUGH BACKING PLATE SLOT AND HOLD ADJUSTER LEVER AWAY FROM SPROCKET BEFORE BACKING OFF BRAKE SHOE ADJUSTMENT

Drum brake adjustment

Troubleshooting the Brake System

Problem	Cause	Solution
Low brake pedal (excessive pedal travel required for braking action.)	• Excessive clearance between rear linings and drums caused by inoperative automatic adjusters	• Make 10 to 15 alternate forward and reverse brake stops to adjust brakes. If brake pedal does not come up, repair or replace adjuster parts as necessary.
	• Worn rear brakelining	• Inspect and replace lining if worn beyond minimum thickness specification
	• Bent, distorted brakeshoes, front or rear	• Replace brakeshoes in axle sets
	• Air in hydraulic system	• Remove air from system. Refer to Brake Bleeding.
Low brake pedal (pedal may go to floor with steady pressure applied.)	• Fluid leak in hydraulic system	• Fill master cylinder to fill line; have helper apply brakes and check calipers, wheel cylinders, differential valve tubes, hoses and fittings for leaks. Repair or replace as necessary.
	• Air in hydraulic system	• Remove air from system. Refer to Brake Bleeding.
	• Incorrect or non-recommended brake fluid (fluid evaporates at below normal temp).	• Flush hydraulic system with clean brake fluid. Refill with correct-type fluid.
	• Master cylinder piston seals worn, or master cylinder bore is scored, worn or corroded	• Repair or replace master cylinder
Low brake pedal (pedal goes to floor on first application—o.k. on subsequent applications.)	• Disc brake pads sticking on abutment surfaces of anchor plate. Caused by a build-up of dirt, rust, or corrosion on abutment surfaces	• Clean abutment surfaces
Fading brake pedal (pedal height decreases with steady pressure applied.)	• Fluid leak in hydraulic system	• Fill master cylinder reservoirs to fill mark, have helper apply brakes, check calipers, wheel cylinders, differential valve, tubes, hoses, and fittings for fluid leaks. Repair or replace parts as necessary.
	• Master cylinder piston seals worn, or master cylinder bore is scored, worn or corroded	• Repair or replace master cylinder
Decreasing brake pedal travel (pedal travel required for braking action decreases and may be accompanied by a hard pedal.)	• Caliper or wheel cylinder pistons sticking or seized	• Repair or replace the calipers, or wheel cylinders
	• Master cylinder compensator ports blocked (preventing fluid return to reservoirs) or pistons sticking or seized in master cylinder bore	• Repair or replace the master cylinder
	• Power brake unit binding internally	• Test unit according to the following procedure: (a) Shift transmission into neutral and start engine (b) Increase engine speed to 1500 rpm, close throttle and fully depress brake pedal (c) Slow release brake pedal and stop engine (d) Have helper remove vacuum check valve and hose from power unit. Observe for backward movement of brake pedal. (e) If the pedal moves backward, the power unit has an internal bind—replace power unit

Troubleshooting the Brake System (cont.)

Problem	Cause	Solution
Spongy brake pedal (pedal has abnormally soft, springy, spongy feel when depressed.)	• Air in hydraulic system • Brakeshoes bent or distorted • Brakelining not yet seated with drums and rotors • Rear drum brakes not properly adjusted	• Remove air from system. Refer to Brake Bleeding. • Replace brakeshoes • Burnish brakes • Adjust brakes
Hard brake pedal (excessive pedal pressure required to stop vehicle. May be accompanied by brake fade.)	• Loose or leaking power brake unit vacuum hose • Incorrect or poor quality brakelining • Bent, broken, distorted brakeshoes • Calipers binding or dragging on mounting pins. Rear brakeshoes dragging on support plate. • Caliper, wheel cylinder, or master cylinder pistons sticking or seized • Power brake unit vacuum check valve malfunction • Power brake unit has internal bind • Master cylinder compensator ports (at bottom of reservoirs) blocked by dirt, scale, rust, or have small burrs (blocked ports prevent fluid return to reservoirs). • Brake hoses, tubes, fittings clogged or restricted • Brake fluid contaminated with improper fluids (motor oil, transmission fluid, causing rubber components to swell and stick in bores • Low engine vacuum	• Tighten connections or replace leaking hose • Replace with lining in axle sets • Replace brakeshoes • Replace mounting pins and bushings. Clean rust or burrs from rear brake support plate ledges and lubricate ledges with molydisulfide grease. **NOTE:** If ledges are deeply grooved or scored, do not attempt to sand or grind them smooth—replace support plate. • Repair or replace parts as necessary • Test valve according to the following procedure: (a) Start engine, increase engine speed to 1500 rpm, close throttle and immediately stop engine (b) Wait at least 90 seconds then depress brake pedal (c) If brakes are not vacuum assisted for 2 or more applications, check valve is faulty • Test unit according to the following procedure: (a) With engine stopped, apply brakes several times to exhaust all vacuum in system (b) Shift transmission into neutral, depress brake pedal and start engine (c) If pedal height decreases with foot pressure and less pressure is required to hold pedal in applied position, power unit vacuum system is operating normally. Test power unit. If power unit exhibits a bind condition, replace the power unit. • Repair or replace master cylinder **CAUTION:** Do not attempt to clean blocked ports with wire, pencils, or similar implements. Use compressed air only. • Use compressed air to check or unclog parts. Replace any damaged parts. • Replace all rubber components, combination valve and hoses. Flush entire brake system with DOT 3 brake fluid or equivalent. • Adjust or repair engine

Troubleshooting the Brake System (cont.)

Problem	Cause	Solution
Grabbing brakes (severe reaction to brake pedal pressure.)	• Brakelining(s) contaminated by grease or brake fluid	• Determine and correct cause of contamination and replace brakeshoes in axle sets
	• Parking brake cables incorrectly adjusted or seized	• Adjust cables. Replace seized cables.
	• Incorrect brakelining or lining loose on brakeshoes	• Replace brakeshoes in axle sets
	• Caliper anchor plate bolts loose	• Tighten bolts
	• Rear brakeshoes binding on support plate ledges	• Clean and lubricate ledges. Replace support plate(s) if ledges are deeply grooved. Do not attempt to smooth ledges by grinding.
	• Incorrect or missing power brake reaction disc	• Install correct disc
	• Rear brake support plates loose	• Tighten mounting bolts
Dragging brakes (slow or incomplete release of brakes)	• Brake pedal binding at pivot	• Loosen and lubricate
	• Power brake unit has internal bind	• Inspect for internal bind. Replace unit if internal bind exists.
	• Parking brake cables incorrrectly adjusted or seized	• Adjust cables. Replace seized cables.
	• Rear brakeshoe return springs weak or broken	• Replace return springs. Replace brakeshoe if necessary in axle sets.
	• Automatic adjusters malfunctioning	• Repair or replace adjuster parts as required
	• Caliper, wheel cylinder or master cylinder pistons sticking or seized	• Repair or replace parts as necessary
	• Master cylinder compensating ports blocked (fluid does not return to reservoirs).	• Use compressed air to clear ports. Do not use wire, pencils, or similar objects to open blocked ports.
Vehicle moves to one side when brakes are applied	• Incorrect front tire pressure	• Inflate to recommended cold (reduced load) inflation pressure
	• Worn or damaged wheel bearings	• Replace worn or damaged bearings
	• Brakelining on one side contaminated	• Determine and correct cause of contamination and replace brakelining in axle sets
	• Brakeshoes on one side bent, distorted, or lining loose on shoe	• Replace brakeshoes in axle sets
	• Support plate bent or loose on one side	• Tighten or replace support plate
	• Brakelining not yet seated with drums or rotors	• Burnish brakelining
	• Caliper anchor plate loose on one side	• Tighten anchor plate bolts
	• Caliper piston sticking or seized	• Repair or replace caliper
	• Brakelinings water soaked	• Drive vehicle with brakes lightly applied to dry linings
	• Loose suspension component attaching or mounting bolts	• Tighten suspension bolts. Replace worn suspension components.
	• Brake combination valve failure	• Replace combination valve
Chatter or shudder when brakes are applied (pedal pulsation and roughness may also occur.)	• Brakeshoes distorted, bent, contaminated, or worn	• Replace brakeshoes in axle sets
	• Caliper anchor plate or support plate loose	• Tighten mounting bolts
	• Excessive thickness variation of rotor(s)	• Refinish or replace rotors in axle sets
Noisy brakes (squealing, clicking, scraping sound when brakes are applied.)	• Bent, broken, distorted brakeshoes	• Replace brakeshoes in axle sets
	• Excessive rust on outer edge of rotor braking surface	• Remove rust

Troubleshooting the Brake System (cont.)

Problem	Cause	Solution
Noisy brakes (squealing, clicking, scraping sound when brakes are applied.) (cont.)	• Brakelining worn out—shoes contacting drum of rotor	• Replace brakeshoes and lining in axle sets. Refinish or replace drums or rotors.
	• Broken or loose holdown or return springs	• Replace parts as necessary
	• Rough or dry drum brake support plate ledges	• Lubricate support plate ledges
	• Cracked, grooved, or scored rotor(s) or drum(s)	• Replace rotor(s) or drum(s). Replace brakeshoes and lining in axle sets if necessary.
	• Incorrect brakelining and/or shoes (front or rear).	• Install specified shoe and lining assemblies
Pulsating brake pedal	• Out of round drums or excessive lateral runout in disc brake rotor(s)	• Refinish or replace drums, re-index rotors or replace

starwheel with a brake adjusting spoon. Move the end of the adjusting spoon upward to move the adjusting screw starwheel downward and contract the adjusting screw. Back off the adjusting screw starwheel until the wheel spins freely with a minimum of drag. Keep track of the number of turns the starwheel is backed off.

6. Repeat this operation for the other side. When backing off the brakes on the other side, the adjusting lever must be backed off the same number of turns to prevent side-to-side brake pull.

7. Repeat this operation on the other set of brakes.

8. When all brakes are adjusted, make several stops, while backing the car, to equalize all of the wheels.

9. Road test the car.

Brake Pedal

TRAVEL

The pedal travel is the distance which the pedal moves toward the floor from the fully released position. Inspection should be made with the brake pedal firmly depressed and when the brake system is cold. The brake pedal travel should be 2¼" (1975-84), 2¾" (1985 and later) or 3⅓" (hydro-boost).

NOTE: *If equipped with power brakes, be sure to pump the brakes 3 times with the engine Off, before making the travel check.*

1. Under the dash, remove the pushrod-to-pedal clevis pin and separate the push rod from the brake pedal.

2. Loosen the push rod adjuster lock nut, then adjust the push rod.

3. After the correct travel is established, reverse the removal procedure.

Brake Light Switch

REMOVAL AND INSTALLATION

The brake light switch on cars with cruise control is of a different design. If your car has cruise control, make sure you use the required, special switch.

1. Disconnect the electrical connector at the front of the switch.

2. Have an assistant depress the brake pedal downward all the way. Pull the switch out of the tubular clip in the bracket located in front of the brake pedal.

3. Remove the old clip from the hole in the metal bracket.

4. Install a new clip into the bracket. Insert the new switch until the body of the switch seats on the clip.

5. Have your assistant release pressure on the pedal. Pull the pedal out until it rests against its internal stop (this will adjust the switch).

6. Plug the electrical connector in securely. Test the system.

Master Cylinder

REMOVAL AND INSTALLATION

On cars with power brakes, the master cylinder can be removed without removing the vacuum booster from the car.

1. Disconnect the hydraulic lines from the master cylinder. Cap the lines to prevent leakage or contamination of the brake fluid.

2. If the car is equipped with non-power brakes, disconnect the pushrod from the brake pedal by removing the clevis pin.

3. Remove the master cylinder attaching nuts and remove the master cylinder.

4. To install a non-power master cylinder, position the cylinder against the firewall with the pushrod inserted into the driver's compartment.

5. Torque the master cylinder attaching nuts to 28 ft.lb. Attach the pushrod to the brake pedal with the clevis pin.

6. On power brake systems, position the master cylinder over the pushrod and torque the nuts to 28 ft.lb.

7. Install the hydraulic lines.

8. Bleed the brake system as outlined in this chapter.

OVERHAUL

Century and Regal use either a Bendix or a Delco-Moraine master cylinder. The repair kits may differ slightly, but procedures are the same. Pay particular attention to the specifics of the instructions that come with the kit.

1. Remove the master cylinder from the car.

2. Remove the mounting gasket and boot, and the main cover, and purge the unit of its fluid.

3. Secure the cylinder in a vise and remove the pushrod retainer and secondary piston stop bolt found inside the forward reservoir.

4. Compress the retaining ring and extract it along with the primary piston assembly.

5. Blow compressed air into the piston stop screw hole to force the secondary piston, spring, and retainer from the bore of the cylinder.

6. Check the brass tube fitting inserts and if they are damaged, remove them. Leave undamaged inserts in place.

7. If replacement is necessary, thread a 6-3 × ⅝" self-tapping screw into the insert. Hook the end of the screw with a claw hammer and pry the insert free.

8. An alternative way to remove the inserts is to first drill the outlet holes to $^{13}\!/_{64}$" and thread them with a ¼"-20 tap. Position a thick washer over the hole to serve as a spacer, and then thread a ¼"-20 × ¾" hex head bolt into the insert and tighten the bolt until the insert is freed.

9. Use denatured alcohol and compressed air to clean the parts. Light rust may be removed with crocus cloth.

10. Replace the brass tube inserts by positioning them in their holes and threading a brake line tube nut into the outlet hole. Turn down the nut until the insert is seated.

11. Check the piston assemblies for correct identification and, when satisfied, position the replacement secondary seals in the twin grooves of the secondary piston.

12. The outside seal is correctly placed when its lips face the flat end of the piston.

13. Slip the primary seal and its protector over the end of the secondary piston opposite the secondary seals. The flat side of the seal should face the piston's compensating hole flange.

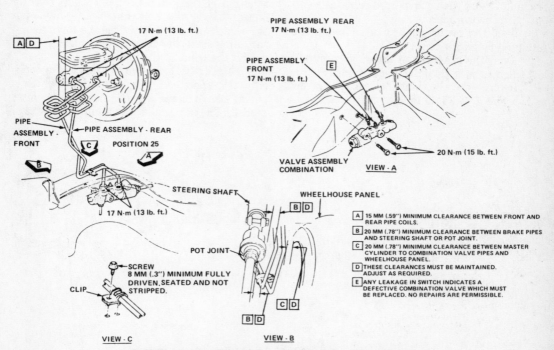

Typical master cylinder and combination valve mounting

RESERVE COVER
RESERVOIR DIAPHRAGM
RESERVOIR
RESERVOIR GROMMET
MASTER CYLINDER BODY
SPRING
SPRING RETAINER
PRIMARY PISTON ASSEMBLY
PRIMARY SEAL
SECONDARY PISTON
SECONDARY SEAL
LOCK RING

Typical disassembled view of master cylinder, 1978 and later shown, other years similar

14. Replace the primary piston assembly with assembled pieces in the overhaul kit.

15. Moisten the cylinder bore and the secondary piston's inner and outer seals with brake fluid. Assemble the secondary piston spring to its retainer and position them over the end of the primary seal.

16. Insert the combined spring and piston assembly into the cylinder and use a small wooden dowel or pencil to seat the spring against the end of the bore.

17. Moisten the primary piston seals with brake fluid and push it, pushrod receptacle end out, into the cylinder.

18. Keep the piston pushed in and snap the retaining ring into place.

19. Relax the pressure on the pistons and allow them to seek their static positions.

20. Replace the secondary piston stop screw and torque it to 25-40 in.lb.

21. Replace the reservoir diaphragm and cover.

NOTE: *Overhaul of the main cylinder portion of power master cylinders is the same as that for manual cylinders.*

Power Brake Booster

REMOVAL AND INSTALLATION

1. Disconnect the booster pushrod from the brake pedal arm by removing the retaining clip, and sliding the eyelet end of the pushrod off of the pin on the brake arm.

2. Disconnect the master cylinder from the booster.

3. Remove the attaching nuts and remove the booster from the firewall.

4. Install the booster on the firewall and torque the nuts to 22-33 ft.lb.

5. Connect the master cylinder to the booster.

6. Connect the booster pushrod to the brake pedal arm by installing the retaining clip, and sliding the eyelet end of the pushrod on the pin on the brake arm.

Hydro-Boost

Hydro-Boost differs from conventional power brake systems, in that it operates from power steering pump fluid pressure rather than intake manifold vacuum.

The Hydro-Boost unit contains a spool valve with an open center which controls the strength of the pump pressure when braking occurs. A lever assembly controls the valve's position. A boost piston provides the force necessary to operate the conventional master cylinder on the front of the booster.

A reserve of at least two assisted brake applications is supplied by an accumulator which is spring loaded on earlier and pneumatic on later models. The accumulator is an integral part of

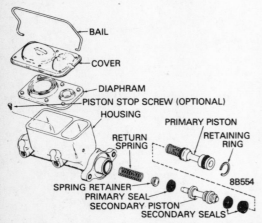

BAIL
COVER
DIAPHRAM
PISTON STOP SCREW (OPTIONAL)
HOUSING
RETURN SPRING
PRIMARY PISTON
RETAINING RING
SPRING RETAINER
PRIMARY SEAL
SECONDARY PISTON
SECONDARY SEALS
8B554

Disassembled view of master cylinder—Diesel V8

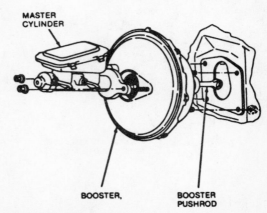

MASTER CYLINDER
BOOSTER,
BOOSTER PUSHROD

Removing power booster

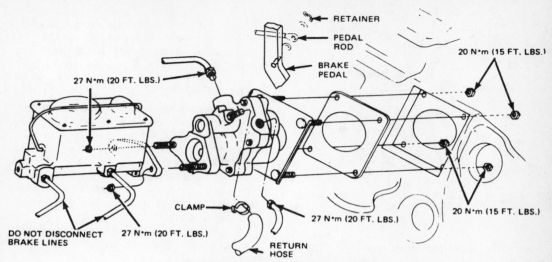

Removing and installing the Hydroboost

the Hydro-Boost II unit. The brakes can be applied manually if the reserve system is depleted.

All system checks, tests and troubleshooting procedure are the same for the two systems.

1. Turn the engine off and pump the brake pedal 4 or 5 times to deplete the accumulator.

2. Remove the nuts from the master cylinder, then move the master cylinder away from the booster, with brake lines still attached.

3. Remove the hydraulic lines from the booster.

4. Remove the retainer and washer at the brake pedal.

5. Remove the attaching nuts retaining the booster fastened to the cowl and the booster.

6. To install, place the booster into position, reconnect the hydraulic lines, reconnect the to the brake pedal and torque the booster-to-cowl nuts to 15 ft.lb. and the master cylinder-to-booster nuts to 20 ft.lb. Bleed the power steering and hydro-booster system.

Combination Valve

The combination valve used on Century/Regals is a three-function valve. It serves as a metering valve, balance valve, and brake warning switch. There are two different valves, one manufactured by Bendix and one manufactured by Kelsey-Hayes. Both valves serve the same function and differ only in minor details. In any case, all combination valves are non-adjustable and must be replaced if they are found to be defective.

REMOVAL AND INSTALLATION

1. Disconnect all the brake lines at the valve. Plug the lines to prevent contamination and loss of fluid.

2. Disconnect the warning switch wiring connector from the valve switch terminal.

3. Remove the attaching bolts and remove the valve.

4. Install the valve in the reverse order of removal.

5. Bleed the entire brake system after valve installation.

Brake Hoses

Brake hoses are rubber covered flex hoses designed to transmit brake pressure from the metal tubes running along the frame to the calipers in front and wheel cylinders in the rear. The calipers and wheel cylinders are unsprung (ride along with the wheels) and the metal brake lines coming from the master cylinder are suspended by the vehicle's springs, along with the frame and body. The flex hoses permit the hydraulic force of the brake fluid to be transmitted to the wheels even though they are moving up and down in relation to the frame. The flexing can cause the hoses to wear, especially if the surface of a hose should rub against the frame or a suspension component. Inspect the hoses frequently and replace them if the rubber cover has cracked or deteriorated otherwise or, of course, if there is any sign whatsoever of leakage.

REMOVAL AND INSTALLATION

Front

1. Remove the through bolt that fastens the hose to the caliper. Remove the washers, noting that there is one on either side of the fitting at the end caliper end of the hose, and disconnect the hose.

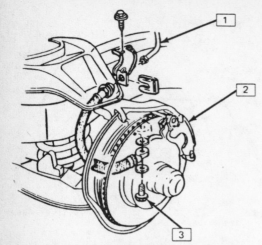

Front brake hose installation typical of 1986–87 models

2. If there is a clip retaining the connection at the frame, remove it. Then, unscrew the flare fitting located on the pipe running along the frame, using a backup wrench on the flats on the fitting at the end of the brake hose. Remove the brake line.

3. Install in reverse order, using new washers and torquing the connection at the caliper to 33 ft.lb. Bleed the system thoroughly.

Rear

1. Remove the clips at either end of the hose. Unscrew the flared fitting located on the pipe running along the frame, using a backup wrench on the flats on the fitting at the end of the brake hose. Do the same with the flared fitting on the wheel cylinder end.

2. Install in reverse order. Bleed the system thoroughly.

Brake Bleeding

The hydraulic system must be bled any time one of the brake lines is disconnected or air enters the system. There are two ways to bleed the system; pressure bleeding or manual bleeding. Both procedures will be given here, although pressure bleeding requires the use of some fairly expensive equipment (a pressure tank) and is seldom used by do-it-yourselfers. Both methods are equally effective.

The correct bleeding sequence is: left rear wheel cylinder, right rear, right front, and left front.

PRESSURE BLEEDING

1. Clean the top of the master cylinder, remove the cover, and attach the pressure bleeding adapter.

2. The spring loaded plunger on the front of the proportioning valve must be depressed while bleeding. Wire or tape can be wrapped around the valve to hold the plunger in.

3. Check the pressure bleeder reservoir for correct pressure and fluid level, then open the release valve.

4. Fasten a bleeder hose to the wheel cylinder or caliper bleeder nipple and submerge the free end of the hose in a transparent receptacle.

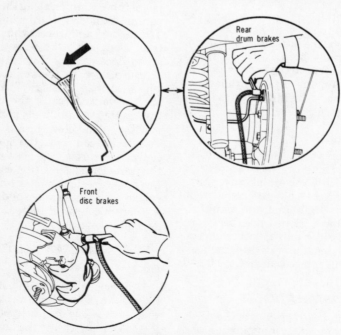

Bleeding the hydraulic brake system

The receptacle should contain enough brake fluid to cover the open end of the hose.

5. Open the wheel cylinder or caliper bleeder nipple and allow the fluid to flow until all bubbles disappear and an uncontaminated flow exists.

6. Close the nipple, remove the bleeder hose and repeat the procedure on the other wheel cylinders according to the sequence.

MANUAL BLEEDING

An alternative to the pressure method of bleeding requires two people to perform; one to depress the brake pedal and the other to open the bleeder nipples.

1. Clean the top of the master cylinder, and then remove the cover and fill the reservoir.

2. The spring loaded plunger of the front of the proportioning valve must be depressed while bleeding. Wire or tape can be wrapped around the valve to hold the plunger in.

3. Attach a bleeder hose and a clear container as in the pressure bleeding procedure.

4. Have the assistant depress the brake pedal to the floor, and then pause until the fluid flow stops and the bleeder nipple is closed.

5. Allow the pedal to return and repeat the procedure until a steady, bubble-free flow is seen.

6. Tighten the nipple and move on to the other wheels in sequence.

7. Frequently check the master cylinder level during this procedure. If the reservoir runs dry, air will enter the system and the bleeding will have to be repeated.

FRONT DISC BRAKES

CAUTION: *Brake shoes contain asbestos, which has been determined to be a cancer causing agent. Never clean the brake surfaces with compressed air! Avoid inhaling any dust from any brake surface! When cleaning*

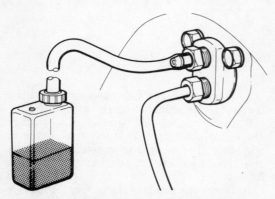

Bleeder hose attachment—rear drum brakes

Lining inspection—front disc brakes

any brake surface, use a commercially available brake cleaning fluid.

Front disc brakes on all Century/Regal models are of the single piston floating caliper type. This type of brake is constructed of a large single casting with the piston in the inboard section of the casting. The caliper assembly is mounted directly to the steering knuckle with two allen head bolts. The caliper is free to slide on the sleeves at the inboard ears and at the bolt at the outboard ears.

Disc Brake Pads

INSPECTION

The pads can be inspected for wear by removing the wheel and inspecting the pads through the opening in the top of the caliper. Later models have a wear sensor which squeals when the brakes are worn beyond their limits. Make sure linings are as thick as required by the manufacturer's specifications as shown in the Brake Specifications chart *or as thick as required by state inspection regulations, whichever is thicker!*

REMOVAL AND INSTALLATION

1. Siphon off ⅔ of the brake fluid from the master cylinder.

NOTE: *During this procedure, you will push the caliper piston back into its bore. This will cause a full master cylinder to overflow.*

2. Jack the car up and support it with jackstands. Remove the wheel(s). Once each wheel is removed, install two lug nuts to retain the disc.

3. Unscrew the two allen head caliper mounting bolts and then slide them out of the caliper just far enough to allow the caliper to be pulled off its mounts and away from the disc. Place the caliper where it won't be supported by the brake hose. Make a wire hook and suspend it from the spring.

4. The outboard pad has been clinched in place via two ears near the outer diameter of the caliper assembly (near the top of the pad). Force the pad downward or away from the outer diameter of the assembly to bend these ears straight and release the tabs which hold the pad against the caliper at the inner diameter (the bottom of the pad). Then, remove the outboard pad.

5. Install a C-clamp on the caliper so that the solid side of the clamp rests against the back of the caliper housing and the inner end of the screw rests against the lining of the inboard pad.

6. Tighten the clamp until the piston moves into its bore far enough to allow the inner brake pad to rest against the caliper. Make sure the caliper piston's outer surface is flush with the surface of the caliper housing. Remove the clamp. Remove the inner pad.

7. Remove the pad support spring clip from the piston.

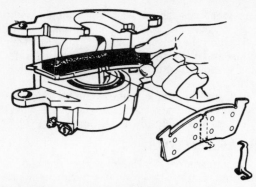

Installing the shoe support spring on the inboard spring

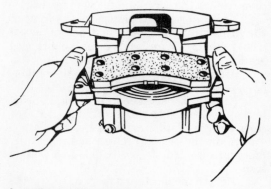

Installing the inboard shoe

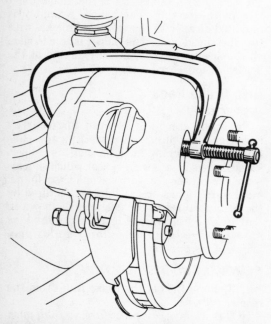

Bottom the piston in its bore with the use of a C-clamp

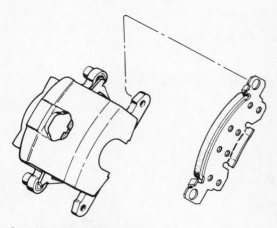

Installing the outboard shoe

8. Remove the two bolt ear sleeves and the four rubber bushings from the ears.

9. Brake pads should be replaced when they are worn to within $\frac{1}{32}''$ of the rivet heads or whenever they reach the minimum thickness specified by state inspection regulations, *whichever is thicker*.

10. Check the inside of the caliper for leakage and the condition of the piston dust boot.

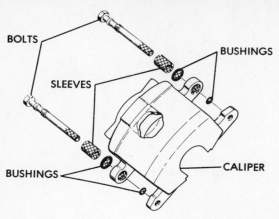

※※ LUBRICATE AREAS INDICATED

Lubricate the sleeves and bushings

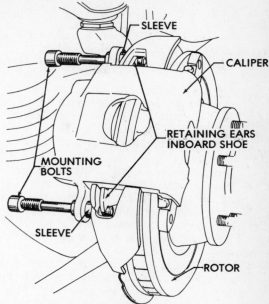

Installation of mounting bolts

11. Lubricate the two new sleeves and four bushings with a silicone spray.

12. Install the bushings in each caliper ear. Install the two sleeves in the two inboard ears.

NOTE: *On models with wear sensors, make sure the wear sensor is toward the rear of the caliper.*

13. Position the outboard shoe with the ears of the shoes over the caliper ears and the tab at the bottom engaged in the caliper cutout. Make sure it lays flat against the caliper.

14. Postion the inboard shoe retaining spring onto the the shoe. Then, snap the retaining spring into the piston inside diameter. The wear sensor, on those cars so-equipped, will now be at the leading edge of the shoe when the wheel is rotating in the normal, forward direction. Check that this is so.

15. With the two shoes in position, place the caliper over the brake disc and align the holes in the caliper with those of the mounting bracket.

CAUTION: *Make certain that the brake hose is not twisted or kinked.*

16. Install the mounting bracket bolts through the sleeves in the inboard caliper ears and through the mounting bracket, making sure that the ends of the bolts pass under the retaining ears on the inboard shoe.

17. Tighten the bolts into the bracket and torque to 35 ft.lb. Make sure there is adequate fluid in the master cylinder by filling it to within ¼" of the top with approved fluid. Pump the pedal several times until it gets hard to depress it. Have someone maintain moderate (50 lbs.) pressure on the pedal as you perform the next procedure. Clinch the upper ears of the outer shoes on both sides by positioning channel lock pliers with one jaw on top of the upper ear and one jaw in the notch on the bottom of the shoe opposite the upper ear.

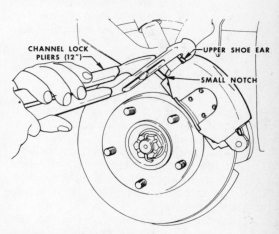

Cinching the outboard shoe

18. Install the front wheel and lower the car.

19. Again add fluid to the master cylinder reservoirs so that they are ¼" from the top.

20. Test the brake pedal by pumping it to make sure there is a 'hard" pedal. Check the fluid level again and add fluid as necessary.

WARNING: *Do not move the vehicle until a "hard" pedal is obtained. Bleed the brakes if necessary (that is, if the pedal is soft and spongy).*

Disc Brake Calipers
REMOVAL, INSTALLATION AND OVERHAUL

1. Perform Steps 2-4 of the procedure for pad replacement. Then, remove the inner pad. Fi-

nally, Remove the pad support spring clip from the piston.

2. Remove the caliper from the hanger. Disconnect the brake hose and plug the line.

3. Remove the U-shaped retainer from the fitting.

4. Pull the hose from the frame bracket and remove the caliper with the hose attached.

5. Clean the outside of the caliper with denatured alcohol.

6. Remove the brake hose and discard the copper gasket.

7. Remove the brake fluid from the caliper.

8. Place clean rags inside the caliper opening to catch the piston when it is released.

9. Apply compressed air to the caliper fluid inlet hole and force the piston out of its bore. Do not blow the piston out, but use just enough pressure to ease it out.

WARNING: *Do not place your fingers in front of the piston in an attempt to catch or protect it when applying compressed air. This could result in a serious injury.*

10. Use a screwdriver to pry the boot out of the caliper. Avoid scratching the bore.

11. Remove the piston seal from its groove in the caliper bore. Do not use a metal tool of any type for this operation.

12. Blow out all passages in the caliper and bleeder valve. Clean the piston and piston bore with fresh brake fluid.

13. Examine the piston for scoring, scratches or corrosion. If any of these conditions exist the piston must be replaced, as it is plated and cannot be refinished.

14. Examine the bore for the same defects. Light rough spots may be removed by rotating crocus cloth, using finger pressure, in the bore. Do not polish with an in and out motion or use any other abrasive.

15. Lubricate the piston bore and the new rubber parts with fresh brake fluid. Position the seal in the piston bore groove.

16. Lubricate the piston with brake fluid and assemble the boot into the piston groove so that the fold faces the open end of the piston.

17. Insert the piston to the bottom of the bore. (This will require a force of 50-100 lbs.) Seat the boot lip around the caliper counterbore. Proper seating of the bore is very important for sealing out contaminants.

18. Install the brake hose into the caliper using a new copper gasket.

19. Lubricate the new sleeves and rubber bushings. Install the bushings in the caliper ears. Install the sleeves so that the end toward the disc pad is flush with the machined surface.

NOTE: *Lubrication of the sleeves and bushings is essential to ensure proper operation of the sliding caliper design.*

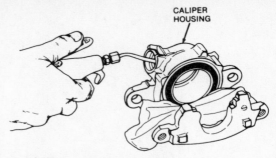

Removing the piston from its bore

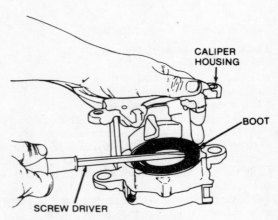

Removing the dust boot from the bore

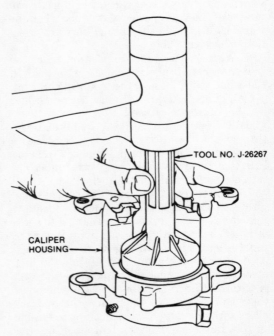

Seat the boot lip around the caliper counterbore

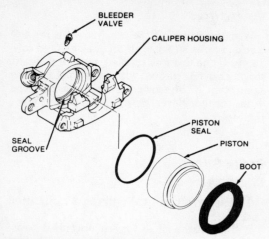

Disassembled view of caliper

20. Install the shoe support spring in the piston.

21. Install the disc pads in the caliper and remount the caliper on the hub. (See "Disc Brake Pad Removal and Installation").

22. Reconnect the brake hose to the steel brake line. Install the retainer clip. Bleed the brakes (see "Brake Bleeding").

23. Replace the wheels, check the brake fluid level, check the brake pedal travel, and road test the vehicle.

Brake Disc

REMOVAL AND INSTALLATION

1. Raise the car, support it with jackstands, and remove the wheel and tire assembly.

2. Remove the brake caliper as previously outlined.

3. Remove the dust cap and remove the cotter pin and the bearing retaining nut. Remove the outer wheel bearing and place it in a clean location.

4. Remove the wheel bearing, hub, and disc assembly from the spindle.

5. Installation is in the reverse order of removal. Adjust the wheel bearing as described below.

INSPECTION

1. Check the disc for any obvious defects such as excessive rust, chipping, or deep scoring. Light scoring is normal on disc brake rotors.

2. Make sure there is no wheel bearing play by performing Steps 1-3 of the wheel bearing adjustment procedure below. Then, check the disc for runout as follows:

3. Install a dial indicator on the caliper so that its feeler will contact the disc about one inch below its outer edge.

4. Turn the disc and observe the runout reading. If the reading exceeds 0.002", the disc should be replaced.

5. Check the caliper thickness with a vernier caliper or other appropriate tool. Minimum

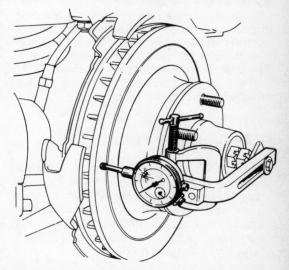

Checking the rotor for lateral runout using a dial indicator

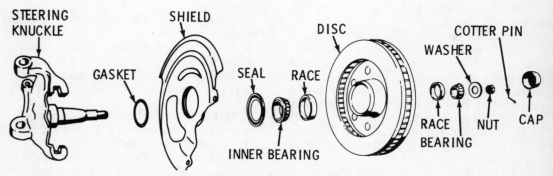

Exploded view of knuckle and hub assembly

thickness dimensions are cast into the disc. Restore the wheel bearings to normal adjustment as described below.

Wheel Bearings
ADJUSTMENT

1. Jack up the car and support it at the lower control arm.
2. Remove the hub dust cover, spindle cotter pin, and spindle nut.
3. While spinning the wheel, snug the nut down to the seat bearings. Do not exert over 12 ft.lb. of force on the nut.
4. Back the nut off ¼-½ a turn. Line up the cotter pin hole in the spindle with a hole in the nut.
5. Insert the cotter pin. Endplay should be 0.001-0.005″. If play exceeds this tolerance, the wheel bearings should be replaced.

REMOVAL, INSTALLATION AND PACKING

1. Jack up the car and support it. Remove the wheel and tire assembly.
2. On disc brake cars, remove the hub and disc as an assembly. Remove the caliper mounting bolts and wire the caliper out of the way.
3. Remove the outer bearing from the hub. The inner bearing assembly will remain in the hub and may be removed after prying out the inner seal. Discard the seal.

REAR DRUM BRAKES

CAUTION: *Brake shoes contain asbestos, which has been determined to be a cancer causing agent. Never clean the brake surfaces with compressed air! Avoid inhaling any dust from any brake surface! When cleaning any brake surface, use a commercially available brake cleaning fluid.*

Brake Drums
REMOVAL AND INSTALLATION

1. Raise the rear of the car in the air and support it with jack stands.
2. Remove the wheel and tire assemblies.
3. Make sure the parking brake is not on.
4. It may be necessary to back off the brake adjustment to remove the brake drum. The drum is held in place by the wheel and can be removed by simply sliding it off the wheel studs. If the drum is stubborn and you have backed the brake adjustment off, tap the drum with a hammer in several places. Don't beat on it. Just tap it.
5. Installation is in the reverse order of removal. Adjust the brakes after installation.

INSPECTION

With the drum off the car, inspect it for any cracks, scores, grooves, or an out-of-round condition. If the drum is cracked, replace it. Light scoring can be removed with emery cloth or fine sandpaper. If the scoring is extensive, have the drum turned. Never have a drum turned more than 0.060″.

Brake Shoes
INSPECTION

1. Remove the brake drum as outlined earlier.
2. Inspect the shoes for any obvious defects.
3. If there are no obvious defects, measure the remaining limits to see if the shoes are still usable. Generally speaking, a lining thickness of around $\frac{3}{32}$″ is acceptable for a bonded brake shoe. On a riveted brake shoe, a lining depth of $\frac{3}{32}$″ is also acceptable. Measure a riveted shoe at one of the rivets. Don't measure it at the edge. Measure a bonded shoe at the edge.
4. Check to make sure the shoes are wearing evenly all the way around. If they aren't, replace them.
5. Reinstall the brake drum and wheel and tire.

REMOVAL AND INSTALLATION

NOTE: *If you have not installed brake shoes before, it is a good idea to leave one set of brake shoes (the shoes on one side) intact as a reference.*

1. Remove the wheel and tire. Remove the brake drum.
2. Free the brake shoe return springs, and the actuating link and guide.
3. Remove the brake shoe holddown springs, the adjuster lever and return spring and the parking brake lever strut and spring.
4. Spread the shoes to clear the ends of the wheel cylinder, then remove the brake shoes as an assembly.
5. Disconnect the parking brake cable from the operating lever.
6. To install, first connect the parking brake cable to the lever.
7. Position the shoe assemblies on the backing plate. Install the holddown pins and springs.
8. Install the adjuster and the primary-to-secondary shoe spring and the actuating link.
9. Install the shoe return springs.
10. Once the brake shoes are installed, install the brake drum. Install the tire and wheel and adjust the brakes.

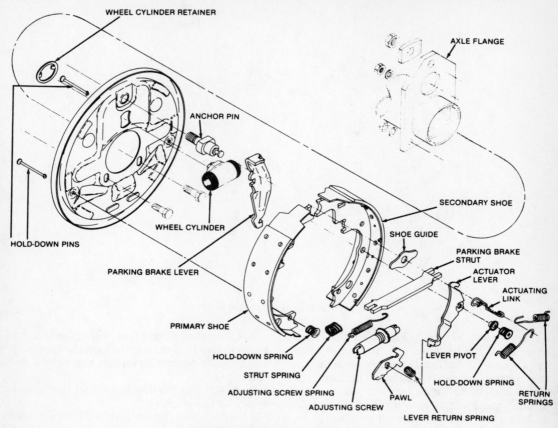

Drum brake assembly—1978 and later

Wheel Cylinders

REMOVAL AND INSTALLATION

1. Remove the brake shoes.
2. Loosen the brake line on the rear of the cylinder but do not pull the line away from the cylinder or it may bend.
3. Remove the bolts and lockwashers (1975-77) or retaining clip, (1978 and later) that attach the wheel cylinder to the backing plate and remove the cylinder.

4. Position the new wheel cylinder on the backing plate an install the cylinder attaching bolts and lockwashers.
5. Attach the metal brake line by reversing the procedure given in Step 2.
6. Install the brakes.

OVERHAUL

Since the travel of the pistons in the wheel cylinder changes when the new brake shoes are installed, it is possible for previously good

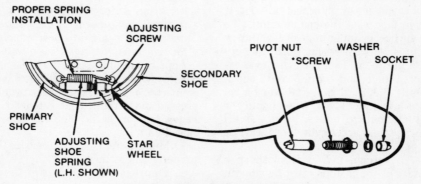

Adjusting screw—disassembled view

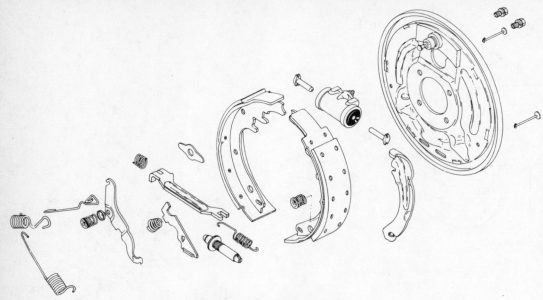

Drum brake assembly—1975–77

wheel cylinders to start leaking after new brake shoes are installed. Therefore, to save yourself the expense of having to replace new brakes that become saturated with brake fluid and the aggravation of having to take everything apart again, it is strongly recommended that wheel cylinders be rebuilt every time new brake shoes are installed. This is especially true on high mileage cars.

1. Remove the brakes.

2. Place a bucket or old newspapers under the brake backing plate to catch the brake fluid that will run out of the wheel cylinder.

3. Remove the boots from the ends of the wheel cylinders.

4. Push one piston toward the center of the cylinder to force the opposite piston and cup out the other end of the cylinder. Reach in the open end of the cylinder and push the spring, cup and piston out of the cylinder.

5. Remove the bleeder screw from the rear of the cylinder, on the back of the backing plate.

6. Inspect the inside of the wheel cylinder. If it is scored in any way, the cylinder must be honed with a wheel cylinder hone or fine emery paper, and finished with crocus cloth if emery paper is used. If the inside of the cylinder is excessively worn, the cylinder will have to be replaced, as only 0.003″ of material can be removed from the cylinder walls. When honing or cleaning the wheel cylinders, keep a small amount of brake fluid in the cylinder to serve as a lubricant.

7. Clean any foreign matter from the pistons. The sides of the pistons must be smooth for the wheel cylinders to operate properly.

8. Clean the cylinder bore with alcohol and a lint-free rag. Pull the rag through the bore several times to remove all foreign matter and dry the cylinder.

9. Install the bleeder screw and the return spring in the cylinder.

10. Coat new cylinder cups with new brake fluid and install them in the cylinder. Make sure that they are square in the bore or they will leak.

11. Install the pistons in the cylinder after coating them with new brake fluid.

12. Coat the insides of the boots with new brake fluid and install them on the cylinder. Install the brakes.

PARKING BRAKE

ADJUSTMENT

NOTE: *Be sure that the parking brake does not drag. An overtightened, dragging parking brake on a car with automatic brake adjusters will result in an extremely short life for rear brake linings.*

Adjustment of the parking brake is necessary whenever the rear brake cables have been disconnected or the parking brake pedal can be depressed more than eight ratchet clicks under heavy foot pressure. The car should first be raised on a lift.

1. Make sure that the service brakes are properly adjusted.

2. Depress the parking brake pedal two ratchet clicks.

Brake Specifications

All specifications in inches (in.) unless noted

Year	Model	Wheel Lug Nut Torque (ft. lbs.)	Brake Disc			Brake Drum			Master Cyl. Bore	Wheel Cyl. or Caliper Bore	
			Original Thickness	Minimum Thickness	Maximum Run-out	Original Inside Dia.	Maximum Wear Limit	Maximum Machine o/s		F	R
'75	All	70–80	1.040	.965	.004	9.50 ①	9.590 ③	9.560 ④	1⅛	2¹⁵⁄₁₆	⅞ ②
'76–'77	All	70–80	1.040	.965	.004	11	11.090	11.060	1⅛	2¹⁵⁄₁₆	¹⁵⁄₁₆
'78–'79	All	70–80	1.040	.965	.004	9.5	9.590	9.560	1⅛	2½	¹⁵⁄₁₆
'80–'85	All	70–80	1.040	.965	.004	9.5	9.590	9.560	1⅛	2½	¾
'86–'87	All	100	1.043	.980	.004	9.5	9.590	9.560	¹⁵⁄₁₆	—	¾

NOTE: Minimum lining thickness is 1/32 in. of lining thickness above rivet head (riveted linings) or 2/32 in. of lining remaining over backing plate (bonded linings). Minimum lining thickness may differ due to variations in local inspection codes. Inspection codes must always take precedence! Note also that drums cannot be machined unless they clean up by the time they reach the Maximum Machine Oversize. Maximum Wear Limit refers to the point at which the drum must be discarded due to wear alone. Do not machine a drum past the Maximum Machine Oversize!

F—Front
R—Rear
① Station Wagon—11"
② Station Wagon—¹⁵⁄₁₆
③ Station Wagon—11.090
④ Station Wagon—11.060

3. Loosen the jam nut on the equalizer adjusting nut. Tighten the adjusting nut until the rear wheel (left rear wheel, 1978-85) can be turned rearward by hand, but not forward.

4. Release the ratchet one click; the rear wheel should rotate rearward freely and forward with a slight drag.

5. Release the ratchet fully; the rear wheel should turn freely in either direction.

Front Cable

REMOVAL AND INSTALLATION

1975-85

1. Raise the car in the air and support it.

2. Remove the adjusting nut from the equalizer underneath the car.

3. On cars built in years through 1985, remove the retainer clip which attaches the cable to the frame.

4. Disconnect the cable from the pedal assembly.

5. Remove the front brake cable.

6. Installation is in the reverse order of removal.

1986-87

NOTE: *New parking brake cables on late model cars are coated with plastic to protect them from corrosion. Be careful in handling them to prevent contact of the coating with any sharp tools or sharp edges along the un-*
derbody. Even slight damage to the coating could cause the cable to rust through later.

1. Raise the car and support it securely on jackstands.

2. Clean and lubricate the threads on the adjusting rod on either side of the nut. Loosen the adjusting nut and then disconnect the front cable at the connector at the rear cables.

3. Where the cable is connected to the frame, compress the fingers of the retainer and release the cable from it.

4. Lower the car. Remove the lower rear bolt from the wheelhouse panel and then pull the panel out for access.

5. Depress the retainer fingers and disconnect the cable at the parking brake pedal assembly.

6. Position the cable housing into the pedal assembly and then connect the cable, making sure the retainer fingers are fully seated.

7. Perform the rest of the installation procedure in exact reverse order. Adjust the parking brake.

Left Rear or Right Rear Parking Brake Cable

REMOVAL AND INSTALLATION

1. Raise the car and support it securely. Clean and lubricate the threads on the adjusting rod on either side of the nut. Loosen the adjusting nut.

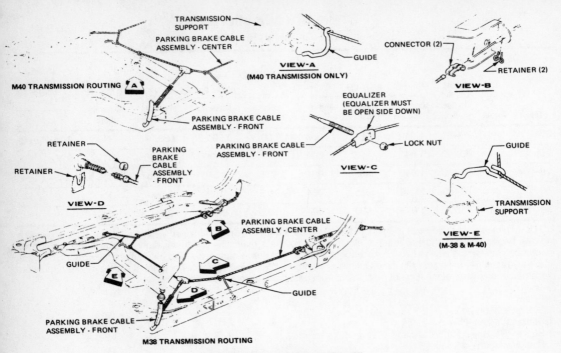

Parking brake cables—1975–77

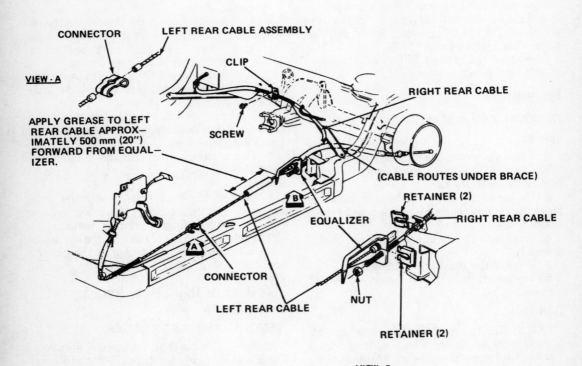

Parking brake cables—1978 and later

2. If removing the left side cable, compress the retaining fingers at the equalizer and loosen the cable; then, detach it at the connector and equalizer. If removing the right side cable, detach it from the retainers at the frame and from the clip on the axle housing.

3. Remove the tire wheel and brake drum associated with the cable you are replacing or, if you are removing both cables, remove them on both sides.

4. Remove the primary shoe return spring and parking brake strut associated with the cable you are replacing or, if you are removing both cables, remove them on both sides.

5. Depress the retaining tangs and then disconnect each cable you are removing at the backing plate. The left side cable may now be removed. Remove the right side cable by removing the adjusting nut and removing it with the equalizer.

6. Install a new cable in exact reverse order. Make sure all connectors that use retaining fingers become securely seated. Adjust the parking brake.

Body and Trim

10

EXTERIOR

Doors

REMOVAL AND INSTALLATION

CAUTION: *Removing a door is a simple operation, but it requires careful handling of a heavy object that is awkward to handle. You must have a helper who will hold the door and ensure that it does not get out of control, which could hurt someone or strip the threads of the mounting bolts. Put a floor jack or other adjustable means of holding the door underneath before starting, so that the helper must only keep the door from tipping as you remove the fasteners.*

The easiest and best way to remove the door is to remove the bolts that fasten the door assembly to the hinges, rather than attempting to remove the bolts fastening the hinges to the body. This is true because it is much easier to gain access to these bolts.

1. If the car has power operated components in the doors (electric windows or motor operated mirrors), remove the trim panel (see the appropriate procedure later in this chapter), and lift the watershield out far enough to reach the electrical connectors. Then, disconnect these connectors. Detach the rubber wire conduit and pull the harness coming from the body out of the door.

2. Very precisely use a sharp scribe to mark the relationship between the door and the door hinges so that you can remount it without the need to adjust it.

3. Open the door all the way and, with the help of another person and using a floor jack or other means, support the door.

4. Remove both the upper and lower bolts attaching the door to the outer portions of the hinges. Remove the door.

5. To install, first install the mounting bolts and turn them in until they are nearly ready to clamp the hinge to the door. Then, position the door carefully so that the matchmarks line up. Tighten the bolts alternately top and bottom until the door is tightly held in position. Torque the bolts to 15-21 ft.lb.

6. Reverse the remaining procedures to complete the installation.

ADJUSTMENT

Doors are made adjustable by using floating plates inside both the doors and hinge pillars. Always mark locations of bolts before loosening them and beginning adjustment. It is best to remove the door lock striker to permit the door to hang free and then close the door so you can observe exactly how it fits onto the body.

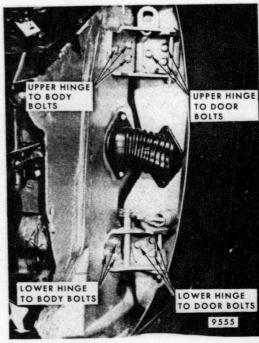

Front door attachment

CHILTON'S
AUTO BODY REPAIR TIPS

Tools and Materials • Step-by-Step Illustrated Procedures
How To Repair Dents, Scratches and Rust Holes
Spray Painting and Refinishing Tips

With a little practice, basic body repair procedures can be mastered by any do-it-yourself mechanic. The step-by-step repairs shown here can be applied to almost any type of auto body repair.

TOOLS & MATERIALS

You may already have basic tools, such as hammers and electric drills. Other tools unique to body repair — body hammers, grinding attachments, sanding blocks, dent puller, half-round plastic file and plastic spreaders — are relatively inexpensive and can be obtained wherever auto parts or auto body repair parts are sold. Portable air compressors and paint spray guns can be purchased or rented.

Auto Body Repair Kits

The best and most often used products are available to the do-it-yourselfer in kit form, from major manufacturers of auto body repair products. The same manufacturers also merchandise the individual products for use by pros.

Kits are available to make a wide variety of repairs, including holes, dents and scratches and fiberglass, and offer the advantage of buying the materials you'll need for the job. There is little waste or chance of materials going bad from not being used. Many kits may also contain basic body-working tools such as body files, sanding blocks and spreaders. Check the contents of the kit before buying your tools.

BODY REPAIR TIPS

Safety

Many of the products associated with auto body repair and refinishing contain toxic chemicals. Read all labels before opening containers and store them in a safe place and manner.
• Wear eye protection (safety goggles) when using power tools or when performing any operation that involves

the removal of any type of material.
• Wear lung protection (disposable mask or respirator) when grinding, sanding or painting.

Sanding

1 Sand off paint before using a dent puller. When using a non-adhesive sanding disc, cover the back of the disc with an overlapping layer or two of masking tape and trim the edges. The disc will last considerably longer.

2 Use the circular motion of the sanding disc to grind *into* the edge of the repair. Grinding or sanding away from the jagged edge will only tear the sandpaper.

3 Use the palm of your hand flat on the panel to detect high and low spots. Do not use your fingertips. Slide your hand slowly back and forth.

WORKING WITH BODY FILLER

Mixing The Filler

Cleanliness and proper mixing and application are extremely important. Use a clean piece of plastic or glass or a disposable artist's palette to mix body filler.

1 Allow plenty of time and follow directions. No useful purpose will be served by adding more hardener to make it cure (set-up) faster. Less hardener means more curing time, but the mixture dries harder; more hardener means less curing time but a softer mixture.

2 Both the hardener and the filler should be thoroughly kneaded or stirred before mixing. Hardener should be a solid paste and dispense like thin toothpaste. Body filler should be smooth, and free of lumps or thick spots.

Getting the proper amount of hardener in the filler is the trickiest part of preparing the filler. Use the same amount of hardener in cold or warm weather. For contour filler (thick coats), a bead of hardener twice the diameter of the filler is about right. There's about a 15% margin on either side, but, if in doubt use less hardener.

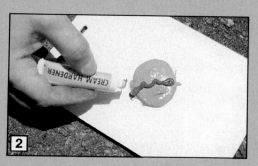

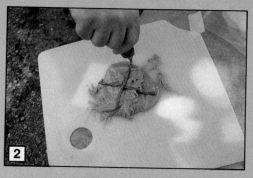

3 Mix the body filler and hardener by wiping across the mixing surface, picking the mixture up and wiping it again. Colder weather requires longer mixing times. Do not mix in a circular motion; this will trap air bubbles which will become holes in the cured filler.

Applying The Filler

1 For best results, filler should not be applied over ¼" thick.

Apply the filler in several coats. Build it up to above the level of the repair surface so that it can be sanded or grated down.

The first coat of filler must be pressed on with a firm wiping motion.

Apply the filler in one direction only. Working the filler back and forth will either pull it off the metal or trap air bubbles.

REPAIRING DENTS

Before you start, take a few minutes to study the damaged area. Try to visualize the shape of the panel before it was damaged. If the damage is on the left fender, look at the right fender and use it as a guide. If there is access to the panel from behind, you can reshape it with a body hammer. If not, you'll have to use a dent puller. Go slowly and work the metal a little at a time. Get the panel as straight as possible before applying filler.

1 This dent is typical of one that can be pulled out or hammered out from behind. Remove the headlight cover, headlight assembly and turn signal housing.

2 Drill a series of holes 1/2 the size of the end of the dent puller along the stress line. Make some trial pulls and assess the results. If necessary, drill more holes and try again. Do not hurry.

3 If possible, use a body hammer and block to shape the metal back to its original contours. Get the metal back as close to its original shape as possible. Don't depend on body filler to fill dents.

4 Using an 80-grit grinding disc on an electric drill, grind the paint from the surrounding area down to bare metal. Use a new grinding pad to prevent heat buildup that will warp metal.

5 The area should look like this when you're finished grinding. Knock the drill holes in and tape over small openings to keep plastic filler out.

6 Mix the body filler (see Body Repair Tips). Spread the body filler evenly over the entire area (see Body Repair Tips). Be sure to cover the area completely.

7 Let the body filler dry until the surface can just be scratched with your fingernail. Knock the high spots from the body filler with a body file ("Cheesegrater"). Check frequently with the palm of your hand for high and low spots.

8 Check to be sure that trim pieces that will be installed later will fit exactly. Sand the area with 40-grit paper.

9 If you wind up with low spots, you may have to apply another layer of filler.

10 Knock the high spots off with 40-grit paper. When you are satisfied with the contours of the repair, apply a thin coat of filler to cover pin holes and scratches.

11 Block sand the area with 40-grit paper to a smooth finish. Pay particular attention to body lines and ridges that must be well-defined.

12 Sand the area with 400 paper and then finish with a scuff pad. The finished repair is ready for priming and painting (see Painting Tips).

Materials and photos courtesy of Ritt Jones Auto Body, Prospect Park, PA.

REPAIRING RUST HOLES

There are many ways to repair rust holes. The fiberglass cloth kit shown here is one of the most cost efficient for the owner because it provides a strong repair that resists cracking and moisture and is relatively easy to use. It can be used on large and small holes (with or without backing) and can be applied over contoured areas. Remember, however, that short of replacing an entire panel, no repair is a guarantee that the rust will not return.

1 Remove any trim that will be in the way. Clean away all loose debris. Cut away all the rusted metal. But be sure to leave enough metal to retain the contour or body shape.

2 Grind away all traces of rust with a 24-grit grinding disc. Be sure to grind back 3-4 inches from the edge of the hole down to bare metal and be sure all traces of paint, primer and rust are removed.

3 Block sand the area with 80 or 100 grit sandpaper to get a clear, shiny surface and feathered paint edge. Tap the edges of the hole inward with a ball peen hammer.

4 If you are going to use release film, cut a piece about 2-3″ larger than the area you have sanded. Place the film over the repair and mark the sanded area on the film. Avoid any unnecessary wrinkling of the film.

5 Cut 2 pieces of fiberglass matte to match the shape of the repair. One piece should be about 1″ smaller than the sanded area and the second piece should be 1″ smaller than the first. Mix enough filler and hardener to saturate the fiberglass material (see Body Repair Tips).

6 Lay the release sheet on a flat surface and spread an even layer of filler, large enough to cover the repair. Lay the smaller piece of fiberglass cloth in the center of the sheet and spread another layer of filler over the fiberglass cloth. Repeat the operation for the larger piece of cloth.

7 Place the repair material over the repair area, with the release film facing outward. Use a spreader and work from the center outward to smooth the material, following the body contours. Be sure to remove all air bubbles.

8 Wait until the repair has dried tack-free and peel off the release sheet. The ideal working temperature is 60°-90° F. Cooler or warmer temperatures or high humidity may require additional curing time. Wait longer, if in doubt.

9 Sand and feather-edge the entire area. The initial sanding can be done with a sanding disc on an electric drill if care is used. Finish the sanding with a block sander. Low spots can be filled with body filler; this may require several applications.

10 When the filler can just be scratched with a fingernail, knock the high spots down with a body file and smooth the entire area with 80-grit. Feather the filled areas into the surrounding areas.

11 When the area is sanded smooth, mix some topcoat and hardener and apply it directly with a spreader. This will give a smooth finish and prevent the glass matte from showing through the paint.

12 Block sand the topcoat smooth with finishing sandpaper (200 grit), and 400 grit. The repair is ready for masking, priming and painting (see Painting Tips).

Materials and photos courtesy Marson Corporation, Chelsea, Massachusetts

PAINTING TIPS

Preparation

1 SANDING — Use a 400 or 600 grit wet or dry sandpaper. Wet-sand the area with a ¼ sheet of sandpaper soaked in clean water. Keep the paper wet while sanding. Sand the area until the repaired area tapers into the original finish.

2 CLEANING — Wash the area to be painted thoroughly with water and a clean rag. Rinse it thoroughly and wipe the surface dry until you're sure it's completely free of dirt, dust, fingerprints, wax, detergent or other foreign matter.

3 MASKING — Protect any areas you don't want to overspray by covering them with masking tape and newspaper. Be careful not get fingerprints on the area to be painted.

4 PRIMING — All exposed metal should be primed before painting. Primer protects the metal and provides an excellent surface for paint adhesion. When the primer is dry, wet-sand the area again with 600 grit wet-sandpaper. Clean the area again after sanding.

Painting Techniques

Paint applied from either a spray gun or a spray can (for small areas) will provide good results. Experiment on an old piece of metal to get the right combination before you begin painting.

SPRAYING VISCOSITY (SPRAY GUN ONLY) — Paint should be thinned to spraying viscosity according to the directions on the can. Use only the recommended thinner or reducer and the same amount of reduction regardless of temperature.

AIR PRESSURE (SPRAY GUN ONLY) — This is extremely important. Be sure you are using the proper recommended pressure.

TEMPERATURE — The surface to be painted should be approximately the same temperature as the surrounding air. Applying warm paint to a cold surface, or vice versa, will completely upset the paint characteristics.

THICKNESS — Spray with smooth strokes. In general, the thicker the coat of paint, the longer the drying time. Apply several thin coats about 30 seconds apart. The paint should remain wet long enough to flow out and no longer; heavier coats will only produce sags or wrinkles. Spray a light (fog) coat, followed by heavier color coats.

DISTANCE — The ideal spraying distance is 8″-12″ from the gun or can to the surface. Shorter distances will produce ripples, while greater distances will result in orange peel, dry film and poor color match and loss of material due to overspray.

OVERLAPPING — The gun or can should be kept at right angles to the surface at all times. Work to a wet edge at an even speed, using a 50% overlap and direct the center of the spray at the lower or nearest edge of the previous stroke.

RUBBING OUT (BLENDING) FRESH PAINT — Let the paint dry thoroughly. Runs or imperfections can be sanded out, primed and repainted.

Don't be in too big a hurry to remove the masking. This only produces paint ridges. When the finish has dried for at least a week, apply a small amount of fine grade rubbing compound with a clean, wet cloth. Use lots of water and blend the new paint with the surrounding area.

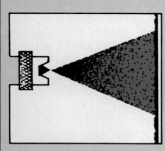

WRONG

Thin coat. Stroke too fast, not enough overlap, gun too far away.

CORRECT

Medium coat. Proper distance, good stroke, proper overlap.

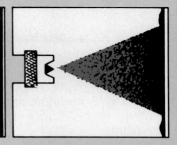

WRONG

Heavy coat. Stroke too slow, too much overlap, gun too close.

How to Remove Stains from Fabric Interior

For rest results, spots and stains should be removed as soon as possible. Never use gasoline, lacquer thinner, acetone, nail polish remover or bleach. Use a 3' x 3" piece of cheesecloth. Squeeze most of the liquid from the fabric and wipe the stained fabric from the outside of the stain toward the center with a lifting motion. Turn the cheesecloth as soon as one side becomes soiled. When using water to remove a stain, be sure to wash the entire section after the spot has been removed to avoid water stains. Encrusted spots can be broken up with a dull knife and vacuumed before removing the stain.

Type of Stain	How to Remove It
Surface spots	Brush the spots out with a small hand brush or use a commercial preparation such as K2R to lift the stain.
Mildew	Clean around the mildew with warm suds. Rinse in cold water and soak the mildew area in a solution of 1 part table salt and 2 parts water. Wash with upholstery cleaner.
Water stains	Water stains in fabric materials can be removed with a solution made from 1 cup of table salt dissolved in 1 quart of water. Vigorously scrub the solution into the stain and rinse with clear water. Water stains in nylon or other synthetic fabrics should be removed with a commercial type spot remover.
Chewing gum, tar, crayons, shoe polish (greasy stains)	Do not use a cleaner that will soften gum or tar. Harden the deposit with an ice cube and scrape away as much as possible with a dull knife. Moisten the remainder with cleaning fluid and scrub clean.
Ice cream, candy	Most candy has a sugar base and can be removed with a cloth wrung out in warm water. Oily candy, after cleaning with warm water, should be cleaned with upholstery cleaner. Rinse with warm water and clean the remainder with cleaning fluid.
Wine, alcohol, egg, milk, soft drink (non-greasy stains)	Do not use soap. Scrub the stain with a cloth wrung out in warm water. Remove the remainder with cleaning fluid.
Grease, oil, lipstick, butter and related stains	Use a spot remover to avoid leaving a ring. Work from the outisde of the stain to the center and dry with a clean cloth when the spot is gone.
Headliners (cloth)	Mix a solution of warm water and foam upholstery cleaner to give thick suds. Use only foam—liquid may streak or spot. Clean the entire headliner in one operation using a circular motion with a natural sponge.
Headliner (vinyl)	Use a vinyl cleaner with a sponge and wipe clean with a dry cloth.
Seats and door panels	Mix 1 pint upholstery cleaner in 1 gallon of water. Do not soak the fabric around the buttons.
Leather or vinyl fabric	Use a multi-purpose cleaner full strength and a stiff brush. Let stand 2 minutes and scrub thoroughly. Wipe with a clean, soft rag.
Nylon or synthetic fabrics	For normal stains, use the same procedures you would for washing cloth upholstery. If the fabric is extremely dirty, use a multi-purpose cleaner full strength with a stiff scrub brush. Scrub thoroughly in all directions and wipe with a cotton towel or soft rag.

FRONT DOORS

1. If the door requires for and aft or up or down adjustment, loosen the body hinge pillar adjustments. Shift the position of the door with the help of an assistant and a floor jack. Then, tighten the bolts. When the position fore and aft and up and down is correct, torque the bolts to 15-21 ft.lb. If you have to move the door to the rear, replace the door jamb light switch.

2. If the door must be adjusted in or out, loosen the bolts attaching the door at the hinge pillar attachments. Shift the position of the door with the help of an assistant and a floor jack. Then, tighten the bolts. When the position in or out is correct, torque the bolts to 15-21 ft.lb.

REAR DOORS

1. If the door requires in or out or significant up or down adjustment, loosen the body side, center pillar hinge adjusting bolts. Shift the position of the door with the help of an assistant and a floor jack. Then, tighten the bolts. When the position in or out and up and down is correct, torque the bolts to 15-21 ft. lbs.

2. If the door requires fore or aft or a slight

up or down adjustment, loosen the body side, center pillar hinge adjusting bolts. Shift the position of the door with the help of an assistant and a floor jack. Then, tighten the bolts. When the position is correct, torque the bolts to 15-21 ft. lbs. If you have to move the door to the rear, replace the door jamb light switch.

Door Locks

REMOVAL AND INSTALLATION

1. Make sure the window is up all the way. Then, remove both the upper and lower portions of the trim pad.

2. Going in through the largest access hole, disengage the rod connecting the remote control to the lock as follows:

   a. Use a flat bladed screwdriver to slide the spring clip out of engagement. The clip must be slid on the lock lever until the ends of the clip no longer engage with the grooved section of the end of the lock rod. You don't need to remove the clip from the lock lever. There is a slot in the rear side of the clip so it can shift on the lock lever even though the lockrod passes right through it.

   b. Pull the lockrod out of the lock lever.

3. If the car has electric locks, remove the solenoid.

4. Remove the three screws mounting the lock onto the door lock pillar section of the door and remove the lock. On some models, it may be necessary to remove the inside remote handle and then remove the lock and its connecting rod together. On four door models, it will be necessary to remove the lock, then separate the lockrod from the lock on a workbench, and install the rod onto the new lock.

5. Install in exact reverse order. Torque the lock mounting screws to 7-12 ft.lb.

Hood

REMOVAL AND INSTALLATION

1. Raise the hood. Cover the fenders with some sort of protective pads. This is necessary to protect the paint because the hood will often

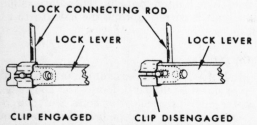

To disengage the spring clips attaching the lockrod to the door lock levers, slide them along the road as shown until the ends of the clip are no longer engaged with the grooved end of the rod

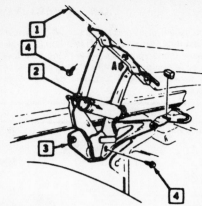

1. Hood assembly
2. Balance spring
3. Hood hinge
4. Hood mounting bolts. Torque to 20 ft. lbs.

Removing the hood. Remove the bolts shown. At installation, torque to the figure shown.

contact these areas during removal or installation procedures.

2. On models equipped with an underhood light disconnect the lamp wiring.

3. Very precisely use a sharp scribe to mark the relationship between the hood and the hood hinges so that you can remount it without the need to adjust it.

4. Support the hood, especially at the front, in a secure manner. Remove the bolts on either side that fasten the tops of the hinges to the underside of the hood. Remove the bolts starting at the front and moving toward the rear to help avoid placing stress on the assembly. Make sure the hood is securely supported to help prevent bending of it as you work.

5. When all the bolts are removed, lift the rear of the hood off the hinges and then lift the unit off the car.

6. To install the hood, carry it from either side and position it over the engine compartment in its normal position. Raise the front and position it at the right angle to the upper surfaces of the hinges. Pass all the bolts through the upper hinges and start them into the lower side of the hood. Do not tighten them, but leave plenty of clearance to adjust the position of the hood on the hinges.

7. Carefully shift the hood on both hinges simultaneously to align the matchmarks. Then, tighten the mounting bolts, torquing to 20 ft.lb. Close the hood and check its fit in the body and the alignment of the hood latch. If necessary, readjust the hood alignment as described below. Reconnect the underhood light wiring, if the car is so equipped.

ALIGNMENT

1. Close the hood and check its fit in the body and the alignment of the hood latch. If necessary, loosen *all* the mounting bolts just slightly and shift the adjustment in the correct direction.

2. Repeat this procedure until the hood latches smoothly and securely and all gaps between the hood and body are of equal width. Torque the mounting bolts to 20 ft.lb.

Trunk Lid

REMOVAL AND INSTALLATION

1. Raise the trunk lid. Cover the fenders with some sort of protective pads. This is necessary to protect the paint because the trunk lid will often contact these areas during removal or installation procedures.

2. On models equipped with an underhood light disconnect the lamp wiring.

3. Very precisely use a sharp scribe to mark the relationship between the trunk lid and the hinges so that you can remount it without the need to adjust it.

4. Support the trunk lid, especially at the rear, in a secure manner. Remove the bolts on either side that fasten the sides of the hinges to the underside of the trunk lid. Remove the bolts starting at the rear and moving toward the front to help avoid placing stress on the assembly. Make sure the trunk lid is securely supported to help prevent bending of it as you work.

5. When all the bolts are removed, lift the rear of the trunk lid off the hinges and then lift the unit off the car.

6. To install the trunk lid, carry it from either side and position it over the luggage compartment in its normal position. Raise the rear and position it at the right angle to the upper surfaces of the hinges. Pass all the bolts through the trunk lid and start them into the side of the upper hinges. Do not tighten them, but leave plenty of clearance to adjust the position of the trunk lid on the hinges.

7. Carefully shift the trunk lid on both hinges simultaneously to align the matchmarks. Then, tighten the mounting bolts, torquing to 20 ft.lb. Close the trunk lid and check its fit in the body and the alignment of the trunk lid latch. If necessary, readjust the alignment. Reconnect the underhood light wiring, if the car is so equipped.

Adjustment

All adjustments (fore and aft and up and down) are made by loosening the hinge strap-to-lid attaching bolts. Loosen *all* the bolts before adjusting the position of the lid to avoid springing it and to make adjustment easier.

Slide the hood back and forth, locating both sides as required; then tighten the bolts. No side-to-side adjustment is provided.

If the hood has adjustable rear bumpers and it does not sit level, loosen the locknuts and turn the bumper screws up or down as necessary. Retighten the locknuts. You may find it helpful to close the trunk lid and measure the gap between the hood and body with a finely calibrated ruler.

Station Wagon Tailgate

REMOVAL AND INSTALLATION

NOTE: *To perform this procedure, you will need a length of rod $3/16''$ in diameter and 12'' long. You will also need new, service hinge pins and retaining rings.*

1. First, rotate the tailgate up and down until the torque rod tension has been eliminated. This occurs at a point near the vertical position of the gate, when spring tension is not required to keep the gate under control. You should be able to feel the point at which there is no longer significant weight to be supported as you raise the gate, and stop there.

WARNING: *Proceed carefully with the next step in case there is still some tension in the torque rod.*

2. Mark the position of the torque rod assist link on the rear body pillar, and then remove it.

3. Open the tailgate and support it in the horizontal position. When the gate is securely supported, disconnect the support cables at the sides of the gate.

4. Place the length of rod against the point of one of the hinge pins. Strike the rod hard with a hammer to force the pin out of the hinge. You have to shear the retaining ring tabs to do this. Repeat this on the hinge on the other side. Then, remove the tailgate.

5. Install the new retaining rings in the grooves in the new hinge pins, positioning the rings so the tabs point toward the heads of the pins. To install, first align the gate to the body and so the hinge halves fit together properly. Then, tap the new hinge pins into position in the same direction in which the original pins were installed. Reverse the remaining procedures, installing the torque rod assist link in the same position, according to the markings made earlier.

ALIGNMENT

Adjust the tailgate horizontally by loosening all the hinge-to-body bolts, repositioning the gate, and then retightening the bolts. Make sure to retain all the shims in position, unless the gate is too close to or too far from the body.

If it is necessary to move the tailgate bottom

in or out, loosen the hinge bolts and add or subtract shims between the hinge and body.

Windshield

REMOVAL AND INSTALLATION

NOTE: *To install a new windshield, you will have to use an adhesive service kit. The GM part No. is 9636067 or you can shop for an equivalent. You will also need: an alcohol base solvent; an adhesive dispensing gun GM part No. J-24811 or equivalent; a commercial type of razor knife; a hot knife; black weatherstrip adhesive; two side support spacers; if the windshield has an embedded antenna, a butyl strip; lower support spacers; masking tape. The area in which you work must be at room temperature to ensure timely curing of adhesive.*

1. Place protective coverings around the areas of the body around the glass.
2. Remove the trim moldings around the windshield. These are retained by wire clips. You can carefully pry these moldings out until the clip ends are visible. The ends can be pried away from retaining grooves in the body to free them and permit removal of the moldings.
3. Remove the windshield wiper arms as described in Chapter 6. If it looks like lower glass stops will interfere with removal of the windshield, remove them too.
4. If the car has an embedded antenna, disconnect the wiring connector at the bottom center of the windshield.
5. With the razor knife, cut the adhesive material built up along the edge of the windshield all around. Run the knife right along the edge of the windshield to do this, cutting as close as possible.
6. Install the foam sealing strip to the new windshield, as follows:
   a. Remove the backing paper from the sticky side of the strip.
   b. Apply the strip to the windshield, using the original windshield as a guide. Check to make sure that the new strip will not obscure the view of the serial number mounted to the top of the dash.
   c. Trim the strip as necessary with a sharp knife to remove excess.
7. Inspect all the retaining clips which fasten the moldings to the body. Clips must not be bent away from the body more than $\frac{1}{16}''$. If possible, bend the clips back into the proper configuration; otherwise, replace them.
8. Locate the lower support spacers for the glass as shown in the illustration. Then, carefully position the new glass on these spacers, resting on the original adhesive. See Step 15 for pointers on getting the glass safely into the right position. Check the relationship between

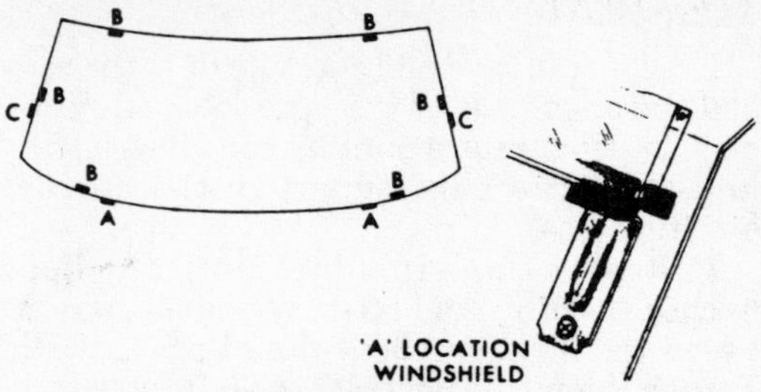

Locate the support spacers for the new windshield as shown.

the glass and adhesive mounting material on the pinchweld flange. Mark these areas so that later, when you apply additional adhesive, you can fill in any gaps and ensure proper mounting and sealing of the glass. Gaps must not exceed $\frac{1}{8}''$.

9. Now, apply masking tape to both sides of the windshield with the inside edge on the glass and the outside edge on the adjacent body pillar. Then, slit the tape with the knife. (This will provide a guide for proper positioning of the windshield later).
10. If the car has an imbedded antenna, mark the location of either end of the butyl strip, mark the location of either end of the strip with the masking tape. On cars with this type antenna only, after the glass is removed in the next step, replace the butyl strip originally used to fill the gap between the windshield and body in this area. It should be approximately 8″ long.
11. Now, remove the glass from the opening. Apply masking tape to the inside of the glass $\frac{1}{4}''$ inboard from the edge of the glass, across the top and down both sides. This will make clean up easier. Make sure not to apply the tape farther in than this to keep it from being visible after installation.
12. Clean the glass around the edge of the inside surface by wiping it with a clean cloth dampened with the alcohol. Make sure the glass dries without application of heat before installation.
13. Apply the *clear* primer as follows, depending on the type of antenna used:
    a. Normal antenna: Apply the primer around the entire periphery of the glass edge *and* $\frac{1}{4}''$ inboard on the inner surface. Allow the primer to dry five minutes.
    b. Embedded antenna: Apply the clear primer just as for the plain windshield; around the entire periphery of the glass edge *and* $\frac{1}{4}''$ inboard on the inner surface. But, avoid getting any of the primer at all into the area marked by the tape in Step 10. Allow the primer to dry five minutes.
14. Apply a smooth bead of adhesive material over the entire *inside edge only* of the glass where the primer was applied in the step above.

Make sure the bead is continuous and smooth.

15. Make sure the front windows/windwings are open. Now, with a helper, carry the glass over to the car. Put one hand on the inside of the glass and one on the outside. Tilt the glass until it is horizontal. One person at a time can hold one hand to support the inside of the glass while reaching around the body pillar to grab the glass with the other. Once the glass is held with both hands (one inside the pillar and the other outside), tilt the glass into position, position the glass on the lower supports and, using the tape markers made above, line the glass up in the right position and then drop it straight into place. Press the glass down firmly to squeeze the adhesive material slightly. Avoid too much squeeze-out, as this will cause an ugly appearance. Paddle on additional adhesive, if necessary, to ensure a full and effective seal, utilizing marks made in Step 8 and inspecting for any other areas of poor seal, as well. If the car has an embedded antenna, one place additional material must be applied is at the edges of the butyl sealing strip.

16. Watertest the windshield with a *gentle* spray from a garden hose. *A hard spray will disturb adhesive.* Use warm water, if you can (it finds leaks more readily). Paddle extra adhesive in to seal any areas that leak and then retest them.

17. Once all leaks have been stopped, cement a rubber spacer between both the right and left sides of the windshield and the body metal to retain the windshield tightly in its present position as the adhesive cures.

18. Install the moldings. Remove clean-up masking tape from the inner surface of the glass and install/connect any remaining parts. Make sure the vehicle sits for six hours at room temperature before moving it so that the adhesive is properly cured.

Rear Window Glass

Since the glass is bonded and sealed in the same manner with the same adhesives, proceed exactly as described above, with one exception. On many rear window installations, you cannot reach around inside the car with one hand in order to support and handle the glass. In these cases, you will have to use special suction cup devices to handle the glass. Be careful to ensure adequate seal of the cups for safe handling.

INTERIOR

Door Panels

REMOVAL AND INSTALLATION

NOTE: *You can use a special tool GM Part No. BT-7323 or equivalent to disengage the* clips fastening the inner panel to the door on front, rear, and lower edges. You'll also need a rubber mallet.

1. Remove the inside handles by removing the two attaching screws. These are usually Phillips head screws and accessible from underneath via recesses.

2. Unscrew and remove the inside door locking knob. If the car is equipped with a strap type door pull handle, pull the escutcheons out of the centers of the strap mounts on either end to reveal the mounting screws. Since these screws pass through the door panel and into the metal shell of the door behind, remove them.

3. If the car has a remote control mirror, remove the remote mirror escutcheon and then disengage the end of the mirror control cable from the escutcheon.

4. If the car has a switch cover plate in the armrest, remove the screws securing the cover plate and disconnect the switch connectors and, if the car has one, the cigar lighter connectors from the wiring harness.

5. If the car has remote control cover plates, remove the attaching screws and remove the cover plates. Then, remove the screws (which were under the cover plate) which secure the cover plate to the inner panel.

6. If the car has integral armrests, remove the screws inserted through the pull cup and into the armrest hanger support.

7. If the car has electric switches located in the door trim panel, disconnect the wiring harness at the switch. If the car has courtesy or reading lamps in the panel, disconnect the wiring harness at the lamp.

8. Use a special tool or flat bladed screwdriver to carefully pry the panel out from the door, going around the periphery to release all the clips from the inner door.

9. To remove the panel, first push it slightly downward and then pull it outward to release it from the inner door at the beltline. Then, lift the panel upward to release it at the top of the door, where it hangs over.

10. To install, first check that all trim retainers are securely installed and are undamaged. If any require replacement:

a. Start the retainer with a ¼" cutout into the attachment hole in the trim panel.

b. Rotate the retainer until the flange that has the ¼" cutout is inside the attachment hole.

11. Connect all electrical connectors.

12. Pull the inside door handle inward and position the inner panel near the door, passing the handle through the handle hole in the panel. Then, lift the panel slightly and install the retainers over the top of the inner door.

13. Position the inner panel so all retainers line up with the holes in the inner door. Start

one into the retainer hole to ensure alignment and hold. Then, use a rubber mallet to tap all the retainers into the corresponding holes in the inner door.

14. Install all the remaining items in reverse order.

Door Glass and Window Regulator

The glass and related regulator parts (the glass guide) are removed as an assembly and the glass is then separated from the regulator and rebonded on a bench. The regulator itself works through a metal tape, and is removed separately from the window and guide parts.

REGULATOR REMOVAL AND INSTALLATION

1975-83 Models

NOTE: *To perform this operation, you will need a ¼" drill and a rivet tool such as GM J-29022 or equivalent and aluminum ¼" x ½" peel type rivets. You will also need a soft adhesive to reseal the water deflector, a center punch and cloth-backed tape.*

1. Remove the door inner panel as described above.
2. Remove the interior pad and peel the water deflector off the soft sealer.
3. With the glass up all the way, tape the glass to the upper door frame.
4. Remove the lower sash channel bolts.
5. Use the punch to drive out the centers of the regulator mounting rivets. Then, drill the remaining portions of the rivets out with the ¼" drill.
6. If the car has electric windows, disconnect it from the wiring harness at the connector.
7. Pull the window regulator out through the access hole in the inner panel.
8. Position the new regulator in the door in reverse of the removal procedure. Install the rivets with the rivet tool.
9. The remainder of installation is the reverse of the removal procedure.

1984-87 Coupe Style Cars

NOTE: *Mark the locations of all attachments prior to loosening them. To perform this operation, you will need a ¼" drill, U nuts (part Nos. 3916700 or 3982098 or equivalent and ¼-20 x ½" attaching screws Part Nos. 9419723 or equivalent. You will also need a soft adhesive to reseal the water deflector, a center punch, two rubber wedge doorstops, and cloth-backed tape. All attachments must be torqued to 90-125 in.lb.*

1. Remove the door armrest cover, the upper and lower trim panels, insulator pad (if the car has one), and the water deflector.

2. Crank the window up or down until it is in the middle of its travel, Then, wedge the two doorstops between the window and the inner door panel at the beltline, one at the front and one at the rear, to hold it in this position vertically.
3. Mark the location of each of the inner panel cam attaching screws (two screws located right at the center of the door) and then remove them.
4. Mark the locations of the vertical guide attaching screws, remove them, and then remove the vertical guide through the access hole. These are two small screws located right under the locking button and a large bolt located directly below the forward upper screw near the bottom of the door.
5. If the regulator is electrically powered, disconnect the disconnect the wiring harness connector at the regulator motor.
6. Drive out the regulator attaching rivet center pins with the center punch and then drill out the rivets with the ¼" drill. On cars with manual windows, these are four rivets below the regulator handle; on cars with electric windows, there are five rivets located above and forward of the large opening in the lower/forward part of the door.
7. Remove the rear nut attaching the lower sash channel cam to the glass on cars with electric windows.
8. Slide the regulator or regulator and motor rearward it disengage its rollers from the lower sash channel cam. Then, remove the regulator through the largest access hole in the inner door panel.
9. Install the U-nuts over the each regulator attaching hole so that the integral nut is located on the outboard side of the regulator backplate.
10. Installation is in exact reverse order. Use the ¼-20 x ½" screws to attach the regulator to the inner panel, torquing them to 90-125 in.lb.

1984-87 Sedan Style Cars

NOTE: *To perform this procedure, you will need duct tape, a center punch, a ¼" drill bit, U-nuts Part No. 3916700 or 3982098 or equivalent and four (manual) or five (electric) screws dimensioned ¼-20 x ½" screws. You will also need a soft adhesive to reseal the water deflector, a center punch, and cloth-backed tape. All attachments must be torqued to 90-125 in.lb. The location of every attachment should be marked before removal.*

1. Remove the armrest, covers, and upper and lower trim panels from the door.
2. Remove the insulator pad and inner panel water deflector.
3. Prop the window up all the way and tape it to the upper frame to hold it there.

4. Mark their locations and then remove the five inner panel cam attaching screws (located at the front and rear of the hole in the rear of the door); remove the inner panel cam.

5. Remove the inside remote rod connecting the handle to the lock. If the car has electric windows, disconnect the wiring harness connector at the window regulator motor.

6. Use the center punch to drive out the regulator attaching rivet center pins and then drill them out with the ¼" drill.

7. Turn and maneuver the regulator so its rollers disengage from the lower sash channel cam. Then, slide the regulator or regulator and motor assembly to the rear and then turn it as necessary and pull it out through the rear access hole.

8. Install the U-nuts over the each regulator attaching hole so that the integral nut ends up on the outboard side of the regulator backplate.

9. Install the regulator in exact reverse order, using the ¼-20 x ½" screws to attach the regulator to the inner panel, and torquing them to 90-125 in.lb.

WINDOW REMOVAL AND INSTALLATION

1975-83 Models

CAUTION: *If the glass is being removed because of breakage or a crack, wear gloves as you handle it to protect yourself from cuts.*

1. Remove the door inner panel as described above.

2. Remove the interior pad and peel the water deflector off the soft sealer.

3. With the glass up all the way, tape the glass to the upper door frame.

4. Remove the bolts that hold the lower sash channel to the regulator sash.

5. Reattach the regulator handle without fastening it and use it to run the regulator all the way down. Remove the regulator sash by rotating it 90° and pulling it out.

6. Support the glass in a secure manner and then remove the tape. When the glass is free, lower it carefully all the way.

7. Now, disengage the front edge of the glass from the front glass run channel. Slide the glass forward, tilt it slightly, and remove the guide

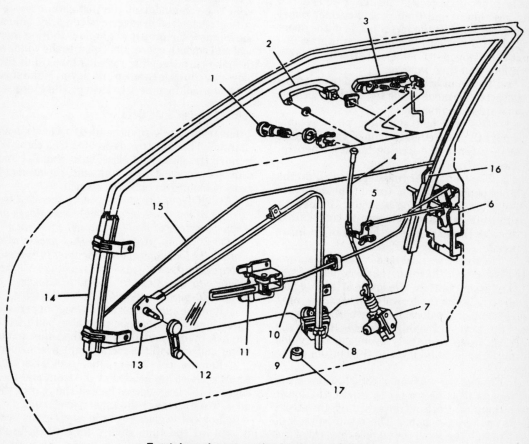

Front door glass operating hardware—typical

from the retainer in the run channel located in the rear leg of the door frame.

8. Now, tilt the glass forward and remove it from the door.

9. On a workbench, unbolt the lower sash channel from the glass and bolt it onto the new glass.

10. Install in reverse order. Use the following method to install the guide retainer:

a. Install the glass and raise it about half way.

b. Supporting the glass with one hand on the lower edge, rotate it rearward to snap the guide into the retainer.

1984-87 Coupe Style Cars

CAUTION: *If the glass is being removed because of breakage or a crack, wear gloves as you handle it to protect yourself from cuts.*

NOTE: *When performing this procedure, mark the locations of all attachments to avoid confusion during reassembly. Torque all fasteners to 90-120 in.lb. You will also need a soft adhesive to reseal the water deflector.*

1. Remove the armrest and cover, upper and lower inner door panels, insulator pad (if the car has them), and then peel the inner panel water deflector off the metal frame of the door.

2. Roll or electrically maneuver the glass until it is halfway down. Mark all attaching screw locations and then remove:

a. The front belt stabilizer and trim retaining screw, located at the top of the door just forward of the middle.

b. The rear belt stabilizer pin assembly screws (2), located at the top of the door just to the rear of the locking button. Then remove the pin itself.

c. The front up-travel stop, located on the inner panel at the top/front of the door.

d. The rear up-stop assembly, located on the glass at the bottom and accessible through the large hole in the rear of the inner panel.

3. The upper vertical guide attaching screws are located near the top of the door, just in front of the locking button; the lower attaching bolt is directly below the forward upper screw near the bottom of the door. Remove both the upper and the lower attaching screws/bolt from the vertical guide and then disengage the guide from the rollers and lay it in the bottom of the door.

4. Change the position of the glass, lowering or raising it as necessary to expose the lower sash channel attaching nuts through the access holes in the inner panel. These will be accessible through the small round hole forward of the large opening in the top/center of the door, and

through the triangular hole just below and forward of the locking button. Remove the nuts.

5. *Holding the glass securely,* separate the glass from the lower sash channel cam. Then, *carefully* remove the glass as follows:

a. Raise the glass slowly and then slide it to the rear.

b. Tilt the top of the glass inboard (toward the center of the car) until the front up stop roller clears the front loading hole at the inner panel beltline reinforcement.

c. Now, tilt the glass 45° to the rear and then raise it slowly so the glass attaching screws clear the beltline loading holes.

To install:

a. First start the rear vertical edge of the glass into the door with the glass at a 45 degree angle so the glass attaching screws clear the loading holes.

b. Tilt the top of the glass inboard slide the assembly rearward, , and then lower the glass through the front loading hole at the beltline reinforcement so as to clear the up stop roller.

c. Lower the glass and align the screw attachments with the holes on the lower sash channel cam.

6. The remainder of the installation procedure is performed in reverse of removal. Adjust the window for proper alignment and weather seal and smooth operation. Operate the window to make sure the glass remains inboard of the blow-out clip as it runs up and down. Make sure to tighten all fasteners to the specified torque.

1984-87 Sedan Style Cars

The front door glass is bonded to a lower sash channel. This, in turn, is welded to a cam. To remove the glass, the glass, sash channel and cam are removed as a unit and replacement glass is bonded in on a workbench.

CAUTION: *If the glass is being removed because of breakage or a crack, wear gloves as you handle it to protect yourself from cuts.*

NOTE: *When performing this procedure, mark the locations of all attachments to avoid confusion during reassembly. Torque all fasteners to 90-120 in.lb. You will also need a soft adhesive to reseal the water deflector.*

1. Remove the armrest and cover, upper and lower inner door panels, insulator pad (if the car has them), and then peel the inner panel water deflector off the metal frame of the door.

2. Remove the inner panel cam attaching screws. These are located at the front and rear edges of the large access hole at the rear of the door. Then, remove the inner panel cam.

3. Lower the glass ¾ of the way, tip the nose downward and then slide it forward to disengage the rear roller. Then, raise the nose to

bring the bottom of the glass to a 45 degree angle and disengage the forward roller by sliding the glass to the rear.

4. Remove the glass by lifting it outboard of the upper door frame. Move the window regulator up and down as required for clearance as you work the glass out.

5. Installation is the reverse of removal. Make sure to tighten the fasteners to the specified torque.

Electric Window Motor
REMOVAL AND INSTALLATION
1975-83 Models

NOTE: *To perform this operation, you will need a drill and $^3/_{16}$" drill bit, and $^3/_{16}$" rivets.*

1. Remove the door inner panel as described above.

2. Remove the interior pad and peel the water deflector off the soft sealer.

3. With the glass up all the way, tape the glass to the upper door frame.

4. Remove the regulator and glass as described above.

5. Disconnect the electrical connector. Drill out the rivets that attach the motor to the door and then remove it.

6. Install the motor, and then mount it with the new rivets. Reconnect the electrical connector.

7. Install the window and regulator as described above.

1984-87 Models

CAUTION: *This procedure cannot be performed safely unless the glass is both intact and attached securely to the regulator. This is because the normal weight of the assembly is required to counteract the force of a counterbalance spring during the time the motor is out of position. If the spring is not restrained by this weight, the mechanism may move violently upward in such a way as to cause personal injury. It is also absolutely necessary to perform Step 2 carefully and effectively for the same reasons.*

NOTE: *To perform this procedure, you'll need a ¾" hole saw, cloth-backed tape, waterproof tape, and Part No. 1052349 Lubriplate Spray Lube A® or the equivalent (to lube the motor drive gear and sector teeth). The lubricant you use must be approved for use in temperatures down to at least -20°F.*

1. Remove the door trim panel, insulator pad and inner water deflector. Raise the window all the way.

2. Tape the window securely to the top door frame to keep the glass from dropping when the motor is removed.

3. There are three dimples in the inner door panel. These are to make access holes for the motor attaching bolts. Center the hole saw over each dimple and drill a hole in each.

4. Remove the motor attaching bolts, disconnect the wiring connector, and then remove the motor through the access hole.

5. Lubricate the motor drive gear and regulator sector teeth with the specified lubricant.

6. Install the regulator motor onto the regulator, carefully meshing the motor pinion gear teeth with the sector gear teeth before installing the three motor attaching bolts. Holding the motor in position so the teeth are properly meshed, install the three mounting bolts and then torque them to 90-125 in.lb.

7. Use the waterproof tape to seal any holes outside the water deflector sealing area and then install the trim.

Power Seat Motor
REMOVAL AND INSTALLATION
Two-Way Power Seats

1. If the seat will move, shift it to a position near the middle of its travel.

2. Remove the nuts that attach the seat adjuster to the floor and then tilt the seat forward for access.

3. On the full width seat, disconnect both power cables at the motor.

4. Disconnect the wiring harness at the motor.

5. Remove the screws that secure the motor support to the seat frame. Remove the motor with the support attached. Then, remove the screws that attach the motor to the support bracket and remove the motor from the bracket.

6. Installation is the reverse of removal. Make sure you test the motor for proper operation to the extremes of travel in both directions.

Six-Way Power Seat Permanent Magnet Motor

1. Unbolt the seat from the floor of the car. Place it upside down in a location where the upholstery is protected from dirt.

2. Disconnect the wires going to the motor at the motor control relay.

3. Remove the two mounting screws that attach the motor mounting support to the seat. Remove the three screws attaching the transmission to the motor.

4. Now, move the motor outboard or away from the transmission far enough to disengage it from the rubber coupling that connects it to the transmission, and remove it.

5. Installation is the reverse of removal.

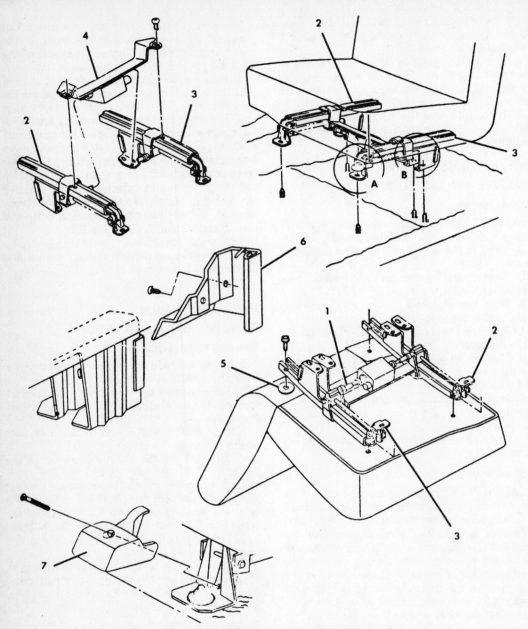

A typical two-way power seat motor installation

Headliner

Cars with deluxe trim use a formed type of headliner that, as a replacement part, comes in two pieces. The headliner cover must be glued to the foundation. This is an extremely difficult operation requiring the use of a number of special tools. It would best be left to a competent automotive upholstery shop. Only the procedure for the standard headliner, which is relatively straightforward, are included here.

REMOVAL AND INSTALLATION

NOTE: *On wagons, you will need a special tool J-2772 or equivalent to remove the headliner.*

1. Remove the following items from the roof of the car:
    a. Courtesy lamps.
    b. Sunshade supports.
    c. Coat hooks.
    d. Upper quarter trim finishing panels.

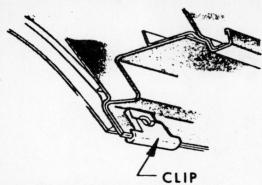

One type of headliner attaching clip

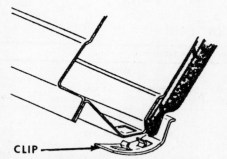

A second type of headliner attaching clip

e. Side roof rail moldings.

f. Windshield and back window garnish moldings.

g. Shoulder strap retainers.

h. Windshield side garnish molding.

i. Roof mounted assist straps.

j. Sun roof trim finishing lace (if the car has a sunroof).

k. Twin lift-off panel roof garnish moldings (if so-equipped).

2. Disengage tabs or clips on each side of the headlining from the attaching slots. On wagons, use the tool J-2772 at one end of the molding and pry the molding loose from the retainer.

3. Then, on sedans move the entire assembly far enough rearward to provide clearance for its front to be pulled out through the front door opening, and remove it. On wagons, remove the headlining through the body rear opening.

If the replacement lining does not have an insulator cemented to the upper surface, carefully remove the insulator from the original headlining. Then, spot cement the insulator to the replacement headlining to hold it in position during installation.

CAUTION: *Load the assembly into the car very carefully as excessive flexing can cause permanent deformation.*

4. On all sedans, install the rear portion of the headlining through the right front door opening, holding it diagonally. On wagons, put it in through the tailgate opening.

5. Engage the headlining at the tabs to retain it temporarily to the roof. Install the side roof rail attaching clips.

6. Align the headlining so that the cutouts for the sunshades and dome lamp line up. Install these two types of accessories, but do not fully tighten the mounting screws.

7. On wagons, align the finishing molding at the centerline of the roof and engage it with its retainer. Install the complete molding on both the right and left sides.

8. Install all other hardware removed in Step 1. You can shift the headliner in that area slightly to fit each item into place.

9. Fully tighten the sunshade and dome lamp mounting screws.

Mechanic's Data

General Conversion Table

Multiply By	To Convert	To	
	LENGTH		
2.54	Inches	Centimeters	.3937
25.4	Inches	Millimeters	.03937
30.48	Feet	Centimeters	.0328
.304	Feet	Meters	3.28
.914	Yards	Meters	1.094
1.609	Miles	Kilometers	.621
	VOLUME		
.473	Pints	Liters	2.11
.946	Quarts	Liters	1.06
3.785	Gallons	Liters	.264
.016	Cubic inches	Liters	61.02
16.39	Cubic inches	Cubic cms.	.061
28.3	Cubic feet	Liters	.0353
	MASS (Weight)		
28.35	Ounces	Grams	.035
.4536	Pounds	Kilograms	2.20
—	To obtain	From	Multiply by

Multiply By	To Convert	To	
	AREA		
.645	Square inches	Square cms.	.155
.836	Square yds.	Square meters	1.196
	FORCE		
4.448	Pounds	Newtons	.225
.138	Ft./lbs.	Kilogram/meters	7.23
1.36	Ft./lbs.	Newton-meters	.737
.112	In./lbs.	Newton-meters	8.844
	PRESSURE		
.068	Psi	Atmospheres	14.7
6.89	Psi	Kilopascals	.145
	OTHER		
1.104	Horsepower (DIN)	Horsepower (SAE)	.9861
.746	Horsepower (SAE)	Kilowatts (KW)	1.34
1.60	Mph	Km/h	.625
.425	Mpg	Km/1	2.35
—	To obtain	From	Multiply by

Tap Drill Sizes

National Coarse or U.S.S.

Screw & Tap Size	Threads Per Inch	Use Drill Number
No. 5	40	.39
No. 6	32	.36
No. 8	32	.29
No. 10	24	.25
No. 12	24	.17
1/4	20	8
5/16	18	F
3/8	16	5/16
7/16	14	U
1/2	13	27/64
9/16	12	31/64
5/8	11	17/32
3/4	10	21/32
7/8	9	49/64

National Coarse or U.S.S.

Screw & Tap Size	Threads Per Inch	Use Drill Number
1	8	7/8
1 1/8	7	63/64
1 1/4	7	1 7/64
1 1/2	6	1 11/32

National Fine or S.A.E.

Screw & Tap Size	Threads Per Inch	Use Drill Number
No. 5	44	.37
No. 6	40	.33
No. 8	36	.29
No. 10	32	.21

National Fine or S.A.E.

Screw & Tap Size	Threads Per Inch	Use Drill Number
No. 12	28	15
1/4	28	3
6/16	24	1
3/8	24	Q
7/16	20	W
1/2	20	29/64
9/16	18	33/64
5/8	18	37/64
3/4	16	11/16
7/8	14	13/16
1 1/8	12	1 3/64
1 1/4	12	1 11/64
1 1/2	12	1 27/64

Drill Sizes In Decimal Equivalents

Inch	Decimal	Wire	mm
1/64	.0156		.39
	.0157		.4
	.0160	78	
	.0165		.42
	.0173		.44
	.0177		.45
	.0180	77	
	.0181		.46
	.0189		.48
	.0197		.5
	.0200	76	
	.0210	75	
	.0217		.55
	.0225	74	
	.0236		.6
	.0240	73	
	.0250	72	
	.0256		.65
	.0260	71	
	.0276		.7
	.0280	70	
	.0292	69	
	.0295		.75
	.0310	68	
1/32	.0312		.79
	.0315		.8
	.0320	67	
	.0330	66	
	.0335		.85
	.0350	65	
	.0354		.9
	.0360	64	
	.0370	63	
	.0374		.95
	.0380	62	
	.0390	61	
	.0394		1.0
	.0400	60	
	.0410	59	
	.0413		1.05
	.0420	58	
	.0430	57	
	.0433		1.1
	.0453		1.15
	.0465	56	
3/64	.0469		1.19
	.0472		1.2
	.0492		1.25
	.0512		1.3
	.0520	55	
	.0531		1.35
	.0550	54	
	.0551		1.4
	.0571		1.45
	.0591		1.5
	.0595	53	
	.0610		1.55
1/16	.0625		1.59
	.0630		1.6
	.0635	52	
	.0650		1.65
	.0669		1.7
	.0670	51	
	.0689		1.75
	.0700	50	
	.0709		1.8
	.0728		1.85

Inch	Decimal	Wire	mm
	.0730	49	
	.0748		1.9
	.0760	48	
5/64	.0768		1.95
	.0781		1.98
	.0785	47	
	.0787		2.0
	.0807		2.05
	.0810	46	
	.0820	45	
	.0827		2.1
	.0846		2.15
	.0860	44	
	.0866		2.2
	.0886		2.25
	.0890	43	
	.0906		2.3
	.0925		2.35
	.0935	42	
3/32	.0938		2.38
	.0945		2.4
	.0960	41	
	.0965		2.45
	.0980	40	
	.0981		2.5
	.0995	39	
	.1015	38	
	.1024		2.6
	.1040	37	
	.1063		2.7
	.1065	36	
	.1083		2.75
7/64	.1094		2.77
	.1100	35	
	.1102		2.8
	.1110	34	
	.1130	33	
	.1142		2.9
	.1160	32	
	.1181		3.0
	.1200	31	
	.1220		3.1
1/8	.1250		3.17
	.1260		3.2
	.1280		3.25
	.1285	30	
	.1299		3.3
	.1339		3.4
	.1360	29	
	.1378		3.5
	.1405	28	
9/64	.1406		3.57
	.1417		3.6
	.1440	27	
	.1457		3.7
	.1470	26	
	.1476		3.75
	.1495	25	
	.1496		3.8
	.1520	24	
	.1535		3.9
	.1540	23	
5/32	.1562		3.96
	.1570	22	
	.1575		4.0
	.1590	21	
	.1610	20	

Inch	Decimal	Wire & Letter	mm
	.1614		4.1
	.1654		4.2
	.1660	19	
	.1673		4.25
	.1693		4.3
	.1695	18	
11/64	.1719		4.36
	.1730	17	
	.1732		4.4
	.1770	16	
	.1772		4.5
	.1800	15	
	.1811		4.6
	.1820	14	
	.1850	13	
	.1850		4.7
	.1870		4.75
3/16	.1875		4.76
	.1890		4.8
	.1890	12	
	.1910	11	
	.1929		4.9
	.1935	10	
	.1960	9	
	.1969		5.0
	.1990	8	
	.2008		5.1
	.2010	7	
13/64	.2031		5.16
	.2040	6	
	.2047		5.2
	.2055	5	
	.2067		5.25
	.2087		5.3
	.2090	4	
	.2126		5.4
	.2130	3	
	.2165		5.5
7/32	.2188		5.55
	.2205		5.6
	.2210	2	
	.2244		5.7
	.2264		5.75
	.2280	1	
	.2283		5.8
	.2323		5.9
	.2340	A	
15/64	.2344		5.95
	.2362		6.0
	.2380	B	
	.2402		6.1
	.2420	C	
	.2441		6.2
	.2460	D	
	.2461		6.25
	.2480		6.3
1/4	.2500	E	6.35
	.2520		6.
	.2559		6.5
	.2570	F	
	.2598		6.6
	.2610	G	
	.2638		6.7
17/64	.2656		6.74
	.2657		6.75
	.2660	H	
	.2677		6.8

Inch	Decimal	Letter	mm
	.2717		6.9
	.2720	I	
	.2756		7.0
	.2770	J	
	.2795		7.1
	.2810	K	
9/32	.2812		7.14
	.2835		7.2
	.2854		7.25
	.2874		7.3
	.2900	L	
	.2913		7.4
	.2950	M	
19/64	.2953		7.5
	.2969		7.54
	.2992		7.6
	.3020	N	
	.3031		7.7
	.3051		7.75
	.3071		7.8
	.3110		7.9
5/16	.3125		7.93
	.3150		8.0
	.3160	O	
	.3189		8.1
	.3228		8.2
	.3230	P	
	.3248		8.25
21/64	.3268		8.3
	.3281		8.33
	.3307		8.4
	.3320	Q	
	.3346		8.5
	.3386		8.6
	.3390	R	
11/32	.3425		8.7
	.3438		8.73
	.3445		8.75
	.3465		8.8
	.3480	S	
	.3504		8.9
	.3543		9.0
	.3580	T	
	.3583		9.1
23/64	.3594		9.12
	.3622		9.2
	.3642		9.25
	.3661		9.3
	.3680	U	
	.3701		9.4
	.3740		9.5
3/8	.3750		9.52
	.3770	V	
	.3780		9.6
	.3819		9.7
	.3839		9.75
	.3858		9.8
	.3860	W	
	.3898		9.9
25/64	.3906		9.92
	.3937		10.0
	.3970	X	
	.4040	Y	
13/32	.4062		10.31
	.4130	Z	
	.4134		10.5
27/64	.4219		10.71

Inch	Decimal	mm
	.4331	11.0
7/16	.4375	11.11
	.4528	11.5
29/64	.4531	11.51
15/32	.4688	11.90
	.4724	12.0
31/64	.4844	12.30
	.4921	12.5
1/2	.5000	12.70
	.5118	13.0
33/64	.5156	13.09
17/32	.5312	13.49
	.5315	13.5
35/64	.5469	13.89
	.5512	14.0
9/16	.5625	14.28
	.5709	14.5
37/64	.5781	14.68
	.5906	15.0
19/32	.5938	15.08
39/64	.6094	15.47
	.6102	15.5
5/8	.6250	15.87
	.6299	16.0
41/64	.6406	16.27
	.6496	16.5
21/32	.6562	16.66
	.6693	17.0
43/64	.6719	17.06
11/16	.6875	17.46
	.6890	17.5
45/64	.7031	17.85
	.7087	18.0
23/32	.7188	18.25
	.7283	18.5
47/64	.7344	18.65
	.7480	19.0
3/4	.7500	19.05
49/64	.7656	19.44
	.7677	19.5
25/32	.7812	19.84
	.7874	20.0
51/64	.7969	20.24
	.8071	20.5
13/16	.8125	20.63
	.8268	21.0
53/64	.8281	21.03
27/32	.8438	21.43
	.8465	21.5
55/64	.8594	21.82
	.8661	22.0
7/8	.8750	22.22
	.8858	22.5
57/64	.8906	22.62
	.9055	23.0
29/32	.9062	23.01
59/64	.9219	23.41
	.9252	23.5
15/16	.9375	23.81
	.9449	24.0
61/64	.9531	24.2
	.9646	24.5
31/32	.9688	24.6
	.9843	25.0
63/64	.9844	25.0
1	1.0000	25.4

GLOSSARY OF TERMS

AIR/FUEL RATIO: The ratio of air to gasoline by weight in the fuel mixture drawn into the engine.

AIR INJECTION: One method of reducing harmful exhaust emissions by injecting air into each of the exhaust ports of an engine. The fresh air entering the hot exhaust manifold causes any remaining fuel to be burned before it can exit the tailpipe.

ALTERNATOR: A device used for converting mechanical energy into electrical energy.

AMMETER: An instrument, calibrated in amperes, used to measure the flow of an electrical current in a circuit. Ammeters are always connected in series with the circuit being tested.

AMPERE: The rate of flow of electrical current present when one volt of electrical pressure is applied against one ohm of electrical resistance.

ANALOG COMPUTER: Any microprocessor that uses similar (analogous) electrical signals to make its calculations.

ARMATURE: A laminated, soft iron core wrapped by a wire that converts electrical energy to mechanical energy as in a motor or relay. When rotated in a magnetic field, it changes mechanical energy into electrical energy as in a generator.

ATMOSPHERIC PRESSURE: The pressure on the Earth's surface caused by the weight of the air in the atmosphere. At sea level, this pressure is 14.7 psi at 32°F (101 kPa at 0°C).

ATOMIZATION: The breaking down of a liquid into a fine mist that can be suspended in air.

AXIAL PLAY: Movement parallel to a shaft or bearing bore.

BACKFIRE: The sudden combustion of gases in the intake or exhaust system that results in a loud explosion.

BACKLASH: The clearance or play between two parts, such as meshed gears.

BACKPRESSURE: Restrictions in the exhaust system that slow the exit of exhaust gases from the combustion chamber.

BAKELITE: A heat resistant, plastic insulator material commonly used in printed circuit boards and transistorized components.

BALL BEARING: A bearing made up of hardened inner and outer races between which hardened steel ball roll.

BALLAST RESISTOR: A resistor in the primary ignition circuit that lowers voltage after the engine is started to reduce wear on ignition components.

BEARING: A friction reducing, supportive device usually located between a stationary part and a moving part.

BIMETAL TEMPERATURE SENSOR: Any sensor or switch made of two dissimilar types of metal that bend when heated or cooled due to the different expansion rates of the alloys. These types of sensors usually function as an on/off switch.

BLOWBY: Combustion gases, composed of water vapor and unburned fuel, that leak past the piston rings into the crankcase during normal engine operation. These gases are removed by the PCV system to prevent the build-up of harmful acids in the crankcase.

BRAKE PAD: A brake shoe and lining assembly used with disc brakes.

BRAKE SHOE: The backing for the brake lining. The term is, however, usually applied to the assembly of the brake backing and lining.

BUSHING: A liner, usually removable, for a bearing; an anti-friction liner used in place of a bearing.

BYPASS: System used to bypass ballast resistor during engine cranking to increase voltage supplied to the coil.

CALIPER: A hydraulically activated device in a disc brake system, which is mounted straddling the brake rotor (disc). The caliper contains at least one piston and two brake pads. Hydraulic pressure on the piston(s) forces the pads against the rotor.

CAMSHAFT: A shaft in the engine on which are the lobes (cams) which operate the valves. The camshaft is driven by the crankshaft, via a belt, chain or gears, at one half the crankshaft speed.

CAPACITOR: A device which stores an electrical charge.

CARBON MONOXIDE (CO): a colorless, odorless gas given off as a normal byproduct of combustion. It is poisonous and extremely dangerous in confined areas, building up slowly to toxic levels without warning if adequate ventilation is not available.

CARBURETOR: A device, usually mounted on the intake manifold of an engine, which mixes the air and fuel in the proper proportion to allow even combustion.

CATALYTIC CONVERTER: A device installed in the exhaust system, like a muffler, that converts harmful byproducts of combustion into carbon dioxide and water vapor by means of a heat-producing chemical reaction.

CENTRIFUGAL ADVANCE: A mechanical method of advancing the spark timing by using flyweights in the distributor that react to centrifugal force generated by the distributor shaft rotation.

CHECK VALVE: Any one-way valve installed to permit the flow of air, fuel or vacuum in one direction only.

CHOKE: A device, usually a moveable valve, placed in the intake path of a carburetor to restrict the flow of air.

CIRCUIT: Any unbroken path through which an electrical current can flow. Also used to describe fuel flow in some instances.

CIRCUIT BREAKER: A switch which protects an electrical circuit from overload by opening the circuit when the current flow exceeds a predetermined level. Some circuit breakers must be reset manually, while other reset automatically

COIL (IGNITION): A transformer in the ignition circuit which steps of the voltage provided to the spark plugs.

COMBINATION MANIFOLD: An assembly which includes both the intake and exhaust manifolds in one casting.

COMBINATION VALVE: A device used in some fuel systems that routes fuel vapors to a charcoal storage canister instead of venting them into the atmosphere. The valve relieves fuel tank pressure and allows fresh air into the tank as fuel level drops to prevent a vapor lock situation.

COMPRESSION RATIO: The comparison of the total volume of the cylinder and combustion chamber with the piston at BDC and the piston at TDC.

CONDENSER: 1. An electrical device which acts to store an electrical charge, preventing voltage surges.
2. A radiator-like device in the air conditioning system in which refrigerant gas condenses into a liquid, giving off heat.

CONDUCTOR: Any material through which an electrical current can be transmitted easily.

CONTINUITY: Continuous or complete circuit. Can be checked with an ohmmeter.

COUNTERSHAFT: An intermediate shaft which is rotated by a mainshaft and transmits, in turn, that rotation to a working part.

CRANKCASE: The lower part of an engine in which the crankshaft and related parts operate.

CRANKSHAFT: The main driving shaft of an engine which receives reciprocating motion from the pistons and converts it to rotary motion.

CYLINDER: In an engine, the round hole in the engine block in which the piston(s) ride.

CYLINDER BLOCK: The main structural member of an engine in which is found the cylinders, crankshaft and other principal parts.

CYLINDER HEAD: The detachable portion of the engine, fastened, usually, to the top of the cylinder block, containing all or most of the combustion chambers. On overhead valve engines, it contains the valves and their operating parts. On overhead cam engines, it contains the camshaft as well.

DEAD CENTER: The extreme top or bottom of the piston stroke.

DETONATION: An unwanted explosion of the air fuel mixture in the combustion chamber caused by excess heat and compression, advanced timing, or an overly lean mixture. Also referred to as "ping".

DIAPHRAGM: A thin, flexible wall separating two cavities, such as in a vacuum advance unit.

DIESELING: A condition in which hot spots in the combustion chamber cause the engine to run on after the key is turned off.

DIFFERENTIAL: A geared assembly which allows the transmission of motion between drive axles, giving one axle the ability to turn faster than the other.

DIODE: An electrical device that will allow current to flow in one direction only.

DISC BRAKE: A hydraulic braking assembly consisting of a brake disc, or rotor, mounted on an axle, and a caliper assembly containing, usually two brake pads which are activated by hydraulic pressure. The pads are forced against the sides of the disc, creating friction which slows the vehicle.

DISTRIBUTOR: A mechanically driven device on an engine which is responsible for electrically firing the spark plug at a predetermined point of the piston stroke.

DOWEL PIN: A pin, inserted in mating holes in two different parts allowing those parts to maintain a fixed relationship.

DRUM BRAKE: A braking system which consists of two brake shoes and one or two wheel cylinders, mounted on a fixed backing plate, and a brake drum, mounted on an axle, which revolves around the assembly. Hydraulic action applied to the wheel cylinders forces the shoes outward against the drum, creating friction and slowing the vehicle.

DWELL: The rate, measured in degrees of shaft rotation, at which an electrical circuit cycles on and off.

ELECTRONIC CONTROL UNIT (ECU): Ignition module, module, amplifier or igniter. See Module for definition.

ELECTRONIC IGNITION: A system in which the timing and firing of the spark plugs is controlled by an electronic control unit, usually called a module. These systems have not points or condenser.

ENDPLAY: The measured amount of axial movement in a shaft.

ENGINE: A device that converts heat into mechanical energy.

EXHAUST MANIFOLD: A set of cast passages or pipes which conduct exhaust gases from the engine.

FEELER GAUGE: A blade, usually metal, of precisely predetermined thickness, used to measure the clearance between two parts. These blades usually are available in sets of assorted thicknesses.

F-Head: An engine configuration in which the intake valves are in the cylinder head, while the camshaft and exhaust valves are located in the cylinder block. The camshaft operates the intake valves via lifters and pushrods, while it operates the exhaust valves directly.

FIRING ORDER: The order in which combustion occurs in the cylinders of an engine. Also the order in which spark is distributed to the plugs by the distributor.

FLATHEAD: An engine configuration in which the camshaft and all the valves are located in the cylinder block.

FLOODING: The presence of too much fuel in the intake manifold and combustion chamber which prevents the air/fuel mixture from firing, thereby causing a no-start situation.

FLYWHEEL: A disc shaped part bolted to the rear end of the crankshaft. Around the outer perimeter is affixed the ring gear. The starter drive engages the ring gear, turning the flywheel, which rotates the crankshaft, imparting the initial starting motion to the engine.

FOOT POUND (ft.lb. or sometimes, ft. lbs.): The amount of energy or work needed to raise an item weighing one pound, a distance of one foot.

FUSE: A protective device in a circuit which prevents circuit overload by breaking the circuit when a specific amperage is present. The device is constructed around a strip or wire of a lower amperage rating than the circuit it is designed to protect. When an amperage higher than that stamped on the fuse is present in the circuit, the strip or wire melts, opening the circuit.

GEAR RATIO: The ratio between the number of teeth on meshing gears.

GENERATOR: A device which converts mechanical energy into electrical energy.

HEAT RANGE: The measure of a spark plug's ability to dissipate heat from its firing end. The higher the heat range, the hotter the plug fires.

HUB: The center part of a wheel or gear.

HYDROCARBON (HC): Any chemical compound made up of hydrogen and carbon. A major pollutant formed by the engine as a byproduct of combustion.

HYDROMETER: An instrument used to measure the specific gravity of a solution.

INCH POUND (in.lb. or sometimes, in. lbs.): One twelfth of a foot pound.

INDUCTION: A means of transferring electrical energy in the form of a magnetic field. Principle used in the ignition coil to increase voltage.

INJECTION PUMP: A device, usually mechanically operated, which meters and delivers fuel under pressure to the fuel injector.

INJECTOR: A device which receives metered fuel under relatively low pressure and is activated to inject the fuel into the engine under relatively high pressure at a predetermined time.

INPUT SHAFT: The shaft to which torque is applied, usually carrying the driving gear or gears.

INTAKE MANIFOLD: A casting of passages or pipes used to conduct air or a fuel/air mixture to the cylinders.

JOURNAL: The bearing surface within which a shaft operates.

KEY: A small block usually fitted in a notch between a shaft and a hub to prevent slippage of the two parts.

MANIFOLD: A casting of passages or set of pipes which connect the cylinders to an inlet or outlet source.

MANIFOLD VACUUM: Low pressure in an engine intake manifold formed just below the throttle plates. Manifold vacuum is highest at idle and drops under acceleration.

MASTER CYLINDER: The primary fluid pressurizing device in a hydraulic system. In automotive use, it is found in brake and hydraulic clutch systems and is pedal activated, either directly or, in a power brake system, through the power booster.

MODULE: Electronic control unit, amplifier or igniter of solid state or integrated design which controls the current flow in the ignition primary circuit based on input from the pickup coil. When the module opens the primary circuit, the high secondary voltage is induced in the coil.

NEEDLE BEARING: A bearing which consists of a number (usually a large number) of long, thin rollers.

OHM: (Ω) The unit used to measure the resistance of conductor to electrical flow. One ohm is the amount of resistance that limits current flow to one ampere in a circuit with one volt of pressure.

OHMMETER: An instrument used for measuring the resistance, in ohms, in an electrical circuit.

OUTPUT SHAFT: The shaft which transmits torque from a device, such as a transmission.

OVERDRIVE: A gear assembly which produces more shaft revolutions than that transmitted to it.

OVERHEAD CAMSHAFT (OHC): An engine configuration in which the camshaft is mounted on top of the cylinder head and operates the valve either directly or by means of rocker arms.

OVERHEAD VALVE (OHV): An engine configuration in which all of the valves are located in the cylinder head and the camshaft is located in the cylinder block. The camshaft operates the valves via lifters and pushrods.

OXIDES OF NITROGEN (NOx): Chemical compounds of nitrogen produced as a byproduct of combustion. They combine with hydrocarbons to produce smog.

OXYGEN SENSOR: Used with the feedback system to sense the presence of oxygen in the exhaust gas and signal the computer which can reference the voltage signal to an air/fuel ratio.

PINION: The smaller of two meshing gears.

PISTON RING: An open ended ring which fits into a groove on the outer diameter of the piston. Its chief function is to form a seal between the piston and cylinder wall. Most automotive pistons have three rings: two for compression sealing; one for oil sealing.

PRELOAD: A predetermined load placed on a bearing during assembly or by adjustment.

PRIMARY CIRCUIT: Is the low voltage side of the ignition system which consists of the ignition switch, ballast resistor or resistance wire, bypass, coil, electronic control unit and pick-up coil as well as the connecting wires and harnesses.

PRESS FIT: The mating of two parts under pressure, due to the inner diameter of one being smaller than the outer diameter of the other, or vice versa; an interference fit.

RACE: The surface on the inner or outer ring of a bearing on which the balls, needles or rollers move.

REGULATOR: A device which maintains the amperage and/or voltage levels of a circuit at predetermined values.

RELAY: A switch which automatically opens and/or closes a circuit.

RESISTANCE: The opposition to the flow of current through a circuit or electrical device, and is measured in ohms. Resistance is equal to the voltage divided by the amperage.

RESISTOR: A device, usually made of wire, which offers a preset amount of resistance in an electrical circuit.

RING GEAR: The name given to a ring-shaped gear attached to a differential case, or affixed to a flywheel or as part a planetary gear set.

ROLLER BEARING: A bearing made up of hardened inner and outer races between which hardened steel rollers move.

ROTOR: 1. The disc-shaped part of a disc brake assembly, upon which the brake pads bear; also called, brake disc.
2. The device mounted atop the distributor shaft, which passes current to the distributor cap tower contacts.

SECONDARY CIRCUIT: The high voltage side of the ignition system, usually above 20,000 volts. The secondary includes the ignition coil, coil wire, distributor cap and rotor, spark plug wires and spark plugs.

SENDING UNIT: A mechanical, electrical, hydraulic or electromagnetic device which transmits information to a gauge.

SENSOR: Any device designed to measure engine operating conditions or ambient pressures and temperatures. Usually electronic in nature and designed to send a voltage signal to an on-board computer, some sensors may operate as a simple on/off switch or they may provide a variable voltage signal (like a potentiometer) as conditions or measured parameters change.

SHIM: Spacers of precise, predetermined thickness used between parts to establish a proper working relationship.

SLAVE CYLINDER: In automotive use, a device in the hydraulic clutch system which is activated by hydraulic force, disengaging the clutch.

SOLENOID: A coil used to produce a magnetic field, the effect of which is produce work.

SPARK PLUG: A device screwed into the combustion chamber of a spark ignition engine. The basic construction is a conductive core inside of a ceramic insulator, mounted in an outer conductive base. An electrical charge from the spark plug wire travels along the conductive core and jumps a preset air gap to a grounding point or points at the end of the conductive base. The resultant spark ignites the fuel/air mixture in the combustion chamber.

SPLINES: Ridges machined or cast onto the outer diameter of a shaft or inner diameter of a bore to enable parts to mate without rotation.

TACHOMETER: A device used to measure the rotary speed of an engine, shaft, gear, etc., usually in rotations per minute.

THERMOSTAT: A valve, located in the cooling system of an engine, which is closed when cold and opens gradually in response to engine heating, controlling the temperature of the coolant and rate of coolant flow.

TOP DEAD CENTER (TDC): The point at which the piston reaches the top of its travel on the compression stroke.

TORQUE: The twisting force applied to an object.

TORQUE CONVERTER: A turbine used to transmit power from a driving member to a driven member via hydraulic action, providing changes in drive ratio and torque. In automotive use, it links the driveplate at the rear of the engine to the automatic transmission.

TRANSDUCER: A device used to change a force into an electrical signal.

TRANSISTOR: A semi-conductor component which can be actuated by a small voltage to perform an electrical switching function.

TUNE-UP: A regular maintenance function, usually associated with the replacement and adjustment of parts and components in the electrical and fuel systems of a vehicle for the purpose of attaining optimum performance.

TURBOCHARGER: An exhaust driven pump which compresses intake air and forces it into the combustion chambers at higher than atmospheric pressures. The increased air pressure allows more fuel to be burned and results in increased horsepower being produced.

VACUUM ADVANCE: A device which advances the ignition timing in response to increased engine vacuum.

VACUUM GAUGE: An instrument used to measure the presence of vacuum in a chamber.

VALVE: A device which control the pressure, direction of flow or rate of flow of a liquid or gas.

VALVE CLEARANCE: The measured gap between the end of the valve stem and the rocker arm, cam lobe or follower that activates the valve.

VISCOSITY: The rating of a liquid's internal resistance to flow.

VOLTMETER: An instrument used for measuring electrical force in units called volts. Voltmeters are always connected parallel with the circuit being tested.

WHEEL CYLINDER: Found in the automotive drum brake assembly, it is a device, actuated by hydraulic pressure, which, through internal pistons, pushes the brake shoes outward against the drums.

ABBREVIATIONS AND SYMBOLS

A: Ampere

AC: Alternating current

A/C: Air conditioning

A-h: Ampere hour

AT: Automatic transmission

ATDC: After top dead center

μA: Microampere

bbl: Barrel

BDC: Bottom dead center

bhp: Brake horsepower

BTDC: Before top dead center

BTU: British thermal unit

C: Celsius (Centigrade)

CCA: Cold cranking amps

cd: Candela

cm^2: Square centimeter

cm^3, cc: Cubic centimeter

CO: Carbon monoxide

CO_2: Carbon dioxide

cu.in., in^3: Cubic inch

CV: Constant velocity

Cyl.: Cylinder

DC: Direct current

ECM: Electronic control module

EFE: Early fuel evaporation

EFI: Electronic fuel injection

EGR: Exhaust gas recirculation

Exh.: Exhaust

F: Fahrenheit

F: Farad

pF: Picofarad

μF: Microfarad

FI: Fuel injection

ft.lb., ft. lb., ft. lbs.: foot pound(s)

gal: Gallon

g: Gram

HC: Hydrocarbon

HEI: High energy ignition

HO: High output

hp: Horsepower

Hyd.: Hydraulic

Hz: Hertz

ID: Inside diameter

in.lb.; in. lb.; in. lbs: inch pound(s)

Int.: Intake

K: Kelvin

kg: Kilogram

kHz: Kilohertz

km: Kilometer

km/h: Kilometers per hour

kΩ: Kilohm

kPa: Kilopascal

kV: Kilovolt

kW: Kilowatt

l: Liter

l/s: Liters per second

m: Meter

mA: Milliampere

mg: Milligram

mHz: Megahertz

mm: Millimeter

mm^2: Square millimeter

m^3: Cubic meter

MΩ: Megohm

m/s: Meters per second

MT: Manual transmission

mV: Millivolt

μm: Micrometer

N: Newton

N-m: Newton meter

NOx: Nitrous oxide

OD: Outside diameter

OHC: Over head camshaft

OHV: Over head valve

Ω: Ohm

PCV: Positive crankcase ventilation

psi: Pounds per square inch

pts: Pints

qts: Quarts

rpm: Rotations per minute

rps: Rotations per second

R-12: A refrigerant gas (Freon)

SAE: Society of Automotive Engineers

SO$_2$: Sulfur dioxide

T: Ton

t: Megagram

TBI: Throttle Body Injection

TPS: Throttle Position Sensor

V: 1. Volt; 2. Venturi

μV: Microvolt

W: Watt

∞: Infinity

<: Less than

>: Greater than

Index

Chilton's Repair & Tune-Up Guides

The Complete line covers domestic cars, imports, trucks, vans, RV's and 4-wheel drive vehicles.

RTUG Title	Part No.
AMC 1975-82	7199
Covers all U.S. and Canadian models	
Aspen/Volare 1976-80	6637
Covers all U.S. and Canadian models	
Audi 1970-73	5902
Covers all U.S. and Canadian models.	
Audi 4000/5000 1978-81	7028
Covers all U.S. and Canadian models including turbocharged and diesel engines	
Barracuda/Challenger 1965-72	5807
Covers all U.S. and Canadian models	
Blazer/Jimmy 1969-82	6931
Covers all U.S. and Canadian 2- and 4-wheel drive models, including diesel engines	
BMW 1970-82	6844
Covers U.S. and Canadian models	
Buick/Olds/Pontiac 1975-85	7308
Covers all U.S. and Canadian full size rear wheel drive models	
Cadillac 1967-84	7462
Covers all U.S. and Canadian rear wheel drive models	
Camaro 1967-81	6735
Covers all U.S. and Canadian models	
Camaro 1982-85	7317
Covers all U.S. and Canadian models	
Capri 1970-77	6695
Covers all U.S. and Canadian models	
Caravan/Voyager 1984-85	7482
Covers all U.S. and Canadian models	
Century/Regal 1975-85	7307
Covers all U.S. and Canadian rear wheel drive models, including turbocharged engines	
Champ/Arrow/Sapporo 1978-83	7041
Covers all U.S. and Canadian models	
Chevette/1000 1976-86	6836
Covers all U.S. and Canadian models	
Chevrolet 1968-85	7135
Covers all U.S. and Canadian models	
Chevrolet 1968-79 Spanish	7082
Chevrolet/GMC Pick-Ups 1970-82 Spanish	7468
Chevrolet/GMC Pick-Ups and Suburban 1970-86	6936
Covers all U.S. and Canadian $^1/_2$, $^3/_4$ and 1 ton models, including 4-wheel drive and diesel engines	
Chevrolet LUV 1972-81	6815
Covers all U.S. and Canadian models	
Chevrolet Mid-Size 1964-86	6840
Covers all U.S. and Canadian models of 1964-77 Chevelle, Malibu and Malibu SS; 1974-77 Laguna; 1978-85 Malibu; 1970-86 Monte Carlo; 1964-84 El Camino, including diesel engines	
Chevrolet Nova 1986	7658
Covers all U.S. and Canadian models	
Chevy/GMC Vans 1967-84	6930
Covers all U.S. and Canadian models of $^1/_2$, $^3/_4$, and 1 ton vans, cutaways, and motor home chassis, including diesel engines	
Chevy S-10 Blazer/GMC S-15 Jimmy 1982-85	7383
Covers all U.S. and Canadian models	
Chevy S-10/GMC S-15 Pick-Ups 1982-85	7310
Covers all U.S. and Canadian models	
Chevy II/Nova 1962-79	6841
Covers all U.S. and Canadian models	
Chrysler K- and E-Car 1981-85	7163
Covers all U.S. and Canadian front wheel drive models	
Colt/Challenger/Vista/Conquest 1971-85	7037
Covers all U.S. and Canadian models	
Corolla/Carina/Tercel/Starlet 1970-85	7036
Covers all U.S. and Canadian models	
Corona/Cressida/Crown/Mk.II/Camry/Van 1970-84	7044
Covers all U.S. and Canadian models	

RTUG Title	Part No.
Corvair 1960-69	6691
Covers all U.S. and Canadian models	
Corvette 1953-62	6576
Covers all U.S. and Canadian models	
Corvette 1963-84	6843
Covers all U.S. and Canadian models	
Cutlass 1970-85	6933
Covers all U.S. and Canadian models	
Dart/Demon 1968-76	6324
Covers all U.S. and Canadian models	
Datsun 1961-72	5790
Covers all U.S. and Canadian models of Nissan Patrol; 1500, 1600 and 2000 sports cars; Pick-Ups; 410, 411, 510, 1200 and 240Z	
Datsun 1973-80 Spanish	7083
Datsun/Nissan F-10, 310, Stanza, Pulsar 1977-86	7196
Covers all U.S. and Canadian models	
Datsun/Nissan Pick-Ups 1970-84	6816
Covers all U.S and Canadian models	
Datsun/Nissan Z & ZX 1970-86	6932
Covers all U.S. and Canadian models	
Datsun/Nissan 1200, 210, Sentra 1973-86	7197
Covers all U.S. and Canadian models	
Datsun/Nissan 200SX, 510, 610, 710, 810, Maxima 1973-84	7170
Covers all U.S. and Canadian models	
Dodge 1968-77	6554
Covers all U.S. and Canadian models	
Dodge Charger 1967-70	6486
Covers all U.S. and Canadian models	
Dodge/Plymouth Trucks 1967-84	7459
Covers all $^1/_2$, $^3/_4$, and 1 ton 2- and 4-wheel drive U.S. and Canadian models, including diesel engines	
Dodge/Plymouth Vans 1967-84	6934
Covers all $^1/_2$, $^3/_4$, and 1 ton U.S. and Canadian models of vans, cutaways and motor home chassis	
D-50/Arrow Pick-Up 1979-81	7032
Covers all U.S. and Canadian models	
Fairlane/Torino 1962-75	6320
Covers all U.S. and Canadian models	
Fairmont/Zephyr 1978-83	6965
Covers all U.S. and Canadian models	
Fiat 1969-81	7042
Covers all U.S. and Canadian models	
Fiesta 1978-80	6846
Covers all U.S. and Canadian models	
Firebird 1967-81	5996
Covers all U.S. and Canadian models	
Firebird 1982-85	7345
Covers all U.S. and Canadian models	
Ford 1968-79 Spanish	7084
Ford Bronco 1966-83	7140
Covers all U.S. and Canadian models	
Ford Bronco II 1984	7408
Covers all U.S. and Canadian models	
Ford Courier 1972-82	6983
Covers all U.S. and Canadian models	
Ford/Mercury Front Wheel Drive 1981-85	7055
Covers all U.S. and Canadian models Escort, EXP, Tempo, Lynx, LN-7 and Topaz	
Ford/Mercury/Lincoln 1968-85	6842
Covers all U.S. and Canadian models of FORD Country Sedan, Country Squire, Crown Victoria, Custom, Custom 500, Galaxie 500, LTD through 1982, Ranch Wagon, and XL; MERCURY Colony Park, Commuter, Marquis through 1982, Gran Marquis, Monterey and Park Lane; LINCOLN Continental and Towne Car	
Ford/Mercury/Lincoln Mid-Size 1971-85	6696
Covers all U.S. and Canadian models of FORD Elite, 1983-85 LTD, 1977-79 LTD II, Ranchero, Torino, Gran Torino, 1977-85 Thunderbird; MERCURY 1972-85 Cougar,	

continued on next page

RTUG Title	Part No.
1983-85 Marquis, Montego, 1980-85 XR-7; LINCOLN 1982-85 Continental, 1984-85 Mark VII, 1978-80 Versailles	
Ford Pick-Ups 1965-86 Covers all $1/_2$, $3/_4$ and 1 ton, 2- and 4-wheel drive U.S. and Canadian pick-up, chassis cab and camper models, including diesel engines	6913
Ford Pick-Ups 1965-82 Spanish	7469
Ford Ranger 1983-84 Covers all U.S. and Canadian models	7338
Ford Vans 1961-86 Covers all U.S. and Canadian $1/_2$, $3/_4$ and 1 ton van and cutaway chassis models, including diesel engines	6849
GM A-Body 1982-85 Covers all front wheel drive U.S. and Canadian models of BUICK Century, CHEVROLET Celebrity, OLDSMOBILE Cutlass Ciera and PONTIAC 6000	7309
GM C-Body 1985 Covers all front wheel drive U.S. and Canadian models of BUICK Electra Park Avenue and Electra T-Type, CADILLAC Fleetwood and deVille, OLDSMOBILE 98 Regency and Regency Brougham	7587
GM J-Car 1982-85 Covers all U.S. and Canadian models of BUICK Skyhawk, CHEVROLET Cavalier, CADILLAC Cimarron, OLDSMOBILE Firenza and PONTIAC 2000 and Sunbird	7059
GM N-Body 1985-86 Covers all U.S. and Canadian models of front wheel drive BUICK Somerset and Skylark, OLDSMOBILE Calais, and PONTIAC Grand Am	7657
GM X-Body 1980-85 Covers all U.S. and Canadian models of BUICK Skylark, CHEVROLET Citation, OLDSMOBILE Omega and PONTIAC Phoenix	7049
GM Subcompact 1971-80 Covers all U.S. and Canadian models of BUICK Skyhawk (1975-80), CHEVROLET Vega and Monza, OLDSMOBILE Starfire, and PONTIAC Astre and 1975-80 Sunbird	6935
Granada/Monarch 1975-82 Covers all U.S. and Canadian models	6937
Honda 1973-84 Covers all U.S. and Canadian models	6980
International Scout 1967-73 Covers all U.S. and Canadian models	5912
Jeep 1945-87 Covers all U.S. and Canadian CJ-2A, CJ-3A, CJ-3B, CJ-5, CJ-6, CJ-7, Scrambler and Wrangler models	6817
Jeep Wagoneer, Commando, Cherokee, Truck 1957-86 Covers all U.S. and Canadian models of Wagoneer, Cherokee, Grand Wagoneer, Jeepster, Jeepster Commando, J-100, J-200, J-300, J-10, J20, FC-150 and FC-170	6739
Laser/Daytona 1984-85 Covers all U.S. and Canadian models	7563
Maverick/Comet 1970-77 Covers all U.S. and Canadian models	6634
Mazda 1971-84 Covers all U.S. and Canadian models of RX-2, RX-3, RX-4, 808, 1300, 1600, Cosmo, GLC and 626	6981
Mazda Pick-Ups 1972-86 Covers all U.S. and Canadian models	7659
Mercedes-Benz 1959-70 Covers all U.S. and Canadian models	6065
Mereceds-Benz 1968-73 Covers all U.S. and Canadian models	5907

RTUG Title	Part No.
Mercedes-Benz 1974-84 Covers all U.S. and Canadian models	6809
Mitsubishi, Cordia, Tredia, Starion, Galant 1983-85 Covers all U.S. and Canadian models	7583
MG 1961-81 Covers all U.S. and Canadian models	6780
Mustang/Capri/Merkur 1979-85 Covers all U.S. and Canadian models	6963
Mustang/Cougar 1965-73 Covers all U.S. and Canadian models	6542
Mustang II 1974-78 Covers all U.S. and Canadian models	6812
Omni/Horizon/Rampage 1978-84 Covers all U.S. and Canadian models of DODGE omni, Miser, 024, Charger 2.2; PLYMOUTH Horizon, Miser, TC3, TC3 Tourismo; Rampage	6845
Opel 1971-75 Covers all U.S. and Canadian models	6575
Peugeot 1970-74 Covers all U.S. and Canadian models	5982
Pinto/Bobcat 1971-80 Covers all U.S. and Canadian models	7027
Plymouth 1968-76 Covers all U.S. and Canadian models	6552
Pontiac Fiero 1984-85 Covers all U.S. and Canadian models	7571
Pontiac Mid-Size 1974-83 Covers all U.S. and Canadian models of Ventura, Grand Am, LeMans, Grand LeMans, GTO, Phoenix, and Grand Prix	7346
Porsche 924/928 1976-81 Covers all U.S. and Canadian models	7048
Renault 1975-85 Covers all U.S. and Canadian models	7165
Roadrunner/Satellite/Belvedere/GTX 1968-73 Covers all U.S. and Canadian models	5821
RX-7 1979-81 Covers all U.S. and Canadian models	7031
SAAB 99 1969-75 Covers all U.S. and Canadian models	5988
SAAB 900 1979-85 Covers all U.S. and Canadian models	7572
Snowmobiles 1976-80 Covers Arctic Cat, John Deere, Kawasaki, Polaris, Ski-Doo and Yamaha	6978
Subaru 1970-84 Covers all U.S. and Canadian models	6982
Tempest/GTO/LeMans 1968-73 Covers all U.S. and Canadian models	5905
Toyota 1966-70 Covers all U.S. and Canadian models of Corona, MkII, Corolla, Crown, Land Cruiser, Stout and Hi-Lux	5795
Toyota 1970-79 Spanish	7467
Toyota Celica/Supra 1971-85 Covers all U.S. and Canadian models	7043
Toyota Trucks 1970-85 Covers all U.S. and Canadian models of pickups, Land Cruiser and 4Runner	7035
Valiant/Duster 1968-76 Covers all U.S. and Canadian models	6326
Volvo 1956-69 Covers all U.S. and Canadian models	6529
Volvo 1970-83 Covers all U.S. and Canadian models	7040
VW Front Wheel Drive 1974-85 Covers all U.S. and Canadian models	6962
VW 1949-71 Covers all U.S. and Canadian models	5796
VW 1970-79 Spanish	7081
VW 1970-81 Covers all U.S. and Canadian Beetles, Karmann Ghia, Fastback, Squareback, Vans, 411 and 412	6837

Chilton's Repair Manuals are available at your local retailer or by mailing a check or money order for **$14.95** per book plus **$3.50** for 1st book and **$.50** for each additional book to cover postage and handling to:

Chilton Book Company
Dept. DM
Radnor, PA 19089

NOTE: When ordering be sure to include your name & address, book part No. & title.

Land Rover
Defender

First published in 2000 as *You & Your Land Rover Ninety, One Ten & Defender*
This revised and expanded edition published May 2010

British Library cataloguing-in-publication data:
A catalogue record for this book is available from the British Library.

ISBN 978 1 84425 710 2

Library of Congress catalog card number 2010921617

Published by Haynes Publishing, Sparkford, Yeovil, Somerset BA22 7JJ, UK

Tel: 01963 442030 Fax: 01963 440001
Int. tel: +44 1963 442030 Fax: +44 1963 440001
E-mail: sales@haynes.co.uk
Website: www.haynes.co.uk

Haynes North America Inc.
861 Lawrence Drive, Newbury Park, California 91320, USA

Printed and bound in the USA

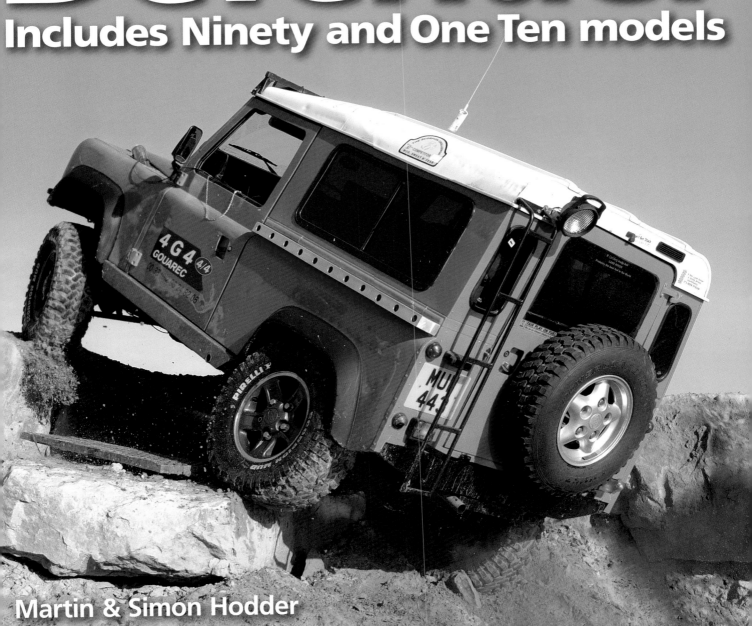

Haynes Enthusiast Guide

Land Rover

Defender
Includes Ninety and One Ten models

Martin & Simon Hodder

LAND ROVER DEFENDER
CONTENTS

ACKNOWLEDGEMENTS

The information contained in this book relies substantially on the personal knowledge, experience and many articles written by us in a number of publications but principally – where more recent topics are concerned – in Land Rover enthusiast.

Coverage of vehicles introduced in the 2000s is essentially based on first-hand experience gained by Simon at various launch events organised so efficiently by Land Rover and through driving vehicles owned by various individuals. It is important to remark that every type of vehicle presented in these pages has been driven by the authors.

Thanks are due also to our expert colleague James Taylor for the information contained in his invaluable collection of reference books on the Land Rover marque.

Our photographs come from a number of sources. Many are the work of Simon, especially those depicting more recent vehicles. There are also numerous contributions from Nick Dimbleby and a fascinating assortment of practical photos from Dave Barker.

To everyone who has helped, or who has provided images, we extend a heartfelt 'Thank you'.

Martin and Simon Hodder

March 2010

← ← **Martin Hodder relaxes beside the Series IIA he was 'joined at the hip to' for many years, although he now enjoys the comfort of a 2001 Range Rover 4.0 Bordeaux.**

← **Simon tries to look at ease standing with his 1991 Range Rover 3.9 Vogue SE. He also has on his driveway an early Discovery and a 1980 Lightweight.**

INTRODUCTION
THE PURE HONESTY OF LAND ROVERS

Passion is something you would expect to be associated with Ferrari, not Land Rover, so why is it that anything from the Solihull factory attracts devotion which is the envy of all other car makers? Why have all Land Rovers been so revered for more than half a century? How is it that countless thousands would choose a Defender any day, rather than a sleek roadburner from Modena, Stuttgart or Munich?

The simple answer is that Defenders – from the very first to the most recent – are no-nonsense, intensely honest vehicles that do everything asked of them without protest. They incorporate all that Land Rover has learned since 1948, and are the culmination of that experience, giving them off-roading capability without equal and on-road performance which, although definitely not in the supercar league, is well up to the job of daily commuting and long-distance holiday motoring.

Yet the appeal goes even further. The coil-sprung utility has a purposeful, workmanlike shape which makes no concessions to modern aerodynamic design. There's no mistaking a Defender, because it looks like no other vehicle, save the generations of 'working' Land Rovers whose distinctive outline has skipped easily from one decade to the next, from one series to the following one.

Defenders have always sat happily among the other products of Land Rover, sharing a technological philosophy with the Discovery and Range Rover which is unique to Soilhull. In the simplest, most basic analysis, only the bodies are different.

In writing this book we have not attempted to provide the detail of every last nut and bolt, each minute change, which took Land Rover from the first Series I to the birth of the One Ten in 1983, and from there to the introduction of the electronically sophisticated Td5 and the even more complex versions that have come subsequently.

Rather, we have set out to add to the enjoyment shared by so many of the entire Defender family, from inception to the present-day, with a book which is a mixture of celebration, information and confirmation. Celebration of the vehicles themselves, information to assist with purchase and ownership, and confirmation that the Defender is, indeed, all those things it is said to be.

Of course, it would have been wrong to produce a book on the Defender without looking back at the beginnings of the breed, and then charting the family's development through the years. The One Ten was an all-new vehicle when it was introduced, yet it took advantage of every lesson along the way, both from all the preceding Land Rovers and the Range Rover. You cannot write in depth about the Defender, already with a lifespan of 27 years, without looking also at those earlier machines.

In tracing the vehicles that led to the Defender we have deliberately focused on the highlights, those aspects which have had the most bearing on each succeeding model in turn: through to

↑ **No other vehicle in the world has such a varied following as the Defender. From battered old farm utility to pampered and shining show winner, Land Rover's workhorse model does it all. (Simon Hodder)**

↑ The unrivalled capability of the Defender series optimises the enjoyment of off-roading activities, whether you're having an easy run on a green lane, or indulging in the more serious side of the pastime. (Nick Dimbleby)

→ The Defender remains popular with search and rescue organisations. Seen here on a training exercise, this 110 belongs to the Severn Area Rescue Association. (Simon Hodder)

the One Ten and Ninety, and from there the Tdi-powered Defenders to the 21st century Td5 and then the Puma-powered models.

We have attempted to present information which is genuinely helpful. For example, the section dealing with the build up from prototype to launch of the first coil-sprung utility models helps to understand the present vehicle, while the detailed rundown of all engine types employed in the Defender family tells in detail what to expect from each, and hopefully will assist buyers in avoiding engines not suitable to their use of the vehicle.

The development of the enthusiast movement is explained, because without this there would be no need for a book of this kind, while the chapters dealing with ownership and preparation for off-roading reflect the progression from owner to enthusiast which is the inevitable consequence of buying a Land Rover.

This book is about the coil-sprung utilities. Yet they cannot be viewed in isolation. Land Rover enthusiasm covers everything and runs in families, as evidenced by the fact that my eldest son Simon

has joined me in producing this book and my second son Cameron is also an enthusiast.

My own Land Rover ownership over the years has included leaf-sprung models, a 1983 One Ten V8, several Range Rovers, Discoverys and Freelanders. My last classic Range Rover was a beautiful 1991 3.9 Vogue SE, which Simon bought from me several years ago. Since then I have stuck with 38A Range Rovers and on my driveway now (along with a 'mint' classic Mercedes S-class car!) is my 2001 Range Rover 4.0 Bordeaux limited edition.

As well as his Range Rover, Simon has a rather weary 1989 Tdi Discovery and a Lightweight that could be brought back to its former pristine condition with a bit of hard work, not to say spare time! Cameron has an immaculate Freelander Td4 for family transport.

So, for all Land Rover enthusiasts like the Hodder clan, we hope very much you will enjoy this book, even if you don't drive a Defender. And for those who are not quite so sated with the magic elixir of Solihull we would like to think the following pages will be interesting, helpful and stimulating.

CHAPTER 1
FROM WORKER TO CULT MACHINE

Not everybody finds it easy to understand why Land Rovers should excite enthusiasm. Discoverys and Range Rovers, certainly, but surely all other products of the world's most revered off-road manufacturer are noisy, uncomfortable, slow, thirsty and old-fashioned?

Well, yes, many of them are … up to a point.

But there's another side to the coin. Discoverys, Range Rovers, and Freelanders apart, all Land Rovers have about them an air of no-nonsense, down-to-earth, tough simplicity. They are honest about what they are, not knowing the meaning of pretentiousness; and although they were never intended to project an image of any kind, they make, in fact, the kind of lifestyle statement that other motor manufacturers would kill for. These days, this is what *sells* motor cars.

It's fascinating to observe how Land Rovers were making these statements long before the concept of a 'lifestyle image' even existed. In the 1940s, '50s and '60s they were working machines which looked the part, with purposeful, clean-cut lines shouting toughness, versatility, and ability at everyone who saw them. They were among the first post-war vehicles to have a clearly identifiable image: there was no mistaking a Land Rover, either as a vehicle or for the things of which it was capable. If you drove one, you were associated with the hard realities of life in the remote out-doors; today, we call it lifestyle.

Then, in 1970, the Range Rover was thrust into the world, with a sleek, classic shape which was, at the same time, very evidently from the same gene pool as its working brothers. Since then, all utility Land Rovers have continued with the original family appearance which began in 1947 with the Series I, while all the luxury vehicles which have followed the original Range Rover have been carved in that vehicle's image. Thus two distinct family lines have been perpetuated. Yet crossing over between the two and linking them together is the familiarity of form you get between close cousins.

This master-stroke of family likeness which has been achieved at Solihull does not, in itself, explain why there's an enthusiast movement for Land Rovers without equal in any other single marque. But when you remember the other qualities of toughness and capability, and mix them into the pot with the looks and reputation, you begin to find the reasons why there's such a worldwide passion for anything and everything to have emerged from the factory at Lode Lane on Birmingham's south-eastern extremity.

First enthusiasts

That there would be an enthusiast movement centred on Land Rovers was inevitable from the day it was decided to put them into production. The first seeds of this passion were sown by the Willys Jeep, bought in large numbers when surplus

← No longer just seen as a simple utility vehicle, an increasing number of Defenders now have custom paint jobs, luxury interiors and highly tuned engines. (Simon Hodder)

DID YOU KNOW?
See the joins

One of the more interesting vehicles within the extraordinary collection of rare and significant Land Rovers which form the fascinating Dunsfold Collection, at Dunsfold, Surrey, is a Ninety which, at first glance, looks very much like any other member of the Defender family. However, far from being commonplace, it is the second prototype and the very first of the line to be built with the production wheelbase of 92.9in (2.36m). Registered CWK 40Y, it shows clearly where the bodywork was extended from a Series III 88-inch, while inspection of the chassis from the rear wheel arches reveals the welding which was necessary in reducing a chassis from a One Ten down to the wheelbase length with which the Ninety was subsequently built.

This priceless vehicle is not locked away in a centrally heated museum but is used regularly. I have driven it on several occasions, one of which was a hard-working off-road session during which it absorbed a considerable amount of punishment with typical ease – living proof that Land Rovers, no matter how rare, are meant to be used.

↑ The original Land Rover, with its 80-inch wheelbase and stark simplicity, soon became a familiar sight on Britain's roads, and remains an extremely appealing vehicle. (Simon Hodder)

wartime vehicles began to go on sale in 1945–6, primarily as working machines. Naturally, among the new owners were people who, despite petrol shortages, enjoyed the fun that Jeeps brought to motoring and who loved the thought of driving where other vehicles could not venture.

Then along came the Land Rover. Because it was a little more square cut, it had a more purposeful look about it than the Jeep which had inspired it, and was undeniably just as useful – if not a touch more so – when taken off the tarmac. Moreover it was British, from one of the world's most respected motor manufacturers.

The Land Rover was an incredibly appealing vehicle, and not all of this attraction could be explained in a logical manner. It was introduced as a working vehicle, for agriculture, forestry, and industry, but the interest in it went far beyond those definitions, and it wasn't long before motoring journalists were thinking, and writing, beyond the confines of the vehicle's advertised role.

In July 1948 the weekly magazine *Motor* published, in two instalments, an extremely entertaining account of an expedition on some

of the ancient routes in Mid-Wales in a Land Rover. This was the first off-roading story to be written involving a Land Rover and, given *Motor*'s great influence at the time, will have played a not inconsiderable part in extending the horizons of a vehicle which went into production that very month.

It was with the publication of these two articles that Land Rover's unique enthusiast movement was born, although nobody could have realised it at the time. Those first published words about the joys of off-roading in a Land Rover presaged something which over the next half-century and beyond would involve hundreds of thousands of people around the world, building with their enthusiasm a self-contained industry serving their needs, and ensuring the preservation of older models.

In June 1948, *Motor*'s E. H. Row and Joseph Lowrey, plus a photographer identified simply as Ross, drove their borrowed Land Rover from the factory and headed westward out of Birmingham. In complete contrast to today's well-equipped off-road enthusiasts, their only recovery aids for this first Land Rover leisure foray into a part of Wales seen as demanding even now, were a length of rope and, as it was described, 'a driving pulley for the power take-off for bollarding the car out if we did get stuck'.

Well, they did get stuck, and on one occasion had to recruit the assistance of 'five burly Welsh farmers' to help them out of a bog by hauling on the tow rope because there was nowhere to secure the rope for their 'bollarding'. They took the Land Rover down a track, never before driven in a motor vehicle, not even the Jeep owned by one of the helpful farmers, with one of the party walking ahead to mark the edge, from which there was a precipitous drop. At the bottom they crossed the Towy river, thought hitherto not to be possible, then had to retrace their route because even the Land Rover could not get through the trees on the far side of the valley.

On the second day they made several ascents of Dunlop's Dividend, a particularly steep, hairpin-strewn climb near the village of Brechfa. The last climb was made with nine people somehow crammed in and on the Land Rover, five of them farmers. Indeed, *Motor*'s expedition must have served as a superb promotional event for the

Rover Motor Company, because the reports commented on the great interest shown in the vehicle by farmers at every stop.

More importantly – because farmers would in due course buy Land Rovers anyway, especially as times became gradually less harsh – the two articles in this opinion-forming motoring magazine told the world that the Land Rover was a car people could enjoy. There were already motorists who enjoyed cross-country driving for fun, doing surprisingly well in cars as ordinary as Austin Sevens, and this first account of an off-roading journey in a Land Rover was a significant milestone for the recently-launched four-wheel drive from Solihull.

By 1955 the Series I had become fully established as a working vehicle and, perhaps to the surprise of many at Rover, was already a part of the motoring scene, having developed a passionate following with people who wanted the extra capability and character that ordinary cars just could not bring them.

Probably the first major expedition undertaken by a privately owned Land Rover finished in

↓ **In all its forms the Defender family has always displayed the unmistakeable general outline that has lived for more than half a century in the 'working' Land Rovers. (Nick Dimbleby)**

London in the summer of that year. Just as the off-roading trip to Mid-Wales was to establish the Land Rover as the ideal vehicle for mountain track driving, this year-long trek showed the world that when it came to extended overlanding the Land Rover was the vehicle to use.

Started just six years after the Land Rover was introduced, this trailblazing journey was the most extensive trip, other than circumnavigation, that it is possible to make – all the way from Australia to Britain. It began on the island of Tasmania, off Australia's south-eastern coast, and for good measure began with a sightseeing tour around most of Australia, before sailing to Ceylon. From there, the route wound through India, then directly west through the Middle East, from Istanbul into Europe, and finally across the Channel back to Britain.

The three people – two men and a woman – who made this journey had fitted the Land Rover 80-inch with a special body providing sleeping space, and towed a trailer which had been specially constructed so that it could be fitted on to the Land Rover's bonnet for sea crossings, thereby avoiding extra shipping costs.

The adventure was fully reported in *Motor* in August 1955. The entire journey, even more arduous then than now because of the lack of metalled roads, was undertaken without serious mechanical difficulties, punctures being the chief problem. As is the case with Land Rover expeditions today, the vehicle was pressed into use on several occasions to rescue the stranded vehicles of other travellers.

There's nothing more demanding than an overland trip from Australia to Britain, especially when it begins with a grand tour Down Under,

and the fact that three people did just this in an 80-inch Land Rover in 1954–5 added fuel to the fire as far as the enthusiast movement was concerned.

The One Ten's first adventure

An off-roading adventure with a One Ten in the Western Highlands of Scotland was reported in detail in a motoring magazine in the same week as the new Land Rover was introduced at the Geneva Motor Show in March 1983.

The Trident Green V8 County Station Wagon CWK 20Y was driven by *Autocar* a couple of weeks before the launch in a bid to find out just how good the new vehicle was. The journey included 85mph (137kph) motorway cruising and, after the short ferry crossing to Skye, some driving on one of the island's tracks – during which the journalists got themselves stuck, requiring rescue.

Later, they drove part of General Wade's Military Road, an epic cross-country route, which the team entered near Fort Augustus at the southern end of Loch Ness. On reaching impossibly deep snow they decided to turn round, only to get one wheel stuck in a very deep pothole with the chassis sitting on ice. The only way out was to jack up each corner in turn, using the standard wheel-change jack, and build up the surface beneath the wheels.

Despite the problems which, they failed to admit, were mostly of their own making, they rated the new vehicle very highly. It was, in fact, a far-sighted story to publish; even before the One Ten was officially launched, it had been apparent to *Autocar* that this was just the sort of use people would be putting it to in the years to come.

It was a good and prophetic first for the magazine.

Model mania

The press was universally enthusiastic about the Land Rover, which undoubtedly encouraged the feeling of warmth many motorists also felt towards it. In 1955 the *Woodworker* magazine showed in great detail how to make an extremely realistic wooden model.

Model making was an important component of the hobby scene in the days before television ruled our lives, and the *Woodworker* Land Rover model would not have been devised and published had the editor not felt there was an enthusiastic following for the vehicle. The model, constructed in plywood and hardboard, was exceptionally realistic. The overall length wasn't given, but the sides were 1ft 2in (0.36m) long, making it quite large.

Since those days, interest in model Land Rovers has kept pace with the enthusiast movement generally, reflecting popular passion for the vehicle. By the time the One Ten appeared in 1983 Land Rover models had been well established in their own right for several decades, and self-build modelling remains very much part of the Land Rover world. However, today's do-it-yourself enthusiasts use kits with parts prefabricated in plastic and white metal. The detail can be impressive: recent introductions include 1/76 scale models of the British Army's Defender XD Wolf, with such options as Fitted-for-Radio or non FFR, right- or left-hand drive, and alternative 'handed' windscreen wipers.

That the model scene mirrors the general enthusiasm for Land Rovers, and in some ways provides a barometer of enthusiasm for the real thing, is evidenced by the mini-industry which has developed around it. Commercial leader of the Land Rover model world is David Mitchell, who runs the world's largest dedicated-marque model business in parallel with his Landcraft off-road training centre at Bala in North Wales. Dave has a stock list of more than 500 items – all of them Land Rovers – and sells to customers around the world. The business developed from his own interest in miniature Land Rovers which, in turn, had grown out of a life-long involvement with the vehicles. The earliest Land Rover model of which Dave is aware is a Dinky version of a Mersey Tunnel Police Series I 80-inch, produced when the 80-inch was in production. There may be even older ones.

The Series I has always been the most popular model within the range, followed by the Lightweight, and remains so despite a growing passion for models of the Defender range – itself the most popular type of Land Rover with today's enthusiasts.

↑ **Whether it is the compact 90 or the spacious 110, the County Station Wagon is the most civilised version of the Defender, proving that Land Rovers do not have to be uncomfortable. (Nick Dimbleby)**

Competition

The dual facts that the Association of Land Rover Clubs (ALRC) celebrated its 50th birthday in 1998, and that its member clubs are almost exclusively for Land Rover enthusiasts, says a great deal about the longevity of the Land Rover enthusiast movement. True, at one time there were far more saloon car owners represented beneath the ALRC's umbrella, but it is inescapable that the association would have long since disappeared but for the passion of Land Rover owners.

Competition has always played an important role for such enthusiasts. Indeed, it was the use of Land Rovers in off-road trials from about 1950 onwards which sparked the first truly active beginnings of the enthusiast movement. These car trials, like their two-wheel counterparts, are practically as old as motor vehicles, but they became especially popular in the years between the First and Second World Wars.

This passion for pitting machine and driver against terrain chosen for its difficulty was quick to return after the war, adding a sense of excitement

to the dreariness of the late 1940s. Within a few months of the first Land Rovers coming into general ownership in the second half of 1948, it was apparent that in any form of competition involving off-road hill climbs and mud, the Land Rover was, quite literally, in a class of its own. It didn't take long for special competitions for the four-wheel drive vehicles to come into being. Remember, except for the Jeep there were no other 4x4s available, and by now a great many Jeeps had fallen by the wayside because of the lack of spare parts.

The original Land Rover, despite its lack of power, was a brilliant trials car. The degree of traction was astonishing to people more accustomed to Austin 7 specials and the like, while the high ground clearance and tiny, 80-inch wheelbase gave it a niftiness through tightly marked sections, often over tree roots and rocks, which competitors loved.

Land Rovers developed, first to the 86-inch and then 88-inch Series Is, then Series IIs, IIAs and IIIs, and then into the ultimate incarnation of the breed, the Ninety. But, throughout, the original 80-inch remained the favourite of triallers, although many different, and always more powerful, engines were experimented with.

The ultimate trials car, however, was not destined to arrive until someone had the inspiration to fit a Rover V8 engine into a Series I 80-inch chassis. It is not known when this was done for the first time, although it was certainly before the launch of the Range Rover in 1970.

Passion for the V8 as a trials engine intensified when people realised just how supreme the Range Rover was in off-road situations. In turn, the Range Rover made life easier for trials enthusiasts, for much-modified versions of that vehicle's permanent four-wheel drive transmission were transplanted into many a trialler, overcoming the hitherto almost insurmountable problem of finding a transmission that was tough enough to survive the torque of the V8 in competition, yet was suitable for four-wheel drive.

For many years it was this passion for the Series I and, of course, other Land Rovers as competitive machinery which drove the enthusiast movement. The machines' capabilities drew trials enthusiasts to them, while the spin-off was a growing general interest in Land Rovers for off-road enjoyment.

⬇ **This challenge-prepared 90 is nearing the limit of what is possible. A few more degrees and it would be in danger of tipping onto its nose! (Simon Hodder)**

Then, in the 1960s, the interest in recreational vehicles began to develop in its own right as owners started to look upon the motor car as more than the functional machine it had been in the decade or so following the end of hostilities in 1945. To begin with the Land Rover had it all its own way, and a great many Series IIs and IIAs were bought by people eager to extend their leisure time with camping, caravanning, and boating, for which the Land Rover was perfect, but by the time the Range Rover appeared on the scene there was also considerable 4x4 choice from the USA and Japan.

However, the Range Rover refocused attention on Solihull machinery, and the growing movement was given a big shot in the arm by wild enthusiasm for the new vehicle. You had to be pretty well-off to afford one – in its first year the Range Rover cost £2,000 (compared with £1,300 for an MGB

GT) – but the rave reviews stimulated many less well-off buyers into choosing Series III Station Wagons instead.

By 1980 Land Rover devotees were among the most passionate of all motorists. However, it was the Defender family which would have the most positive impact on Land Rover enthusiasm. I remember very clearly returning from the 1983 Geneva Motor Show, launch pad of the One Ten, positively burning with praise for what Land Rover had achieved. This, in turn, spurred me to persuade my employers, IPC, to allow me to launch Britain's first full-scale, glossy, 4x4 magazine, *4-Wheel Drive*, to compete with David Bowyer's *Overlander* newsletter, itself about to be turned into the glossy publication *Off-Road*. My own launch, in 1984, coincided more or less with the introduction of the Ninety.

The mid-1980s were a great turning point for

↑ **From early days the Series I has been a favourite machine for trials competitors, where agility and excellent ground clearance are important. (Nick Dimbleby)**

the Land Rover movement, which was already a force to be reckoned with. Though the two new magazines were not dedicated solely to Land Rovers the Solihull marque inevitably dominated both. And in enthusiast terms the Ninety has shown itself to be the most significant vehicle produced by Land Rover. A number of specialist companies dedicated to supplying parts for older models also made their first appearance at this time, and some of them, such as John Craddock, have since grown into world-renowned organisations.

The two specialist magazines were a natural marketplace for four-wheel drive enthusiasts and the traders who relied on them, and served to stimulate further the growing interest in off-road driving for fun, and recreational 4x4 vehicles.

But other events also encouraged growing interest in four-wheel drive. By 1985 the 4x4 products of Japanese manufacturers were being promoted heavily and were selling well, considerably raising the profile of off-road vehicles. This process in turn would, in due course, be good for the Land Rover movement. Most of the Far Eastern vehicles were good products, with high standards of comfort, light

DID YOU KNOW?

On Safari

Africa was always a principal destination for Land Rovers, but when South Africa imposed 100 per cent duty on imported vehicles in a bid to deter massive imports from Japan, Solihull faced a serious problem. The way round this was for completely knocked-down (CKD) kits to be assembled at a large plant in Cape Town, and it was from here that the basic vehicles for some strange-looking special safari Land Rovers, capable of seating 16, were supplied for conversion by local specialists. A particularly popular series was constructed on 110-inch and 127-inch chassis, many with 6x6 modification by Safari Centre of Johannesburg.

The curiosity value alone must have worked wonders for the image of Land Rover. But, on a more practical level, many thousands of fairly wealthy individuals have been introduced to the capability and reliability of Land Rovers by being ferried around the unforgiving terrain of southern Africa on Defender-based vehicles. That sort of experience tends to leave a lasting impression.

controls, good looks, and excellent engines and gearboxes.

Yet, for all the appeal of Japanese 4x4s – the Mitsubishi Shogun, in particular, being quite capable of out-performing Land Rovers (but not the Range Rover) in all respects other than

difficult off-roading – enthusiasm for Land Rovers remained unaffected. Many users of working Land Rovers, farmers in particular, switched to Mitsubishi, Daihatsu, and Isuzu at about this time, as did plenty of people in the Range Rover marketplace, but within a few years they would mostly have returned to Solihull machinery.

All this time club membership was growing quite rapidly. Competition, which had done so much to establish the Land Rover enthusiast movement, began to take second place to fun off-roading, with a steady influx of Land Rovers on to Britain's network of green lanes, and the establishment of purpose-designed off-road driving centres. The first off-road driving schools began to do quite well.

Then, in 1987, the world's first specialist Land Rover magazine appeared in the form of *Land Rover Owner*. The new publication was both a measure of

how far the enthusiast movement had come, and the catalyst for much of the rapid growth thereafter.

The magazine came at just the right time. The One Ten and Ninety had been around for four and three years respectively, and were popular with enthusiasts, many of whom used the new vehicles to replace their old Series IIIs. In other cases the sheer attractiveness and capability of the coil-sprung Land Rovers brought fresh faces into the fold.

From this point on the Land Rover's dedicated followers grew rapidly in numbers, the movement getting a further shot in the arm with the running of the first Land Rover show at Billing Aquadrome, Northampton, in 1990. Organised by the original management team of *Land Rover Owner*, headed by the dynamic Richard Green, this annual event has ever since brought together countless thousands of enthusiasts in the

↑ **The Defender 110 is an ideal vehicle for expeditions to the difficult terrain of northern and Saharan Africa. (Nick Dimbleby)**

↖ **Well before the launch of the first of the Defender family, greenlaning had been a popular form of off-roading for owners of leaf-sprung Land Rovers. Comfort levels were not up to those of the later coil-sprung vehicles, though. (Nick Dimbleby)**

The Range Rover was a success from the start, stimulating further interest in Land Rovers generally, as well as exceeding expectations in its own right. The original body lines, as in this very early example, were destined to remain fundamentally unchanged until the first series went out of production a quarter of a century later. (Nick Dimbleby)

→ This is the first prototype of the Ninety, with a 90-inch wheelbase, and now lives alongside the second prototype, which had the production wheelbase of 92.9in, at the Dunsfold Collection in Surrey. (James Taylor)

celebration of all things Land Rover. The show, and the magazine with which it was associated, played a major role in cementing the various factions of the movement into a cohesive whole, particularly in its first five years.

'Billing', as it is known by Land Rover people worldwide, is by far the largest and most important event of its type. As a single-marque jamboree it has no equal.

enthusiast-owned Discoverys over recent years.

And, as ever, the Range Rover remains highly popular. Attend any gathering of Land Rover people and there will always be an assortment of Range Rovers – maybe ancient, and obviously well past their best, sometimes alongside nearly new 'mark IIs'.

That the enthusiast movement has been important to the sales of more modern Land

Into the future

It is an inescapable fact that the Defender series of vehicles has been particularly significant in the development of the Land Rover movement. There's the obvious appeal to the keen off-roader, of course, but the sheer usefulness of the range, and the family-carrying ability of the One Ten in particular, makes them especially suitable for anybody who enjoys the outdoor life. Many a camping or caravanning family has bought a Defender 110 purely because of its appeal as a lifestyle-related vehicle, and has then found within weeks that they've become enthusiasts.

The Discovery, too, has been important, with many owners finding unexpected enthusiasm after years of driving large, but extremely bland, estate cars and other 4x4s. Existing enthusiasts, too, have taken to this vehicle, in some cases adding, say, a five-year-old Discovery to, perhaps, a Series Land Rover. The Billing Show, always a barometer of ownership, has seen a marked increase in

Rovers is beyond doubt. Land Rover itself, at one time slow to even acknowledge the existence of enthusiasts, now makes much of its heritage and is eager to participate at major events.

There seems little doubt that the movement will continue to flourish, and that the Defender will remain central to it. With greater emphasis than ever before on environmental issues, it is possible that some off-roading activities may come under pressure, but this is unlikely to harm the movement in any way.

It is thought that the massive success of the Freelander, which seems set to introduce more people to Land Rover ownership than any other model, will be generally good for both club memberships and general enthusiasm, as owners seek to explore the more-extensive capabilities of the Defender – the ultimate Land Rover.

In some ways, the enormously appealing Defender is safeguarding the future of the movement. It will surely continue in this role for many years to come.

The Discovery is enormously popular with enthusiasts, who admire its unique mixture of comfort, space, off-roading ability and value-for-money. Here, the off-road stability is being put to the test. (Nick Dimbleby)

CHAPTER 2
LEGENDS ARE MADE OF THIS

The birth of Land Rover is one of the most oft-repeated stories in the history of motoring. It's a tale of inspiration and determination, of great timing and imaginative engineering and, above all, it's a story about making the most out of difficult circumstances. Yet for all that, the story of the subsequent success of first the machine, and then the Land Rover marque, is perhaps even more remarkable.

The original Land Rover was thrown together extremely rapidly, based to no small degree on the Second World War's ubiquitous Jeep. Using whatever components happened to be available within the Rover organisation, in a factory in which production was otherwise virtually at a standstill, the Land Rover was intended as no more than a stop-gap earner to tide the company over until real money began pouring into its coffers when the post-war world woke up to the enormous attractions of Rover cars. But, as is often the way, subsequent events failed to stick to the script.

Demand for the Land Rover exceeded all expectations by a very long way, while there were very few buyers for Rover's cars, which were little more than reawakened pre-war models. The Land Rover became better, but the cars failed to pull themselves out of the high-quality, yet stuffy mould which, before the war, had served the company well. The Land Rover production lines became ever more important to Rover's precarious finances, and the short-term lifespan intended for the utility machine evolved into permanence.

The Jeep's influence

The true beginning of the Land Rover story does not go back to the advent of four-wheel drive technology in the earliest days of the 20th century, nor to the all-terrain tanks of the First World War, but to the best-known and best-loved vehicle of the Second World War: the Jeep.

The wartime Jeep was to have a profound and permanent influence because it inspired the development of four-wheel-drive motoring throughout much of the world. Most importantly, in the post-war period the Jeep's qualities were to lead to the Land Rover. For that reason alone the Jeep's story is one which should not be forgotten or overlooked.

Entering service in 1941, the Jeep was the result of a far-sighted decision by the US military that, because it seemed inevitable that America would be drawn into the war raging in Europe, there would be enormous advantages in having a lightweight, general purpose, four-wheel-drive vehicle. As everybody knows, the resultant vehicle became known as the 'Jeep' because of its 'General Purpose' (GP) classification. Prototypes were built with astonishing speed, in order to meet the urgency dictated in its specification requirement of June 1940. Quickest to appear was that of the Bantam Car Company, closely followed by Willys-

← The humble Series I went through more than 60 years of evolution to become today's Defender. This famous and beautifully preserved example is owned by Land Rover, and is seen here being driven at Eastnor Castle. (Simon Hodder)

DID YOU KNOW?
Speed limit
The fact that the first Land Rovers could hardly exceed 50mph (80kph) was not at all a problem for drivers of the day, and the performance of the vehicles should be viewed in this context.

The Land Rover had been classified by the authorities as a commercial vehicle, although to be truthful there had been considerable uncertainty as to its proper place in law. In the post-war period all commercial vehicles were limited to a maximum speed of 30mph (48kph), and woe betide the driver of any commercial who went faster. Consequently, Land Rovers trundled along at the same speed as coal delivery lorries and the like. However, by the 1950s people were beginning to question the 30mph limit for light commercial vehicles and, although it was very rare to see any car – other than the occasional Jaguar – doing more than about 55mph (88kph) Land Rover drivers in particular were starting to feel aggrieved. An appeal to the Law Lords in 1956 against a speeding conviction settled the matter, and Land Rovers were decreed to be car-type vehicles, thus freeing them from the 30mph restriction.

↗ This is the machine
which played an important
part in the Second World
War, the Willys Jeep,
and which inspired the
creation of the Land Rover
during 1947. (James Taylor
Collection)

Overland, and Ford. In the event, Bantam was unable to meet production requirements, despite coming up with the best design, and Willys got the contract, although many of the Bantam's features were incorporated. Though Ford was beaten by Willys because the latter's engine was better, Ford nevertheless produced a quarter of a million Jeeps under licence, compared to the 360,000 built by Willys by the end of the war.

Wartime service wasn't the end of the Jeep story in America, with non-military versions proving popular amongst various user groups from 1945 onwards. In Britain, though, there was no prospect of buying a foreign-built vehicle at the time – or at least, not a new one.

Jeeps had been a very familiar sight on British roads throughout America's participation in the war, and people liked them. More to the point, many British servicemen had seen them in action, and had been highly impressed. Many of the Jeeps which survived the war were sold off in Britain at the end of hostilities, and such was the vehicle's reputation and usefulness – especially to farmers, whose only means of cross-country transport hitherto had been by tractor or horse

– that any Jeep in working order was sure to find a buyer.

One was snapped up by Maurice Wilks, not just a farmer but also Rover's Chief Engineer, who found the little truck perfect in the mud of his rain-soaked Welsh farm. The story goes that Maurice's brother Spencer asked what he would do when the Jeep wore out, spares not being available, and Maurice promptly stated he would buy another Jeep. 'Why don't we build our own?' one is alleged to have said to the other.

One problem, and there were many, was that Rover's Board still saw its future in cars, and they didn't want to commit themselves to anything which might get in the way of car production once they had a new medium-sized saloon ready. But the huge Solihull factory – German bombers had destroyed the company's principal factory and head offices in Coventry in 1940 – could not sit idle. It had to start producing something, and was obliged to play a role in the all-important export drive, one of the few ways of bringing desperately needed foreign money into Britain.

Following the conversation between Maurice and Spencer Wilks, Rover's Gordon Bashford

← Originally it was thought that a centre-steer design would simplify production because it would be suitable for left- and right-hand-drive markets. However, the prototype showed it was not such a good idea, and the concept was dropped. (James Taylor Collection)

↓ The machine which started the legend was simply called a Land Rover, and only became known as Series I when the second series was introduced in April 1958. Originally, it was seen merely as a stop-gap vehicle, providing production in an otherwise little-used factory amid the austerity of post-war Britain. (Nick Dimbleby)

went off to buy a couple of surplus Jeeps …
and the Land Rover story began. Maurice Wilks
reputedly came up with the new vehicle's name
during that same fortuitous conversation.

Rapid popularity

Given the extremely enthusiastic following the Jeep
had built up in its own short but important lifetime,
it is not at all surprising that the Land Rover would
quickly achieve enormous popularity, which in turn
developed into a cult status similar to that enjoyed
by the Willys Jeep.

Under the direction of Robert Boyle – but with
Maurice Wilks keeping a fatherly eye on everything –
the design of the Land Rover began to take shape in
the second quarter of 1947. It was a stop-gap vehicle,
remember, so expensive tooling was not part of the
plan, and this dictated the welded steel chassis and,
for production vehicles, simply formed body panels
with a marked absence of curves. Steel was a rare
commodity and supplies were mainly restricted to
guaranteed export business, so only the chassis and
mechanical parts would be steel; on the other hand,
there was plenty of aluminium which, although much
more expensive than steel, had the extra advantage
of being easier to work by hand.

In order to make it possible to utilise a single
production line for both home and export orders
it was felt that a centre-steer vehicle would be
ideal, so this was the format of the first prototype
completed in mid-1947. The Jeep influence at this
stage was quite profound, with an open, door-less
body, curved wings and wheel arches, and even a
Jeep chassis – although this was because Rover's
own design wasn't yet complete.

By the time the first pilot build vehicles were
emerging from Solihull, very early in 1948, things
had changed considerably. Gone were centre
steering, curved wings, and some of the wheel
arch sweep, along with the feeble 1,389cc engine
of the prototypes, which had been used in the
pre-war Rover 10. It was these pilot build Land
Rovers which were used to launch the vehicle at
the Amsterdam Motor Show in April 1948, and
to demonstrate the usefulness of Rover's new
utility machine at agricultural shows around Britain

→ **Solihull has known
plenty of milestones. This
photograph shows the
factory celebration for
the 250,000th model built.
(James Taylor Collection)**

during the following few months. Full production commenced in July 1948, an amazing achievement for traditionally slow-moving Rover.

As far as most customers were concerned, the first production vehicles were the same as the ones they'd seen in demonstrations. They were pick-ups, finished in light green, but significant differences included re-routeing the exhaust to the right-hand side instead of the left, non-galvanised chassis, and bolt-on front bumper. Power came from a slightly modified version of the 1,595cc inlet-over-exhaust engine developed for the P3 saloon, as was the gearbox, with the useful addition of a step-down ratio and permanent four-wheel drive with a freewheel system in the front driveline.

Nobody knew it, but this was the forerunner of the entire family, the patriarch which would establish the Land Rover as the principal go-anywhere working vehicle throughout much of the world. Its immediate success, and the passions it aroused, surprised most of those who had been connected with its development, not least Rover's Board of Directors.

Prophetically, Rover's Chairman announced a few days before Christmas 1948 – a time when good news was hard to come by in austerity-stricken post-war Britain – that the level of orders already received pointed to the possibility of Land Rover output exceeding the company's car production figures. A year later it had done just that.

Direct line

Today's Defender is a direct descendant of the 1948 Land Rover, and it's a great tribute to the original design that you could place a Land Rover built in 2010 in a time machine, take it back to 1948, and see it recognised instantly. The appearance of the original machine might have been a product of necessity and austerity, but it's a shape which has stood the test of time better than that of any other motor vehicle.

The square-cut lines of a Land Rover denote a functionality which is unique, and which in the Land Rover is very much more than skin deep. Today's Land Rover is altogether more competent than the vehicle which started it all – and so it should be after more than five decades of steady development – but the 1948 Land Rover was

↑ **Land Rover tried very hard to project the Series I as a vehicle suitable for hard work on the farm. This photograph shows a 107-inch earning its keep. (James Taylor Collection)**

→ **Although quite a snug fit, there was ample working space around the 1.6-litre engine in the early Series I 80-inch models. (James Taylor Collection)**

just as capable of doing everything asked of it as today's Td5 or Puma.

Nobody really knows for sure, but it is quite probable that when Maurice Wilks appointed Robert Boyle to head up the small project team which gave the world the Land Rover, he thought no further than giving farmers like himself a vehicle which would make life easier. It was only as the project began to take shape that the export potential began to dawn – hence the attempt, initially, to produce it with central steering – and it was only after the Amsterdam Motor Show launch that the vehicle's appeal to other user groups, including private individuals, started to show through.

It's tempting, today, to relate everything to the way things are done now, with car makers producing vehicles aimed at clearly identified, and verified, market sectors. That a single individual had the idea for a vehicle, and that the vehicle itself then attracted the user groups to it, seems remarkable. But that's the way things were when the Land Rover came into being.

Again, seen from today's perspective the original Land Rover might seem a pretty uninspiring vehicle. The inlet-over-exhaust 1,595cc

engine gave it a top speed of around 50mph (80kph), with 40-45mph (65–72kph) cruising, and it was extremely basic: you paid extra for doors, side-screens, canvas roof for the cab, passenger seat, and starting handle. But the price until October 1948 was only £450, and even the huge jump from this to £540 including the extras, left the vehicle within the 'affordable' category for most potential users. There's also the point that, at the time, even many everyday cars could not pass 60mph (96kph) and were seriously lacking in creature comforts.

The simplicity and functionality appealed greatly to a small number of motoring journalists who were among the first non-Rover people to drive the Land Rover. On 30 April 1948 *Commercial Motor* wrote in glowing terms, under the headline 'A maid-of-all-work for the farmer', about the outstanding features of this new Rover. The magazine was enthusiastic about the sturdiness of the engine, and commended Rover for giving the vehicle such an excellent cooling system with the needs of stationary work in mind. In its detailed description of the transmission it commented on the wisdom of the freewheel device incorporated into the front drive from the transfer box. Rover was also praised for providing, uniquely, three auxiliary power points: at the front for a mechanical winch; the main power take-off provision at the rear; and the central power take-off facility for powering portable plant carried inside the vehicle.

Less concerned with the pure working nature of the Land Rover was *Autocar*, whose first description of the vehicle, also on 30 April 1948, contained a number of far-seeing comments. 'So much has been said and written in the past about the so-called People's Car, much of it nonsense, that the advent of a really practical British vehicle which goes far beyond that over-publicised proposal should be hailed with genuine acclamation', stated one of Britain's most-respected magazines. The article went on to: 'If the world has to be strictly economical for years to come, is not this the sort of car that most of us need, one that is entirely practical and essentially usable?'

Comments like this led to considerable early interest in the Land Rover, which grew to fever pitch over the next few months as potential users were able to view the few demonstrators available and, if they were very lucky, to have a brief test drive. By the end of that year the future of the Land Rover was beginning to look very secure.

On the farm

The massive enthusiasm generated within a few months of the first Land Rovers becoming available illustrates vividly just how right the vehicle was, and how timely was its introduction. Yet it was in some ways less useful on the farm than Land Rover's advertising would have you believe.

The most outstanding of post-war agricultural innovations was the much-loved Ferguson tractor, produced in very large numbers by Standard from 1946, which gave farmers the working power they needed at the time. This could pull ploughs, harrows, rollers, and harvesting binders, and had power-take-off and pulley drive (for threshing machines, pumps, circular saws, etc). Rover attempted to portray the Land Rover as being capable of most of these same

↓ **This publicity photograph was taken for the launch of the Series II 109-inch, a wheelbase destined to become highly popular around the world, accounting for three-quarters of Land Rover sales. The 109-inch was introduced towards the end of Series I production, for the 1957 model year. (James Taylor Collection)**

Levels of purchase tax varied in the austere years following the Second World War but were, to put it mildly, punitive. As late as 1959 (a year after the introduction of the Series II), the price differential between basic Land Rovers, which did not attract purchase tax, and Station Wagons, which did, was considerable:

Model	Basic body	Station Wagon
88-inch	£650	£1,049
109-inch	£730	£1,219

Most of the extra cost of the Station Wagons was purchase tax, a factor which inhibited sales and actually influenced manufacturing decisions. In the first year of Land Rover production, a very pretty Station Wagon was built on the 80-inch chassis and introduced at the Commercial Motor Show in October 1948. Despite having very pleasant lines, seating for seven, winding windows in the front doors and other refinements, purchase tax pushed the price so high that few customers were found, and the vehicle was discontinued in 1951.

duties, but, in truth, it could not plough and wasn't much use for much of the other field work that tractors and horses took in their stride. Though by the early 1950s horses were beginning to fade out from heavy work, they were replaced by tractors, not Land Rovers.

However, since the owners of most smaller farms could not afford to run two cars (many couldn't afford even one), Land Rovers began to replace some of their existing vehicles – including wartime Jeeps as they wore out. This is how the Land Rover started to become a permanent feature of British rural life. Only on large farms, which in 1948–50 were few and far between, were Land Rovers bought to work alongside tractors.

In truth, it didn't take very long for Rover to realise that the new vehicle had limited appeal as an agricultural machine, although it was continually promoted as such, and orders came in from a much wider selection of buyers than had been expected. This encouraged Rover to introduce its Station Wagon at the 1948 Commercial Motor Show. This was a delightful seven-seater based on the standard 80-inch chassis, but it only lasted until 1951, principally because of its high price.

Important early developments were the dropping of the freewheel for the 1951 model year, replacing it with a dog clutch, and the facility of two-wheel drive in high gears as an alternative to the permanent four-wheel drive in low ratios. Another key move, during 1951, was the introduction of a 1,997cc engine, derived from the original 1.5-litre unit. But this engine was not used for long, and a new unit with the same dimensions was introduced in late 1953, overshadowed by the launch at the same time of the more useful 86-inch model (which replaced the 80-inch) and the all-new 107-inch vehicle, available initially only as a pick-up.

Pointing the way forward, a second seven-seat Station Wagon was introduced in 1954, based on the more practical 86-inch body. This was followed two years later by the very appealing ten-seat Station Wagon built on the 107-inch frame.

In late 1956 both wheelbase types gained an extra two inches, the resulting 88-inch and 109-inch versions being destined to remain in service until they were replaced by the Ninety and One Ten vehicles, which later became the Defender. The reason for the extra length was the introduction, although not until June 1957, of Land Rover's first diesel engine, a 2,052cc unit specially developed by Rover for its 4x4.

So, with a choice of petrol and diesel engines, 88-inch and 109-inch chassis, and different body types, the legend of the Land Rover was firmly in the making. And this was before the end of the first series.

Birthday party

The tenth birthday of the Land Rover was celebrated in great style, and what better way to acknowledge the huge success of Rover's 'stop-gap', production-filling, post-war vehicle than with the introduction of a second version?

The Series II, launched in April 1958, was 1.5in (38mm) wider and looked a little sleeker, with some slight curves to parts of the body to reduce the hard angularity of the Series I, more shaping to the bonnet panel, lower body sides hiding the exhaust pipe and chassis sides, and neater door hinges. There was no mistaking it for a Land Rover – indeed, you had to know your Land Rovers to be able to tell it was a different vehicle – and in making the new model so like the one it replaced Solihull's designers and engineers had laid the groundwork for one of the vehicle's more important characteristics for the physical similarity of the entire Land Rover family, from Series I to Defender, has proved an important factor in ongoing enthusiasm for the marque.

Of course, things had to change mechanically, and at Land Rover changes have very often been for the better, unlike many car companies. The key development introduced with the Series II was the use of the 2,286cc petrol engine, giving 25bhp more than the 2-litre unit it replaced and, as time would tell, immense reliability and ruggedness.

The new engine was, in fact, a development of the 2,052cc diesel unit. It was to prove a crucial power plant for Land Rover, and lived long enough to be used in the One Ten in 1983 and in Series IIIs produced for two years after that. Unfortunately, early buyers of 88-inch Series IIs had to make do with the old petrol engine until supplies had been used up, although the

new engine was fitted in the 109-inch. And if you wanted a Station Wagon, you had to make do with the old-model 107-inch because the 109-inch Series II Station Wagon was not ready until several months later.

The Series II was more than a re-engined and (slightly) restyled version of what had gone before. Its extra width made it more stable on side slopes and gave it a better steering lock. The ride, too, was better. The Series II gave way to the Series IIA in early Autumn 1961. A very significant introduction at the same time – but not the reason for the IIA designation, which was to permit a new chassis numbering system throughout Rover – was the upgrading of the diesel to 2,286cc, giving it more power and torque and much better reliability.

Other than the introduction of the Forward Control version on the 109-inch chassis, little of importance happened to the 88-inch and 109-inch utilities, other than the introduction of the 2,652cc six-cylinder engine option for the long wheelbase

↓ One of the less well-known engines in the Land Rover story is the six-cylinder 2,652cc IOE unit introduced for the 1967 model year in the Series IIA 109-inch. (James Taylor Collection)

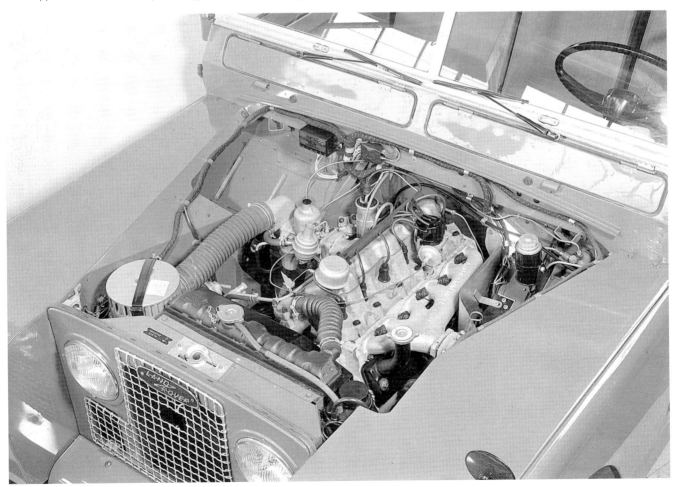

↑ The Range Rover, with its long-travel springs and extreme axle articulation, set new standards of off-road performance from its first days, as this shot of the amazing vehicle displays. It was to be 13 years after the Range Rover's launch before this sort of performance would be possible with a utility model. (Nick Dimbleby)

in 1967. This engine remained an option in the subsequent Series III until the Stage 1 V8 was introduced in 1980.

Range Rover's influence

The Range Rover was launched in June 1970 and was destined to have a profound effect on the fortunes of Land Rover as well as a major impact on the leisure four-wheel drive market. Last, but not least, it would greatly influence the technical thinking of the fourth generation of 'working' Land Rovers in 13 years' time.

Although Solihull's production lines had been turning out Land Rovers for 22 years, the Range Rover was the company's first genuinely new vehicle since the Series I. It would revolutionise 4x4 thinking so much that by the time production of what was then known as the Classic finally ceased in 1996 it was still the undisputed class leader.

It came on to the market a full year before the Series IIA Land Rover gave way to the Series III, yet not one aspect of the Range Rover's advanced technical specification was used in the Series III – although, if Solihull had wished to take the plunge, it could have continued the Series IIA for another couple of years, and then brought out a mechanically advanced Series III. This was not to be, however, and it was left entirely to the Range Rover to establish the principles of low-rate long-travel coil springs, extreme axle articulation, permanent four-wheel drive, and high standards of performance and comfort.

Land Rover's reluctance to apply the benefits of the Range Rover to the utility range can be explained by the conservatism of the markets the latter served, and by a shortage of cash. Both are good reasons, but the fact remains that Solihull had, in the Range Rover, the basis for entirely fresh thinking in its range of 'working' models. Nobody will ever know how much harm was done by not moving faster.

Growing enthusiasm

By the time the Series III was introduced in September 1971 there was already, as we have seen, an enthusiast movement. Furthermore, the launch of the Range Rover in 1970 had resulted in a great deal of marque awareness among groups not in the 'front line' of Solihull's customers.

Only the reasonably well-off could afford a Range Rover, but people were now looking towards Land Rover for everyday and leisure vehicles. The Series IIA had been quite difficult for some people to drive, with its absence of synchromesh on the lower two gears, but there were no such problems with the all-synchro Series III. The dash, too, was more car-like, and although all versions were now fitted with a 9.5-inch heavy-duty clutch, the pedal operating pressure was reduced considerably.

At the time the Series III arrived in the showrooms Land Rover had manufactured nearly 800,000 vehicles. Some 75 per cent of annual production was being exported, and although many of the overseas markets were still more than happy with the simple nature of the Land Rover, the situation was destined to change, both at home and abroad, as the end of the 1970s approached.

At the beginning of the decade there was little opposition to the Land Rover, either as a working or a leisure vehicle, but as the 1980s loomed, on the horizon there were genuine alternatives, and Japan was getting in on the 4x4 act. Those people who had been happy to use a Series III as an everyday commuter and weekend 'fun' car were beginning to realise that nimbler and easier-to-drive

↓ Although introduced after the Range Rover, the Series III Land Rover remained a very basic machine. The concessions to more car-like qualities included an improved dash and all-synchro gearbox. (Nick Dimbleby)

four-wheel vehicles might now be available.

On the other hand, the Land Rover enthusiast movement was gaining strength, and continued to do so with increasing force throughout the life of the Series III. There's little doubt that the more car-like qualities of the third generation Land Rover helped to bring people into Land Rover ownership but, at the same time, there was also a groundswell of interest in Series IIs and IIAs. Series Is became simultaneously even more popular as triallers, many being fitted with V8 engines, while others were drawn into the burgeoning classic car scene.

The final important event of the pre-coil-sprung Land Rovers was the introduction in February 1979 (but for overseas markets only) of the V8-powered 109-inch Series III, which was not available to British buyers until 1980. Known as the Stage 1 V8, this high-powered Series III was a direct result of massive Government investment in the then British Leyland Corporation under the Ryder Plan, and was a replacement for the six-cylinder model, whose engine had not been as successful as hoped.

The Stage 1 Land Rover showed the way forward, with the use of the Range Rover's permanent four-wheel drive and lockable centre differential, and it created a lot of interest with user groups who were desperately in need of more power than the four-cylinder engines could ever give, and better reliability under heavy-use conditions than the inlet-over-exhaust six-cylinder unit. It made an immediate impact in the 4x4 leisure market, especially in the highly attractive County Station Wagon form, and showed that Land Rover could compete – and beat – the rest of the world when it came to go-anywhere vehicles suitable to the new type of buyer.

Good though it was, however, the Stage 1 V8 did not lead directly to the first of the new generation of Land Rovers. Instead, all the lessons learned since 1948 with the utility vehicles, along with the technical developments which had made the Range Rover one of the world's most notable and successful 4x4s, would go into the melting pot from which an entirely new type of Land Rover would emerge in 1983.

↓ The first factory-produced Land Rover with good road-going performance was the Stage 1 V8, available only in the 109-inch version, and retaining the leaf springing of the rest of the Series III models. (Nick Dimbleby)

Specifications

Dates are for model years.

SERIES I 80-INCH (1948–54)

Engine (1948–51)	1,595cc IOE four-cylinder
Power	50bhp @ 4,000rpm
Torque	80lb ft @ 2,000rpm
Engine (1952–4)	1,997cc IOE four-cylinder
Power	52bhp @ 4,000rpm
Torque	101lb ft @ 1,500rpm
Transmission (1948–50)	Permanent four-wheel drive with front driveline freewheel; four-speed gearbox with transfer box
Transmission (1950–4)	Selectable four-wheel drive in high-ratios; permanent four-wheel drive in low; four-speed gearbox with transfer box
Steering	Recirculating ball, worm-and-nut system
Suspension	Live axles front and rear with semi-elliptic leaf springs and hydraulic dampers
Brakes	Hydraulic drums all round, with transmission parking brake
Dimensions	Wheelbase 80in (2.03m); track (front and rear) 50in (1.27m); length 123in (3.12m); width 61in (1.55m); height (1948–51) 70.5in (1.79m), (1951–4) 73.5in (1.87m)

SERIES I 86-INCH (1954–6)

As for 80-inch except: wheelbase 86in (2.18m); length 140.7in (3.57m); width 62.6in (1.59m); height 76in (1.93m).

SERIES I 107-INCH (1955–8)

As for 1954 80-inch except: wheelbase 107in (2.72m); length 173.5in (4.41m); width 62.6in (1.59m); height (basic model with hood) 83.5in (2.12m).

SERIES I 88-INCH (1957–8)

As for post-1952 80-inch except: 2,052cc ohv four-cylinder diesel engine option with 51bhp @ 3,500rpm and 87lb ft torque @ 2,000rpm; wheelbase 88in (2.23m); length 140.75in (3.57m); width 62.6in (1.59m); height 76in (1.93m).

SERIES I 109-INCH (1957–8)

As for 88-inch except: wheelbase 109in (2.77m); length 173in (4.39m); height 83.5in (2.12m).

SERIES II 88-INCH (1958–61)

Engine (petrol)	2,286cc ohv four-cylinder
Power	70bhp @ 4,250rpm
Torque	120lb ft @ 2,500rpm
Engine (diesel)	As Series I
Transmission	As Series I
Suspension	As Series I
Brakes	As Series I
Dimensions	Wheelbase 88in (2.23m); track 51.5in (1.31m); length 142.4in (3.62m); width 64in (1.63m); height 77.5in (1.97m)

SERIES II 109-INCH

As for 88-inch except: wheelbase 109in (2.77m); length 175in (4.44m); height 81in (2.06m).

SERIES IIA (1962–71)

Engine (petrol)	As Series II
Engine (diesel)	2,286cc ohv four-cylinder
Power	60bhp @ 4,000rpm
Torque	103lb ft @ 1,800rpm
Transmission	As Series II
Suspension	As Series II
Brakes	As Series II
Dimensions	As Series II

SERIES IIA 109-INCH

As for Series II 109-inch and, mechanically, Series IIA 88-inch except (from 1967): 2,625cc IOE six-cylinder engine option with 83bhp @ 4,500rpm and 128lb ft torque @ 1,500rpm.

SERIES III 88-INCH (1972–84)

As for Series IIA except: five-bearing crankshaft for four-cylinder engines from 1980; all-synchro gearbox.

SERIES III 109-INCH

As for 88-inch; dimensions as Series IIA; six-cylinder engine discontinued in 1980.

SERIES III 109-INCH V8 (1979–85)

As for standard 109-inch except: 3,528cc ohv V8 engine with 91bhp @ 3,500rpm and 166lb ft torque @ 2,000rpm; permanent four-wheel drive with lockable centre differential.

CHAPTER 3
BIRTH OF THE ONE TEN AND NINETY

A crucial step forward

It is true to say that Land Rover should have developed coil-sprung utility vehicles long before they did. The great success of the Range Rover was in no small part due to its extremely competent suspension and drive train, and there's no reason at all why Solihull's management should not have seen the way forward much earlier.

By the mid-1970s the Range Rover had established itself, and had proved very quickly that the combination of low-rate, long-travel coil springs, permanent four-wheel drive, good brakes, and plenty of power was virtually unbeatable. Yet Land Rover felt constrained by the traditionalism of much of its market, particularly in developing countries, and by the resistance to change of its core United Kingdom agricultural market. Furthermore, throughout the 1970s the company's military customers around the world seemed more than happy with the Series III.

There was no carved-in-stone plan to replace the Series III, and the various experimental projects which were based on different versions of the Range Rover chassis and its suspension and running gear were largely half-hearted, and not all of them were what might be deemed official. True, there were reasons for not rushing into a new vehicle, but with hindsight most of these were more in the nature of excuses.

The entire Rover organisation has been afflicted at various times by spells of complacency, arrogance, and ignorance – sometimes simultaneously. This has also been true of Land Rover, albeit to a lesser extent, but has here applied more to certain key individuals at specific periods rather than to Land Rover as a company.

Shortage of funds for investment in new vehicles is the reason usually trotted out to explain Land Rover's failure to bring out new models when, clearly, they have been needed. And, of course,

it's true, because Land Rover was always having to prop up the parent company, which failed consistently in the post-war years to come up with cars which the general public wanted. Even the much-vaunted P6, excellent model that it was, wasn't able to generate sufficient cash to ensure future investment. Much of that burden was shouldered by Land Rover, just as it had been before and has been subsequently.

Despite that, the automotive world was moving on so rapidly by the mid-1960s that the Series III should have had only a short life, and maybe should never have existed at all. It was launched after the Range Rover and the fact that, firstly, it was actually introduced, and secondly, that it soldiered on until the mid-1980s, doesn't say much for Land Rover's planning. It's not unreasonable to point an accusing finger at Land Rover and ask why it was not ready to replace the Series IIA with the first generation of the Defender family by the mid to late 1970s, instead of coming up with the Series III which, other than its all-gear synchromesh, was little better than the IIA.

When they finally arrived, the One Ten and Ninety used the Range Rover's suspension and transmission, and variations on its chassis. Even the body was a reworking of that used for the Series IIA and III. If this was the correct answer in 1983 – and history has proved that it was – then it would also have been the right solution in the 1970s.

In the event, this is how it happened …

DID YOU KNOW?
Playing safe
When the One Ten was introduced, Land Rover said the Series III would remain in production for five more years. Whether or not they meant it, this statement was probably intended to placate traditionalists and reassure military users. Series III production actually ceased just two years later.

Mixed motivations

From the viewpoint of the British market, the introduction – let alone the development – of the fourth series of 'working' or utility Land Rovers was done in a manner which was difficult to understand. The short wheelbase version of the then current Series III was by far the most popular with the principal users in the UK, who were somewhat mystified when the first of the coil-sprung generation was unveiled at the 1983 Geneva Motor Show.

There was an initial reaction among important user groups which didn't bode well for sales of the One Ten, as the new Land Rover was known. While those motoring journalists who had driven it wrote about it with enormous enthusiasm, and even those who had simply looked at it were glowing in their praise, Britain's farmers were not easily swayed by such opinions. They could not understand why the only wheelbase available was 110in (2.79m) when mostly they purchased short wheelbase models; they were perplexed that the same 2,286cc petrol and diesel engines which frustrated them in their

Series IIIs had been carried over; and, generally speaking, were not taken in by the fact that they could have a 3.5-litre V8 if they wished.

But what this key sector of the home market didn't know, and probably would not have been impressed by even if they had, was that the decision to introduce the new vehicles with the long wheelbase version had been taken with the worldwide market in mind.

Land Rover was, of course, obliged to think globally – most of its export sales were currently 109-inch models – and not simply in terms of its principal UK buyers, and time has proved that the introduction of the coil-sprung Land Rovers was, indeed, done with the right models, which were destined to remain fundamentally unchanged for a very long time. However, that is not to say that the birth of the One Ten, followed a year later by the Ninety, was all part of a carefully laid-down marketing strategy within the corridors of power at Solihull. Indeed, it is no exaggeration to say that the story behind the introduction of coil springs to utility Land Rovers is a typical example (for Rover/ Land Rover/British Leyland) of a catalogue of

⇩ **From the beginning, the Range Rover showed the way forward, yet traditionalism, and the lack of a definite plan for the future development of the Land Rover, delayed the introduction of the luxury vehicle's mechanical and suspension advantages into the utility vehicles. (Nick Dimbleby)**

← As this prototype shot shows, the development of the One Ten avoided anything revolutionary as far as appearance was concerned. Indeed, by using Range Rover technology for the mechanical side of the new Land Rover, just about everything was tried and tested. (James Taylor Collection)

missed opportunities, dead ends, and pure chance, such as characterised the conglomerate into which Rover and Land Rover had been poured.

There was never a plan, as such, to replace the Series III with a completely new model at a particular point in time. It was more a case of it being obvious that a replacement would be needed, and that coil springing would have to be part of the package – or even the basis of it – and that more power was essential.

Part of the reason it happened the way it did was an acute shortage of cash for new Land Rover models, despite the soar-away success of the Range Rover. The make-or-break Rover SD1 car was scheduled for launch in 1976 and £27 million – then a massive amount – was to be poured into the project, including a new factory. Inevitably, this impacted heavily on Land Rover's intentions and actions in the middle years of the decade.

The Ryder Report of 1975 recommended huge investment in Land Rover vehicles, and one high-profile result was the first effort at modernising the 109-inch Series III by fitting it with the V8 as an option in 1979. Known as the Stage 1 because it represented the first stage in the investment

DID YOU KNOW?
Robot workers
Land Rover used robot technology for the first time for the welding of the One Ten's chassis. This contained more than 400 welds and the 16 Asea robots achieved new levels of consistency, quality and productivity.

programme, the resultant vehicle had a flat front (because of the positioning of the engine) and permanent four-wheel drive. However, it was not the direct antecedent of the One Ten as some observers have subsequently concluded.

It was the Range Rover rather than a utility Land Rover that showed the way forward, and in 1976 – three years before the Stage 1 came on the scene – a first prototype of a new-generation Land Rover had been assembled using a standard 100-inch Range Rover chassis and a greatly cut-about Series III 109in body. The following year, another prototype was cobbled together – which is not a glib phrase, but a reflection of the way it actually happened – using a Range Rover chassis cut down from 100in (2.54m) to 90in (2.29m).

However, this V8-powered second prototype was seen essentially as a military vehicle, which it

Stronger door
Because of the door-mounted spare wheel, a third hinge was added to the rear door of the Station Wagon for extra strength, with a higher mounting point for the wheel which hitherto had to be removed when towing.

was hoped would replace the 88-inch Lightweight. But then the whole project was sideswiped by a decision to go back to a 100-inch plan, because it was hoped to produce an appropriate 100-inch chassis vehicle for an important order from the Swiss Army. This deal never happened, but more than 70 100-inch prototypes were built before the idea of producing a Land Rover based on the standard Range Rover chassis was abandoned in 1986 – which was three years after the launch of the One Ten.

Common sense suggested otherwise, but Land Rover was still hankering for some form of 100-inch vehicle as a replacement for the 88-inch. But there was also the question of the 109-inch model. Would it remain as it was, but with a revised chassis design, or would it be wiser to make a fresh

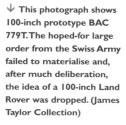

↓ **This photograph shows 100-inch prototype BAC 779T. The hoped-for large order from the Swiss Army failed to materialise and, after much deliberation, the idea of a 100-inch Land Rover was dropped. (James Taylor Collection)**

start? As it happened, there was already a 110-inch Range Rover chassis for ambulance conversions, and a 109-inch body, slightly modified, was mated with it in 1978, producing the very first version of the One Ten.

Development progressed, with Range Rover chassis characteristics very much to the fore, including the 5in (127mm) wider track – compared with the Series III – of the Range Rover's axles, which were given additional strength. The chassis itself was made a lot tougher, with deeper side members becoming its most noticeable characteristic. It was decided early on that the Series III replacement would also feature permanent four-wheel drive.

The question of gearboxes, however, was not quite so straightforward. An excellent five-speed gearbox, the LT77, had been developed for the Rover SD1, but was not considered man enough for the V8 engine, especially with low ratios raising stress levels, leaving only the four-speed Range Rover unit (LT95) for the V8. Perhaps surprisingly, it was also decided to provide selectable four-wheel drive as an option with the diesel and four-

cylinder petrol models. Maybe it was thought this would find favour with traditionalists.

As the project progressed and the One Ten took shape there were increasing misgivings about the 100-inch wheelbase idea, and Land Rover looked again at the once-abandoned 90-inch chassis for the short wheelbase model. So another prototype was built, again with a 90-inch axle-to-axle measurement.

Although 2in (50mm) longer than the 88-inch it was considered too short for the increasing demands being put on the very popular short wheelbase working machine, and was out-of-step with the (mainly Japanese) opposition. One more prototype was therefore assembled, but this time the chassis was stretched to 92.9in (2.36m) – destined to become the production measurement. Because of the long time-gap between the very first 90-inch chassis and these two more recent ones, most people look on these as being 90-inch prototypes one and two.

With the wheelbases established there was now the question of styling. One major influence was the flat-front look of the Stage 1, which had to be retained in V8 versions because of the position of the engine, which in turn pushed the front ancillaries and radiator further forward; but it was a look which people liked. Another factor which contributed considerably to the final styling was the cost of the additional tooling which would be involved if the Series III body width was to be extended. Instead, deformable wheel arch eyebrows took care of the extra axle width.

The large one-piece windscreen, seat design, instrumentation, and various detail aspects came together with welcome smoothness, as did the pre-production programme, and the launch date was set. The Stage 2 Land Rover, representing the second stage of the investment programme which had begun with the Stage 1 V8, was on its way.

The new Land Rover

For the first time, the Land Rover stand was one of the principal features of the prestigious Geneva Motor Show in March 1983. The world's press always visit Geneva in strength, such is the importance of the event, and the star of the

Solihull display, the first coil-sprung Land Rover, was one of the talking points around the show's halls and bars.

It was, for Land Rover, an historic event. Other than the Range Rover, the new vehicle was Solihull's first all-new model since the Series I, and although the One Ten's heritage was clearly evident in its styling – even to those with only a passing interest it could be nothing other than a Land Rover – its degree of innovation was described by some pundits as revolutionary.

Land Rover confirmed pre-Geneva announcements that the One Ten was to be sold first in Britain and Switzerland, followed by the rest of Europe, then the Middle East and the remainder of the world. It was not, as many had expected, an immediate replacement for the 88-inch and 109-inch Series IIIs which would, the company stated, remain in production for at least five more years.

The One Ten was available in five body types: soft-top, hardtop, pick-up, high capacity pick-up, and Station Wagon, plus a chassis cab for specialist conversions. The County Station Wagon variant, pioneered with the Series III, featured self-levelling rear suspension (optional on other models), cloth seats with head restraints, and tinted glass.

The One Ten's chassis was robot-built at Land Rover's Garrison Street factory, in which £7 million had been invested. It was based on the Range Rover frame, but strengthened as in the early prototypes, with a centre depth of more than 7.5in (190mm), and modified for the three engine options.

The coil springing produced a dramatic improvement in on-road ride comfort and a considerable boost in off-road performance through its much longer travel. With 7in (178mm) of vertical travel at the front and 8.25in (209mm) at the rear, suspension travel was up by 50 per cent and 25 per cent respectively. The gas-filled, oil-damped, self-energising Boge

Hydromat rear strut was an important innovation, retaining full vertical movement of the rear coils, even under maximum load.

The Land Rover front beam axle was located by forged steel leading radius arms and a Panhard rod. The rear Salisbury axle was given tubular trailing links to control fore-and-aft movement, while an A-frame mounted centrally on the axle controlled lateral movement. Standard on the County Station Wagon was a rear-mounted anti-roll bar, carefully designed, according to Land Rover's engineering people, so as not to seriously restrict rear suspension travel.

The problem of braking shortcomings apparent on previous Land Rovers was addressed quite early in the development programme, and the new vehicle was given 11.8in (300mm) discs at the front and 11in (279mm) drums behind.

Power-assisted steering was listed as an option for the first time on a 'working' Land Rover; and although the company's traditional recirculating ball system was retained, redesigned linkage made it lighter – even without assistance – and a lot more precise. The coil springs permitted a 5ft (1.5m) tighter turning circle than the 109-inch.

→ **Nearly three-quarters of all Land Rovers sold worldwide in the 1970s and early 1980s were long-wheelbase models, like this 109-inch, which is why Land Rover launched the One Ten before the Ninety. (Nick Dimbleby)**

First engines

The familiar 2,286cc petrol and diesel engines were given a slight power boost for the One Ten. The petrol unit was improved with a revised camshaft, redesigned inlet and exhaust manifolds, and twin choke Weber 32/34 DMTL carburettor, although all this achieved was to take power from 70 to 74bhp at 4,000rpm. Diesel power was still unacceptably feeble, with only 60bhp at 4,000rpm and 103lb ft of torque at 1,800rpm. But at least the diesel now had a solenoid cut-out in the ignition, rather than the manual system on previous vehicles, giving a more modern way of stopping it.

Customers who wanted real power could opt for the familiar 3,528cc all-alloy Rover V8, which,

although in a lower state of tune than in the Range Rover, gave 114bhp at 4,000rpm and a healthy 185lb ft of torque at 2,500rpm. As with the Range Rover, there were two Zenith Stromberg CD carburettors.

The transmissions developed during the prototype period were unchanged. The new LT77

five-speed gearbox had been strengthened for use with the four-cylinder engines, while the V8 retained the now out-of-date four-speed LT95 'box from the Range Rover. It desperately needed an overdrive, but instead of being offered as a factory-fitted option it was only available as an aftermarket fitment from Fairey.

The five-speed gearbox was mated with the new, separate, LT230R transfer box, first used with the still-new automatic Range Rover, but the four-speed unit had the familiar integral transfer box from the manual Range Rover. With both gearboxes the transmission was the permanent four-wheel drive type with lockable centre

↑ **This 1989 Ninety has the 2.5-litre four-cylinder petrol engine, developing 83 bhp at 4,000rpm and 133lb ft of torque at 2,000rpm. (Simon Hodder)**

differential (again from the Range Rover), but for those die-hards who wanted it there was also a Series III-type selectable four-wheel drive as an optional extra.

Enter the Ninety

Despite the popularity of the Series III (and before it the Series II and IIA) 88-inch in Britain, it was an inescapable fact that 70 per cent of Land Rovers sold worldwide in the early 1980s were long wheelbase versions – which is why Land Rover had no option but to introduce the One Ten first. But it was only a year before the second coil-sprung utility appeared, the 92.9in (2.36m) Ninety … and already a number of changes had occurred.

Most important of these was the use of the

newly developed 2.5-litre diesel engine. It took power up to 67bhp at 4,000rpm – still mediocre, but any improvement was worth having – while torque was now 114lb ft at 1,800rpm.

The selectable 4×4 option was not offered on the new vehicle; virtually nobody had wanted it in One Ten form. And although you could still buy a One Ten with a V8 engine, the 3.5-litre unit was not available with the Ninety, even optionally, at the time of its launch.

The Ninety had Land Rover axles front and rear, without the option of a self-leveller, and without the One Ten County's anti-roll bar on the short wheelbase model's equivalent. Axle location and suspension arrangements were those pioneered the previous year, and there was the same power steering option.

On its introduction, the One Ten hadn't fully lost all traces of the vehicle it was destined to replace, because it had SIII-type sliding windows on the front doors. However, the Ninety came along with modern winding windows – but still without single-piece front doors – and these were installed in the One Ten at the same time. Body styles for the Ninety were shorter equivalents of the One Ten's, with the obvious exception of the high capacity pick-up only available with the longer wheelbase.

While the Ninety was received ecstatically by all who drove it, there was one reservation: the lack of a V8 meant that on-road performance and towing ability were restricted by the asthmatic and now ancient petrol engine and the still inadequate diesel. But just over a year after the Ninety's launch things began to happen, showing that Land Rover was indeed listening to its customers and was trying very hard to make its new vehicles the very best in all respects. In May 1985 the Ninety was given V8 power, the first time the 3.5-litre unit had been used in a short-wheelbase model, other than one which had been tried in the mid-1960s and a number of experimental 88-inch V8s in the 1970s. The Stage 1 V8, six years earlier, had been produced only with the 109-inch chassis. But now, the Ninety finally had the same high-power option as the One Ten, with ignition being upgraded to electronic type for better starting and more reliable tune.

The V8 gearbox was changed – at last – for the five-speed Santana-built LT85. Now both these mighty Land Rovers had a maximum speed better than 85mph (137kph), and could cruise all day at 75–80mph (120–128kph), provided you could afford the fuel. Consumption was a tad better than it had been with the four-speed

↓ **This impressive-looking machine is a 1983 One Ten County Station Wagon, registered CWK 37Y. The author owned an identical 1983 vehicle in the mid-1980s, but found the thirst of the V8 engine difficult to live with. (James Taylor Collection)**

DID YOU KNOW?
It's a wind-up
Other than those in the Range Rover, the front windows introduced with the launch of the Ninety in 1984 were Land Rover's first wind-up type.

→ **This is how it was for the first generation of One Ten V8s. Note the old Range Rover four-speed gearbox. All other One Tens had five gears, and although permanent four-wheel drive was standard, selectable four-wheel drive could be specified. Not many customers took that route however, and it was soon dropped. (Dave Barker)**

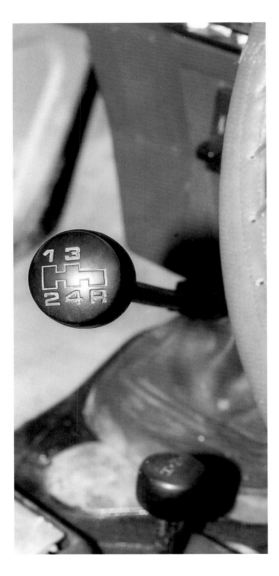

↗ **The adoption in 1985 of the five-speed gearbox for V8 models made a big difference to the Land Rover at cruising speed. This is the Range Rover version. (Dave Barker)**

gearbox on the One Ten, but you were doing well to get 15mpg, and it could be as bad as 12mpg with a degree of enthusiasm.

Petrol engine changes didn't stop with the V8 Ninety, however. In the autumn of 1985 the four-cylinder petrol option for both vehicles changed to a 2,495cc derivative of the old petrol engine. It was, in fact, remarkably similar in many respects to the 2.5-litre diesel unit, introduced at the Ninety's launch, although it did not include the diesel's change-over from chain auxiliary drive to toothed belt. The power increase was welcome, with 83bhp at 4,000rpm, and 133lb ft of torque at 2,000rpm.

With these improvements the new vehicles were well and truly on the motoring map. The four-cylinder engines now produced reasonable

power, while word soon got around the important agricultural market in Britain that the coil springing really did make a significant difference to ride quality, and that much quieter running, even with the all-important (to farmers) diesel engine, meant you could hold a conversation at 50mph (80kph) — virtually impossible in a Series III diesel.

It had been very important for Land Rover to get the new utilities right before they went on the market, and this had been achieved, especially with the 2.5-litre four-cylinder engines. Importantly for many overseas markets, the traditional mechanical simplicity had been retained, facilitating servicing and even major repairs in remote locations and with a minimum of equipment.

Specifications

LAND ROVER ONE TEN (1983)

Engine	3,528cc petrol V8 overhead valve
	Bore/stroke: 88.9mm/71.7mm
	Compression ratio: 8.13:1
	Carburettors: Two Zenith Stromberg
Power	114bhp @ 4,000rpm
Torque	185lb ft @ 2,500rpm
Steering	Recirculating ball with optional power assistance
Transmission	Four-speed permanent four-wheel drive with transfer box and lockable centre diff
Suspension	Front, beam axle with leading arms and Panhard rod, coil springs and telescopic dampers; rear, beam axle with trailing arms, central A-frame, coil springs, and telescopic dampers; self-levelling rear strut standard on County, optional on other models
Brakes	Front, 11.8in (300mm) discs; rear, 11in (279mm) drums; vacuum servo
Dimensions (County)	Wheelbase 110in (2.79m); track 58.5in (1.49m); length 180.3in (4.58m); width 70.5in (1.79m);
	height 80.1in (2.03m); ground clearance 8.5in (216mm); turning circle 42ft (12.81m); unladen weight 4,105lb (1,864kg); max payload 2,619lb (1,189kg)
Tyres	6.50 x 16 on 5.5in rims
Fuel capacity	17.5gal (79.5l)
Max speed	86mph (138kph)
0–60mph (0–96kph)	15.1sec
Consumption	12–17mpg

Other engines

	2,286cc petrol overhead valve
	Bore/stroke: 90.47mm/88.9mm
	Compression ratio: 8.0:1
	Carburettor: Weber 32/34 DMTL
Power	74bhp @ 4,000rpm
Torque	120lb ft @ 2,000rpm
	2,286cc diesel indirect-injection overhead valve
	Bore/stroke: 90.47mm/88.9mm
	Compression ratio: 23:1
Power	60bhp @ 4,000rpm
Torque	103lb ft @ 1,800rpm
Transmission	Five-speed permanent four-wheel drive (selectable 4x4 optional)

LAND ROVER NINETY (1984)

Engine	2,286cc petrol (as One Ten)
	2,495cc diesel indirect-injection overhead valve
	Bore/stroke: 90.47mm/97mm
	Compression ratio: 21:1
Power	67bhp @ 4,000rpm
Torque	114lb ft @ 1,800rpm
Transmission	Five-speed permanent four-wheel drive (no selectable 4x4 option, which was also dropped on One Ten)

Remaining specifications as for One Ten except for following key points:

- rear brake drums 10in (254mm);
- tyres 6.00 x 16 or, on County, 205 x 16 radial;
- no self-leveller option;
- wheelbase 92.9in (2.36m);
- length 146.5in (3.72m);
- height 77.6in (1.97m) (CSW);
- fuel capacity 12gal (54.5l).

Key innovations

- First use of coil springs
- First of use of disc brakes
- First five-speed gearbox
- First use of self-leveller
- First one-piece windscreen
- First power-steering option

CHAPTER 4
THE DEFENDER ARRIVES

Land Rover had no intention of standing still after the initial engine and transmission shortcomings of the new coil-sprung utilities had been rectified during the first couple of years. Customer feedback had identified some strongly felt demands for further improvement but, to be fair, Solihull's development people were very much on the ball and were working on a number of changes. Top of the list was the inadequacy of the 2.5-litre normally aspirated diesel engine, a long way short of the target where power was concerned. But there had also been comments about certain aspects affecting convenience and comfort. It has often been said that the One Ten and Ninety were given a post-launch facelift, and although this is perhaps an overstatement, the non-mechanical changes were nevertheless important.

Despite its upsizing to 2.5 litres in 1984, the diesel engine produced only 67bhp, a power figure at least a decade out of date when you consider the advances being made in diesel engines outside Land Rover. With a heavy load on board it made the performance of the One Ten in particular something of a joke; towing a heavy trailer, which is a task Land Rovers have always been designed for, meant extremely slow going, with much use of second and even first gear on hills. Land Rover's answer was to fit the Ninety and One Ten with a turbocharged development of the 2.5-litre diesel unit from October 1986, identifying models thus equipped with a rear-door badge proclaiming 'TURBO' for 1987 models, changing to 'turbo' for 1988. The full designation was Diesel Turbo.

Using the code name Project Falcon, this engine had been under development for two years before its introduction at the end of 1986, and was part of a general engine improvement programme. Although it has become fashionable in recent years to criticise this original turbo diesel – much of the adverse comment coming from people unable to look at it from the perspective of 1986

– its introduction was a turning point of great significance for Land Rover. As we now know, it turned out to be a stop-gap engine presaging the introduction of the much-improved 200 Tdi. But although Land Rover knew it would have to come up with an altogether better engine as a long-term solution to its general diesel shortcomings, when the Diesel Turbo went into production it was not known how long it would have to be used and precisely what would replace it.

Project Gemini, which was to lead to the 200 Tdi, had begun several months after the instigation of Project Falcon towards the end of 1984. The principal driving force behind Gemini, of course, was to come up with a world-class diesel for all of Solihull's vehicles, but, right up to the point just prior to it going into production, there remained a strong lobby within Rover for a bought-in turbocharged diesel engine; not everybody had the confidence that Land Rover was capable of developing a new-generation power unit.

Stop-gap it may have been, but contrary to a widely held notion, the 2.5-litre Diesel Turbo introduced in late 1986 was not a bolt-on conversion. True, the new engine was based on the existing 2.5-litre unit, itself only introduced at the end of 1983, but considerable research and re-engineering lay behind it. Land Rover had developed a new cylinder block with integral turbocharger oil feed and drain, along with a revised crankshaft which had been given cross

← During the last few years before the introduction of the Defender name, Land Rover was improving the vehicles consistently, but before the Tdi was available no significant upgrade was possible. (Nick Dimbleby)

> **DID YOU KNOW?**
>
> **Air power**
>
> The air intake position for the Diesel Turbo models was unique. The intake grille was positioned high up in the left-hand side towards the front, between the top rear of the wheel arch eyebrow and the door pillar. This can be used to distinguish a Diesel Turbo model, even if it has subsequently been fitted with a different engine. (Many now have Tdi units.)

↑ **This badge proclaimed Land Rover's first turbocharged diesel engine, the 2.5-litre Diesel Turbo. The name was used in this way to avoid confusion with the VM-powered Range Rover. (James Tayor Collection)**

drillings in order to improve the lubrication of the bearing journals. The company had also introduced completely new pistons and piston rings, while nimonic exhaust valves were used to cope with the much higher combustion temperatures associated with turbocharging.

For the turbocharger, Land Rover had gone to Garrett. The unit used with the new engine was the AiResearch T2, with an integral wastegate limited to 10psi. Diesel injection was with a DPS self-priming pump with boost control capsule and cold start timing retard system.

Because of the increased temperatures, along with the additional power output, the cooling system was uprated from that used in pre-turbo vehicles. In part this was accomplished with a standard-fitment oil cooler, but the viscous fan was

improved and new heat shielding developed.

Much of the work during the development of the new engine had concentrated on improving bottom-end torque and minimising turbo lag. It certainly paid off, because the new engine produced 85bhp at 4,000rpm (the old engine gave 67bhp). More importantly for a working, off-roading 4×4, the torque figure was improved from 114lb ft to 150lb ft, but still at 1,800rpm.

Important for many of Land Rover's export customers was the fact that the new engine would run perfectly well on very low cetane numbers (as low as 4C), and would perform well at high altitude.

The effect of this engine development work could be felt immediately you opened the throttle. For the first time a diesel-powered Land Rover had reasonable acceleration and acceptable maximum (75mph, or 121kph) and cruising speeds. With the aerodynamics of a brick, neither the Ninety nor the One Ten could ever be a road-burner, but the new engine gave the Ninety a 0–60mph (0–96kph) acceleration time of a touch over 22 seconds. Not Porsche-like, it's true, but compare this with the V8 Ninety's 0–60mph time of 14.2 seconds, and maximum speed of 83mph (133kph). Better still, look at the 29 seconds achieved by the four-cylinder petrol version of the Series III.

The 1986 Motor Show was also the platform for other important improvements to the Ninety and One Ten. Until now the utility vehicle V8 engines had continued to use carburettors, whereas the Range Rover had gone over to fuel injection, which took power to 165bhp. For the 1987 model year the switch was made from twin Strombergs to a pair of SUs and this, along with a new camshaft, took the power output to 134bhp – more, incidentally, than Range Rover V8s had been producing before their switch to injection. The increase in performance was welcomed by customers, although they still had to contend with high fuel consumption. The V8 is a thirsty unit, particularly so when used with the Ninety and One Ten, and there was nothing of significance to be done about it.

Apart from an important switch to new one-piece doors, other changes didn't amount to very much. However, one particularly sensible modification was the relocation of the radio panel, from just in front of the gear lever to a recessed position in the centre of the fascia. This spelled the end of channel changing whenever you swapped gears, although it took away a chunk of already sparse oddments space.

Door trims were improved, along with locking buttons and door handles, a new filler cap, and County Station Wagons were given a fresh set of

↑ **For 1988 Defenders the dash was redesigned, giving the radio (where fitted) a far more suitable position. (James Taylor Collection)**

decals, the third since launch. The Ninety County was given enamelled five-spoke Rostyle wheels, giving it a less utilitarian appearance.

The changes for the 1988 model year were mostly cosmetic, perhaps the biggest surprise being that the 'new' models were shown, not at the traditional Motor Show (more correctly the London Motorfair), but in December at the Royal Smithfield Show. Much of the emphasis in this late 1987 exhibition was on the County Station Wagons, which Land Rover wanted to popularise as much as possible in advance of the launch of the Discovery, scheduled for the autumn of 1989. It was obvious that the forthcoming vehicle would attract some buyers who would otherwise choose the County Station Wagon, so it made sense to make the CSW as attractive as possible.

The 1988 models became the first Land Rovers ever to depart from the traditional galvanised finish for the bumpers, in favour of black paint. On County Station Wagons the black bumper – which looked very strange at first – was complemented with body-colour grille, headlamp surrounds, and wheel arch eyebrows. On other models these parts were black. The County set also gained yet another side decal design and, far more usefully, a new type of Britax sunroof, offered as an extra on other models. Interiors became a little more car-like with revised trim, and there were better window seals.

Smithfield was again chosen the following year to announce the 1989 models, but the changes were few, with much fiddling of decals once more, and Rostyle wheels becoming an all-model

↑ The Station Wagon variant of the One Ten and Ninety was a very attractive vehicle, as this pre-Defender photograph shows and its popularity increased markedly in later years. (Nick Dimbleby)

→ The black-bumper County Station wagon of 1989 was a departure from Land Rover's normal policy, and the unusual shade attracted more than its fair share of criticism from traditionalists. (James Taylor Collection)

← After the 1989 models, the company decided not to display the Land Rover name on the plate above the grille, anticipating the full switch to Defender, which was announced at the 1990 Motor Show. (Nick Dimbleby)

option within the Ninety range (they were already standard on the County Station Wagons). Most noticeable was the redesign of the upper body sides for hardtops and Station Wagons, on which the rivet heads were no longer exposed. This certainly made the County types more visually appealing.

Not much happened the following year either, although the adoption of the now-familiar green oval Land Rover badge in its position on the radiator grille brightened the front somewhat. The plate above the grille was now without the Land Rover name, instead simply reading '90' or '110'.

The most important aspect of these 1990 models was that they were the last Land Rovers not to have a separate name. Since the inception of the marque in 1948 all utility models had been known simply as Land Rovers, but this was about to change for good – causing no little controversy along the way.

Defender was about to arrive.

DID YOU KNOW?
Sales patter
The introduction of the Diesel Turbo engine in late 1986 made a big difference to the appeal of the Land Rover throughout the world, but especially in Europe, where diesel power was, and remains, a much favoured option.

During the first half of the decade Solihull had been losing out to the Japanese, particularly in its traditional markets, but the decline was reversed in 1987, as sales figures clearly show. The Diesel Turbo was one reason for this, but another was that growing disenchantment with the old, leaf-sprung models had reached the point where it was inevitable that customers would try other products. That the new Land Rovers were worlds better than their predecessors was not without doubt, but it needed a growing awareness of this among customers, coupled with the realisation that most of the Japanese vehicles were far less suitable – which could only be gained by using them – for people to consider switching back to Land Rover. All this took time, of course, but it clearly demonstrates that the Ninety and One Ten were introduced not a moment too soon; any later, and Land Rover's utility sales would have nosedived, possibly without any chance of recovery.

The 127

It is often forgotten that the 127 dates back as far as the One Ten – or rather the designation does, because it was the end of 1983, rather than the spring, when the extra-long-wheelbase variant first became available.

The Special Projects department started considering the One Ten as the basis for special conversions, principally by authorised aftermarket conversion companies, shortly before the official launch of the coil-sprung Land Rover. At about the same time it was noted that there ought to be a market for a model with a high-capacity pick-up rear body and a four-door, five-man cab up front, and it was put to Special Projects that the way forward would be to produce the vehicle with a special, 135-inch chassis.

There was no problem in constructing a cab but, because the suggested extra-long chassis was not a viable proposition, it ended up as a 127-inch derivative of the One Ten frame carrying a shortened version of the rear body for the normal high-capacity pick-up. It was called the Crew Cab.

Up to mid-1985, all production vehicles were hand-converted from standard One Ten chassis by Solihull's Special Projects department. This was not the way things had been done in the past, when companies such as Spencer Abbott would have been responsible for production versions of vehicles such as the Crew Cab – but it was the way it would work from now on.

Under the dynamic managing directorship of Tony Gilroy, Land Rover was becoming much more cost-conscious and profit minded. One effect of this was the reorganisation of Special Projects into a new division known as Special Vehicle Operations. It was part of SVO's job to take back in-house much of the hitherto farmed-out aftermarket conversion work, and it was within this new regime that the original Crew Cab spawned a complete family of vehicles based on the 127-inch chassis. From the second half of 1985 they would be badged as the Land Rover 127.

As well as the 127 Crew Cab, SVO also developed many other variations of the basic box body. With four variations to the basic body – short or long (depending on whether or not it

was to be used with the Crew Cab) and high or low – it was not at all difficult for Land Rover to produce just about anything customers wanted for military or civilian use.

When the original One Ten and Ninety became Defender 110 and 90 the SVO 127 was renamed the Defender 130. This was not because, as some owners had thought at the time, there was any increase in wheelbase; it was simply the result of an understandable desire to have nice, easy numbers throughout the whole family of utility vehicles.

At the same time, output of all 127-inch vehicles was switched to the production line, providing more economical build for this increasingly popular variant and, at the same time, giving a bit of welcome elbow room within SVO – which was renamed again in 1992, when it became Land Rover Special Vehicles.

↑ Four box body variations of the 127/130 were produced, offering customers the choice of short or long body (depending on whether the normal or Crew Cab was used), with tall or short sides. Further special variations have been built by companies such as Foley Specialist Vehicles. (Nick Dimbleby)

← This is the badge of the Range Rover Turbo D from which Land Rover was obliged to differentiate with the name of the Diesel Turbo Ninety and One Ten. (James Taylor Collection)

CHAPTER 5
THE DEFENDER: Tdi TO Td5

Before the arrival of the Discovery in September 1989, any suggestion that a 'working' Land Rover might have a name all its own would have seemed as far-fetched as Land Rover Ltd being able to produce a world-beating diesel engine. The Discovery dispelled any fears about the diesel engine ... but what about the idea that a Land Rover might be called something other than a Land Rover?

There were two very good reasons for introducing a name for the utility models. With only a two-vehicle range prior to the Discovery – Land Rover and Range Rover – names hadn't mattered a great deal, but in the run-up to the Discovery's introduction the marketing people felt compelled to find a suitable label for the Ninety and One Ten. It would avoid confusion and tie everything down rather neatly.

The second point they had to consider was the high value of the Land Rover name as a notable motoring marque. The company name, therefore, would be much better reserved for use in its corporate sense, and, regardless of other considerations, this meant that it would no longer be acceptable for a vehicle produced by Land Rover Ltd to be known as, simply, a Land Rover.

Several explanations have been given for the use of the Defender name. Land Rover said at the time that the alternative was Attacker, and it was also stated that Defender 'came from nowhere' during a session in a Boston bar involving visitors from head office and their North American subsidiary hosts. It's neither clear how many 'possibles' were listed, nor is it known whether there were any serious misgivings at Land Rover about the new name.

Defender was catapulted into the public eye at the Birmingham International Motor Show in September 1990. I was there on Press Day with the rest of the media and recall clearly the surprise expressed at the choice of name, the real joy at the use of the 200 Tdi diesel engine in the 'working'

vehicle range ... and the indifference to the modest list of other improvements.

Exteriors were decked out in bright decals, making much of the Defender name, but were otherwise very much 'as you were'. Inside, there was at last a cubby box available between the outer pair of front seats, which had each been moved inboard an inch to give more elbow room, and cloth seat coverings were now an option. Land Rover also tried to excite visitors with the news that courtesy lights had at last been fitted to a utility Land Rover and the wash-wipe programme had been improved.

However, compared with the importance of the new engine, and what at the time seemed a strange choice of name, it would have taken a major internal makeover to arouse any real interest. Those who knew their Land Rovers were pleased that the old LT85 Santana gearbox had been replaced with a revised version of the LT77, specially strengthened for the V8 and therefore

DID YOU KNOW?
Name games

Land Rover's marketing people were surprised by the strong reaction against their use of the word 'Defender'. It was considered to be too military, and had been chosen with the popularity of Land Rovers for military and paramilitary use in mind. It was seen as completely out of step with the other names in use within Solihull's group of vehicles: Discovery and Range Rover. Many complained that it was too reminiscent of ugly scenes from the streets of Northern Ireland, in which Land Rovers were usually prominent, and some orders were cancelled as a result. Many journalists, otherwise impressed with the new vehicle, were outspoken in their criticism of the name. People wrote letters to newspapers and complained on radio phone-ins that they didn't want to drive around in a vehicle which had been named expressly for the Army, and Land Rover received sacks of mail on the subject.

But the protests were short-lived. The Defender was far too good a vehicle not to be bought simply because of its name – which Land Rover, anyway, had no intention of changing.

the utilities the benefits of Discovery's engine. As my description of the development of the Tdi (below) shows, one of the factors behind the project which led to the Tdi was the absolute necessity for Land Rover to have a top-flight diesel in order to be able to make an impact on European markets – which were diesel dominated – with the 'working' models.

The Tdi exceeded all expectations, and it was an enormous achievement that a company the size of Land Rover, a very small player in the big boy's world of car manufacture, was able to produce a diesel engine not bettered by anything in its class. It transformed the 90 and 110, and probably averted serious difficulties at Land Rover. Market conditions, which included real competition for the Station Wagons from the Discovery, and the excellent qualities of the Toyota Hi-Lux pick-up truck, which made it a genuine 'working' vehicle competitor, led to falling sales throughout the early 1990s. Without the Tdi engine it is practically certain that the Defender would have been in trouble. In its Defender application the Tdi was nevertheless given less power and torque than the Discovery: 107bhp at 3,800rpm and 188lb ft at 1,800rpm.

Very little happened over the next few years, with changes restricted to detail in the brake systems and a different steering wheel. One improvement appreciated by drivers, though, was the better gear selection with the LT77S gearbox introduced in 1992 models.

Solihull caused a stir in 1993 when it introduced its first addition to the Defender range in the shape of the 90SV, aimed squarely at the market for weekend fun vehicles. It picked up the theme of the Cariba, a concept vehicle which the company had played around with some six years earlier, and was a glamorised pick-up with County cab, a full roll cage, other 'lifestyle' adornments, and no choice of engine. It was the Tdi or nothing!

The 90SV ('SV' standing for Special Vehicles) was built exclusively for the home market, with no left-hand drive option, and could have been far more popular than it was. But the conversion from standard pick-up was done, one-at-a-time, by the Special Vehicles department, which kept the price up and numbers down. Much was made of the 90SV having disc brakes all-round, instead of the Defender's system hitherto of discs at the front

↑ **In naming the utility range Defender, Land Rover broke the no-model-name tradition which had stood since 1948. The choice of such a military-sounding name caused an outcry for a month or so, but the world soon became accustomed to it, and it is now difficult to think of calling these vehicles anything else. (Nick Dimbleby)**

possessing more than adequate reserves for the new diesel. However, it was the Tdi we all wanted to talk about.

This engine had already been used in the Discovery for a year before it first appeared in the Defender, and had received nothing but praise from motoring writers and users alike. Most importantly it had proved reliable, although some problems would develop as time marched on, and it was without doubt a major factor in the Discovery's amazing first-year success story. It was not, however, an engine which had been developed especially for the Discovery and then shifted over to the Defender production line in order to give

→ Responding to a growing interest in 'lifestyle' motoring, Land Rover produced the Cariba concept vehicle in the 1980s, picking up the theme with the introduction of the 90SV in 1993. (James Taylor Collection)

↓ The 300 Tdi engine succeeded the 200 Tdi, which was launched in 1989. Both these 2.5-litre turbocharged, direct injection units were world beaters and remain in many ways the best off-roading power units ever constructed. (Nick Dimbleby)

and drums at the rear. However, this now became standard on all Defenders, the harmonisation of braking arrangements with the Discovery making good sense for Land Rover, and even better sense for its customers.

At the same time as the 90SV was launched, the seven-seat County Station Wagon was reintroduced, making a particularly attractive version of the 90, although the desperate lack of space when all seven seats were occupied reduced its practicality somewhat. There was room for three more in the new ten-seat 110 County Station Wagon, while the 12-seater continued as before.

Defenders took another important step forward in March 1994 when several key changes were announced, some of which affected all vehicles in the Solihull line-up. The central theme was a new diesel engine. Although the 200 Tdi had been well-received and was genuinely a world-beating engine, it had its shortcomings. For a start it was noisy, although when compared with its Diesel Turbo predecessor it was remarkably refined. While its hard-sounding beat was a characteristic of direct injection diesels, it had been decided at an early stage that the original unit needed improving. Some reliability problems had developed as well, further justifying development work.

The engine revealed in the spring of 1994 was much more than a simple revision of the original Tdi. Its name, the 300 Tdi, was simply a marketing label because there was no change in capacity, no increase in power or torque, and no change

Td5 worries

Conrico International – the export organisation which supplies Land Rovers to many Third World territories, often in connection with aid work – was so worried about the possibilities of electronic problems immobilising the Td5 in arduous conditions that it persuaded Land Rover to continue supplying the new Defender with the old Tdi engine.

In the past their technical simplicity has enormously enhanced the usefulness of Land Rovers in remote areas, and this persisted with the Defender right through to the end of Tdi production. It was Conrico's view, based on experience, that operation in areas requiring frequent deep wading, along with mud and exceptionally high humidity, was likely to make electronic control systems less than dependable.

It's one thing suffering an electronics-related breakdown when you can call out the AA, and quite another when your life can be at risk when a vehicle becomes immobilised and the nearest support garage might well be several hundred miles of difficult track away. Furthermore, Conrico had to point out to Land Rover that the purchase of expensive diagnostic and tuning equipment was not in any way a practical proposition throughout most of the territories concerned. As a result the Td5 engine was vetoed by Conrico, whose Defenders consequently became Td5/Tdi hybrids.

Many enthusiasts echoed Conrico's concerns and originally declined to take the Td5 on arduous expeditions, aware that any failure of the electronic systems could leave them stranded. A limp-home system in the Td5 permits the engine to run at 1,200rpm in the event of a systems crash, but this would clearly be of little use in the middle of the Sahara.

It didn't prevent the Td5 becoming an enthusiasts' machine, as has happened also with the later Puma-powered Defender, which is even more electronically reliant.

in the basic philosophy of the 200 Tdi. However, a great deal of work had been done, resulting in 208 new components, many of them fundamental to the operation of the engine. These included cylinder head, exhaust manifold, turbocharger, injectors, pistons, conrods, timing belt, alternator, and water pump.

The result was astonishing, especially to the thousands of everyday users who had been more than happy with the first Tdi. The new engine was a much neater installation, a great deal smoother, and noticeably quieter, and while it couldn't make the diesel-powered Defender as civilised as a V8, the difference now was much less than anyone who had driven an original One Ten back in 1983 would have believed possible.

Along with the new engine – fitted to Discoverys and Range Rovers in exactly the same tune – was a new gearbox, the R380, which gave smoother and slicker changes, had synchromesh on reverse, and a revised double-H gate. Also making life easier was a reworked clutch mechanism which reduced the pedal operating pressure to acceptable levels at last.

The Defender, an excellent vehicle from the beginning, was now unbelievably good. With the introduction of the 300 Tdi engine its usefulness as an everyday car, even for people with very long commuting journeys, was beyond doubt. In County form, especially as a 110, it was a serious rival even for the company's own Discovery. It only required

a look around any supermarket car park to see just how popular it was becoming as a non-working utility vehicle.

The trend in this direction continued with 1996 models, when front and rear anti-roll bars were offered as options, along with Freestyle wheels and BF Goodrich All Terrain tyres. In part this was due to requirements for the NAS (North American Specification) vehicles. NAS influence could also be seen in a special-edition 300 Tdi 90, the Defender 90 Eastnor, produced for the French market.

During this model year, Land Rover won a most important military order for the Defender XD, or Wolf, which not only stamped the seal of approval on the Defender from the most demanding of all users, but also did more than anything else to guarantee its continued existence. The British MoD contracted for 8,800 vehicles, and this in turn sparked off orders from other countries.

Improvements for 1997 and 1998 were restricted to detail and to the choice of wheels, with interior trim receiving even more attention; and with 1998 being Land Rover's 50th anniversary year, it was no great surprise to find Collectors' Edition vehicles for all model ranges, Defender's allocation being the Defender V8 50, introduced in June. Based very much on American model policy, this was a 90 County Station Wagon with 4-litre injected V8, ZF automatic transmission, and full external roll cage. Air conditioning was standard and there was considerable attention to external and internal trim – without doubt, the best pre-Td5 Defender to be built.

And, yes, the new-breed Defender was waiting in the wings, because with the 1998 models the first series of Defenders had run its course. Enthusiasts throughout the world held their breath.

The Defender Td5

The first new Defender since the advent of the Tdi engine represented a great technical advance over the old model, but the electronic nature of these advances initially caused concern among some user groups.

The Td5 looked very much like any other recent Defender – indeed, only enthusiasts noticed the tiny air vents between the front sidelights and direction indicators, and the

elongated indicator repeaters – but the differences were huge. Most important was the introduction of the five-cylinder direct injection diesel engine, another triumph of engineering for Solihull and an enormous step forward in terms of power, torque and refinement compared with the 300 Tdi. It produced 122bhp at 4,200rpm, a useful increase over the Tdi, and 195lb ft of torque at 1950rpm compared with 188lb ft at 1800rpm.

The Td5 was very much an engine of the 21st century and had been planned to provide diesel power for Solihull vehicles for many years to come. It was fully monitored and controlled by an electronic control unit (ECU), and there was electronically controlled injection by individual camshaft-driven pumps for each cylinder. There was also an electronic system to improve the matching of engine and drive train speeds, reducing

↑ **Land Rover's 200 Tdi was one of the first small-capacity direct injection diesels to go into mass production. It was a much more suitable engine for the various 4x4 applications at Solihull than anything from the opposition. (Dave Barker)**

← **The 300 Tdi Defender. Although the engine retained the same power and torque characteristics of the 200 Tdi, it was substantially re-engineered, and was significantly quieter and smoother. A revised gearbox, the R380, was introduced with the new engine. (Nick Dimbleby)**

the onset of shunt and snatch, further assisted with a new type of dual-mass flywheel.

The throttle pedal travel was short for an off-road vehicle, in which reasonably long travel is usually required for smooth operation in low ratios. With the Td5 the engine management system adjusted the tune of the engine with low range selected, changing the response of the engine to throttle action and electronically 'elongating' the action.

All these features were standard. As options you could also have Land Rover's excellent ABS system – one of the very few to have full off-road effectiveness – and electronic traction control (ETC), which operates in conjunction with the ABS. With these fitted, the Defender's traction is unbelievably good over all forms of terrain, permitting it to maintain headway when only one wheel is gripping, something you can otherwise only achieve with locking differentials on both axles used in conjunction with a centre diff lock.

The Td5 was also brought up to date with revised instrumentation, which included a very useful 'water in fuel' indicator, giving advance warning of diesel degradation. There was better seat trim and improved sound insulation too.

Clearly this latest Defender was the best so far. The electronics did not give the feared problems and users were happy; most of them could not imagine the Defender getting any better than the Td5 – but, of course, nobody knew that the Puma version would be coming along.

Tdi development

Long before the Defender was planned, Land Rover had known it would have to do something about its diesel engine. There was a project to produce a diesel version of the V8 (Iceberg, aborted in late 1983). This was followed by Project Falcon, which was to turbocharge the existing diesel, newly enlarged to 2.5 litres, and there was also Project Beaver, in which the 2.4-litre Italian VM unit would be fitted to the Range Rover.

The Falcon engine was announced in October 1986 and was warmly received; and, of course, the VM unit was fitted to the Range Rover, but without the resounding success a better engine would have enjoyed. Both projects had, anyway, been viewed as short-term solutions.

↑ The Defender Td5, with five-cylinder direct injection turbo diesel engine, represents a technological step forward. However, the degree of electronic sophistication was at the time an unknown quantity with regard to severe off-roading, and the vehicle's use in remote Third-World territories.
(Nick Dimbleby)

← The engine bay of the Defender Td5 was a far cry from the cluttered, untidy appearance of the turbocharged diesel, the Diesel Turbo. The five-cylinder was, at the time, the smoothest ever Land Rover-made diesel unit.
(Dave Barker)

The really important project was Gemini, which commenced in the early part of 1985. This was the key part of the strategy being developed by powertrain chief John Bilton, who was convinced that the way forward in the European 4x4 market was with a new generation of diesel engines. He knew that Ford, Audi, and Fiat were working on small-capacity direct injection units (a system hitherto popular only with HGV engines). He knew, too, that direct injection for car (and 4x4) use was by no means proven, but nevertheless took a gamble by selecting this as the way forward for Gemini.

Although the fuel economy benefits of direct injection were well proven, so too was the much greater combustion noise and lack of refinement. However, Bilton knew that work on two-spring, or dual-rate, injection was being carried out by both

Bosch and by Lucas/CAV. He thought that this was where the breakthrough would come. Eventually, Land Rover opted for the Bosch injection system for what was to become the 200 Tdi, although Lucas/CAV had also figured prominently in the development programme.

The two-spring Bosch system provides a rising-rate return spring for the injectors. This slows the initial rate of injection and controls the rate of rise of combustion pressure, which has a significant effect on diesel 'knock', particularly on start-up, always the bugbear of the direct system. But the new engine would not work as a high-revving (in diesel terms) car power unit without a considerable re-think on the combustion chambers, compared with the design currently employed by Land Rover.

To sort this out, Bilton went to AVL in Graz, Austria, at the time the world's leading diesel consultants, and way ahead of the game in direct injection technology and know-how. AVL gave Land Rover what was needed to make the combustion process work as required, and were also extensively involved in improving reliability and durability.

Development work was carried out at Solihull. The new engine shared the dimensions of the then existing 2.5-litre turbo diesel, around which it was generally based. But it was given a new block, pistons, and conrods, and the direction of water flow through the block was reversed, although, interestingly, it was able to be machined on the

same line as the existing (pre-Tdi) unit. The Diesel Turbo's crankshaft was retained – just about the only component which was – although the cold rolling process was improved. The most dramatic change was in the cylinder head, cast in aluminium alloy and produced in a completely new CNC (computerised numerical-controlled) machining centre. The straightforward two valves per cylinder, pushrod operated system was retained.

Overall, the engine was 45lb (20kg) lighter than the turbo diesel. It produced virtually the same power, and more torque at lower rpm, than the VM then being used in the Range Rover, and it was apparent that this unit would, indeed, be suitable across the range, as had been the intention all along.

Turbocharging experience gained with the Diesel Turbo proved invaluable, although it was a long time before the development team was satisfied it had a set-up capable of producing the desired power/torque/reliability characteristics. In the event, the Garrett T25 turbocharger, coupled with an efficient intercooler, proved capable of doing the job remarkably well.

More than two million test miles were put into the new engine in all manner of vehicles, and history has endorsed it as one of the British motor industry's more significant engines.

It was only nine months before the launch of the Discovery in 1989 that it was finally decided to use the Gemini engine for this vehicle and,

↑ For many years, the One Ten was a mainstay machine for the British Ministry of Defence, just as the Defender has been. The normally aspirated version of the 2.5 diesel engine virtually pioneered the use of diesel for Land Rovers used by the British armed forces. (Nick Dimbleby)

← The Defender V8 50 was produced as a limited-edition model in celebration of Land Rover's 50th anniversary. It featured a 4-litre fuel-injected V8 and, for the first time in a UK production model, automatic transmission. (Nick Dimbleby)

← The Defender XD, or Wolf, was a specially strengthened version which rapidly became a favourite with a number of military customers. More than 8,000 are in service with the British forces. (Nick Dimbleby)

↓ A number of Ninetys were used by British forces in the Gulf War; because they were in some ways scaled-down versions of the famed Pink Panthers (109-inch vehicles nicknamed 'Pinkies') it was not surprising the Ninetys were dubbed 'Dinkies'. (Nick Dimbleby)

subsequently, in all diesel-powered Solihull models. As John Bilton said at the time, 'There was a lot of pressure during the development of the 200 Tdi to opt for a bought-in engine.'

Military models

The One Ten went into military service in Britain in 1985, closely followed by the Ninety and then, after a while, the 127. The first overseas military order came from Holland in 1984.

Diesel power for the British forces was pioneered by the One Ten with the 2.5-litre normally aspirated diesel, and diesel subsequently becoming a near-standard type of engine for British military Land Rovers.

The most common form of the One Ten in the British forces was always the soft-top, and a GS (General Service) version was the first to be developed at Solihull. Other types rapidly followed, including the Shortland armoured car variant along with other armoured bodies, often to special order.

A notable development on the basic One Ten

during the 1980s was the DPV (Desert Patrol Vehicle) to replace the SAS Pink Panthers, while the 1990s saw the production of the V8-powered SOV (Special Operations Vehicle) for the US Rangers. This came about from the Americans seeing Land Rovers in action during the Gulf War, and deciding that they'd like their own.

The Ninety, with its reduced load-carrying capacity, has been much less popular with the world's armed forces. Many observers thought it would take over from the Series III Lightweight for airborne operations but, in fact, the One Ten largely assumed those duties. That's not to say Ninetys have not seen service, because considerable numbers have been ordered for communications and other duties not requiring the carrying capability of the One Ten. Most, but not all, military Ninetys have been hardtops. The Land Rovers which so inspired the Americans during the Gulf War were diesel Ninetys, rapidly converted into scaled-down versions of the Series IIA Pink Panthers, and instantly dubbed 'Dinkies' by the squaddies who used them.

However, the Defender series saw the re-

↓ The Wolf, or Defender XD, had to be given a much stronger chassis, tougher body-to-chassis mountings and a detachable roll cage before it was acceptable to the Ministry of Defence. Mechanically, these Land Rovers are as near-standard as possible, something which has characterised military Land Rovers throughout the company's history. (Nick Dimbleby)

company's heritage and image. NAS Defenders gradually improved in specification and safety features – such as air bags and roll cages in order to comply with Federal regulations – and were all V8-powered, progressing to the 3.9-litre injected version of the long-lived ex-Buick engine in 1995.

For 1997 the specifications were upgraded for the last time. These models were given the 4-litre version with GEMS engine management and OBD II on-board diagnostics, but their most significant feature was that they became the first of Solihull's utility vehicles to be line-fitted with automatic transmission. From the end of 1998 the North American market also received the new Td5.

Defender from 2001

Following the decision by Land Rover not to announce any changes to the Defender range for the 2001 model year, enthusiasts waited eagerly to hear what would be new for the 2002 models, improvements for which were introduced at the Frankfurt Motor Show on 11 September 2001.

Among a varied list of alterations there were – as expected – no modifications to the Td5 engine, which remained the standard power plant world-wide. However, it was stated that the 300 Tdi would once again be offered as an alternative engine for non-European markets, a continuing acknowledgement of the concerns in some regions about the standard unit's reliance on a sophisticated electronic management system. With the changes, the Defender range acquired central locking and optional electric front windows. Practical revisions included improvements to the heater system and the wiper mechanism. An optional cold-climate pack of heated front seats and heated windscreen also became available.

An important change to the 90 Station Wagon was the deletion of the bulkhead in order to improve cabin space and to allow the front seats to recline further. From this model year, all Defenders were fitted with a radio preparation kit, and a radio-cassette unit became standard for some markets.

A new model derivative was the County Double Cab, with body-coloured wheelarch eyebrows, tinted glass, Techno cloth trim and a radio-cassette player. The County specification also

↑ **North American Specification (NAS) Defenders have always featured a number of differences compared with those destined for the European market. They have all been powered by the V8 petrol engine although, with the introduction of the Td5 at the end of 1998, American customers have had to accept diesel power. (Nick Dimbleby)**

emergence of the short-wheelbase Land Rover as a fighting machine alongside the 110 and 130, as a result of Project Wolf, in which a new breed of military 4x4 was developed. The first vehicles were provided for battlefield trials in 1993, following which modified and strengthened second-generation Wolf vehicles were eventually ordered at the beginning of 1996. Land Rover decided these tougher-than-usual variants should have a name, and they settled on Defender XD (eXtra Duty), otherwise known as the Wolf. They have subsequently proved extremely popular around the world.

A great deal of work went into developing these special military Defenders. They have stronger chassis, tougher body-to-chassis mountings, reinforced body, and removable roll cage over the rear body. Although they have been kept as standard as possible mechanically, XDs have a tougher rear axle and four-pinion differential to cope with the extra loading.

The Wolf, or XD, is extremely popular with its users, especially those whose job it is to drive them and fight with them. The product of entirely fresh thinking at Solihull regarding military Land Rovers, it has ensured the continuation of a fine tradition of manufacturing vehicles for defence and police forces around the globe.

The Defender in the USA

Although the Discovery proved popular in the USA, it was important for Land Rover to sell Defenders as well in order to enforce the

now included side and rear steps, plus front and rear mud flaps; white metallic paint and Freestyle alloy wheels with 238/85 tyres became options.

2003 models

Black carpeting became standard for all Defenders for the 2003 model year. An equally minor change, but one of great usefulness nonetheless, was the inclusion of load-retention rings in Hard Tops and Station Wagons. Still on the practical side, it was at long last decided to use a single key to operate the ignition and door locks, while the security of the locks themselves was improved.

Vehicles fitted with cubby boxes between the front seats would, from now on, have twin integrated cup holders provided as a standard part of the cubby box. And while on the subject of internal items, it was announced there would be an optional ICE head unit with single-slot CD player and up to four speakers. ABS with four-wheel Electronic Traction Control would remain an option throughout the series.

The range itself was extended, with a new top model, known as the Defender SE. Entry-level models would be called the Defender E, while Defender S types replaced the County range. S and SE versions were given remote central locking and electric front windows as standard.

← This might look just like any other silver Defender, but it is in fact one of the limited edition X-Techs, of which only 100 were sold in the UK. (Simon Hodder)

The Defender SE announcement was a further sign of the appeal of Defenders as luxury leisure vehicles, and Land Rover's desire to maximise its penetration into the more discerning sectors of the market. It would be available in five different versions: a Hard Top or Station Wagon on the 90 and 110 chassis, or a Double Cab (introduced the previous year) on the 110 chassis. External distinguishing features were Brunel gunmetal finish on the grille and headlamp surrounds and the side runners, and smoked lenses for the side and front turn indicators. The Brunel gunmetal was repeated inside the vehicle on the switch panel. Control knobs and steering wheel were covered with black leather, and the seats were upholstered with black leather and ripstop trim. Standard fitment on these models was the cold-climate pack of heated windscreen and heated front seats, and the tail door on Hard Tops and Station Wagons was given a mesh storage pocket.

↓ **The SVX was released as a limited edition to mark Land Rover's 60th anniversary. They might not be the most practical of the Defender special editions, because the spare wheel and storage lockers take up most of the available space in the rear load area, but they are certainly very stylish! (Simon Hodder)**

Defender X-Tech

Limited-edition 'specials' have played an important role in Land Rover's marketing for many years, and various types have appeared around the world to meet specific requirements in individual countries. The Defender 90 Hardtop X-Tech SE was one of the first of the new millennium, and was a striking machine with strong appeal to an important, but perhaps relatively small, sector of the marketplace.

It actually went on sale in September 2000, with an initial build of a mere 50 units. Land Rover said it was aimed at 'extreme sports enthusiasts, requiring a vehicle that will not only carry their equipment, and get them there, but stand out in any crowd'. It was, the company declared, 'a true working vehicle, with youthful, fresh appearance for those with an active lifestyle'.

On its introduction the Td5-engined X-Tech was priced at £20,175 on the road, with standard

Specifications

LAND ROVER DEFENDER 90 200 TDI

Engine	2,495cc diesel direct injection four-cylinder
	Bore/stroke: 90.47mm/97mm
	Compression ratio: 19.5:1
Power	107bhp @ 3,800rpm
Torque	288lb ft @ 1,800rpm
Steering	Recirculating ball with power assistance
Transmission	Five-speed permanent four-wheel drive with transfer box and lockable centre diff
Suspension	Front, beam axle with leading arms and Panhard rod, coil springs and telescopic dampers; rear, beam axle with trailing arms, central A-frame, coil springs and telescopic dampers
Brakes	Front, 11.8in (300mm) discs; rear, 11in (279mm) drums; vacuum servo
Dimensions	Wheelbase 92.9in (2.36m); track 58.5in (1.49m); length 146.5in (3.72m); width 70.5in (1.79m); height 77.6in (1.97m) (hardtop); unladen weight 3,734lb (1,695kg); max payload 1,556lb (706kg)
Wheels/tyres	16in/205 16 (standard)
Fuel capacity	12gal (54.5l)
Max speed	84mph (135kph)
0–60mph (0–96kph)	17.4sec
Consumption	23–27mpg

LAND ROVER DEFENDER 90 TD5

Engine	2,492cc diesel direct injection five-cylinder
	Bore/stroke: 84.45mm/88.95mm
	Compression ratio: 19.5:1
Power	122bhp @ 4,200rpm
Torque	195lb ft @ 1,950rpm
Transmission	Five-speed permanent four-wheel drive with transfer box and lockable centre diff; electronic traction control optional (with ABS)
Wheels/tyres	16in/7.50 R16 (standard)
Fuel capacity	13.2gal (60l)
Max speed	85mph (137kph)
0–60mph (0–96kph)	16sec
Fuel consumption	24–28mpg

Suspension, steering, and dimensions as before, except: unladen weight 3,836lb (1,741kg); max payload 1,350lb (613kg) (hardtop).

ABS and ETC, and unique sculpted wheels. It was finished in Blenheim Silver, and carried the County Pack, including tinted glass, sunroof, rear step and radio-cassette. Inside was a cubby box, aluminium gear knob and leather-trimmed steering wheel.

Defender Black

Perhaps even more striking that the X-Tech, the Defender Black limited edition was, as the name suggests, an all-black vehicle, and it certainly caused a stir when unveiled at an international motor exposition at London's Canary Wharf in June 2002. Land Rover announced a plan to build 100 examples based on the Defender 90, and 150 on the 110 Double Cab. Both were priced at £24,995, with a specification including the Td5 engine, ABS and four-wheel ETC, although the target market was described vaguely as 'a new breed of owners'. A well-heeled new breed, no doubt.

For their money, purchasers bought a vehicle with leather trim, single-slot CD player, air conditioning, alloy wheels, chequer plate on the wing tops and sides, side protection rails, and distinctive chrome-detailing inside. Enthusiasts had been given plenty of time to save for the Defender Black, because a prototype had been displayed at the Land Rover Marque Day 13 months before the launch.

CHAPTER 6
THE Td5 GENERATION

By 2002 Land Rover had made a number of changes to the Td5 Defenders, many of which the company called 'Quality Actions', aimed at sorting out some of the known issues with earlier models. Visually, everything looked pretty much the same as before.

The rear door, well known as an area prone to corrosion, was now a one-piece pressing, made from zinc-coated steel, resulting in much improved corrosion resistance. Despite the fact that it looked much the same as ever, this was a welcome upgrade. The door hinges, catches and numerous other fittings throughout the vehicle were also improved to combat corrosion, and, at the request of customers worldwide, central locking and electric windows became available, although these remained an optional extra.

Welcome as these improvements were, the fact that the engine in Land Rover's basic utility model now relied entirely on a modern suite of electronics generated a degree of scepticism from some quarters. As time passed, however, the system proved to be very reliable.

Although many adventurers still preferred to enter remote areas with Tdi-powered Defenders, the Td5 was gaining a solid reputation. The electronics, even when exposed to high temperatures, dusty environments and deep water, were clearly not going to prove the Achilles heel that some had feared.

Refinements to the Td5 models continued, and, by the time the 2004 models went on sale, journalists were using headlines like 'As good as it's going to get' amid continued rumours that the Defender line would soon be axed.

In the top-end XS models, drivers could benefit from such comforts as heated leather seats and air conditioning, although the air conditioning hardware was still an obtrusive, bolt-on item taking up valuable leg room for front seat occupants. Land Rover's base utility model was rapidly becoming anything but!

The new centre dash in 2005 models put switches in a more ergonomic position, and the bulkhead behind the front seats was finally replaced with an unobtrusive tubular brace, giving the interior a much more car-like feel. The last Td5 Defenders would look virtually identical to the first ones, but under the skin they had been vastly improved.

Electronic opportunities

The Td5's engine management system opened up a whole new world of opportunity to enthusiasts looking for extra performance. Land Rover engines had always left the factory in a conservative state of tune, and the Td5 was no exception. Almost as soon as these latest models went on sale, tuning specialists began offering upgrades.

Over the next few years a whole tuning and performance industry grew up, and the Defender began to appeal to a different type of owner, not interested in off-roading at all but in seeing how quick they could make Solihull's big old utility go!

By upgrading the turbocharger and intercooler, and by altering the ECU's fuel map, the performance of the Td5 can be improved substantially. By doing these things, and by fitting a modified cylinder head, enthusiasts have shown

← With the introduction of the Td5 engine, Defenders relied more heavily than ever before on electronics. Initial worries about the ability of these systems to cope with the off-road environment proved unfounded. (Simon Hodder)

DID YOU KNOW?
Selectable four-wheel drive
When the One Ten was introduced in 1983 Land Rover announced that, in addition to the vehicle's much vaunted permanent four-wheel-drive system, selectable four-wheel drive was available to those who wanted it. The extra-cost option for the four-cylinder models included freewheeling front hubs and was designed to appeal to die-hard customers. Few, if any, took up this option and it was deleted rather quickly... and quietly.

← This is what the electronic brain of a Td5 looks like with the lid off. No surprise then that you are advised not to get it wet! It lives under the driver's seat, so if water gets in under the doors when you are wading, that's exactly what could happen. Patch cables are available that allow it to be repositioned in the roof lining above your head, which seems like a very sensible precaution for serious off-roaders. (Simon Hodder)

↑ This subtle-looking 90 houses one of the most powerful Td5s in the world. When we photographed it, it was producing 208bhp as measured on a rolling road. It feels more like a sports car than a Defender, thanks to a specially prepared cylinder head, a variable-vane turbocharger and a remapped ECU. (Simon Hodder)

that the Td5 can be coaxed into producing as much as 208bhp and 332lb ft of torque, representing a huge increase over the standard engine. Ultimately, the limiting factor would appear to be the diesel injectors, which can only be made to push so much fuel into the engine. Once that limit is reached, finding more power is almost impossible without fitting higher capacity injectors, but at the time of writing, none are available.

Driving a 90 with an engine like this is a fairly brutal experience. With the coil springs reduced in height by some two inches to improve cornering stability, and running on low profile tyres, the ride is very firm, and the acceleration is something that you simply don't expect from a Defender.

But not all tuning is about speed. Remapping the electronic management system to produce a wider, flatter torque curve, aimed at making the Defender a better tow vehicle, and to improve its drivability in off-road situations, is far more common practice, and has been shown to be a worthwhile exercise, especially if you regularly tow large trailers or caravans.

↓ **This 90, seen here making a four-wheel power slide, has been chipped, which means that the software contained within the engine's electronic control unit has been customised by a specialist engine tuner (in this case Bell Auto Services, based near York). The result is a very punchy drive, thanks to a considerable increase in torque. (Simon Hodder)**

Limited edition specials

During the lifetime of the Td5 Defender, a number of limited edition specials were produced, aimed primarily at boosting sales, and we'll look at some of the more important ones aimed at the UK market here.

In 1999, 150 Heritage Defender 90s were made, featuring Atlantic Green paint, a grey plastic grille designed to remind people of the early wire mesh grilles on Series Land Rovers, and a leather interior trim.

In 2001 the Tomb Raider special hit the market, with 900 being made available worldwide, 250 of which were destined for the UK market. They were all presented in Bonatti Grey, with chequer plate on the body along with an external roll cage covered in spot lights. These vehicles were inspired by the extremely successful Tomb Raider movie, which featured a similarly modified Defender, albeit briefly, and they caused quite a stir when they first appeared at the Land Rover shows.

The Defender Black limited edition was announced at the Canary Wharf International Motor Expo on 10 June 2002. There were 100

→ Thanks to its modular construction, the Defender lends itself particularly well to conversions of this type. The extra length and axle allow for greater loads to be carried. (Simon Hodder)

↓ This six-wheeled Td5 fire tender protects lives at the Goodwood aerodrome, one of the busiest grass airstrips in the country. The Defender is one of the few vehicles that combines all the attributes needed for this role. (Simon Hodder)

→ The Defender has always been a working vehicle, and these two are certainly doing that! The workers are using cherry pickers to clear tree branches from around high voltage power lines, so their lives very much depend upon their Land Rovers. (Simon Hodder)

vehicles based on the 90, and 150 based on the 110 Double Cab. Costing £24,995 both versions featured black paint, leather trim, single-slot CD player, air conditioning and alloy wheels. Other features included chequer plating to the wing tops and body sides, leather trimmed steering wheel, chrome instrument bezels and alloy knobs for the gear and transfer box levers.

From 1 September 2003, the Defender G4 went on sale in the UK, equipped with A-frame protection bars, rear light guards, Black Mogul fabric seats, Boost 16-inch alloy wheels, windscreen protection bar, and chequer plating on the wing tops and sills. Only 150 vehicles were made for UK consumption, all powered by the Td5.

November 2003 saw the introduction in the UK of 100 examples of the Defender X-Tech. Based on the Defender 90, the X-Tech came in Zambezi Silver, with headlamp surrounds and grille in Brunel gunmetal finish. These Defenders

had a long list of special features, both inside and out, and came at an on-the-road price of £21,995.

Finally, available at the end of 2005, the Defender Silver came in both 90 and 110 Station Wagon form, and as a 110 Double Cab. An A-frame bar, driving lamp kit, hinged lamp guards, sump guard, black chequer plate, half-leather seats, CD player and towing pack set these 300 examples apart from standard models.

End of the line

The long list of limited edition specials helped bolster Defender sales, but emission rules within the EU were becoming ever stricter, and by the beginning of 2007 the Td5 engine would be replaced by a much more modern diesel, fitted to a thoroughly revamped version of the Defender, aimed at keeping production alive for several more years.

↓ Heritage special edition Defenders did not all come in Atlantic Green, as this dark Bronze Green 110 model shows. (Simon Hodder)

↑ This 110 is owned and used by Alpha 4x4 Weddings and Funerals, who specialise in providing a caring and professional Land Rover based service to enthusiasts all over the UK. The Defender holds such an important place in people's hearts that they seem the obvious means of transport for two of the most significant two journeys we will make. (Simon Hodder)

→ This Td5-powered 90 has been extensively modified to allow it to compete in winch challenge events. The long travel suspension system helps keep all the wheels on the ground, increasing stability and traction over extreme ground. (Simon Hodder)

CHAPTER 7
ENTER THE PUMA

Many motoring journalists, not to mention enthusiasts, were convinced that development of the Defender would end with the Td5 models. It was widely rumoured that Land Rover could not justify investing large sums of money in a vehicle that had a limited future production life.

To prove these commentators wrong, on 12 February 2007 the first full production model of a new generation of Defenders rolled off the line at Solihull. It was a low-key affair, and this first vehicle was no commemorative special. It was simply a white 110 truck cab with a canvas tilt.

The authors had seen this new Defender five months earlier, when lead designer for the project, Dave Saddington, gave us a guided tour of one of the design mock-ups at Gaydon. It was clear that the exterior was to remain pretty much the same as the Td5 models, which of course pleased Defender fans all over the world when the news got out. Some significant changes were made, though.

One of the signature features on the Defender has always been the fresh air vents on the bulkhead, beneath the windscreen. Indeed, these were present on the very first Land Rovers back in 1948. In redesigning the dashboard, however, the design team chose to do away with them – the pressings in the bulkhead remain, just not punched through. This legacy feature helps retain the Defender's traditional appearance, although in fact the decision had more to do with keeping costs down than anything else.

The most notable change was the introduction of a large bulge on top of the bonnet, needed to accommodate the new engine, which was taller than the outgoing Td5.

Engine and transmission

The new engine is in fact a modified Ford 2.4-litre Duratorque diesel, used with huge success in the Transit van. This led to some people referring to the new model rather unkindly as the Transit-engined Defender, although Land Rover engineers had, of course, spent considerable time and effort ensuring that this already-proven engine was up to the rigours of life in the Defender. Particular attention had been given to improve waterproofing and oil delivery at the extreme off-road angles that Defenders are typically exposed to.

Use of the Ford Duratorque engine made absolute sense. Ford owned Land Rover at the time, and adapting this robust and powerful engine for life in the Defender was hugely cheaper than designing something from scratch. It was also the first non-Land Rover engine to be factory fitted to the Defender since production began.

The Duratorque engine is the most advanced ever to appear in a production Defender. It has four valves per cylinder, driven by twin overhead camshafts. In common with most modern diesels it has a cast iron block with alloy cylinder heads, along with a single turbocharger and common-rail diesel injection. It's a strong engine, producing 360Nm (265lb ft) of torque at just 2,000rpm, and a healthy 120bhp at 3,500rpm, making it eminently suitable for the Defender. The combined fuel economy figure for the 90 Station Wagon is a respectable 28.3mpg.

← The Defender can be driven almost anywhere, straight out of the showroom, and the 2007 models are no different. This one is tackling some of the deep mud holes at Eastnor Castle. (Simon Hodder)

DID YOU KNOW?
The puny first diesel
In contrast to the more recent power units, the first diesel engine offered with the One Ten was never going to win any friends for its power. The four-cylinder 2286cc unit was, like its petrol counterpart, carried over from the Series III and both had been 'improved'. The diesel, however, was slightly less powerful than it had been before, producing only 60bhp and 103 lb ft of torque. This was, remember, an engine offered for the largest and heaviest utility Land Rover produced so far.

There's still no option for an automatic gearbox, but there are now six forward gears. This has allowed for a wide spread of gear ratios, with first gear being lower than Defender owners have been used to. Pulling away from a standstill is now effortless, even when towing a trailer with the maximum permitted weight of 3,500kg.

Land Rover resisted the temptation to formally name the engine in Defender configuration for marketing or badging purposes, but it was known as the Puma engine during the development, and this name has become widely used.

Interior

The interior of the current Defender is very different from the older Td5 models. The dashboard is now a one-piece design, and incorporates a new heating and ventilation system. This new dashboard features none of the squeaks and rattles that came as standard in previous models, and incorporates a very car-like set of plastic fresh air vents that work extremely well. The new air conditioning unit, when fitted, is unobtrusive and extremely efficient.

Changing European statutory requirements dictated another big alteration. From 2007 all seats had to be forward facing, and be fitted with full three-point seat belts. The rear seats are set higher than those in the front, which Land Rover refer to as 'stadium seating', to give rear passengers a better view through the front window. Despite the change to forward facing rear seats, the 110 Station Wagon still comes with a 7-seat option.

The rear seats still fold out of the way when not in use, and one of the design requirements

↑ The dashboard was completely redesigned for 2007. It takes many cues from the Discovery 3 and the Range Rover Sport, but retains a welcome utility feel. Overall it is much more car-like than any previous Defender dash, reflecting the needs of most modern customers, who want utility and comfort in the same package! (Simon Hodder)

← European laws now require all seats to be forward facing, with proper seat belts for all occupants. A clever mounting system allows these seats to be swung out of the way when not in use. In the 90 the system permits the retention of much of the load space found in previous versions. (Simon Hodder)

called for there to be enough room to fit a domestic fridge and all its packaging in the load bay. Despite the ever-increasing sophistication of the Defender family, Land Rover remains committed to retaining its practicality.

Into the future

The Defender is now more refined than ever before. The interior has an almost car-like quality about it, and the Puma engine is up to 30 per cent quieter than the old Td5, making life much more pleasant for the occupants. These changes reflect the fact that this rugged, versatile and supremely capable utility vehicle now appeals to a great many people

who want to buy one for what it stands for and not necessarily for what it can do.

Changes in legislation have dictated a number of changes to the Defender, but one constant element is the hugely strong steel chassis, the box section, ladder frame design of which still makes it one of the most adaptable vehicles of its kind in the world.

Will the Defender continue to evolve over the coming years? History shows that every time someone predicts that a particular revision will be the final one, they are proved wrong within a few short years. So, despite the fact that the Defender line will have to end one day, we reckon there's plenty more to come from those brilliant people at Land Rover, and from the most recognisable vehicle in the world. Long live the Defender!

↑ From most angles the 2007 Defender looks much like any other. Land Rover designers were very conscious of the fact that they would be treading on thin ice if they took too many liberties with this iconic shape! (Simon Hodder)

→ A Land Rover Experience 110 Defender seen here taking people for a gentle off-road drive at Eastnor Castle. Despite the new laws requiring forward facing rear seats for all passengers, the 110 can still seat 7 adults in comfort. (Simon Hodder)

← The latest Defender was eagerly awaited by its devotees. This early 110 model took part in Land Rover's 60th anniversary parade at Gaydon in May 2008, and attracted a lot of attention as it was driven past thousands of people lining the route. (Simon Hodder)

DID YOU KNOW?
Defender air con in 1992
After a break of 18 years Land Rover returned to the US market with a special edition of the 200 Tdi Defender in 1992. Standard specification included air conditioning, then still a rarity in Britain but essential for US buyers.

← The Ford-derived 2.4-litre Duratorque engine, coupled with the new six-speed gearbox, makes the latest Defenders better at towing large loads than ever before. First gear is lower than on previous models, which makes pulling away from a standstill effortless. (Simon Hodder)

↑ The Defender has taken more than 60 years to evolve into its current form. How much longer will the line continue? (Simon Hodder)

→ The latest Defenders are just as capable off-road as their predecessors. Land Rover engineers spent a lot of time ensuring that the electronic systems were waterproofed. (Simon Hodder)

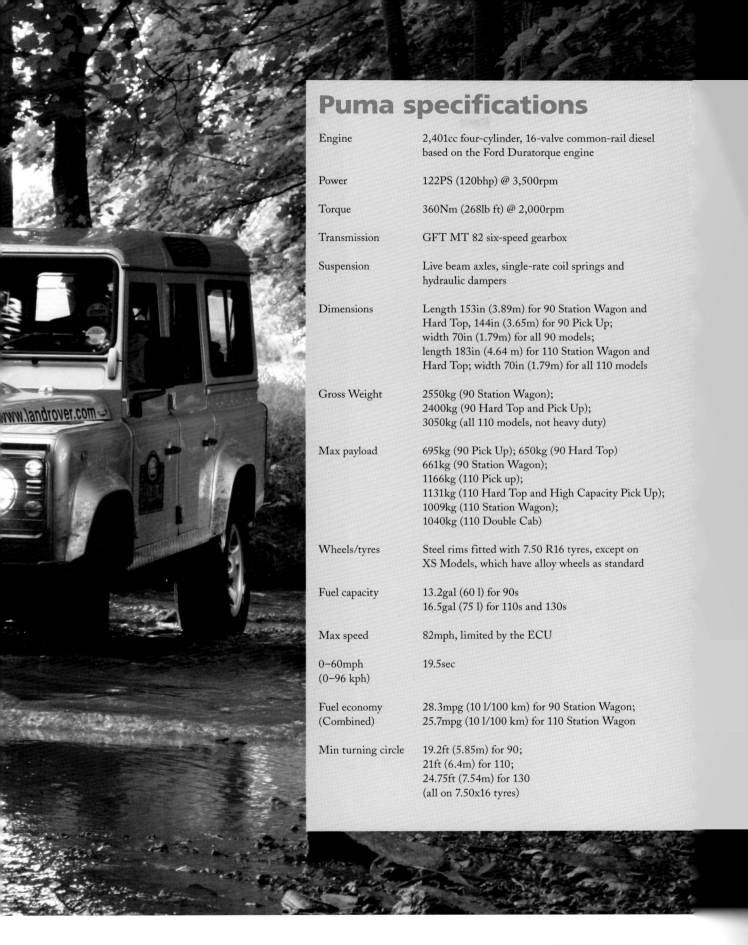

Puma specifications

Engine	2,401cc four-cylinder, 16-valve common-rail diesel based on the Ford Duratorque engine
Power	122PS (120bhp) @ 3,500rpm
Torque	360Nm (268lb ft) @ 2,000rpm
Transmission	GFT MT 82 six-speed gearbox
Suspension	Live beam axles, single-rate coil springs and hydraulic dampers
Dimensions	Length 153in (3.89m) for 90 Station Wagon and Hard Top, 144in (3.65m) for 90 Pick Up; width 70in (1.79m) for all 90 models; length 183in (4.64 m) for 110 Station Wagon and Hard Top; width 70in (1.79m) for all 110 models
Gross Weight	2550kg (90 Station Wagon); 2400kg (90 Hard Top and Pick Up); 3050kg (all 110 models, not heavy duty)
Max payload	695kg (90 Pick Up); 650kg (90 Hard Top) 661kg (90 Station Wagon); 1166kg (110 Pick up); 1131kg (110 Hard Top and High Capacity Pick Up); 1009kg (110 Station Wagon); 1040kg (110 Double Cab)
Wheels/tyres	Steel rims fitted with 7.50 R16 tyres, except on XS Models, which have alloy wheels as standard
Fuel capacity	13.2gal (60 l) for 90s 16.5gal (75 l) for 110s and 130s
Max speed	82mph, limited by the ECU
0–60mph (0–96 kph)	19.5sec
Fuel economy (Combined)	28.3mpg (10 l/100 km) for 90 Station Wagon; 25.7mpg (10 l/100 km) for 110 Station Wagon
Min turning circle	19.2ft (5.85m) for 90; 21ft (6.4m) for 110; 24.75ft (7.54m) for 130 (all on 7.50x16 tyres)

CHAPTER 8
THE WORLD'S BEST OFF-ROADER

There is no other generally available, off-the-shelf, dual-purpose vehicle with the off-roading capabilities of the Land Rover Defender. It is the natural choice for serious off-road competition and the favoured machine for a large proportion of the world's recreational off-roaders. Even in the USA, where there's a tradition of fine, home-grown 4x4s and where the Defender's penetration into the market has been relatively small, 90s figure strongly when groups of enthusiasts take to the hills.

The reputation for being able to cope with extremely rough terrain was established with the very first Land Rovers, which were more capable off the tarmac than the only alternative four-wheel drive vehicle available, the ex-military Willys Jeep. The American vehicle was good, but the Land Rover had the edge.

The Land Rover legend developed with its growing popularity around much of the globe as a working vehicle. Farmers, construction workers, and forestry teams took them everywhere, while adventurous individuals used them for weekend fun and, occasionally, trans-continental expeditions. If you wanted to drive where other road-going machinery couldn't go, you went by Land Rover.

Solihull improved the vehicles constantly as they progressed through Series II, IIA, and III, but it became increasingly apparent from the mid-1970s onwards that two principal aspects would have to be put right if they were to retain their great popularity: the engines were old-fashioned and inadequate, and the leaf spring suspension was too firm and somewhat restricting in off-road situations. The launch of the One Ten in 1983, followed the next year by the Ninety, mostly rectified these shortcomings. Coil springing totally overcame the criticisms relating to the earlier suspension and, as the new series progressed, the engines also became much more suitable.

In the face of growing numbers of increasingly good 4x4s from the USA and the Far East, it was not true to say that Series IIIs stood head and shoulders above the rest when it came to off-roading, as earlier models had; but the original One Ten and Ninety put this right at a stroke. And with better engines, culminating in the 200 Tdi introduced with the adoption of the Defender name, it became ever-more difficult for other vehicles to rival the utility Land Rovers over rough ground. In fact, the only opposition came from, firstly, the Range Rover, and then the Discovery.

Awkwardly for Land Rover, right from its launch in 1970, the Range Rover had been a superior off-roader to the tail-end Series IIA and, from 1971, the Series III. The company promoted the Series III, as it had all previous Land Rovers, as the 'go-anywhere vehicle, unbeatable on farm, track or mountain', yet anyone who had driven a Range Rover off-road knew very well that it would keep going long after a Series III had been brought to a standstill.

The Range Rover was the world's best off-roader – but only until 1983.

The Defender reigns

The development of the new-generation utility Land Rovers was not the most scientific project the automotive world has ever known, and it began much later than it should have done with somewhat less enthusiasm than it might have had. That it resulted in such excellent vehicles,

← You can take a completely standard Defender straight out of the showroom and drive it over some of the world's toughest off-road terrain. This particular vehicle has been modified to help it compete in extreme off-road competitions. (Simon Hodder)

> **DID YOU KNOW?**
> **Transfer box**
> The transfer box got its name because, in a 4x4, it provides the mechanism by which power is transferred from the normal gearbox to the prop shafts for the front and rear axles. Its other role of providing a step-down system for low ratios doesn't really have anything to do with its name.

destined to take Land Rover into the 21st century, would be something of a surprise to any present-day motor industry analyst.

Like most 4x4s, the Defender is a compromise. But whereas other all-terrain vehicles are designed principally for road work, usually with compromised off-road ability, Land Rover's tradition ensured that the original Ninety and One Ten would be, firstly, working off-road utilities, and secondly, road-going light trucks.

The Range Rover had already proved that, despite being principally a road-going estate car, there need be little, if any, compromise in off-roading capability, and the Discovery and

second-generation Range Rover have continued the theme. But only the Solihull factory has been able to achieve that fine blend.

It was different with the Defender family, which had to be capable of the same hard work in the same unforgiving conditions as had the earlier Series Land Rovers. You can have a true working vehicle which is acceptable on the road but, as the Japanese had found, it is much more difficult to design a road-going vehicle with high levels of passenger comfort which is also capable of carrying loads of rubble, barrels of oil, or dead sheep.

In many ways, the vehicle which comes closest to the concept of the working Land Rover is the Toyota Hi-Lux 4x4 pick-up truck, but even this, good as it is, is nowhere near as capable in bad conditions as a Land Rover. And that is perhaps the best illustration of what Land Rover achieved when the One Ten was in the design stage.

Solihull didn't take the easy way out when the Range Rover's chassis, suspension and transmission were used for the One Ten. There

↓ **Not very practical on a cold day, but at least everything is easily accessible!** (Nick Dimbleby)

Off-road strengths

was no way of improving on the systems which had been developed in the late-1960s and, as time has proved conclusively, nothing better has emerged since. By marrying these crucial aspects of chassis and suspension design to the type of bodies used for previous generations of utility models, Land Rover was able to come up with a working vehicle which could operate in conditions which would stop anything else. By refusing to compromise on the working nature of the vehicles, Land Rover knew that the One Ten and Ninety and, in time, the Defender, would be less car-like on the road than most other 4x4s.

In making these decisions the people at Solihull were completely correct, as history has proved. And it is because of this resolute approach that the Defender has become so universally popular with the enthusiast movement. For countless thousands of faithful disciples the Defender, in all its forms, with its square-cut and workmanlike lines, its unrivalled off-road ability, and its instant recognisability, is the world's most important vehicle. The fact that design compromises resulted in it being noisy, thirsty, and comparatively slow has merely added to its appeal.

The secret of the Defender lies in the strength of its chassis, its long-travelling coil suspension, the refusal of Land Rover to be tempted away from beam axles, and its permanent four-wheel-drive transmission. Closely following these features in importance has been a succession of excellent engines: firstly the V8, then the progressively better 200 and 300 Tdi diesels. Of all these characteristics it is the springing and axles which give the Defender its great capability over rough ground. Indeed, only the Range Rover and Discovery, which have near-identical arrangements, are able to compete.

To understand the advantages given by the Defender's suspension, it is necessary first to look at the drawbacks of other forms of springs and axles. It also helps to appreciate that the single, most important aid to traction when off-roading is to keep all four wheels in firm contact with the surface; the most common cause of becoming immobile, other than when a muddy surface fails to enable the tyre treads to grip, is when one or more wheels lose contact with the surface, or

↑ The most significant improvement achieved with the introduction of the Defender family was the dramatic increase in axle articulation resulting from the switch from leaf to coil springs. Axle articulation is the single most-important consideration in pre-traction-control vehicles, followed by engine torque characteristics. (Nick Dimbleby)

→ Although Land Rover had used leaf springs from the beginning, the limitation they impose on axle articulation meant that none of these vehicles could match the off-road performance of the Ninety and One Ten. (Dave Barker)

↓ This photograph shows the Defender beam axle very clearly. As well as working brilliantly with the springing, the axle casing itself is enormously strong, and protects the half shafts from accidental damage. (Simon Hodder)

DID YOU KNOW?

Traction control

The electronic traction control, or ETC, introduced as an optional extra with the Defender Td5 relies on the ABS system for its operation. If there's a fault with the ABS, you lose ETC as well.

fail to exert sufficient pressure to permit the tyres to transmit enough torque to maintain forward movement.

Anyone with experience of, say, a Series IIA or III Land Rover will be aware of two principal shortcomings when off-roading, both of which are

related to the suspension design. Firstly, leaf springs restrict the extent of axle articulation which, in turn, limits the vertical movement of the wheels when encountering holes or upward obstructions; secondly, the way in which the springs are fixed to the underside of the body, by shackle assemblies, forms an obstruction which can easily make such firm contact with the ground that it immobilises the vehicle.

To a lesser or greater degree these factors also apply to many non-Land Rover four-wheel drive vehicles. Most manufacturers stuck resolutely to leaf springs long after Solihull had proved that coil springing was much better for off-roading and, even today, some are still using them. It's a sign, of course, that much of the opposition was not particularly interested in providing exceptional off-road capability in vehicles which, in some cases, were otherwise very good.

By switching to long-travel low-rate (or 'soft') coil springs, Land Rover was able to increase very considerably the axle articulation. With the use of this system in the One Ten Solihull provided 7in (178mm) of wheel travel at the front and 8.25in

(210mm) at the rear, an improvement of 50 per cent and 25 per cent respectively over the Series III. The coil springs had the second advantage of greatly reducing the shocks which are inevitable when off-roading, even when doing it correctly and driving very slowly, and improving the on-road ride to a quite remarkable degree.

When Land Rover was developing the Range Rover it resisted the temptation to use independent suspension, either at the front alone or on all four wheels. By sticking to beam axles, which are rigid from end-to-end, and which were used in all the Series vehicles, a further advantage

↓ **The use of beam axles in Land Rovers is considered by some to be rather out-of-step with modern automotive thinking. Yet it is precisely this aspect of design, along with the use of long-travel low-rate springs, which gives the Land Rover its advantage over the opposition, where independent suspension rules the day. (Nick Dimbleby)**

by retaining them in its new breed of utilities and, at the same time, introducing the long-travel coils which had proved so effective in the Range Rover, the Defender series was given a suspension system which transformed the capabilities of the 'working' vehicles. However, a suspension system of this type, when used with vehicles which are sometimes very heavily loaded over the roughest terrain imaginable, is subject to extreme forces, sometimes in several directions simultaneously. It is therefore imperative for axle location to be properly and robustly controlled, with a suspension-to-body mounting system capable of taking extreme punishment. Anyone who has stripped-down or replaced sections of a Defender's suspension system will know just how well this has been achieved, and how these vehicles are capable of withstanding the stresses involved in heavy-duty off-roading.

The front axle is located by long, forged steel leading radius arms which prevent the axle from moving forwards and backwards, and a Panhard rod which prevents sideways movement. The radius arms run back from each axle end to the chassis and are bolted in position through bushes which permit the vertical movement of the arms as the wheels move up and down. These arms are particularly strong and provide much of the front-end strength for which the Defender's suspension is renowned.

The springs at their lower end are mounted directly to the top of the axle, and are held by particularly tough chassis brackets at the top – a far stronger arrangement than, for example, the MacPherson strut system used on saloon cars, which would not be able to cope with the extreme loadings encountered in off-roading.

Land Rover pioneered an excellent rear suspension arrangement with the Range Rover and this, too, was carried over into the One Ten and Ninety. Fore and aft movement of the axle is firmly located with tubular trailing lower links running from the chassis to the axle, while lateral movement is controlled by an A-frame, which consists of twin upper links running upwards and backwards centrally from the axle and bolted to the chassis on either side. A system of bushes permits full wheel movement.

A further refinement was the fitment on some long-wheelbase models of a Boge self-

↑ In designing the rear suspension of the One Ten, Land Rover incorporated the Boge self-levelling strut which had been pioneered on the Range Rover with great success. It was offered as standard only on Station Wagons, but many were fitted as options to other versions. (Dave Barker)

was gained and this was duly carried over into the Defender series.

There are two benefits of solid, beam axles when off-roading. The first is that ground clearance remains more constant beneath the differential than it does with independently sprung axles which, because of their action, can sometimes reduce effective ground clearance. The second, related, advantage is that with beam axles the wheels are less likely to take up the odd angles they adopt over rough ground with independent action. Land Rover tyres therefore mostly have the tread in line with the ground.

By using beam axles in earlier vehicles Land Rover had made the most of its leaf springs, but

levelling strut, a self-energising device linking the centre of the axle to the chassis. Effectively, it's a third suspension unit designed to permit full movement of the rear springs when the vehicle is heavily loaded. Unfortunately, however, over the years many owners have neglected to replace worn-out self-levellers, with the result that load-carrying 110s can be inhibited off-road because of restricted spring movement. With the unit operating correctly even an overloaded vehicle retains most, if not all, of its axle articulation.

The Defender's transmission also has a lot to do with its off-road capability. Because it is a permanent four-wheel drive system, there isn't the need to manually select 4x4 when the going gets tough, as is the case with most rival vehicles. Torque from the engine is delivered via the main gearbox to a transfer gearbox, which provides the choice of high or low range, and from there to front and rear propeller shafts. A centre differential within the transfer gearbox permits different rotation speeds between the two prop shafts, thereby preventing the build-up of stresses in the transmission (transmission

↑ **With just one wheel spinning, a Defender will usually come to a halt if the centre differential has not been locked because of the way all torque transfers to the wheel offering** least resistance. Locking the centre differential maintains drive to the other axle and, if both those wheels are gripping, keeps the vehicle on the move. (Dave Barker)

wind-up) which would otherwise be inevitable when cornering because of the smaller turning radius taken by the rear axle. Each axle has conventional differentials.

The centre diff, another aspect of the Defender range first used in the Range Rover, can be locked by moving the secondary gear lever (used for selecting high or low ratios) over to the left. When this is done the front and rear prop shafts are effectively locked together. Without this facility, simply losing grip with one wheel would bring a Defender to a standstill. This happens because whenever a wheel loses traction all the torque for that axle takes the line of least resistance and moves to the spinning wheel; the

↑ **In Defenders the small lever used for selecting high or low ratios is also used to lock the centre differential which, by locking the front and rear prop shafts into a 'solid' drive unit, helps to keep the vehicle going when drive is lost on one axle. Locking or limited slip axle differentials are not fitted by Land Rover, but can be added if required. (Nick Dimbleby)**

Engines for off-roading

As well as the Defender's excellent suspension and transmission, the third factor which greatly affects its off-road performance is the engine and, more specifically, its torque characteristics and whether it is petrol or diesel.

Outright brake horse power is of little advantage when off-roading, although clearly it makes a difference to main road performance. Rather, it is torque which is required for off-roading and for heavy-duty towing work, and the lower the revs needed to produce maximum torque the more it can be made to work for you.

A further point regarding engines concerns the difference between petrol and diesel when it comes to off-road reliability and performance. Initially, the One Ten came with either 2.25-litre petrol and diesel engines, both low on power and torque, or the tried and tested 3.5-litre petrol V8. The Ninety came without a V8 option to start with, having the good old 2.25-litre petrol and the newly enlarged 2.5-litre diesel. The 2.5 diesel was a little better than the one it replaced, but not much, although it wasn't a bad off-road unit.

The V8 had proved itself an excellent off-road engine in the Range Rover, and in the early days

other wheel is simply starved of power. Without a centre diff, or with the unit in its 'free' position, all torque from the gearbox would go to the prop shaft feeding the axle with the spinning wheel, leaving the other axle without power. By locking the centre diff the loss of traction to just one wheel only deprives that axle of driving ability. Because the two prop shafts are locked, they both continue to turn at the same speed and, provided both wheels on the second axle are gripping, the vehicle will continue to move. However, if traction is lost by one wheel on each axle, the vehicle will stop, regardless of the centre diff. This can only be overcome by the fitment of locking, or limited slip, diffs to replace the standard axle units (see Chapter 12).

→ **With the centre diff lock engaged, a Land Rover will cross with ease the sort of ditches which will almost certainly stop other types of vehicle not possessing the axle articulation of the Defender. Ditches must never be tackled head-on. (Nick Dimbleby)**

of the Defender family was the preferred option for enthusiasts. At the time it was introduced for the Ninety, in 1985, it produced 114bhp; more importantly, its torque figure was 185lb ft at 2,500rpm. For off-roading you need to get your torque at a slower engine speed than this, but even at 2,000rpm the torque was better than the opposition could manage. The drawback of the V8, as with all petrol engines, has always been the great difficulty of waterproofing the electrical system sufficiently to prevent misfires or complete stoppage when there's deep water about. A diesel will run completely submerged, provided there's a high-level air intake. Not so a petrol unit.

The introduction of the 2.5-litre Diesel Turbo in late 1986 at last gave the One Ten and Ninety the right engine to match the rest of their off-road superiority. It was not as good as the Tdi would prove to be a few years later, but with this engine the Land Rovers had the combination of diesel dependability for off-road work, and decent power and torque figures. It's worth taking a look at the figures for Land Rover and its competitors at the time the Diesel Turbo took over from the normally-aspirated engine, and to compare all these with the 200 Tdi.

	Power	Torque
	(bhp@rpm)	(lb ft@rpm)
Land Rover 3.5 V8	114 @ 4,000	185 @ 2,500
Land Rover 2.5 D	67 @ 4,000	114 @ 1,800
Land Rover 2.5 DT	85 @ 4,000	150 @ 1,800
Daihatsu Fourtrak 2.8 TD	87 @ 3,600	155 @ 2,200
Isuzu Trooper 2.2 TD	74 @ 4,000	125 @ 2,500
Mercedes 300 3.0 GD	80 @ 4,000	126 @ 2,400
Mitsubishi Shogun 2.4 TD	84 @ 4,200	148 @ 2,000
Nissan Patrol 3.2 D	95 @ 3,600	160 @ 1,800
Toyota Landcruiser 4.0 D	99 @ 3,500	171 @ 1,800

From 1990

Land Rover 2.5 Tdi	107 @ 3,800	188 @ 1,800

↑ **Extreme caution must be exercised when driving in water without a high-level air intake. The slightest amount of water entering the inlet system can damage an engine very seriously; diesels are best for wading because of the lack of an electrical ignition system. (Nick Dimbleby)**

This table clearly shows the massive strides that have been made by Land Rover in the progression from its first turbocharged engine to, eventually, the Tdi. Examination of the torque figures highlights the difference between Land Rover, from the 2.5 DT onwards, and most of the competition. Only the Shogun, with its excellent engine, and the huge Toyota, have similar torque characteristics, but even these are sidelined from 1990 onwards with the appearance in the Defender of the Tdi. And it is worth noting the Tdi's torque superiority over even the Rover V8.

Driving experience

Only by driving different vehicles off-road can you appreciate the superiority of the Defender. During the mid-1980s my own V8 One Ten County Station Wagon, one of the earliest, was used as everyday transport and for off-road fun. At the same time my work enabled me to gain considerable off-roading experience in Mitsubishi Shoguns, Daihatsu Fourtraks, a Mercedes G-Wagen, and an Isuzu Trooper. The experience was most illuminating and gave me an early, yet permanent, appreciation of the superiority of the Defender series.

As has been explained, the Land Rover gains its principal advantage from its suspension and beam axle arrangement, but in practice it's the way everything performs which makes the difference. Take a simple and frequently encountered obstacle, such as a ditch crossing. Unless the surrounding terrain makes it impossible, a ditch should always be crossed diagonally, so that only one wheel risks being out of contact with the surface at a time as it drops into the depression. The long travel of a Land Rover's coil springs with the associated extreme axle articulation means that a Defender will frequently cross such an obstacle with ease. With the centre diff lock engaged you stand a good chance of 'walking' the vehicle through in first gear low ratios and the diesel engine running at tickover ... even if there's a ridge on one side of the ditch, or the sides of the obstacle are particularly uneven, very muddy, or both.

But it is far less easy with a vehicle fitted with leaf springs, or with short-travel coils and, probably, independent front suspension. The suspension

may cause the front diff to dig in with one wheel pushed up as far as it will go and the other dangling uselessly on the end of its spring.

Climbing awkward, tight, rocky sections is another example where a lack of axle articulation, reduced ground clearance because of independent suspension, and poor throttle response at low revs will stop you. But a Land Rover diesel, especially a Tdi, will take it with ease, climbing with no or very little throttle input (in first low) as the tyres resolutely clamber over each rock. If you need some power for a particularly steep section, it comes immediately you apply just a touch more

↑ On a muddy hill climb like this the excellent torque characteristics of the Tdi engine give the best chance of getting to the top. Engines which produce their maximum torque at a higher engine speed are unable to produce the smooth and controllable power flow needed in these situations. (Nick Dimbleby)

DID YOU KNOW?
Gearing down
It's not a practical proposition to produce a standard gearbox containing all the gear ratios required in an off-roader, and neither would it be practical to use a gearbox with ten or more forward speeds. Apart from the difficulties of using it, such a gearbox would be potentially dangerous if any of the extra-low ratios were selected inadvertently.

Experts and expeditions

Being built on an enormously strong chassis gives the Land Rover a huge advantage over other off-roaders. The chassis imbues massive strength to the entire structure, it reduces under-body vulnerability, it gives uniquely strong mounting points for the suspension, and it facilitates the addition of winches and recovery points with ruggedness impossible in monocoque structures.

Heavy duty winches are essential for extreme off-roading, and for much expedition work. To fit one to a Land Rover Defender you can, if you wish, bolt it directly to the front bumper, a solid steel affair which is, in turn, bolted to the main chassis frame. Consequently a winch recovery with a Land Rover passes the stresses through the chassis without any of it affecting the body. It is, in fact, possible to suspend a Defender on a suitably strong cable without any risk of damage – television advertising some years ago which showed a Defender being winched up a near-vertical dam retaining wall at a Welsh reservoir involved no trickery, just some unseen safety measures.

The most dramatic way to recover a stranded vehicle from impossibly deep mud, or a bog, is to use the kinetic energy recovery system. This

↑ **A clear illustration of the lack of structural strength in the upper bodywork of Land Rovers. (Nick Dimbley)**

→ **The most spectacular form of vehicle recovery is the kinetic energy (or KERR) method, whereby a stretchable rope between the stuck and recovery Land Rover is coiled on the ground before the recovery vehicle takes off at high speed, literally plucking the immobile machine from its mud trap. (Dave Barker)**

throttle, and you remain fully in control.

If hampered by less pliant independent suspension and, again, with ground clearance possibly being reduced by vertical movement of the wheels, it's far less straightforward. Furthermore, if the engine doesn't produce sufficient torque unless it's turning at 2,000rpm or more – and this is very often the case – you're obliged to tackle the section with quite a bit of throttle, and consequently, more speed than you'd like.

Muddy hill climbs can be very difficult, whatever vehicle you're driving, but the torque of the Land Rover Tdi engine gives you the best chance of success in many situations. For example, if it's dangerous to attempt the climb quickly – speed is sometimes the best answer with mud – the only solution is to tackle it at modest speed, but in a relatively high gear, such as third or even fourth (low ratios). The Tdi will cope with this because it produces lots of torque without requiring a heavy right foot. Many other engines, though, will not let you do this and will simply stall.

involves a stretchable but very strong rope being attached to the front of the stranded vehicle and to the rear of the one doing the recovery, which is positioned with its rear just a few feet from the one which is stuck. The rope is loosely coiled between the two, the recovery vehicle takes off as rapidly as possible, and the energy stored within the tightly stretched rope yanks the stuck Land Rover clear.

It's all very dramatic, and not a little dangerous, but would be impossible with vehicles not possessing the chassis strength of the Land Rover. To do this, the recovery rope must be attached to a strong point on the front of the first Land Rover, which is usually a pair of recovery attachments known as JATE rings, first developed for military use. These are bolted to the main chassis legs and the incredible stresses involved pass through the attachments and into the chassis. Usually, the rope will be attached to the recovery Land Rover's towball or pintle, although this can only be done when the towball is in line with the forces involved, and the tow bar is properly attached to the rear crossmember. Provided there's no deep rust on the crossmember or rear chassis the vehicle has no problem with the forces involved.

It's because of its chassis, and the way the towing equipment is connected directly to it, that a Land Rover can tow incredibly heavy loads. Naturally, there are strict laws governing towing in normal circumstances, but it is not unusual for Defenders to be called on to tow fully loaded heavy trucks for short distances. Police patrols do it regularly with Defenders, Range Rovers, and Discoverys when broken-down HGVs need moving urgently. For more normal towing work with caravans and horseboxes Defenders are ideal. The torque of the Tdi or V8 engine copes easily with this sort of work, while the size, weight, and design of the vehicles makes them just about the best tow cars imaginable.

For more adventurous travelling, such as long-haul overland trips through Third World territories, Land Rovers have been the way to go since the birth of the marque in 1948. The Defender 110 Tdi is the perfect expedition vehicle, offering excellent mechanical reliability, long range, spacious accommodation, and almost unrivalled load-carrying capability. These factors, along with the Defender's all-terrain prowess and, with an expedition-style roof rack, more than ample space for a roof-top tent, make it the preferred choice for a high proportion of long-distance trekkers.

↓ **What the well-equipped expedition vehicle is wearing. Thorough vehicle preparation is essential before any trip to the Sahara, Middle East, or further, and items such as a full expedition roof rack, under-body protection, water and fuel containers are essential. (Nick Dimbleby)**

CHAPTER 9
TESTING TIMES

Motoring journalists have been supportive of Land Rover since its earliest days, when they wrote with undisguised enthusiasm about the very first model. Solihull's first all-new vehicle since those times, the Range Rover, was also greeted with massive praise, which has continued to the present day. And so, too, has been the Defender, which, although falling beyond the everyday remit of most car publications, has received wide coverage in Station Wagon form in all the mainstream motoring magazines. Almost without exception the comments have been favourable, even when written by journalists who didn't fully understand the vehicle, as has sometimes been the case.

Land Rover has always understood the importance of first-hand road tests of its vehicles. Going back to 1948, it made early production models available to journalists, and this has been the company's policy ever since.

Although part of Rover, then British Leyland, then Rover Group, BMW, Ford and finally Tata, Land Rover itself has always been a small company when compared with mainstream manufacturers and, consequently, has never been able to justify a large fleet of press vehicles. But it has always done its best to make test vehicles available to newspapers, magazines, and television shows. Positive press comment is the best form of promotion a car maker can have, and it speaks volumes for the confidence within Land Rover that vehicles have been made available to such a wide variety of media outlets. It's reassuring, too, that in recent years Solihull has loaned Defenders to the enthusiast press, knowing very well that the vehicle is setting out to take part in an off-road event in France, for example, with a high chance of bodywork damage.

Yet it's the mainstream motoring press, read by knowledgeable motorists and by potential buyers in search of unbiased information, that has always been the most meaningful for Land Rover. Here's what writers around the world have said about the Defender series, from pre-Defender days to the Tdi.

Launch week

In the week of March 1983 when the new coil-sprung Land Rover was launched, *Autocar* carried a fully descriptive article packed with detail. The magazine clearly recognised the great importance of the One Ten and went to great lengths to make sure its readers fully understood the technical background. There wasn't a great deal of editorial comment to be found amid the factual information, but what there was showed considerable under-standing and not a little foresight:

'The concept of the One Ten is to combine the traditional ruggedness, reliability and longevity of the Land Rover with the better riding, better handling, more sophisticated suspension system of the Range Rover. Land Rovers have been around since 1948, Range Rovers since 1970; the One Ten is long overdue.

'Its introduction could not have been delayed much longer. The demand for four-wheel drive vehicles in the developing world is still strong, and more and more manufacturers are muscling in on the 4x4 market with vehicles that have as good or better off-road capability than the traditional Land Rover yet offer more car-like, more comfortable passenger accommodation. While Land Rover Ltd's own Range Rover still offers probably the best compromise of on-road refinement and off-road ability, it is expensive, particularly when compared with its adequately competent competition, notably that offered by the Japanese.

'Land Rover have shied away from making the One Ten too car-like. It is still very much a

↑ From the very earliest days of the One Ten and Ninety, motoring journalists were writing enthusiastically about the capabilities of the new vehicles. (Nick Dimbleby)

utility machine, and Land Rover want it to look that way. Hence passenger accommodation is little changed, and the cab remains functional, retaining such primitive features as sliding windows, and under-screen flap fresh air ventilation.

'Functional it may be, but there can be no doubt that the One Ten is a vast improvement, boosting Land Rover's competitiveness in an increasingly hard-fought sector of the market. The improvement in on-road ride alone should be enough to regain the loyalty of many who might have been tempted to buy foreign in the search for a reasonably priced utility with reasonable levels of refinement. The One Ten also has considerably better off-road capability.'

Specialist view

The first reference to the new One Ten in a specialist magazine came in the May 1983 issue of *Overlander*, then Britain's only off-road publication. Again, as befits the importance of the vehicle, the write-up was largely technical, but there were

some observations as well, Brian Hartley's closing comment being particular prophetic:

'The One Ten can only be really appreciated from the driving seat. It is there that all regular and seasoned Land Rover, and for that matter, Range Rover drivers had better prepare for a severe case of culture shock.

'The One Ten's on- and off-road driving manners came as something of a revelation to one who was weaned on the 'old' type Land Rovers (the One Ten having aged the original vehicle at a stroke). Taken as a whole the driving experience was more impressive than either the Range Rover or the Mercedes G-Wagen. The latter vehicle in particular is going to have a hard time against the One Ten in every aspect except the passenger compartment.

'It would require far harsher conditions than those we encountered to really test the mettle of the One Ten, but I would happily put money on its coil sprung rump to match any of the competition, from whatever continent, in an all-out off-road test, including its own stable mates.

'Could it be, I wonder, that we are witnessing the birth of a new legend?'

V8 Pick-Up

The same writer was at it again in January 1984. This time *Overlander* was doing a full test on a One Ten V8 High-Capacity Pick-Up, and a little bit of aggravation became mixed with a lot of praise:

'The cab leaked a lot. The passenger side had two distinct leaks, one from behind the plush pressed felt headlining and the other from behind the dash scuttle. From other sources I believe this is not an isolated case and does not bode well for the long-term future of the trim in particular.

'Off-road the One Ten behaved exactly as you would expect a vehicle with its breeding. Laden or unladen it took every-thing in its stride. Ditches and sharp hummocks, which are usually the real stoppers for leaf-sprung vehicles, were taken with ease, keeping the driver and, just as important, the load on an even keel. It also allowed any such obstacles to be taken gently, rather than 'with a run', again resulting in a softer ride for whatever or whoever was being carried.

'At 14mpg the consumption was better than I had expected as the vehicle had been used hard for stop/start runs, off-road testing and full loads. The 4-cylinder versions would probably be better on fuel consumption, but with those sort of payloads the lack of power would be painfully evident.

'One thing is certain, in its class the V8 One Ten HCPU has no competitor in terms of off-road performance.'

Early adventures

Two of the earliest off-roading stories involving the new vehicles were those in *Autocar* in March 1983, detailing a journey to Scotland which was made before the launch of the One Ten, and an excellent feature in the rival weekly *Motor* in September the following year, in which the new Ninety was put through its paces.

Autocar's article was, in fact, part of a feature introducing the One Ten, in which the journalists managed to get the vehicle bogged down within feet of starting their drive along a track in Skye, and hopelessly cross-axled on General Wade's

↓ **When the Ninety came along it was greeted with even more enthusiasm than the One Ten. *Motor* magazine carried out an exhausting trip with one using some of the most difficult ancient roads in Wales. (Nick Dimbleby)**

↑ The Defender has always had considerable appeal as an everyday vehicle. Its excellent road-going performance went down very well with *Autocar* when it tested a V8 in 1985. (Nick Dimbleby)

military road in the Western Highlands when reversing. Nonetheless, the article was in general extremely complimentary, although it did include a comment about finding a limit to the One Ten's ability which, although true, should have been accompanied by an admission of the journalists' own recklessness in failing to take due care where they took the vehicle. Competent off-road drivers would not have got stuck where *Autocar* did.

The feature by *Motor* on the Ninety was altogether different. It was written by freelance Phil Llewellyn, who does know what he's doing, and involved driving a 2,286cc petrol-engined Ninety for several days along very challenging ancient tracks in some of the remotest parts of Wales. Sensibly, Llewellyn and photographer Tim Wren were accompanied by a winch-equipped One Ten.

In an excellently written and stimulating feature the capabilities of the Ninety and One Ten were thoroughly endorsed after driving through some of the most difficult green lanes anywhere – one seven-mile (11km) stretch took seven hours, which is a good measure of the sort of test the Ninety was put to. There was plenty of winching, but the magazine didn't contain a single note of criticism

about either of the two vehicles, both of which had proved much better than expected. Unlike some other journalists who drove the new Land Rovers with the old four-cylinder petrol engine, Llewellyn accepted the lack of power as a characteristic of the unit and drove accordingly, both on- and off-road. It would be interesting to know by how much more he'd have enjoyed it with a V8 or, looking to the future, a Tdi.

V8 Ninety

The lack of a V8 option for the Ninety on its introduction was the source of considerable dissatisfaction, but when the big petrol engine did come along in the short-wheelbase model it was greeted with great joy. Among the magazines covering the extension of the V8 option, plus five-speed gearbox, into the Ninety was *Autocar*, with a short but enthusiastic piece published on 8 May 1985:

'The short wheelbase Land Rover is now available with 3.5-litre V8 engine and five-speed gearbox, giving vastly improved on-road performance and refinement and exhilarating off-road ability.

'The big change is under the bonnet. Twitch the engine into life and there is a satisfying burble from the big exhaust pipe. Twin Zenith Stromberg 175 CDSE carbs hiss gently beneath the cylinder banks. Engage first, step on the pedal and – by Land Rover standards anyway – the car rockets forwards. The most impressive feature is that on a long run it is quite easy to get 90mph up on the speedometer, and to cruise at 85mph on part throttle.

'Off-road the V8 Ninety must now rival the Range Rover as the Best Off-road car in the World. Permanent 4wd with central differential lock, all round long travel coil spring suspension follows the Range Rover pattern, and the short wheelbase and steeper angles of approach and departure mean even better ability on tortuous terrain.

'It's not all good news. Big power in a chunky car means a thirst for fuel. We measured consumption at 13.2mpg, though, in fairness to the car, we drove it hard during its short stay with us – fast on the motorway or in low ratio on the rough. A less exuberant owner should get around 15mpg, and 17mpg could be available to someone with particularly light feet.'

Enter the turbo

Before the Tdi there was the Diesel Turbo. In March 1987, soon after the turbocharged 2.5-litre diesel had been introduced, *Autocar* carried out a full road test on a Ninety County Station Wagon fitted with the new engine:

'When turbocharging the 2.5-litre diesel, Land Rover's engineers were not concerned with outright performance – rather they wanted an engine with plenty of low and mid-range pulling power and no significant turbo lag. With a peak output of 85bhp at 4,000rpm though, the Land Rover has more power than the Mitsubishi Shogun and Isuzu Trooper turbo diesels, and only 2bhp less than Daihatsu's 2.7-litre unit. It also produces a good deal more torque than most of its competitors and, at 1,800rpm, peak torque occurs lower down the rev band.

'The end result is an engine that has a remarkable ability to pull from low rpm with no discernible turbo lag in normal use. Hence the Ninety feels quite rapid on the road with a broad spread of power.

'Power doesn't come for free, and the turbo diesel's extra horses have taken their toll on the fuel consumption. An overall figure of 18mpg doesn't sound impressive at first, and indeed it is bettered by several of the Land Rover's Japanese competitors. The figure does reflect the hard time the Land Rover was given during its time with us … the average owner could certainly expect to attain 20mpg.

'Off-road ability is still at the heart of the success of the Land Rover range, in contrast to some of its competitors where highway comfort is the main attraction. The Ninety turbo diesel does not disappoint in that respect and is surpassed in off-road ability only by V8-engined versions. The car seems almost unstoppable, and once a gear has been selected to tackle an obstacle the driver can concentrate on the task of selecting the right line.

↓ **Whether it is a caravan, horsebox or conventional trailer, Defenders are excellent towing vehicles. (Nick Dimbleby)**

'The Ninety is a superb off-roader that is equally at home on the road, with good handling and an excellent ride. In County guise it offers virtually the same equipment levels as its Japanese rivals and at £12,783 it is priced competitively with them. If conversation is not high on the list of priorities it would make an excellent motorway cruiser for a large family.

'For a long time in the '70s, Land Rover traded on its reputation and little else. The steady stream of improvements started with the One Ten have brought it bang up to date though, and with the latest Ninety the company has demonstrated you no longer need to be merely a patriot to buy a Land Rover.'

The first Tdi

Although a very worthwhile improvement, the first turbocharged engine was not in the same league as the second, the all-new 200 Tdi. This entered service with the Discovery in 1989, then went to the utility production line the following year, transforming what were now known as the Defender 90, 110, and 130. One of the early Defender Tdi write-ups was in Car. What did this no-nonsense, hard-hitting publication have to say?

'Apart from the grille name badges and nasty Defender door decals, what is new is the switch to the excellent direct injection 2.5-litre Tdi diesel introduced on the Discovery.

In its first year the 200 Tdi has proved remarkably reliable and engineers claim it matches the specific fuel consumption of the best truck diesels.

'The horsebox frequently hitched to the back of a Discovery isn't lightweight, but Land Rovers traditionally work harder for their living, drivers revving them for long periods in low gears. For this reason the peak has been taken off the power curve, leaving the Land Rover on 107bhp at 3,800rpm, compared with the Discovery's 111bhp at 4,000rpm. Torque is now 188lb ft at 1,800rpm, instead of 195lb ft for the sister vehicle.

'Stand next to the Tdi at idle and it barely registers as an oil-burner, so suppressed is the diesel 'knock'. But the most convincing improvement comes when the Land Rover 110 County is faced with a long incline, something which would have had its predecessor wheezing and dawdling. The new engine neither struggles nor kicks up a din.

'Off-road it would take a full load to dampen the Tdi's remarkable eagerness. Even climbing the steepest inclines the engine feels strong and lusty, not simply dependable. Downhill braking in bottom gear is infinitely reassuring. The workhorse's worthy new lease of life has not come too soon.'

Digging deep

While Car's readers were noting these comments, the enthusiasts who had bought the latest issue of Land Rover Owner were reading a slightly deeper analysis of the Defender Tdi, this time a 90:

'It was easy with Discovery to be dazzled by the new body on the Range Rover chassis and the strikingly roomy and well-

↓ **The interior of the 90 Tdi impressed** Land Rover Owner, **while the Tdi engine was described as a 'milestone' for the entire Land Rover range. (Nick Dimbleby)**

↑ **Even before the advent of the Tdi, the County Station Wagon was a force to be reckoned with.** *Autocar* **was very impressed with a Diesel Turbo version tested in 1987. (Nick Dimbleby)**

designed interior and not spend enough time looking under the bonnet. Yet it was there, as users will by now have found out, that was perhaps the most impressive part of the whole launch package – the 2.5-litre, turbo charged, intercooled, direct injection diesel, designated 200 Tdi.

'For the first time, a diesel-engined Land Rover, yielding affordable economy, can easily keep up with – and even be ahead of – other car traffic and find itself in the fast lane of an autoroute at an easy and comfortable 75mph cruise.

'As with Discovery, revs and a lot of gear changing are not essential. The extraordinary torque of the Tdi makes fifth gear a useable gear rather than a gear you get into only after accelerating to the speed you want in fourth.

'The power steering of the Defender is admirably suited to its role, both in lightness and gearing. Of the two, the gearing and 'speed' of the steering was the more valued attribute.

'The suppleness of the Range Rover-type all-coil suspension was soon proven when I took it off-road. Even this suspension,

however, will eventually run out of movement and when it did the centre diff lock got me out of trouble – but only just. Land Rover still do not offer an across-the-axle differential lock, so it was possible in extreme situations to get diagonal wheels spinning while the vehicle was suspended on the wheels at the other two corners.

'With the Defender the Land Rover utility models have quietly stepped into a new era of their long career and the steady evolution is apparent throughout the machine. The advent of the Tdi diesel – that actually has fractionally more torque than the V8 – is a milestone for the whole Land Rover range.'

Export drives

Throughout its history Land Rover has depended on overseas sales for a sizeable proportion of its income. Australia has always been a good market for Solihull's products, so what did the Australian press, renowned for being outspoken, make of the switch from leaf springs to coil-sprung utilities? Here are some of the comments made by *Motor Manual* magazine in February 1985:

'The Land Rover as we have come to know it, is dead. In its place is the all-new 110, which is really a Range Rover that looks like a Land Rover.

'Despite a number of changes, and continuing refinement, the Landie gradually gave way to the Japanese product swamping the world market. The time came when old ideas had to be replaced by newer ones.

'The County Wagon is, of course, to be the main focus of JRA's (Australian importer) Land Rover efforts. A new one million dollar assembly facility at Moorebank in NSW will build all the 110s with the exception of the petrol County which will be initially imported.

'The alloy V8 won't be the only power plant available in the County, as the Isuzu 3.8-litre diesel used in previous Land Rovers is listed as an option. Turbocharging for the 3.8 is a predictable extension soon.

'Off-road the 110 feels like a Range Rover, yet it doesn't. The long wheelbase adds something to the ride quality that is balanced out by the fact that the springs, while retaining long-travel characteristics, are slightly firmer.

'Steep, rutted climbs are more comfortable in a 110 than most because you've got that long-reaching suspension keeping all four wheels in contact with the ground.

'The 110 is as comfortable and secure a way of going off-roading as anything else we know. It's a top-class bush track cruiser that will both get you there safely, and leave you relatively refreshed at the end of the day.

'The new Land Rover is very competitive with the Japanese in value for money – and way ahead for all-round ability. Long live the British!'

Problems, problems

One of Land Rover's traditional weaknesses has been poor build quality, and the Defender series has been affected just as much by this as any other Solihull vehicle. The journalist who tested a One Ten for the Australian *4x4* magazine in July 1985 had plenty to complain about:

'During the test the ash tray self destructed and the dashboard as a whole had more rattles than a millionaire's baby. One door wouldn't lock at all, the passenger side front door would not open from the outside and the driver's door would not open from the inside.

'The dust sealing around the rear door was abysmal, and the exterior mirror mounts were too flexible – the mirrors vibrated, and made it almost impossible to get a clear picture of what was coming up behind.

'I'm told that the clunks and thuds from the transmission are built in to both the 110 and the Range Rover. They also have the same ultra slow gear change problem. There's no such thing as a snap change.

↑ The Australian publication *Motor Manual*, wrote with great enthusiasm about the new range of coil-sprung Land Rovers, describing them as 'top class bush track cruisers'. (Nick Dimbleby)

'Travelling at any speed above 60kph with both the front windows down produces wind buffeting of a high order. In fact, it's impossible to keep a peaked cap on one's head unless you do the straps up to a point that would do justice to a well applied tourniquet.'

However:

'The 110 took everything in its stride … Regardless of the conditions the ride was, to say the least, comfortable … The V8 engine was superb, delivering smooth power throughout the range … The quietness of the motor is a big plus for the 110 … The Landy 110 is surprisingly nimble off-road despite its size.

'Apart from a little mishap in deep ruts, the 110 felt invincible. Hot but invincible. There seems to be an excessive amount of exhaust heat transferred through the floor, and driving in bare feet was almost out of the question.'

Out of Africa

South Africa was also important to Solihull, and in March 1990 *Car South Africa* reported on a test involving a V8 One Ten County Station Wagon. Included among the comments, which were generally favourable, was a much-heard cry for axle diff locks as well as the built-in lockable centre diff. Unfortunately, local taxation makes Land Rovers costly in South Africa.

'The rich-on-character V8 provides the One Ten Station Wagon with enough urge to go with the latest semi-civilised body treatment. The test model was fitted with the 'Hiline' trim, which includes an oddments bin between the front seats, metallic paint, air conditioning and power steering, cord cloth upholstery, carpeting and radio/tape combo.

'After venturing into slippery marsh we concluded that we would have preferred a diff lock on each of the axles as well as the centre diff lock, because when both front and rear sets of wheels are on slippery ground power tends to spin out of a wheel on each axle, leaving the vehicle bogged down.

'The fact that the vehicle relies heavily on imported parts, despite being produced at Leyland's Blackheath plant, pushes the price up to R104,390, which is a tough one to swallow.

But if you are serious about travelling off-road, this one had better be on your shopping list.'

Spicy sport

Until 1982, the Camel Trophy used Range Rovers for the annual combination exercise of impossible driving conditions, bridge building, and other tasks in remote parts of the tropics, switching to Series IIIs for 1983. Then, to publicise and celebrate the new Land Rover, One Tens were used for the fifth anniversary event in Brazil. One of the few British magazines to report on the Trophy was *4-Wheel Drive* in its December 1984 issue:

'Diesel engines were chosen for the 20-vehicle strong convoy – fuel economy, low down torque and the ever present danger of fire made this the only choice. The units were the now

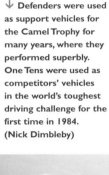

⬇ Defenders were used as support vehicles for the Camel Trophy for many years, where they performed superbly. One Tens were used as competitors' vehicles in the world's toughest driving challenge for the first time in 1984. (Nick Dimbleby)

superseded 2.3-litre engines.

'Finally, incredibly, everybody got through and the Trophy was finished. Damage to people? Remarkably, none. Damage to vehicles? Considerable. All of them sustained incredible wounds.

'It goes without saying that there is hardly a straight body panel between them, but other maladies include bent chassis, bumpers split like sardine cans and a range of other parts ripped or broken off. But they kept going.'

90 for the USA

Our final word comes from that great American institution *Car and Driver*, which wrote about the first US-certified (or North American Specification) 90 in its February 1994 issue. Land Rover North America had invited the press to the wilds of Wyoming for a taster:

'The Brits at Land Rover in the motherland thought their American pals were off their nut when they asked for a US-certified version of the rugged little Defender 90.

But those boys at Lanham, Maryland, at Land Rover North America know their off-road play toys. Didn't the 500 Defender 110s they brought in a year ago sell instantly? There was no question. They wanted the 92.9-inch wheelbase Tonka truck of dirt diggers in their stateside stable.

The cabin is Spartan; the knobs and the door handles are industrial-looking. The Brits were loathe to use US rubber but are so impressed by these [BF Goodrich Mud Terrains].

Four-wheel disc brakes and four-wheel coil-spring suspension are the kind of equipment we have come to expect from Land Rover, the kind that sets it apart from the competition. The long-travel coils provide exceptional articulation in rugged terrain; it's really neat to watch a Defender 90 from the rear as it climbs a rocky hill with its front and rear wheels angling in different directions.

The best option you can choose [if you decide to buy] is an off-road vehicle permit, because not to take this brilliant brute off-road would be a tragedy. It would be like getting your most coveted toy for Christmas and never taking it out of the package.'

↑ **Land Rovers have been used as workhorses in Africa since the earliest days.** *Car South Africa* **considered the Defender series well worth considering for off-road work in the hostile environment of southern Africa. (Nick Dimbleby)**

ENGINES

A surprising number of engines have been used to power Defenders and their predecessors since the advent of the One Ten in 1983. However, not all have suited these otherwise excellent vehicles. A full appraisal of the qualities, shortcomings, fuel consumption, and reliability of all engine types is given in Chapter 11, but the information below forms part of the outline information package with which all would-be buyers should arm themselves.

Original choice was either the good old 3.5-litre petrol V8 or the venerable 2,286cc four-cylinder petrol and diesel units carried over from the Series III, and the Series IIA before that. The V8, of course, is also an old engine, but has always been an excellent power unit, albeit a very thirsty one.

The 2.5-litre diesel and petrol engines followed, before the 2.5 petrol option was dropped and the diesel acquired a Garrett turbocharger, becoming the Diesel Turbo. Then came the first of the Tdi family, the 200 Tdi, which in turn was followed by the 300 Tdi and finally the Td5 and Puma types.

↑ The 3.5-litre V8 engine was fitted as a standard unit for several years. It is the most appealing engine in many ways, but be prepared for 14–16mpg fuel consumption. Sometimes it is even worse than that. (Dave Barker)

← The 110 County Station Wagon is the best Defender choice for those who want to enjoy family motoring in comfort. This is the most civilised model in the entire range. (Nick Dimbleby)

↑ **Ex-military vehicles are usually worth checking out, especially if you are on a tight budget, because most have been very well maintained mechanically, although bodywork condition varies greatly. (Nick Dimbleby)**

Other than the Td5 and Puma, which are both completely new-generation units with an excellent mix of power, torque, and refinement, the best of these units for most people is the 300 Tdi. This had the same power and torque as the 200 Tdi from which it was developed, but was more reliable and less noisy.

The original turbocharged engine, the Diesel Turbo, has been described as 'the worst engine made by Land Rover', but this is unjust. True, the Diesel Turbo proved to have long-term reliability problems, and was never in the same league as the first of the Tdis, but the fact that a Ninety or One Ten has one of these engines should not in itself put you off if the price is right.

Non-turbo 2.5-litre diesels are now quite rare in civilian vehicles, although numerous ex-military 90s and 110s have them. If you can put up with the lack of pace and, again, the asking price is appropriate, don't be put off. It is, in fact, a pretty good off-road engine.

The V8 is, in these days of very high fuel prices, a specialist engine because of its great thirst. However, if an LPG conversion can be justified, running costs work out much the same as for a Tdi.

ENGINE RUNDOWN

Puma: The best Defender engine so far, despite not being a Land Rover 'original' but of Ford origin.

Td5: Excellent with no inherent reliability problems; early worries about electronics have proved unfounded.

300 Tdi: Best of the Tdi engines.

200 Tdi: Still going strong in very many good-value vehicles.

V8: Great thirst, but best for heavy-duty towing.

Diesel Turbo: Long-term reliability problems, but now found in inexpensive vehicles. Good off-road engine.

Non-turbo 2.5 diesel, 2.25 diesel, 2.5 and 2.25 petrol: The 2.5 diesel's not too bad, although slow, and the 2.5 petrol, which was a pretty good engine, is now rare. The rest are best left alone, except when the vehicle's very cheap and an engine transplant is viable.

Buying

WHERE TO BUY

There have never been so many sources for used Land Rovers, although this presents its own problems. Knowing just where to begin the search can be one of the most difficult parts of the whole exercise. They turn up just about everywhere, although there's a tendency for particular types of Land Rover, or Land Rovers which have been used for specific purposes, to be sold at clearly identifiable places, and advertised through particular publications.

Generally speaking, there's a greater risk when buying any vehicle privately, because there's very little, if any, comeback if the vehicle is subsequently found to have been misrepresented. Despite this risk, however, private advertisements in local papers can be the source of good, honest machines, and it also pays to look for them in less obvious places – a number of years ago I spotted a Range Rover for sale in Horse & Hound and, after checking it out, bought for a very fair price what turned out to be a truly excellent five-year-old vehicle.

The principal sources are:

Land Rover franchised dealers: Vehicles are covered by a good warranty and nearly always in excellent order. But they are only ever very recent vehicles, and are always higher-priced than elsewhere.

Specialist Land Rover dealers: Usually described and sold honestly, vehicles from such sources are often the best bet. These dealers have a reputation to maintain within the general Land Rover movement.

General used car dealers: Occasionally the source of gems, although you need to watch out for badly neglected ex-farm Land Rovers which have been traded-in. Prices range from fair to 'you must be joking'.

General 4x4 traders: These can be a good source, and it's always an encouraging sign if a vehicle on offer was traded for a more modern or higher specification one by the previous owner. Prices are usually reasonable.

Internet: Most, if not all, specialist Land Rover dealers and other 4x4 traders now have websites with regularly updated stock lists.

↓ **Specialist dealers are usually the best source of used Land Rovers. This late-model 300 Tdi was spotted at Four plus 4 in Leeds, and represents the best of the Tdi Defender range. (Dave Barker)**

→ **Never buy a vehicle if the vendor cannot produce the V5 registration 'logbook'. If you are told it has been sent for, either arrange to come back when it has arrived, or walk away altogether.**
(Dave Barker)

military dealers. Prices for some private sales can be very ambitious.

Ex-military dealers: The place to go for a Land Rover released from the military but not yet civilian registered. Mostly, they are very honest people and prices are reasonable. Beware, though, because some released Land Rovers are in awful condition.

CHECKOUT

Before examining a vehicle talk to the vendor about how it has been used, when it last changed hands, what work has been carried out, and why it is being sold. Clearly, this applies more to private sales, but it is worth asking the same questions even if it's a dealer sale, because sometimes much of the history is known.

Inspect the paperwork carefully, checking that the name of the registered keeper on the V5 'log book' tallies either with the identity of the person selling it or, if it's a dealer sale, what you're being told. Note how long the vehicle has been owned by the vendor (or currently registered owner). If it is only a short time – less than a year – you need to know why it is being sold so quickly.

Look for proof of purchase, and inform the vendor you'll carry out a check for outstanding hire purchase, etc, with a company such as AA Data Check or HPI. This will tell you if there are any prior claims on ownership and whether it is logged as having been an insurance write-off.

Ask to see previous MoTs, which are a very reliable check on the mileage displayed on the distance recorder, and see if there's evidence of regular servicing and repairs. Many Land Rovers are maintained by enthusiastic owners, and there may be no paperwork to support their hard work, but vehicles which have been dealer maintained should have the evidence to support it.

If the vehicle's reasonably new, and certainly if it is being sold by a Land Rover dealer, the service book should be fully stamped up, and there should also be invoices for additional work.

INITIAL INSPECTION

An initial, general look around will tell you much about the vehicle, the way it has been used, and the amount of care it's received. It's worth doing this before checking it out in detail because a preliminary check will sometimes tell you it's not worth spending any more time on it.

There are also special internet sites for used vehicles, such as eBay, but special care is vital when considering a purchase.

Auctions: Here you take the greatest risk for the chance of the best bargain. Auctions are the place to go if you know what you're looking for and how to check it out. Prices are usually very good.

Local newspapers: Land Rovers privately owned, but not necessarily by enthusiasts, often find their way into local papers. However, as with all private sales it is crucial to check legal ownership as well as the condition of the vehicle. Prices can be good because bargaining is often fruitful.

Trader publications: These are the biggest single source of used Land Rovers, but are also the place that some people try to unload unhealthy/dodgy machines. They are nevertheless really worth trying, although you'll look at loads before buying. Prices are all over the place.

Specialist Land Rover magazines: These are not the Mecca for private sales you'd imagine, although they are the place to look for fully-prepared off-roaders and expedition vehicles being sold privately, and for specialist and ex-

Does it look genuinely clean, or does it show signs of having been hurriedly washed down for your visit? Walk around the Land Rover and look along the panels and the sill area beneath the doors. A few dents are inevitable with older vehicles, but lots of dents and gouges may well indicate a hard life off the tarmac, or careless ownership.

Is the interior tidy? If it has carpets and they are scuffed and muddy it has most likely been off-roading, and/or not enjoyed the benefit of overmats. Are the seats dirty or torn? Is the headlining intact? Is the dashboard clean, or covered with dirt?

Open the bonnet and look around. If it is filthy, with wires hanging loose, it has been neglected. Low coolant and hydraulic levels, along with pitch black oil on the dipstick, perhaps at a low level, tell the same story (although the oil in diesel engines blackens very quickly).

A Land Rover which fails these initial tests isn't worth buying. There are plenty about, so walk away – but if the early signs are encouraging, dig deeper.

← Land Rovers which are used off-road inevitably pick up some knocks and dents along the way, although it should not stop you buying if everything else is satisfactory and the price is right. This example shows damage to the gearbox crossmember. (Dave Barker)

↓ A badly rusted rear crossmember will almost certainly mean MoT failure and must be replaced. Some surface rusting is inevitable on older vehicles, but never forget that this part of the chassis takes all the strains of towing. (Dave Barker)

↑ **The fact that Land Rovers are constructed with aluminium alloy body panels does not mean there is no chance of corrosion. Electrolytic reaction between the body skin and supporting steel frame causes corrosion like this, especially on door bottoms. (Dave Barker)**

HISTORY

It helps to know how the vehicle has been used in the past. Some Station Wagons are used as crew buses on large construction sites, and have a tough time of it. Boating enthusiasts often use Land Rovers for hauling vessels up slipways, with frequent immersion in salt water. And although Land Rovers are designed for off-road use, too much of it causes premature wear to most mechanical components, puts great strain on steering, suspension parts, and wheel bearings, leads to premature chassis rusting, and plays havoc with the interior.

On the other hand, a Land Rover which has been used for everyday family transport or as a status-symbol company car is unlikely to present any of these problems. But if it has clocked up a high mileage in a short time, it is likely to have been driven flat out from dawn to dusk, leading to the possibility of premature engine wear.

CHASSIS

The most important part of any Land Rover is the chassis, an enormously strong box-section construction which, although resisting the passage of time well, inevitably falls victim to rust over the years. Original chassis are not galvanised, although some replacements are.

The chassis must be inspected very carefully. Look first for dents and gouges caused by contact with rocks off-road. The odd dent is to be expected, especially on older models, but lots of them point to a very hard life. Damage like this turns readily to rust, so look for corrosion or, much worse, evidence of filler, which is totally unacceptable. Repair sections or plates welded into position are okay, but bear in mind that if a chassis has got to the point where entire sections have already been repaired, a full replacement will not be too far away. And that's a big, expensive job.

The rear of the chassis can be more prone to corrosion than the front, while the rear crossmember frequently rusts before the main chassis rails. This is a principal load bearing section, and takes all the stresses of towing, so must be in perfect order. Outriggers, too, rust quite readily, especially those at the bulkhead.

From the point of view of the corrosion inspection, the bulkhead can be included with the chassis. Although it is more than likely that any serious rust will be restricted to the footwell area, which is relatively easy to repair, it is possible that the bulkhead itself is corroded on very early vehicles. Check from inside the cab and from beneath and above the engine bay. Bulkhead replacement is a major exercise.

BODYWORK

The body skin is aluminium alloy, which doesn't rust but is subject to corrosion as the result of electrolytic action where the alloy is in contact with steel. This happens on quite recent vehicles – although it shouldn't – and shows itself as bubbling beneath the paint and crumbly white powder. Virtually all Defenders will display some degree of this corrosion at various points around the body. If it's relatively slight it can be ignored, but extensive bodywork corrosion will need remedial work at some time, which may well include some reskinning and replacement of the underlying steel framework.

The doors should be inspected closely, starting with the hinges and working all the way round, inside and out. The earliest One Tens had Series

← This is one of the front coil springs of a 90. The low-rate (or 'softness') and long-travel design transformed the comfort of Land Rover utility vehicles and made them unbeatable off-road. (Dave Barker)

↙ The earliest One Tens had Series III type doors which were in two pieces and had sliding windows. Wind-up windows were introduced concurrently with the launch of the Ninety in 1984, and one-piece doors came a little later. (Dave Barker)

III-type two-piece front doors, with sliding glass. These are worth retaining if you buy one of these now-rare vehicles, but they don't wear very well and are likely to need complete replacement at some time.

The rear doors take a lot of punishment from road dirt and badly secured loads, while the hinges wear prematurely if the spare wheel is rear-door mounted. Very often, rear window wash-wipers and heating elements don't work, so check them.

SUSPENSION

Land Rover suspension is extremely tough, but with older vehicles, and those which have done a lot of off-roading, or have regularly carried very heavy loads, some problems can be expected. The bushes throughout the system wear, leading to a general sloppiness which is readily noticed during a test drive. Fortunately, replacement is not particularly expensive, and is something anyone buying an older coil-sprung Land Rover should be prepared for.

The springs are huge, tough units which stand the test of time well, but will inevitably lose their strength eventually. If the Land Rover sags on one

→ Prop shaft universal
joints take a pounding on
any vehicle which uses
them, but they have a
particularly tough life on
Land Rovers which are
used off-road. Use of low
ratios imposes high torque
levels, while immersion in
mud and sand can cause
premature wear.
(Dave Barker)

side, or sits down at the front or rear, or has a
general soggy, woolly feel to the ride and handling,
it may well need new springs and shock absorbers.
Fortunately again, springs are not expensive and,
along with the dampers, are easy to replace.

An important part of the rear suspension on
some 110-inch vehicles – but not fitted to all of
them – is the Boge self-levelling strut. It is self-
energising and is designed to permit full rear
suspension travel even when heavily loaded. It is
difficult to test accurately because the unit only
works when the vehicle is moving, but, depending
on the general state of the coil springs, you may be
able to notice if the rear of the Land Rover droops
noticeably with a couple of people sitting as close
as possible to the rear door as you drive along.
The self-leveller can be dispensed with, in which
case higher-rate rear springs are needed, unless the
vehicle is not going to be heavily loaded.

STEERING
Another cause of poor handling is wear in the
steering system, usually the ball joints, although
it can be difficult to decide, without jacking the

vehicle up, whether the sloppiness is caused by
steering, suspension, or both. In most cases it's
both! However, worn steering joints, or even wear
in the steering box itself, is no reason to turn away
from an otherwise good Land Rover.

While checking the steering, it is important to
examine the chrome-plated front swivels. With
time these develop surface pitting, particularly after
plenty of off-roading in abrasive conditions, causing
leaking to occur. The only cure is replacement.

The power steering system is tough, but should
be checked for leaks before and after the test
drive, and for noise-free operation on the move.

TRANSMISSION
Some free-play is to be expected in the permanent
four-wheel-drive transmission, mostly coming from
gradually developing wear in the propshaft universal
joints, but eventually it becomes unacceptable. If it's
bad you'll notice clunks and free play as you take
up the drive when starting off and when changing
gear. If you're not sure when test driving, replicate
heavy traffic by travelling slowly in first gear, on
and off the throttle; this is when the wear is most
annoying and inconvenient.

→ The steering swivel
assembly protects the
complex inner mechanisms
from everyday road dirt,
winter mud, and the
rigours of off-roading.
Eventually, the chrome-
plated swivels become
pitted and then start to
leak lubricant; examine
closely before buying.
(Dave Barker)

Wear develops right through the system, and with a differential on each axle plus one between the front and rear propshafts, plus the transfer gearbox, let alone the main gearbox and front constant velocity joints, there are plenty of places for things to go wrong.

Test for smooth changes in all gears by going up and down through the gearbox, and check that it doesn't jump out of gear when accelerating and on the over-run. Select low ratios and repeat the exercise, but don't be too alarmed if the high-low selector is rather stiff in operation, particularly on a vehicle where there's been no need to use low ratios. Engage the diff lock, the operation of which is confirmed by a warning light on the dash, but don't drive around on any firm surface with the diff lock engaged: this can cause serious transmission damage.

Make sure the handbrake will hold the vehicle on an incline, but don't apply it on the move. Land Rovers have transmission brakes, in the form of a drum brake on the rear prop shaft, and must be used only at a standstill.

Check beneath the vehicle for oil leaks from the axle differentials and main and transfer gearboxes.

↑ While the original 2.3 petrol engine was inadequate, the 2.5-litre unit derived from it was somewhat better and is quite usable even today. This 2.5 is still working hard on an everyday basis. (Dave Barker)

← Proving the longevity of Ninetys and One Tens, there are still many around with the Diesel Turbo engine (shown here), while a number of ex-military vehicles have the normally-aspirated version of the now very old 2.5-litre diesel. (Dave Barker)

ENGINE

Clearly, the older the vehicle the more allowance must be made for age, and the basic characteristics of the unit. For example, the 2.5 non-turbo and its turbocharged development used in the Diesel Turbo are both noisy and unrefined compared with the 200 Tdi, while the 300 Tdi is even quieter and smoother.

The 2.5 diesel and 2.5 Diesel Turbo are both reliable engines, although the Diesel Turbo has been unfairly labelled as a particularly unsatisfactory unit. It is true, though, that many Diesel Turbos have failed to reach much more than 65,000 miles (105,000km) or so without major overhaul.

With both these pre-Tdi engines check carefully for serious oil leaks, particularly from seals, and with the Diesel Turbo look for oil blown into the air cleaner, and evidence of cracks in the head or block (water in the oil, and oil in the coolant).

The 2.5-litre diesel engines have timing belts, and if there is no hard evidence of belt replacement recently, budget for doing it if you buy the vehicle. Whenever there's doubt, timing belts should always be replaced – it's a great deal less costly and less inconvenient than rebuilding most of the engine if it fails the first time you drive it.

Most, if not all, of these older diesels usually blow out a cloud of blue or white smoke on start-up, but this should disappear quickly. If it persists, there's trouble.

On the move the non-turbo diesel will be noisy and sluggish, while the Diesel Turbo is noisy and fairly lively. If the latter fails to accelerate reasonably well (bearing in mind its 0–60mph or 0–96kph time when new was about 22 seconds), and will not cruise happily at 65mph (105kph), there's something wrong with it. However, don't expect too much, because maximum speed was never better than 75mph (120kph), compared with the 68mph (109kph) of the non-turbo.

The 2.25 petrol engine was the same unit being used in contemporary Series IIIs when the One Ten was launched and, although a reasonably smooth engine, it was always a little rattly and inclined to puff out a bit of blue smoke.

Listen for timing chain rattle, and check for excessive crankcase pressure by looking for smoke, as opposed to wispy fumes, from the oil filler

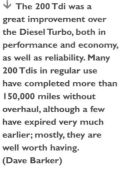

↓ **The 200 Tdi was a great improvement over the Diesel Turbo, both in performance and economy, as well as reliability. Many 200 Tdis in regular use have completed more than 150,000 miles without overhaul, although a few have expired very much earlier; mostly, they are well worth having. (Dave Barker)**

cap. Again, as with the diesels, some blue exhaust smoke is to be expected on start-up and very often on the over-run. The engine was built to run on leaded petrol, and will now require either lead replacement fuel, or the use of approved lead replacement additives with unleaded petrol.

The short-lived 2.5-litre petrol engine was similar in many ways, although more powerful and more suited to the vehicle. These are found only rarely, and should be checked out in the same way as the smaller engine.

Smoothest and quietest of the lot was the 3.5-litre petrol V8, but most have deteriorated with age. In good order the V8 should be quiet and smooth at tickover, building to a lusty roar at high revs. Unfortunately, many have suffered from poor maintenance, something they don't like at all; if a V8 runs rough, this is probably why, and if it's smoking as well the wear has spread to pistons, rings, bores, and bearings. A rebuild can be expensive.

Best all-round engines for the entire Defender family are the Tdis. Both are excellent engines, with ideal power and torque characteristics for the host vehicles. They provide perfectly acceptable road-going performance, and excel in off-road situations. Many have been retro-fitted into pre-Tdi Ninetys and One Tens, so they can crop up in the earliest of the family.

Some 200 Tdis have developed quite advanced wear at around 65,000 miles (105,000km) or so, while far more have gone on past 150,000 miles (240,000km) without protest. Some of the premature wear can be blamed on use, so it is worth finding out as much as you can about the way the Land Rover has been driven. For example, some people have chosen Defenders as company cars, perhaps switching from much faster BMWs and Volvos in order to display something different in the company car park. In many cases, drivers have tried to compensate for the relatively poor performance by accelerating to full revs for every gearchange and driving the engine flat out on the open road. Sometimes, this has proved too much, particularly for earlier Tdis. Consequently, be on the lookout for engines which have developed valve and piston wear (blue exhaust smoke and/or serious oil leaks), turbocharger wear, intercooler problems, and cracked blocks and heads.

↓ **Many 300 Tdi engines have required a modification to the cambelt pulley system to overcome a fault in some (but not all) of these engines which caused premature cambelt wear and the risk of belt breakage. (Nick Dimbleby)**

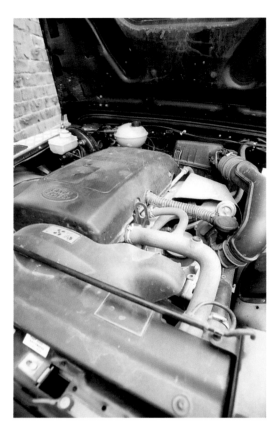

→ Introduced in late-1998 the Td5 diesel engine has won many friends, especially among owners who regularly cover high mileages. The electronic management system raises a question mark over off-road activities which involve regular immersion in very deep water. (Dave Barker)

Timing belt changes are, of course, crucial. Find out when one was last done. Many vehicles with 300 Tdi engines have required a modification to the timing belt drive pulleys because of a production fault which caused the belt to run slightly out of line. Other than this, the 300 Tdi has proved more reliable long-term than the 200 Tdi, and problems are few.

The five-cylinder Td5 diesel engine was introduced in 1998, bringing unprecedented power and refinement to diesel-powered Land Rovers. The engine itself is successful, but buyers intending to indulge regularly in extreme off-roading, especially where it involves a lot of deep water wading, need to be aware that Td5 Defenders have a sophisticated electronic engine management system, and that ECUs and their associated components do not mix well with water.

But it's not just water that electronic systems don't like. Some Td5s have suffered from engine oil finding its way into the injector wiring loom. This results in a misfiring engine because command signals from the ECU never reach the affected injectors, so they don't open to let fuel

into the combustion chambers.

It has to be said that this problem mainly affected earlier Td5s, and most of them will have been sorted out by the time they've reached the second-hand market, but if you come across an engine that appears to be running roughly, this is probably why.

INTERIOR

The seating in the Defender family is either of the hard-wearing cloth used as standard in Station Wagons, or is the less appealing vinyl-covered type found in the utility models. Paradoxically, the cloth is often the longer living of the two because of its greater resistance to tearing, but the fact that the plastic type can be hosed down gives it the practical edge when there's a lot of mud about.

Many enthusiast owners fit waterproof overcovers – an excellent way of preserving cloth seats if the Land Rover is used on a farm or construction site or is off-roaded – but take a good look at the condition of the seats beneath the covers.

'Working' Land Rovers usually have no carpeting, but if you're looking at Station Wagons check the state of the carpets. Nearly all Land Rovers leak rainwater at various points around the roof and side windows, and this doesn't do the carpets and seats much good. Condensation is also a problem, especially with basic van-type bodywork not fitted with headlinings or sidewall insulation.

Spotter's guide

1983

One Ten introduced. Bodywork virtually identical to later models, but first-year vehicles easily identifiable by their two-piece, Series III-type front doors with horizontally sliding windows. Wheel arch eyebrows were all body-coloured. Five body types: soft-top; Hard Top; pick-up; High-Capacity Pick-up; Station Wagon/County Station Wagon. Engines: 2,286cc petrol; 2,286cc diesel; 3,528cc V8 petrol. Transmissions: Five-speed permanent four-wheel drive or optional selectable four-wheel drive with four-cylinder engines; four-speed permanent four-wheel drive with V8.

When it comes to four-cylinder petrol engines you're more likely to come across the 2,495cc derivation of the old unit, which commenced production in late-Summer 1985. In this engine the power is about 12 per cent better at 83bhp, and the torque is a more respectable 133lb ft at 2,000rpm. The larger engine was used for all versions of the One Ten and Ninety from Autumn 1985, and is a better alternative than the earlier version. It only adds a few miles per hour on to top speed because, with the very poor aerodynamics of these vehicles, it takes a lot of extra power to squeeze out any more than 70mph (112kph). The comfortable cruising speed is about 65mph (105kph), but there's an improvement in noise levels compared with the 2.3 and, while it doesn't provide the ambience of the V8, it's not at all bad.

This engine is better, too, for all those jobs which the 2.3 struggles with, such as heavy towing, and is a better off-road engine too. It's not perfect, but the differences are there to be admired.

The 2.5 is a longer-living engine than the 2.3, partly because its extra power means it doesn't work quite so hard to do any particular task, but

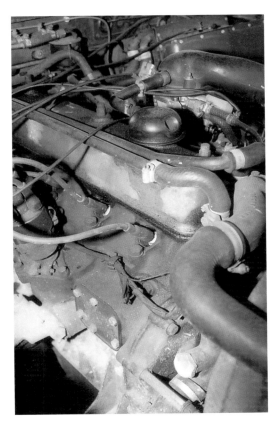

← The 2,286cc petrol engine was carried over from the Series III, which in turn had taken it from the Series II and IIA. It is reliable and rugged but does not have sufficient power for regular use; the 2.5-litre engine developed from it is better. (Dave Barker)

↓ It is extremely important to know in advance the sort of driving you will be doing in a Defender before making any purchase decisions. (Nick Dimbleby)

overall gearing, or drops the engine speed, by 21.8 per cent), showed no consumption difference at a steady 60mph, although normal driving on main roads took the average from 17.5mpg without overdrive, to 19.9mpg with it.

Another worry is the use of these engines without leaded petrol, important to prevent valve seat recession. Although a number of lead-replacement additives have been approved for use in Britain and elsewhere, their effectiveness over long-term operation with engines which, of necessity, have to work quite hard, is not clear. The situation is exactly the same with the lead-replacement petrols which are now widely available.

The only good news in this respect is the limited availability in the UK of traditional four-star petrol, a concession made available principally for the historic car movement; but filling stations able to provide it are few and far between. Only 120 sources of leaded petrol were listed throughout Britain in June 2000. (At the time of writing a fully updated list was published in every issue of Classic Car Weekly.)

↑ **There are a lot of Defenders out there that have had an engine transplant. If you're considering buying such a vehicle, make sure the job has been done properly, paying particular attention to the engine mounts and wiring. Make sure you check that the engine matches the one listed on the registration document. (Simon Hodder)**

also because it is a more modern unit. Unlike the 2.5-litre diesel with which it is closely related, the 2.5-litre petrol retained chain drive for the camshaft, which adds to its appeal and longevity.

Running costs of all these engines are quite high, and there's the added problem these days that there isn't a type of petrol which fully suits them. On longer journeys, where more use can be made of fifth gear, it's possible to achieve a best consumption figure of about 23mpg, but that's only likely if cruising speed is kept well down. Everyday use, including stop-start town driving, is likely to achieve no better than 18–19mpg.

These are not economical units and a good idea of their thirst can be found in some steady-speed fuel consumption tests carried out on a Series III 88-inch (comparable information with the same engine in the One Ten and Ninety is not available), in which at a steady 60mph (96kph) the Series III gave 14.8mpg. While a Ninety would be a little better because of its overdrive fifth gear, the difference would not be more than a couple of miles per gallon. Indeed, another test on a Series III, in which the same vehicle was compared with and without a Fairey overdrive unit (which raises the

PETROL V8

For many people the V8 is the only engine to have in a Land Rover. It is smooth and powerful and, for some, there's nothing like the burble of a V8 for bringing a tingle to the back of the neck.

The 3.5-litre Rover V8 engine began life with Buick in 1961, so is the longest-lived power unit in Land Rover's line-up. Even the latest versions are descended directly from the American original. It was first used in utility Land Rovers in the Stage 1 Series III 109-inch, and was the star in the original list of engine options for the One Ten in 1983. The V8 continued as an option in the One Ten and Ninety (although it wasn't offered with the first Ninetys) and then for a short while in Defenders. It has been dropped from the production line, though, as Land Rover increasingly standardised on Tdis, and was not available at all with the Td5 series.

In its original form in the first One Tens it came just as it did with the then-current Range Rover, although with less power, and still used four-speed transmission while all the other One Tens had five gears. Even in this form, it was a delightful engine for the One Ten, giving good performance from its 114bhp and 185lb ft of torque, with an 80mph (129kph) cruising speed which was then simply astonishing in a Land Rover.

The downside was its enormous appetite for fuel, with 12mpg being commonplace, and for most owners this took the edge off the enjoyment. I owned one of the very early One Tens and found its consumption very much worse than the Range Rover – with identical engine and transmission – which followed it. I could get 19 or sometimes 20mpg from the Range Rover, but never more than 14mpg from the One Ten.

The situation improved with the Santana-built five-speed LT85 gearbox introduced in 1985, when the V8 also became part of the Ninety engine list, and it is this combination which most V8 buyers will encounter these days. Because of the V8's thirst and, at least in Britain, extremely high fuel prices, V8 Land Rovers are not as popular as they once were, and to a degree prices reflect this.

If you're not bothered about the fuel cost, or don't plan on doing many miles annually, perhaps using your Land Rover only for recreation, the V8 is still a very worthwhile option. And if you are

intending to cover long distances, it's well worth considering an LPG conversion, the cost of which can be recouped in a year or two with LPG being roughly half the cost of petrol.

The V8 engine gives the utility Land Rovers a level of mechanical refinement which isn't possible with any of the diesels, not even the Td5. Along with this there's a top speed of just about 90mph (144kph) and 85mph (137kph) cruising … if you don't mind watching the fuel gauge moving downwards. At 14 seconds acceleration to 60mph (96kph) this is at least three seconds quicker than the Tdi, and there's an overall lustiness about the performance which feels most un-Land Rover-like.

Fuel consumption, however, remains the bugbear of the V8. In a road test of a V8 Ninety in Autocar in 1985 the magazine recorded an overall figure of 13.2mpg, commenting that average driving should take it to 14.5mpg, and a gentle approach would extend it to 17mpg.

It's a mistake to buy a V8 Land Rover in the belief that because it's a large-capacity engine it must be reliable. The Rover V8 can indeed be reliable over very high mileages, but only when oil

↓ If you are doing a lot of commuting and other long-distance driving the V8 will cost you dearly because of its great thirst. However, it is the most pleasant of all Land Rover engines. (Nick Dimbleby)

↑ The pre-turbocharger 2.5-litre diesel is a reasonable engine for off-road use, but is hopelessly out of its depth in modern traffic conditions. The earlier 2,286cc diesel is suitable only for removing to make way for a good engine! (Nick Dimbleby)

changes and other servicing routines are carried out to the book. Therefore, try to assure yourself that the engine has been properly maintained before you buy, and keep the schedules going religiously afterwards.

In most respects the V8 is a very good off-road engine, although the fact that it needs 2,500rpm to produce maximum torque gives it very different characteristics to, say, the Tdi units – which provide a higher torque figure than the V8 at only 1,800rpm.

Something which many enthusiasts admire about the V8 is its extremely smooth power delivery. When used in conjunction with a stripped-out 90 it has a good power-to-weight ratio. It's universally popular with enthusiasts involved in speed-related off-road competition, when it is normally used in conjunction with automatic transmission.

The big problem with the V8 is the vulnerability of all petrol engines to water, and it takes a great deal of effort to waterproof a V8 satisfactorily … and even then you can never be really sure that a few drops won't short out one of the plugs, or find their way into the distributor.

NON-TURBO DIESELS

The 2,286cc diesel engine, like the petrol unit of the same size, was carried over into the One Ten. However, it was replaced by the 2.5-litre version in February 1984, so its lifetime in the new vehicle was brief, and it was never used in the Ninety.

That the old diesel was used for a such a short time is a cause for celebration. With only 60bhp available it was never powerful enough for Series IIIs, even though it was a popular choice, but to put it in an all-new Land Rover in the 1980s is something of which Solihull's management should have been ashamed.

Because of its brief use in the One Ten, only a handful of survivors remain. The best thing that can be said is that any of these remaining 2.25-litre diesels are inevitably going to be cheap and, therefore, ideal candidates for engine transplants. Even at a give-away price, to buy a One Ten with this engine with the intention of using it will certainly result in severe disappointment.

The 2,495cc unit was developed from the five-bearing 2,286cc engine without a great deal of effort by Land Rover. The increase in capacity and power was achieved by lengthening the stroke, while a new DPS injector pump provided more accurate fuel metering and helped improve fuel consumption. Cold starting was improved, too, with more advanced glow-plugs.

Yet for all this, maximum power was only 67bhp and torque a modest 114lb ft, albeit at the extremely useful 1,800rpm which is a feature of Land Rover diesels. Having maximum torque so low in the rev range means that towing is not quite as hard-going as the maximum power figure would suggest, while in off-roading situations there's surprisingly good response to limited throttle input. It's a tough, slogging engine capable of pulling a Ninety or One Ten through deep mud, up slippery hills, and over difficult rocky sections with relative ease.

It's on the open road that you notice the limitations which are inevitable with only 67bhp on tap. Maximum speed is just about 70mph (112kph), which is about 10mph (16kph) better than the 2.25 diesel-powered Series III with which it is most frequently compared. It will actually cruise at 70mph, provided there are no inclines and no headwind, and with a decent tailwind will reach 80mph (129kph). To maintain the 70mph cruise, or anything like it, lots of use needs to be made of fourth gear.

The achievement of this engine was to make the new Land Rovers acceptable for road use and to give them the ability to keep up (well, almost) with other traffic. Even when used very hard during a road test for Motor in 1986 it returned an overall fuel consumption figure of 21.8mpg, and most owners can expect to get 23mpg in normal use, which is better than the earlier, smaller engine.

DIESEL TURBO

The considerably reworked 2.5-litre diesel which emerged as the Diesel Turbo at the end of 1986 provided Land Rover with a crucial shot of adrenalin, and enabled Solihull to hold its head above water in terms of increasingly important diesel power until the first Tdi came along.

Looked at today, the Diesel Turbo appears crude, unsophisticated, noisy, and of questionable reliability, but when it was introduced it was hailed as an important step forward. It was used until the introduction of the Tdi to the Defender in 1990, and the large numbers produced means that plenty are still in use today.

Because the vehicles fitted with this engine are

now all more then 19 years old, and because of its acknowledged inferiority to the Tdi, Ninety and One Ten Diesel Turbos are usually very affordable. Consequently it's an engine which purchasers at the budget end of the Defender range may well end up with.

In designing the engine – it was far more than a 2.5 with a turbocharger bolted on – Land Rover engineers were much more concerned with pulling power than with outright performance. Yet anybody who has driven both the normally-aspirated 2.5 and the Diesel Turbo cannot fail to be impressed with the difference.

The turbocharged engine boosted maximum speed by about 5mph (8kph) over the non-turbo 2.5, taking it to 75mph (121kph), which is also a realistic cruising speed. The earlier engine would also cruise at maximum speed (as would the engine before it), but it took only the slightest upward slope or headwind to knock it back to 60mph (96kph), whereas although the Diesel Turbo is easily dislodged from 75mph, it will nevertheless keep up 70mph (113kph) with relative ease.

Although there's no rev counter, maximum speed with the turbocharged engine equates to

↑ The Diesel Turbo engine is not an attractive unit to look at compared with the Tdi, but it works well enough and was much better than the normally aspirated unit which preceded it. The turbocharger can suffer from lack of lubrication if oil changes are not carried out to schedule. (Dave Barker)

↑ **Defenders are excellent tow vehicles, and many are bought with caravanning holidays in mind. Some are even converted into mobile homes. (Nick Dimbleby)**

3,750rpm in fifth gear, just below the peak power point of 4,000rpm. The engine is governed to 4,250rpm. This gives the Ninety and One Ten quite brisk acceleration to 50mph (80kph), which is reached in 14 seconds. However, so much power is required to accelerate the very un-aerodynamic vehicle beyond this point that it takes a further eight seconds to reach 60mph.

In everyday use, this makes the Diesel Turbo an easy engine to live with in terms of performance and general usefulness, while its low-down lugging ability (quite a breakthrough for Land Rover at the time, considering the general state of turbocharger technology in the early 1980s) makes it a very handy off-road engine.

It may be noisy compared with the Tdi, and the under-bonnet layout really is a mess compared with more modern engines, but it is only the long-term reliability which lets it down in any significant way, especially when you take into account the present-day purchase price of Diesel Turbo Land Rovers. Its principal weak points are the cylinder head, which develops cracks, and the pistons, which are also inclined to crack and, sometimes, to lose chunks altogether.

Despite this, if the engine is in good condition when it's first bought, and is then used with a degree of respect – which means avoiding long spells at near-maximum rpm, paying meticulous attention to coolant temperatures and levels, and always changing the oil at the recommended interval, or before – it should give long and reliable service.

THE TDI ENGINES

There is no doubt that these are the best of all Defender engines prior to the Td5, and that in many respects both the 200 Tdi and 300 Tdi are preferable to the V8 petrol engine. They develop a little more torque than the carburettor-fed 3.5-litre V8, the most important consideration in a Land Rover, and travel nearly twice as far on each gallon of fuel.

The 200 Tdi was a genuine breakthrough when it was first introduced with the launch of the Discovery in 1989. It was an all-new engine, and the first of Land Rover's diesels to feature direct injection, with its advantages of power and economy. It was introduced into the newly named Defenders in 1990, in a slightly lower state of tune than in the Discovery. However, the Defender's 107bhp was only 4bhp less than in the Discovery, and the torque, at 188lb ft, was 10lb ft less. According to Land Rover this was done to slightly reduce the stresses when running continuously at maximum rpm in low gears, which they considered a significant feature of the everyday life of Defenders.

Whatever the reason, the new engine was significantly more powerful than the Diesel Turbo, and had 25 per cent more torque – improvements which transformed diesel-powered Land Rovers and which, today, make even the earliest 200 Tdi Defender a delightful vehicle to drive.

With Tdi power, Defenders have a maximum speed of 85mph (137kph) and will cruise all day at 75–80mph (121–129kph). The slowing-down effect of hills and headwinds is very much reduced, although a combination of a long motorway incline, headwind, and a heavily loaded vehicle can bring you down to fourth gear.

More than absolute speed, it's the liveliness of the Tdi which impresses the most. The 0–60mph (0–96kph) time is about 17 seconds, which means that although you won't beat hot hatchbacks away from the lights, the Defender is able to mix it with the rest of the traffic and, on the open road, to cruise at the same speed as most other cars. Gone are the days of crawling along in lines of HGVs.

Although owners have towed caravans, horseboxes, and other trailers with all previous diesel engines, the Tdi is the first one to be able to do it with consummate ease. The combination of Tdi engine and Defender weight and size makes it a perfect tow vehicle for caravan touring holidays, as countless owners have been delighted to discover for themselves.

The 200 Tdi is, generally, a reliable unit. Some have developed problems with cracks in their blocks at fairly low mileages (60–70,000 miles, or 96–112,000km) while others have gone on past 200,000 miles (322,000km) with no trouble at all. Mostly, they are reliable for 120,000 miles (193,000km) or so, but top-end overhauls are not uncommon soon after.

The 300 Tdi does not appear to have the same problems. Although performance remains the same, it was considerably re-engineered from the 200 Tdi and, as well as being quieter and smoother, appears to have no longer-term problems. Both engines, of course, require strict attention to routine service schedules.

One problem which has caused difficulties for 300 Tdi owners has been caused by incorrect alignment of the pulleys for the camshaft drive belt, leading to premature wear and, in some cases, total belt failure with varying degrees of engine damage. This did not affect all 300 Tdi engines, and the units in question have in all probability been rectified by now, although Land Rover has been most reluctant to acknowledge the problem and some dealers have been less than forthcoming with information to their customers.

The new gearbox introduced with the 300 Tdi gave much improved gear selection with more logical gear positions, and is a sweeter unit all-round. At the same time, revisions to the clutch mechanism reduced operating pressures; drivers no longer develop massive muscles in their left leg in stop-start conditions.

The Tdi engines produce commendable economy when one takes into account the shape and weight of the vehicles in which they are fitted, and the fact that many owners work these engines extremely hard in order to make the most of the inevitably limited performance of Defenders. It is

↓ **Although both the Td5 (shown here) and the Puma-engined Defender produce maximum torque at slightly higher engine speeds than the Tdi models, they are superb off-road machines. They're even more so with the electronic traction aids that began to become commonplace with these versions. (Nick Dimbleby)**

→ The Td5 engine's complexity can be off-putting to DIY enthusiasts, although the management system ensures it retains its all-round tune much more satisfactorily than previous diesels. (Dave Barker)

↓ Until the Td5 came along the interior of the later Tdi County Station Wagons (seen here) was as close as you could get to luxury in a Defender, while retaining the essential functionality. The Puma interior brought more luxury, but the workmanlike feel continued. (Nick Dimbleby)

quite possible to achieve 25mpg on a regular basis, and as much as 28mpg on long journeys with a little bit of restraint. However, when used very hard consumption can be as much as 22mpg.

THE TD5 AND PUMA

Significantly smoother than the Tdi and with 122bhp on hand, the 2.5-litre five-cylinder turbocharged engine specially developed by Land Rover has shown yet again that it's not only the giants of car making who can come up with world-class engines. Although it's more powerful, the Td5's 195lb ft of torque at 1,950rpm is the same as the Tdi's, but at 150rpm more, so there's just a little less punch at very low revs.

The engine is a delight to live with, combining the refinement of saloon car diesels with the power you need in a Land Rover. Economy is just a fraction better than the Tdi, although the difference is too slight to notice on a day-to-day basis. The engine has proved to be free from reliability problems.

Although the 2.4-litre Puma engine produces its maximum torque at a slightly higher engine speed than the Td5, this is not at all noticeable

from the driver's seat. This Ford unit, suitably and well modified for fitment in the Defender, provides all the 'grunt' the demanding off-road enthusiast requires. Along with that goes a level of refinement that Defender owners didn't even dream about back in the Tdi days.

Both engines are heavily reliant on electronic control systems – an inevitability these days – yet there have been no problems relating to electronics other than those where owners have not taken due care in waterproofing these components when extreme wading has been on the menu. Used properly, these are the most reliable power units yet.

Body options

Although the type of body and level of trim has less bearing on the pleasure derived from a Defender than making the right engine choice, it helps greatly if you get it right. Clearly, a Pick-up body makes no sense for anyone wishing to use a Defender for family transport, but it is surprising how many people buy a 90 when a 110 would

be altogether better, or choose a County Station Wagon when their hobby is off-roading in as much mud as possible.

The County Station Wagon is the easiest to live with and should be the preferred choice for anyone wishing to combine commuting with family holidays. But if finances don't run to full CSW specification, which carries a substantial price premium, it's possible to create your own by buying a basic Hard Top, installing windows, soundproofing, carpets, and headlinings, and then fitting aftermarket seats of your choice into the newly created rear passenger area. This is most commonly done with 90s.

Noisiest of all Land Rovers are Hard Tops in their basic, ex-factory form. The bare sides, rear wheel arch areas and floor transmit noise from the exhaust, transmission, suspension and tyres, and suffer badly from condensation for much of the year – uncomfortably so in winter.

Pick-up bodies appeal to many, especially if working loads need to be carried and there's no family to worry about. However, the open truck bed provides no security for luggage or for off-roading equipment, unless secure steel containers are bolted to the truck floor.

↑ **Pick-up, or Truck Cab versions of the 90 and 110 invariably begin life as working vehicles on farms or construction sites. They are attractive vehicles, but need extra-careful checking because of the risk of prior abuse, and are not the most practical of Land Rover models. (Nick Dimbleby)**

CHAPTER 12
MODIFICATION AND PREPARATION

Good though the Defender is in its standard specification, a lot can be done to make everyday life with a Land Rover more enjoyable and to prepare it for off-road activities and long-haul expedition work. Whatever you're planning to do with your Land Rover, though, there's usually no need for any sort of modification to Tdi engines, gearboxes, transmissions, or bodywork in order to obtain better performance. However, there is a massive choice of 'bolt-on' equipment for various types of off-roading, including safety fitments such as roll cages, wheels and tyres, and special expedition items. And, uniquely to Land Rovers, it is always possible to discard an early type of engine and fit in its place a Tdi, later diesel or petrol V8, thereby upgrading performance at a stroke.

Greenlaning

For very many green lane outings there's no need to change anything at all on even the most standard Land Rover. This is particularly so during the drier parts of the year when you're unlikely to find any sections bad enough to cause difficulties. Even in the winter months there's plenty of greenlaning which doesn't require special equipment and, because of today's environmental situation and the political sensitivity of many routes, any tracks which might prove particularly difficult in bad weather and would result in surface damage should not be driven.

The greatest individual aid to traction for green lane outings is the use of all-terrain or mud-terrain tyres: any enthusiast with a Defender fitted with general-purpose road-biased tyres should invest in a set of tyres more suited for off-road work. It has become fashionable to fit mud-terrain tyres on 4x4s regardless of whether they'll ever be taken off-road, but this is not the most sensible approach. Mud terrains might give the impression you're a

hard off-roader, but unless you're likely to have a use for them, it's better to choose a less aggressive tread pattern.

Mud terrains will give you a better chance of coping with deep mud and some (but by no means all) slippery climbs, but there's a downside to them: when being used on wet tarmac the very characteristic of their design which makes them so good in mud – the widely-spaced, large tread blocks – means you have less rubber in contact with the road than with other tyre types. Consequently, stopping distances are increased in wet conditions.

Therefore the sensible tyre choice for anyone likely to go greenlaning without getting involved in very severe conditions is an all-terrain type, with relatively large tread blocks combined with a less-open overall pattern. These tyres are surprisingly effective and are well capable of dealing with most conditions the enthusiast is likely to encounter. Furthermore, they wear better than the mud-terrain type when vehicles are used principally on the road. On the other hand, if your greenlaning

← **Modifying your vehicle can become a hobby in its own right. For many, it's as much about customising the appearance as it is about enhancing off-road capability. (Simon Hodder)**

> **DID YOU KNOW?**
> ### 3.9-litre diesel
> Enthusiasm among Australians – always great fans of Land Rovers – for the early One Ten was aided greatly by the 3.9-litre diesel option, an attractive alternative to the V8, which was never offered in Britain. The engine was the Isuzu 4BD1 direct-injection four-cylinder unit which, although no road-burner, produced 97bhp at 3,200rpm, some 50 per cent more than Land Rover's own diesel, and almost as much torque as the V8, its 188lb ft coming at a very useful 1,800rpm.
>
> In 1986 the 3.9 diesel was given the same five-speed gearbox as the V8, with identical ratios other than lower overall gearing in the high-range transfer. The main gearbox ratios suited the diesel much less than it did the V8, and the first four gears were much the same as they had been before the new gearbox. Fifth, however, became a genuine overdrive, much appreciated on some of Australia's never-ending, dead straight outback roads.

→ Mud-terrain tyres are available under various brand names and are the best choice for serious off-roading where deep mud is a persistent problem. Otherwise, a less-aggressive, all-terrain tread pattern can be the best bet. (Nick Dimbleby)

↓ Owners of 90s fitted with rear anti-roll bars find that the vehicle's behaviour on the road is much better than non-roll bar Defenders, but the bar restricts articulation of the rear axle slightly, so for serious off-roading, it pays to remove it altogether. (Dave Barker)

and other off-roading activities involve driving in deep mud on a regular basis, it would be pointless to fit any other type of tyre than a mud terrain. Bear in mind, however, that mud tyres are not at all effective in sand.

Some Defenders are fitted with anti-roll bars and drivers who clock up high road-going mileages often ask if they'd be better removing the rear anti-roll fitment. The answer is to leave it in place. The bar gives better handling on the road and, with extensive road use, would be missed if it wasn't there. Off-road, the anti-roll bar restricts axle articulation, but in most greenlane situations you can avoid requiring the full potential articulation. It's only when your off-roading becomes more demanding that the restriction imposed by the anti-roll bar creates problems.

Wading plugs

One aspect of which owners should be aware is that all Land Rovers have a drain hole in the clutch housing between the engine and gearbox; those

which have a camshaft belt drive also have one at the bottom of the drive belt housing. Engines such as the V8, the 2.25 petrol and diesel units, and the 2.5 petrol have chain-driven camshafts which do not require a drain. These holes permit oil to drain away in the event of an oil leak in this area, and should therefore be left clear in normal use.

However, whenever the vehicle is likely to be immersed in water or mud which may reach the drain holes, wading plugs should be screwed in to prevent ingress. It is important to do this because water or liquid mud or sand entering the holes can cause serious damage.

The plugs should be removed afterwards, at the very latest two or three days after they've been fitted. Where vehicles are operated in conditions requiring the continuous use of wading plugs, they should be removed every few days to permit any oil to drain away.

Wading plugs are available from all Land Rover dealers, and many accessory and parts shops, and should be carried in a handy spot inside the Land Rover, along with a 13mm or half-inch spanner.

Serious off-roading

Anyone who plans to use a 90 or 110 for off-roading in demanding conditions needs to ensure the vehicle is properly equipped. Again, the first and easiest 'modification' is to ensure that the tyres are suitable. The choice will almost certainly be the mud-terrain type, of which there are many types available. Check out the relative qualities and prices of different makes by going to an off-road tyre specialist.

The next consideration should be whether or not to equip the Land Rover for use in water deeper than the non-adapted maximum depth of roughly the height of the uppermost section of the wheel rim. Entering water much deeper than this carries with it a significant risk of it getting into the air intake system and, consequently, damaging the engine. So, if you're ever likely to get serious about off-roading, or you want to be able to cope with water whenever it occurs – such as flooded roads – it really pays to be permanently prepared.

Deep wading is challenging and can be fun, but it can also do a lot of damage and is potentially dangerous. It's wise to equip your Defender so that

it can cope with deep water, but it is best to avoid it if at all possible!

Because they have no ignition system diesel engines will keep running in deep water, but only if you have an adequate high-level air intake and a fully-sealed air system. It takes only a tiny amount of water to be sucked in because of inadequate

sealing to destroy the engine. Consequently, your first purchase must be a good-quality high-level intake (snorkel) which is suitable for the 2.5-litre turbocharged engine in the Land Rover. It should reach roof height, or slightly more, and must be substantial enough to take the knocks of off-roading. It will need firm attachment to the A-post beside the windscreen.

With the snorkel, buy suitable piping (flexible and solid) to link it to the air filter box, and make sure you have a good supply of high-quality clips to secure all joints, possibly using a suitable silicone sealant as well to ensure a total seal throughout the system. The air filter box itself will need additional sealing. Silicone applied round the rim of the base will seal it solidly when the top is in position, but it makes sense to also seal round the join with heat-resistant tape. All the breather tubes from the axles and gearboxes must be extended so they pass up the outside of the snorkel tube.

There's not much more you need to do for occasional deep wading, which should be restricted to wheel arch height if at all possible. You can go deeper – indeed, a diesel Land Rover will run with the engine fully submerged – but then you'll

↑ This is the hole in a five-speed gearbox into which the wading plug screws. Wading plugs should be fitted whenever the vehicle is to be used in water or deep mud and, if not removed immediately, should be taken out within a day or two. They must not be left in for normal running, because the hole permits the escape of small quantities of oil. (Dave Barker)

be damaging the alternator and probably the turbocharger.

Virtually nothing can be done to stop water coming in through the door seals, so part of your preparation should be to replace any carpets with rubber mats. If you go really deep you'll soak the seats – even waterproof covers won't protect them if they're under water.

A strong plastic bag, or even an old coat, draped over the radiator grille, will reduce the flow of water on to the fan, and will also protect the radiator from floating debris or, in winter, chunks of ice. And don't forget to fit those wading plugs!

Diesel-engined Land Rovers are the only type suitable for deep wading because of the absence of a distributor, high-tension plug leads, and spark plugs. Without a high-level air intake Land Rover's maximum wading depth advice must be followed, and even then it is possible that a petrol-engined vehicle might short out. It is extremely difficult to make a petrol engine's electrics fully waterproof.

Given the proper precautions all diesel Land Rovers are capable of similar wading performance. However, great care must be exercised with the Defender Td5 because of its total reliance on a

sophisticated electronic management system. It has not yet been fully established whether the management system and its ECU, the electronic traction control (ETC) 'black box' and other electronics will withstand regular immersion, but the general feeling is that they won't. Water-proofing them to a satisfactory level is likely to prove extremely difficult, especially in the case of the management system. You might think you've got away with it after one or two outings, but long-term reliability will almost certainly suffer. The best advice is to forget about serious wading in the Td5; deep water is especially unkind to vehicles bristling with electronics.

The next consideration should be a winch, essential for any serious off-road outings and all expedition work, and very reassuring for even light-hearted greenlane outings. The most popular type is the electric winch, which takes current from the Land Rover's battery (see later) and, via a low-geared electric motor, provides power to the drum on which the steel winching cable is stored. A less well-known alternative is the hydraulic type, such as the Milemarker, which takes its operating power from the vehicle's power steering pump.

Several makes of electric winch are available. All of them are well-made, they all have similar characteristics within certain power bands, and all the models sold in Britain will fit easily to a 90 or 110. In most cases you can buy the winch complete with a winch mounting bar which replaces the front bumper. Alternatively, winches may be mounted on the bumper which, because of its rugged construction and the way it attaches directly to the front sections of the chassis, will comfortably handle all the stresses involved with winching.

When choosing a winch it pays to buy the most powerful available. This is not so much because you will necessarily need all the pulling power it will provide, but because it improves the speed of operation of a heavy recovery. An electric winch operating close to its capacity can be used for only a few minutes before it must be rested to cool it down. If, for example, the winch is only running at half capacity the operating periods will be longer than a fully-loaded unit – but rest intervals will still be needed if the pull is a long one.

An hydraulic winch is also very easily fitted to a Land Rover. The hydraulic pressure which operates

↑ **A high-level air intake must extend to the roofline of the vehicle, and all joints between the base of the intake and the inlet manifold, including the edges of the air box, must be totally sealed and checked before every off-roading session. (Nick Dimbleby)**

← **Deep wading such as this can only be done with a vehicle which has been specially prepared. Most important is the fitment of a high-level air intake, or snorkel, and the extension of breather tubes from gearboxes, etc. It is virtually impossible to waterproof a petrol engine to cope with deep water, so diesels win every time. (Nick Dimbleby)**

↑ Winch operation must
be done with great care,
and wherever possible
should involve an assistant
(the 'winch master')
who controls the entire
operation from a position
where the winch is clearly
visible. Winches can be
dangerous, while at all
times it is crucial to keep
well away from winch
cables under tension.
(Nick Dimbleby)

it comes from the vehicle's power steering pump via a straightforward adaptation. Although the actual line speed of a top-flight hydraulic winch, such as the Milemarker, is slower than an equivalent electric type, a long and difficult recovery with a hydraulic unit can actually be faster. This is because the winch does not heat up, so can run continuously until the recovery is complete, and the line speed is constant.

As well as a winch, a Land Rover being prepared for serious off-roading should also be fitted with special recovery attachments at the front (if they're not part of a special winch mounting bar), Most effective are JATE rings, developed originally by the British Army for airborne operations. These are bolted through the longitudinal chassis sections. The towing equipment takes care of rear recovery … but only as long as it is in perfect condition, and the rear crossmember and all the chassis are free of rust damage.

Although Land Rovers are exceptionally tough vehicles, the upper body has no structural strength and a roll-over can have nasty consequences. Many enthusiasts now fit roll cages to Hard Top bodies for peace of mind, and if you own, say, an ex-military 110 soft-top a roll cage is highly recommended.

Any soft-top vehicle without a roll cage or rollover bar relies entirely on the windscreen surround to support it and protect its occupants if it turns over. The windscreen structure of a Land Rover is not designed for that purpose, which means the occupants are likely to be crushed if

something goes wrong and the vehicle flips on to its top.

When deciding on roll-over protection there's the choice of a full-blown cage or the simpler single-bar anti-roll arrangement. If you're likely to become involved in competitive trialling at CCV (cross-country vehicle) level you will have to invest in a fully approved roll cage, but for normal use the single-bar type may well suit you best.

Don't be tempted to make one up for yourself with a few lengths of tubing, in the belief that a cheap DIY job will do just as well. It won't, because there's no substitute for the knowledge of metal strengths, stress points and safe design which you get when you buy recognised, professional items.

There are plenty of cages and bars on the market, especially designed for Land Rovers. You can get excellent protection with the single-bar type, the best of which have immensely strong bracing sections for bolting or welding directly on to the chassis; the main bar structure also connects directly to the chassis. With one of these fitted the rollover protection is much better than with a standard Hard Top Land Rover, which is why enthusiasts also fit them to roofed vehicles. For soft-tops, the rollover bar can be supplied to precise dimensions to allow the normal canvas hood to fit snugly over it.

For the ultimate in protection, even if you don't have competition in mind, a tailor-made full roll cages is the answer. Some are made by specialist workshops, although the best-known are the Safety Devices range, with so many variations that you're sure to find just what you want.

Full cages provide a higher degree of safety to driver and passengers – which is why they're compulsory for competition – but are somewhat more expensive and can be considerably more difficult to fit. However, anyone who has examined the roll cage inside a Camel Trophy Discovery needs no further advice on the amount of protection it provides.

Removing and replacing a canvas top will be no more difficult with a roll cage or anti-roll bar fitted. Indeed, most enthusiasts find that the extra support provided by the protective steelwork makes the canvas a little tighter all round, and less inclined to flap when surrounded by lorries on motorways.

The tubing should be wrapped in special impact-

154 LAND ROVER DEFENDER

→ The one weak point of a Land Rover is the upper body, which does not possess the structural strength to withstand a roll over. Many enthusiasts fit full or partial roll cages as a sensible safety precaution while, for competition use, they are compulsory. (Nick Dimbleby)

↓ One of the few acceptable forms of heavy recovery is the JATE ring, an extra-strong attachment which should be bolted through the main chassis frames near the front of the vehicle. For heavy-duty recovery they should be used as a pair, connected via a bridle arrangement to equalise forces throughout the chassis. (Nick Dimbleby)

absorbing sleeving to protect heads, arms, and bodies from direct contact with the steel in an accident or when bouncing about off-road. This is available from roll cage suppliers.

Cross-axle lockers

One of the few complaints made by off-roading enthusiasts is that Land Rovers are not fitted with any means of locking either or both of the axle differentials in order to maximise traction. Even with the centre differential between the front and rear prop shafts locked a Land Rover will be immobilised in any situation which leads to loss of traction by one wheel on both axles. Being able to lock either of the axle diffs, or having a limited slip arrangement on either or both axles, minimises the chances of becoming stuck.

Fortunately, various aftermarket systems are available, most of which can be home-fitted by competent DIY owners. It is possible, at one extreme, to fit manually operated lockers to both axles or, at the other, to have a limited slip

→ These are the dashboard switches for operating an ARB differential lock, which is engaged by air pressure fed from an on-board compressor. The system is extremely effective. (Dave Barker)

differential operating on just one. The full locking system will get you through just about anything, but even the limited slip diff will make a profound difference to a Land Rover's ability to cope with mud, slippery hills, snow, and ice.

Perhaps the most popular differential conversion is to fit ARB air lockers, which replace the standard Rover axle differential. Normal diff action is retained until the locking system is activated by a compressed air system, when it forms a solid link across the axle. Most owners fit just one ARB unit, usually to the rear axle, but it is possible to have them front and rear for extreme conditions. The unit is supplied as a complete differential, with the additional option of the compressor and fitting kit.

Another commonly used device is the Torson Gleason differential conversion, which can be used on either or both axles. This again allows normal differentiation while the tyres are gripping, but proportions the torque according to the available traction whenever grip is lost. It's a good system, but relies on the driver stabbing at the brake pedal whenever grip has been lost and the vehicle has stopped, in order to prompt the unit to transfer torque. It therefore has the disadvantage that in most cases you'll come to a standstill before grip is restored.

A third type is the Detroit Locker which is more correctly an 'unlocker' than a 'locker'. On-road, the Detroit Locker differential remains locked in all normal situations while driving in a straight line, but automatically unlocks when the mechanism detects that the vehicle is cornering. However, this only happens on a trailing throttle; the moment that power is reapplied, the mechanism again 'locks'. This means that, when off-roading, the unit is already locked regardless of the terrain, and remains locked unless a corner is taken without throttle input, which when off-roading is extremely unlikely.

There's also the Truetrac limited slip differential to consider. This is not a locker, as such, because it never locks an axle as a solid piece but, when one wheel is spinning, it permits sufficient torque to be transmitted to the gripping wheel to pull you through in most cases. The Truetrac may be used on either, or both axles, and for extreme effectiveness can be used on the front with, say, a Detroit locker on the rear.

Other off-roading add-ons

Under-body protection is essential for serious off-roading in order to prevent rocks and other projections damaging the differentials, steering mechanism, sumps, and other vulnerable areas. It is also very advisable to fit steel sill protectors, which are bolted to the chassis and run along each side of the vehicle beneath the doors – an area which takes a lot of punishment in extreme situations. The manufacture and sale of the various guards and shields has become very big business; along with winches and roll cages they have proved popular with owners who want their Land Rovers simply to look the part, as well as those who intend to use them in anger.

Popular under-body items are bolt-on differential guards, steering guards, and axle guards, manufactured either in heavy duty aluminium alloy or steel. All these items, along with sill protectors, are easy to fit at home.

Many enthusiasts fit specialist springs and shock absorbers to cope with the punishment of off-roading, and it is not at all unusual to replace the standard suspension bushes with a plastic set which, some people believe, provide better handling in extreme conditions, along with longer bush life.

Because electric winches impose severe battery drain, even with a high-output alternator running flat-out, it is quite usual to fit a second battery along with a split-charge device. Another option is to replace the standard battery with an Optima spiral-wound type which, with a rating of 850 amps, has enormous reserves of power and can cope with heavy-load, long-running winching operations.

Off-road competition

Anyone wishing to become as proficient as possible in all aspects of off-roading could well consider trying their hand at events like trialling, winching competitions, and other competitive activities which are available through the Land Rover club movement. These are excellent ways to hone off-roading techniques, although in order to take part in many types of competition you need to be fairly proficient in the first place.

Trialling is the logical place to start. Increasing

↑ Many off-road enthusiasts fit under-body guards to protect steering components, differentials and sumps from violent (and often catastrophic) impact with rocks. A wide choice of protection is available and it is all easy to fit on a DIY basis. (Nick Dimbleby)

numbers of events are being organised for novice drivers with standard, road-going vehicles. These are often called Tyro or Novice trials, and you can compete in any kind of everyday vehicle. They're classified as RTV (road-taxed vehicle) events.

Most local and regional Land Rover clubs organise a variety of competitions, with beginners' trials becoming ever more popular with recent converts to off-roading. Generally you need to be a club member to take part, although there's often a no-obligation opportunity for first-timers, giving them a chance to try it out before becoming committed to the club world. It's enormous fun, with masses of help and advice on hand from more experienced enthusiasts.

Provided you understand the basics of off-road driving (such as choosing the right gear, throttle control, reading the way ahead, vehicle placement, etc) and you fully understand the vehicle's controls, you can enjoy events like this without damaging your vehicle or yourself. You'll be certain to improve your skill level in all respects. You'll learn rapidly how to manoeuvre through narrow spaces while at the same time dealing with side slopes,

deep holes, rocks, tree roots, and mud; you'll rapidly find out how to choose the most suitable gear for difficult and/or slippery climbs; coping with awkward obstacles will become second nature; and the natural apprehension when driving through water will soon disappear.

One great advantage of trialling – which in itself is a wonderful pastime – is that you can watch how others tackle the same obstacles as yourself. Seeing how fellow competitors manage to make it look easy, or make a complete mess of a section you took in your stride, is a great way to learn.

Once you've got this far you might find yourself developing a healthy interest in winching … enough to start thinking about activities such as challenge events. Clearly, competitions like this are not for novices – though some clubs organise winching contests suitable for people with limited experience – but even if you don't take part, there's a lot to be learned by watching how more-skilled enthusiasts do it. To watch a team winch their Land Rover up an impossibly steep hillside, perhaps starting from a muddy river, can be truly inspirational. You'll be given a live demonstration of what so far may have been theory for you: the selection of anchor points; connecting the winch cable to tree strops and ground anchors; effective use of guidance signals; and sensitive control of the winch motor.

It's a big step from being a casual observer to a competitor in something like the Warn Challenge, but the way to do it is to progress through club events until you feel ready for the toughest tests. Obviously, the more demanding winching contests are suitable only for specialised off-road vehicles. Mostly people use 90s fitted with state-of-the-art winches (sometimes with a second one rear-mounted), heavy-duty recovery attachments, mud-terrain tyres, snorkels, and locking differentials.

The ultimate off-roading competition was, at one time, the Camel Trophy. That event is now defunct, and over its last few years had changed into more of an outdoor lifestyle occasion rather than the all-action, driving and winching orientated contest it was in its heyday. Some of the challenges which made the Camel trophy so attractive to Land Rover, as a showcase for its vehicles, crop up in occasional events held in the same style.

↓ Trials competition is an excellent way to put off-roading skills to the test. There are categories for most types of vehicle, short and long-wheelbases, road-legal (RTV) and competition specials (CCV). (Nick Dimbleby)

Expeditions

Increasingly, European-based Land Rover enthusiasts are stretching their off-roading adventures into parts of north and north-west Africa, heading for the challenges of the Sahara desert and Atlas mountains. Others, even more adventurous, head even further afield.

An expedition to, for example, the Sahara is not something to be undertaken lightly. The environment is always hostile, and can be lethal, and despite the close proximity of the region's northernmost parts to southern Spain, few of the everyday benefits of the 21st century are present. That said, there's no reason why anybody with reasonable off-roading ability and with a Land Rover in good mechanical condition should not head south, cross from Spain to Morocco, and enjoy a bit of real adventure.

It is quite feasible to embark on such a journey with a standard vehicle – after all, the locals manage perfectly well with ordinary cars, many of them seemingly on the verge of extinction. However, they're not planning on living out of their vehicles for weeks on end and, mostly, their

desert driving is restricted to established hard-surfaced roads.

A group of two or three enthusiast-driven Land Rovers taking an extended tour around the mountains and deserts of northern Africa can usually manage without major modifications, but deserts are dangerous places, and it's better to be prepared. If you're travelling alone, or intend venturing into the real wilderness of the region, you must be properly equipped and your vehicle fully suitable for the conditions it will encounter.

The most important pre-expedition check is the cooling system, which has to be able to cope with high-load, slow-speed work in ambient temperatures of 40–45°C, and sometimes more. You may need assistance in the form of a second fan, especially with vehicles more than about five years old, and if you're hitting the Sahara in summer it would be wise to fit one, regardless of the state of the cooling system. Electric fans can be fitted easily to back up the existing one, but another option is to discard the existing fan altogether and use a pair of smaller ones instead. This will increase the airflow through

↑ **You have to be pretty serious to become involved in winching competitions. However, it is great fun, despite being exceptionally hard work, usually in terrible conditions. (Nick Dimbleby)**

the radiator, using a larger area of the rad to do so, and thereby giving more cooling efficiency.

A high-level air intake, or snorkel, is a worthwhile fitment for expedition use. There's the obvious benefit of deep wading – remember that flash floods can cause major problems in mountainous areas, even in desert regions – plus the additional benefit of considerably less sand and dust being drawn in when the air intake is at roof height. It means you'll spend less time worrying about the state of the air filter.

If you don't already have one, give serious consideration to a winch. You must have one for solo expeditioning, and at least one vehicle in a group of two or three should be winch-equipped. Choosing one with its own bumper assembly, complete with strong points for a high-lift jack, and specialist towing attachments, saves the bother of adding these separately. But if you don't fit a winch it is essential to have JATE rings fitted to the front of the chassis, and to have a rear tow bar capable of (a) pulling other vehicles and (b) pulling

↑ **Taking your Defender through deep water can be great fun, but before you do it's a good idea to fit a raised air intake. That way, there's no risk of water entering your engine and causing very expensive damage. (Simon hodder)**

CHAPTER 13
LOOKING AFTER YOUR LAND ROVER

Because there are so many different engines in the various types of Ninety, One Ten, and Defender, it is not possible in the space available here to provide specific information on routine servicing. However, full details are provided in the relevant Workshop Manuals, the *Haynes Service and Repair Manual* for the series, and the *Haynes Restoration Manual*.

This chapter in no way attempts to replace or even supplement the level of information available in these publications. It comprises, instead, an advisory approach on matters relating to the general care of vehicles in the Defender family. The importance of routine maintenance, and the implications of failure to adhere to service schedules, are spelled out. There's guidance on some of the more usual if not necessarily routine work, and there's an overview of bodywork inspection and renovation.

As well as that, some of the technical concerns associated with ownership of these versatile and complex machines are looked at, from the point of view of the owner who is, perhaps, less experienced than some when it comes to Land Rovers.

Routine maintenance

As with all vehicles, it is crucial to carry out inspection and servicing precisely to the recommended schedules. This applies to all aspects of the vehicle, not just the engine, and in a Land Rover includes steering, transmission, and suspension inspection which is not required in some other vehicle types but which, in all of the Defender series, is essential for correct operation.

The V8 petrol engine, Diesel Turbo, Tdi and later units are especially sensitive to servicing requirements. If servicing is carried out correctly with high-quality materials the life of these engines will be prolonged considerably.

Particularly susceptible to lax servicing, the V8's working life can be shortened very considerably if oil change intervals are extended or ignored altogether, and/or poor-quality oil is used. The consequential blocked or restricted oilways inhibits the supply of oil to the camshaft and valve gear, leading to premature camshaft wear, noisy and worn hydraulic tappets, and poor running. On the other hand, a V8 which has been treated properly throughout its life can go on to give trouble-free operation over an extremely high mileage.

All the turbocharged engines are vulnerable to the effects of infrequent oil changes and inappropriate lubricants. Again, this leads to premature wear, especially in 200 Tdis, which can be prone to crankcase pressurisation because of rapid wear caused by inadequate oil changes. Another result, in all the turbo engines, is premature turbo wear because of oil starvation resulting from partially blocked oilways. It is crucial, too, that coolant levels, radiator performance, and water pump operation are fully up to the mark in all vehicles with these engines.

The V8 produces a great deal of heat which must be properly dispersed if the all-aluminium unit, and particularly the cylinder heads, is not to be damaged. Head gasket problems with the V8 are nearly always caused by under-performing coolant, and it doesn't take long for a blown head gasket to cause serious problems, firstly to the

← **There's more to looking after a Land Rover than washing and waxing it. They do require more maintenance than a typical family car, but looking after them is part of the fun. This one is being serviced by Dave Rogers at High Peak 4x4, but you can very easily service them on your driveway. (Simon Hodder)**

> **DID YOU KNOW?**
> **Auto Defender... in 1989**
> The lack of an automatic option for Defenders was lamented by many, yet it is not widely known that a professional conversion was available back in 1989. Watford Land Rover dealers Harris-Mayes offered their own high-quality V8 auto conversion using a ZF four-speed 'box. The cost of the job on a new vehicle was £3,250 plus VAT. We believe some are still around.

→ A lack of routine oil changes can lead to premature camshaft wear in any engine, but especially Land Rover V8s. This camshaft had developed pronounced early wear because the vehicle's owner neglected servicing requirements. (Dave Barker)

The condition of the radiator must be checked after every off-roading expedition. Mud and other debris blocks the airways through the radiator and, if not removed, can lead to extreme overheating in a very short time, with disastrous consequences.

This attention to the cooling system is equally important with Tdi engines. Land Rover diesels are usually very well cooled, which is why a Tdi can be left to tick over for ages without any noticeable increase in coolant temperature, but if anything goes wrong overheating can occur rapidly, again with dire results.

Bodywork renovation

Detailed renovation and restoration advice is provided in the *Haynes Restoration Manual*. It is appropriate here to point out some of the things which go wrong with Land Rovers leading to a need for restoration or, in more extreme cases, replacement.

Front wings are vulnerable on all vehicles, especially so when a Land Rover is used for off-roading. They are easily removed and replaced by anyone with a few basic tools.

The sill strip beneath the doors is extremely vulnerable to off-roading damage, but consists of simple panels held in place with screws and brackets. When replacement becomes necessary it makes sense to consider one of the tough, steel replacement kits specially designed for off-road enthusiasts. These not only resist impact, and

↑ Whenever vehicles are used off-road there is a possibility of damaged or blocked radiators, leading to possible coolant loss and, in the case of mud blockages, almost certain overheating. Aggressive wading risks damage to the radiator from debris in the water unless the grille is covered to protect the delicate radiator behind it. (Dave Barker)

head itself, and also to other areas because of the probable pollution of water with oil, and oil with water.

The coolant level must therefore be checked regularly, and a careful watch maintained on the temperature gauge, especially when operating in hot-weather conditions and/or when towing. As with all modern engines the coolant must be the prescribed mixture of water and antifreeze, which should be checked annually; the use of water alone leads to blocked water channels and does not lubricate the water pump without antifreeze.

therefore retain their appearance, but they also prevent damage to the door bottoms.

Rear doors on Hard Tops and Station Wagons suffer badly from the effects of road dirt, while the hinges wear prematurely because of the substantial weight of the door-mounted spare wheel and tyre. Bolts and hinges can be replaced, or the door can be reskinned or replaced completely. The front and rear side doors suffer badly from the effects of aluminium corrosion through an electrolytic process, and the steel frames rust with equal enthusiasm. The doors are dismantled quite easily and can be replaced partially as required or as complete units

Although the chassis of Land Rovers are extremely durable, they all develop rust with time. Enthusiast-owned vehicles which have regularly been immersed in mud or which have been bounced over rocks will develop chassis rust faster than those which lead a more sheltered life.

While the rear of the chassis is, in some ways, more likely to rust, the front of the vehicle is also vulnerable. Some rust-prone sections, such as the front crossmember, are easy to repair — especially so the crossmember, which is held in place with bolts. Other sections, such as outriggers, will require cutting away before replacements are welded in place. At the same time the area around the outrigger join, along with the entire front-to-rear length of the main chassis frames, should be examined closely and replacement parts welded in as required. The rear crossmember is particularly vulnerable to rust and, because it carries all the

stresses of towing, must be checked with particular care, along with the ends of the chassis rails to which it attaches. When replacing, always use a crossmember with extension legs which fit over the ends of the chassis to ensure the strongest possible repair.

Brakes

Replacement of brake pads for front and rear (where discs are fitted) is straightforward and won't cause any problems to anyone who has carried out such work on other vehicles. One important point to remember is that shims might be fitted to the rear of the brake pads. If so, make sure the right shims go back in the right place. Another point to bear in mind is that split pins are used to secure the caliper retaining pins, and new split pins must be fitted whenever removal has been necessary.

The front brake caliper can be removed, perhaps for work on the front suspension, without disturbing the hydraulic connections. Alternatively, it can be taken off the vehicle altogether. Rear calipers (where used) do not have a flexible hose, so cannot be removed without disturbing the hydraulic system. Models prior to 1994 were fitted with rear drum brakes, and although shoe replacement is a more protracted job than fitting

← **The front wings of any vehicle used for off-roading are liable to damage, and the aluminium panels of Land Rovers are virtually impossible to panel beat back into shape. Replacement sections are easy to fit, and are not expensive. (Dave Barker)**

↓ **The sill panels of 90s and 110s are vulnerable to damage from rocks, earth banks and tree debris. Sill protectors, like this one fitted to a 90, bolt to the chassis and protect the lower door area, as well as retaining the good looks of the sill area, even after heavy-duty off-roading. (Dave Barker)**

↑ **There's nothing complicated about the front disc brakes used on Defenders, although some have shims fitted behind the pads, which must be replaced with care when renewing pads.** (Dave Barker)

pads to a disc system, there's nothing particularly difficult about it. The important thing, especially if you're not doing this sort of job every day, is never to attempt to rush any work on the braking system.

Non-routine mechanical work

Neither spring nor shock absorber replacement requires any special skills and, to be fair, neither does much of the work you might need to do on the steering linkage, suspension joints, anti-roll bar bushes, and so on. However, there are jobs which are much more difficult and not for the novice, unless there's someone to help (despite the excellence of Workshop Manuals). This includes engine removal and stripdown, gearbox removal, clutch work, steering box and front swivel pin assembly replacement or overhaul, and front and rear hub overhaul and replacement.

Technical topics

FUEL SAVERS

The heavy fuel consumption of all Land Rovers is a worry to many owners who find their vehicles more expensive to run than they had expected. Naturally, the V8-powered models are the worst offenders, but some people also become concerned with the amount of diesel consumed by Tdis, the most efficient of all Land Rover diesels other than the much newer TD5.

Too many owners who are new to Land Rovers fail to check out the likely fuel consumption before they take the plunge for the first time. It should be obvious that anything weighing two tons or more, with appalling aerodynamics, complex and energy-sapping transmission and, more often than not, off-roading tyres, will not be cheap to run. In all cases the burden can be eased slightly, but it must be remembered that a 90 or 110 simply cannot be as economical as a Discovery or Range Rover fitted with the same engine.

The worst fuel consumption of all is found with early One Tens fitted with the 3.5-litre petrol engine and four-speed gearbox. It is just a little better with later One Tens, which had five-speed transmission, and with all V8 Ninetys, which had five gears. The best consumption you can expect with early One Tens is 13–15mpg, but even later versions and Ninetys will rarely, if ever, return better than 14–17mpg.

So what can be done?

Firstly, all Land Rover V8s will run on unleaded fuel without difficulty, and usually without adjustment of the ignition timing. Many owners mistakenly believed in the past that four-star was necessary – sometimes because they had been misinformed when buying – and in these non-four-star days some owners are even using lead replacement fuel additives. This is not necessary.

An electric cooling fan instead of the standard viscous-coupled unit provides a very slight saving, while synthetic lubricants in the engine and transmission can reduce drag. However, you've got to be doing a high mileage in order to achieve any financial benefits with these.

Swapping those mean-looking mud-terrain tyres for road-bias rubber is worth doing if you spend all your time on tarmac, but not if you enjoy off-roading.

← The rear crossmember takes all the stresses of towing and must therefore be rust free, other than perhaps the inevitable surface blemishing. The tow hitch assembly should also be inspected carefully on a regular basis. (Dave Barker)

But there are actions you can take which cost very little and which will optimise consumption. Spark plugs need to be in perfect condition, the distributor and the rest of the ignition system must be functioning at full efficiency, timing must be spot-on, the air filter clean, and the carburettors checked for wear and leaks, and properly balanced. Replacing an early standard ignition with an electronic system, such as Lumenition, can itself improve consumption by at least 1mpg, which is worth doing when the base figure is about 14mpg.

There's less you can do with diesels, and even the Tdi engine can produce a consumption figure no better than 22–23mpg when worked hard in a Defender, improving to a very best of perhaps 28mpg on a long journey. On average, a Tdi will give somewhere between 24 and 27mpg.

It is crucial with diesels to ensure that the injectors are functioning at 100 per cent efficiency, with spot-on timing and no defects in the pump.

This can only be checked and, if necessary, set up with professional equipment, but is worth doing from time to time.

With the Diesel Turbo and 200 and 300 Tdi it's vital that the turbocharger is functioning correctly and that waste gate and pressure sensing lines are not contaminated with oil. Air leaks sometimes occur with turbochargers and it's inevitable that, with time, the turbo will develop problems, resulting in a very noticeable performance drop and an increase in fuel consumption. Turbochargers cannot be repaired at home, but various specialist companies provide exchange renovation schemes at a lower cost than a new unit. Intercooler problems with Tdis can also have a marked effect on consumption and performance.

DEFENDER OVERDRIVE

Another tried and tested way of improving fuel consumption is to fit an overdrive, popular with owners of earlier Land Rovers and a wide range of classic cars but, until recently, not an option for the Defender owner. An overdrive unit built by GKN Driveline and available through a limited number of UK specialists now makes it possible for owners of five-speed Defenders to increase substantially the overall gearing of their vehicles.

The unit bolts directly to the LT230 transfer box and is compatible with the LT77 and R380 gearboxes. It reduces engine revs by 28.3 per cent and can produce a 20 per cent saving in fuel, depending on type of use. It is most beneficial in Defenders which are used regularly for long

← In order to get the best possible fuel consumption from the thirsty V8 everything must be in top order. Spark plugs need to be changed at the recommended intervals to avoid them ending up like this, causing poor starting, and raising fuel consumption. (Dave Barker)

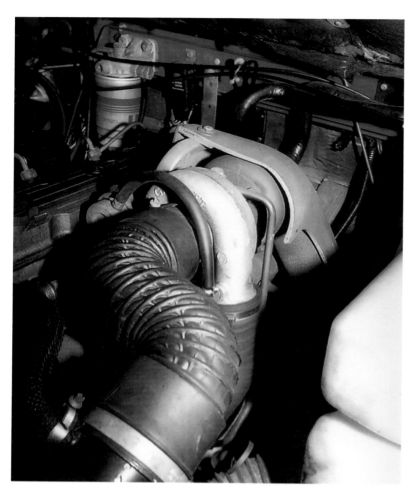

GET CONVERTED

A third way of reducing fuel costs with 2.5-litre and 3.5-litre petrol vehicles is to have them converted to LPG. The conversion gives virtually the same economy and performance from a fuel which is roughly half the price of petrol. Other advantages include full dual-fuel capability, which enables you to continue using petrol whenever necessary and, with both gas and petrol tanks full, a much extended range. There are also disadvantages, however. The large LPG tank inhibits the load-carrying capability of a 90, although it's much less of a problem with a 110, and LPG refuelling centres are still difficult to find in some areas, especially out of normal working hours.

The cost of conversion varies and it pays to get at least a couple of quotes before going ahead. And bear in mind that a little-used Land Rover, even with a V8 engine, would probably take several years to repay the cost of conversion. For high-mileage users it's nevertheless attractive on a cost basis, provided the availability problem can be overcome.

TRANSFER SWAP

Gearbox conversions are less common than engine transplants, and transfer box conversions even more so. However, one way of raising the overall gearing of, say, a Ninety fitted with the 2.5-litre petrol engine is to replace the standard transfer box with one from a Discovery or pre-viscous coupled Range Rover. This raises the gearing by about 15 per cent, which provides a small boost to fuel economy and makes cruising a little more restful. However, anyone considering this should not do so if larger diameter tyres are already fitted, and should not fit larger tyres afterwards, because this would make the gearing uncomfortably high for the engine and considerably reduce the ability to make full use of fifth gear. Nor is it an option if the Land Rover is to be used heavily loaded, or if any towing is contemplated.

The conversion itself is straightforward, although two holes will be needed for the handbrake brackets. These should be drilled and tapped before the transfer box is installed.

Another conversion which can be carried out is with the Borg-Warner chain-driven unit

↑ **The turbocharger must always be functioning correctly. Wear is inevitable over high mileages, especially where oil changes have been neglected. Reconditioned units are less expensive than new replacements and perform equally well. (Dave Barker)**

road journeys when, as well as the fuel saving, the reduction in mechanical noise because of the reduced engine speed makes a significant difference to overall comfort levels. The cost on introduction in 1999 was about £1,000 including VAT. Anybody regularly using a Defender for long-distance travel would soon recoup this.

The GKN overdrive is fitted through the floor by removing the centre seat. The job is straightforward and can be accomplished without special mechanical knowledge or equipment. Selection is via a button switch on the gear knob which activates the unit's hydraulic operating system, giving a smooth and positive shift into or out of overdrive. It defaults to direct drive in the event of a problem with the electrical or hydraulic systems.

It's a tough, long-lasting fitment easily capable of withstanding the heavy use to which many Defenders are subjected. Supplying agents provide a full back-up service.

from later Range Rover classics. However, the dimensions are different and the unit will not fit straight in without a certain amount of modification beneath the vehicle. But almost anything is possible with Land Rovers!

SPARE WHEEL TIPS

The factory-fitted standard spare wheel position for members of the Defender family is on the rear door. This doesn't suit everybody and there's always the problem that the considerable weight of the wheel and tyre causes premature wear of the door hinges. There's only one approved alternative mounting position, but one or two other methods of carrying the spare are worth considering.

Anyone not wishing to use the rear door to carry the spare, for whatever reason, can buy a bonnet mounting kit. There are drawbacks, however, because a bonnet-mounted spare inhibits forward visibility, particularly in some off-roading situations, such as when cresting a steep hill. The weight of the spare also makes it difficult to lift the bonnet, and requires the use of a sturdy additional prop (a length of timber or steel) to ensure it won't accidentally fall on you when you're working beneath it. Furthermore, the weight causes extra wear of the bonnet hinges and release mechanism, especially with regular off-roading.

↑ The best position for the spare wheel and tyre is on the rear door, although the extra weight leads to premature wear of the door hinges. Fortunately, they are not difficult or expensive to replace. (Dave Barker)

← An alternative to the rear door position for the spare wheel is to use a bonnet mounting kit. However, the wheel and tyre impairs vision, especially when driving off-road, and makes the bonnet extremely heavy to lift. (Dave Barker)

perhaps when using an alternative position. The parts can be obtained as a complete kit from Land Rover dealers, or you can use one of the swing-away kits sold by a number of accessory specialists.

SMOKE SIGNALS

Among the many myths about Land Rover engines is that they are bound to smoke, and that the normally aspirated diesel engines are sure to smoke more than petrol units. However, this isn't an across-the-board statement of truth because there is always a reason for engines to produce smoke. Older units are more inclined to smoke, of course, but there's still a reason behind the annoying habit.

So, to dispel one belief, diesel engines (normally aspirated or turbocharged) do not produce, as a breed, any more smoke than their petrol-fuelled counterparts. Their fumes can be more visible, and it is the colour of the smoke which gives the strongest clues as to their cause.

The majority of higher-mileage diesel engines will puff a little black smoke when starting from cold. However, if it's more than a modest mini-cloud it suggests that the injectors are either worn or badly adjusted. The good news is that they are easily removed for replacement or servicing.

If the smoke is white the cause is almost certainly an excess of fuel, which is usually due to problems with the distributor pump, or its timing.

When you see blue or blue-tinged smoke on start-up or when accelerating after being on over-

Other positions worth considering include inside the vehicle, if you don't need the space, or on an expedition-style roof rack if you're strong enough to lift it up there and get it down when required.

It's not unknown for previous owners to have removed the rear door mounting components,

run, it is most probably caused by wear in the valve guides and seals (see the section on start-up smoke below). If blue smoke doesn't disappear from the exhaust after start-up and persists while you're driving, it's almost certain you have wear in the bores and that the pistons and piston rings have also developed serious wear. There may even be broken piston rings.

The most serious of these problems is cylinder wear. To check for it, remove the engine breather cap while the unit is running and then slowly increase the revs. If the bores, pistons, and rings are worn beyond normal tolerances they will allow the crankcase to pressurise, blowing oil mist or smoke out of the cap. And if that happens you're facing a major stripdown.

START-UP SMOKE

Owners of older Land Rovers have always accepted a large puff of smoke when starting the engine as something to expect. If this happens with a more modern vehicle it can be worrying, especially to those with limited mechanical knowledge. Of course, the more modern engines used in Ninetys and One Tens (except for the four-cylinder petrol and normally aspirated diesel units) do not usually smoke unless there is something seriously wrong with them. Or do they?

Any engine which has done more than about 80,000 miles (129,000km) can develop start-up smoking, and this does not necessarily mean a major overhaul is due, a breakdown is rapidly heading your way, or MOT failure is imminent. In most cases, the smoke is caused by nothing more serious than worn valve stem seals. When these seals have become worn they allow a small amount of oil to drop down from the rockers when the engine is stationary, past the seal, and down to the back of the valves. The moment you start the engine this oil is burnt off and produces a smoke cloud.

This wear can develop without you being aware of it, but will gradually get worse until the oil seals have to be replaced. This usually involves cylinder head removal, which is not particularly complicated, although there's obviously more to it with the twin heads of the V8 engine.

CAMBELT DILEMMA

Whenever buying a used diesel-engined Land Rover – no matter whether it's a pre-Tdi 2.5-litre engine or a 200 or 300 Tdi – it's essential to examine the service history closely, if there is one. The history will help you decide whether or not to proceed with the purchase: the more complete the service story, the more faith you can have in the vehicle's mechanical side.

One aspect to be looked for above all others, once you have actually decided to go ahead, is information relating to cambelt changes. If there's any uncertainty at all, and especially if there is no service history, budget for a belt replacement before you begin using the Land Rover.

← Even a dense, black cloud does not necessarily mean serious trouble. It can mean the engine is being 'over-fuelled', signifying a problem with the injector pump, the timing or the injectors, or perhaps all three. If there is no reliable record of the cambelt of a Tdi engine having been changed recently, it is essential to do this immediately after buying. The better specialist dealers will do it as a matter of course when preparing a vehicle for its new owner. This shows the cambelt arrangement in the 300 Tdi. (Dave Barker)

↑ **One of the worst enemies of any Land Rover used for off-roading is accumulated mud and sand around the underside of the vehicle. Always power wash thoroughly after off-road outings, getting the water into all the hidden areas and the awkward upper sections of the chassis. Do not forget to blast away at the brakes in order to clean muck away from discs and calipers. (Dave Barker)**

BRAKE PROBLEMS

The brakes of Defenders which are used regularly off-road, especially where deep mud is involved, can wear faster than usual, and sometimes unevenly, even though the vehicle may not do too much road driving. The cause is the abrasiveness of some of the stuff the vehicle gets immersed in, pistons and pads 'sticking' because of mud, and the devastation caused to any moving parts whenever sand is driven through. Front brakes are particularly vulnerable, and sometimes there can be considerable variation in the wear rate of the front pads.

A difference of 5mm or more in the friction material qualifies as an excessive difference in pad wear rate. As well as the 'sticking' of pads and pistons, this can also be caused by a badly worn or rough disc surface on the side of the worst-worn pad (which can result from off-roading). Inferior quality pads can also have uneven wear rates.

The state of the discs is easily checked simply by looking at them. If there's any deep scoring – often caused by off-roading – or corrosion, or the disc is unevenly worn in any way at all, the only cure is to fit new discs. As with the replacement of brake pads, discs should only ever be replaced as a pair.

Correct operation of the piston can be checked by removing the normally worn pad and getting an assistant to gently apply the footbrake so that the pistons can be seen to emerge equally and steadily from the caliper. Take great care with this, though, because if you overdo it the piston could pop out of the bore.

After 'opening' the pistons, retract them using a lever or a pair of grips, checking that the resistance felt from each one appears to be equal. If it's not, the caliper must be checked professionally, or you may decide to simply invest in a new one.

Finally, never buy cheap or unknown brake components. Uneven wear is one thing, but pad break-up or some other failure could lead to total loss of braking.

Because off-roading is unkind to brakes and other components, the underside of the vehicle should be power-washed after every session, including the brakes, which should be inspected carefully on a very regular basis. It is not enough to rely on the normal service schedules.

If a cambelt has gone beyond its recommended replacement point it will be worn, and could fail at any time. You get no warning of failure; one moment the engine's running perfectly and the next it's stopped, often with a loud bang. A broken belt invariably means some degree of engine damage, which can be severe – so don't risk it.

You don't have the same problem with V8s, of course, because they have chain drive for the single camshaft. With these engines it's essential to listen for a front-end rattling noise, which indicates a worn chain. Although V8 timing chains will continue to run with a rattle, sometimes for years, any appreciable increase in noise means that replacement is due.

Index

Page numbers in *italics* refer to illustrations.